Television and the American Family

LEA's Communication Series
Jennings Bryant/ Dolf Zillmann, General Editors

Selected titles in Mass Communication (Alan Rubin, Advisory Editor) include:

Alexander/Owers/Carveth • Media Economics: Theory and Practice, Second Edition
Harris • A Cognitive Psychology of Mass Communication, Third Edition
Moore • Mass Communication Law and Ethics, Second Edition
Price • The V-Chip Debate: Content Filtering From Television to the Internet
Sterling/Bracken/Hill • Mass Communications Research Resources: An Annotated Guide
Van Evra • Television and Child Development, Second Edition

For a complete list of other titles in LEA's Communication Series,
please contact Lawrence Erlbaum Associates, Publishers

TELEVISION AND THE AMERICAN FAMILY

SECOND EDITION

33 , 147

Edited by

Jennings Bryant
Institute for Communication Research
The University of Alabama

J. Alison Bryant
Annenberg School for Communication
University of Southern California

LEA
2001

LAWRENCE ERLBAUM ASSOCIATES, PUBLISHERS
Mahwah, New Jersey   London

Lawrence Erlbaum Associates, Inc., Publishers
10 Industrial Avenue
Mahwah, New Jersey 07430

Cover design by Kathryn Houghtaling Lacey

Library of Congress Cataloging-in-Publication Data

Television and the American family / edited by Jennings Bryant, J. Alison Bryant.—2nd ed.
       p. cm.
   Includes bibliographical references and index.
   ISBN 0-8058-3421-4 (cloth)—ISBN 0-8058-3422-2 (pbk.)
       1. Television and children—United States.   2. Television and family—United States.
   3. Television serials—United States.   I. Bryant, Jennings.   II. Bryant, J. Alison.

   [HQ784.T4 T44632000]
   306.85'0973—dc21   00-037528

Books published by Lawrence Erlbaum Associates are printed on acid-free paper, and
their bindings are chosen for strength and durability.

Printed in the United States of America
10 9 8 7 6 5 4 3 2 1

For our wife and mother Sara,
our son and brother Todd,
and our daughter and sister Adrienne

Contents

PART VII: PUBLIC POLICY ISSUES

Preface

The first edition of *Television and the American Family* was published in 1990, the second in 2000. Few things have changed more in the decade that separates these editions than the two institutions whose integration is the topic of this book.

Television circa 1990 is practically extinct. Its manifold faces of industry, technology, and social institution have morphed into forms that could not have been imagined a decade ago. It is now digital television, enhanced TV, WebTV, DirecTV, and a myriad of other variations on the theme—and that's only one dimension of one of its faces, the technological side. The social, structural, ownership, and other faces of television have changed at least as much as its technological infrastructure.

The American family is not extinct, but the form of the American family that most people envision actually has become rather rare. A recent survey from the National Opinion Research Center, entitled "The Emerging 21st Century Family," details just how radical changes to the family have been. The following are a few of the most notable transformations:

- Whereas two decades ago most American households included children, today, kids are in just 38% of homes
- Whereas two married parents with children comprised the most common type of family unit a generation ago, in the year 2000, that type of family can be found only in about one in four households
- The most typical household today is that of an unmarried person with no children; such homes account for a third of all U.S. households, a share that has doubled since the 1970s
- Whereas three out of four adults were married a generation ago, only slightly more than half of them are today
- The average age when marriage occurs has increased; men and women marry approximately 4 to 5 years later than they did in the 1960s
- Divorce rates more than doubled between the 1960s and the 1980s, although the divorce rate actually declined slightly in the 1990s
- The number of women giving birth out of wedlock has increased dramatically over the past generation, from 5% of births to nearly 33% of births

- The portion of children living with a single parent has jumped over a generation from 1 out of 20 to about 1 out of 5 children (Welna, 1999).

So when we talk about the American family today, we are no longer talking about mom and dad and sis and junior (Welna, 1999).

Despite all of these changes to the institutions of both television and family, some things have remained remarkably consistent across the decade. One is the mutually symbiotic relationship of the American family and television. Obviously television is dependent on families both for viewership and for the purchase of the wares it hawks, but a recent report from the Kaiser Family Foundation, entitled *Kids & Media @ The New Millennium* (Rideout, Foehr, Roberts, & Brodie, 1999), indicates that the American family has continued its strong reliance on television as well. The following were among the numerous noteworthy findings of this report:

- American children spend the equivalent of a full-time work week using media
- Many parents do not appear to exercise much oversight of their children's media use
- Traditional media—especially television—continue to dominate children's media use time
- Black and Hispanic children spend significantly more time using media—especially television—than do White children
- Although boys and girls spend approximately the same amount of time each day using media, girls listen to more music, and boys watch more television and play more video games
- Children in single-parent homes watch more television than do those in two-parent homes (Rideout et al., 1999).

Another consistent element across the decade is that families continue to have a love–hate relationship with television. Although we obviously rely on television for information and entertainment, we also continue to lambaste television for the harmful effects we think it has on our families. Bold claims for antisocial effects and quieter claims for beneficial effects from using television abound.

Fortunately, research evidence has almost managed to keep pace with the perennially popular questions and flamboyant accusations about television and family. A primary purpose of this volume is to organize and present this important research.

This volume is divided into seven sections. In Part I, Introduction and Overview, Margaret Andreasen provides invaluable grounding for the research evidence that follows. She presents normative data that lay our groundwork, establishes the parameters of our territory of inquiry, and provides perspectives that offer context for subsequent sections in "Evolution in the Family's Use of Television: An Overview."

In Part II, Uses of Television by the American Family, four chapters are designed to facilitate readers' understandings of how we use the ubiquitous medium of television and its appendages. In "Television Use in Families With Children," Jennifer Kotler, John Wright, and Aletha Huston utilize fairly large brush strokes to indicate how various factors, including developmental and familial variables, relate to varying patterns of television use. David Atkin focuses on how the new media environment is altering family usage of television and other media in "Home Ecology and Children's Television Viewing in the New Media Environment." James Walker and Robert Bellamy have taken a leading role in conducting research into how those seemingly innocent little remote controls that hide in chairs and under sofas have unobtrusively changed the way we use television. They report that and related research in "Remote Control Devices and Family Viewing." Carolyn Lin does the same for other important extensions of television in "The VCR, Home Video Culture, and New Video Technologies."

More than our usage of television changed. In Part III, Attitudes Toward Television, Dan Brown and Tammy Hayes trace the evolution of public and private attitudes toward this volatile medium in a chapter entitled "Family Attitudes Toward Television."

Part IV, Portrayals of American Families on Television, presents a sampling of research findings in what is undoubtedly the most frequently explored tradition of research into television and family. James Robinson and Thomas Skill set the stage for this section with "Five Decades of Families on Television: From the 1950s Through the 1990s." More specialized assessments are provided by Mary Strom Larson in "Sibling Interaction in Situation Comedies Over the Years," Katharine Heintz-Knowles in "Balancing Acts: Work/Family Issues on Prime-Time TV," and Jannette Dates and Carolyn Stroman in "Portrayal of Families of Color on Television." William Douglas offers a detailed and critical assessment of the way families are portrayed on television in "Subversion of the American Television Family," and Jennings Bryant, Charles Aust, Alison Bryant, and Gopakumar Venugopalan present two clinical assessments in their chapter that asks, "How Psychologically Healthy are America's Prime-Time Television Families?"

Probably the area that fosters more public concern about television than any other is the social and psychological impact of television. This is explored in Part V, Meanings and Effects. Alison Alexander launches this section by exploring "The Meaning of Television in the American Family." Walter Gantz explores several critical issues regarding the complicated meaning and place of television in modern domestic life in "Conflicts and Resolution Strategies Associated With Television in Marital Life." Building on the highly influential research tradition of "fright reactions" to media, Joanne Cantor and Marie-Louise Mares examine the "Effects of Television on Child and Family Emotional Well-Being." Concluding this section is a chapter by Nancy Signorielli and Michael Morgan that utilizes the well-known binoculars of the cultivation hypothesis, "Television and the Family: The Cultivation Perspective."

Recognizing the impact of television on the family is one thing, doing something about it is another. Part VI, Mediating Television's Impact, presents three chapters that address ways to influence the effects of television. Nancy Buerkel-Rothfuss and Rick Buerkel, in "Family Mediation," and Erica Weintraub Austin, in "Effects of Family Communication on Children's Interpretation of Television," take more general but quite comprehensive looks at the issue of family mediation of television. In "Mediating Advertising Effects," David Boush focuses exclusively on advertising, the dominant support system for American television.

The final portion of this volume, Part VII, Public Policy Issues, addresses the evolution and impact of public policy in the area of television and family. Alison Bryant, Jennings Bryant, Lisa Mullikin, James McCollum, and Curtis Love restrict their treatment to a specialized form of television programming in "Curriculum-Based Preschool Television Programming and the American Family: Historical Development, Impact of Public Policy, and Social and Educational Effects." Marina Krcmar covers public policy issues more broadly in "The Effect of Television Policy on Children and Families."

Throughout the preface, we discussed changes and consistencies in the American family. One final note in this vein should be added, and that regards editorship. The first edition of *Television and the American Family* had one editor (JB), who continues to serve as the senior editor for this edition. He dedicated the first volume to his family, including his eldest child Alison. Illustrating the amount of change that can take place in the prototypical American family in a decade is the amount of change that has taken place in the Bryant family. Alison (JAB) represents a new generation of communication scholars and takes her rightful place as co-editor of the second edition. That's what has changed. What has stayed the same is that we have remained best friends throughout the decade.

REFERENCES

Rideout, V. J., Foehr, U. G., Roberts, D. F., & Brodie, M. (1999). *Kids & media @ the new millennium.* Menlo Park, CA: Kaiser Family Foundation.
Welna, D. (Reporter). (1999, November 24). University of Chicago survey on the changing American family. *All things considered.* Washington, DC: National Public Radio.

I

Introduction and Overview

Evolution in the Family's Use of Television: An Overview

Margaret Andreasen
University of Wisconsin-Madison

Evolution transforms human psyches so slowly and inconspicuously we may live lifetimes without recognizing mutations that take humankind along a new path. Social structures, like the family, adapt to changing circumstances more readily. But the development of technology is sometimes so rapid that many find the changes incomprehensible. And by the time we grasp the importance of a mechanism, it is obsolete.

In considering the family's use of television, we encounter all three evolutionary types: Humans, still responding with "fight-or-flight" responses, have changed little over the centuries; social structures like families have undergone major transformation since World War II; and marvelous telecommunications technology that was born yesterday—or this morning—forces us into new ways of knowing.

DEFINING PARAMETERS

When analyzing the American family's use of television more than a decade ago, researchers and ordinary citizens disagreed about what constituted a family and about the nature and length of the relationships necessary to establish family ties (Andreasen, 1990). The traditional

views of family systems too often seemed irrelevant to the living, interacting familial units that no longer resembled mother, father, Dick, Jane,
Sally, along with the appropriate two family pets. Although there is still
some definitional disagreement, most concede that diversity in family
structure is the norm (Schwartz & Scott, 1997). Currently, if individuals
regard themselves as linked in a familial system, most researchers are
willing to accede to that identification.

Now, however, we find confounding definitions of *television* that com-
plicate our examination of family television use. A decade ago, most researchers regarded cable access, satellite dishes, remote control devices,
and videocassette recorders (VCRs) as accouterments of the medium,
rightly discussed along with the television set itself in an analysis of family television consumption.

Although many families relied on their VCRs to facilitate home viewing of movies that might otherwise be missed, the VCR provided another
very significant function; the time-shifting of television programs. Recording specific programs enabled family members to replay those shows at
times convenient for viewers instead of when television VIPs scheduled
the programs to glean the largest target audience. Regarded as neither a
new medium nor an additional media channel, the VCR simply made television viewing more convenient.

If the rubric *television viewing* appropriately includes the consumption of time-shifted programs, does it apply to those that, in addition,
undergo a shifted *locus*? If, for example, family members view a television program on a computer monitor instead of on a television screen, are
they consuming television? Some commentators would say "Yes." Barry
Schuler, the president of America Online's Interactive Services Group,
planning to bring "AOL TV" to market sometime in 2000, observed his
product would "not take your TV and turn it into a computer monitor. . . .
This is about enhanced TV" (Tedesco & Colman, 1999, p. 11).

On the other hand, the point of consumer access is the computer, and
corporations that collect television programs and make them available
on the Internet may have created a new medium. Mark Cuban, the president of the currently prominent "aggregator of video," Broadcast.com,
argued against considering such program access an extension of television. Although Broadcast.com now carries programming from more than
40 television stations, Cuban rejected the notion that this service is
another cable television channel "because the Internet isn't TV. It's a new
medium" (Tedesco, 1999, pp. 20–21).

Those of us already getting news stories online from CNN, NBC, ABC,
and *The New York Times* would probably agree with Cuban. When we use
our computers to access news originating with other media channels, we
don't imagine that we are watching cable television or believe that we
are reading newspapers. And just as we view these news consumption

experiences as computer mediated, so also when we use our television monitors as tablets for e-mail messages via WebTV, our access to an e-mail channel is the computer, not television.

As video aggregating and streaming increase, however, we are less likely to define media channels individually and will likely see the conglomerated information source as the hybrid it is, a melding of television and computer technology, that provides computer convenience. It will also reward television stations with larger audiences, particularly for daytime special event or news coverage (Tedesco, 1999, p. 22).

Perhaps the most conspicuous and broadly distributed example of the merging of computer technology and television, however, is WebTV. Using a television set, a phone line, and Microsoft WebTV technology (selling at Best Buy for as little as $69 in 1999), plus a keyboard, viewers can connect to the World Wide Web (WWW) at the touch of a button. The television screen serves as the Internet monitor, and subscribers to WebTV's monthly service have easy access to the Web. Consumers, however, who invest $199 can obtain WebTV Plus Internet Browser with Web Picture-in-Picture, thereby having the option of watching television at the same time as they access the Internet. The potential for simultaneous consumption of two media channels here suggests the weakness of technology-based distinctions between the two.

The demarcations between these media channels are likely to disappear as merging technologies in the home make interactive television the norm. Now there are about 35 million online homes with access technology, but that number is expected to increase to nearly 57 million in 2002 (Tedesco, 1999, p. 24). Moreover, as consumers grow accustomed to video and audio on the Web sites they visit most frequently, and as technological advances diminish the barriers created by limited broadband carriage and poor computer monitor quality, long-form entertainment will be commonly available via the computer system alone, or projected on larger high density, high quality digital television screens. Family members will be able to access pay-per-view movies, along with other entertainment programs as well as electronic shopping originating with either television networks or the Internet on either their computer monitors or television screens.

In addition, new computerized scanning recorders can be attached to television sets. These personal video recorders (PVR) will scan all television programs available to a household for specific shows, content, personalities, or topics. The computer units, equivalent to hard disks, for example, ReplayTV (introduced in 1999 for about $700 to $1,500) and Tivo (for about $500 to $1,200), find and record the user selected items for playback at the convenience of the individual or family making the selection. The unit can store between 14 and 20 hours of programming and can "record many shows at the same time" (Carter, 1999, p. C1). Consumers can then connect their traditional VCR to the PVR to build video libraries. In effect, these devices enable the viewer to function as the programmer. Cable and broadcast channels provide the programs, but viewer goals and taste determine which programs will appear and when they will be viewed on a particular television set in a household.

There is much speculation about the effects PVRs will have on family viewing habits. Traditional channel surfers may find watching recorded programs somewhat confining. Those who hate commercials may find the ease of skipping them facilitated by the PVR a joy. This feature, however, has concerned all those dependent on sales for television's commercial operation, as well as the product and service advertisers. On the other hand, both ReplayTV and Tivo need investors and may compromise consumer interests in exchange for financial support. For example, "a senior PVR executive said his company had expressed a willingness to disable its commercial skipping capability in exchange for deals with networks and advertisers" (Carter, 1999, p. C4).

The possible effects of this technology on families' television viewing are broad. It may be that most in-home viewing will be of deliberately selected recorded programs, which would preclude chance or ill-considered exposure to programs inappropriate for children or to shows promoting values antithetical to those parents espouse. If the technology enables consumers to avoid commercials, we can expect more subtle in-program commercials and product placements as advertisers promote sales indirectly. In some respects, this approach may be more detrimental than the obvious commercial is. Adults and children alike have come to recognize the commercial's sales pitch for what it is. That identification will become more difficult for those children and adults who already have trouble distinguishing television fiction from documented fact as in-program product promotions further blur these distinctions.

It is likely that in the future, the PVR will be built into television sets. If this comes to pass, we can expect that the merging of technologies will alter once again how we define and use television. Although a few scholars have argued that most households around the world will never have access to computer technology (Lockard, 1997), Americans' passion for electronic toys makes it likely that here, at least, media systems will commonly include computer technology.

So what is television? For the purposes of examining the family's use of the medium in this chapter, I focus on the television consumption experience. A *television set* is the appliance available in 99.4% of American households (Nielsen, 1998), that, along with remote control devices, VCRs, programming devices, and any concomitant technologies, stimulates for any or all family members the home television experience instead of the sense of using a computer. Essential to the former experience might be some minimum physical distance between the viewer and the screen so that even if content is controlled by a single individual, image consumption could conceivably be shared. Most often the audio component of messages, at least those not limited to headphone reception, should facilitate shared listening. The American television viewing experience would also incorporate the opportunity for those watching to identify the purveyors of the content being consumed, although in-program placement of products could make that difficult to accomplish.

Perhaps most important, however, in this chapter, television consumption is regarded as one-way: Viewers can choose to view programs or portions of them, but can neither interact with message senders beyond casting an e-mail vote in a television poll nor technologically interact with video content. Interactive TV has been touted broadly, but it is not yet present in many homes. As Tedesco and Colman (1999) observed, interactive television has great potential, but it is a market "substantially short on development" (p. 11). Consequently, it is assumed here that television viewing permits choosing and rejecting television messages, but for most people, it does not technically facilitate true interactivity or the simultaneous manipulation and restructuring of minimal video units. However common interactivity will be in homes of the future, today most Americans find the television viewing experience as selective or passive, not interactive.

Rather than speculate about which medium dominates a video–computer hybrid in a given television exposure, I am assuming that media convergence and medium dominance are less important than the experience family members have when they view television. The viewing intentions of family members, as well as the social, emotional, and physical histories they bring to the viewing experience, mediate its outcomes.

Nonetheless, we need to note that what television content enters the home may be determined by the technological sophistication of both the media consumer and the equipment in the household. A television set today is not just a box with an on–off switch and channel changer. And those sets without cable or direct satellite access and lacking supplemental video recording and computerized programming options do not provide a full range of video choices.

Technical advances that merge television with the computer, however, may limit as well as expand the range of programs watched in a given household. Should a dominant family member use a PVR to personalize the media content that comes into the home, other family members may discover that their television options decrease.

A child's choices may be reduced by protective parental control and a programmable V-chip, "V" for the television violence the chip might exclude from the home environment. The chip, a federally mandated technology that reads codes attached to transmitted video material, enables parents to block reception of programs that the parents find inappropriate for child viewing. Fifty percent of television sets with 13-inch or larger screens sold after July 1, 1999, had to contain the V-chip. All new sets were to include the technology by January 2000 (McConnell, 1999).

All potential television content, then, may not be available to all family members. Our concern, therefore, is not with all the video options a family might have. *Television viewing* encompasses the watching and/or listening behavior that actually takes place in a household when an individual, alone or in the company of family members, chooses and attends to broadcast and cablecast messages appearing on a television monitor.

TELEVISION IN THE HOME

When television was first introduced in the United States and shortly thereafter became a necessary home appliance, it had a prominent status that dictated its location in the household. It took up residence in the 1950s in the home's "best" space, the living room, and then moved into its own domain, the family room, in the late 1950s, 1960s, and 1970s. Television sets subsequently proliferated as television transformed itself into an everywhere appliance (Andreasen, 1990). During the remainder of the century, bedrooms, kitchens, even occasional whirlpool-endowed bathrooms, made room for the set.

Accompanying and encouraging this appliance migration and proliferation, however, was a changing vision of the American home. As the nation's wealth increased, so did home ownership, rising from about 64% during the period between 1985 and 1994 to 66.3% in 1998 (Study: "U.S. Homeownership," 1999). With the increasing wealth of many homeowners, the maxim that an individual's home was his castle was applied almost literally. The size of the average American home grew from 1,100 square feet in the 1950s to 1,400 square feet in the 1970s to 2,000 square feet in the 1990s (de Graaf & Boe, 1997). Over the last generation, then, whereas family size decreased about 20%, house size increased about 50% (Pedersen, 1999). Greater living space, along with a move to three- and four-car garages, facilitated increased accumulation of objects and toys geared to the penchants and pastimes of individuals rather than the recreational interests of the entire family. The larger house also provided opportunities for family members to achieve privacy, not only for sleeping and bathing, but also for hobbies, entertainment, and personal pursuits. In such an environment, family members could separate, even avoid each other, much of the time.

The new residences—sometimes referred to as "tract mansions"—frequently incorporated activity zones into their designs. Master bedroom suites and children's wings were not uncommon, as family rooms gave way to the "adults' room" and the "kids' room." Interior designer Christopher Lowell observed on his syndicated television program *Interior Motives* that the family room had been "relegated to the kitchen" (April 6, 1999).

Media rooms were included in newer homes or added to older structures where spaces were made to accommodate "media centers." Thus, in addition to the many smaller and sometimes older television sets located in private or semiprivate areas of the home, Americans were beginning to recreate the "electronic hearth," so revered in the 1950s, in a central location. Now, however, the electronics provided multimedia contact and a central viewing screen far larger than television had formerly made available. Instead of the 19-inch screen common in 1980, Americans were more likely to purchase sets with screens in the 25- to 27-inch range, selling in 1999 at between $250 and $900. Also growing in popularity at the end of the century was stereo projection television with a screen 41 to 80 inches in size, available for $1,200 to $4,000 (Circuit City, 1999).

The most exciting innovation for home viewing, however, was the high definition digital television image. Providing a much sharper picture than formerly possible, but at a much higher cost—$5,000 to $7,000 for a home receiver ("HDTV arrives," 1999), this equipment accompanied the advance to digital broadcast signals mandated by the FCC, an operation in progress at the turn of the century. The home electronic hearth, in addition to the latest television digital technology, was likely to include computer, disc and cassette video and audio recording-playback equipment. The sophistication of options was limited only by market availability and by consumers' pocketbooks. Cable and direct satellite subscription, the latter competing more effectively with cable after January 1, 2002, when pending legislation will require satellite companies to carry local market signals, could ensure the broadest range of entertainment options (Albiniak, 1999a).

The well-outfitted media center in 1999 represented a major family expense. It provided an entertainment focus, however, that would be hard for family members to resist. Although program content could still be the strongest variable affecting where family members might view television, image and sound quality available at a technologically sophisticated home media center might once again draw family members together. But as Siepmann observed in 1950, sitting in the same room to view a television program does not a family make. Moreover, with almost three fourths of all television homes making room for two or more television sets and an average of 2.82 sets present in multiset households (Television Bureau of Advertising, Inc., 1996), watching a favorite program in isolation or with similarly aged siblings or peers was possible.

And such viewing might be preferable to watching a show chosen by another family member, even in an expensive media center. When fellow viewers are compulsive channel surfers, and one in-home study revealed that viewers using a remote control device averaged 36.6 channel changes per hour (Kaye & Sapolsky, 1997), viewing any vintage television set not controlled by another person is attractive. Cable service to a home provided the same broad program selection to all television sets in a household, and about two thirds of American television homes sub-scribed to cable (Nielsen, 1998).

Just as family members may differ from one another in program choice, they may also differ in their abilities to master electronic sys-tems. Although manufacturers simplified video control technology, it still challenges some viewers. Even with program codes appearing with pro-gram titles in television listings and with streamlined remote control devices, some individuals had difficulty programming their VCRs. Older persons with failing vision or arthritic hands were especially vulnerable to programming difficulties and preferred to view older but more familiar systems rather than new super video technology. We can assume, there-fore, that individual viewing of older television monitors in relatively pri-vate spaces coexists with group viewing of "the best set."

THE FAMILY ENTERING THE 21ST CENTURY

Beliefs regarding family values and political judgments about what con-stitutes a family continue to shape our sense of family structure. But demographic data demonstrate likewise that nostalgic definitions of fam-ily are not necessarily the basis for actual family units or for intrafamily interactions. In 1997, for example, 32% of families with children under 18 were headed by one parent, up from 28% in 1990, and 22% in 1980 (U.S. Bureau of the Census, 1998). Also in 1997, 5.5% of America's children lived in homes headed by a grandparent, up from 4.9% in 1992 (*Los Angeles Times* Syndicate, 1999). Moreover, at the end of the century, the marriage rate was 43% lower than it had been 40 years earlier. In 1996, at its lowest rate in recorded history, 49.7 marriages occurred per 1,000 unmarried women; in 1960, 87.5 marriages per 1,000 unmarried women had taken place (Fletcher, 1999).

For the purposes of this chapter, then, we accept a broad definition of *family*. Families are systems bound by ties of blood, law, or affection, and, like all systems, they require cohesiveness and adaptability for their survival. Because change is a constant, we assume that development and change occur both within the family and external to it, and that family members need to monitor, identify, and adjust to these alterations to maintain family function. Whatever the familial structure, the system must provide caring, protection, and intimacy for its members in order to buttress the unit's physical and emotional health and longevity (Schwartz & Scott, 1997).

Just as family structures were varied at the end of the 20th century, so also were families' ability to thrive. Family resilience was enhanced, however, by strong intrafamily communication, appropriate parental child-rearing skills, economic security, physical health, and limited external and internal stressors (Schwartz & Scott, 1997; Stafford & Bayer, 1993).

Within the family system, demands on parental time and resources have been particularly acute during the last two decades. Adults, many of them baby boomers, have found themselves in the "sandwich generation" (Roots, 1998). Attempting to care for their adolescent children, these adults simultaneously have tried to meet the needs of their own declining parents. A lengthened life span has provided older adults with more time as grandparents, but it has also strained their personal resources and left them needing their adult children's financial, emotional, and physical support. Meanwhile adolescence also lengthened. Children in their 20s were now less likely than in the past to have established their own families and to have settled into careers. Labeled by one commentator as the "boomerang generation," these young adults still sought support and nurturing from their parents (Okimoto, 1989).

Perhaps what has challenged families most, however, was the requirement that adults juggle employment and child-care roles. In 1977, fewer than half the employed males with children under 18 had employed spouses; by 1997, two thirds did. In 75% of dual-earner couples in 1997, both partners worked full-time, an increase from the 66% of 20 years earlier (Bond, Galinsky, & Swanberg, 1998, pp. 35–36). In 1997, almost 20% of employed workers were single parents (Bond et al., 1998, p. 30), and, in light of welfare reform provisions enacted in the 1990s, that percentage will continue to grow. The net result of these changes is that parents' homemaking and family nurturing accommodates an employer's schedule, and by the end of a work day, parental energy is frequently low. Bond et al.'s study (1998) reported that more than 25% of the employees surveyed said their jobs "often" or "very often" left them "emotionally drained," and 36% "often" or "very often" felt "used up" at the end of the workday (p. 7). Workers also reported that job stress affected their family life. They said the stress accounted for their coming home in a bad mood or left them too tired to do things with their families. More than onethird of workers interviewed reported that within the preceding 3 months, they had felt unable to cope with all they had to do (p. 59).

In spite of the overprogrammed nature of their lives, most respondents highly valued their families. Among the employed individuals interviewed in 1997, 85% reported they were "very satisfied" or "extremely satisfied" with their marriages or primary relationships, and 69% described themselves as "very satisfied" or "extremely satisfied" with family life (Bond et al., p. 61). The report of statistical data and surveys compiled by Rutgers University's National Marriage Project paints a gloomier portrait. These respondents were not limited to employed individuals, and their answers to questions regarding marital happiness revealed that such emotional satisfaction was declining. The percentage of married people reporting they were "very happy" in their marriages dropped from 53.5% between 1973 and 1976 to 37.8% in 1996 (Fletcher, 1999).

The Rutgers project uncovered another potentially negative trend. Whereas in the period immediately after World War II, 80% of the children grew up in homes with two biological parents, in 1996, only about 60% of children had that home environment (Fletcher, 1999). When two parents share childrearing chores, neither parent is so likely to be overwhelmed by the work. When one parent alone takes on all the tasks associated with homemaking and childrearing, children are likely to get less parental attention. They are, for example, less likely to be read to. They are more likely to have difficulty performing daily tasks, like eating and dressing, and if the single parent is a mother, 49% of them are likely to be living in poverty (Federal Interagency Forum on Child and Family Statistics, 1999, pp. 45, 57, 12). But we need not measure the success of family life in terms of vulnerabilities; we can instead consider marital longevity and the health and happiness of family members.

At the end of the 20th century, Americans regarded love and companionship as the primary reasons for marriage and family life. After love, a term with many meanings, (listed as the reason by 36% of respondents) and companionship (the reason given by 12%), the most common motivations for marriage listed in a survey published in 1991 were; desire for children (12%), happiness (9%), money (5%), habit or convenience (5%), and dependence (3%) (Patterson & Kim, 1991). Given the free choice that accompanies most Americans' decisions to marry and the nature of the reasons mentioned, we might expect marriages in the United States to be characterized by high levels of compatibility that would in turn encourage the unions' longevity.

Yet, a 1996 survey of respondents in 21 countries revealed that on a compatibility index, American couples demonstrated lower levels of compatibility than did their counterparts in Turkey, Spain, Nigeria, Ireland, and Sweden. Moreover, marriages in Japan, where compatibility scores were lowest, had high levels of longevity (Kristof, 1996). Perhaps a couple's expectations regarding a legal union are a better predictor of its persistence than is love or even compatibility.

There is not universal agreement on this point. Whereas some social critics believe that marriages fail because of a general moral decline that manifests itself in selfish behavior, an unwillingness to commit and assume responsibility for that commitment, others point to an erosion of the legal, social, and economic barriers to divorce (Glenn, 1993).

Most social critics nonetheless agree that unrealistic expectations of marriage contribute to disillusionment, and that wedding finery does not frame the relationship in terms of future marital responsibility. Increasing numbers of individuals are attempting to prevent that cause for marital disappointment by developing prenuptial contracts that specify not only the disposition of financial matters in case of divorce, but also establish rules of conduct for the marriage itself. Such a document and the communication required to compile it, some couples believe, will minimize marital conflict (Schwartz & Scott, 1997, pp. 205–206).

Whatever they expect of the legal union, most Americans marry at least once, although fewer Americans are marrying today than ever before, about 85% now compared with 94% in 1960 (Fletcher, 1999). Demographers assume that about half these marriages will last until one partner dies (Bedard, 1992; Fletcher, 1999).

There are some indications, however, that marriage may be less vulnerable to dissolution now than it was 20 years ago. First, the divorce rate, having climbed fairly steadily since the early 1960s, reached a plateau and even declined after the mid-80s (National Center for Health Statistics, 1995). Second, men and women are waiting longer to marry, the median age in 1998 for men being 26.7 years, and for women, 25. The median age at which men married in 1980 was 24.7 and in 1960, 22.8. Women in 1980 had a median age at marriage of 22; in 1960, it was 20.3 (U.S. Bureau of the Census, 1999). Older partners may enter marriage with greater maturity. Also, because the highest divorce rates occur among men 20 to 24 years of age and women 15 to 19 years of age, postponing marriage may not only increase the likelihood of a permanent unmarried state, but may also presage a continuation of the downward trend in the divorce rate.

Regardless of the age at which a couple marries, family life requires stamina. Just maintaining a household involves many chores, and research indicates that when both parties are employed, inequity in the division of household labor results in psychological distress for the partner doing the greater share. Bird (1999) reported that wives in her study were more likely than their husbands to be depressed and also to take credit for most of the housework; 70%, compared to the 36.7% husbands claimed to have done. The wives' employment status, however, also predicted distress. Full-time homemakers who did 80% of the housework were among the least distressed respondents (Bird, 1999).

The most important and perhaps riskiest task that a couple can take on, however, is the rearing of children. Parenting a very young child requires implementing strategies to ensure the child's health and safety. Parents are also responsible for teaching children society's rules and norms and for encouraging moral development. At all stages of a child's development, parents need to encourage in their offspring a spirit of cooperation and compliance, a response that too often seems elusive (Forehand, 1977). Eisenberg (1992), for example, found that conflict occurs between mothers and 4-year-olds an average of 1.5 times every 5 minutes.

Although children at other stages of development may be more compliant, teenagers' need for independence makes their efforts at writing their own life scripts particularly hard for parents. And teens recognize that parents may have trouble controlling adolescents, a fact that seemingly does not cheer them. When a U.S. House Education Subcommittee conducted hearings into juvenile violence in 1999 after two students killed 12 of their classmates and one teacher before committing suicide at Colorado's Columbine High School, one teen, a Columbine survivor, told the legislators that neither parents nor schools nor legislators could control high school students: "You cannot change or control teen behavior" (Adam Campbell, as cited in "Testimony," 1999). The speaker's demeanor indicated he was not heartened by his own words ("Testimony," 1999).

Perhaps more disconcerting, however, is the fact that parents may be too stressed themselves or too pressed for time to listen to and to understand well the adolescents they are attempting to mentor. Half the nation's 31 million teenagers, between 12 and 19 years old, have divorced parents, and almost twothirds have both parents employed outside the home (Kantrowitz & Wingert, 1999).

Not only do parents' busy schedules discourage intrafamily communication, but so also do the teens' own regimens. In addition to school, homework, part-time jobs, and monitoring younger siblings in their parents' absence, these teens are negotiating for social status with high-school peers. Nonetheless, they spend an average of 3½ hours alone daily. The combination of pressure and isolation may leave them angry and without mature guidance (Kantrowitz & Wingert, 1999). Ninety percent of Americans recently polled now say that parents are not spending enough time with their teens. And 56% of teens claim they have few sources of support that can help them avoid trouble (Adler, 1999). It would seem then that some of America's teens are floundering in spite of relative wealth and education.

Every generation has its own set of social rules and evolves its own jargon that may not be comprehensible to members of other age cohorts. Teenagers today, however, share a culture that is more highly encrypted than that of earlier age groups. Parents may find their children's music unintelligible, or even tasteless and violent. Parents under these circumstances may be unable or unwilling to work at translating the messages the music carries.

Increasingly, the consumption of all media is a solitary enterprise; families do not gather to share an evening with Lucy or the Waltons or Huxtables. Teenagers watch about 11 hours of television each week, and their program selections are not likely to coincide with their parents' choices. So today, when teen boys watch their favorite program, *The Simpsons,* and teen girls consume their most preferred fare, *Dawson's Creek* (Kantrowitz & Wingert, 1999, p. 39), they probably are not watching television with parents at their sides. This cultural segregation does little to promote family cohesiveness and mutual understanding. Co-director of the Institute on Violence and Destructive Behavior in Oregon, Hill Walker, observed that children now live in "almost a virtual reality without adults" (Leland, 1999, p. 45). And much of that virtual reality is unfamiliar to parents. As one teenager noted, "TVs raise children now more than parents do. . ." (Leland, 1999, p. 46). Parents who neither know their children nor the media they consume have little opportunity to recognize symptoms of trouble, to prevent viewing of inappropriate programs, or to intervene in antisocial or destructive responses to media exposure.

It would be a mistake, however, to assume that parents are able to apply omnipotent interventions in dealing with their children. The family is not a unidirectional system. Children do affect the behavior of their parents, just as parents influence the development of children. Stafford and Bayer (1993) described the internal working of the family system in terms of communication patterns that constitute a "spiral of recursive feedback loops" (p. 122). And researchers, classifying family systems on the basis of their dominant communication and behavior patterns, observed that most family systems provide for child intercession as well as parental intervention, thereby disallowing a simple unidirectional family model (Chaffee, McLeod, & Atkin, 1971; Fitzpatrick, Marshall, Leutwiler, & Krcmar, 1996; Krcmar, 1998; Ritchie, 1991). Regardless of the internal norms families establish, however, they are subject to the exigencies of social forces. The boundaries of the "recursive feedback loops" extend beyond the household, so that the family is not an island unto itself.

When we take for granted, though, that the images we see on television accurately represent the world beyond the home, we could be wrong. The social reality television presents, even in news and public affairs programs, may create a false impression. If, for example, we were to draw conclusions about the juvenile crime rate or the number of child victims of criminal violence from television's attention to such events during the first half of 1999, we would surmise that never before had there been so much juvenile crime in the United States. In fact, the rate reached a peak in 1993 (Federal Interagency Forum on Child and Family Statistics, 1999, p. 40). And whereas the media producers concentrated on youth violence, they had less time for other events that would affect family life.

Actual pressures from outside the family system then and subsequently include the state of the economy, quality of education available to children of all ages, community values, and employment opportunities. Public policy that affects taxes, human rights, and health care affects families. In the aftermath of violent episodes in schools across the country, Americans in 1999 also considered how regulation of media content and guns could affect families. Too often, though, the world portrayed on television was an environment that seemed unresponsive to familial needs. And that environment was making its presence felt in the family system every day as media messages presenting fact and fantasy flooded into private and public spaces in American homes.

But in spite of television violence, most teens neither rejected their parents nor held them hostage. And most adolescents inspired parental and community pride. These children, too, had access to media and were exposed to television's version of reality. Are we mistaken then to argue that television has been responsible for weakening family ties? Perhaps. But more media channel options targeted to age and interest-specific audiences have encouraged a narrow viewer focus and have discouraged awareness of other group's needs and goals. Age gaps were difficult to overcome when family members shared knowledge and values. But when media use discouraged the sharing of message content and instead promoted loyalty to social cohorts outside the family system or to values antithetical to those parents held, familial communication was likely to suffer.

TELEVISION IMAGES AND THEIR EFFECTS ON FAMILIES

Since the Surgeon General's report *Television and Behavior: Ten Years of Scientific Progress and Implications for the Eighties* (Pearl, Bouthilet, & Lazar, 1982) appeared, Americans have had reason to believe that television violence could prompt children's aggressive behavior. In addition to the theoretical bases for such a belief provided by Bandura's social learning theory and Gerbner's proposition that heavy television viewers would adopt a social reality that reflects the skewed world portrayed on television (Bandura, 1994; Gerbner, Gross, Morgan, & Signorielli, 1986), we have had a compilation of significant research data. Specific studies documented in the 1982 report demonstrated the effects television had on children. Since then, few scholars have been willing to attribute specific violent acts to viewing particular television programs, but researchers have associated rowdy and aggressive activity with children's previous viewing of violent television content and have observed that such aggressive behavior can become a life-long pattern ("National Television Violence Study," 1994–1995, p.4).

For a long time, parents have been concerned about violent portrayals on television, but they have also worried about presentations of promiscuous and unsafe sexual behavior as well as sexually suggestive language. If any persons thought that the V-chip mandate might encourage the industry to censor itself, they were wrong. After the advent of the V-chip, program content did not improve. In fact, the Parents Television Council's examination of network program content revealed that in November 1998, sexual references and rude language had increased (Knight Ridder Newspapers, 1999). The V-chip might help parents prevent objectionable content from appearing on specific television screens in the home, but it did little to improve the content of programs in general.

Parents may be a little less anxious about sexual content now than in the past because their concern of late has focused more clearly on violence. In May 1999, the National Institute on Media and the Family released research findings that showed for the first time that parents worried more about the amount of violence their children encountered on television and in movies and video games (81%) than about the amount of sexual content to which children were exposed (Gentile, 1999).

Regardless of the level of concern parents felt, in most homes, television was available and was used much of the time. Data from the National Institute on Media and the Family have shown that 40% of families always or often had the set turned on during meals. And 38% of respondents said that their children could watch television in their own bedrooms (Gentile, 1999).

There was, moreover, a correlation between children's school performance and the time the television set was on in the household. Children who did poorly in schools more often came from families where the television set was on during meals, or the set was on for greater periods of time even when no one was watching. On the other hand, children who watched less television than the national average of 25 hours per week were more successful in school, as were children who engaged in family games or other activities that did not involve electronic media (Gentile, 1999).

Children's sense of well-being is also affected by exposure to television. As researchers like Joanne Cantor have learned more about the frightening effects of television images on children at various stages of development, parents have had new reason to worry. Decades of nightmares and self-protective behaviors can follow exposure to graphically portrayed violence (Cantor, 1998).

Given the hundreds of scholarly studies that justify concerns about television's effects on children, many found it hard to understand the May 1999 presidential order for a joint Federal Trade Commission and Justice Department probe to examine the causes of juvenile violence and the role of the media in developing antisocial or violent behavior problems (Albiniak, 1999b). The President's call seemed unnecessary to some because so much data had already been collected ("Many researchers say link is already clear. . .," 1999).

In spite of the decline in juvenile crime, the 1998–1999 rash of school shootings and the extensive television coverage of events at Columbine High School sounded alarms. From April 20 into June 1999, the nation mourned, attributed blame, and demanded action. In addition to prompting the President's mandate for research, these killings gave rise to public dialog on television and radio talk shows, Internet chat rooms, newspaper editorial pages, as well as to conversation in bars and on buses across America. A nation obsessed with presidential impeachment, sexual scandal, and war in Yugoslavia only a few months earlier now focused on its children.

In the process, many sought culprits to take responsibility for the violence. Blame was directed primarily at parents, schools, the entertainment industry, and the National Rifle Association. Although neurological exams of adults with histories of violent episodes of rage showed that 36% of the perpetrators have minimal brain dysfunction, and in spite of biological factors' link to "elevated aggression" (Kashani & Allan, 1998, p. 6), few commentators attempted to link the tragedy to the killers' biology or genetic makeup. So also little was said about the accessibility and effectiveness of mental health care in this country. Instead, following the Colorado shootings, the airwaves rang with simple analyses and single-focus solutions: Irresponsible media had portrayed violent behavior for children to emulate; gun lobbies had fought gun control and thereby allowed the easy distribution of weapons to children; parents had not properly controlled their children, and those who hadn't should be punished; student massacres could not occur in properly secured schools, and so the country needed increased police monitoring of schools and metal detectors in school buildings. In many ways, these reactions provided a case study of a public's sense of impotence in a situation that required comprehension and solution.

As television coverage of the national debate over juvenile violence continued during May and June 1999, certain themes involving media recurred: Television portrayal of violence was rampant; antisocial behavior and crime stories were featured in both television news and entertainment programs; both television channels and TV sets had proliferated so widely that it was difficult, if not impossible, for parents to monitor viewing behavior; and no matter how much television viewing encouraged violent behavior, children's use of the Internet might pose an even greater risk.

Although the Internet has been criticized in the past for the adult content it made available to children, the fact that the teenage Colorado killers had access to recipes for bombs on Websites now focused attention on and criticism of this telecommunications medium along with television and movies. First, children's solitary Internet use was difficult to monitor, and the content of the Websites children consulted was not neatly presented for parental perusal in a newspaper schedule along with television listings. But parents' inability to monitor Internet consumption might not be the medium's greatest threat. What could make Internet use more dangerous than television, in spite of large television screens that can bring blood and fury into our homes, is the manner in which we consume the two media.

We still talk about "watching television." Even when we empathize with characters in television presentations, we are spectators. And as television has become so common in our households, we attend to it in the way we attend to most other phenomena in our lives—piecemeal. We have become a nation of "multitaskers" (Weeks, 1999). For a long time, we've observed that people try to do two or three things at once (Robinson, 1977). Now, though, technology is leading us along that path. We consume media as we perform many other tasks: We wake up to clock radios that force us to process information before we brush our teeth; we eat breakfast as we pack school lunches and watch Katie Couric question the President. And in the process, we learn to shift mental gears quickly. The problem is not simply that we have too many chores to perform in the time available, although that, too, is the case. Paul LeBlanc, president of Vermont's Marlboro College, attributes this attentional style to the "velocity of information" we have to process and to the technology that beams this information to us. The need to absorb and make sense of so much information from so many sources "makes it harder to process sequentially" (Weeks, 1999).

It is most likely that juggling tasks and media content prevents our heavy investment for a long period of time in any one activity, person, or situation. Deutsch argued that such juggling "limits our social interactions in the world" (Weeks, 1999). We are focused on our own thought processes and on specific chores, not on persons or ideas that transcend those tasks. The formats of commercial American television, moreover, prevent continuous sequential processing; commercials interrupt story lines and shift viewer focus. Thus, television viewing involves tuning in and out; the screen's images thereby have less power to obsess the viewer.

Using a personal computer, on the other hand, tends to be a solitary enterprise, often occurring in spaces that preclude interactions with family members. The solitary PC user experiences few distractions. Although multitasking is a computer operation, the individual accessing information sources must do so in a sequential manner. The computer, in other words, invites concentration and persistence and may, consequently, produce an effect more intense than that of television.

Video games, though, may be the most affecting medium because they require attention and involvement. Violent games like "Doom" and "Mortal Kombat" require a particularly toxic kind of involvement; winning depends on killing figures representing opponents. Here the player is not merely a spectator, but he or she actually perpetrates the violent or lethal act, only on the screen to be sure. But playing the game encourages focus and an emotional commitment to win. This sort of consumption behavior is more involving than that generally occurring when television programs are "watched." Even violent programs on large screens do not direct children to participate as virtual killers.

Television viewing on its own, however, can have negative effects. It is an addictive behavior for a portion of the population (McIlwraith, 1998). And children are likely to remain inactive as they watch the screen, sufficiently so that in 1999, the Surgeon General of the United States concluded that television viewing is hazardous to children's health because it contributes to obesity (Associated Press, 1999). Children's time spent with television, however, has declined. A University of Michigan Panel study reported that boys and girls in 1997 watched 1½ hours on weekdays, a drop from 2 hours each weekday in 1981. Boys' weekend viewing in 1997 was just over 2½ hours daily, whereas in 1981, they viewed 3 hours per day on weekends. Girls' daily weekend viewing in 1997 was just under 2½ hours, an increase from 2 hours in 1981 (Panel Study of Income Dynamics, 1998). The reason for this shift seems to have less to do with children's disenchantment with television programs than it does with the fact that children are now spending more time in school and other structured environments. With more mothers in the workforce, children's days are more tightly programmed, with the result that children in 1997 had less free time than in 1981; it dropped from 40% to 25% of the child's day (Panel Study of Income Dynamics, 1998).

With fewer hours of viewing, children were nonetheless exposed to video violence. An analysis of television programs for 1994–1995 revealed that 57% of programs contained violence, and one third of these included nine or more violent interactions. In one fourth of these encounters, a gun was used. Perhaps most disturbing, though, is that plot contexts for violent action did not punish the perpetrators of violence (National Television Violence Study, 1998), Bandura's learning theory suggests that children can surmise that behavior that is punished should be avoided, but in a world where cruelty or violence is unpunished, bad behavior may seem admirable. When the perpetrator is attractive, the child might even conclude that punishment would be inappropriate. If the context of violent episodes suggests that the end justifies the means or that the recipient of the violence "deserves what he got," viewers are more likely to perceive violence as a norm and are also more likely to behave aggressively after exposure to the message (Krcmar, 1998; Paik & Comstock, 1994).

Research has shown, moreover, that when children see and focus on difficult negative consequences that follow poor decisions and high-risk behavior, they are inclined to avoid acts associated with such penalties. The study, undertaken by researchers at the University of California–Santa Barbara in conjunction with Court TV, AT&T, and AOL-Time Warner, compiled video clips of court cases involving teenagers and showed them to children in randomly chosen California classrooms. The exposure was accompanied by assignments in writing and class discussion. Before-and-after tests revealed that viewing the clips and participating in the ancillary activities correlated with changed attitudes and behavior. UCSB researcher Barbara Wilson noted that this "Choices and Consequences" curriculum "reduced middle school kids' teasing, swearing and getting into fights with other kids" (Albiniak & McConnell, 1999, p. 17). The results illustrate that children who see punishment associated with antisocial behavior tend to avoid such behavior. Although viewing television at home is different from watching video at school, the similarities are great enough for us to be concerned about television messages that fail to relate poor decisions to their negative consequences.

Even programs that are nonviolent, however, give children too little benefit for the time they invest. The Annenberg Public Policy Center of the University of Pennsylvania, tracking children's television since 1996, observed that there are 12% more programs aimed at children now than in 1998, but that about 21% of children's fare has little or no educational value. In prime time hours, when children are most likely to watch television, only 6% of programs for children are available. It is no surprise, then, that parents have indicated enthusiasm for the V-chip: A large majority (84.1%) "strongly" or "somewhat" favor the technology, and 51.4% say they would use the V-chip "often" (McQueen, 1999).

The new technology will not eliminate the larger problem posed by the manner in which society treats its villains. One of the results of real malevolent and brutal behavior in America today is media attention. Violence confers fame upon aggressors. It is possible that some teenagers, enticed by the "romance of risk," may view antisocial behavior as a means to establishing an identity and gaining personal recognition (Erikson, 1968; Ponton, 1997). As Kantrowitz and Wingert (1999) observed, although "teenagers may claim they want privacy . . . they also crave and need attention . . ." (p. 38). If violent acts and antisocial behavior attract media coverage, and media recognition accords status, adolescents do not need to look far for publicized and violent role models. With exposure to television's presentation of successful aggressors, a few teenagers, feeling alone, anonymous, and impotent, may explore a violent path to personal identity and social recognition. Too often, no one in or outside those adolescents' families diagnoses signals of potential violence in time to prevent it.

Perhaps, then, we should not be surprised that in the 4 weeks following the Columbine High School tragedy and the massive media coverage attending it, an *Education Week* analysis showed more than 350 students were arrested on "charges related to threats against schools, school officials, or their classmates . . . . at least 30 incidents involved an actual bomb or weapon" (Drummond & Portner, 1999). In hundreds of other cases, schools were closed or routines disrupted by threats of violence. Although school officials and police may have been more alert after the Littleton tragedy than ever before to minimal indicators of potential trouble in schools nationwide, the educators interviewed reported that they could not recall another month in which so many threats occurred (Drummond & Portner, 1999). Whatever the motivation of these would-be offenders, they gained their knowledge most probably from television, and copied media-publicized violent acts.

These events suggest that children are vulnerable to negative role models viewed on television, and that parents need to monitor children's exposure to such content. When the viewing is accompanied by Internet access, parents may need to intervene in their children's computer use also. Internet contacts that promote the negative role models children have seen on television may buttress the penchant to copy antisocial behavior in much the way that writing and discussion supported the messages regarding self-control children acquired in the "Choices and Consequences" program reported earlier.

TELEVISION AND CULTURE

Just as television technology needs to be examined in the context of family life and the telecommunications environment, so also television program content deserves analysis in the context of cultural values. As political figures and religious leaders attempted to define the moral landscape at the end of the century, current events and these new definitions provided the general public with conflicting messages. All sides, however, argued for the responsibility of families to instill virtue and self-discipline in children. And parents, perplexed about how to accomplish that end, nonetheless, sought to achieve it.

A lot of parental concern about television had been mobilized in the 1990s in advocacy for the V-chip, and during this decade, parents also strongly supported antitobacco, antialcohol, and antiillicit drug campaigns. The problems that substance abuse could cause the entire family were clear, and although some might disagree about the best ways to counter these ills, there was little disagreement about their negative effects.

But in 1998 and 1999, social problems seemed out of control, and, more important, their etiology was unclear. It was possible to blame cigarette manufacturers' profit motive for the promotion of cigarettes to young people, but untangling the causes for the misuse of the Internet or for children killing children or for parents' inability to parent was much harder. The issues seemed more complex, and the sides were not neatly delineated. The result was broad, public disagreement about what the nation's problems were and about how to solve them. The political face of these "culture wars" became apparent during President Clinton's impeachment hearings in the winter of 1998–1999 as television and public radio carried live and taped accounts and denouncements of presidential misbehavior. If parents were confused about how to maintain family cohesiveness and adaptability earlier in the decade, television talk shows during this period probably did not help.

Television provided the backdrop against which much of this cultural battle was waged. Culture was not neatly defined by ethnic background or socioeconomic status as in the past (Martin & Flores, 1998). Although age could be a critical predictor of culture club membership (e.g., "baby boomer," "Generation-Xer"), cultural groups were more likely to be defined by a set of values, by religious beliefs, or by specific dress codes and interpersonal styles. Whatever differences separated even small groups were no longer played out on in private, but also gained media exposure and longevity. With a greater number of television channels having time to fill and competing with one another, prickly opinions could be viewed most times of the day and night. During the presidential impeachment hearings and following the Colorado school shootings, television commentators, citizens, and legislators criticized specific popular values, parental styles, and media presentations for national divisions as well as for antisocial behavior.

Families that could use these television exposés as an impetus to a discussion of the family's own values may well have benefited from the events. But the tone of much of the media presentations was confrontational and even hostile. Although parents, not children, were the primary consumers of this television content, there is reason to believe that parents could be affected. The programs communicated at least two negative assumptions. First, the expression of anger is permissible, even admirable. Programs, like *The Capitol Gang*, did little to teach the anger management skills sorely needed at the end of the century, nor did they encourage public civility. Second, distinctions between genuine debate and frivolous entertainment are unimportant. With both television personalities and public servants demonstrating combative behavior, the differences between real emotion and that produced for television audience appeal had already grown hazy. As entertainers like Ronald Reagan, Sonny Bono, and professional wrestler Jesse Ventura had been elected to public office, Americans may have come to expect flare to accompany political acumen.

Although the audience for controversy and confrontation was large, most media consumers were wary of talk-show conflict that became physically violent. *The Jerry Springer Show,* for example, attracted attention from and disapproval by the Chicago City Council when program content escalated from verbal abuse to physical assault.

When legislators and families considered televised violence, they did so primarily in terms of its impact on children, not on adults. Congress, ignoring the many and varied contributors to a violent society, sought to eliminate violence by considering legislation that would protect children and affect two cultural staples; guns and the media. Media industry supporters argued that it was not the media presentations themselves, but rather children's access to them, that might be problematic. In a flurry of Washington hearings televised during May and June of 1999 by C-Span and covered with varying degrees of thoroughness by other television outlets, the U.S. Senate and Congress promoted various solutions. Offerings that would change the status quo, however, had little success at that time. Sen. Ernest Hollings (D-NC), for example, proposed a bill that would have delayed violent television programs to late night hours so that children might watch nonviolent television during their primary viewing hours. The Hollings measure was defeated (Albiniak, 1999b).

One of the more colorful speakers in these debates was Rep. Tom DeLay (R-Tex.) who argued that "broken homes," along with television, video games, day care, birth control, and abortion were responsible for the nation's malaise. Not a single-issue man, Rep. DeLay even went on to implicate classroom presentations of the theory of evolution in the problem, as he sought to weaken proposals to make gun acquisition more difficult.

DeLay conceded that winning the culture war was a very important goal, although key House votes in June 1999 had ostensibly dealt with regulating media content and strengthening gun control: "Culture won . . ." as media regulation and stricter gun control lost (Henneberger, 1999). A "culture vote" that DeLay and most of the Congress supported was one granting schools federal permission to post the Ten Commandments, a move of dubious constitutionality that provided even more dubious protection against juvenile violence. Whereas for some, the foundation of these culture wars was clearly political, DeLay attributed the success of his side to a concern about values progressing from the Presidential impeachment, which he helped to engineer (Henneberger, 1999). DeLay's success, however, probably had less to do with the genuine soundness of his arguments than it did with his appearance, both in front of a Congressional audience and on camera. He was a television personality.

The style of the culture wars made them prime television commodities. Talk shows that gleaned ratings from adversarial bickering gave air time to the contenders. *Rivera Live*, for example, in a program focusing on juvenile violence pitted USC law professor Susan Estrich, who argued for early intervention, gun control, and a strengthening of the juvenile justice system, against Liberty University Chancellor Jerry Falwell, who supported the posting of everyone's version of the Ten Commandments and more youth ministers to guide teenagers (June 22, 1999). The importance of the issues and the celebrity of the players on these nationally presented, confrontational talk shows may have given televised bickering greater respectability. Yet, the combatants wore makeup, and the battle was a television production. In 1999, regardless of the topic, the show went on.

If we accord credence to Bandura's social learning model and ask what lessons televised conflict, whether verbal or physical, might teach children as well as adults, we can conclude that all could learn that putting the opponent down is the way to win and that winning is everything. Some might argue that this was a lesson taught by political debates decades ago or by situation comedies like *Roseanne*, but the more recent television battles seemed focused on seamier behavior and more personal issues.

American society may encourage rough and even hard-hearted modes of problem solving, but in earlier periods, the citizenry was shocked and mobilized by television glimpses of the violence visited upon civil rights proponents in the South and upon Vietnam nationals in our most unpopular war. Today, however, ratings for television wrestling are climbing, and reports of road rage are common. And neither fantasy violence nor real mayhem seems to inspire much social protest. We might need to ask whether televised confrontation has made society as a whole insensitive to the differences between genuine violence and conflict that is merely theatrical.

When in 1998 the Federal Communications Commission implemented the coding system for television programs to guide parents in choosing acceptable programs for children, that system included a distinction between "fantasy violence" and "violence." A May 1999 survey done by the National Institute on Media and the Family revealed that 57% of parents did not understand all of the television ratings symbols (Gentile, 1999), but labels like "violence" and "fantasy violence" suggest that the categories themselves are fuzzy. We have assumed that young children have trouble distinguishing reality from television fiction, but that older children can. Yet, as reality takes on the terror of the horror movie, as the United States increases efforts to find life in outer space, as the *X-Files'* quirky view of reality entices young and old alike, we may have to reevaluate society's ability to distinguish between television's fantasy portrayals and its documentation of events of the day. If we cannot be sure that society as a whole makes such clean distinctions, we may be assuming too much when we expect parents to teach their children to differentiate between the imaginary and the real.

What is perhaps more perplexing than television's modeling of negative behavior, however, is the set of programs purporting to portray virtue. Whereas, in fact, problem solving may involve painful concessions and intelligent anger management, television rarely portrays such struggles. Difficulties are instead resolved by the touch of an angel. The endearing characters in *Seventh Heaven* are a happily married couple with six beautiful children. The mother is not employed outside the home; the father is a minister; the children are all healthy and smart; and sweet reason wins the day. This ideal family has great audience appeal, but its virtue may be hard for many children to find or replicate in their own experience, in spite of the program's willingness to deal with genuine social issues. Fantasy virtue is an insufficient model for real families in an imperfect world.

Television presentations, even the news, have always relied on a narrative line. Yet, it has been and continues to be important for viewers to be able to distinguish fact from fiction, real virtue from "let's pretend," and the possibilities for heroic behavior from easy fixes. Television, along with its technological concomitants, can create a "virtual realty" for American families, but producers of television programs and Internet messages might do better to consider real families along with real virtue.

These concerns, however, need to be viewed in light of the many fears associated with television over the last half century. For much of this time, social critics have worried about the effects of the medium's presentation of violence and sex, its promotion of material values, as well as its potential for addiction (Andreasen, 1990). Contemporary families have the means to both reap the possible benefits of television and avoid its negative consequences. But to do so, families need to remain alert to the medium's changing content and its evolving role in the household. As television programming and technology increasingly satisfy narrow audience segments and appeal to sectarian values, parents will have to identify and choose program content that embodies the family's culture, bonds family members, and presents issues honestly.

CONCLUSION

Television is an electronic medium that we can increasingly control with the aid of the V-chip and the PVR. We may even be able to affect the medium's evolution. In the past, technology was invented, promoted, and sold to consumers. But television in its new media context will lend itself to a variety of uses and users. It can now accede to the purposes of individual families and evolve with concomitant technology in accord with family media consumption goals and behavior. Parents can examine the role they desire for communications technology in the family system and use a PVR or any other media components to create the information and entertainment package deemed best for the family. Although the marketplace may promote the acquisition of new communications technology, no family is compelled to adopt every innovation any more than it is required to consume media messages that undermine family strengths. In the future, media centers and their use could well evolve in the home to meet individual families' specific needs.

A family needs assessment will have to direct this evolutionary process. When parents are stressed or children are lonely or angry, television, however much it amuses or informs, does not eliminate these problems. Intrafamily communication may help, and well-chosen television messages may give some impetus to that communication. Parents, considering family needs, are in a position to determine how television and ancillary technologies might contribute to the family's culture and well-being.

REFERENCES

Adler, J. (1999, May 10). The truth about high school. *Newsweek*, pp. 56–58.

Albiniak, P. (1999a). Sat TV gets closer to local. *Broadcasting & Cable, 129*(22), 11.

Albiniak, P. (1999b). Washington demands answers. *Broadcasting & Cable 129*(21), 22–26.

Albiniak, P., & McConnell, B. (1999). Washington watch: TV teaches consequences. *Broadcasting & Cable, 129*(29), 17.

Andreasen, M. (1990). Evolution in the family's use of television: Normative data from industry and academe. In J. Bryant (Ed.), *Television and the American family* (pp. 3–55). Hillsdale, NJ: Lawrence Erlbaum Associates.

Associated Press. (1999, April 23). Surgeon General: Turn off TV, it's unhealthy. *The Capital Times*, p. 10A.

Bandura, A. (1994). Social cognitive theory of mass communication. In J. Bryant & D. Zillmann (Eds.), *Media effects* (pp. 61–90). Hillsdale, NJ: Lawrence Erlbaum Associates.

Bedard, M. (1992). *Breaking with tradition: Diversity, conflict, and change in contemporary American families*. Dix Hills, NY: General Hall.

Bird, C. (1999). Gender, household labor, and psychological distress: The impact of the amount and division of housework. *Journal of Health and Social Behavior, 40*(1), 32–45.

Bond, J., Galinsky, E., & Swanberg, J. (1998). *The 1997 national study of the changing workforce*. New York: Families and Work Institute.

Campbell, A. (1999, May 4). *Testimony before the U.S. House Education Subcommittee.* C-Span.

Cantor, J. (1998). *Mommy, I'm scared.* New York: Harcourt Brace.

Carter, B. (1999, July 5). Will this machine change television? *The New York Times,* pp. C1, C4.

Chaffee, S., McLeod J., & Atkin, C. (1971). Parental influences on adolescent media use. *American Behavioral Scientist, 14,* 323–340.

Circuit City, *Television: Compare prices* Online. Available: www.circuitcity.com.

de Graaf, J., & Boe, V. (Producers). (1997). *Affluenza* [videotape]. (Available from Public Broadcasting & KCTS Television, Portland, OR)

Drummond, S., & Portner, J. (1999, May 26). Arrests top 350 in threats, bombscares. *Education Week, 18*(37), 1, 12–13.

Eisenberg, A. (1992). Conflicts between mothers and their young children. *Merrill-Palmer Quarterly, 38,* 21–43.

Erikson, E. (1968). *Identity: Youth and crisis.* New York: Norton.

Federal Interagency Forum on Child and Family Statistics. (1999). *America's children: key national indicators of well-being, 1999.* Washington, DC: U.S. Government Printing Office.

Fitzpatrick, M., Marshall, L., Leutwiler, T., & Krcmar, M. (1996). The effect of family communication environments on children's social behavior during middle childhood. *Communication Research, 23*(4), 379–406.

Fletcher, M. (1999, July 2). Fewer getting married nowadays. *The Capital Times,* pp. 1A, 14A.

Forehand, R. (1977). Child noncompliance to parental requests: Behavior analysis and treatment. In M. Hersen, R. M. Eisler, & P. M. Miller (Eds.), *Progress in behavior modification* (Vol. 5, pp. 111–247). New York: Academic Press.

Gentile, D. (1999, May 6). *MediaQuotient [tm] study reveal relationship between family media habits and school performance, attitude, behavior* [Online]. Available: www.mediafamily.org

Gerbner, G., Gross, L., Morgan, M., & Signorielli, N. (1986). Living with television: The dynamics of the cultivation process. In J. Bryant & D. Zillmann (Eds.), *Perspectives on media effects* (pp. 17–40). Hillsdale, NJ: Lawrence Erlbaum Associates.

Glenn, N. D. (1993, May). What's happening to American marriage? *USA Today Magazine,* p. 10.

HDTV arrives. (1999, March). *Consumer Reports,* pp. 13–16.

Henneberger, M. (1999, June 21). Tom DeLay holds no gavel, but a firm grip on the reins [Online]. Available: www.nytimes.com

Kantrowitz, B., & Wingert, P. (1999, May 10). How well do you know your kid? *Newsweek,* pp. 36–40.

Kashani, J., & Allan, W. (1998). *The impact of family violence on children and adolescents.* Thousand Oaks, CA: Sage.

Kaye, B., & Sapolsky, B. (1997). Electronic monitoring of in-home television RCD usage. *Journal of Broadcasting & Electronic Media, 41*(2), 214–215.

Knight Ridder Newspapers. (1999, May 30). Objectionable content rose after TV ratings began. *Wisconsin State Journal,* p. 4F.

Krcmar, M. (1998). The contribution of family communication patterns to children's interpretations of television violence. *Journal of Broadcasting & Electronic Media, 42*(2), 250–264.

Kristof, N. (1996, February 11). Who needs love? In Japan many couples don't. *The New York Times,* p. A6.

Leland, J. (1999, May 10). The secret life of teens. *Newsweek,* pp. 45–50.

Lockard, J. (1997). Progressive politics, electronic individualism and the myth of virtual community. In D. Porter (Ed.), *Internet culture* (pp. 219–232). New York: Routledge.

Los Angeles Times Syndicate. (1999, July 1). Number of kids raised by grandparents grows. *The Capital Times,* p. 12A.

Lowell, C. (Host & Creative Consultant). (1999). *Interior Motives* [television program]. In W. G. Longstore Productions, Inc. & All American Television (Producers), Bethesda, MD: Discovery Communications, Inc.

Many researchers say link is already clear media and youth violence. (1999, May 10). [Online]. Available: www.intelihealth.com

Martin, J., & Flores, L. (1998). Colloquy: Challenges in contemporary culture and communication research. *Human Communication Research, 25*(2), 293–299.

McConnell, B. (1999). Gore presses for V-chip use. *Broadcasting & Cable, 129*(18), 19, 22.

McIlwraith, R. (1998). "I'm addicted to television": The personality, imagination and TV watching patterns of self-identified TV addicts. *Journal of Broadcasting & Electronic Media, 42*(3), 371–386.

McQueen, A. (1999, June 28). Study questions value of kids' TV. *Wisconsin State Journal,* p. 1A.

National Center for Health Statistics. (1995). Advance report of final divorce statistics, 1989 and 1990. *Monthly vital statistics report, 43*(9). Rockville, MD: Author.

National television violence study, 1994–1995: Executive Summary. (1998) Studio City, CA: Mediascope, Inc.

Nielsen Media Research, Inc. (1998, September). *U.S. TV household estimates.* Northbrook, IL: A.C. Nielsen Company.

Okimoto, J. (1989). *Boomerang kids.* New York: Pocket Books.

Paik, H., & Comstock, G. (1994). The effects of television violence on anti-social behavior: A meta-analysis. *Communication Research, 21,* 516–546.

Panel Study of Income Dynamics. (1998). Children's time, *Child Development Supplement.* Ann Arbor, MI: University of Michigan Institute for Social Research.

Patterson, J., & Kim, P. (1991). *The day America told the truth: What people really believe about everything that really matters.* Englewood Cliffs, NJ: Prentice-Hall.

Pearl, D., Bouthilet, L., & Lazar, J. (Eds.), (1982). *Television and behavior: Ten years of scientific progress and implications for the eighties.* (DHHS Publication No. ADM 82-1196). Washington: U.S. Government Printing Office.

Pedersen, D. (1999, May 10). Lessons from Paducah. *Newsweek,* p.35.

Ponton, L. (1997). *The romance of risk.* New York: Basic Books.

Rathbun, E. (1999). Internet will be the only network, *Broadcasting & Cable, 129*(18), 43.

Ritchie, L. (1991). Family communication patterns: An epistemic analysis and conceptual reinterpretation. *Communication Research, 18,* 548–565.

Robinson, J. (1977). *How Americans use time.* New York: Praeger.

Roots, C. (1998). *The sandwich generation: Adult children caring for aging parents.* New York: Garland Publications.

Schwartz, M., & Scott, B. (1997). *Marriages & families: Diversity and change.* Upper Saddle River, NJ: Prentice-Hall.

Siepmann, C. (1950). *Radio, television and society.* New York: Oxford University Press.

Stafford, L., & Bayer, C. (1993). *Interaction between parents and children.* Newberry Park, CA: Sage.

Study U.S. homeownership hit 66% in '98. (1999, June 21). *L.A. Times* [online]. Available: www.latimes.com

Tedesco, R. (1999). Who'll control the video streams? *Broadcasting & Cable, 129*(10), 20–24.

Tedesco, R., & Colman, P. (1999) AOL invades TV sets. *Broadcasting & Cable, 129*(21), 11.

Television Bureau of Advertising, Inc. (1996). *Trends in television* [pamphlet]. New York: Author.

Television: Compare prices. (Online). Circuit City.

Testimony before the U.S. House Education Subcomittee. (1999, May 4). Washington, DC: C-SPAN.

U.S. Bureau of the Census. (1998). Current population reports. In *Statistical Abstract of the United States* (p. 65). Washington, DC: U.S. Department of Commerce.

U.S. Bureau of the Census. (1999, January 7). Estimated median age at first marriage, by sex: 1890 to the present. *Current population reports* (Series P200–514).

United States Department of Commerce, Economic & Statistics Administration, U.S. Census Bureau, the Official Statistics. *Grandparents raising grandchildren* [Online]. Available: http://www.census.gov/press-release/cb98-ff.10.html [1998, September 3]

Weeks, L. (1999, June 4). Multi-tasking: Are we forgetting something? *The Capital Times*, p. 3D.

II

Uses of Television by the American Family

Television Use
in Families With Children

Jennifer A. Kotler
John C. Wright
Aletha C. Huston
University of Texas at Austin

The television set has become an important member of the American family. Fewer than 1% of American families have no television set (Kaiser Family Foundation, 1998). Television can bring family members together or it can isolate them; it can teach positive, educational messages or it can relay antisocial, frightening information; it can be an arena in which to negotiate taste, values, and preferences, or it can be the battleground for family arguments. It can detract from meaningful family interaction, or it can provide an attractive distraction from family conflict. Television can be the friendly babysitter, the annoying houseguest, or the default activity when nothing more interesting is available.

During the approximately 50 years that television has been available in the United States, the medium has changed continuously. At its inception, television led to slight increases in the time families spent together, probably because they were jointly watching their single black-and-white set that offered only a few channels (Maccoby, 1964). Near the end of the century, 80% of American families had two or more sets (Stranger, 1998); nearly 60% of adolescents and about 30% of preschool children have a television set in their bedroom, allowing more separation of family members when they watch television. On average, children watch 2 to 3 hours of broadcast or cable television, selecting from many channels, and they view about 1 hour of videotapes on the weekdays and slightly more during the weekend days (Kaiser Family Foundation, 1998; Stranger, 1998).

The content has also changed. Broadcast television has shown high levels of violence for many years, but since the late 1970s, there have been significant increases in explicit sexual content and reality programs showing violence; cable and videotapes allow levels of explicit violence and sexuality that exceed the standards of broadcast television (Huston, Wartella, & Donnerstein, 1998; Huston & Wright, 1997). At the same time, new FCC regulations have supported the production and broadcasting of more educational programs for children (Huston & Wright, 1998). The technology, industry structure, and content of television are moving targets that will continue to change, seemingly with ever-increasing momentum.

Our purpose in this chapter is to describe how children incorporate this diverse medium into their lives as they develop from infancy through adolescence and to offer some understanding of the many roles that television plays in family life. We first examine individual differences in patterns of viewing; then we discuss how parents and families use television and how they socialize their children's television viewing habits.

The television viewing of individuals and families occurs in an ecological context that includes many social institutions (e.g., school, work, the television industry) and such macrosocial influences as culture and socioeconomic status (Bryant & Anderson, 1983, Huston & Wright, 1997). Highly educated and economically advantaged families watch less television than do families with less education and lower economic status, probably in part because they have more alternatives (Comstock, 1991). African American families watch more television than European Americans do even when socioeconomic status is controlled (Brown, Childers, Bauman, & Koch, 1990; Comstock, 1991). Although less is known about other ethnic groups, there is evidence that Hispanic families watch more television than do European Americans (Comstock & Cobbey, 1982). Thus, ethnic and cultural patterns, education, and economic status contribute to television use by children and families.

CHILD CHARACTERISTICS

Aside from habit, expectation, and lack of funds for alternative entertainment media, however, individual differences in age, gender, intellectual ability, and personality in part determine the amount and the type of programming children watch.

Age

Age is, of course, not a cause of developmental change but rather an index of both maturation and cumulative experience. Age changes in television viewing may result from changing cognitive abilities and knowledge about the world, and also from such age-correlated events as attending school. On average, viewing time increases from preschool to entry into elementary school, where viewing declines then increases to a peak in late childhood and early adolescence. There is some reduction during adolescence (Comstock, 1991; Ridley-Johnson, Chance, & Cooper, 1984). Preschool children spend more of their viewing time watching videos than do adolescents (Mares, 1998).

Preschool children spend the majority of their viewing time watching educational programs, cartoons, and nonanimated child and family programming (Scantlin, Kotler, Bickham, Wright, Vandewater, & Huston, 1999). Early exposure to high rates of slapstick violence in cartoons is in part balanced by the excellent educational and informative programming for preschoolers aired on PBS and cable channels. By first or second grade, children watch fewer informative programs and more situation comedies than when they were younger (Huston, Wright, Marquis, & Green, 1999; Scantlin et al., 1999). However, because cartoons are popular with this age group, they see a great deal of violence (Eron, Huesmann, Brice, Fischer, & Mermelstein, 1983; Wober, 1988). Toward the end of elementary school, children become interested in dramatic and "reality-based" programs (Cantor & Nathanson, 1997). By the middle of the teens, adult entertainment programming dominates the list of favorites. Adolescents spend the greatest proportion of their viewing hours watching comedies (Hawkins, Reynolds, & Pingree, 1991). This shift toward adult programming is accompanied by diversification in preferences (Comstock, 1991).

Within these broad developmental changes, individual differences in the total amount of television viewed and in the types of programs viewed are highly stable from age 2 or 3 onward. Children who watch a lot of television during their early years are likely to be heavy viewers later, and early viewers of educational programs (or cartoons) are likely to be relatively frequent viewers of such programs at later ages (Huston, Wright, Rice, Kerkman, & St. Peters, 1990; Tangney & Feshbach, 1988; Wright & Huston, 1995).

Gender

One might expect television to be more appealing to boys than to girls because the majority of major characters are male, and the violent, adventure content themes that prevail in many programs are sex stereotyped.

Nonetheless, the findings are inconsistent. In some studies, boys watched more (Desmond, Hirsch, Singer, & Singer, 1987; Eron et al., 1983; Huston et al., 1990); in others, girls watched more (Lyle & Hoffman, 1972); in still others, there were no consistent differences (Huston et al., in press; Ridley-Johnson et al.,1984; Tangney & Feshbach, 1988). The discrepancies may be due to the different ages studied or to variations in the types of programming that are most appealing to girls and boys.

Compared to boys, girls generally watch less violent programming (Ridley-Johnson et al., 1984; Van der Voort, 1986) and are more likely to enjoy family shows (Ridley-Johnson et al., 1984). Girls choose programs portraying relationships and sexual conent more than do boys (Greenberg, Linsangan, & Soderman, 1993). Boys serve as a larger audience for cartoons, westerns, crime, action–adventure, and sports programming (Comstock, 1991; Desmond et al., 1987). Boys' proclivity toward violent content may indicate an interest in programs that feature justice restoration rather than a preference for violence per se (Cantor & Nathanson, 1997). Boys are also more likely than girls to replay action scenes on videotapes whereas girls tend to replay scenes that induce positive affect or that are physically attractive (Mares, 1998). The forms of television programs as well as their content are sex stereotyped, and even young children know the production conventions and formal features that mark programming designed for boys versus that designed for girls (Huston, Greer, Wright, Welch, & Ross, 1984).

Intelligence and Academic Success

Because most television content is assumed to be relatively undemanding intellectually, it might be less appealing to bright children than to those of average or low intelligence. Children who do well in school may choose to spend their time in homework or other pursuits rather than in watching television. At the same time, many believe that heavy viewing may lead to reduced intellectual functioning and school performance. Either causal direction leads to a prediction that highly intelligent and achieving children will watch less than do other children. With respect to intelligence, the data are inconsistent. Some studies find that at certain ages, brighter children watch *more* television than their average peers, presumably because brighter children tend to engage in more of many activities (Abelman, 1987).

Highly achieving children do watch less television than low achievers. In a meta-analysis of 23 studies of the relation of television viewing to school achievement, the average correlation was –.06. The relation was curvilinear, with the best students watching about 10 hours a week (Williams, Haertel, Walberg, & Haertel, 1982). As viewing increased beyond 10 hours a week, achievement declined dramatically. Comstock

(1991), using an analysis of the California Assessment Study, found a linear, negative relationship, and other studies have suggested that viewing more than 30 hours a week is associated with low achievement (Neuman, 1988; Potter, 1987).

When academically successful children do watch television, they choose content that is more likely to be beneficial than that preferred by low achievers. Low achievers like more violent programs and identify more with violent characters, as compared to their more successful peers (Huesmann, Lagerspetz, & Eron, 1984), and children of average intelligence watch more violent television than do brighter children (Wiegman, Kuttschreuter, & Baarda, 1992). Gifted preschool children are more likely to watch educational programs than cartoons and entertainment programming compared to children of average intelligence (Abelman, 1987). Hence, it appears that intelligence and achievement may lead children to select different types of program content.

At the same time, these correlations may reflect the influence of program content on academic and intellectual functioning. Longitudinal studies have provided evidence that viewing educational programs is associated with increases in vocabulary (Rice, Huston, Truglio, & Wright, 1990), school readiness (Wright & Huston, 1995), and later adolescent academic achievement (Collins, Wright, Anderson, Huston, Schmitt, & Linebarger, 1997), and viewing violence is associated with low school performance (Huesmann et al., 1984).

Personality and Affect

Personality characteristics influence the types of program content that are most appealing. Boys and girls with aggressive tendencies are drawn to violent television (Atkin, Greenberg, Korzenny, & McDermott, 1979; Cantor & Nathanson, 1997; Wiegman, et al., 1992). When given choices between programs with parental advisories regarding violent content and ones without advisories, aggressive children more often chose programs with advisories (Cantor & Harrison, 1996). Those who are heavy viewers in general and who watch more violent television also have problematic interpersonal relationships, suffer from emotional and behavioral problems, are less trusting of others, and are less popular with peers (Huesmann et al.,1984; Ridley-Johnson et al, 1984; Sprafkin & Gadow, 1986).

Conversely, fearful children avoid programs with violence or frightening content. Children who reported having been frightened by television portrayals in the past were less likely to choose a program with a cautionary parental advisory than a program without an advisory warning (Cantor & Harrison, 1996). Children with severe anxiety symptoms were less likely to watch violent television than were controls (Bruce, 1995, cited in Cantor & Nathanson, 1997).

FAMILY INFLUENCES ON CHILDREN'S TELEVISION USE

Children's patterns of television use are developed from birth in the family context. Parents and siblings influence the amount and kind of television exposure for young children by their patterns of viewing, by regulating or encouraging viewing, and by more general family characteristics such as parental attitudes, communication style, and general climate in the household.

Context of Use: Who Watches What With Whom?

In the 1950s, television brought families together; it was viewed by some as a sort of electronic hearth forming the center of home. By the 1980s, the entire family rarely sat down together to watch television (McDonald, 1986). Very young children watch television with their parents, but children are more likely to watch television with their siblings than with their parents (Van Evra, 1998). Siblings influence the types of programs to which children are exposed. Those with older siblings are drawn away from educational programs at earlier ages than are first born or only children. Conversely, having a younger sibling helps prolong the child's viewing of educational preschool programs like *Sesame Street* (Piñon, Huston, & Wright, 1989).

When parents do view with children, they often determine what is watched. Mothers and children say that fathers have the strongest claim to the set (Lull, 1982). Children are drawn into watching what their parents are watching more frequently than parents accommodate to or join in watching children's fare. The majority of time that young children spend watching programs intended for adults is spent coviewing with parents (Wright, St. Peters, & Huston, 1990). As children get older, however, the balance of influence shifts; when adolescents and parents view together, the adolescent often influences the programs chosen (Dorr, Kovaric, & Doubleday, 1989).

Parents who believe that television influences children's development (positively and/or negatively) view with their children for more hours than parents who do not see the medium as a powerful influence. However, this coviewing may be due to similar viewing preferences and habits. For example, voluntary coviewing with parents is more common among older than younger children (Dorr et al., 1989), and parent coviewing with young children is more frequent during programs that are aimed at a general audience than during programs that are created for child audiences (St. Peters, Fitch, Huston, Wright, & Eakins, 1991). Coviewing of videos, however, was least likely to occur with older male children in one study (Mares, 1998).

When coviewing occurs, it presents an opportunity for parents and children to discuss and evaluate television content. When parents attempt to cultivate critical viewing skills, they can help children understand or question content messages; enhance the educational value of the viewing experience; and moderate some of the adverse effects of violent or frightening programs (Austin, 1993; Austin, Roberts, & Nass, 1990; Desmond et al., 1987; Huesmann, Eron, Klein, Brice, & Fischer, 1983).

Most coviewing, however, is not directed by parents' intent to educate and inform (Fabes, Wilson, & Christopher, 1989; Weaver & Barbour, 1992). In fact, parent–child coviewing could increase vulnerability to television's negative influence because the parent's mere presence can imply an endorsement of specific messages that may not be appropriate or healthy for young viewers (Van Evra, 1998). For example, in families where teenagers watched a lot of television with their parents but had very few rules about viewing, the adolescents were more likely to see the world as a scary place and to hold more gender-typed attitudes than did youngsters whose parents had rules about viewing or who watched less often with their children (Rothschild & Morgan, 1987). Because children watch general audience and adult programs with their parents more often than child programs, and because this joint viewing is often based more on similar interests rather than on a need on the part of a parent to mediate the viewing experience, it is likely that coviewing does not necessarily set the occasion for an educational experience.

Family Tension, Parenting Values, and Communication Style

The social atmosphere in the family can influence both television consumption and its effects. Family decisions and conflicts about how much television to watch, what programs to watch, and when to watch them are indicators of how decisions and control about other topics are practiced. Parents with negative attitudes about television report high family cohesion, expression and participation in intellectual and recreational activities (Christopher, Fabes, & Wilson, 1989). Parents who usually reason with children to elicit self-control, and who rarely use verbal threats of punishment for noncompliance are the ones whose children seem to be the most affected by prosocial television content and least affected by antisocial content (Abelman, 1985). Children in families that stress deference and conformity (socio-oriented), rather than questioning of ideas and critical thinking (concept oriented), watch more television and discuss it less with their parents. Concept-oriented families are more selective in their viewing habits than are socio-oriented families (Lull, 1982).

Mothers who focus on control are less likely to engage their children in discussion about television content than are mothers who are more idea oriented (Austin, 1993). Similarly, Messaris and Kerr (1983) found that mothers with high control orientation were more likely to provide directive comments or advice about television than were mothers who were less controlling in general.

There are hints that television is used for escape and compensation in families with high levels of conflict. Children in highly conflictual and tension-filled households watch slightly more television and more videos than do children in households with less discord (Morgan, Alexander, Shanahan, & Harris, 1990; Rosenblatt & Cunningham, 1976). Television may serve as an outlet or a way of avoiding social interaction and conversation for those who have difficulty interacting with each other. Children whose parents are physically punitive or who are insensitive to their developmental needs watch more television as well (McLeod & Brown, 1976; Tangney, 1988) perhaps as a way of avoiding interaction with an erratic and difficult parent. Boys whose parents use withdrawal of affection as their primary disciplinary technique watch more television than boys whose parents use other forms of discipline (Desmond et al., 1987).

Particular types of programs may provide escape from family difficulties. Children whose parents hold dysfunctional attitudes toward parenting (unrealistic age expectations, role reversal) watch more fantasy, violence, more superhero and loner programs than do children whose parents do not hold such attitudes (Tangney, 1988). These children avoid programs that are cognitively demanding or that portray positive social interactions. Parent–child conflict is also related to adolescents' viewing of violence (Chaffee & McLeod, 1972). Tangney (1988) argued that children who have difficult relationships with their parents may be drawn to violent and fantasy fare and may avoid positive family and relationship programming because it may be too emotionally taxing to see positive portrayals of family life when their current situation is much more troubled. Surprisingly, parents' aggressiveness was not related to the amount of violent television that children watched in a longitudinal study by Huesmann, Lagerspetz, and Eron (1984).

Parental Regulation of Television

The most direct way parents can intervene in children's television use is by regulating what, when, and how much the child watches. Parents can select programs, make rules, organize time, or place restrictions on their children's television use. Estimates of the actual percentage of parents who actively regulate their children's television, however, vary from study to study (Dorr & Rabin, 1995; Stranger, 1998). When parents do regulate, they probably do so because the child is unable or unwilling to monitor his or her viewing in accordance with parental wishes, or is ignorant of those wishes and of how to discriminate acceptable from unacceptable content.

Some parents regulate time with television because they are concerned about the total amount of time their children spend viewing, the time of day it is viewed, or its interference with other activities (Stranger, 1997). Parents who impose time limits on television say they do so to promote healthier and more creative activities (St. Peters et al., 1991). They may set absolute limits on the amount that children are allowed to watch, for example, 1 hour on weekdays and more on weekends. Others require completion of certain tasks before viewing (e.g., homework, and chores), and require a standard bedtime.

Most parents who regulate, however, say they are concerned about content; therefore, they restrict particular programs or categories of program (Stranger, 1997). Some ban specific channels (e.g., MTV, HBO); others prohibit specific genres (e.g., soap operas, horror movies); still others restrict on a program-by-program basis.

From the inception of television until the early 1980s, parents worried most about television violence, especially murder, and there was relatively little concern with children's exposure to sex (Blood, 1961; St. Peters et al., 1991). Although violence is still a primary concern, parents are now distressed about sex, explicit language, and frightening content, programming that is politically, socially, or religiously objectionable, and programs that they think will cause adverse reactions in the child (Kaiser Family Foundation, 1998; St. Peters et al., 1991). These concerns have increased substantially during the past few years with the increasing variety of viewing fare available.

Since the late 1970s, the television industry has given more information about the appropriateness of TV content for children. For most of this period, warnings were placed at the beginning of a show indicating that it might be unsuitable for children. More recently, industry ratings have been developed that denote the age for which a program is appropriate, and some stations label the type of objectionable content it may include. Large-scale studies have indicated that between 33% and 54% of parents say that they use the rating systems to guide their children's viewing (Kaiser Family Foundation, 1998; Stranger, 1997, 1998). In one survey, 70% of parents of children ages 2 to 17 were aware that the networks provide information on the screen about the appropriateness of programs for people of different ages, but many did not accurately associate a rating with its meaning. Many parents said they favored the V-chip, an electronic device in television sets that will allow them to block out content rated by the industry as to violence, sexual content or innuendo, or appropriateness of language for certain age ranges (Stranger, 1998), but, a majority in another study said that they probably would not purchase such a device to add to their present set (Kaiser Family Foundation, 1998).

Regulation and Child Characteristics.   Regulation varies depending on characteristics of the child. Regulation declines as children get older (Atkin, Greenberg, & Baldwin, 1991; Gross & Walsh, 1980; Kim Baran, & Massey, 1988). Some studies found that parents tend to control girls' viewing more than boys' viewing (Gross & Walsh, 1980; Ridley-Johnson et al., 1984; Sneegas & Plank, 1998). Others showed that boys are more likely to receive parental intervention than are girls (Abelman, 1987); and still others demonstrated no sex differences in parental control (Atkin et al., 1991; Kim et al., 1988).

Techniques of regulation vary with children's intelligence. Parents of gifted children were more likely to discuss program content with their children than to prohibit viewing. Parents of children of average intelligence were more likely to simply forbid certain programming (Desmond, Singer, Singer, Calam, & Colimore, 1985). There is some evidence that school achievement is positively correlated with parental control over television (Lin & Atkin, 1989) but the direction of causality could function in either or both direction.

The Relationship Between Parental Regulation and Children's Television Use.   Because of the correlational nature of most regulation studies, it is unclear whether parents regulate viewing in response to their child's television habits, or whether parental regulation is responsible for the child's television consumption. That is, regulation may be proactive or primarily reactive to perceived child behavior. Both effects can operate concurrently. A second problem is that children may respond to parental control with an improvement in desired viewing habits, or attempted control may arouse reactance and resistance.

Many investigations show that high control is associated with desired viewing habits. These findings suggest that parental control induces children to watch less television overall, to watch better programming when they do watch, and to be more discriminating viewers (Brown et al., 1990; Desmond, Singer, & Singer, 1990; St. Peters et al., 1991; Stranger, 1997).

In a few investigations, however, high control was not associated with positive child viewing outcomes. These findings are subject to two quite different interpretations. It may be that high control induces children to watch undesired content as a reaction against the parent (Krcmar, 1996; Tangney, 1988). Because most children like television, and many see its use as a discretionary right, they frequently think that selecting television programs is a domain in which their parents' intervention should be minimized. Accordingly, older children wishing to protect their growing autonomy may be likely to react to television restriction in an oppositional manner. This phenomenon is called *psychological reactance* (Brehm, 1966). Boys in late childhood and adolescence are especially likely to be attracted to programs that are meant for an adult audience and that have parental advisories (Cantor & Harrison, 1996; Cantor, Harrison, & Nathanson, 1997). Even when children are aware that there are rules prohibiting programs with certain ratings, many say that they watch such programs anyway (Kaiser Family Foundation, 1998). This effect is even stronger for children who think their parents are highly controlling in general (Krcmar, 1996).

On the other hand, parents may have been sampled at a moment when they were reacting to undesirable viewing with a regimen of increased control (Abelman, 1987; Atkin et al., 1991). Thus, the relationship could be a marker of flexibility, sensitivity, and responsiveness of parents. Only longitudinal data could tell us if parents are tracking viewing with regulation only when needed, or if children are responding oppositionally to high control and favorably to reduced control.

Still another possibility is that the child does not require regulation because the parent finds the pattern of viewing acceptable. Some parents are confident of potential control without needing to exercise it very often (Lewis, 1981). Part of being a sensitive parent is knowing when to become less directive as children show signs of developing appropriate choices (Baumrind, 1991).

Encouragement to View

Parents regulate children's viewing by encouraging particular times or programs that they find educational or appropriately entertaining as well as by restricting viewing. In a study of young children, encouragement and restriction were independent of one another (St. Peters et al., 1991). Parents who encouraged viewing had children who watched more educational television and who coviewed with parents more than children whose parents did not encourage viewing.

Video technology has provided another means of regulation by allowing parents to select appropriate programming for their children. By providing children with a vast library of videos, parents can guide viewing, at least for young children. Videos also overcome the very real problem that there are many time periods in which child audience programming is not available on broadcast or cable television. Redirecting attention toward acceptable alternatives that the child likes may keep conflicts to a minimum while entertaining the child with appropriate programming (Blood, 1961; Jordan, 1990).

Just as broadcasters are providing warnings about negative content, the FCC now requires stations to label programs that are "educational and informative" for the child audience. Because "children" are defined as ages 0 to 16, some have worried that these labels would be counterproductive, leading children and adolescents to avoid programs carrying them. In one survey, about 50% of 10- to 17- year- olds reported that labeling a program "educational" would not drive viewers away and might actually attract them. Only about a 20% of children surveyed said that they would be less likely to view a program that they knew was educational (Stranger, 1997).

CONCLUSION

The role of television as a companion of children and as a family member has evolved since 1940s, and it will continue to do so as changes such as digital television, fusing of television with interactive media, and other technologies transform the way children use media. There is little doubt that the array of available content will continue to increase, and that regulation of children's exposure will become increasingly difficult. As choice increases, it is critically important to understand the individual and family patterns that guide children's use of electronic media. The information reviewed in this chapter suggests certain groups of children who may be especially vulnerable to violent and other negative content: males in middle to late childhood, children who have difficult interpersonal relationships, children who are academically unsuccessful, and children who are undiscriminating in their viewing habits. These vulnerabilities may be exacerbated in families with dysfunctional parenting attitudes, high stress, a great deal of conflict, or where parents exercise too much or too little control over what their children watch on television.

Technological changes and increased variety can also enhance the positive uses of television. Thus far, preschool children are the age group who watch educational and prosocial television and who get the most out of these programs. Older children who do well academically and socially, and who come from families where they are encouraged to explore educational activities and ask questions freely, also use television to good advantage.

Because some children are at greater risk than others for developing poor viewing habits, and because parents are often unable or unwilling to curb such use, it is especially critical that the television industry and the policy leaders who regulate the broadcasting industry continue to find ways to make sure that prosocial and educational television are easily recognizable and readily accessible to all, along with appropriate advice and advisories to parents about regulation and encouragement of media use.

REFERENCES

Abelman, R. (1985). Styles of parental disciplinary practices as a mediator of children's learning from prosocial television portrayals. *Child Study Journal, 15,* 131–145.

Abelman, R. (1987). Child giftedness and its role in the parental mediation of television viewing. *Roeper Review, 9,* 217–220.

Atkin, C., Greenberg, B., Korzenny, F., & McDermott, S. (1979). Selective exposure to televised violence. *Journal of Broadcasting, 23,* 5–13.

Atkin, D. J., Greenberg, B. S., & Baldwin, T. F. (1991). The home ecology of children's television viewing: Parental mediation and the new video environment. *Journal of Communication, 41,* 40–52.

Austin, E. W. (1993). Exploring the effects of active parental mediation of television content. *Journal of Broadcasting and Electronic Media, 37,* 147–158.

Austin, E. W., Roberts, D. F., & Nass, C. I. (1990). Influences of family communication on children's television-interpretation processes. *Communication Research, 17,* 545–564.

Baumrind, D. (1991). Effective parenting during the early adolescent transition. In P. A. Cowan & E. M. Hetherington (Eds.), *Family transitions: Advances in family research series research* (pp. 111–163). Hillsdale, NJ: Lawrence Erlbaum Associates.

Blood, R. O. (1961). Social class and family control of television viewing. *Merrill-Palmer Quarterly, 7,* 205–222.

Brehm, J. W. (1966). *A theory of psychological reactance.* New York: Academic Press.

Brown, J. D., Childers, K. W., Bauman, K. E., & Koch, G. G. (1990). The influence of new media and family structure on young adolescents' television and radio use. *Communication Research, 17,* 65–82.

Bryant, J., & Anderson, D. R. (Eds.). (1983). *Children's understanding of TV: Research on attention and comprehension.* New York: Academic Press.

Cantor, J., & Harrison, K. (1996). Ratings and advisories for television programming. In National Television Violence Study (Vol. 1, pp. 361–410). Thousand Oaks, CA: Sage.

Cantor, J., Harrison, K., & Nathanson, A. I. (1997). Ratings and advisories for television programming. In Center for Communication and Social Policy (Ed.), *National Television Violence Study* (Vol. 2, pp. 267–322). Thousand Oaks, CA: Sage.

Cantor, J., & Nathanson, A. I. (1997). Predictors of children's interest in violent television programs. *Journal of Broadcasting and Electronic Media, 41,* 155–167.

Chaffee, S. H., & McLeod, J. M. (1972). Adolescent television use in the family content. In G. A. Comstock & E. A. Rubenstein (Eds.), *Television and social behavior* (Vol. 3, pp. 149–172) Washington, DC: Government Printing Office.

Christopher, F. S., Fabes, R. A., & Wilson, P. M. (1989). Family television viewing: Implications for family life education. *Family Relations, 38,* 210–214.

Collins, P. A., Wright, J. C., Anderson, D. R., Huston, A. C., Schmitt, K., & Linebarger, D. (1997, April). *The relations of early television viewing to adolescent academic achievement.* Paper presented at the Society for Research in Child Development, Washington, DC.

Comstock, G. (1991). *Television and the American child.* Orlando, FL: Academic Press.

Comstock, G., & Cobbey, R. E. (1982). Television and the children of ethnic minorites: Perspectives from research. In G. L. Berry & C. Mitchell-Kernan (Eds.), *Television and the socialization of the minority child* (pp.245–260). New York: Academic Press.

Desmond, R. J., Hirsch, B., Singer, D., & Singer, J. (1987). Gender differences, mediation, and disciplinary styles in children's responses to television. *Sex Roles, 16,* 375–389.

Desmond, R. J., Singer, J. L., & Singer, D. G. (1990). Family mediation: Parental communication patterns and the influences of television on children. In J. Bryant (Ed.), *Television and the American family* (pp. 293–309). Hillsdale, NJ: Lawrence Erlbaum Associates.

Desmond, R. J., Singer, J. L., Singer, D. G., Calam, R., & Colimore, K. (1985). Family mediation patterns and television viewing: Young children's use and grasp of the medium. *Human Communication Research, 11,* 461–480.

Dorr, A., Kovaric, P., & Doubleday, C. (1989). Parent–child coviewing of television. *Journal of Broadcasting and Electronic Media, 33,* 35–51.

Dorr, A., & Rabin, B. E. (1995). Parents, children and television. In M. H. Bornstein, (Ed.),

Handbook of parenting: Vol 4. Applied and Practical Parenting (pp. 323–351). Mahwah, NJ: Lawrence Erlbaum Associates.

Eron, L. D., Huesmann, L. R., Brice, P., Fischer, P., & Mermelstein, R. (1983). Age trends in the development of aggression, sex typing, and related television habits. *Developmental Psychology, 19,* 71–77.

Fabes, R. A., Wilson, P., & Christopher, F. S. (1989). A time to reexamine the use of television in family life. *Family Relations, 38,* 337–341.

Greenberg, B. S., Linsangan, R., & Soderman, A. (1993). Adolescents' reactions to television sex. In B. S Greenberg, J. D. Brown, & N. L. Buerkel-Rothfuss (Eds.), *Media, sex and the adolescent* (pp. 196–224). CressKill, N.J: Hampton Press.

Gross, L. S., & Walsh, R. P. (1980). Factors affecting parental control over children's television viewing: A pilot study. *Journal of Broadcasting, 24,* 411–419.

Hawkins, R. P., Reynolds, N., & Pingree, S. (1991). In search of television viewing styles. *Journal of Broadcasting & Electronic Media, 35,* 375–383.

Huesmann, L. R., Eron, L. D., Klein, R., Brice, P., & Fischer (1983). Mitigating the imitation of aggressive behaviors by changing children's attitudes about media violence. *Journal of Personality & Social Psychology, 44,* 899–910.

Huesmann, L. R., Lagerspetz, K., & Eron, L. D. (1984). Intervening variables in the TV violence–aggression relations: Evidence from two countries. *Developmental Psychology, 20,* 746–775.

Huston, A. C., Greer, D., Wright, J. C., Welch, R. , & Ross, R. (1984). Children's comprehension of televised formal features with masculine and feminine connotations. *Developmental Psychology, 20,* 707–716.

Huston, A. C., Wartella, E., & Donnerstein, E. (1998). *Measuring the effects of sexual content in the media: A report to the Kaiser Family Foundation.* Menlo Park, CA: Kaiser Family Foundation.

Huston, A. C., & Wright, J. C. (1997). Mass media and children's development. In W. Damon, I. Sigel, & K. A. Renninger (Eds.) *Handbook of child psychology: Vol. 4.) Child psychology in practice* (5th ed., pp. 999–1058). New York: Wiley.

Huston, A. C., & Wright, J. C. (1998). Contributions of television toward meeting the informational and educational needs of children. *The Annals of the American Academy of Political and Social Science, 557,* 9–22.

Huston, A. C., Wright, J. C., Marquis, J., & Green, S. (1999). How young children spend their time: Television and other activities. *Developmental Psychology, 35,* 912–925.

Huston, A. C., Wright, J. C., Rice, M. L., Kerkman, D., & St. Peters, M. (1990). Development of television viewing patterns in early childhood: A longitudinal investigation. *Developmental Psychology, 26,* 409–420.

Jordan, A. B. (1990). A family systems approach to the use of the VCR in the home. In J. R. Dobrow (Ed.), *Social and cultural aspects of VCR use.* (pp.163–179). Hillsdale, NJ: Lawrence Erlbaum Associates.

Kaiser Family Foundation. (1998, May). *Parents, children and the television ratings system.* Menlo Park, CA: Author.

Kim, W. Y., Baran, S. J., & Massey, K. K. (1988). Impact of the VCR on control of television viewing. *Journal of Broadcasting and Electronic Media, 32*(3), 351–358.

Krcmar, M. (1996). Family communication patterns, discourse behavior, and child television viewing. *Human Communication Research, 23,* 251–277.

Lewis, C. C. (1981). The effects of parental firm control: A reinterpretation of findings. *Psychological Bulletin, 90,* 547–563.

Lin, C. A. & Atkin, D. J. (1989). Parental mediation and rulemaking for adolescent use of television and VCRs. *Journal of Broadcasting and Electronic Media, 33,* 53–67

Lull, J. (1982). How families select TV programs: A mass-observational study. *Journal of Broadcasting, 26,* 801–811.

Lyle, J., & Hoffman, H. R. (1972). Children's use of television and other media. In E. H. Rubinstein, G. A. Comstock, & J. P. Murray (Eds.), *Television and social behavior* (Vol. 4, pp. 129–256). Washington, DC: Government Printing Office.

Maccoby, E. E. (1964). Effects of the media. In M. Hoffman & L. W. Hoffman (Eds.), *Review of child development research* (Vol. 1, pp. 323–348). New York: Russell Sage Foundation.

Mares, M. L. (1998). Children's use of VCRs. *The Annals of the American Academy of Political and Social Science, 557,* 120–132.

McDonald, D. G. (1986). Generational aspects of television coviewing. *Journal of Broadcasting & Electronic Media, 30,* 75–85.

McLeod, J. M., & Brown, J. D. (1976). The family environment and adolescent television use. In J. D. Brown (Ed.), *Children and television* (pp. 199–233). Beverly Hills, CA: Sage.

Messaris, P., & Kerr, D., (1983) Mothers comments about television: Relation to family communication patterns. *Communication Research,* 10, 175–194.

Morgan, M., Alexander, A., Shanahan, J., & Harris, C. (1990). Adolescents, VCRs, and the family environment. *Communication Research, 17,* 83–106.

Neuman, S. B. (1988). The displacement effect: Assessing the relation between television viewing and reading performance. *Reading Research Quarterly, 23,* 415–439.

Piñon, M. F., Huston, A. C., & Wright, J. C. (1989). Family ecology and child characteristics that predict young children's educational television viewing. *Child Development, 60,* 846–856.

Potter, W. J. (1987). Does television viewing hinder academic achievement among adolescents? *Human Communication Research, 14,* 27–46.

Rice, M. L., Huston, A. C., Truglio, R., & Wright, J. C. (1990). Words from Sesame Street: Learning vocabulary while viewing. *Developmental Psychology, 26,* 421–428.

Ridley-Johnson, R., Chance, J. E., & Cooper, H. (1984). Correlates of children's television viewing: Expectancies, age, & sex. *Journal of Applied Developmental Psychology, 5,* 225–235.

Rosenblatt, P., & Cunningham, M. (1976). Television watching and family tensions. *Journal of Marriage & The Family, 38,* 105–111.

Rothschild, N., & Morgan, M. (1987). Cohesion and control: Adolescents' relationships with parents as mediators of television. *Journal of Early Adolescence, 7,* 299–314.

Scantlin, R. M., Kotler, J. A., Bickham, D. S., Wright, J. C., Vandewater, E. A., & Huston, A. C. (1999). *An analysis of American children's use of electronic media.* Poster presented at the biennial meeting of the Society for Research in Child Development, Albuquerque, NM.

Sneegas, J. E., & Plank, T. A. (1998). Gender differences in pre-adolescent reactance to age-categorized television advisory labels. *Journal of Broadcasting & Electronic Media, 42,* 423–435.

Sprafkin, J., & Gadow, K. D. (1986). Television viewing habits of emotionally disturbed, learning disabled, and mentally retarded children. *Journal of Applied Developmental Psychology, 7,* 45–59.

St. Peters, M., Fitch, M., Huston, A. C., Wright, J. C., & Eakins, D. J. (1991). Television and families: What do young children watch with their parents? *Child Development, 62,* 1409–1423.

Stranger, J. D. (1997). *Television in the home 1997: The second annual survey of parents and children.* Philadelphia PA: The Annenberg Public Policy Center.

Stranger, J. D. (1998). *Television in the home 1998: The third annual national survey of parents and children.* Philadelphia, PA: The Annenberg Public Policy Center.

Tangney, J. P. (1988). Aspects of the family and children's television viewing content preferences. *Child Development, 59,* 1070–1079.

Tangney, J. P., & Feshbach, S. (1988). Children's television viewing frequency: Individual differences and demographic correlates. *Personality and Social Psychology Bulletin, 14,* 145–158.

Van der Voort, T. H. A. (1986). *Television violence: A child's eye view.* Amsterdam: North Holland.

Van Evra, J. (1998). *Television and child development (2nd ed.).* Mahwah, NJ: Lawrence Erlbaum Associates.

Weaver, B., & Barbour, N. (1992). Mediation of children's televiewing. *Families in Society, 73,* 236–242.

Wiegman, O., Kuttschreuter, M., & Baarda, B. (1992). A longitudinal study of the effects of television viewing on aggressive and prosocial behaviors. *British Journal of Social Psychology, 31,* 147–164.

Williams, P. A., Haertel, E. H., Walberg, H. J., & Haertel, G. D. (1982). The impact of leisure-time television on school learning: A research synthesis. *American Educational Research Journal, 19,* 19–50.

Wober, M. (1988). The extent to which viewers watch violence-containing programs. *Current Psychology: Research & Reviews, 7,* 43–57.

Wright, J. C., & Huston, A. C. (1995, June). *Effects of educational TV viewing of lower income preschoolers on academic skills, school readiness, and school adjustment one to three years later.* Report to Children's Television Workshop, Center for Research on the Influences of Television on Children, University of Kansas, Lawrence, KS.

Wright, J. C., St. Peters, M., & Huston, A. C. (1990). Family television use and its relation to children's cognitive skills and social behavior. In J. Bryant (Ed.), *Television and the American family* (pp. 227–251). Hillsdale, NJ: Lawrence Erlbaum Associates.

Home Ecology and Children's Television Viewing in the New Media Environment

David J. Atkin
Cleveland State University

The 1999 mass murder of 15 students in Littleton, Colorado reignited debates concerning the impact of emerging media on children and the role parents play in controlling access to and uses of these newer, more virulent content environments. In particular, the killers were reportedly heavy users of such new media as video games (e.g., "first-person shooter" games like "Doom"), graphic movie rentals (e.g., *Natural Born Killers*), and the Web (e.g., hate group pages detailing bomb-making tips). Acknowledging the latter's influence only hours after the Colorado attack, AOL pulled down Web sites posted by the gunmen, members of the Trenchcoat Mafia.

These tragic shootings not only illustrate how the introduction of new voice, video, and data channels has altered the media and cultural landscape in the United States, but they also underscore the importance of family viewing and mediation patterns for child development. Of course, the media are but one of several inputs that can determine a person's behavior, often working in conjunction with peer influences (e.g., gangs) and parental supervision, which can mediate uses of violent media forms. Given the wide scope of these developmental influences, this chapter examines media uses in the context of Bronfenbrenner's (1979) theory of ecologically embedded niches, extending past applications of that model to new media environments (Atkin, 1994; Atkin, Greenberg, & Baldwin, 1991).

A home ecology-based approach is useful, because today's youth represent the first generation to grow up in a multimedia environment. In addition to cable television and videocassette recorders (VCRs), families must now contend with a "fifth medium"—the Internet—that presents a paradigm shift in American television viewing. At the approach of a new millennium, nearly 90% of Americans owned a VCR, 66% subscribed to cable, nearly 40% owned a computer, and 30% (62 million) of adults surfed the Web (Maguire, 1988).

Thus, as Levy (1989) observed, the rapid diffusion of these technologies presages a "video revolution," presenting viewers with unprecedented choice and control over their viewing environment (see also Charney & Greenberg, in press; Greenberg & Lin, 1989; Lin, 1990, 1992, 1993, 1994a; Lin & Jeffres, 1998; Morgan, Alexander, Shanahan & Harris, 1990; Rubin & Bantz, 1989; Rubin & Rubin, 1989). Although this technological convergence blurs the lines between various electronic media (e.g., Dholakia, Mundorf, & Dholakia, 1996; Lin & Atkin, in press), the present chapter focuses on the influence of this "media revolution" on television viewing.

In this way, we draw from several bodies of literature to aid in the exploration of a theoretical framework applicable to the new media environment. Synthesizing this literature offers tremendous advantages for an exploratory review like this, which seeks to chronicle emergent theoretical elements.

AN OVERVIEW OF BRONFENBRENNER'S CONCEPTION OF HOME ECOLOGY

Even before the video revolution, the issue of television's impact on children was one of the most widely researched topics in the social sciences (e.g., Bryant & Zillmann, 1986). Research suggests that parental mediation of television viewing can enhance TV's prosocial effects (e.g., Corder-Bolz, 1980) and ameliorate its negative influence (e.g., Brown & Linne, 1976). Yet, although early studies provide a good profile of new media adopters, remarkably little work has addressed the influence of new video on family interaction (Brown, Childers, Bauman, & Koch, 1990).

Bronfenbrenner's model of ecologically embedded niches was selected as the starting point for this investigation, owing to its unique latitude for incorporating dynamically changing program environments and the ways in which they impact audience viewing. Scholars (Atkin et al., 1991) imported Bronfenbrenner's model to communication to help contextualize parental mediation of children's viewing in the new media environment. Those components can be summarized as follows:

1. A *mesosystem*, involving interrelations among two or more settings in which the developing person actively participates (e.g., the child's relations among home media environments, school and peer groups).

2. An *exosystem*, involving one or more settings that do not involve the developing person as an active participant, but in which events occur that affect, or are affected by, what happens in the setting containing the developing person (e.g., television).

3. A *microsystem*, or pattern of activities, roles and interpersonal relations experienced by the developing person in a given setting with particular physical and material characteristics (e.g., interpersonal interaction in the home).

4. A *macrosystem*, involving consistencies, in the form and content of lower order systems (micro, meso, and exo) that exist, or could exist, at the level of the subculture or the culture as a whole, along with any belief systems or ideology underlying such consistencies.

5. An *ontogenic system*, which comprises the child's individual psychological competencies for development (citing Bronfenbrenner, 1979, pp. 222–226).

Given that television enters the home via an external source, Bronfenbrenner (1979) placed television as "a second-order effect, in this case operating not completely within a microsystem but rather across ecological borders as an exosystem phenomenon" (p. 242). Later work placed new video in the context of a mesosystem (intersection) of (a) the distinctive demography of new technology adopters (encompassing the macrosystem), (b) new program environments (creating different exosystems), and (c) family uses of those technologies (within the microsystem). It is useful, then, to see how new media impact family viewing across these contexts.

The Exosystem: A Profile of Changing Media Content and Use Patterns

Researchers began to focus on family accommodations to differential content settings during the 1980s (Atkin, Heeter, Baldwin, 1989; Greenberg, Heeter, & Lin, 1988). That work characterized "traditional" and "new" media in terms of their relative potential for offensive programming, so that the viewing audience for each could be contrasted. The present analysis draws from Webster's (1986) admonition to contrast television services along content dimensions "so as to make polar the factors affecting audience behavior and their relevance to social theory" (p. 68). As Atkin (1994) noted, the exosystem concept thus allows us to conceive of television as a dynamically changing variable—not simply as a common denominator for mass audiences. "More than any other setting, the exosystem influences and is influenced by public and private policy decisions, especially where the media are concerned" (p. 25).

Webster's work is representative of several conceptualizations that see broadcast television content limited to a relatively narrow range of discourse, one that is motivated by two factors; the need to maximize audiences (and please advertisers) by providing inoffensive, lowest common demoniminator fare with the widest possible audience appeal, and the duty that broadcasters, as licensed public trustees, have to avoid offending audiences (e.g., with indecent programming). The high courts have upheld the selective enforcement of indecency regulations against broadcasters (*FCC v. Pacifica*, 1977), as opposed to wire-based telecommunication providers (*HBO v. FCC*, 1977) on several grounds. Chief among them is the state interest in protecting children from indecent material aired over the ubiquitous broadcast airwaves (see, e.g., Atkin, 1994, 1997). Because the Internet does not share this ubiquitous nature (Morris & Ogan, 1996), indecency restrictions under the Communication Decency Act were found unconstitutional (U.S. appeals ruling on Internet porn, 1999).

Webster (1986) defined broadcast television as a conventional medium that uses a relatively small number of channels to deliver content that is inoffensive, universally available, and unvarying across channels on a fixed timetable. This stands in contrast to new video media, which open the distribution system to potentially unlimited channel and content capabilities (e.g., VCRs and cable).

Or, in the parlance of diffusion theory, new media represent more discontinuous applications of the familiar television technology. Diffusion research focuses on the adoption process, providing profiles of those who are relatively earlier to adopt new products and services (Rogers, 1995, in press). For instance, Krugman (1985) noted that VCRs represent a dynamically discontinuous innovation, insofar as they engender a separate purchase for hardware and software. Neuendorf, Atkin, and Jeffres (1998) later argued that the Internet is perhaps the most discontinuous of all new media, owing to the virtual requirement of computer ownership and the financial and operational barriers that must be overcome by adopters. Figure 3.1 reflects this new relative ordering of media discontinuity.

For the present case, we're more interested in profiling these media with regard to content environments, as opposed to effort expended by adopters. Research shows that the availability of uncut adult (or R-rated) movies is a primary motivation for subscription to premium cable services (Albarran & Umphrey, 1994; Ducey, Krugman, & Eckrich, 1983; Heeter & Greenberg, 1988; Jacobs, 1995; LaRose & Atkin, 1991). Although most basic cable services are self-censors in matters relating to indecent fare, adult themes in music video provide a basis for some parental concerns over program appropriateness (Atkin et al., 1989; "Attorney General," 1986; Brown et al., 1990).

As Lin (Chap. 5, this volume) details, VCRs are the most widely diffused potential modality for adult fare. In particular, they provide avenues for

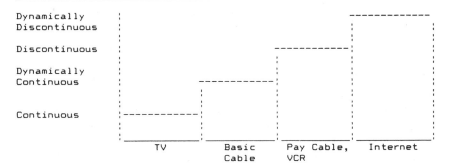

FIG. 3.1.   An updated adaptation of Krugman's (1985) model of relative discontinuity of media content.

peer viewing, allowing teens to explore antiauthority identities and a greater degree of viewing freedom in the United States (Heeter & Greenberg, 1988; Jordan, 1990; Levy, 1989; Lin, 1992, 1993, 1994a; as well as in Europe (e.g., Johnsson-Smagardi & Roe, 1986; Roe, 1987).

The significance of this rapidly changing environment becomes manifest for families, as these new outlets present new windows on the world that offer heretofore unseen glimpses into adult-oriented realms. Even before the widespread diffusion of the Internet, policymakers expressed concern about the impact of emerging video technologies on children during the 1980s, given that the vast majority of video releases carried an R rating (Attorney General, 1986). Although parental mediation has not yet been investigated in the realm of Internet, popular press accounts detail reports of obscene web sites, pedophiles sharing information with children via e-mail, and the like (see Reagan, in press). One of the few content analyses of cyberspace found, among other things, that 35% of all images in a USENET sample featured an erect penis, and 33% featured fetishes (Mehta & Plaze, 1997). Exposure to some of this material can be controlled through such screening programs as NetNanny, which we discuss later.

Screening devices notwithstanding, the removal of social-system controls—such as the indecency restrictions with broadcast fare—reinforces the need for parental screening of child viewing (Lin & Atkin, 1989). This leaves parental mediation of viewing as a last line of defense in this "brave new world" of emerging media. In order to gain a better understanding of this media selection process, it is useful to explore perspectives on media selection in the multimedia environment.

A Changing Mesosystem: Family Uses of the New Media

The media substitution hypothesis posits that audience members may substitute the use of a functionally similar medium for a more conventional option (e.g., Lin, 1994a). This perspective dates to Lasswell's (1948) seminal work, which foretold the displacement of radio by television as the most widely adopted mass entertainment medium. More recent research suggests that the arrival of new cable channels displaces viewership of traditional TV viewing (Henke & Donohue, 1989; Lin, 1994a). As Lin's review (Chap. 5, this volume) recounts, other investigations characterize prerecorded video playbacks on a VCR as a replacement for movie-outing activity (e.g., Childers & Krugman, 1987), particularly for children (e.g., Lin, 1993).

New Video Media.   Studies of children's time expenditures (see Kotler, Wright, & Huston, this volume) suggest that American children today spend less time watching TV than they did in the early 1980s. Even so, TV viewing ranks among the top three or four activities for children (behind sleep and school). According to a study reported in the *Washington Post*, children average about 90 minutes with television on weekdays, down from 2 hours in 1981 (Vobejda, 1998). This viewership nevertheless continues to dwarf time spent studying (21 minutes per weekday), reading (76 minutes per weekday), and most particularly, using computers (30 minutes per week for 6-year-olds and 72 minutes per week for 12-year-olds).

Many of the pioneering studies on the influence of new media on family viewing, chiefly addressing cable and VCRs, found very little disruption in viewing patterns in either the United States (Levy, 1989) or Europe (e.g., Roe, 1989). For instance, Greenberg and Lin (1988) found that half of the British population had at least one extra feature among a range of alternatives (including home computers, teletext, and VCRs). The latter technology was most widely diffused, but it has not produced substantially increased volumes of viewing. Even teletext, an information-oriented off-air progenitor of online news services, generated relatively little displacement of traditional media use.

Summarizing empirical findings from several European countries, Schoenbach and Becker (1989) maintained that the first decade of this media revolution yielded little evidence of dramatic, long-term reductions of time devoted to nonmedia behaviors. They found instead a rather consistent pattern of increasing specialization in the uses of all media, not only in the new ones. Those authors concluded that the new media do not create new audience interests; rather, they provide the means by which existing interests or needs can be satisfied. Although a raft of subsequent studies further profiled the dimensions of audience activity, selectivity, and viewing in new media environments, most failed to uncover any evidence of wholesale displacement of old media by new media (e.g., Abelman, Atkin, & Rand, 1997; Atkin, 1995; Atkin, Jeffres, Neuendorf, 1998; Atkin, Neuendorf, & Jeffres, 1998; Jeffres & Atkin, 1996; Jeffres, Atkin, &

Neuendorf, 1995; Lin, 1993, 1994a; 1999; Neuendorf et al., 1998; Perse & Courtright, 1993; Perse & Dunn, 1998; Rubin & Bantz, 1989; Rubin & Eyal, in press). Because research traditions addressing these emerging video media are relatively mature, it is useful to focus on influences accompanying the less familiar Internet medium.

The Internet.   As personal computers (PCs) and TV media converge, programmers are looking for the releasing touch that will help them harness the potential of the Internet as an entertainment and marketing vehicle for children. As Lin (1999) noted, this nascent medium's capability encompasses a continuum, ranging from interactive information retrieval, to one-on-one interpersonal, group, and mass communication modes; that is, television allows the audience to gaze into a "visual window" on the world initially, but the Internet enables them to reach beyond that window threshold and communicate with the world within. Lin's own work is representative of many prototypical Internet studies exploring marketing applications accompanying Internet diffusion. Even so, remarkably little work has explored social impacts of Internet use, in either theoretical or empirical terms.

Price Waterhouse (1997) projected that Web revenue would increase to more than $30 billion by the year 2000, defining it as

> . . . hypertext multimedia system that links computer resources around the world. Innovative uses of the Internet/Web and on-line services involve interactive databases, three-dimensional graphics, virtual reality, animation, audio/video, Java applets, and other emerging technologies. (p. 437)

Commentators (Atkin, Jeffres, & Neuendorf, 1998; Stipp, 1998) maintained that exotic "electronic superhighway" conceptions of the Internet are being replaced by a new paradigm; the convergence of "old" media with the computer. Yet, as Perse and Dunn (1998) noted, a focus on social impacts may be "premature" until we understand how and why people use computer technology. They found that media uses and gratifications (e.g., information seeking) were key predictors of PC use. Kiesler's (1997) widely reported Internet study, conducted at Carnegie Mellon, suggested that users of the Internet become lonely and socially withdrawn. Other studies (Finn, 1998; Kang & Atkin, 1999) have refuted this conception.

Diffusion-based research on the computer—a prerequisite for home adoption of the Internet—attributes low adoption levels to such entry barriers as cost and technology complexity (e.g., Lin, 1998). Despite the considerable hype surrounding the growth of the Internet, media substitution mechanisms are not so readily apparent between traditional-mediated and computer-mediated communication channels, even when the channels under comparison provide similar content. Industry research on adults, for instance, showed that audience use of online services has little effect on their patronage of television, newspapers, and other traditional news sources (Jessell, 1995; Klopfenstein, in press). Similarly, academic studies (Jeffres & Atkin, 1996; Perse & Dunn, 1998) failed to find any significant correlations between interest in using online services on the Internet and other traditional mass media. Even so, other studies report a slight reduction of television viewing time among online users (e.g., Atkin, Jeffres, & Neuendorf, 1998; James, Wotring, & Forrest, 1995; Lin, 1999).

Drawing from past work on content substitution, it is likely that the Internet will compete with other networks for children's programming and advertising inputs—as well as for their leisure—over time. These relationships between media could, of course, prove to be complementary or orthogonal. As Jeffres and Atkin (1996) noted, a complementary relation reflects a situation where the use of one medium makes the utility of another medium more complete. For instance, because the VCR allows for time-shifting of television program viewing, it complements the television viewing experience (Lin, 1993, Chap. 5, this volume). In many respects, online applications provide a similar enrichment function for computer use (Atkin, Jeffres, & Neuendorf, 1998; Perse & Dunn, 1998).

Yet, because the online media have yet to achieve the visual quality of print media, or the audiovisual quality of television and film, their use remains orthogonal to television. In that regard, online content is perhaps perceived as a desirable functional supplement for meeting children's gratification expectations associated with traditional media use, but it is not yet a functional displacement for them.

In a rather obvious case of complementarity, Internet usage presupposes computer ownership, now found in over 40% of U.S. households. According to a study by Jupiter Communications (1997), online access presently encompasses 6.5% of children ages 2 to 17. That number is expected to grow to 31.4% by 2002, at which time the share of children using online services from home (20 million) should approach the national average for all ages, which is 35%. Also, the number of online homes in the United States is projected to grow to 45 million by the end of 2002, up from a 1996 base of 15 million. Some 23% of posttoddlers with online access are expected to use it by that time, as are most of their teenage counterparts. As Table 3.1 details, that represents a 15-fold percentage increase from 1996 to 2002, encompassing 47% of all children.

The Jupiter Communication study is representative of several that document lower Internet use levels among younger children, a phenomenon that they attribute to the complexity of computer technology. That study also reported that over 40% of child respondents indicated they watch

TABLE 3.1
Industry Estimates of the Number of Children Online, 1996–2002

Year	Total US Children Age 2–12 (millions)	Total Children Online	Access Only From Home	Access Only From School	Percent Online
1996	42.7	1.4	1.4	0.0	3%
1997	43.1	2.7	2.6	0.1	6%
1998	43.3	5.1	4.6	0.5	12%
1999	43.4	7.9	6.7	1.2	18%
2000	43.6	11.5	9.0	2.5	26%
2001	43.6	15.9	11.6	4.3	36%
2002	44.3	20.9	14.9	6.0	47%

Note. From Jupiter Communications, 1997.

less television because of their online activities, which contradicts non-displacement findings in studies addressing adults (e.g., Jeffres & Atkin, 1996). Jupiter Communications further reported that almost 12% of 13- to 17-year olds with access used online services in 1996, compared with only 4.2% of 2- to 12-year-olds with access; they projected that classroom access climbed from 1.5 million in 1996 to more than 20 million by 2002.

Indeed, even the perception that the Internet might cut into television viewing time could greatly impact the $800,000,000 that children's advertisers spend on TV each year. Research by Nickelodeon has indicated that children's viewership—measured in persons using television (PUTs)—is down 13% from Fall 1998–Fall 1999 (Katz, 1999). Most of this decline was at the expense of broadcast TV, as basic ratings actually increased .2% during that same period, as average weekly viewership of basic cable increased from 3.98 hours in 1996 to 4.55 hours in 1998. That study also documented that the average child watched 19.49 hours of TV per week in 1998, down from 20.5 hours in 1996.

As ad agency executive Gary Carr noted (cited in Katz, 1999), "(O)ne theory is that kids are using the Internet more . . . we've seen that TV ratings in homes with computers are a little lower" (p. 39). As computer and Internet applications reach the "take-off" phase of their diffusion, it will be interesting to see how these viewership numbers are influenced as more services come online.

Ontogenic Dimensions

Although an extended discussion of media effects exceeds the scope of this chapter, it is worth noting that the studies reviewed here typically explain at most only one third of the variance in media adoption, use, and mediation. The ontogenic realm presents the most promising line of attack for broadening this explanatory scope, as scholars rooted in the communibiological perspective continue to make dramatic advances in explaining human communication behavior (e.g., Beatty & McCroskey, 1998). Although relatively nascent in the mass communication realm, communibiology applies the principles to neurobiology to communication processes.

For example, scholars have found that temperament accounts for a wide degree of variance—often approaching 80% or better—in areas like communication apprehension. Specific subcomponents of temperament might include such personality measures as introversion, extroversion, and neuroticism (worrying about others' opinions), all of which can help inform the study of media use (e.g., Finn, 1998). A preliminary study of companion digital TV technologies, for instance, found that adoption intentions were explained by variables relating to mood management with humor and depression (Atkin, Neuendorf, Jeffres, & Skalski, 2000); the perceived increases in interactivity provided by new media should thus attract those seeking a wider range of media stimulation.

Given the past success of similar work on biological influences on media use (e.g., Check & Guloien, 1989; Zillmann & Bryant, 1988), researchers should consider broadening applications of the communibiological paradigm to the study of audience adoption and use beyond the Internet realm, mentioned earlier. For instance, Garbarino's (1999) review noted that only one third of teens are drawn to violent video games, movies, and recordings . . . but virtually all of them are boys. Are boys simply made differently? Garbarino's own work pointed to a strong interaction between testosterone and consumption of the more violent images available on music, video, and computer/online media.

Although there is a dearth of published research on uses and effects of violent (first-person shooter, or FPS) video games, several bills before Congress—offered in the wake of the Columbine High shootings—authorize the allocation of funds for such work. Industry research suggests that violent games account for only about 7% of the $5.5 billion industry, and 90% those games are purchased by adults.

This returns us to the issue of parental mediation, which has been more widely studied in the ontogenic realm with television. As Abelman, Lin, and Atkin (in press) noted, Bronfenbrenner's framework can aid in the study of family interaction with media, particularly for special IQ populations:

> Researchers might fruitfully move to consider, for instance, the mediating influences of family size (microsystem) or race and class dimensions (macrosystem) on televiewing across the ontogenic classifications . . . Even within the level of exosystem (media environment) variables, it will be important to consider

characteristic uses of new media—such as VCRs, cable and computers—across special populations . . . (in press)

These authors further noted that almost 3 million youngsters in the United States are currently classified as emotionally disturbed (ED), learning disabled (LD), or mentally retarded (MR) by their local school district of education, and an additional 1 million of the school-aged population could be classified as intellectually gifted or intellectually gifted with a learning disability. Their own meta-analysis uncovered a dearth of work on the influence of new media on exceptional children.

Abelman et al. (in press) echoed Baran's (1972) call to employ broad-based, integrative frameworks to help contextualize the many characteristics and experiences that make lower IQ children particularly susceptible to the influence of television (e.g., low self-esteem, a history of failure, little social contact, and high dependence). Both studies underscore the utility of Bronfenbrenner's work in helping frame the study of television.

Turning to developmental influences, perhaps the most extensive application for research on television in the ontogenic context involves research on educational TV. As other chapters in this volume detail, scores on the SAT have dropped 50 to 60 points since the 1960s, as time spent with TV increased. Recent research in this tradition has investigated the impact of new media on scholastic performance, finding little influence of cable (Barnes & Kelloway, 1978) or of VCR use (Roe, 1989) and some learning benefits associated with computer use (e.g., Kiesler, 1997).

Work on family viewing suggests that gifted children receive higher levels of mediation than do general child audiences (Abelman & Petty, 1989). Even so, Salomon (1984) concluded that these children have "the most negative views of the medium, expend the least mental effort in processing a presented program, and show the poorest inference-making performance" (p. 62).

There's a paucity of literature addressing television's influence on other special population (e.g., LD, ED, MR) groups, despite the relatively important role that television could play for these groups. Owing to the dearth of work assessing influences of new media use, it is useful to examine a mesosystem (linkage) involving psychological determinants of subscribership to emerging exosystems defined by new media.

A New Mesosystem: Individual and Family Motives for Media Adoption

In addition to the ontogenic dimensions of media use, researchers have investigated more specific motivations for new media adoption and use. Chief among them is added diversity with program fare for cable households (Heeter & Greenberg, 1988). Clearly, cable viewers are not as satisfied with television in its traditional form, and seek to make greater use of the medium (Ducey et al., 1983; Jacobs, 1995; LaRose & Atkin, 1988; Metzger, 1983). These viewing segments vary in accordance with their consumption attitudes toward video as well. Approximating a relatively more innovative consumer, cable subscribers are more willing to take risks with purchases. VCR owners are also more open to new ideas (Levy, 1981, 1989) than are their broadcast counterparts, who seem content with traditional fare (Krugman, 1985; Lin, 1994a).

With regard to specific cable household types, basic subscribers seek greater program variety than do traditional viewers, but not as much as pay subscribers (Becker, Dunwoody, & Rafaeli, 1983; Heeter & Greenberg, 1988; Lin, 1994a; Metzger, 1983). They also reside between pay and nonsubscribers in terms of their receptiveness to new ideas (Atkin, 1993; Krugman & Eckrich, 1982; Lin, 1994a).

Although classic work on diffusion suggests that innovators have a higher I.Q. than nonadopters across general product categories, few such differences have been found in the media context (Rogers, 1995). Consistent with diffusion theory, research has suggested that demographic differences between adopters and nonadopters of new media have been levelling over time (Jacobs, 1995; LaRose & Atkin, 1988; Sparkes & Kang, 1986). Such adoption is more strongly a function of communication needs (e.g., shopping; see Jeffres & Atkin, 1996), as highly motivated viewers are more avid media adopters (e.g., Lin, 1993). The most comprehensive line of research in new media adoption addresses the link between audience uses and gratifications (Eighmey, 1997; Lin, 1998; Newhagen & Rafaeli 1996; Perse & Dunn, 1998).

Although it does not address intraindividual competencies for development in the classical sense, uses and gratifications theory is germane here given its ability to reflect individual differences shaping media use. The tradition posits that audience media use is associated with a set of psychological motives, including surveillance, entertainment, personal identity, escape, and companionship (Rubin, 1983). These motives prompt the audience to purposefully select certain media/contents in order to satisfy a set of psychological needs behind those motives (e.g., Katz, Blumler, & Gurevitch, 1974); they've also been empirically linked with distinct channel selection decisions and viewing content choices as well as with varying viewing levels and viewing gratifications obtained (e.g., Palmgreen, Wenner, & Rosengren, 1985; Perse & Courtright, 1993).

The significance of these uses and gratifications variables to the media adoption and mediation process can be explained in terms of diffusion theory. For instance, Lin (1998) found that more strongly motivated audiences are also more likely to be adopters or "likely adopters" of new media. The most frequently cited motives for using electronic bulletin boards include informational learning and socialization (James et al., 1995). Surveillance needs are a strong predictor of potential adoption of news and information services via pioneer online services (Lin, 1994b).

As mentioned earlier, a primary motivation for new media adoption includes a desire for program diversity with program fare (Heeter & Greenberg, 1988), as cable viewers are not as satisfied with television in its traditional form, and seek to make greater use of the medium (Ducey et al., 1983; LaRose & Atkin, 1988; Metzger, 1983). Moreover, consistent with diffusion research, earlier cable adopters are more innovative consumers and are more willing to take risks with purchases (Krugman, 1985; Lin & Jeffres, 1998).

Pay cable subscribers are the most demanding viewers in their appetite for program variety, followed by basic, and finally, traditional viewers (Albarran & Umphrey, 1994; Becker et al., 1983; Heeter & Greenberg, 1988; Metzger, 1983). These groups are similarly ordered in terms of their receptiveness to new ideas (Atkin et al., 1991; Krugman & Eckrich, 1982).

Other work has affirmed that adoption of emerging technologies such as cable, videotext, PCs, and CDs, was best predicted by the adoption of functionally similar technologies that fulfill similar communication needs (e.g., Reagan, 1996) and positive user attitudes toward them. These underlying similarities can form the basis for media technology adoption clusters (Atkin, 1993), which Reagan et al. (1995) later retermed *technology repertoires.*

Looking at motivations for the adoption of the most discontinuous medium, the Internet, Katz and Aspden (1997) suggested that the desire for sociopersonal development was the primary explanatory factor. Miller (1996) concluded that babyboomers primarily utilized the Internet services for information retrieval purposes, whereas their younger counterparts typically pursued offerings unique to the Internet (e.g., use music and entertainment or download photos, video clips, and music clips).

Although the linkage between audience motivations and exposure to new media content is well established, implications for parental mediation have not been fully explored in that context. Research on the diffusion of adult-oriented services suggests that adopters tend to be more highly educated, opposed to censorship, and open to new ideas (Atkin, 1997; Thompson, Chaffee, & Oshagen, 1990). As we discuss shortly, the pervasity of adult-oriented content in new media outlets does not prompt greater mediation in subscriber households (e.g., Atkin et al., 1989, 1991).

Bronfenbrenner's (1979) conception obviously predated the new media revolution, and his brief discussion of family interaction with television was limited to traditional environments. He did, however, echo early findings that TV reduces family interaction, which can only be resuscitated

by parental supervision of viewing. Bronfenbrenner's exosystem concept was selected as a starting point here, given its latitude to express
content variability in emerging media environments. It is helpful, then,
to examine the social systems factors that drive new media adoption.

The Macrosystem: Social Status Influences On Media Adoption and Use

Although the media literature does not address the full range of factors
impinging on child development, several social locators have been investigated in relation to new media uses. The macrosystem represents the
broadest ecological component, subsuming intrasocietal contrasts involving cultural beliefs, values, and attitudes that influence new media adoption, consumption, and mediation behaviors. Bronfenbrenner (1979) described this element in terms of "various socioeconomic, ethnic, religious,
and other subcultural groups, reflecting contrasting belief systems and
lifestyles" (p. 26).

The role of socioeconomic status is perhaps the most widely researched macrosystem dimension, dating to seminal studies of viewing
(Bower, 1963; Chaffee, McLeod, & Atkin, 1971). This work suggested that
social status is inversely related to viewing time and predictive of mediation (Himmelweit, Oppenheim, & Vince, 1958; Himmelweit & Swift, 1976;
Rossiter & Robertson, 1975; Schramm, Lyle, & Parker, 1961). Despite this
upper middle-class ethos favoring parental control over viewing (Brown
& Linne, 1976), social status is predictive, paradoxically, of the adoption of these new media environments (Krugman, 1985; LaRose & Atkin,
1988, 1991).

The apparent crosspressures prompted by class-driven dynamics moti-
vating mediation alongside greater adoption of these "brave new media"
may be changing as their penetration increases, however. In particular,
researchers (Lin & Atkin, 1989) found socioeconomic status to be one of
the least predictive variables for child viewing behavior in the new media
environment.

Focusing on other social locators, early cable adoption research found
basic cable families were younger, wealthier, and larger, relative to traditional families (Krugman, 1985; LaRose & Atkin, 1988; Webster 1983).
Ethnicity represents another macrosystem determinant of viewing, with
African American households spending the most time with TV (AC Nielsen,
1998; Brown et al., 1990; Greenberg & Dervin, 1970) while indicating similar levels of mediation (Blosser & Heintz, 1988; Greenberg & Dominick,
1969). In new media environments, rulemaking decreases as viewing increases (Atkin et al., 1991; Lin & Atkin, 1989).

Although there is a dearth of work investigating the influence of ethnicity in new media environments, adoption studies have shown that
African American and Hispanic households are less likely than their White

counterparts to have access to cable, VCRs, and computer media (Atkin et al., 1998b; Brown et al., 1990; Krugman, 1985). The confluence of findings suggests that ethnicity is not as consistent a predictor as income in determining cable adoption (Jacobs, 1995; LaRose & Atkin, 1991).

Focusing on computer applications, children clearly do not enjoy the same type of access to the Internet that they do for television. Early studies have suggested that families adopting pioneer computer bulletin board services also approximate the demographic profile of general "innovators," whose personal attributes include younger age and both greater income and higher education (Atkin & LaRose, 1994; Dutton, Rogers, & Jun, 1987). More recent studies of Internet users indicate a similar trend (Atkin et al., 1998a; Katz & Aspden, 1997). A national survey (Price Waterhouse, 1997) found that these adopters' median household income fell between $50,000 and $75,000.

In further profiling interactions between macrosystem variables and new media use, the following section examines how these factors interact with media use.

Microsystem: Parental Mediation in the New Media Environment

Bronfenbrenner (1979) casted video programming as an exosystem component because it influences interactive processes in the home, or microsystem. In that regard, as Atkin (1994) noted, it represents a mesosystem (intersection) of (a) the distinctive demography of new technology adopters (encompassing the macrosystem), (b) new program environments (creating different exosystems), and (c) family uses of those technologies (within the microsystem). This section reviews parental mediation behaviors elicited by ontogenic concerns over the impact of programming, which is exercised in the microsystem.

As other chapters in this volume detail, television as an exosystem "houseguest" may motivate mediation behaviors, including (a) debriefing (or helping interpret) program content; (b) instilling general modes of responding so that the child can interpret similar events in the future, and (c) restraining the child from viewing potentially distressing material (Mander, 1983).

Research compendia (e.g., Kotler, Wright, & Huston, Chap. 2, this volume) conclude that few microsystem factors consistently predict mediation. This may stem from the difficulty in categorizing the many different permutations of those factors occurring from family to family (see Austin, Chap. 18, this volume; Krcmar, 1996).

Even though research in traditional environments found that families with lower income and education view more TV than upscale families, the latter's affinity for cable and VCRs has reversed that trend. The sparsity of viewing regulations among pay cable and VCR settings indicates that children in that exosystem watch more programming in all of its various forms, including R-movies (Atkin et al., 1989; Heeter & Greenberg, 1988).

As other chapters in this volume detail, research indicates that parental mediation activities are influenced by the number of parents (e.g., Corder-Bolz, 1980; Huston, Zillmann, & Bryant, 1994) and siblings within a given household (e.g., Atkin et al., 1991). Family uses and responses to TV may, in turn, be influenced by macrosystem (e.g., social class) variables. Such mediation is more likely to occur in families with gifted children, where perceptions of television's effects are also greater (Abelman & Petty, 1989).

Although the previous section presents an upscale profile of pay cable subscribers, these families also tend to be larger and younger than either their traditional or basic counterparts (Heeter & Greenberg, 1988; Krugman & Eckrich, 1982; Lin, 1994a; Webster, 1983). As one might imply from their subscription behavior, pay viewers also view television as a more important source of entertainment and spend more time with the medium.

As Lin's chapter (this volume) details, VCRs also enhance home entertainment, in addition to interpersonal communication (e.g., Rubin & Bantz, 1987). Family mediation in this context can enhance the decision-making process accompanying tape rental (Cohen & Cohen, 1989; Rubin & Rubin, 1989), facilitating family cohesion and home entertainment activity (Lin, 1990).

Lower technology outlets can also confound the mediation process in new video homes, whose richer exosystem is also likely to include a TV set for children (Brown, Bauman, Lentz, & Koch, 1987). At present, over half of U.S. television households have two or more television sets, a factor that can spread parental supervisory resources thinly.

Another such microsystem resource includes the number of parents in the home, as households with two working parents (or a single working parent) also mediate VCR use less frequently than their dual-parent counterparts (Brown et al., 1990; Lin & Atkin, 1989). This family communication may be motivated by VCR use, including the refinement of technical competence (Cohen & Cohen, 1989) and interpersonal adjustments to the "transient needs" of each family member (Rubin & Rubin, 1989).

Thus, as Lindlof, Shatzer, and Wilkinson (1988) noted, these divergent interests in VCR uses among the family necessitate the articulation of a family dialectic. Parental control over child viewing can perhaps be most easily managed via management of VCR libraries (Heintz, 1990). Despite the increased potential for control, VCR homes are less likely to exercise it (Lin & Atkin, 1989). Specifically, indecent (R-rated) movies on pay cable are "often" watched by adolescents from VCR homes as compared to "sometimes" watched by non-VCR teens (Kim, Baran, & Massey, 1988).

Similarly, verbal and other parental mediation behaviors have been found less frequently in basic cable (Haefner, Hunter, & Wartella, 1986) and pay cable (Atkin et al., 1989) homes, despite their relatively greater potential for offensive content ("Attorney General," 1986). In that regard, new video media allow teens to circumvent parental controls and pursue idiosyncratic subcultures (Roe, 1987). Lin (1990, chap. 5, this volume) noted that VCRs can also help strengthen peer bonds, especially in the case of video parties. Anecdotal evidence addressing Web use, discussed at the onset, suggests that online media present similar capabilities for unsupervised child access.

Internet Mediation and Use. Focusing on microsystem determinants of Internet access, several studies have addressed the "gender gap" in computing, where only 5% of the Internet users were women in 1994. Recent work suggests that this gap is decreasing, as the percentage of girls online jumped to 31% in 1996 and to above 40% in 1998 (Klopfenstein, in press).

Although there is a dearth of academic work on parental mediation of Web use, press reports suggest that parents are concerned that their children might use the new medium to view sexually explicit web pages or to correspond with pedophiles (see Kiesler, 1997). One such report outlined how school-aged children inadvertently encounter graphic images of child sex, simply by typing in the rather innocuous address of "boys.com" or "girls.com." Even so, a Carnegie Mellon University panel study of family Internet use (Manning, Scherlis, Kiesler, Kraut, & Mukhopadhyay, 1997) concluded that ". . . families aren't big consumers of sexual information on the Internet"; in particular: "Forty-two percent read a sexually oriented newsgroup . . . The group that sampled sexually oriented newsgroups included three fourths of the teenage boys, almost half of the teenage girls, a third of the adult men, and a fifth of the adult women" (p. 68).

As home PC penetration increases, however, the bulk of child access to Internet sites will occur at home. Aside from electronic screening programs like NetNanny, parents can facilitate supervision of a minor's use of the Internet by placing host terminals in a central location, perhaps in a room without doors. Electronic screening devices are not quite a panacea for Internauts seeking to filter out offensive material, however, as many programs might inadvertently screen out nonprurient web pages on such topics as safe sex. Given that less intrusive filtering devices, including credit card numbers, were also found unconstitutional, it is clear that the last line of defense in Internet use lies with parental supervision.

MERGING THE NESTED SETTINGS

These various findings can be viewed, on balance, in the context of interlinkages among the nested settings in which they occur. It is useful, then, to expand and update ecological perspectives on family accommodations to new media to reflect emerging online modalities. We begin by reaffirming the assumption that new media can feature different types of programming, initially attracting audiences distinctive from those of traditional broadcasting. This in turn presents new opportunities for viewing and for parental mediation. Integrating these various and several findings within the context of Bronfenbrenner's model (1979), Atkin (1994, p. 30) offered the following typology of ecological settings governing parental mediation of media use:

Microsystem:
- Children, if left unregulated, will view a greater variety and duration of programming across a wider range of times.
- Parents will more closely mediate viewing in households with younger (i.e., preteen) and female children, because they are perceived as more "vulnerable" to the influence of TV.
- Mediation levels will be lower where supervisory resources are stretched, as in multichild and dual-income or single-parent households.

Exosystem:
- New video programmers cannot maximize profits through inoffensive "mass audience" fare, and therefore offer more indecent fare in order to appeal to more specialized audiences.
- Children from new video households will have access to a wider range of programming than their traditional video counterparts.

Macrosystem:
- In traditional video settings, lower S.E.S. households typically watch more television and engage less frequently in mediation.
- New video households, generally higher in S.E.S., tend to watch more than traditional video households; parental mediation is largely unidentified in these settings.

Integrating these input factors, Atkin (1994) offered a formula for the determination of mediation that accounts for the varying levels of discontinuity accompanying different media:

$$\text{Likelihood of action} = \frac{\text{Expected benefit from intervention}}{\text{Effort required to intervene}}$$

Updating that framework here, the expected benefit might be a function of the harms avoided by blocking children from exposure to, say, web pages fostering racial hatred. But, as Meyrowitz (1986) argued, mediation is not strictly a function of need. Given that most parents find mediation (or confrontation) in the context of family viewing to be "painful," parents won't intervene in cases where required parental effort is great. In the parlance of diffusion theory, this effort might be maximized in cases when perceived barriers to parental learning (e.g., mastering HTML) are greatest.

Of course, parents could easily limit access by discontinuing the innovation or severely curtailing family access. The disadvantage of that approach, however, is that parents would need to restrict their own access to the medium as well. These types of trade-offs enhance the desirability of electronic screening devices (e.g., cable lockboxes for cable).

CONCLUSION

The advantage of an ecological perspective such as Bronfenbrenner's (1979) is its ability to accommodate diverse regulatory, media, family, and social influences on child media use and development. Integrating findings addressing exo-, micro-, macro-, and ontogenic-system components, the present chapter summarizes the nascent phase of research on new media in each context. The complexity of these relationships can only be complicated by ongoing changes in the home media environment, the investigation of which presents a daunting challenge for future research.

Now, a decade further along in the video revolution, the observations of early commentators (Atkin et al., 1989, 1991; Heeter & Greenberg, 1988) hold true; the complex interaction among mesosystem factors precludes any clear projections on the influence of new online media on child development. Using work on the initial diffusion of cable and VCRs as a guide, we might expect that new PC-TVs will reinforce existing patterns of family viewing. Parents may indicate adopting this technology for the same reasons they purchased more "continuous" TV adjuncts a decade ago— the enhanced content and control they provide for children's viewing.

Of course, the increased facility that VCRs offer for parental control did not translate into action, given that mediation of viewing was infrequent and selective in those households. It remains to be seen whether the increased facility for offensive fare invites greater parental control and mediation in Internet households.

Just as film was heralded as a potentially harmful new medium during the 1920s (Wartella & Reeves, 1985), emerging channels like the Internet will continue to attract parental concern. This phenomenon has perhaps been most vividly demonstrated by the attention given to Internet influences in the Littleton Colorado shootings, mentioned earlier. When commentators ask why these various school shootings accelerated during the 1990s, they will likely point to shortcomings in the regulation of exosystem influences ranging in scope from media content to gun sales. To the extent that these new media forms lend rise to a new gun subculture, macrosystem variables are also important, particularly as the child develops. And ontogenic dimensions can help explain why girls, who also have access to violence-laden exosystems, are less likely to use and be influenced by it. The fact that parents can now be charged for the crimes of their children, however, underscores the degree to which society holds microsystem factors paramount. Given the wide complex interaction of these factors, Bronfenbrennber's (1979) model provides a suitable framework for later study, even though our discussion is limited to media factors here.

Clearly, as other chapters in this volume detail, the media are generally neutral in their own right. Even the Internet, with its potential for offensive content, remains primarily a publishing medium. Computer games also possess a great potential for proactive educational purposes, in addition to the darker applications outlined earlier. But the latter forms of interactive participation provide a more compelling agent for media effects than graphic violence in other modalities (e.g., film), given their elicitation of user involvement. Further research should proceed on that point.

Drawing from past work, we can project that social concern and parental guidance will peak when a technology first arrives. Over time, though, a social acclimation to the technology should prompt these concern levels to dissipate as families become more familiar with it. To the extent that high technology households are more upscale, per diffusion theory, media use adoption motives can overpower class-driven (macrosystem) imperatives encouraging parental mediation.

Thus, just as demographics have yielded diminished returns—relative to psychographics and media use—in studies of product adoption (e.g., Krugman, 1985), class-driven theories of mediation need to be constantly reevaluated as newer media and content forms come online. Given convergence of these media functions on the emerging information grid, the current methods of gauging family mediation practices may need to be completely revamped.

Although research on the use and mediation of computer/online uses is virtually nonexistent, we can again obtain clues about emerging mediation forms by drawing from preliminary work on cable and VCR use. For instance, much of that work suggests that parents are more likely to restrict child access than to engage in proactive mediation (e.g., to enhance learning). As the ongoing transformation of media continues to blur traditional elements of the media mix, audiences will need to cope with increases in both channel capacity and content diversity, particularly in its more virulent forms.

On balance, this chapter extends past work on family uses of television, providing important linkages to new media among such concepts as diffusion theory, media uses, and substitution. The "convergence" of telephony, computing, and traditional mass media thus presents new control opportunities as well as challenges to parents seeking to monitor their children's viewing. As Lin (1994a) suggested, technological freedom has "emancipated" audience members from the long-term passive role of "TV viewer," to assume a more active role as "TV users" with increased control over their video media environment. These relations can only be complicated by ongoing changes in the home media environment, the investigation of which presents a promising opportunity for future research. Further work should extend this link between changing viewing options and family viewing and mediation patterns as more media services come online.

REFERENCES

Abelman, R., Atkin, D., & Rand, M. (1997). What viewers watch when they watch TV: Affiliation change as a case study. *Journal of Broadcasting & Electronic Media, 41*, 360–379.

Abelman, R., Lin, C., & Atkin, D. (in press). Selected media effects on special populations. In R. Carveth & J. Bryant (Eds.), *Meta-analyses of media effects.* Hillsdale, NJ: Lawrence Erlbaum Associates.

Abelman, R., & Petty, G. R. (1989). Child attributes as determinants of parental television-viewing mediation: The role of child giftedness. *Journal of Family Issues, 10*, 251–266.

Albarran, A. B., & Umphrey, D. (1994). Marketing cable and pay cable services: Impact of ethnicity, viewing motivations, and program types. *Journal of Media Economics, 7*, 47–58.

Atkin, D. (1993). Uses of cable TV amidst a multimedia environment. *Telematics & Informatics, 10*, 51–60.

Atkin, D. (1994). An integrative perspective on parental mediation of children's TV viewing habits across traditional and new program environments. *World Communication, 23*, 22–34.

Atkin, D. (1995). Interest in computer-mediated information services among college students. *Telematics & Informatics, 12*, 1–9.

Atkin, D. (1997). Assessing the need for Stern indecency measures: Audience perceptions of indecency controls across telecommunication media. *Proteus*, 19–25.

Atkin, D., Greenberg, B. S., & Baldwin, T. F. (1991). The home ecology of children's television viewing: Parental mediation and the new media environment. *Journal of Communication, 41*, 88–99.

Atkin, D., Heeter, C., & Baldwin, T. (1989). How presence of cable affects parental mediation. *Journalism Quarterly, 66*, 558–563.

Atkin, D., Jeffres, L., & Neuendorf, K. (1998). Understanding internet adoption dynamics. *Journal of Broadcasting & Electronic Media, 42*, 475–490.

Atkin, D., & LaRose, R. (1994). An analysis of the information services adoption literature. *Advances in Telematics, 2*, 91–110.

Atkin, D., Neuendorf, K., & Jeffres, L. (1998). Reassessing public support for public access cablevision: A faded passion? *Telematics & Informatics, 15*, 67–84.

Atkin, D., Neuendorf, K., Jeffres, L., & Skalski, P. (2000, May). *Predictors of audience interest in adopting digital television.* Paper presented to the International Communication Association, Acapulco.

Attorney General's Commission on Pornography. (1986). Washington DC: Government Printing Office.

Baran, S. J. (1973). TV and social learning in the institutionalized MR. *Mental Retardation, 11* (3), 36–38.

Barnes, S. G. & Kelloway, K. R. (1978). *Cable TV viewership: An examination of innovative behavior.* Unpublished manuscript Memorial University of Newfoundland Working Paper, 78–14.

Beatty, M. J., & McCroskey, J. C. (1998). Interpersonal communication as temperamental expression: A communibiological paradigm. In J. C. McCroskey, J. A. Daly, M. Martin, & M. J. Beatty (Eds.), *Personality and communication: Trait perspectives* (pp. 41–68). Cresskill, NJ: Hampton Press.

Becker, L. B., Dunwoody, S., & Rafaeli, S. (1983). Perceptions of television content. *Journal of Broadcasting, 27,* 127–140.

Blosser, B. J., & Heintz, K. E. (1988, May). *Rules for television viewing: An examination of ethnic differences and parent–child consensus.* Paper presented at the annual conference, International Communication Association, New Orleans.

Bower, R. T. (1973). *Television and the public.* New York: Holt, Rinehart & Winston.

Bronfenbrenner, U. (1979). *The ecology of human development.* New York: Russel Sage Foundation.

Brown, J. D., Bauman, K. E., Lentz, G. M., & Koch, G. (1987, May). *Young adolescents' use of radio and television in the 1980s.* Paper presented at the International Communication Association, Montreal.

Brown, J. D., Childers, K. W., Bauman, K. E., & Koch, G. (1990). The influence of new media and family structure on young adolescent television and radio use. *Communication Research, 17,* 65–82.

Brown, J. R., & Linne, O. (1976). The family as a mediator of television's effects. In R. Brown (Ed.), *Children and television* (pp. 184–198). Beverly Hills, CA: Sage.

Bryant, J., & Zillmann, D. (1986). *Perspectives on media effects.* Hillsdale, NJ: Lawrence Erlbaum Associates.

Chaffee, S. H., McLeod, J. M., & Atkin, C. K. (1971). Parental influences on adolescent media use. *American Behavioral Scientist, 14* (3), 323–340.

Charney, T., & Greenberg, B. S. (in press). Uses and gratifications of the Internet. In C. Lin & D. Atkin (Eds.), *Communication technology and society: Audience adoption and uses of the new media.* Cresskill, NJ: Hampton Press.

Check, J. V. P., & Guloien, T. H. (1989). Reported proclivity for coercive sex following repeated exposure to sexually violent pornography, nonviolent dehumanizing pornography, and erotica. In D. Zillman & J. Bryant (Eds.), *Pornography: Research advances and policy considerations* (pp. 159–184). Hillsdale, NJ: Lawrence Erlbaum Associates.

Childers, T., & Krugman, D. (1987). The competitive environment of pay-per-view. *Journal of Broadcasting & Electronic Media, 31,* 335–342.

Cohen, A., & Cohen, L. (1989). Big eyes but clumsy fingers: Knowing about and using technological features of home VCRs. In M. Levy (Ed.), *The VCR age* (pp. 135–147). Newbury Park, CA: Sage.

Corder-Bolz, C. R. (1980). Critical television viewing skills for elementary schools. *Television and children, 3* (3), 34–39.

Dholakia, R. R., Mundorf, N., & Dholakia, N. (1996). *Infotainment technologies in the home: Demand side perspectives.* Hillsdale, NJ: Lawrence Erlbaum Associates.

Ducey, R., Krugman, D., & Eckrich, D. (1983). Predicting market segments in the cable industry: The basic and pay subscribers. *Journal of Broadcasting, 27,* 155–161.

Dutton, W. H., Rogers, E., & Jun, S. (1987). The diffusion and impacts of information technology in households. *Oxford surveys in information technology* (Vol. 4, pp. 133–193). New York: Oxford University Press.

Eighmewy, J. (1997). Profiling user responses to commercial web sites. *Journal of Advertising Research, 37,* 59–66.

Federal Communications Commission v. Pacifica Foundation, 438 U.S. 728 (1977).

Finn, S. (1998, May). *Computer attitudes and personality traits: A uses and gratifications approach to computer technology research.* Paper presented to the International Communication Association Conference, Montreal.

Garbarino, J. (1999). *Lost boys.* New York: The Free Press.

Greenberg, B. S., & Dervin, B. (1970). *Use of the mass media by the urban poor.* New York: Praeger.

Greenberg, B. S., & Dominick, J. R. (1969). Race and social class differences in teenagers' use of television. *Journal of Broadcasting, 13,* 1331–1334.

Greenberg, B. S., Heeter, C., & Lin, C. (1988). Playboy viewing styles. In C. Heeter & B. S. Greenberg (Eds)., *Cableviewing* (pp. 191–206). Norwood, NJ: Ablex.

Greenberg, B. S., & Lin, C. (1988). *Teletext use in the U.K.* London: IBA.

Haefner, M. J., Hunter, L. S., & Wartella, E. A. (1986). *Parents, children and new media: Expectations, attitudes and use.* Paper presented to the International Communication Association, Chicago.

Heeter, C., & Greenberg, B. S. (1988). *Cableviewing.* Norwood, NJ: Ablex.

Heintz, K. E. (1990). VCR libraries: Opportunities for parental control. In J. Dobrow (Ed.), *Social and cultural aspects of VCR use* (pp. 147–162). Hillsdale, NJ: Lawrence Erlbaum Associates.

Henke, L., & Donohue, T. (1989). Functional displacement of traditional TV viewing by VCR owners. *Journal of Advertising Research, 29* (3), 18–25.

Himmelweit, H., Oppenheim, A.M., & Vince, P. (1958). *Television and the child.* London: Oxford University Press.

Himmelweit, H., & Swift, B. (1976). Continuities and discontinuities in media usage and taste: A longitudinal study. *Journal of Social Issues, 32* (4), 133–156.

Home Box Office, Inc. v Federal Communications Commission, 567 F. 2d 9 (D.C. Cir. 1977), *cert. denied,* 434 U.S. 829, 98 S. Ct. 111, 54 L. Ed. 2d 89.

Huston, A. C., Zillmann, D., & Bryant, J. (1994). Media influence, public policy, and the family. In D. Zillmann, J. Bryant, & A Huston (Eds.), *Media, children, and the family* (pp. 3–18). Hillsdale, NJ: Lawrence Erlbaum Associates.

Jacobs, R. (1995). Exploring determinants of cable television subscriber satisfaction. *Journal of Broadcasting & Electronic Media, 39,* 262–274.

James, M. L., Wotring, C. E., & Forrest, E. (1995). An exploratory study of the perceived benefits of electronic bulletin board use and their impact on other communication activities. *Journal of Broadcasting & Electronic Media, 40,* 318–330.

Jeffres, L., & Atkin, D. (1996). Predicting use of technologies for communication and consumer needs. *Journal of Broadcasting & Electronic Media, 40,* 318–330.

Jeffres, L., Atkin, D., & Neuendorf, K. (1995). The impact of new and traditional media on college student leisure preferences. *World Communication, 24,* 67–73.

Jessell, M. (1995, November 6). Internet begins to cut into TV viewing. *Broadcasting & Cable,* 113.

Johnnson-Smagardi, U., & Roe, K. (1986). *Teenagers in the new world:* Video recorders, video games and home computers (Report No. 2). Lund: Department of Sociology.

Jordan, A. (1990). A family systems approach to the use of the VCR. In J. Dobrow (Ed.), *Social and cultural aspects of VCR use* (pp. 163–179). Hillsdale, NJ: Lawrence Erlbaum Associates.

Jupiter Communications. (1997). *The 1997 online kids report.* New York: Author.

Kang, M. & Atkin, D. (1999). Exploring the role of audience uses and gratifications in the adoption of multimedia cable. *Telematics & Informatics, 16* (4), 59–76.

Katz, E., Blumler, J. G., & Gurevitch, M. (1974). Utilization of mass communication by the individual. In J. G. Blumler & E. Katz (Eds.), *Uses of mass communications* (pp. 19–34). Beverly Hills, CA: Sage.

Katz, J., & Aspden, P. (1997). Motivations for and barriers to Internet usage: Results of a national public opinion survey. *Internet Research, 7,* 170–188.

Katz, R. (1999, January 3). Kids may be toddling away from television. *Variety,* p. 39.

Kiesler, S. (1997). *Culture of the Internet.* Mahwah, NJ: Lawrence Erlbaum Associates.

Kim, W.Y., Baran, S., & Massey, K. K. (1988). Impact of the VCR on control of television viewing. *Journal of Broadcasting & Electronic Media, 32,* 351–358.

Klopfenstein, B. (in press). The Internet and Web as communication media. In C. Lin & D. Atkin (Eds.), *Communication technology and society: Audience adoption and uses of the new media.* Cresskill, NJ: Hampton Press.

Krcmar, M. (1996). Family communication patterns, discourse behavior and child television viewing. *Human Communication Research, 23,* 251–277.

Krugman, D. (1985). Evaluating the audiences of the new media. *Journal of Advertising, 14* (4), 14–19.

Krugman, D., & Eckrich, D. (1982). Differences between cable and pay cable viewers. *Journal of Advertising Research, 22,* 423–429.

Lasswell, H. (1948). The structure and function of communication in society. In L. Bryson (Ed.), *The communication of ideas* (pp. 37–51). New York: Harper.

LaRose, R., & Atkin, D. (1988). Intentions to disconnect cable service: The role of customer satisfaction variables. *Journal of Broadcasting & Electronic Media, 32,* 403–413.

LaRose, R., & Atkin, D. (1991). An analysis of pay-per-view versus other movie delivery modalities. *Journal of Media Economics, 4,* 3–17.

Levy, M. (1981). Home video recorders and time-shifting. *Journalism Quarterly, 58,* 31–37.

Levy, M. (1989). *The VCR age.* Beverly Hills, CA: Sage.

Lin, C. A. (1990). Audience activity and VCR use. In J. Dobrow (Ed.), *Social and cultural aspects of VCR use* (pp. 75–92). Hillsdale, NJ: Lawrence Erlbaum Associates.

Lin, C. (1992). The functions of the VCR in the home leisure environment. *Journal of Broadcasting & Electronic Media, 36,* 345–351.

Lin, C. A. (1993). Exploring the role of VCR use in the emerging home entertainment culture. *Journalism Quarterly, 70,* 833–842.

Lin, C. A. (1994a). Audience fragmentation in a competitive video marketplace. *Journal of Advertising Research, 34,* 1–17.

Lin, C. A. (1994b). Exploring potential factors for home videotex adoption. In J. Hanson (Ed.), *Advances in telematics* (pp. 111–124). Norwood, NJ: Ablex.

Lin, C. A. (1998). Exploring personal computer adoption dynamics. *Journal of Broadcasting & Electronic Media, 42,* 95–112.

Lin, C. A. (1999). Predicting online service adoption likelihood among potential subscribers: A motivational approach. *Journal of Advertising Research, 39*(1). 79–89.

Lin, C., & Atkin, D. (1989). Parental mediation and rulemaking for adolescent use of television and VCRs. *Journal of Broadcasting & Electronic Media, 33,* 53–67.

Lin, C., & Atkin, D. (Eds.). (in press). *Communication technology and society: Audience adoption and uses of the new media.* Cresskill, NJ: Hampton Press.

Lin, C., & Jeffres, L. (1998). Factors influencing the adoption of multimedia cable technology. *Journalism & Mass Communication Quarterly, 75,* 341–352.

Lindlof, T. R., Shatzer, M., & Wilkinson, D. (1988). Constructing rituals of extension through family television viewing. In J. Lull (Ed.), *World families watch television* (pp. 237–259). Newbury Park, CA: Sage.

Maguire, T. (1998, December). Web nets the masses. *American Demographics,* p. 18.

Mander, M. S. (1983). *Communications in transition.* New York: Praeger.

Manning, J., Scherlis, W., Kiesler, S., Kraut, R., & Mukhopadhyay, T. (1997). Erotica on the Internet: Early evidence from the homenet trial (pp. 68-69). In S. Kiesler (Ed.), *Culture of the internet* (pp. 53–67). Mahwah, NJ: Lawrence Erlbaum Associates.

Mehta, M. D., & Plaze, D. (1997). Pornography in cyberspace: An exploration of what's in usenet. In S. Kiesler (Ed.), *Culture of the internet* (pp. 53–67). Mahwah, NJ: Lawrence Erlbaum Associates.

Metzger, G. (1983). Cable Television Audiences. *Journal of Advertising Research, 23* (4), 41–47.

Meyrowitz, J. (1986). *No sense of place.* New York: Ablex.

Miller, T. E. (1996, July). Segmenting the Internet. *American Demographics,* p. 48.

Morgan, M., Alexander, A., Shanahan, J., & Harris, C. (1990). Adolescents, VCRs and the family environment. *Communication Research, 17,* 83–106.

Morris, M., & Ogan, C. (1996). The Internet as mass medium. *Journal of Communication, 46,* 39–50.

Neuendorf, K., Atkin, D., & Jeffres, L. (1998). Understanding adopters of audio information services. *Journal of Broadcasting & Electronic Media, 42,* 80–95.

Newhagen, J. E., & Rafaeli, S. (1996). Why communication researchers should study the Internet: A dialogue. *Journal of Communication, 46,* 4–13.

Nielsen Media Research, Inc. (1998, February). *Media News.* New York: Author.

Palmgreen, P., Wenner, L. A., & Rosengren, K. E. (1985). Uses and gratifications research: The past ten years. In K. E. Rosengren, L. A. Wenner, & P. Palmgreen (Eds.), *Media gratifications research: Current perspectives* (pp. 11–37). Beverly Hills, CA: Sage.

Perse, E., & Courtright, J. (1993). Normative images of communication media: Mass and interpersonal channels in the new media environment. *Communication Research, 19,* 451–484.

Perse, E., & Dunn, D. (1998). The utility of home computers and media use: Implications of multimedia and connectivity. *Journal of Broadcasting & Electronic Media, 42,* 435–456.

Price Waterhouse (1997). *Technology Forecast: 1997.* Menlow Park, CA: Author.

Rafaeli, S. (1986). The electronic bulletin board: A computer-driven mass medium. *Computers and the Social Sciences, 2,* 123–136.

Reagan, J. (1996). The "repertoire" of information services. *Journal of Broadcasting & Electronic Media, 40,* 112–121.

Reagan, J. (1995) (in press). The difficult world of predicting telecommunication innovations: Factors affecting adoption. In C. Lin & D. Atkin (Eds.), Communication technology and society: Audience adoption and uses of the new media. Cresskill, NJ: Hampton Press.

Roe, K. (1987). Adolescents' video use. *American Behavioral Scientist, 30,* 522–532.

Roe, K. (1989). School achievement, self-esteem, and adolescents' video use. In M. Levy (Ed.), *The VCR age.* Newbury Park, CA: Sage.

Rogers, E. (1995). *Diffusion of innovations.* New York: Free Press.

Rogers, E. (in press). The information society in the next millennium: Captain's log, 2001. In C. Lin & D. Atkin (Eds.), *Communication technology and society: Audience adoption and uses of the new media.* Cresskill, NJ: Hampton Press.

Rossiter, J. R., & Robertson, T. S. (1975). Children's television viewing: An examination of parent–child consensus. *Sociometry, 38,* 308–326.

Rubin, A. (1983). Television uses and gratifications: The interactions of viewing patterns and motivations. *Journal of Broadcasting, 27,* 37–51.

Rubin, A. M., & Bantz, C. R. (1987). Utility of videocassette recorders. *American Behavioral Scientist, 30,* 417–185.

Rubin, A., & Bantz, C. (1989). Uses and gratifications of videocassette recorders. In J. Salvaggio & J. Bryant (Eds.), *Media uses in the information age: Emerging patterns of adoption and use* (pp. 181–195). Hillsdale, NJ: Lawrence Erlbaum Associates.

Rubin, A., & Eyal, K. (in press). The videocassette recorder in the home media environment. In C. Lin & D. Atkin (Eds.), *Communication technology and society: Audience adoption and uses of the new media.* Cresskill, NJ: Hampton Press.

Rubin, A. M., & Rubin, R. (1989). Social psychological antecedents of VCR use. In M. Levy (Ed.), *The VCR age* (pp. 92–112). Newbury Park, CA: Sage.

Salomon, G. (1984). Investing effort in television viewing. In J. P. Murray and G. Salomon (Eds.), *The future of children's television* (pp. 53–82). Boys Town, NE: The Boys Town Center.

Schramm, W., Lyle, J., & Parker, E. B. (1961). *Television in the lives of our children.* Stanford, CA: Stanford University Press.

Schoenbach, K., & Becker, L. B. (1989). The audience copes with plenty: Patterns of reactions to media changes. In L. Becker & K. Schoenbach (Eds.), *Audience responses to diversification: Coping with plenty* (pp. 198–212). Mahwah, NJ: Lawrence Erlbaum Associates.

Sparkes, V., & Kang, N. (1986). Public reactions to cable television: Time in the diffusion process. *Journal of Broadcasting & Electronic Media, 30,* 213–222.

Stipp, H. (1998, July). Should TV marry PC? *American Demographics,* 16–21.

Striesand, B. (1999, June 14). Lawyers, guns, money. *U.S. News & World Report,* pp. 56–57.

Thompson, M. E., Chaffee, S. H., & Oshagen, H. (1990). Regulating pornography: A public dilemma. *Journal of Communication, 40,* 73–83.

U.S. appeals ruling on Internet porn. (1999, April 4). *Cleveland Plain Dealer,* p. A2.

Vobejda, B. (1998, November). Less time for child's play. *Washington Post Weekly Edition,* p. 34.

Wartella, E., & Reeves, B. (1985). Historical trends in research on children and the media: 1900–1960. *Journal of Communication, 35* (3), 118–135.

Webster, J. (1983). The impact of cable and pay cable television on local station audiences. *Journal of Broadcasting, 27,* 119–125.

Webster, J. (1986). Audiences of the new media. *Journal of Communication, 36,* 78–108.

Zillmann, D., & Bryant (1988). Pornography's impact on sexual satisfaction. *Journal of Applied Social Psychology, 18,* 438–453.

Remote Control Devices and Family Viewing

James R. Walker
Saint Xavier University

Robert V. Bellamy, Jr.
Duquesne University

There are several generally accepted truisms about television as an industry and as an important social force in the lives of families. First, television can affect behaviors, often in negative ways, depending on its content and the contexts of its use. Second, children are the most affected and deserve protection through some combination of parental/guardian actions, industry self-regulation, and governmental policies. Finally, the television industry is in a period of rapid change as a result of technological diffusion and regulatory change (Walker & Ferguson, 1998).

These truisms are reflected in the continuing discussions and actions of researchers, policymakers, and concerned citizens. Most recently, combined government and generally coerced industry action led to a television content ratings system and the introduction of V-chip technology that will allow parents or guardians to restrict their children's access to some undesirable content. Earlier regulatory actions included "Family Viewing Time," limitations on advertising in children's programming, and minimum children's television standards (Kunkel, 1990). These actions, in turn, are part of a long history of restricting children's access to media.

The continuous content regulation concerns are occurring in a radically changed television industry. Gone forever is the first generation of television, when the "Big 3" network oligopoly presented similar program options to 90% or more of all prime-time viewers. Today, the Big 4 networks compete against other niche-broadcast networks and a wide variety of cable and satellite delivered alternatives. In this environment, the cumulative viewing audience for the Big 4 often trails the cumulative cable audience. But industry restructuring is not the only source of change. Family viewing has changed as well.

In its first generation, the three commercial television networks competed in a one-set-per-family environment and that set was the focal point of media interaction for most families. In 1960, there was slightly more than one set per U.S. household. The medium's second generation saw the development of strong competition from the Fox network, cable, independent stations, and VCRs with remote control devices (RCDs) facilitating the selection of these new alternatives (Bellamy & Walker, 1996). By 1990, there were an average of two receivers per home (Copeland & Schweitzer, 1993). Now, approximately three in four (74%) U.S. households have more than one set, and nearly one in four (24%) has three or more sets (*Broadcasting & Cable Yearbook*, 1998, p. xxxi). Children and teens control many of these additional sets. According to industry sources, one third of all 6- to 7-year-olds have their own sets as do approximately 60% of all teenagers (Spring, 1999).

Just as radio before it, television has become increasingly an individual medium. In the developing third generation of television (Bellamy & Walker, 1996), the medium's content will continue to shift to more targeted programming. The "family viewing hour" may become the "narrowcast minute." Specialized networks, videotapes and discs, video games, and computer–television interfaces will offer more focused content of varying lengths to relatively small and demographically desirable viewing segments.

The diffusion of such television technologies as videocassette recorders (VCRs)/video disc players and RCDs has had enormous impact on industry structure and undoubtedly reflects a more active audience. Because substantial numbers of viewers use these tools actively to construct personalized television environments, it is more likely that they come into conflict with those sharing a common viewing experience than would have been the case in an era of limited channels and control.

THE SIGNIFICANCE OF RCD RESEARCH

Given the rapid increase in video alternatives in U.S. homes, there are three major reasons for our emphasis on RCDs. First, the RCD is available in virtually every U.S. household to control television program selection (Klopfenstein, 1993). Second, the RCD is an essential navigation tool for the increasing number of video options, encouraging both viewer content selectivity and content avoidance (Perse, 1998). Finally, the RCD is a "subversive" technology that has changed the way millions of viewers watch television (Bellamy & Walker, 1996). RCD grazing (channel surfing) has challenged an industry built on the notion that a relatively passive audience could be created with few channels and sold in bulk to advertisers. As Robinson and Godbey (1997) concluded:

> The VCR did not seem to make much of a dent in regular viewing habits, although cable and remote controls may have changed channel surfing into the most exercise many Americans now get. (p. 153)

RCDs and Family Viewing Interactions

The rapid diffusion of RCDs has important implications for the study of family viewing. Alexander (1990) divided family viewing into four types of interactions; control of program selection, interpretation of program content, maintenance of the family system, and interpretations outside the viewing context. She argued that family viewing research must move beyond considerations of simple program reception, acknowledging that mass and interpersonal communication blend in family viewing. In this chapter, we focus on the impact of RCDs on the control of program selection and their impact on the family system, specifically, the possible reduction of family viewing. In particular, we examine who controls the RCD in families, how families with contrary communication patterns approach RCD control differently, and what RCD uses are related to individual viewing.

RCDs greatly facilitate program selection and thus can be seen as a tool for parental control of program content. In family viewing situations, one parent or the other can control the RCD and thus limit program options. However, in the absence of parental control, the RCD also increases exposure to the vast array of distribution channels now available. Because many young children and a majority of teens now have their own receivers (Spring, 1999), the RCD appears to function as both a source of parental control and of childhood exploration.

RCDs have another major control function; controlling interaction with content. For example, watching a prerecorded program on a VCR while using the RCD to "zip" through all advertising, promotions, and program openings and endings is a different content interaction than "surfing" from one program source to another to construct an individual programming mix. In a family viewing context, the former behavior may be encouraged, whereas the latter viewing behavior may drive family members to their own sets.

In the following discussion, we pursue two objectives; (a) to provide an analytical review of the existing empirical literature on the RCD's role in family and group television viewing environments, and (b) to propose future lines of research on the impact of RCD use on family viewing.

RCDs and Family Viewing: Key Questions and Answers

We have organized our review of the research on RCD uses and gratifications and family viewing around seven questions addressed in prior research.

1. In family viewing situations (parents & children), who controls the RCD?
2. Besides gender and family role, what other variables account for differences in which family member controls the remote?
3. In same-gender adult viewing situations, who controls the remote?
4. How do other viewers react to RCD domination?
5. When the viewing situation (group or individual) is unknown, what individuals are more likely to control the remote?
6. Is frequent remote control use related to viewing alone?
7. What gratifications of remote control use are most associated with group viewing and with individual viewing?

Because RCD research that focuses specifically on family and group viewing is limited, we also incorporate findings from studies of individual RCD use that are relevant to these questions.

In Family Viewing Situations (Parents & Children), Who Controls the RCD? The popular stereotype of father in his "Archie Bunker" easy chair "hogging" the remote for most of the evening has some support in the research literature. Both qualitative (Cornwell et al., 1993; Krendl, Troiano, Dawson, & Clark, 1993; Morley, 1986; Walker, 1996) and quantitative (Copeland, 1989; Copeland and Schweitzer, 1993; "Remote Controls," 1992) studies of RCD control or dominance within the nuclear family have yielded similar results.

In a study of working-class British families, Morley (1986) used focused interviews of family members to examine routine television viewing. In his limited sample of 18 families, male control was nearly universal. He found that "none of the women in any of the families use the automatic control [RCD] regularly" (p. 148). Using the RCD to dominate program selection was for some men a sign of family dominance. "We discuss what we all want to watch and the biggest wins. That's me. I'm the biggest" (p. 148).

Males found it easier to control viewing because they were more likely to devote full attention to the medium. Women were much more likely to view while performing housework or talking with others. Men were granted the privilege of uninterrupted viewing after their day's out-of-home work was completed. Despite similar daytime work commitments, women must often perform household and family tasks during the prime hours of evening viewing. However, because Morley's findings were based on group interviews, he cautioned that the results may be influenced by group pressures that present family viewing in stereotypic ways over-stating the universal dominance of males. His study was also based on interviews with a demographically homogeneous group of families. In addition, this study is nearly 15 years old, which means that both televi-sion content and viewing environment may be substantially different.

Morley's results were supported in three subsequent observational studies. Cornwell et al. (1993) coded RCD use in 10 diverse households. Each household was videotaped for 36 hours over 6 days. Despite a slightly higher level of RCD use by females for all viewing situations (due to one very active female RCD user), males dominated the RCD in male/female viewing situations, using the RCD 77% of the time. In observing three households, Krendl et al. (1993) found that, after children were sent to bed, fathers dominated the RCD more frequently than mothers. Krendl et al. also noted different patterns of program selection. Mothers typically used printed program guides to select programs, whereas fathers used the RCD to perform orienting searches before selecting a program. This finding is consistent with research that shows males are more adept at visual and females more inclined toward verbal information process-ing (Perse & Ferguson, 1993).

In a study of 31 heterosexual couples who were either married or liv-ing together, Walker (1996) used in-depth interviews and questions with quantitative response options to assess the relationship between gen-der, power, and RCD use. The results of this study provided both qualita-tive and quantitative evidence that males tend to dominant RCD use and program selection. This male RCD dominance makes television viewing a "source of conflict—conflict [for women] between their own enjoyment and the enjoyment of their partners" (p. 820).

Male dominance of RCDs was also reported in one industry and two academic surveys of RCD use in families. In a survey of *Consumer Reports* readers ("Remote Controls," 1992), men were much more active users and twice as likely as women to take charge of the remote. In a telephone survey of 218 university-community families, Copeland (1989) also found that RCDs were most frequently controlled by male heads of households.

Adult males generally held or controlled the remote in 35% of sample homes, whereas adult females controlled it in 26% of homes and children controlled it in 19%. For most other homes, family members took turns using the remote. In childless homes, males dominated 30% and females 19% of the time.

In a subsequent survey of 133 (72 male and 61 female) university students (Copeland & Schweitzer, 1993), male RCD dominance was much more pronounced. Slightly more than 60% of these undergraduates reported that their father was the family member that "usually dominates (holds) the remote control when your family watches television together" (p. 163). The next most dominate group were son(s) (19.6%), with mothers (8.7%) and daughter(s) (6.5%) trailing notably. Significantly, males dominated the RCD in nearly 8 in 10 households.

Finally, in a study of 74 two-parent families using both observations and questionnaires, Lull (1990) found evidence of male dominance in program selection. Although RCD use was not specifically reported, fathers were, in both observations and self-report measures, the most likely to select programs. In 92% of the observed selections, there was no discussion of the father's program choice.

Male dominance in RCD use and program selection reported in these qualitative and quantitative studies is congruous with the socialist feminist explanation of gender differences in RCD use posited by Perse and Ferguson (1993). Men are socialized to control both technology and group situations. Give these social conditions, it is not surprising that they are more likely to control the RCD during family viewing. In group settings, the more socially powerful males dominant program selection by controlling the RCD, the most frequently used device for channel changing.

Besides Gender and Family Role, What Other Variables Account for Differences in Which Family Member Controls the Remote? Although a variety of demographic and psychological variables have been examined in studies of individual RCD uses and gratifications (Bellamy & Walker, 1996), only two studies have specifically examined the factors that account for differences in RCD control within families. Neither of these studies used demographic or psychological variables, focusing instead on family communication patterns. After recording the general pattern of RCD dominance by male family members, Copeland (1989) and Copeland and Schweitzer (1993) examined the relationship between styles of family communication and differences in RCD dominance among families. In the first study, Copeland (1989) employed Family Communication Pattern scales (McLeod & Chaffee, 1972) to distinguish among families with different RCD-dominant members. His results showed that families in which women were more likely to control the RCD were also more likely to be socio-oriented families that limited conflict by mediation. For these families, Copeland suggested that mothers served as mediator, reducing conflict between fathers and children over program selection by controlling the RCD.

In Copeland and Schweitzer's (1993) subsequent study, the McMaster Family Assessment Device (Epstein, Baldwin, & Bishop, 1983) was used to measure family functioning, including patterns of transactions among members. In this study, when daughters dominated the RCD, families exhibited more emotional or direct communication styles than when males (fathers or sons) were the RCD controllers. Also, when the mother was RCD dominant, more emotional or direct communication styles were used more often than when the son(s) were dominant. Finally, when daughters dominated the RCD, families perceived that they had more ability to solve their problems than when either fathers or sons controlled the RCD.

Although examination of the variables related to RCD dominance in families has been limited to family communication variables, ignoring potentially important demographic and psychological variables, the results have been consistent. Male dominance of the RCD seems to be related to a reduction in the family's ability to openly review and address family problems. Although it is unlikely that male RCD dominance causes this situation, it may be symptomatic of other problems in the family that reduce open communication.

In Same-Gender Adult Viewing Situations, Who Controls the Remote?   Walker's (1996) study of viewing couples also examined a small subset of five gay or lesbian couples. As with the heterosexual couples, for the gay couples, a dominant RCD user typically emerged from the dyad, and some resentment was expressed by the RCD-deprived member. However, lesbian couples reported more equal sharing of the RCD and more frequently muted the sound during commercials to facilitate conversation.

How Do Other Viewers React to RCD Domination?   Most RCD studies have evaluated individual use of the RCD, but two studies have reported individual reactions to the use of RCDs by others. First, *Consumer Reports* ("Remote Controls," 1992) reported in a survey of its readers that women were much more likely than men to complain about RCD dominance. Thirty-eight percent of females complained that males "hog" the RCD, whereas only 15% of men grumbled about control of the RCD by women. In addition, more women protested RCD grazing (flipping from channel to channel) by men (66%) than men protested grazing by women (43%). Second, Heeter (1988b) reported that women had higher scores than men on an RCD annoyance item: "How often does someone else change channels when you wish they wouldn't?" Thus, although both genders expressed some concern about RCD "abuse" by the other gender, women were significantly more likely to complain than were men.

When the Viewing Situation (Group or Individual) Is Unknown, What Individuals Are More Likely to Control the Remote? Although research on RCD use during family viewing has been limited to a few studies, numerous studies have examined RCD use by individuals. In these studies, the viewing context (group or individual) has not been specified. However, it is reasonable to assume that findings from these studies apply to many group situations. Several demographic variables, including gender, age, ethnicity, education, and income, and psychological variables, including sensation and novelty seeking, have been associated with individual RCD use. Based on the results of these studies, we suggest that individuals with certain characteristics are more likely to dominate RCD use in group viewing situations.

The demographic variables with the clearest relationship to RCD use are gender and age. As previously indicated, abundant academic and industry studies of individual RCD use that include gender as a variable typically have found higher levels of activity by males (Bellamy & Walker, 1996; Perse, 1998; Perse & Ferguson, 1993). The popular image of the RCD-obsessed male may be overstated, but nearly all studies have shown males are at least somewhat more inclined to click the clicker. These findings are consistent with studies previously reviewed that report male dominance during group viewing. Several studies also have shown a consistent negative relationship between age and RCD activity. Younger viewers are likely to use RCDs more frequently than are older viewers (Bellamy & Walker, 1996). An interaction between age and gender has also been demonstrated, with younger females more closely approximating the RCD activity of their male counterparts, whereas older females use the RCD significantly less than their male cohorts (Perse & Ferguson, 1993).

The relationships between RCD use and education, income, and ethnicity have proven to be very weak. Income and education have usually been unrelated to RCD uses and gratifications (Bellamy & Walker, 1996), whereas studies of ethnic differences in RCD use have found only a slight tendency for minorities (African Americans and Hispanics) to exhibit higher levels of use. The most common finding for these variables has been no significant relationship to various RCD activities or to the gratifications obtained from RCD use.

Four studies have found significant relationships between a variety of psychological variables and RCD activities. Heeter (1988a) found sensate novelty seeking positively correlated with three types of RCD-orienting searches and cognitive novelty seeking positively correlated with exhaustive-orienting searches and channel changing. In an experimental study of RCD use, Bryant and Rockwell (1993) found that viewers' locus of control was related to changing channels with an RCD. Research participants with a high internal locus of control changed channels significantly more frequently than those with a high external locus of control. Wenner and Dennehy (1993) studied the relationships between a variety of RCD activities and gratifications and three psychological variables; desirability of control, sensation seeking, and novelty seeking. Sensation seeking was positively related to RCD dominance, entry scanning, and commercial avoidance. Novelty seeking was positively related to total RCD activity as well as to the specific actions of entry scanning (orienting search) and muting. Desirability of control was negatively related to total RCD use and to muting. Finally, Weaver, Walker, McCord, & Bellamy (1996) found that viewers who scored high on a neuroticism scale were motivated to use the RCD for content avoidance. In group viewing situations, viewers who scored high on a psychoticism scale received gratification from using RCDs to control the viewing of others.

From these studies of individual viewing, a demographic/psychological profile of the frequent RCD user emerges. Heavy RCD users are more likely to be male, younger, and sensation and novelty seekers. Those interested in using RCDs to control content are higher in neuroticism, whereas those who are specifically interested in controlling the viewing of others in group-viewing situations measured higher on the psychoticism scale. Although it is certainly possible for the group dynamics to mediate the influence of these variables on RCD use during group viewing, we suggest that these variables, identified in studies where the viewing context was not specified, are likely to have significant influence on RCD activity in group settings.

Is Frequent Remote Control Use Related to Viewing Alone?   Based on research to date, RCD use increases when viewers watch in isolation. Some RCD uses such as program selection through an orienting search, volume adjustment, and muting during commercials are not necessarily distracting to other viewers in a group. However, many common actions such as grazing (channel surfing) and multiple-program viewing (viewing two or more programs by using the RCD to switch among them) can be very annoying to other viewers in the group. Thus, a major consequence of frequent RCD use may be a reduction in group viewing as other members of the family are driven away by the compulsive grazer. Such activities are frequently reported in press accounts of RCD use. Indeed, a small percentage of RCD users report obtaining gratifications from controlling or annoying others with their RCD use (Walker & Bellamy, 1991; Walker, Bellamy, & Traudt, 1993; Weaver et al., 1996; Wenner & Dennehy, 1993). In addition, one study has related this gratification to higher levels of psychoticism (Weaver et al., 1996).

Because of its potential distraction to others, RCD use is likely to be controlled in group settings and to increase when viewers watch in isolation and are freed from group pressures "to just leave the clicker alone." This conclusion was supported by three studies of RCD use that employed three different methods. Wenner and Dennehy's (1993) survey of undergraduates found positive relationships between estimated time viewing in isolation and four RCD uses; RCD dominance, grazing, multiple-program viewing, and a composite measure of total RCD activity. However, RCD activities that could be easily tolerated or could even enhance group viewing (orienting searches, commercial avoidance, muting) were unrelated to RCD uses. In an observational study, Eastman and Newton (1995) also noted fewer instances of RCD use in group viewing situations, including the amount of channel changing during programs and commercials. Eastman and Newton reported that "with companions—families, spouses, or friends—most RCD holders change channels only at the hourly and half-hourly breaks, if at all, and leave the channel alone during most commercials" (p. 14). Finally, in their assessment of cable television viewing using automatic electronic recording devices, Greenberg, Heeter, and Sipes (1988) found time spent viewing alone was a modest but statistically significant predictor of both channel changing and what we now label as grazing or multiple-program viewing (viewing in segments of 5 minutes or less).

Thus, general RCD activity, grazing, and multiple-program viewing are less common in group viewing situations. Because grazing and multiple-program viewing are initiated by the individual, they maximize the individual's gratification at the expense of other group members. However, RCD uses that may benefit the group or at least not concern it (orienting searches, commercial avoidance, and muting) are not related to the group or individual viewing context. Greenberg et al. (1988) and Eastman and Newton's (1995) studies also support this view, as characteristics associated with grazing and multiple-program viewing, such as in-program channel changing and viewing is short stretches, are associated with viewing in isolation. These studies support the contention that certain RCD activities are disruptive and are not likely to be tolerated by group members for very long. The result of compulsive RCD use during programs may be a reduction in group viewing, as family members are driven to other activities or usage of their own personal televisions.

What Gratifications of Remote Control Use Are Most Associated With Group Viewing and With Individual Viewing? Just as levels of participation in different RCD activities (grazing, multiple-program viewing, commercial avoidance, muting, etc.,) vary from viewer to viewer, the particular gratifications obtained by RCD use may vary. Several earlier studies examined a variety of gratifications derived from RCD activity (Ferguson, 1992; Heeter, 1988a; Heeter & Greenberg, 1988; "How Americans Watch TV," 1989; Umphrey & Albarran, 1993; Walker & Bellamy, 1991; Walker et al., 1993; Wenner & Dennehy, 1993). The results of these studies are summarized elsewhere (Bellamy &

Walker, 1996). More recently, Perse (1998) identified a lack of interest in a program and avoidance of particular content as motivations for channel changing. For our purposes, we classify the gratifications as individual, primarily serving the needs of the RCD user, or group, primarily serving the needs of the group.

Individual gratifications were by far the most common and were more highly valued by RCD users. The most highly valued gratification came from using the RCD to enhance the personal television experience by allowing viewers to get more out of television or to relieve their boredom with current programming (Bellamy & Walker, 1996; Perse, 1998). Closely related was the gratification that comes from allowing the individual to see what else is on. Three content gratifications were also identified; accessing music videos and accessing news (Bellamy & Walker, 1996), and selective avoidance of unpleasant stimuli (Bellamy & Walker, 1996; Perse, 1998). Also, in one study of adult RCD users (Walker et al., 1993), a mixed gratification emerged from the factor analysis that included both accessing news and controlling family viewing in the same factor. As noted earlier, a small percentage of RCD users also claim to gain gratification from annoying others by controlling their viewing (Bellamy & Walker, 1996). Although it is possible that some of these gratifications please both the individual and the group, the focus of the gratification is from the RCD user's perspective (relieving his or her boredom, selection of favorable content, avoidance of unfavorable content). Thus, these common RCD gratifications are more likely to be individually derived.

Although most RCD gratifications appear to focus on individual benefits, one common gratification, commercial avoidance, may have group benefits. Because commercials represent predetermined breaks in programming, a viewer zapping with an RCD may not be as distracting to other viewers. However, not all commercials are offensive and some group members may be annoyed at the deletion of favorite ads. In addition, other viewers may worry about missing program content, if the commercial zapper does not return to the original program in time. To summarize, this brief review of common RCD gratifications appears to reinforce the perception that frequent RCD activity benefits the individual at the expense of the group.

DISCUSSION

Only a limited body of research has examined the use of RCDs by families. Much of that research has centered on the issue of control, with the male head of the household typically taking control of the remote sometimes to the chagrin of other family members. Families where females control the remote have more open communication patterns. In individual studies, heavy RCD users are more likely to be male, young, and to have more interest in sensation or novelty seeking. Some RCD uses (grazing, multiple-program viewing) and gratifications are linked to solitary viewing.

Making technology, such as the RCD, the unit of analysis enables researchers to consider its importance in understanding the dynamics of family television viewing. However, a caution is in order. Often, technological diffusion is given too much credit for changes in human behavior or, perhaps more precisely, potential changes in human behavior. Too often our research pivots around the search for effects produced by technological change without considering the specific functions of specific technologies. Technological change may produce few changes in family viewing, if the change does not help the family meet existing family needs.

Our analysis suggests that RCDs may reduce total family viewing because some RCD uses (grazing, multiple-program viewing) discourage group viewing. However, the need for family viewing may be stronger than the need to engage in these RCD activities. For example, television gives couples and families with children an opportunity to be together physically, providing a context and subject matter to stimulate conversation. Because this companionship function is not an effect of television technology, it is not likely to be altered by the use of a television technology like the RCD. Instead, the use of the technology is likely to be altered to meet the more important companionship function. Clearly, more research is needed to substantiate our analysis.

SUGGESTIONS FOR FURTHER RESEARCH

Rapid changes in the television industry seem likely to continue for several years, because the structure of a new global media industry has yet to solidify. However, the continual increase in channel capacity, limited only by consumer interest in more choice, will increase the power of niche marketing as an industry "driver." Although the short-term result of digitalization and convergence might be a revival of "nuclear family" viewing situations,[1] the long-term expectation is for the family to be only one

---

[1] Continued audience segmentation and the diffusion of high definition digital television (HDTV) may actually be responsible for a brief resurgence in family programming and viewing. Increasing specialization makes the rarer mass-appeal programs more desirable to advertisers seeking a relatively undifferentiated audience (e.g., soft drinks, personal hygiene products, and snack foods). For these advertisers, family appeal programming on broadcast television networks has a chance to become the "cool" alternative in an overly specialized environment. In addition, the high costs of the new generation of HDTV receivers will limit the number of homes with multiple HDTV sets. The family once again may gather around the main receiver as they did with their first black-and-white sets in the 1950s, their first color sets in the 1960s, and their first VCRs and projection TVs in the 1980s.

of many selling niches for the television industry (Andreasen, 1990). In a nation where approximately 60% of all teenagers and a 33% of 6–7-year-olds have their own television sets (Spring, 1999), economic logic dictates that the industry design programming attractive to minors. The success of both Fox and the WB networks can be attributed largely to their ability to commodify the fickle youth audience through their prime-time programming. Thus, an ongoing research agenda needs to reflect this industry change.

Unfortunately for those interested in family viewing, too much of the remote control research to date has been based on self-report measures that reflect the attitudes and perceptions of only one family member. Although there are well-known limitations and strengths of this approach, more group observational studies with larger samples are needed to help us better understand how the RCD functions in the family.

We also need to broaden our studies of family RCD use to include various control devices (the RCD, the computer mouse) in conjunction with other electronic media; VCRs, video games, audio systems, and computers. RCDs may have direct effects on family viewing, but they may also interact with other television or video technologies in significant ways. In addition, both basic quantitative and more in-depth motivational and behavioral studies of young people are needed; no previous RCD studies have examined significant numbers of children and teens. As with other television effects studies, children and youth must be recognized as highly influential in family viewing situations.

The emergence of the RCD in nearly every U.S. household probably has affected all four viewing interactions identified by Alexander (1990). However, the limited research on family viewing and RCDs to date has focused on the control interaction; who has physical control of the RCD in the family viewing environment (Krendl et al., 1993; Morley, 1986). We suggest that Alexander's other three interactions (interpretation, maintenance of the family system, and interactions outside the viewing context) have all been affected by RCD-stimulated changes in industry technology, programming, and marketing. The assumption that prime time is the domain of adult programming control has less legitimacy in an environment where millions of children and teens can use RCDs to make their own programming selections in the comfort and privacy of their rooms. Shared interpretations are also less likely in a television environment characterized by increasing amounts of individual use. Studying alterations in shared interpretations is particularly important, because recent research (Krcmar, 1998) has shown (a) that image interpretation is more important than the image itself in producing television effects, and (b) that "family communication mitigates the relationship between TV viewing and interpretations of TV images" (p. 260).

We need to systematically address the relationship between RCD use and family viewing. Future research should focus on (a) the use of various RCD behaviors (orienting searches, grazing, multiple-program viewing, etc.) in different group situations (whole family, one parent and child, combinations of siblings, family members and nonfamily members), (b) how different conceptions of the role of the RCD by various family members affects group viewing, and (c) the relationship between the amount and quality of family viewing, and the various RCD uses, gratifications, and effects identified in previous research.

If family viewing fulfills certain critical functions in family life, then increased RCD activity during individual viewing sessions may have no effect on family viewing. RCD uses and gratifications may be reserved for private viewing, after family needs have been met. Without more basic research, using the family rather than the individual as the unit of analysis, we will not be able to address this critical issue.

REFERENCES

Alexander, A. (1990). Television and family interaction. In J. Bryant (Ed.), *Television and the American family* (pp. 211–225). Hillsdale, NJ: Lawrence Erlbaum Associates.

Andreasen, M. S. (1990). Evolution in the family's use of television: Normative data from industry and academe. In J. Bryant (Ed.), *Television and the American family* (pp. 3–55). Hillsdale, NJ: Lawrence Erlbaum Associates.

Bellamy, R. V., Jr., & Walker, J. R. (1996). *Television and the remote control: Grazing on a vast wasteland.* New York: Guilford.

Broadcasting & Cable Yearbook. (1998). New Providence, NJ: R. R. Bowker.

Bryant, J., & Rockwell, S. C. (1993). Remote control devices in television program selection: Experimental evidence. In J. R. Walker & R. V. Bellamy, Jr. (Eds.), *The remote control in the new age of television* (pp. 73–85). Westport, CT: Praeger.

Copeland, G. (1989, November). *The impact of remote control tuners on family viewing.* Paper presented at the meeting of Speech Communication Association, San Francisco, CA.

Copeland, G. A., & Schweitzer, K. (1993). Domination of the remote control during family viewing. In J. R. Walker & R. V. Bellamy, Jr. (Eds.), *The remote control in the new age of television* (pp. 155–168). Westport, CT: Praeger.

Cornwell, N. C., Everett, S., Everett, S. E., Moriarty, S., Russomanno, J. A., Tracey, M., & Trager, R. (1993). Measuring RCD use: Method matters. In J. R. Walker & R. V. Bellamy, Jr. (Eds.), *The remote control in the new age of television* (pp. 43–55). Westport, CT: Praeger.

Eastman, S. T., & Newton, G. D. (1995). Delineating grazing: Observations of remote control use. *Journal of Communication, 45* (1), 77–95.

Epstein, N. B., Baldwin, L. M., & Bishop, D. S. (1983). The McMaster family assessment device. *Journal of Marital and Family Therapy, 9,* 171–180.

Ferguson, D. A. (1992). Channel repertoire in the presence of remote control devices, VCRs and cable television. *Journal of Broadcasting & Electronic Media, 36,* 83–91.

Greenberg, B. S., Heeter, C., & Sipes, S. (1988). Viewing context and style with electronic assessment of viewing behavior. In C. Heeter & B. S. Greenberg (Eds.), *Cableviewing* (pp. 123–139). Norwood, NJ: Ablex.

Heeter, C. (1988a). The choice process model. In C. Heeter & B. S. Greenberg (Eds.), *Cableviewing* (pp. 11–32). Norwood, NJ: Ablex.

Heeter, C. (1988b). Gender differences in viewing styles. In C. Heeter & B. S. Greenberg (Eds.), *Cableviewing* (pp. 167–176). Norwood, NJ: Ablex.

Heeter, C., & Greenberg, B. S. (1988). Profiling the zappers. In C. Heeter & B. S. Greenberg (Eds.), *Cableviewing* (pp. 67–73). Norwood, NJ: Ablex.

How Americans watch TV: A nation of grazers. (1989). New York: C. C. Publishing.

Klopfenstein, B. C. (1993). From gadget to necessity: The diffusion of remote control technology. In J. R. Walker & R. V. Bellamy, Jr. (Eds.), *The remote control in the new age of television* (pp. 23–39). Westport, CT: Praeger.

Krcmar, M. (1998). The contribution of family communication patterns to children's interpretations of television violence. *Journal of Broadcasting & Electronic Media, 42,* 250–264.

Krendl, K. A., Troiano, C., Dawson, R., & Clark, G. (1993). "OK, where's the remote?" Children, families, and remote control devices. In J. R. Walker & R.V. Bellamy, Jr. (Eds.), *The remote control in the new age of television* (pp. 137–153). Westport, CT: Praeger.

Kunkel, D. (1990). Child and family television regulatory policy. In J. Bryant (Ed.), *Television and the American family* (pp. 349–68). Hillsdale, NJ: Lawrence Erlbaum Associates.

Lull, J. (1990). *Inside family viewing: Ethnographic research on television's audiences.* London: Routledge.

McLeod, J. M., & Chaffee, S. H. (1972). The construction of social reality. In J. T. Tedeschi (Ed.), *The social influence process* (pp. 50–99). Beverly Hills, CA: Sage.

Morley, D. (1986). *Family television: Cultural power and domestic leisure.* London: Comedia.

Perse, E. M. (1998). Implications of cognitive and affective involvement for channel changing. *Journal of Communication, 48*(3), 49–68

Perse, E. M., & Ferguson, D. A. (1993). Gender differences in remote control use. In J. R. Walker & R. V. Bellamy, Jr. (Eds.), *The remote control in the new age of television* (pp. 169–186). Westport, CT: Praeger.

Remote controls: Can one do the work of many? (1992, December). *Consumer Reports,* pp. 796–99.

Robinson, J. P., & Godbey, G. (1997). *Time for life.* University Park: The Pennsylvania State University Press.

Spring, G. (1999, March 22). ATAS panel eyes kids TV. *Electronic Media,* pp. 4, 52.

Umphrey, D., & Albarran, A. B. (1993). Using remote control devices: Ethnic and gender differences. *Mass Comm Review, 20,* 212–219.

Walker, A. J. (1996). Couples watching television: Gender, power, and the remote control. *Journal of Marriage and the Family, 58,* 813–823.

Walker, J. R., & Bellamy, R. V., Jr. (1991). The gratifications of grazing: An exploratory study of remote control use. *Journal Quarterly, 68,* 422–431.

Walker, J. R., Bellamy, R. V. Jr., & Traudt, P. J. (1993). Gratification derived from remote control devices: A survey of adult RCD use. In J. R. Walker & R. V. Bellamy, Jr. (Eds.), *The remote control in the new age of television* (pp. 103–112). Westport, CT: Praeger.

Walker, J. R., & Ferguson, D. A. (1998). *The broadcast television Industry.* Boston: Allyn & Bacon.

Weaver, J. B., Walker, J. R., McCord, L. L., & Bellamy, R. V., Jr. (1996). Exploring the links between personality and television remote control device use. *Personality and Individual Differences, 20,* 483–489.

Wenner, L. A., & Dennehy, M. O. (1993). Is the remote control device a toy or tool? Exploring the need for activation, desire for control, and technological affinity in the dynamic of RCD use. In J. R. Walker & R. V. Bellamy, Jr. (Eds.), *The remote control in the new age of television* (pp. 113–134). Westport, CT: Praeger.

The VCR, Home Video Culture, and New Video Technologies

Carolyn A. Lin
Cleveland State University

Videocassette recorders (VCRs), seemingly an old communication tech-nology at the end of the 20th century, are more than just a metal box that we take for granted. First introduced in 1975 at a sticker price of $2,500, the Sony Betamax machine symbolized the beginning of a "cultural rev-olution" that changed our relationship with our "window to the world"— the television set—in a most unimaginable manner. The impact of the VCR went far beyond just the way we watch television.

VCRs, for instance, helped bring up a generation of children by "act-ing" as a regular "babysitter" to them ("New Poll Shows," 1988). Accord-ing to a 1996 national survey conducted by MIT, 80% of the public selected the VCR as the most helpful invention that has made life easier ("Survey Rates the VCR," 1996). Above all, when we look back to the technologi-cal achievements and cultural trends pertinent to our family life in the 20th century, VCRs will stand out as one of the most significant contribu-tors to that history.

Even so, the demise of the VCR has been predicted by some industry forecasters (Dennis, 1997), due to the arrival of digital versatile (or video) discs (DVDs). However, such forecasts have yet to be borne out by even the slightest market movement. The future of the VCR, more likely, lies in a move to digital formats—as opposed to outright extinction—in the 21st century; that is, at least until another technology comes along that could be more economical, more user friendly or more versatile than the VCR. This suggests that the VCR will continue to have an impact on our home-based leisure culture in the new millenium.

Past research has shown that our leisure culture at home both evolves and is emancipated by the VCR at the same time. This chapter examines this intriguing VCR phenomenon by focusing on its role in the family viewing environment, in home video culture, and in a new-age visual culture.

THE VCR IN THE HOME

The evolution of the VCR, from a technological novelty during the early days of its introduction to its present status as a "technology appliance" in our home, did not take very long. In 1980, the VCR was owned by 1.1% of television homes in America (A. C. Nielsen Company, 1998). By the end of 1997, that figure had risen to 89%, and the projected penetration ratio by the year 2000 is 93% ("Everything about television," 1998). By comparison, a widely hailed replacement for the VCR, the DVD, was in less than 1% of U.S. households during the same period (Garrett, 1999), suggesting an overestimation of audience acceptance of DVDs in the first 3 years of their market introduction (Sedman, 1998). Other video technologies that can deliver the same content to the audience at home and that are considered strong threats to the survival of the VCR—namely, pay per view (PPV) and video-on-demand (VOD) services—have also fallen short of their projected competitive advantages (Robinson, 1995).

Although digital VCRs have been available on the market without much fanfare for the past decade, the upcoming conversion of the U.S. television system from an analog to a digital format, scheduled to occur during the early 21st century, may change that. VCRs built for the reception and recording of digital signals transmitted by a direct broadcast satellite (DBS) have already entered those households that adopted such DBS services as DirecTV since 1996 ("Hitachi will make VCRs," 1996). Nevertheless, industry experts expect that analog VCR sets will not be replaced by any particular digital video recording and playback units any time soon, even after the digital television broadcast conversion has occurred ("The New Digital Conundrum," 1997). This prediction was made based on the strong audience affinity with the VCR, as it still satisfactorily serves audience video communication needs in conjunction with an analog TV set.

At any rate, whether it is in an analog or a digital format, the VCR appears to be the video appliance of our choice even as we enter the 21st century. The term *technology appliance* or *video appliance,* as described here, refers specifically to a technology such as the VCR that has become a fixture of our visually oriented modern life. If the telephone is the technology appliance that allows us to communicate with one another across distance, then the VCR is the appliance that enables us to make the physical sights, sounds, and events we experience permanently, as preserved through its recording and playback capability.

THE VCR AND THE HOME VIDEO CULTURE

According to Lin (1992), the VCR serves at least three functions in the home video culture: It supplies home entertainment, it displaces other leisure activities, and it provides social utility. Specifically, the reason that the VCR plays a significant role in our home video environment is because it is the very first video communication medium that allows us to "take control" of when, where, how, and what to watch on television or via a television monitor. In essence, VCR use reflects audience choice behavior when it comes to constructing a video-programming environment that one desires at home. Such control and choice are not alien to the audience's nature, albeit it can only be exercised as permitted by the capability of human technology. The net result of this type of audience control and choice inevitably helps draw out or foster an "active audience" (as opposed to a "passive audience") from the perspective of audience behavior (Levy, 1989).

VCR Users as an Active Audience

The active audience paradigm as conceptualized by Blumler (1979) can be seen as an outgrowth of the uses and gratifications perspective, which maintains the idea that the audience is a self-motivated seeker of various psychological gratifications when making media use and content selection decisions. An active audience is supposed to be someone who, given a set of gratification-seeking predispositions and motivations, is more cognitively, affectively, and behaviorally involved with the media use process, starting from the preexposure to the postexposure period (Levy & Windahl, 1984). In the case of television viewing, an active audience may engage in more content or channel choice planning prior to exposure, may become more cognitively and affectively involved with the content during exposure, and may generate more short-term behavioral outcomes postexposure (Lin, 1993).

In parallel fashion, an active VCR user is even more mentally and physically active than an average active TV audience member. For instance, an active VCR user may carefully determine the video title playback and TV program recording choices in advance and may strategically replay fleeting images or zip commercials during recording (Lin, 1990). By the same token, watching movie rentals also enables the VCR user to plan and structure their viewing environment and in effect to become a more attentive or active audience (Krugman & Johnson, 1991). Moreover, a VCR user was also found to be a more active television viewer as compared to a non-VCR user prior, during, and after exposure (Lin, 1990). On the whole, the implications of the VCR user resembling an active audience profile are multidimensional as they relate to the motives, uses, and effects of the VCR experience and how that experience shapes our video culture at home and in society.

VCR Use Motives

The most cited reasons for VCR ownership and uses include the following: (a) record TV shows for later viewing, (b) record a TV show while watching another,(c); play back video rentals, and (d) save money and time from going to the movie theater (Harvey & Rothe, 1985). The first two activities are commonly identified as the "time-shifting" activity. Fundamentally, there are two main motives for VCR ownership—time shift TV programs for later viewing and to watch video rentals. Time shifters, according to Potter, Forrest, Sapolsky, and Ware (1988), are motivated by the value of personal freedom and control over one's viewing schedule. By contrast, source shifters look to the lure of communication modality alternatives and spend a large amount of time watching movie rentals. Other researchers also found parallel support for such a distinction (e.g., Ram & Jung, 1990).

Cohen, Levy, and Golden (1988), however, differentiated the psychological needs gratified by television viewing, cinema attendance, and VCR use. They believed that, whereas the VCR is valued due to its ability to enhance viewing options and satisfaction, cinema attendance tends to help fill available time. Rubin and Bantz (1987) similarly supported the notion of perceived utilities of the VCR as the primary motives for VCR adoption and uses.

A secondary motive for VCR ownership—building a home video library of recorded movies or memorable TV programs, and so forth—reflects the home video culture image some homeowners wish to project to others (Lull, 1988). Other video library builders focus more on constructing a family video album, recording significant family events such as the first steps of a child and weddings; more utility-minded library builders may record learning-related events, such as medical operations, for later discussion and review (Lindlof & Shatzer, 1990).

An additional motive for VCR use—creating a socializing opportunity— projects yet another unique aspect of the VCR function. Rubin and Bantz (1989) proposed a VCR-use model based on an individual's "locus of control." Their model suggested that those audiences whose social affiliation needs are strong due to their life positions may use the VCR as a social tool to gratify such an interpersonal communication need. Lin (1992) indicated that the interpersonal communication that takes place prior to a social event is an interesting phenomenon all on its own, as friends and families discuss what video(s) to get, how to get the video(s), when to show the video(s), and where to hold the video social gathering.

Inviting friends and family to a "video party" or a "video social," is reminiscent of the heyday of television diffusion, when families and friends would gather to watch a significant television event at a TV owner's home. The social utility function of the VCR, as driven by the audience desire to share a visual experience with others, speaks volumes to the yearnings for "family viewing" that was lost due to the entry of multiple TV sets into American homes (Lin, 1992). This family viewing experience is readily viable with the use of the VCR, because although over 73% of homes own more than one TV set, most of them have only one VCR (A. C. Nielsen, 1998).

In sum, the motives for VCR ownership and for VCR use are essentially derived from the audience's fundamental desire to take control over their television viewing environment by customizing their home video culture. This home video culture is best reflected by the audience activity involving VCR use and how that activity is configured into modern family life.

VCR Use Patterns

As the VCR medium matures, its uses also evolve over time to become more of a playback instead of a time-shifting unit, compared to 10 years ago, when these two activities occurred more equally (Sims, 1989). Today, an average VCR household uses its VCR for about 6 hours per week, with 1.52 hours devoted to recording television programs and another 3.5–4 hours playing back primarily prerecorded tapes instead of home recording ("TV Dimensions '98," 1998). As a result of this active use of the VCR in the home, a concern over the potential of video playback displacing television viewing and movie going arose for the television and film industries, respectively.

Nonetheless, the concern over video rental displacing movie outings did not materialize. As indicated by Krugman and Johnson (1991), viewing video rentals is not perceived as the same activity as going to the movies by all video viewers. And even though other studies (e.g., Lin, 1992, 1994) have suggested displacement of other leisure activities due to video rental viewing, movie-going activities were not one of them. Video rentals, in effect, can be regarded as complementary to movie theater patronage, as audiences watch video rentals to make up for missing opportunities to see a feature film at a movie theater.

By the same token, the fear of television networks losing their audience base has been proven as largely unfounded, as an average viewer still spends about 22 hours per week watching television ("TV Dimensions '98," 1998). This lack of a true displacement relationship from the VCR to its host TV set depicts the VCR once again as a medium that complements the traditional television viewing experience (Krugman & Rust, 1993). However, as the majority of home recording was done with prime time network programs (with advertising-sponsored cable TV network programs accounting for the remaining recording), the nature of the active audience did have a negative impact on the viewing of those commercials attached to those home-recorded programs. Through the remote control device, the same active audience that switches channels to graze program offerings (prior and during television viewing), zaps commercials, and concurrently watches multiple channels, acts much the same way when it comes to VCR use.

In particular, an active VCR user/viewer frequently pauses the VCR to zap commercials during recording and fast-forwards the home recording to zip commercials during playback (Henke & Donohue, 1989). Other studies, for instance, have found that viewers zip through commercials during playback because it gives them personal control over their viewing process, which they find to be rewarding (e.g., Sapolsky & Forrest, 1989). Unless the commercials are judged to be interesting enough and worthy of "looking time," those viewers who zap will also most likely zip through commercials during recording and playback (Olney, Batra, & Holbrook, 1990).

Another unique phenomenon "perfected" by the VCR users is the act of repeat viewing. Consider that the nature of television viewing—a temporal process with fleeting images—is essentially altered by a VCR that records and plays back those images. Much like home audio recordings that can be played over and over again on an audiocassette recorder or a programmable CD player, the VCR allows the viewers to review the video recording and hence to possess control over their viewing environment, yet in another innovative manner (Dobrow, 1990). This type of repeat viewing can occur with any prerecorded tapes containing a variety of topics and genres (e.g., science, education, self-help, exercise lessons, movies, etc.), off-air home recordings, and family videos. The VCR, then, can be utilized as a tool for educational purposes in either a formal or informal setting, in addition to being a cultural "entertainment" device.

Within family viewing contexts where children are involved, the VCR use patterns added a new dimension (i.e., family communication via parent–child interaction over video content selection and family viewing activity planning). Children as young as 3 were found to understand the function of the VCR and how to operate it (Lindlof, Shatzer, & Wilkinson,

1988). Moreover, these toddlers were also capable of making demands on their parents about what video titles they would like to watch, when to watch them, and how often to watch them. Such demands place parents in a situation where they have to negotiate and communicate with their children about the types of video titles that they believe are suitable and allowable for their children's consumption. Through this type of parent–child interaction (or even the lack of it), parents can exercise control over what types of video content to which their children should be exposed. In fact, some parents use the VCR as a means for regulating and controlling their children's television and movie viewing diet (Kim, Baran, & Massey, 1988).

These parent–child interaction sessions are not always conflict-free. But they do help increase family communication among members who wish to partake in the video or television viewing content selection and scheduling decision-making process (Lindlof & Shatzer, 1989). This type of family communication, in and of itself, is a desirable event both for keeping the family discussing an issue of shared interest and collaboratively building a home video culture together (Lin, 1992).

These ideal family communication scenarios could occur only if the parents are involved with their children's media consumption decisions. Unfortunately, parental mediation as a social phenomenon is not widespread in our society by any measure. Families with preschool children may practice more parental involvement in terms of helping to select programs (Jordan & Holtz, 1998), even though empirical evidence does not always support such an assumption. For instance, Lindlof and Shatzer (1989) found that parents rarely preview the tapes their children play back. Krendel, Clark, Dawson, and Troiauo (1993) similarly concluded that parents mostly allow children to play tapes by themselves without any particular instructions or rules being given or enforced. Even when parents claimed to have exercised control over their children's video viewing activity, they failed to preview those videos on a regular basis (e.g., Kim, et al., 1988).

But when parents do practice parental mediation in terms of controlling video viewing for young children, such mediation activity is more often structure rather than substance-oriented. For instance, Jordan (1990) found that the VCR, when used for controlling children's viewing time, is utilized as a tool to structure time for the family in terms of when to shift to video viewing, how much of the tape to watch, and how much "idle" time to fill in the day.

This situation appears to worsen when adolescents are present, as studies have shown that parental mediation becomes less frequent for that group. For example, Lin and Atkin (1989) reported that parental mediation activity decreases when children's age increases, when the number of children in the home increases, and when children have their own television sets; but they also discovered that parents selectively make more viewing rules for their male than for their female adolescent children. In a similar vein, Greenberg and Lin (1989) revealed that parental mediation of television viewing did not increase due to the presence of a VCR. And as rule making and rule enforcement on television viewing is infrequent in a majority of the homes, as indicated in other studies (e.g., Atkin, Greenberg, & Baldwin, 1991), this further confirms a lack of parental involvement in their children's VCR-use activity (e.g., Krendel et al., 1993).

In summary, the audience profile of a VCR household reflects an active audience that records programs off-air and replays home recordings and video rentals based on advance planning. Such advance planning arrives due to frequent interpersonal communication and interaction about what programs to record and which video titles to rent. This structural coordination of recording and playback schedules does not necessarily propel increased parental rule making and rule enforcement with regard to the content of the tapes that are replayed by children, especially adolescents. Yet one thing is clear, the VCR liberates the audience from being bound to the rigid television program schedule or the rather laborious ritual of movie-outing activity.

Effects of VCR Use

The first and foremost social effect of the VCR on the American public is the reallocation of home leisure time. Due to VCR use, there is an increase in time spent with both television and family (Harvey & Rothe, 1985) and in the frequencies of family interaction and family viewing (Lindlof & Shatzer, 1990). By contrast, a decrease in cinema attendance (Henke & Donohue, 1989) and other leisure activity participation (Lin, 1992) has also been reported due to VCR use.

Whether the arrival of the VCR represents an evolution or a revolution of the way we approach mass communication as a society, we are living in a "VCR age" (Levy, 1989). Meanwhile, we have also witnessed the first generation of children—the first "videogeneration"—growing up with the VCR in their homes (Lin & Atkin, 1989). As this first videogeneration grows up and reaches adulthood at the beginning of the 21st century, their video media culture may be both similar and different to that of the previous generation.

As the VCR extends the audience's individual ability and technical capability to control and consume desirable electronic media content, the substance and style of the mainstream electronic media content such as network television programs remains relatively stable and consistent (Lin, 1995). The only exception involves the few niche program genres originated by cable television, such as HBO, CNN, ESPN, and MTV in the 1980s and HGTV, travel, and food channels in the 1990s. However, upon closer scrutiny, these niche program genres resemble more of an electronic tube version of a movie theater release, a content-specialized magazine, or a prolonged "sports event" coverage, except for the music video genre.

Hence, it is not surprising to learn that the presence of a VCR in the home does not alter the audience's program choice behavior (e.g., Atkin, Heeter, & Baldwin, 1989). Television viewing level in homes equipped with the VCR and cable television access also was not found to be significantly greater than in those homes that only received traditional broadcast television (e.g., Pinon, Huston, & Wright, 1989).

Consequently, the long-standing media effects established by past research remain largely valid and reliable when applied to this new VCR generation. For instance, Morgan, Shanahan, and Harris (1990), in their cultivation study, concluded that the VCR serves to reinforce instead of mitigate the cultivation effects fermented by heavy television viewing. Furthermore, Morgan and Shanahan (1991) reported that VCR use is mostly irrelevant to the perception of the violent and mistrusting "mean world" phenomenon, as opposed to television viewing. In a similar vein, Perse, Ferguson, and McLeod (1994) also failed to substantiate any unique contribution from VCR use to any single dimension of media cultivation effects of fear and crime.

And even though heavy exposure to MTV videos featuring females as the target of both physical and sexual aggression from their male counterparts is common, the resulting impact on adolescent perception of sex roles and sexual behavior does not appear to deviate from that generated by traditional media exposure (e.g., Strouse, Buerkel-Rothfuss, & Long, 1995). In essence, the lack of a unique "cultivation effect" caused by the VCR use alone seems to be indicative of the complementary relationship of the VCR to the television viewing activity itself. That is, the VCR merely helps facilitate an alternative means of exposure to the content that is being (or was) shown on television or in a movie theater.

On the other hand, this VCR age also extends a different kind of audience orientation that centers on the notion of audience as "user" instead of "viewer" (e.g., Lin, 1990). This notion predates VCR studies, as scholars made the distinction with the selective exposure concept in the 1980s. As Bryant (1989) suggested, the relatively passive term "receiver" somehow does not seem appropriate for selective exposure perspectives (e.g., Bryant, 1989). The user or audience (instead of viewer or audience) concept demarcates an era where television viewing was a one-way communication activity—as opposed to a two-way communication activity—

in which the user is allowed to manipulate the communication process. Users select (or create) the content and the means of content delivery to substantively program and technically manipulate their visual content consumption experience in order to satisfy an array of communication needs ranging from entertainment to instructional learning.

The net effect of this user behavior at one level projects a new form of previously unattainable "cultural individualism" via individualized visual content viewing choice, one that parallels the less onerous choice behavior demonstrated in music and book genre preference due to its audiovisual nature. For instance, both children and adults often own their personal video library collection from which they can retrieve videos for repeat viewing and for social viewing purposes (to entertain their own friends; e.g., Heintz, 1990; Lull, 1988). In a less obvious way, these individual video collections help form various idiosyncratic "video culture clubs" that help shape and reinforce their peer cultures within. This phenomenon further signifies a deeper evolutionary invasion of the popular entertainment culture into our children's socialization process, as the youth culture became an intricate extension of the popular images presented in that visual content through video-related merchandise, music, and fashion. The sociocultural consequences of such an evolutionary process should become apparent as we start to observe the adults of this first video generation.

At another level, the VCR is the first consumer communication technology that challenges its users to deal with relatively complicated technical features in order to successfully operate it. This challenge apparently was met by both adults and children (e.g., Lindlof, et al., 1988), as the user became accustomed to programming their VCR to perform the functions intended. Although no studies have attempted to link VCR use competency with user ability to operate other video technologies, it is obvious that the younger generation is more proficient in their ability to manipulate both the VCR and such video technologies as the video game console and personal computers. An early study did mention a potential scenario of a "media aficionado" (Greenberg & Lin, 1989, p. 87) subgroup among those gadget-rich kids who have access not only to the VCR, but also to video cameras, personal computers, and so forth.

The implications of this technology adoption and its relevant technical orientation in the user or audience are intriguing. For instance, Pool (1983) foresaw "technologies of freedom," where the adoption of technology can help preserve personal freedom of expression and free exchange of ideas from being impeded by institutional and socioenvironmental constraints. If we envision the VCR as a tool that emancipates the viewers to become the users (Lin, 1990), then the VCR can be considered a technology that "frees" its users from being encapsulated by their media and social environment. Hence, the VCR may be regarded as the early catalyst in a revolution that converts the once lackadaisical public into a more avidly technocratic one. The impact of this technological revolution can only be observed in our currently entrenched visual-technical culture in a context that goes beyond what has already been studied with the VCR and its related social activities.

THE VCR AND NEW VIDEO TECHNOLOGIES

At the time of this writing, new video technologies now found in American homes—as well as others yet to arrive—are capable of supplying video images that far surpass anything we could have imagined in past decades. Will the VCR be displaced by any of these newly launched video technologies any time soon? From an historical context, this displacement mechanism between different communication media or channels has not occurred very frequently. And when substitution between an old and a new media technology actually takes place, it typically happens due to the presence of the following three conditions; content superiority, technical superiority, and greater cost-efficiency.

For instance, television replaced radio to become the primary mass entertainment medium (Lasswell, 1948), as it provided superior entertainment content, technically superior visual images, and greater cost-efficiency afforded by home video entertainment. But the radio medium survived by transforming itself into a niche medium. In the case of a complete displacement, an example could be how compact discs made plastic records and record players extinct (Lin, 1999) due to their superior sound quality and superior hardware and software durability (which also translates into greater cost-efficiency in the long run).

The question of when the VCR may be displaced by other newer video technologies on the market is not easily answerable, as the VCR still stands as the video technology preferred by the public. Its companion technology—the video camera—can also perform both recording and playback functions and offers its user even more freedom to both produce and replay visual images. In fact, the video cameras can effectively be considered an ideal "mini-VCR" that is both portable and technically superior. And when a video is interfaced with a personal computer's digital editing software, enabling the user to edit video frames in a nonsequential manner, it is not difficult to see why the VCR (or the video camera) is both a viable and a much appreciated home video technology.

Even though the VCR's life span may surpass everyone's expectation, it will eventually have to compete against the DVD. Some project an eventual displacement between the "old" VCR and the new DVD in the near future (e.g., Dennis, 1997). The newly arrived DVD is a form of digital video on compact disc that is lighter, smaller, and more economical than its older counterpart—the laser disc. Because as it also comes in a programmable format, the DVD possesses more superior audio and video resolution than the VCR (even in its digital form).

Hence, the rivalry between the VCR and the DVD could be similar to the one between digital audiocassette and compact discs, where the compact discs won by default because of the greater availability of existing software and hardware supplies. Nonetheless, digital audiocassette technology survives side-by-side with compact discs due to its recording and replaying capability, one that can only be achieved by a programmable compact disc (and disc player) at a much more costly level. This suggests that the VCR may also coexist with the DVD, as long as the programmable DVD and its companion disc player are less economical than the ubiquitous VCRs.

Such a coexistence relationship between two substitutable media technologies can be considered supplementary in nature. The most clear-cut example can be found in the symbiotic relations between film releases on video and in movie theaters. Given the proper circumstances, the public will choose to visit a movie theater and to enjoy the superior audio-visual presentation of a feature film in its original form. But when such opportunities are not available, the public can turn to video releases and accomplish the same goal in a less technically desirable fashion. Hence, video rentals supplement the public's patronage of theatrical films (Krugman & Johnson, 1991).

In the case of the VCR and the DVD, this supplementary relation may be exercised by the user in a manner that will allow the DVD to become the primary medium for prerecorded video playback, leaving the VCR as the key medium for time-shift recording and home recording playback. The video camera will then remain the main medium for producing and replaying family videos.

The VCR and the CD-ROM share a secondary complementary relationship. This is due to the fact that, as both the CD-ROMs and videocassettes may offer similar infotainment and instructional content, the CD-ROM complements the VCR in that it enhances the video content use experience by allowing "user-content" interactivity. For instance, a videocassette containing a popular children's program such as "Arthur" can often be found in a CD-ROM format, which permits the children to "interact" with the characters in the program.

Other forms of new video technologies that could displace, supplement, or complement the VCR include such aforementioned delivery systems as video-on-demand (VOD) or direct broadcast satellites and even the possible Internet movies that can be downloaded ("Survey Rates the VCR," 1999) and replayed on the PC-TV. The Internet movie delivery mode will not be immediately feasible unless high-speed broadband Internet connection channels become widely available. Yet, if the sudden interest in downloading music recordings through the Internet is any indication, the Internet movie phenomenon may arrive over time.

When and if any of these alternative delivery systems becomes realistically competitive, what then might the future hold for the VCR and its ancillary technologies—the DVD and the CD-ROM? Only time will tell!

CONCLUSIONS

Technology forecasting has long been known as a "dangerous" profession. Yet, certain existing patterns and faded vestiges can often supply intelligent clues to unlock the mystery over what the future may hold. In the present case, the VCR has been proven as a medium that serves multidimensional functions for its users. These functions occur at both a micro and a macrolevel. An examination of these micro and macrolevel effects of the VCR medium may provide the necessary information for peering into the future infrastructure of the home video technology system.

At a micro and individual level, the VCR technology has helped eliminate the environmental constraints associated with home video entertainment imposed by an inflexible television program schedule. In doing so, users have gained the right and freedom to dictate the viewing schedule and the television content that will be consumed through time-shifting. The user is also at liberty to complement television program viewing and supplement movie outings with theatrical video releases through playback activity.

At the family level, the previously mentioned two activities require regular interpersonal communication pertaining to bilateral or multilateral negotiation, coordination, and collaboration between family members who have to share the use of the same VCR, for different purposes at different times. This type of interpersonal communication can bring the family closer together, as members in the family make an effort to keep in touch with each other and to share an agreed-on television viewing ritual, recording schedule, time-shifting routine, and/or rental video repertoire.

From a societal level, the entry of the home VCR has brought about a unique activity that pulls together friends and relatives to watch special video titles in a social event setting. This type of video-enhanced social gathering provides an additional means for friends and families to strengthen their bonds by interacting with each due to the interpersonal communication generated by the video showing itself. It should not be difficult to envision that the individual video culture can be identified in the family video culture, while the family video culture can be traced in the social group video culture. Hence, the home video culture in society is something that gets shaped by and evolves over time.

By contrast, from a macro and individual level, the VCR medium provides the technical freedom to its user that circumvents the rigid television program scheduling structure by inadvertently transforming the user from a "technology novice" to a "technology connoisseur." It accomplishes this by making its user learn how to effectively and correctly operate its somewhat complicated technical features. In aggregate terms, the VCR users might have become the first generations in the 20th century to be technically literate and sophisticated with communication technologies.

This sort of literacy and sophistication, when translated into a family setting, might have helped spur user or audience eagerness to adopt other new communication technologies in the home. As a result, an array of personal as well as mass communication technologies—such as pagers, personal organizers, personal computers, video cameras, video game players, and so forth—were often adopted in identifiable clusters, as distinguished by the communication needs they serve to fulfill (e.g., Lin, 1998; Perse & Courtright, 1993; Rogers, 1995). The continuous diffusion of these various communication technologies in families across the country then pushes both the parents and children in a given household to further their communication technology competency.

When individuals and family members become more technically oriented, communication technology experimenters, users, friends, and relatives alike also join the fray. Eventually, an entire generation of children who grew up programming the VCR to play back their favorite videos or record their must-see television programs also become a generation of communication technology enthusiasts. With that in mind, it is reasonable to assert that the VCR might have started a video revolution, where the users are both motivated and inspired to become increasingly technically capable of controlling their communication environment to attain greater personal freedom and choice.

What then must become of the VCR, the quintessential video medium of the 20th century? The answer may lie in the three media substitution criteria laid out earlier. Namely, it depends on what, if any, home video media technology can offer its user superior content, superior technical benefits, or greater cost-efficiency. If such a technology exists, then the VCRs will also subside, like the low-equity home video technologies they replaced—the various forms of video laser discs and those cumbersome disc players.

But before that potential eventuality is realized, there remain several important areas of VCR research that need scientific attention. These areas include; (a) the social and psychological origins of VCR use, (b) the differences in motives, use patterns, and sociocultural effects of VCRs on different sociological groups, (c) the impact of the VCR on the video technology culture, and (d) the theory or theories that may describe, explain, and predict this all-encompassing video culture phenomenon.

And as long as this home video culture evolution and revolution continue to progress, the public will also proceed to become more sophisticated and critical users of mediated entertainment and information content. Whether this symbolizes the dawn of an "intelligent couch-potato era" remains to be seen and poses yet another interesting topic for future research.

REFERENCES

A. C. Nielsen Company. (1998). *Nielsen report on television*. Northbrook, IL: Author.

Atkin, D. J., Greenberg, B. S., & Baldwin, T. F. (1991). The home ecology of children's television viewing: Parental mediation and the new video environment. *Journal of Communication, 41*, 40–53.

Atkin, D. J., Heeter, C., & Baldwin, T. (1989). How presence of cable affects parental mediation of TV viewing, *Journalism Quarterly, 66*, 557–563, 578.

Blumler, J. G. (1979). The role of theory in uses and gratifications studies. *Communication Research, 6*, 9–36.

Bryant, J. (1989). Message features and entertainment effects. In J. J. Bradac (Ed.), *Message effects in communication science* (pp. 231–262). Newbury Park, CA: Sage.

Cohen, A., Levy, M., & Golden, K. (1988). Children's uses and gratifications of home VCRs. *Communication Research, 15*, 772–780.

Dennis, S. (1997, June 16). Seismic shift for consumers due, says Price Waterhouse. *Newsbytes News Network*, p. 1.

Dobrow, J. R. (1990). The rerun ritual: Using VCRs to re-view. In J. R. Dobrow (Ed.), *Social and cultural aspects of VCR use* (pp. 181–193). Hillsdale, NJ: Lawrence Erlbaum Associates.

Everything about television is more: Sets, viewers, channels, watching. (1998). *Research Alert, 16*, 1–2.

Garrett, D. (1999, January 11). DVD may be heir apparent, but VHS is still king. *Video Business, 19*(2) 4–5.

Greenberg, B. S., & Lin, C. (1989). Adolescents and the VCR boom: Old, new, and nonusers. In M. R. Levy (Ed.), *The VCR age: Home video and mass communication* (pp. 73–91). Newbury Park, CA: Sage.

Harvey, M. G., & Rothe, J. T. (1985). Video cassette recorders: Their impact on viewers and advertisers. *Journal of Advertising Research, 25* (6), 19–27.

Heintz, K. E. (1990). VCR libraries: Opportunities for parental control. In J. R. Dobrow. *Social and cultural aspects of VCR use* (pp. 147–162). Hillsdale, NJ: Lawrence Erlbaum Associates.

Henke, L. L., & Donohue, T. R. (1989). Functional displacement of traditional TV viewing by VCR owners. *Journal of Advertising Research, 29*(2), 18–23.

Hitachi will make VCRs for DirecTV. (1996, May 31). *Nikkei Sangy, Shimbun*, p. 1.

Jordan, A. (1990). A family systems approach to the use of the VCR in the home. In J. R. Dobrow (Ed.), *Social and cultural aspects of VCR use* (pp. 163–179). Hillsdale, NJ: Lawrence Erlbaum Associates.

Jordan, A., & Holtz, J. (1998, November). *Public policy and private practice: Government regulation and parental mediation of children's viewing in the home*. Paper presented at the 84th annual meeting of the National Communication Association, New York.

Kim, W.Y., Baran, S. J., & Massey, K. K. (1988). Impact of the VCR on control of television viewing. *Journal of Broadcasting & Electronic Media, 32*, 351–358.

Krendel, K. A., Clark, G., Dawson, R., & Troiauo, C. (1993). Preschoolers and VCRs in the home: A multiple methods approach. *Journal of Broadcasting & Electronic Media, 37*, 293–311.

Krugman, D., & Johnson, K. F. (1991). Differences in the consumption of traditional broadcast and VCR movie rentals. *Journal of Broadcasting & Electronic Media, 35*, 213–232.

Krugman, D., & Rust, R. (1993). The impact of cable penetration and VCR penetration on network viewing: Assessing the decade. *Journal of Advertising Research, 33*(1), 74–85.

Lasswell, H. (1948). The structure and function of communication in society. In L. Bryson (Ed.), *The communication of ideas* (pp. 37–51). New York: Harper.

Levy, M. R. (1989). Why VCRs aren't pop-up toasters: Issues in home video research. In M. Levy (Ed.), *The VCR age* (pp. 9–18), Newbury Park, CA: Sage.

Levy, M. R., & Windahl, S. (1984). Audience activity and gratifications: A conceptual clarification and exploration. *Communication Research, 11*, 51–78.

Lin, C. A. (1990). Audience activity and VCR use. In J. R. Dobrow (Ed.), *Social & cultural aspects of VCR use* (pp. 75–92). Hillsdale, NJ: Lawrence Erlbaum Associates.

Lin, C. A. (1992). The functions of the VCR in the home leisure environment. *Journal of Broadcasting & Electronic Media, 36*, 345–351.

Lin, C. A. (1993). Modeling the gratification seeking process of television viewing. *Human Communication Research, 20*, 251–271.

Lin, C. A. (1994). Leisure-time reallocation in a video culture. *Mass Communication Review, 21*, 4–16.

Lin, C. A. (1995). Diversity of network prime-time formats during the 1980s. *Journal of Media Economics, 8*, 1–10.

Lin, C. A. (1998). Exploring personal computer adoption dynamics *Journal of Broadcasting & Electronic Media, 42*, 95–112.

Lin, C. A. (1999). Predicting online service adoption likelihood among potential subscribers: A motivational approach. *Journal of Advertising Research 39*(2), 79–89.

Lin, C. A., & Atkin, D. J. (1989). Parental mediation and rulemaking for adolescent use of television and VCRs. *Journal of Broadcasting & Electronic Media, 33*, 53–67.

Lindlof, T. R., & Shatzer, M. J. (1989). Subjective differences in spousal perceptions of family video. *Journal of Broadcasting & Electronic Media, 33*, 375–395.

Lindlof, T. R., & Shatzer, M. J. (1990). VCR usage in the American family. In J. Bryant (Ed.), *Television and the American family* (pp. 89–109). Hillsdale, NJ: Lawrence Erlbaum Associates.

Lindlof, T. R., Shatzer, M. J., & Wilkinson, D. (1988). Accommodation of video and television in the American family. In J. Lull (Ed.), *World families watch television* (pp. 158–192). Newbury Park, CA: Sage.

Lull, J. (1988). Constructing rituals of extension through family television viewing. In J. Lull (Ed.), *World families watch television* (pp. 237–259). Newbury Park, CA: Sage.

Morgan, M., & Shanahan, J. (1991). Do VCRs change the TV picture? VCRs and the cultivation process. *American Behavioral Scientists, 35*, 122–135.

Morgan, M., Shanahan, J., & Harris, C. (1990). VCRs and the effects of television: New diversity or more of the same? In J. R. Dobrow (Ed.), *Social & cultural aspects of VCR use* (pp. 107–123). Hillsdale, NJ: Lawrence Erlbaum Associates.

New poll shows leisure time shrinking. (1988, March 17). *Christian Science Monitor*, p. 8.

Olney, T. J., Batra, R., & Holbrook, M. B. (1990). A three-component model of attitude toward the ad: Effects of the zipping and zapping of television commercials. In S. J. Agres, J. A. Edell, & T. M. Dubitsky (Eds.), *Emotion in advertising: Theoretical and practical explorations* (pp. 269–281). New York: Quorum.

Perse, E., & Courtright, J. (1993). Normative images of communication media: Mass and interpersonal channels in the new media environment. *Communication Research, 19,* 451–484.

Perse, E. M., Ferguson, D. A., & McLeod, D. M. (1994). Cultivation in the newer media environment. *Communication Research, 21,* 79–104.

Pinon, M. F., Huston, A. C., & Wright, J. C. (1989). Family ecology and child characteristics that predict young children's educational television viewing. *Child Development, 60,* 846–856.

Pool, I. de Sola. (1983). *Technologies of freedom.* Cambridge, MA: Belknap Press.

Potter, J., Forrest, E., Sapolsky, B. S., & Ware, W. (1988). Segmenting VCR owners. *Journal of Advertising Research, 28*(2), 29–39.

Ram, S., & Jung, H. (1990). The conceptualization and measurement of product usage. *Journal of the Academy of Marketing Science, 18*(1), 67–76.

Rogers, E. (1995). *Diffusion of innovations,* New York: The Free Press.

Robinson, L. (1995). Point of view. *Video Business, 15*(21), 48.

Rubin, A. M., & Bantz, C. R. (1987). Utility of videocassette recorders. *American Behavorial Scientist, 30,* 471–485.

Rubin, A. M., & Bantz, C. R. (1989). Uses and gratifications of videocassette recorders. In J. Salvaggio & J. Bryant (Eds.), *Media use in the information age: Emerging patterns of adoption and use* (pp. 181–195). Mahwan, NJ: Lawrence Erlbaum Associates.

Sapolsky, B. S., & Forrest, E. (1989). Measuring VCR "ad-voidance." In M. R. Levy (Ed.), *The VCR age: Home video and mass communication* (pp. 148–167). Newbury Park, CA: Sage.

Sedman, D. (1998). Market parameters, marketing hype, and technical standards: The introduction of DVD. *Journal of Media Economics, 11,* 49–58.

Sims, J. B. (1989). VCR viewing patterns: An electronic and passive investigation. *Journal of Advertising Research, 29,* 11–17.

Strouse, J., Buerkel-Rothfuss, N., & Long, E. C. (1995). Gender and family as moderators of the relationship between music video exposure and adolescent sexual permissiveness. *Adolescence, 30,* 505–521.

Survey rates the VCR most helpful invention. (1996, December 21). *Plain Dealer,* p. 11A.

The new digital conundrum. (1997, April 28). *Cablevision, 21*(15), 9–10.

TV dimensions '98. (1998). *Media Dynamics,* p. 1.

III

Attitudes Toward Television

Family Attitudes Toward Television

Dan Brown
Tammy Hayes
East Tennessee State University

This chapter examines research about attitudes of family members and draws inferences about those attitudes from research about families' use of television. The research clusters into main categories examining family attitudes toward television in general, attitudes about living with television, and attitudes about television content. Research about television in general addresses beliefs by family members about whether television is beneficial or harmful and attitudes about the overall quality of television.

The section on living with television surveys the place of television in homes, including physical locations of sets, family attitudes about viewing television together, and attitudes about children's viewing and parents' supervision of viewing. Studying family television use covers attitudes toward and understanding of programs and the use of television in day-care centers.

The section on family attitudes toward television content includes beliefs about program suitability for children and several categories related to television content, including believability and specific content areas. The content areas include violence, sexual content, and alcohol and drugs. A summary raises questions about needs for more research about family attitudes toward television.

FAMILY ATTITUDES ABOUT TELEVISION IN GENERAL

Is Television Harmful or Beneficial?

Do families believe that television brings the family together or that it prevents them from interacting with fellow family members? Early researchers reported that while watching television together, families talked little and focused on the set (e.g., Brody, Stoneman, & Sanders, 1980; Bronfenbrenner, 1975; Maccoby, 1951; Walters & Stone, 1971). Although families did not think of television viewing time as a time for family conversation, they generally believed that watching television brought them together and gave them topics for conversation.

Gunter and Svennevig (1987) and Brown and Bryant (1990) summarized research regarding the effects of television on family life. These studies suggest a receptive attitude by families and children toward television as a teacher and as a model of beliefs about family life and what behavior is appropriate and desirable in the family. These summaries show television as both a positive and negative influence on family life.

The negative factors motivate some people to give up television completely because of fears that viewers may become addicted (Diamond, 1996). McIlwraith (1990, 1998) and Smith (1986) provided the research perspective on whether such fears are warranted, but true addiction seems outside the impact of television. However, negative attitudes about television persist.

Interviews with parents (Zinsmeister, 1997) who removed television from their homes found fears that television encourages passivity among family members of all ages, stifles creativity, reduces interpersonal and physical activity, and introduces overemphasis on sexual matters, particularly among children too young to understand such complex relationships. The interviews also revealed quite a few consistent beliefs about the benefits of the absence of television.

Zinsmeister (1997) wrote that more Americans rate television's influence as negative than those who rate it as positive. He contrasted that condition with 1962 Gallup poll results reporting that twice as many respondents described television as a good influence as those describing it as a bad influence. He added that Americans say that television is getting worse at twice the rate they say that it is improving.

Lieberman (1996) wrote that " . . . many average citizens see television as a threat to their children and their country" (p. 18). He contended that many public opinion polls show that Americans have had enough unsavory content from entertainment media, especially from television, but he contended that the polls barely begin to measure the strength of public outrage. "Most opinion polls show that most people think the entertainment industry shovels too much sex and violence at the audience; according to a survey by Yankelovich Partners, Inc., 8 in 10 Americans have a highly negative opinion of their current entertainment fare" (Diamond, Lavagnino, & Zimmerman, 1996, p. 2754).

Yet, other studies from 1997 and 1998 show positive attitudes toward television. Jordan's (1997) summary of a 1996 Conference on Children and Television included a survey of family relationships with television with responses from 1,205 parents and 308 children. Most parents believed that television was more of a positive than a negative influence on their children and were pleased with the availability and quality of television shows for preschool children. However, parents expressed less satisfaction with television content that was available for children of elementary school years. Parents' most frequent uses of V-chips tended toward identifying quality programs for their children rather than toward blocking out undesirable shows.

Stanger (1998) analyzed telephone interviews conducted in spring 1998. The survey contacted a national probability sample of parents and children in homes with television, including 1,208 parents of children ages 2 to 17 and 300 children ages 10 to 17. Both parents (63.4%) and children of ages 10 to 17 (62.7%) responded that television's impact has been more beneficial than harmful. From previous, similar surveys since 1996, Stanger (1998) found the 1996 proportion of parental belief in a mostly beneficial effect reached its lowest point, 57%, followed by 64.6% the next year.

Television as a negative force in the family involves its relationship with children's involvement with activities other than television. Christopher, Fabes, and Wilson (1989) reported from a survey of 55 parents that parents differed in beliefs about whether television impairs their children's involvement with other activities. Parents' negative attitudes toward television were "significantly and positively related to their reports of family cohesion, expression, intellectual/cultural activities, and participation in active recreation" (Christopher et al., 1989, p. 212). Parents who held negative attitudes about television, more often than other parents, restricted their children's viewing.

Quality of Television

Walsh, Laczniak, and Carlson (1998) addressed a sample of somewhat older than average mothers with high levels of education. The researchers found that these mothers generally held negative attitudes about the quality of television programming directed to children.

Stanger (1998) found low overall perceptions of quality in families' attitudes about television from 1996 to 1998. Only 16% of parents of children ages 2 to 17 held "mainly" or "very positive" views about the quality of television for children. However, about 30% of respondents held negative attitudes. In 1997, 12.5% of parents found "a lot" of good television shows for children, compared with 11.8% in 1998.

Parents are more concerned with what television programs their children watch than with time spent viewing (e.g., Holman & Braithwaite, 1982; Lyle & Hoffman, 1972; St. Peters, Fitch, Huston, Wright & Eakins, 1991; Stein & Freidrich, 1972; Stanger, 1998). Stanger (1998) reported that the proportion of parents responding that they were more concerned about how much television their children watched, rather than what they watched, ranged from a low of 17.1% in 1996 to a high of 22.1% in 1998. Those proportions contrasted with strong responses of concern about what children watched relative to how much they watched, ranging from 71.1% in 1997 to 67% in 1998.

Parents' concern for their children's encounters with media content was greater for television than for all other media. The proportion of parents identifying television as their greatest source of concern for their children declined slightly from 1996 (61%) to 1998 (55.6%), perhaps because the Internet joined the options for the first time in 1998. Except for television, only music (14.9%) and the Internet (12.9%) received mention by more than 3.8% (video games) of parents (Stanger, 1998).

Children showed more positive attitudes about television than did their parents. Although the proportion of parents indicating that television did more good than harm increased from 1996 to 1998, among children ages 10 to 17, that figure achieved its highest degree of support (66%) in 1996 and fell each year to a low of 62.7% in 1998 (Stanger, 1998).

The 1998 proportion of children of ages 10 to 17 describing the quality of television as "mainly positive" or "very positive" reached 31.6%, up from the 1997 figure of 19.1%. Among children in this group, the respective proportions for 1997 and 1998 who agreed that a lot of good television shows for children were available reached 23.7% and 24.2% (Stanger, 1998).

FAMILY ATTITUDES ABOUT LIVING WITH TELEVISION

The Place of Television in Family Homes

Physical Location of Television in Homes. Surveys of family involvement with television show a prominent relationship in terms of numbers of television sets owned, time spent with the medium, and physical place in the home. Parents with more positive views toward television tend to own at least three sets (Christopher et al., 1989). A survey of 66 parents of children ages 3 to 8 found 55% of homes owning multiple sets and 22% with sets in children's bedrooms (Taras, Sallis, Nader, & Nelson, 1990).

Sherman (1996) reported results from multiple surveys of how families use television. A January 1996 survey of 1,287 households with children found that the proportion of families with children under age 18 that owned three or more television sets more than doubled to 48% from 22% in a similar 1981 survey. From a 1995 national sample of 2,886 households, families with children under age 12 revealed that 36% had at least one television set located in a child's bedroom, and 53% of homes with teenage children had television sets in the children's bedrooms. Combining those two groups, television sets in children's bedrooms comprised 20% of all sets. Knowing about television in children's bedrooms is important because of the lack of parental supervision over such viewing.

From a 1995 national sample including 466 households with children under 12, Sherman (1996) reported that education level appeared to influence parents' willingness for children to have television sets in the children's bedrooms. As parents' education level increased, the likelihood of children having sets in their own bedrooms declined. Among households containing a family member with at least a college degree, 24% of children had television sets in their own bedrooms. However, the proportion of that occurrence reached 41% when no one in the household had attained a college degree.

Similar patterns emerged from the 1996 survey (Sherman, 1996). Among households with children under age 12, the presence of a family member with a college degree and children having television sets in their bedrooms occurred in 30% of the homes. With no college degree in the family, children had television sets in their bedrooms in 40% of the homes.

The relationship weakened as children grew into teenagers. Both studies found about 50% of teens with television sets in their bedrooms. In 1995, 54% of homes without a college degree had teenager bedrooms with television sets. Only 49% of homes with a college degree earner had teenager bedrooms with a television set. Sherman (1996) speculated that the increase in proportion of families with teenage children having bedroom television sets might reflect diminishing influence by parents on their teenagers' behavior. Obviously, other interpretations are also plausible.

Sherman (1996) cited evidence that a large proportion of television use occurs in bedrooms, especially in homes with children. In homes with both children under age 12 and teenagers, more than one-third of total television use occurred in bedrooms, reaching 40% during prime time in homes with teenagers. That figure exceeded the comparable use in homes with children under 12 and in homes with no children.

Stanger (1998) reported that 42.3% of the participants' homes included television sets in children's bedrooms, up from 41% in 1996. The increase in proportion of children's bedrooms appeared in two of the three age groups reported by Stanger, as well as in the whole group. Among children ages 2 to 5, the proportion rose from 29% in 1996 to 31.2% in 1998. Television sets became part of 57.7% of adolescents' bedrooms, compared with 55% in 1996. However, among children ages 6 to 11, the proportion declined from 37% in 1996 to 34.5% in 1998.

Stanger (1998) reported that 82.6% of 1,208 households participating in the Annenberg Public Policy Center (APPC) survey in 1998 owned more than one television set. All of those households had children ages 2 to 17. In 1996, the first year of the APPC surveys, 80% of the households owned multiple sets, and the mean number of sets per home ranged upward from 2.4 in 1996 to 2.7 in 1998.

Families Viewing Television Together.   Boorstin (1971) compared the family gathering around television with the cave-dweller's fire that drew people together for "warmth and safety and togetherness" (p. 36). Although family viewing remained the norm in the early 1970s, even in households with as many as four television sets, the growth of multiple-set households brought an increase in solo television viewing (Bower, 1973). This group viewing tends to occur mostly as adult pairs or child groups, but rarely as whole families.

For a detailed review of research regarding attitudes about television and family life, see Brown and Bryant (1990). The review includes findings that modern families seldom watch television as a family unit. Family television viewing patterns seemed more closely related to habits and program preferences than to efforts by families to spend time together, monitor children's viewing, or teach children lessons (Dorr, Kovaric, & Doubleday, 1989; Field, 1988; McDonald, 1985, 1986).

People often see such television images as influencing notions about appropriate family life (Fallis, Fitzpatrick, & Friestad, 1985), despite the overall feeling that such images are inaccurate or unrealistic (Robinson, Skill, Nussbaum, & Moreland, 1985). Attitudes were more closely related to types of programs viewed and viewer characteristics, rather than to the total amount of viewing (Wober & Gunter, 1987). Most couples saw watching television as doing something together and admitted that selecting programs occasionally caused disputes (Gantz, 1985).

St. Peters et al. (1991) supported the findings of Dorr et al. (1989). From a sample of 326 children in Topeka, Kansas, parents' television viewing with their children stemmed from the parents' usual viewing habits, not from the children's habits. Parents who tended to offer more encouragement to children about television viewing of particular shows at particular times tended to watch more television with them.

St. Peters et al. (1991) contradicted the popular notion that children watch adult content that is inappropriate for them primarily because of lack of parental supervision. "In fact, young children are apt to be exposed to situation comedies, crime shows, soap operas, variety shows, and news because they are with their parents, not because they are left alone" (p. 1421).

Nielsen Media Research (as cited in Lazar, 1994) reported in 1990 that children ages 2 to 5 watched television for 28 hours each week, and children ages 6 to 11 watched 24 hours per week. The American Academy of Pediatrics Committee on Communications (as cited in Lazar, 1994) reported that among all the activities of high school graduates, only sleeping occupied more time than watching television.

Stanger (1998) found that children spent more time watching television than any other activity at home. He reported the overall average time that children viewed television as 2.55 hours per day, excluding the viewing of videotapes. Adding the time spent with tapes, children spent 3.5 hours each day watching television. Excluding viewing of videotapes, preschoolers spent 2.6 hours per day watching television, and adolescents spent 2.63 hours per day so occupied. Those groups watched slightly more than did children of elementary school age (2.4 hours). Children's television viewing occupied more than twice as much time as their school homework.

Parents said that they watched slightly less (2.3 hours) television than did their children. Parents frequently (91.1%) said that they "almost always" or "once in a while" join their children in watching television, down slightly from 92.2% in 1997 but up from 89% in 1996. Most parents (61.8%) reported a "great deal" of monitoring of their children's television viewing, down from 65.9% in 1997 and 66% in 1996.

Children's Television Viewing and Parental Supervision.   "Parents' perceptions of television should influence the degree to which they monitor and control television in the family" (Fabes, Wilson, & Christopher, 1989, p. 339). Austin (1993) and the American Academy of Pediatrics (Sege & Dietz, 1994) favored parents' keeping control over children's television viewing. Parents should control children's viewing for a variety of reasons, such as concerns about "obesity, cognitive development, and stereotypes" (Sege & Dietz, 1994, p. 604) as well as for the potential harm from viewing televised violence. Interestingly, Griffore and Phenice (1996) found no differences in the amount of viewing by children regardless of whether families set rules for viewing.

Taras et al. (1990) reported that only 15% of the parents reported regulating their children's viewing of particular television shows. Only 38% of the parents reported frequently discussing television programs with their children, and only 20% agreed that more than half of their children's viewing time was spent with parents engaged in coviewing. However,

65% of mothers in the sample believed that they had a "strong" influence on their children's television viewing selections.

Stanger (1998) reported that 64.9% of parents reported setting rules governing children's television viewing. Figures were similar for 1996 (66%) and 1997 (68.9%). However, nearly one fourth of the parents (23.8%) admitted that their children watch unsuitable shows "a great deal" or "sometimes." Nearly one third (28.1%) of adolescents conceded that they watched programs of which their parents would disapprove.

Attitudes About Using Television Program Ratings

Control by parents of children's access to television has been found to influence children's attitudes about the world, understanding of television content, and social behavior in situations not involving television (Messaris & Sarett, 1981). Parental control over children's viewing also underlies efforts to establish television program ratings similar to motion picture ratings. Attitudes of family members toward program ratings are reflected by the growth of what Jordan called "an ever expanding cottage industry . . . to help parents make more informed choices about what their kids are watching, reading, and playing" (quoted by Susan Miller as cited in Dickinson, 1997, p. C-5).

Most parents (59%) allow their children to watch "whatever they want most or all of the time" (Cantor, Harrison, & Nathanson, 1997, p. 290). However, program ratings support some control over children's television viewing. A fall 1996 national survey (Cantor, Stutman, & Duran, 1997) of randomly chosen members of the National PTA focused on parents' concerns about effects of television viewing and attitudes of parents toward television ratings. The survey included 679 representatively distributed responses from 50 states.

Most parents (89%) considered program ratings as very important or moderately important (Cantor et al., 1997). Parental desire for such ratings did not vary with either age or sex of the children in the family. Almost the same proportion (84%) of parents favored the use of ratings in cartoons, but the degree of concern declined with increasing age of children in the family. Cantor et al. (1997) speculated that the decline reflected a decrease in child viewing of cartoons and a lowered parental concern about cartoon influence as children mature.

Fully 92% of respondents wanted ratings for reality-based programs, including shows about crime and law enforcement. No differences by age or sex of children emerged among parents' concerns (Cantor et al., 1997).

Respondents (80%) wanted a rating system to reveal program contents instead of merely reporting an overall program rating (20%; Cantor et al., 1997). The parents (82%) preferred content information to recommendations about whether programs are acceptable for viewing. They expressed skepticism about subjective ratings of who should see respective programs and showed little trust for program ratings by the television industry. Parents wanted distinct ratings for sexual content, violence, and language. They preferred the content-specific ratings of cable programmers to the ratings used by the Motion Picture Association of America by nearly three to one. Cantor et al. (1997) compared their national PTA survey results with another national survey (Silver & Geier, 1996). Both studies found preferences for content-specific ratings.

Parents participating in the National PTA survey generally differed in their level of concern depending on the ages of their children. They also reflected varying degrees of concern within the same age groups for boys as compared with concern for girls (Cantor et al., 1997).

Parental concern for television violence was greatest for younger children (Cantor et al., 1997). Although no differences appeared in overall concern for boys or girls, more concern emerged for girls as children grew older. Among children ages 3 to 7, parental concern varied considerably about children's violence and fright reactions. Parents of boys were less concerned about fright than about violence, and parents of girls felt the opposite way. Older studies (e.g., Desmond, Hirsch, Singer, & Singer, 1987; Gross & Walsh, 1980) reflected more parental concern for controlling viewing among girls than for boys.

Cantor et al. (1997) found that, among parents of children ages 8 to 12, parents of boys showed more concern about violence and risk taking than did parents of girls. Sex on television strongly concerned parents of both boys and girls in this group. Among parents of children ages 13 to 18, concern for girls exceeded that for boys on all five measures; sex, violence, profanity, risk taking, and fright. This list appears in descending order of concern for this age group. Cantor et al. (1997) concluded that most parents want a television program rating system, and they want one assisting informed independent viewing choices. Parents prefer to make their own judgments about the suitability of television programs for their children.

A few months after a television rating system was voluntarily adopted by broadcasters in January 1997 (FCC, 1997), a survey (Sneegas & Plank, 1998) of 203 fourth-and fifth-grade students in Missouri and California found that 37% of the children could not accurately distinguish between pairs of ratings system codes. The majority (69%) of children reported no parental requirements for using the ratings system, but girls reported more viewing rules than did boys.

Sneegas and Plank (1998) speculated that girls would be more likely than boys to avoid watching programs with prohibitive ratings. They found that girls, more often than boys, avoided shows based on program ratings, watched more shows rated TV-G, and more shows with no content warnings. Boys watched significantly more shows with ratings of TV-14, TV-M, and more shows containing violence and sexual content. Sneegas and Plank reported that boys would be more likely than girls to succumb to forbidden programs with prohibitive ratings.

A 1999 study (Kaiser Family Foundation, 1999) of 1,001 parents found that 90% of parents believed that the television program rating system is "very useful" or "somewhat useful." However, only 52% said that they had ever used program ratings to guide viewing choices, and 39% said that they had used the ratings to block a child's viewing of a program.

Most parents (77%) said that they would use V-chips to prevent their children from seeing objectionable television shows if the devices were in their homes (Kaiser Family Foundation, 1999). Among the children surveyed in 1998, 78% expressed approval of their parents using the V-chips to block programs, and only 35% admitted that they would attempt to defeat the blocking scheme if their parents used it (Albiniak, 1998). Most parents (72%) said that when they buy their next set, they will select a model containing a V-chip (Kaiser Family Foundation, 1999). Nevertheless, many parents' knowledge of the rating system appeared to be weak, with 19% of the parents responding that they had never heard of the rating system, and only 39% responding that they had heard or seen any explanation of it. The respondents did not believe that parents know enough about the rating system to effectively use it.

Attitudes About Television in Day-Care Facilities

Parents and teachers responded before and after a 5-month study of materials accompanying "Mister Rogers' Neighborhood" in day-care centers in Toledo, Ohio (McFarland, 1992). Before the study, 95.5% of parents "strongly agreed" or "somewhat agreed" with the statement: "Television can be used effectively with preschool children." After the study, 100% of answers fell into one of those categories. Before the study, 90.5% of the parents somewhat or strongly disagreed with the statement: "Television has no place in child care." After the study, 91% felt that way. Similar stability occurred with a statement about whether television can change children's behavior. The proportion of parents who strongly or somewhat agreed that "Mister Rogers' Neighborhood" can positively affect preschool children's behavior increased from 89.1% to 100% after the study. However, parents' attitudes about cartoons remained stable around the study, with 41% after the study either somewhat or strongly disagreeing that cartoons can positively affect preschool children. Also, 14% of the parents had no opinion after the study about the influence of cartoons, and 41% somewhat or strongly agreed that cartoons can have positive effects.

FAMILY ATTITUDES ABOUT TELEVISION CONTENT

Preferred Programs for Children

Stanger (1998) reported parents' attitudes about the best programs for young people. Parents easily favored public television (48%) over broadcast network (8.8%) and cable (37.7%) programs. However, support for public television as a source for young people's shows declined slightly from the 57% and 61.1% figures for 1996 and 1997 respectively. Among parents of children ages 2 to 17, parents' favorite 1998 shows for their children were *Barney* (19%) and *Sesame Street* (17%), and no more than 9% of parents named other shows.

These results proved strikingly similar to Beron's (1993) survey of parents of children who attended a day-care facility in Bremen, Indiana. From 23 parents who were asked to rate the top five and bottom five programs for children, *Teenage Mutant Ninja Turtles* was the most frequently named negative show, with twice as many votes as *Cyber Cops,* the second-ranked negatively perceived program. The parents expressed considerable negativity toward cartoons.

Stanger (1998) found that parents believed that the best shows for adolescents included *Home Improvement* (9%) and *Saved by the Bell* (8%). Other shows were tightly grouped and close behind. The adolescents themselves favored *The Simpsons* (15%) and *Home Improvement* (12%) as the best shows for that age group. No other programs were named by more than 8% of the teenagers. Adolescents' favorite 1998 shows were *The Simpsons* and *South Park,* both selected by 8% of the teenagers.

Young people, unlike their parents, did not name public broadcasting as their favorite source of quality programming. However, APPC surveys showed for the first time in 1998, that young people chose broadcast network programs (38.4%) ahead of cable shows (35%). Selection of public television programs by young people as their favorites ranged from a low of 19% in 1996 to a high of 21.9% in 1997, dropping slightly to 20.8% in 1998. Other sources fluctuated considerably in their approval from young people who responded to APPC surveys. In 1997, 12% of young people selected broadcast networks as their favorite programming source, compared with 32% in 1996. During the same interval, the proportion of young people who named cable as their favorite programming source rose from 44% to 62.8% before dropping to almost half that level in 1998 (Stanger, 1998).

Believability of Television

A 1998 survey (Austin, 1993) of 346 adolescents asked a set of questions intended to reveal patterns in parents' attempts to influence their children's interpretations of television. The more parents discussed television content with children, the greater the level of their children's skepticism about television, as measured by questions about whether television news omits important information from stories. Austin cited a Gallup poll as reporting that parents were seven times less likely to discuss offensive television content with their children as they were to turn off the set or to ban the children's viewing of the content.

Stanger (1998) found that most parents and teenagers believe "most" or "all" of both television news and newspaper content. Parents indicated a stronger degree of trust in television news (62%) than in newspapers (53.8%). Teenagers expressed slightly more confidence than their parents in both television (69.6%) and newspaper news (64.3%).

Sherman (1996) suggested that children's tastes in viewing television provide formative elements for their cultures. Children's beliefs in the reality of television portrayals were reportedly associated with the likelihood of their belief in mutual family member support as real (Buerkel-Rothfuss, Greenberg, Atkin, & Neuendorf, 1982). Parental control over children's viewing also influenced children's perceptions about families.

In families where parents exercised strong control over children's television viewing and encouraged the children to watch selected programs, children tended to believe that real family members are supportive of each other. This tendency usually appeared in families in which parents watched television with children and discussed the content with them (Buerkel-Rothfuss et al., 1982).

Adult respondents to a 1998 poll conducted for the National Partnership for Women and Families overwhelmingly (84%) believed that families on television are unlike their own families (Heintz-Knowles, 1998). However, on the whole, children perceived *Full House*, a popular situation comedy, as quite realistic (Weiss & Wilson, 1998). The sample represented boys and girls evenly, with 28% Whites, including mostly lower class children from two grade levels; 77 in K to 2 and 71 from Grades 3 to 5. Respondents saw program segments and photographs of cast members. They believed that most or all real families are similar to the family in the program on three measures of reality; how many families are like the television family, how many families have similar feelings to those of the television family, and how much of what happened on the show happens in real life.

A 1986 to 1987 survey (Rabin, Corr, Kovaric, & Doubleday, 1991) questioned 858 children in the second, fifth, and tenth grades who named *The Cosby Show, Family Ties,* and *Diff'rent Strokes* as their favorite family television programs. A follow-up study in 1989 included 40 adults and used questionnaire responses to evaluate perceived realism of the shows. As expected, beliefs in realism of the shows declined as the viewers' ages increased. However, ethnic matches between viewers and television characters bore no relationship to the perception of realism. The authors observed that, although adults seemed to find popular family television shows to be unrealistic portrayals of reality, television portrayals could be shaping children's perceptions about the world.

Chandler (1997) summarized the research about children's understanding of television, showing that children of various ages believe to different degrees that television content is real. He examined such factors as children's developmental frameworks, their ability to distinguish between real objects and representations of objects, their awareness of the constructedness of television shows, their thinking of television images as showing things from the real world, their ability to assess the possibility of televised concepts as occurring in real life, and their ability to assess plausibility that television portrayals might occur in reality. At first, children probably believe that everything they see on television is real (Fitch, Huston, & Wright, 1993, as cited in Chandler, 1997). As children mature, they learn about the conventions of television and become aware that television content is assembled rather than being something reported from facts. The proportions of respective age groups from which children understood that television programs were fabricated included 15% of 5- and 6-year-olds; 23% of 7- to 9-year-olds; and 19% of 11- and 12-year-olds (Dorr, 1983).

Chandler (1997) found general agreement that 8 years of age is a turning point beyond which children believe progressively less in the reality of television. Chandler cited Fitch et al. (1993) in showing that children's judgments about television reality usually reach par with those of adults by 10 years of age. However, Fitch et al. (as cited in Chandler, 1997) noted that cognitive maturation, rather than experience with television, determined the ability to accurately distinguish between television fantasy and reality. Some studies (e.g., Elliott & Slater, 1980; Greenberg & Reeves, 1976) found evidence that viewers who watch more television are more likely to believe in the reality of television content. However, the direction of any such causal relationship between amount of time spent watching television and belief in its reality is unclear.

Attitudes About Race Portrayals on Television

Most parents (62.9%) agreed that their children see "some" or "a lot" of television characters with whom the children can relate (Stanger, 1998). African American parents (69.7%) and White parents (63.3%) more often expressed satisfaction than did Asian and Hispanic parents (54%).

Parents of preschool children ages (2 to 5) most often found "some" or "a lot" of identifiable characters for their children (69.7%) compared with parents of children ages 6 to 11 (64.6%) and ages 12 to 17 (56.5%). Although parents expressed less confidence than teenagers in television's inclusion and portrayal of minorities and females, both groups appeared to believe that television does a good job in these areas (Stanger, 1998).

More than two thirds of teenagers (68.2%) felt that television offers "some" or "a lot" of characters with whom they can identify. Teens did not show the disparity in approval displayed by their parents, with African Americans (68.8%) and Whites (67.2%) showing similar proportions of identification with television characters as that shown by Asian and Hispanic teens (70.9%). Girls (70%) varied little from boys (66.5%) in this age group in finding identifiable characters, and no differences emerged among children from different age groups. No significant differences emerged by income level of households among either the parents of teenagers or the children in finding some or a lot of identifiable characters (Stanger, 1998).

In May 1998, Children Now released the results of a national poll of 1,200 children ages 10 to 17, including 300 children from each of the four largest racial groups. The study (Children Now, 1998) also included nine focus groups involving children across America and concluded that children of all races become aware very early in life of media stereotypes. Children also believe that these stereotypes influence people's opinions. The children, especially those of color, believed that seeing people of their own races is important. The proportions of respective respondents expressing this belief included heavy support from African Americans (82%), Asians (79%), Latinos (78%), and Whites (67%). Although the children from all races (91%) agreed that enough White main characters appear on television, fewer respondents believed that there are enough main African American characters (57%), Latino characters (20%), or Asian characters (14%).

All the children frequently associated positive characteristics with television's White characters and negative characteristics with characters of minority races. Positive characteristics included having wealth, being well educated, doing well in school, and displaying leadership and intelligence. Negative characteristics included being in financial need, appearing lazy, and acting foolish. The children believed that Whites on television usually play secretaries (79%), bosses (71%), doctors (67%), and police officers (53%). They believed that African Americans on television usually portray criminals (59%) and maids or janitors (35%). The children believed that news media usually portray African Americans and Latinos more negatively than Whites and Asians, especially when the people in the news are young people. The children agreed that television people of all races are shown doing both good and bad. However, they believed that African Americans appear on television doing bad things 35% of the time and good things only 14% of the time. They believed that Whites appear doing bad things only 9% of the time and good things 42% of the time. Although White children (76%) believed that enough people of their race appear on television as newscasters, African American (71%), Latino (63%), and Asian (51%) children wanted more people of their race as newscasters. None of the children's groups, however, indicated that the race of newscasters affected their trust in television news (Children Now, 1998).

Attitudes About Television and Violent Content

The National Television Violence Study reported that violence appeared in 61% of 1996 to 1997 television shows, excluding newcasts and sports (Smith, et al., 1998). The Kaiser Family Foundation (1999) found that 60% of parents who responded to a May 1999 national survey reported a "great deal" of concern about the amount of violence their children see on television, and another 26% were "somewhat" concerned, producing a total of 86% showing some concern. The proportion of parents expressing these degrees of concern increased from 75% of parents who expressed some concern during a similar 1996 survey. The proportion of parents expressing a great deal of concern reached only 39% in 1996.

Hough and Erwin (1997) studied the impact of a variety of factors on children's attitudes toward television violence. Children's attitudes about television violence were not predicted by personal viewer characteristics. Instead, only the number of hours of school day viewing predicted such attitudes. Children who watched more television were more aware of and concerned about violence in television programs. However, Hough and Erwin cautioned that the impact of other variables could have been influenced by the school day viewing behavior.

Children who watched higher amounts of television felt more at risk and were more suspicious than children who watched less television. Those children who watched more television were more likely to think of the world as a scary place. These findings echoed those of Singer, Singer, and Rapacynski (1984). Hough and Erwin (1997) reported feeling encouraged that many of the heavy viewing children seemed aware of the effects that television had on them.

Boys apparently prefer violent television programs, and girls appear to enjoy nonviolent television programs (Van Evra, 1990, 1997). Girls tend to report more emotional responses to violence on television, become more frightened by it, and watch with a lower level of involvement than do boys. Wober (1988) reported that several studies indicated that aggressive young television viewers prefer violent shows, a trend that appeared in most countries from which data are available (Huesman & Eron, 1986).

Attitudes About Television and Sexual Content

As with violence on television, sexual content, as either talk about sex or portrayal of sexual behavior, is a television staple. Sexual content appears in slightly more than half (56%) of all programs and appears in an average of 3.2 scenes per hour among all television shows that contain sexual content (Kunkel et al., 1999). A Kaiser Family Foundation (1999) national survey reported that 66% of parents felt a great deal of concern that their children were exposed to too much sexual content on television, and another 21% were somewhat concerned. These respective figures changed from 43% and 28% in a similar 1996 survey.

In April and May of 1998, a national survey of 1,204 American adults of at least 18 years of age was sponsored by the Kaiser Family Foundation and ABC Television (KFF/ABC, 1998). The survey focused on sex and sexual health and revealed insights about attitudes among American parents about sex on television. Most respondents believed that movies and television show too much casual sex and encourage irresponsible sexual activity. A majority of respondents believed that, to some degree, movies and television images show inaccurate images about sexual life, for example, the notion that frequent changing of sex partners is necessary for great sex; that people can have spontaneous sex without worrying about the consequences; that only thin, beautiful people can have great sex; and that having a normal sex drive means always being in the mood for sex. Little support appeared among the respondents for the belief that movies and television show that older adults can have great sex. Most respondents also expressed the opinion that movies and television content should include, with sexual portrayals, references about safe sex protections.

The KFF/ABC (1998) survey also addressed family conversations about sexual topics as a result of television content. Most respondents reported conversations with children as a result of television shows and news programs, and most of them said the experiences were positive. Just under one third believed that an unwanted conversation occurred with their children about sex after seeing something on television. Most parents reported having switched off the television set and prohibited their children from watching certain shows because of sexual content on television. Although nearly half of the adults said that they asked a health care provider about a sexual topic or spoke with a sexual partner about sex after seeing sexually related television content, not many experimented with new sex activities after seeing sexually oriented television content.

Examining some of these findings (KFF/ABC, 1998) in more detail reveals that 55% of the respondents felt that too much casual sex in movies and television shows contributes a lot in creating problems with unplanned pregnancy and sexually transmitted diseases. Only 6% felt that such portrayals contribute nothing to these problems. When asked about the manner in which television shows sex and nudity, 74% of the people sampled believed that the television practices encourage irresponsible sexual behavior. References in television to portrayals of sexual activity were believed to incur a responsibility to include references to condoms or other methods of safe sex by 77%; only 18% advocated no such need.

Television portrayals of sexuality were considered inaccurate reflections of sex life by 83% of the respondents, among whom 23% said the representations reflected their own sex life "not too well." Another 50% felt that the reflections reflected their sex life "not well at all." Asked about the sexual messages sent by television and movies, only 14% believed that these content types do not send the message that frequently changing sex partners is necessary to having a great sex life. With 2% giving no opinion on that question, 84% expressed their agreement that movies and television promote, to some degree, the idea that having multiple sex partners is necessary to great sex. The respective proportions of respondents who believed that some such influence appears in movies and television content were 14% responding that the notion is portrayed "only a little," 29% "some," and 41% "a lot." Respondents identified several images that occur in movies and television "a lot." These images included portrayals that only thin, beautiful people can have great sex (53%), that having a normal sex drive means always being in the mood for sex (41%), and that people can have spontaneous sex without worrying about the consequences (53%). The latter image was reported by another 25% of respondents as occurring "some" of the time, and 11% indicated that the message is sent "only a little." However, the image that older adults can have great sex received little support. Only 14% answered "a lot" in describing the extent to which movies and television portray that idea. "Some" received the nod of 14% of the sample, "only a little" by 33%, and 19% believed that this image appears "not at all" in movies and television (KFF/ABC, 1998).

In addition to questions about beliefs about the messages conveyed in movies and television, the survey included items about whether television served as a catalyst for conversations among parents and their children. When the respondents were selected on the basis of having at least one child between the ages of 8 and 18, 329 qualified. Among them, 70% reported having had a conversation with a child because of something that appeared in a television show, and 63% had such a conversation based on television news content. The surveyors identified parents who experienced conversations with their children about sexual topics, producing a sample of 257 parents. Questions addressed how the parents felt the last time they had a conversation based on something seen on television. Among these respondents, 65% felt that the conversation was a good opportunity to talk with their children about sexual matters, and only 31% said that the television content raised an issue about which they did not want to have a conversation with their children at the time of the event. Among the parents with at least one child of age 18 or under, 76% of 491 reported forbidding children from watching a particular television program because of sexual content. Other actions based on the entire sample of adults revealed actions taken because of sexual content on television: Sixty percent turned off the television, 46% talked with a health care provider about a sexual topic, 44% talked with a sexual partner about sex, and 13% tried a new sexual activity (KFF/ABC, 1998).

Attitudes About Television and Alcohol and Drugs

Between September 15 and October 13, 1998 the Kaiser Family Foundation and Children Now, with assistance from Princeton Survey Research Associates (PSRA), surveyed parents and children who were members of randomly selected families (Kaiser Family Foundation/Children Now, 1999). The respondents included 880 parents of children ages 6 to 15 and 348 children ages 10 to 15. The sample included 447 parents of children ages 8 to 12, 267 parents of children ages 10 to 12, and 272 parents of children ages 13 to 15. The sample also included 161 children ages 10 to 12 and 187 ages 13 to 15. Parents were asked about what initiated conversations with their children about various topics. The response choices included "something on the news," "something in a TV show, movie, or other entertainment media," and other nonmedia sources. The proportion of parents who believed that these conversations began from media content were higher than the proportions responding that the conversation began because of occurrences not related to media. Although the items in the survey did not separate television responses from other media, television was named as a prominent example of entertainment media in the survey questions (Kaiser Family Foundation/Children Now, 1999).

When asked about conversations with their children about alcohol or drugs, 49% of parents answered that the exchange was prompted by something on the news; and 61% reported that the conversation was prompted by something in a television program, movie, or something in other entertainment media. The other sources in the survey included something in a class or program at school (51%), something that happened in school or in the community (45%), something that happened or was found at home (40%), or something that occurred in a visit to a doctor's office. Apparently, parents believe that the media, especially television, more often than other factors, provide catalysts for parent–child discussions about drugs and alcohol (Kaiser Family Foundation/Children Now, 1999).

In discussing violence with their children, parents also emphasized the media in general, and television in particular, in prompting conversations. Of those responding that prospective catalysts did begin conversations, 67% reported that it was from something on the news, and 70% of the discussions arose from something in a television show, movie, or other entertainment media. Only events at school or in the community (62%) reached these levels among the other sources. School classes (39%), family events or something found at home (27%), and visits to doctors (2%) trailed by large margins. Nonmedia sources lagged behind the news (61%) and entertainment media (68%) in starting conversations about AIDS. None of the other sources were named by more than 44% of the parents. For beginning parent–child communication about sex, only the entertainment media (64%) were named by more than 41% (news) (Kaiser Family Foundation/Children Now, 1999).

The study inquired into the amount of influence that parents believed stemmed from various sources about "issues like sex, drugs, and violence." The parents believed that their own influence was greatest among these sources. Mothers (76%), fathers (63%), friends (66%), and television shows, movies, and other entertainment media (60%) were the only sources that 60% or more of the respondents believed to have "a lot of influence" over children's attitudes about these issues. Other influence sources that failed to rate as high included siblings (49%), schools and teachers (47%), churches, religious organizations, or clergy (35%), the Internet (27%), and magazines (25%). When the children were asked the sources from which children of their own age group find out a lot about issues like sex, drugs, and violence, the respondents chose television shows, movies, or other entertainment media more frequently (49%) than any other source. Friends (47%) ranked second, and schools and teachers (41%) were the only other category named by more than 38% of the children (Kaiser Family Foundation/Children Now, 1999).

Although several sources ranked higher than entertainment media as identified sources of information about drugs and alcohol, television shows, movies, and other entertainment media (24%) ranked first as a frequent source of information about violence. However, older children (13–15) were more likely (27%) to name the entertainment media as the source of information about violence than were the younger children (10–12). Among the younger group, 26% named their mothers as the most frequent source, with the entertainment media (22%) ranking as the second most likely source of information about violence. Information about AIDS and sex tended not to come most often from entertainment media. Only 11% of the children found most of their information from television shows, movies, and other entertainment media, and only 6% named these media as their primary source of information about sex (Kaiser Family Foundation/Children Now, 1999).

SUMMARY

Based on the review of literature appearing in this chapter, family attitudes about television tend to be generally positive. The vast majority of families approve of television, even though a small group of families ban it from their homes. Although families apparently do not tend to talk while watching television, individuals perceive television as providing opportunities for doing something together and supporting family members.

Almost all parents in one study reported believing that television belongs in day-care facilities and can change children's behavior. Children are more likely than parents to approve of television as a positive force and spend more time watching television than they devote to any other activity at home.

Nevertheless, parents express greater concern for television than for any other medium, including the Internet. Parents say that they frequently watch television with their children and usually monitor their children's viewing. However, more than one third of children under age 12 enjoy television sets in their bedrooms, and more than half of teenagers have them. The frequency of television sets located in children's bedrooms suggests parental acceptance of unsupervised viewing by children, and parents with less education tend to be more likely than other parents to consent to the arrangement.

Although Stanger (1998) found that 64.9% of parents said that they set rules for their children's television viewing, Cantor et al. (1997) found that 59% of parents allowed children to control their own viewing. Additional research is needed to clarify this apparent discrepancy. Most parents say that they are more concerned with specific programs that their children watch, rather than the amount of time that the children spend watching television. However, many parents appear to be ignorant of the program ratings system that could support parental supervision of children's viewing.

Almost all parents consider program ratings as important and favor the use of ratings in such programs as cartoons and reality shows, and 78% of children approve of their parents' using V-chips to block objectionable programs. However, most parents are ignorant about the components of the rating system, and only 30% reported that buying a television set with a V-chip within 1 to 2 years is likely (Kaiser Family Foundation, 1999). Furthermore, 38% of parents said that they would not pay $25 extra to obtain a new television set with a V-chip.

Parents prefer public television programs for their young children, but children and teenagers prefer broadcast and cable programs. Research has addressed some programming genres, such as soap operas and cartoons. For example, only 41% of parents in one study reported believing that television cartoons can positively affect preschool children (McFarland, 1992). More information is needed about attitudes of particular groups toward specific program types and how attitudes vary by personal characteristics, family differences, and viewing patterns. For example, additional study is needed regarding attitudes toward television of teenagers, elderly, and minority audiences.

Television portrayals apparently offer a variety of characters with whom children of various races can identify, although Asian and Hispanic parents in particular would like their children to see more characters like themselves. Most preschool and teenaged children perceive that characters like themselves appear on television. Children of all races become aware very early in life of media stereotypes, detect differences in positive or negative portrayals by racial stereotypes, and understand that these stereotypes influence people's opinions about real people.

Parents show considerable concern regarding their children's exposure to television violence and sexual content, and the degree of concern appears to be growing. Children's attitudes about television violence show more concern among heavy viewers than among children who watch less television. Feeling at risk and suspicious of others is associated with heavy television viewing, and heavy viewers readily approve of parental control over their viewing. Only the number of hours of school day viewing predicted such attitudes (Hough & Erwin, 1997). More research is needed about the factors that are associated with such viewing. The impact of televised news coverage of violence on children's attitudes toward television needs additional research.

Most adults believe that movies and television show too much casual sex, show little resemblance to real sex life, and encourage irresponsible sexual activity. Children say that they learn more from the media, including television, about sex, drugs, and alcohol than from any other source. Parents report that television serves as a catalyst for family conversations dealing with sensitive topics such as sexuality, drugs, and alcohol. However, nearly one third of parents report that such conversations were not ones that they wanted at the time that television raised the subject.

Parents tend to believe that they provide the strongest influence on their children's knowledge about sex, drugs, and violence. Children, however, name television shows and other media as providing the most frequent influence, followed by friends, and the combination of schools and teachers. No other category of influence was named by more than 38% of children. Apparently, parents have much to learn about their children's and their own attitudes toward television.

REFERENCES

Albiniak, P. (1998, June 1). Parents taking to ratings. *Broadcasting & Cable, 128*(23), 16.

American Academy of Pediatrics Committee on Communications. (1990). Policy statement: Children, adolescents and television. *Pediatrics, 85*, 1119–1120.

Austin, E. W. (1993, Spring). Exploring the effects of active parental mediation of television content. *Journal of Broadcasting & Electronic Media, 37*(2), 147–158.

Beron, B. (1993, December). *An evaluation of children's television.* East Lansing, MI: National Center for Research on Teacher Learning. (ERIC Document Reproduction Service No. ED 372 770)

Boorstin, D. J. (1971, September 10). Television. *Life*, pp. 36–39.

Bower, R. T. (1973). *Television and the public.* New York: Holt, Rinehart & Winston.

Brody, G. H., Stoneman, Z., & Sanders, A. (1980). Effects of television viewing on family interactions: An observational study. *Family Relations, 29*, 216–220.

Bronfenbrenner, U. (1975). The origins of alienation. In U. Bronfenbrenner & M. A. Mahoney (Eds.), *Influences on human development* (2nd ed., pp. 658–677). Hinsdale, IL: Dryden.

Brown, D., & Bryant, J. (1990). Effects of television on family values and selected attitudes and behaviors. In J. Bryant (Ed.), *Television and the American family* (pp. 253–274). Hillsdale, NJ: Lawrence Erlbaum Associates.

Buerkel-Rothfuss, N. L., Greenberg, B. S., Atkin, C. K., & Neuendorf, K. (1982). Learning about the family from television. *Journal of Communication, 32*(3), 191–200.

Cantor, J., Harrison, K., & Nathanson, A. (1997). *National television violence study, (Vol. 2).* Thousand Oaks, CA: Sage.

Cantor, J., Stutman, S., & Duran, V. (1997). What parents want in a television rating system: Results of a national survey. *Children First: The Website of the National PTA* [online]. Available: http://www.pta.org/programs/tvrpttoc.htm

Chandler, D. (1997). Children's understanding of what is "real" on television: A review of the literature. *Journal of Educational Media, 23*(1), 67–82.

Children Now. (1998, May). *A different light: Children's perceptions of race and class in media.* Paper presented at Children Now's Fifth Annual Children & the Media Conference, Los Angeles, CA. [online]. Available: http://www.childrennow.org/media/race.html

Christopher, F. S., Fabes, R. A., & Wilson, P. M. (1989). Family television viewing: Implications for family life education. *Family Relations, 38*, 210–214.

Desmond, R. J., Hirsch, B., Singer, J. L., & Singer, D. G. (1987). Gender differences, mediation and disciplinary styles in children's responses to television. *Sex Roles, 16* (7/8), 375–389.

Diamond, D. (1996, January). Life without TV: How one family conquered its tube addiction. *Parents, 71*(1), 87–88.

Diamond, E., Lavagnino, D., & Zimmerman, C. (1996, December 21). Big media turn against big media. *National Journal, 28* (51–52), 2754–2755.

Dickinson, J. (1997, June 3). Parental guidance: A variety of media help us set guidelines on kids' TV, movies and computer software. *The Dallas Morning News*, p. C5–C6.

Dorr, A. (1983). No shortcuts to judging reality. In J. Bryant & D. R. Anderson (Eds.), *Children's understanding of television: Research on attention and comprehension* (pp. 199–220). New York: Academic Press.

Dorr, A., Kovaric, P., & Doubleday, C. (1989). Parent–child coviewing of television. *Journal of Broadcasting & Electronic Media, 33*, 35–51.

Elliott, W. R., & Slater, D. (1980). Exposure, experience and perceived TV reality for adolescents. *Journalism Quarterly, 57*, 409–414, 431.

Fabes, R. A., Wilson, P., & Christopher, F. S. (1989). A time to re-examine the role of television in family life. *Family Relations, 38*, 337–341.

Fallis, S. F., Fitzpatrick, M. A., & Friestad, M. S. (1985). Spouses' discussion of television portrayals of close relationships. *Communication Research, 12*, 59–81.

Federal Communication Commission (1997). *V-chip homepage* [online]. Available: http://www.fcc.gov/vchip/

Field, D. E. (1988). Child and parent coviewing of television: Its extent and its relationship to cognitive performance (Doctoral dissertation, University of Massachusetts, 1987). *Dissertation Abstracts International, 48*, 2799B–2800B.

Gantz, W. (1985). Exploring the role of television in married life. *Journal of Broadcasting & Electronic Media, 29*, 65–78.

Greenberg, B. S., & Reeves, B. (1976). Children and the perceived reality of television. *Journal of Social Issues, 32*(4), 86–97.

Griffore, R. J., & Phenice, L. A. (1996). Rules and television viewing. *Psychological Reports, 78*, 814.

Gross, L. S., & Walsh, R. P. (1980). Factors affecting parental control over children's television viewing: A pilot study. *Journal of Broadcasting, 24*, 411–419.

Gunter, B., & Svennevig, M. (1987). *Behind and in front of the screen: Television involvement with family life.* London: John Libbey & Company Ltd.

Heintz-Knowles, K. (1998). *Balancing acts: Work/family issues on prime-time TV.* National Partnership for Women & Families [online]. Available: http://www.nationalpartnership.org/publications/contentanalysis.htm

Holman, J., & Braithwaite, V. (1982). Parental life-styles and children's television viewing. *Australian Journal of Psychology, 34*, 375–382.

Hough, K. J., & Erwin, P. G. (1997, July). Children's attitudes toward violence on television. *The Journal of Psychology, 131*, 411–416.

Huesman, L. R., & Eron, L. D. (1986). *Television and the aggressive child: A cross-national comparison.* Hillsdale, NJ: Lawrence Erlbaum Associates.

Jordan, A. B. (1997, March). Supplement: Children and television: A conference summary *The Annals of the American Academy of Political and Social Science, 550*, 153–168.

Kaiser Family Foundation. (May, 1999). Parents and the V-chip: A Kaiser Family Foundation Survey. [online]. Available: http://www.kff.org/archive/media/entertainment/vchip/vchip_s.pdf

Kaiser Family Foundation/ABC Television. (1998, September). Sex in the 90s: Kaiser Family Foundation/ABC Television 1998 national survey of Americans on sex and sexual health. [online]. Available: http://www.kff.org/kff/library.html?document_key=2120&data_type_key=392

Kaiser Family Foundation/Children Now. (1999, March 1). *Talking with kids about tough issues: A national survey of parents and kids.* Menlo Park, CA: Author.

Kunkel, D., Cope, K. M., Farinola, W. J. M., Biely, E., Rollin, E., & Donnerstein, E. (1999, February). *Sex on TV: content and context* [A biennial report to the Henry J. Kaiser family Foundation]. Report No. 1458. Menlo Park, CA: Henry J. Kaiser Foundation.

Lazar, B. (1994, January). Under the influence: An analysis of children's television regulation. *Social Work, 39*(1), 67–75.

Leichter, H. L., Ahmed, D., Barrios, L., Bryce, J., Larsen, E., & Moe, L. (1985). Family contexts of television. *Educational Communication and Technology Journal, 33*(1), 26–40.

Lieberman, J. I. (1996, May-June). Why parents hate TV. *Policy Review, 77*, 18–24.

Lyle, J., & Hoffman, H. R. (1972). Children's use of television and other media. In E. A. Rubin-
    stein, G. A. Comstock, & J. P. Murray (Eds.), *Television and social behavior* (Vol. 4,
    pp. 129–256). Washington, DC: U. S. Government Printing Office.
Maccoby, E. E. (1951). Television: Its impact on schoolchildren. *Public Opinion Quarterly,
    15,* 421–444.
McDonald, D. G. (1985). Spousal influences on television viewing. *Communication Research,
    12,* 530–545.
McDonald, D. G. (1986). Generational aspects of television coviewing. *Journal of Broad-
    casting & Electronic Media, 30,* 75–85.
McFarland, S. L. (1992). *Extending "The Neighborhood" to child care.* Toledo, OH: Public
    Broadcasting Foundation of Northwest Ohio.
McIlwraith, R. D. (1990, August). Theories of television addiction. In R. McIlwraith (Chair),
    Television addiction: Theories and data behind the ubiquitous metaphor. Symposium con-
    ducted at the annual meeting of the American Psychological Association, Boston, MA.
McIlwraith, R. D. (1998, Summer). "I," addicted to television: The personality, imagination,
    and TV watching patterns of self-identified TV addicts. *Journal of Broadcasting & Elec-
    tronic Media, 42,* 371–387.
Messaris, P., & Sarett, C. (1981). On the consequences of television-related parent–child
    interaction. *Human Communication Research, 7,* 226–244.
Rabin, B. E., Dorr, A., Kovaric, P., & Doubleday, C. (1991, April). *Children's perceived real-
    ism of family television series.* Paper presented at the biennial meeting of the Society for
    Research in Child Development, Seattle, WA.
Robinson, J., Skill, T., Nussbaum, J., & Moreland, K. (1985). Parents, peers, and television
    characters: The use of comparison others as criteria for evaluating marital satisfaction.
    In E. C. Lange (Ed.), *Using the media to promote knowledge and skills in family dynamics*
    (pp. 11–15). Dayton, OH: Center for Religious Telecommunications.
Sege, R., & Dietz, R. (1994). Television viewing and violence in children: The pediatrician as
    agent for change. *Pediatrics, 94,* 600–607.
Sherman, S. (1996, November–December). A set of one's own: TV sets in children's bed-
    rooms. *Journal of Advertising Research, 36*(6), 9–13.
Silver, M., & Geier, T. (1996, September 9). Ready for prime time? *U.S. News & World Report,
    121*(10), pp. 54–62.
Singer, J. L., Singer, D. G., & Rapacynski, W. S. (1984). Family patterns and television view-
    ing as predictors of children's beliefs and aggression. *Journal of Communication, 34*(2),
    73–89.
Smith, R. (1986). Television addiction. In J. Bryant & D. Anderson (Eds.), *Perspectives on
    media effects* (pp. 109–128). Hillsdale, NJ: Lawrence Erlbaum Associates.
Smith, S., Wilson, B., Kunkel, D., Linz, D., Potter, W. J., Colvin, C., & Donnerstein, E. (1998).
    Violence in television programming overall: University of California Santa Barbara
    study. In *National television violence study, (Vol. 3,* pp. 5–220). Thousand Oaks, CA: Sage.
Sneegas, J. E., & Plank, T. A. (1998, Fall). Gender differences in pre-adolescent reactance to
    age-categorized television advisory labels. *Journal of Broadcasting & Electronic Media,
    42,* 423.
Stanger, J. D. (1998, June 22). *Television in the home 1998: The third annual national survey
    of parents and children.* Philadelphia University of Pennsylvania.
Stein, A. H., & Friedrich, L. K. (1972). Television content and young children's behavior. In
    E. A. Rubinstein, G. A. Comstock, & J. P. Murray (Eds.), *Television and social behavior*
    (Vol. 4, pp. 202–317). Washington, DC: U. S. Government Printing Office.
St. Peters, M., Fitch, M., Huston, A. C., Wright, J. C., & Eakins, D. J. (1991). Television and
    families: What do young children watch with their parents? *Child Development, 62,*
    1409–1423.

Taras, H. L., Sallis, J. F., Nader, P. R., & Nelson, J. (1990, March). Children's television-viewing habits and the family environment. *American Journal of the Diseased Child, 144*, 357–359.

Van Evra, J. (1990). *Television and child development.* Hillsdale, NJ: Lawrence Erlbaum Associates.

Van Evra, J. (1997). *Television and child development* (2nd ed.). Hillsdale, NJ: Lawrence Erlbaum Associates.

Walsh, A. D., Laczniak, R. N., & Carlson, L. (1998, Fall). Mothers' preferences for regulating children's television. *Journal of Advertising, 27*(3), 23.

Walters, J. K., & Stone, V. A. (1971). Television and family communication. *Journal of Broadcasting, 15*, 409–414.

Weiss, A. J., & Wilson, B. J. (1998, June). Children's cognitive and emotional responses to the portrayal of negative emotions in family-formatted situation comedies. *Human Communication Research, 24*, 584–610.

Wober, M. (1988). The extent to which viewers watch violence-containing programs. *Current Psychology, 7*, 76–92.

Wober, J. M., & Gunter, B. (1987). Television and social control. Aldershot, Hampshire (UK) Gower.

Zinsmeister, K. (1997, September-October). TV-free: Real families describe life without the tube. *The American Enterprise, 8*(5), 63–72.

IV

Portrayals of American Families on Television

7

Five Decades of Families on Television: From the 1950s Through the 1990s

James D. Robinson
Thomas Skill
University of Dayton

The fictional family on television, in its many forms, has become one of our most enduring benchmarks for making both metric and qualitative assessments of how the American family is doing in the real world. For many in the arena of public policy, the debate frequently points to television as a primary source for what is good or bad about the family institution. Stephanie Coontz (1992) made this point very clearly in her sociological history of American families:

> Our most powerful visions of traditional families derive from images that are still delivered to our homes in countless reruns of 1950s television sit-coms. When liberal and conservatives debate family policy, for example, the issue is often framed in terms of how many "Ozzie and Harriet" families are left in America. (p. 23)

Previous work in this area sought to establish and extend our understanding of how families are portrayed on television (Moore, 1992; Skill & Robinson, 1994; Skill, Robinson, & Wallace, 1987) with an implicit goal of providing a more objective base for public discussion. This chapter strives to enhance our understanding of the trends in televised family configurations as they span 45 years from the 1950s to the 1990s.

Although some voices in the popular media consider many televised family portrayals to be uninvited role models for atypical or dysfunctional family configurations or lifestyles, numerous studies confirm that television is at best a "close follower" of real-world trends and lifestyles. Overall, the data suggest that television is far more likely to reinforce traditional models of family than to promote nonconventional configurations (Gerbner, Gross, Morgan, & Signorielli, 1980; Skill, 1994; Skill & Wallace, 1990; see Signorielli & Morgan, chap. 16, this volume; Skill, Wallace, Cassata, 1990). Examples of such studies include the work of Gerbner and his colleagues (1980). They reported that home, family, and romance are important components of the way characters are portrayed and that these presentations are, for the most part, traditional and stereotypical. With regard to the presentation of marital status, females were more likely to be explicitly shown as married. From 1969 to 1979, only 9% of the female characters could not be coded for marital status—45% were not married, and 46% were married or formerly married. In contrast, fully 24% of male characters were not classifiable in terms of marital status, with 45% not married and only 30% married or formerly married.

Signorielli (1982) studied the portrayal of married, formerly married, and single characters in prime-time network television dramas. The findings revealed that men outnumbered women by three to one and that women were more often portrayed as married and located in a home or family setting. Themes of home, family, marriage, and romance were seen as the domain of females. Overall, television seems to cultivate the impression that marriage is a rather neutral and safe state of existence. Married women, however, were presented as least able to succeed at blending both career and family, a problem almost never encountered by males.

In a study that explored the relationship between social class and happiness across TV families, Thomas and Callahan (1982) examined prime-time programs over a 3-year period beginning in 1978. Results indicated that "for the families portrayed on television, money clearly does not buy happiness and that, in fact, relative poverty does" (p. 186). It was concluded that families of lower socioeconomic status have stronger and more harmonious interpersonal relationships, are likely to have more members with pleasant and agreeable personalities, demonstrate greater levels of good will toward each other, and have better problem resolutions than families with higher socioeconomic status.

Comstock and Strzyzewski (1990) analyzed 29 hours of televised interactions across 41 prime-time network programs. This study examined conflict, jealousy, envy, and rivalry in family interactions. The data indicated more than that 30% of the conflict situations involved parents and children, 19% involved spouses, and 13% involved siblings. Integrative strategies, considered to be a constructive form of conflict because they promotes relational growth and maintenance, were employed most often by mothers and sons. Distributive strategies, considered a destructive form, were most often employed by siblings and spouses. The authors concluded that family conflict and the expression of jealousy occur frequently on prime-time television but that these portrayals are not predominantly antisocial.

In a related investigation, Skill and Wallace (1990) explored the frequency and distribution of assertive power, conformity, and rejection behaviors in prime-time families. The sample for this study consisted of 21 episodes across 18 different programs in which one or more family groups served as the primary story vehicle. The interactions of family members were analyzed by family role (i.e., mother, son, sister, etc.) and by family type (i.e., intact, nonintact, and mixed configurations). Assertive power had five possible manifestations; reward, coercive, legitimate, reference, and expert. This investigation explored the extent to which family members employed one of the five types of power strategies, yielded to the power of others (conformity behaviors), rejected others' attempts to use power (rejection), or engaged in none of the previous behaviors (neutral). More than 2,000 communicative acts were identified in this study, and the findings indicated that intact families engaged in the fewest assertive power and rejection acts of all family types, and in the most conformity acts. In terms of models of family life for the audience, the use of power in this study tended to be more positive than negative. Intact families, for the most part, used power in a compassionate fashion. Nonintact families followed closely, whereas mixed families (programs with both intact and nonintact families as primary story vehicles) were most likely to employ abusive forms of power such as coercion. The data overall suggest that models of family interaction on prime-time television tend to be rather diverse and for the most part, tempered with a sincere concern for the members of their respective families.

Sweeper (1984) content analyzed 93 episodes of family comedy–drama series for the period 1970 through 1980. The focus of the investigation was the comparison of portrayal characteristics of African American and White families. The findings of this study indicate that members of African American families were more likely to come from broken homes than were White family members. Consequently, more African American households were headed by single females. Educational achievement and occupational status were lower for African American family members.

Akins (1986) conducted a comparative analysis of family lifestyles and interactions across two sets of 30 commercial network television programs. One set was developed and aired in the 1960s, the other in the

1980s. The study examined television programs featuring a family with at least one preadolescent child. This investigation focused on the portrayals of family lifestyle and interpersonal interactions, which may serve as possible models for children. The data were analyzed across two program eras to determine if, and to what extent, content themes and interaction patterns of family members had changed during the previous 20 years. The findings suggest that children in the 1980s programs both initiated more interactions and exhibited more numerous interactions with their parents than did children in the 1960s programs. Family members were found to be more supportive and more likely to show concern for each other in the 1980s programs. Conversely, family members in the 1980s shows were also more likely to evade, ignore, withdraw, and oppose one another than were families in the 1960s shows. Similarly, children in the 1980s programs were more likely to both seek information and initiate conflict with adults than were children in the 1960s program. Family members in the 1980s programs exhibited more overt love and caring toward each other, but males in both the 1960s and 1980s shows were portrayed as more interactive than females. Whereas children's interests were portrayed in similar ways across the two programming eras, the concerns, problems, and program themes encountered by children in the 1980s shows were presented as more complex and adultlike than in the 1960s shows.

Skill et al. (1987) systematically analyzed, over a 6-year period (1979–1985), the range and extent of family life configurations in prime-time television across conventional and nonconventional types of portrayals. The findings revealed that prime-time network television tends to reinforce conservative to moderate models of family life. More than 65% of all families presented were found to be conventional in configuration (i.e., oriented toward the nuclear family unit). It was also found that the nonstandard interpretations of family were highly diverse in their configurations and, for the most part, comfortably framed in the less-threatening comedic form.

Moore (1992) adapted definitions developed by Skill et al. (1987) for the analysis of conventional and nonconventional family structures in "successful" family series from 1947 to 1990. Moore studied only those programs on the air for more than one season and excluded shows that featured families in historical settings. Moore employed two broad categories of conventional and nonconventional families with a limited number of subcategories. Of the 115 series analyzed, Moore found that 63% were "conventional" or traditional in configuration. Nonconventional single-parent families were more likely to be headed by fathers, and the most likely reason for "singleness" was the death of a spouse. From 1950 to 1990, Moore found that the portrayal of conventional families steadily decreased from a high of 79% during the 1950s to a low of 58% in the 1980s.

Skill and Robinson (1994) extended Moore's analysis by including all network fictional series featuring a family as a primary story vehicle from 1950 to 1989; by greatly expanding the classification system for types of families, which included 11 *configuration* types, seven *head of household* types, and eight *marital status* types; and by engaging in a decade by decade comparative analysis of families on television with U.S. Census Bureau (1990) statistics on families. This investigation produced some valuable trend analyses of both fictional and real-life families over 40 years. The authors found that married heads of households were the most common configuration across all decades, but the frequency dropped from a high of 69% in the 1950s to a low of 52% in the 1980s. They also found that, across all decades, families on television had very little in common with families in the U.S. Census data. The most glaring difference was the continuing dominance of the single-father household on television. Although the 1990 census revealed the highest level of father-headed households at 3.1%, television had no less than 17% of its families headed by single fathers in every decade. The 1960s had a whopping 28.4%, and the 1980s had 22%.

METHOD

All prime-time fictional series that employed a family configuration as the primary story vehicle airing on the commercial networks (ABC, CBS, Fox, NBC) were included in this study. Multiple sources were used to identify and verify all programs in this investigation. Four primary sources were employed in order to cover the time frame of September 1950 through August 1995. Brooks and Marsh's (1988, 1992) *The Complete Directory to Prime Time Network TV Shows*, Holland's (1991) *BIB Television Programming Source Books*, McNeil's (1984) *Total Television*, and Terrace's (1979) *Complete Encyclopedia of Television Programs* were used to build the database for all programs meeting the inclusion criteria. In addition, the "Fall Preview" issues of *TV Guide* were consulted to verify family demographics for many of the programs in this study. Various program and "fan" web sites also served as useful sources for verifying configuration data in this investigation.

Family Definitions and Category System

Programs selected for inclusion in the study had to meet the minimum criteria of employing, on a regular basis, an identifiable family configuration as the primary story vehicle. A family configuration was defined as a social unit characterized by one or more of the following elements; an adult head of household with dependent children, married couples with dependent children, married couples with adult children, married couples without children, or adults with dependent children sharing domiciles with others. The definition of family was not limited to a legal marital arrangement, nor was the definition of dependent children limited to natural or adopted statuses. Adults who performed parental duties as a head of household were coded as a portrayal of family regardless of legal status.

The decision to include only those programs that featured a family as the primary, recurring story vehicle was based on two factors. Greenberg and his colleagues (Greenberg, Buerkel-Rothfuss, Neuendorf, & Atkin, 1980), in their study of family role interactions, argued that it was important to focus on shows that feature a family as the central unit of interest (i.e., primary story vehicle), because "learning should be most facilitated by those shows which permit vicarious experience with known and familiar characters over time" (p. 162). Likewise, it was hypothesized that if television was to have any impact on public conceptions of how families organize themselves, it would arise from the regular, ongoing portrayal of families cast as protagonists. Those momentary glimpses of a family situation presented as a minor subplot in some larger, unrelated story would not have the same symbolic power and presence as would a family that served weekly as the primary story vehicle for a program.

Classification of families in this investigation involved coding each family on three dimensions; *family configuration, head of household*, and *head of household marital status*. The first dimension, *family configuration,* attempts to characterize the household situation of the primary family in the television program. This dimension consisted of 10 mutually exclusive configurations. A coding hierarchy was employed to insure each program was placed into only one category on each dimension. The hierarchy was as follows; multiple portrayal families, extended families, reconstituted families, nuclear families, single-parent families, empty nest families, childless families, and guardian (male, female, or couple) families.

Multiple portrayal families were defined as families in programs that featured more than one primary family as a story vehicle and where those family configurations consisted of more than one family type (i.e., nuclear, extended, and single-parent in same series). This category included programs such as *Dallas* and *Knots Landing* where numerous family configurations are central to the story. Extended families were defined as households that are populated by family members other than parents and minor children. This category captured the presence of grandparents and other relatives in the family environment. The fact that the family may be headed by single parent or relative was accounted for in the other dimensions. Reconstituted families were defined as families that result from the merging of members from previous marriages through a new marriage. The *Brady Bunch* stands as a prime example of a reconstituted family. Although reconstituted families are frequently a form of nuclear family, it was determined that the distinction should be maintained in coding because such a family does not reflect the traditional characteristics of the nuclear family. Nuclear families were defined as households comprised of both parents and dependent children living in the same home. Single-parent families were defined as households consisting of one parent only with dependent children. Empty nest families were defined as households comprised of married couples whose adult children are involved in the program but do no live in the same home. Childless families were defined as married couples living in the same home without children. Guardian families were distinguished as being headed by males, females, or couples who are responsible for one or more minor children and who are not the parent or parents of the children.

The second dimension, *head of household,* characterizes the relationship of the head of the household with the children (if any) in that household. This dimension consisted of seven categories; parents, father, mother, relative, married couple (if no children in home), multiple portrayals (more than one household with differing configurations), or other (head of household is not related to children).

The third dimension, *head of household marital status,* provides a description of the marital status of the head of household. This dimension consists of eight categories; married, divorced, separated, widower, widow, multiple portrayal (more than one household with differing marital statuses), unmarried, or unclear.

Each program was also coded for type of program (i.e., situation comedy or drama), for the year it first aired and the number of seasons that it aired. Seasons were calculated based on each program's broadcast history. A season begins in September of each year and runs through August of the following year. The actual number of episodes produced was determined for about 85% of the programs in the study. Each program was also coded for network, gender and number of children in the family, and ethnic/racial characteristics of the family.

Intercoder Reliability

Because this study represented a census of television programs featuring families from 1950 to 1995, no sampling procedures were utilized. However, a sample of 60 programs was drawn to test intercoder reliability on family configuration (.90), head of household (.98), marital status (.91), number of children (.91), gender of children (1.0), and family ethnic/racial characteristics (.96). These reliabilities were based on two independent coders using Holsti's (1969) coder agreement formula. Reliabilities were not calculated for network, show type, episodes produced, or year and seasons aired. However, this information was verified for accuracy in coding and checked against multiple published sources for correctness.

RESULTS

During the period September 1950 through August 1995, a total of 630 fictional television series featuring a family aired on four commercial television networks (ABC, CBS, Fox, NBC). Just over 72% of these series were situation comedies, and approximately 28% were dramatic programs. The total number of series featuring families has steadily increased with each decade. The 1950s had the fewest with a total of 85 series; the 1960s had 98; the 1970s had 139; the 1980s had 175; and the first 5 years of the 1990s had 133 series featuring a family as the primary story emphasis. At that rate, over 265 prime-time series featuring a family as the primary story emphasis will have been aired during the 1990s.

Although increase is due in part to the advent of the FOX network and consequently more opportunity for prime-time network programming, the vast majority of the family-centered series were aired on ABC, CBS, and NBC. Only nine of the prime-time series that featured a family prominently in the plot aired on the Fox network. Similarly only 14 such programs shown during the first 5 years of the 1990s were FOX programs. During the 1990s, 30% of these programs were aired on ABC, 31% were aired on CBS, and 27% were aired on NBC. Thus, only about 10% of the family-based series were aired on the FOX network and even after omitting those programs from analyses, an increase in the number of prime-time series prominently featuring families remained.

As the number of series featuring a family central to the plot increased over the decades on television, the dramatic series has become a more common story vehicle. Eighty-five percent of the families on television during the 1950s were in situation comedies, leaving just 15% in dramatic series. In contrast, during the 1960s, the percentage of series featuring a family declined to 77%, and in the 1980s, the number of situation comedies featuring the family increased to 65% of the series. A slight reversal in this trend began in the 1980s, in which 67% of the series featured families in a comedic fashion. During the first half of the 1990s, however, just over 76% of the series featuring the family were situation comedies. Whether this emphasis on the family in prime-time programs continues throughout the 1990s remains to be seen.

Family Characteristics: Children

The number and proportion of families with children has also increased over the last 45 years. During the 1950s, series featuring a childless family were a mainstay on television. In fact, childless families made up 25%

of the family series aired during that time. In the 1960s the number of childless families dropped slightly (24%), and this trend continued into the 1970s (23%) and 1980s (17%). Examination of the first 5 years of the 1990s indicates a dramatic decrease in childless families. Childless families plummeted to 2.3% of the families on series featuring families. This decrease in childless families is one of the most dramatic changes in family configuration over the past 45 years. Although many "real-life" married baby boomers may have been building their careers and delaying parenthood during the 1980s and 1990s, the data indicate that television was not providing many family models that reflected this trend.

Throughout the first 50 years of television, male children have outnumbered female children. The 1950s was a time of fewer children in families and a tendency for boys to outnumber girls when they were part of a series. Of the 120 children during the 1950s, 56% were male. The 1960s saw more children (150), but little change in gender distribution (55% male). The 1970s showed some shifting of emphasis with the total number of children increasing to 255 and males comprising a somewhat more equitable 52% of the siblings. The 1980s was the first decade of the child-oriented family with 316 children on series featuring families. In addition, the 316 children were evenly split between boys and girls. In the first 5 years of the 1990s, however, the percentage of male children reverted back to the proportions of the 1950s and 1960s. Just over 55.4% of the 276 children appearing on family-oriented series were male during the 1990s. If this trend continues, there will be more than 550 children on family focused prime-time series before the end of the 1990s and most of these children will be male.

The size of families on these series has steadily grown since the 1950s. In the 1950s, the average TV family contained 1.8 children. TV family size increased to 2.0 children during the 1960s and 2.4 during the 1970s. During the 1980s, family size dipped slightly to 2.2 children per family, and during the first 5 years of the 1990s, to 2.45 children per family. Whether the role prominence of children on these programs changed is not known and merits further investigation.

Family Characteristics: Ethnic/Racial

Families on television are not ethnically or racially diverse, but there have been significant changes in the racial composition of television over the years. During the 1950s and 1960s, 97% of the families were White (see Table 7.1). During the 1950s, there were two Hispanic families and one Native American family. The first televised African American family did not appear until the 1960s, when *Julia* (1968) aired featuring Diahann Carroll as a widowed African American woman working as a nurse and raising a son. The only other non-White portrayals during this decade was

TABLE 7.1
Families on Television: Ethnic/Racial Composition by Decade

Decade	White	African American	Hispanic	Native American	Asian	Other/ Mixed	N
1950s	97%	0%	2%	1%	0%	0%	85
1960s	97%	1%	0%	0%	0%	2%	98
1970s	84%	14%	1%	0%	1%	0%	139
1980s	87%	6%	2%	1%	0%	4%	175
1990–1995	80.5%	13.5%	0%	0%	0.8%	5.3%	133
Total	87.7%	7.6%	0.6%	0.4%	0.3%	2.5%	630

a drama about an Asian orphan adopted by a single White male (*Kentucky Jones*) and a comedy series featuring a prehistoric family entitled *It's About Time*. The era of the 1970s was the most racially diverse with African American families comprising nearly 14% of all family portrayals. This era also featured two Hispanic families and one Asian family. The decade of 1980s introduced a number of mixed White/African American and African American/Asian families. There were also three Hispanic families and one Native American family on the air during this time. Despite the popularity of *The Cosby Show*, the total number of African American families decreased by 50% during this decade. In the first 5 years of the 1990s, there was a resurgence of African American familes on television. In fact, nearly 14% of the families on series featuring the family were African American. The percentage of White familes was 80.5%, just under 1% were Asian, and the remaining 5.3% were programs with multiple family configurations of different racial backgrounds (e.g., *Married People*) or multiracial families (e.g., *True Colors*).

Family Characteristics: Head of Household

Parents and married couples have been the predominant household leaders for families on television across all decades, but their share of the "family market" diminished in the decade of the 1980s and continued to decline during the first 5 years of the 1990s. During the decade of the 1950s, parents and married couples headed a combined total of 68% of the families on television. Single-fathers and mothers headed a combined total of nearly 24% of the families. By the 1980s, parents and married couples headed a total of 50% of the families. Single fathers and mothers headed 34%. In the first 5 years of the 1990s, only 38.3% of the families were headed by parents or married couples, and 32.3% were headed by single fathers or single mothers. Just over 5% of the remaining single-family configurations were headed by relatives and 2.2% were headed by guardians unrelated to the children.

Since the 1950s, television families have been configured in a variety of different ways (see Table 7.2). Although the decades of the 1980s and 1990s showed an increased number of mothers as heads of single-parent families, fathers remained the most dominant image of single parenthood. During the 45-year span of this study, just under 17% (16.8%) of all families on television were headed by a single male parent. Female single parents headed just over 13% of all families. During the first 5 years of the 1990s, 18% of the families were headed by single fathers and 14.3% of the households were led by mothers. Whereas the images of fathers going it alone might be convenient dramatic device, the reality of this configuration is that mothers are heads of single households by nearly a 7:1 margin over fathers (U.S. Bureau of Census, 1995).

Family Characteristics: Head of Household Marital Status

The number of married people heading households has dropped over the past 45 years, from a high of 68.2% in the 1950s to a low of 39.8% in the 1990s (see Table 7.3). During this time, programs featuring a childless married couples became a rarity on television. Childless households headed by married couples dropped from a high of 24.7% during the 1950s to 2.3% during the first 5 years of the 1990s.

Households headed by widows and widowers became somewhat less common over the past 45 years. During previous eras, widowhood was the most frequent reason for single parenthood on television. In the 1950s, widows and widowers accounted for 15% of the families. In the 1960s, their numbers peaked at a combined total of 26% of all families. In the 1970s, 16% of the families were headed by widows or widowers. In the 1980s, just 13% of the households were headed by widowers and widows. In the first 5 years of the 1990s, widows and widowers decreased to 8.3% of family heads.

TABLE 7.2
Families on Television: Head of Household by Decade

Head of Household	1950s	1960s	1970s	1980s	1990–1995	Total
Parents	43.5%	37.8%	43.9%	39.4%	38.3%	40.5%
Married Couples w/o Children	24.7%	21.4%	18.7%	10.9%	1.5%	14.1%
Father	12.9%	21.4%	13.7%	17.7%	18.0%	16.8%
Mother	10.6%	10.2%	10.8%	16.6%	14.3%	13.0%
Relative	7.1%	6.1%	5.8%	4.0%	5.3%	5.4%
Multiple Portrayals	0.0%	3.1%	5.0%	8.6%	20.3%	8.3%
Other	1.2%	0.0%	2.2%	2.9%	2.3%	1.9%
n	85	98	139	175	133	100.0%

TABLE 7.3
Marital Status of Household Head by Decade

Marital Status	1950s	1960s	1970s	1980s	1990–1995	Total
Married	69.4%	59.2%	63.3%	52.0%	39.8%	55.4%
Widower	10.6%	16.3%	10.1%	8.6%	4.5%	9.4%
Unclear	10.6%	6.1%	6.5%	8.0%	9.8%	8.1%
Widow	4.7%	10.2%	6.5%	4.6%	3.8%	5.9%
Multiple Portrayal	0.0%	3.1%	5.8%	8.0%	20.3%	8.3%
Unmarried	4.7%	5.1%	5.0%	5.1%	5.3%	5.1%
Divorced	0.0%	0.0%	2.9%	10.9%	15.0%	6.8%
Separated	0.0%	0.0%	0.0%	2.9%	1.5%	1.1%
n	85	98	139	175	133	630

Across the first 45 years of television, widowers headed a dispropor-tionate share of the households. In the 1950s and the 1980s, widowers headed nearly twice as many households as widows and a third more in the 1960s and 1970s. During the first 5 years of the 1990s, however, there was an increase in the number of widows heading households. Widow-ers dropped to 4.5% whereas widows made up 3.8% of family household heads.

Although divorced or separated heads of households did not appear on television until the 1970s, by the 1990s, 16.5% of all families were headed by either a divorced or separated parent. The majority of these broken families were from divorces (15%) and not separations. During the 1980s, 14% of all TV families were headed by divorced or separated heads of household. This represents a dramatic change in familes that has remained relatively stable over a 15-year period. Divorce and sepa-ration were unheard of during the earlier years of television.

Family Characteristics: Household Configuration

The status of a family household obviously goes beyond the character-istics that describe the head of the household. Family configuration pro-vides an environmental demography of the home. As Table 7.4 indicates, there is no dominant configuration that characterizes the way families live on television. Even during the "conservative" era of the 1950s, only 38% of the families on television consisted of both parents living in the same home with their children. From the 1960s to the 1990s, the nuclear family remained between 24% and 26% of all families on television, thereby suggesting that this configuration has remained rather stable through-out the years.

One of the most dramatic changes in family portrayals on television has been the increase in multiple family configurations. Until the first

TABLE 7.4
Family Configuration of Household by Decade

Family Configuration	1950s	1960s	1970s	1980s	1990–1995	Total
Nuclear	37.6%	24.5%	25.9%	26.3%	25.6%	27.5%
Extended	17.6%	29.6%	26.6%	29.1%	22.6%	25.6%
Single Parent	14.1%	16.3%	18.0%	21.7%	21.1%	18.7%
Childless	23.5%	20.4%	17.3%	6.9%	2.3%	12.5%
Reconstituted	1.2%	3.1%	2.9%	6.3%	6.0%	4.3%
Guardian (male)	3.5%	3.1%	4.3%	3.4%	2.3%	3.3%
Guardian (female)	2.4%	0.0%	2.2%	1.7%	0.8%	1.4%
Multiple Portrayals	0.0%	1.0%	0.7%	2.3%	18.0%	4.9%
Empty Nest	0.0%	1.0%	0.7%	1.7%	0.0%	0.08%
Guardian (couple)	0.0%	1.0%	1.4%	0.6%	1.5%	1.0%
n	85	98	139	175	133	630

5 years of the 1990s, there were virtually no family series prominently featuring more than one family. In the 1990s, just over 18% of all family-focused series contained multiple family configurations. This means that during the first 5 years of the 1990s, 87.3% of the series featuring familes were configured in one of four ways; nuclear, extended, single parent, or multiple family portrayals. In contrast, during the 1950s, the four domi-nant family configurations were nuclear, childless, extended, and single parent—accounting for 92.8% of the families. Similarly, the four most com-mon configurations of the 1960s were extended, nuclear, childless, and single parent—accounting for 90.8% of the families. During the 1970s, the four most dominant family configurations remained the same—accounting for 87.8% of the families. During the 1980s, a greater number of family con-figurations were used as story vehicles. The three dominant family con-figurations were nuclear, extended, and single parent and accounted for 77.1% of the families. Keep in mind that during this time, only 2.3% of the series contained multiple family configurations.

In addition to the dramatic decrease in childless couples and the huge increase in multiple family configurations, another significant change in the television family was the increase in extended families. Portrayals of extended families includes all households that have family members beyond parents and minor children and during the 1960s and through-out the 1980s, the extended family configuration was more popular in fic-tional television than was the nuclear family.

In the 1950s, 18% of the familes had extended family members living in the same home. In the 1960s, this category grew to 30% of the family series, dropping to 27% in the 1970s, and then rising to 29% in the 1980s. During the first 5 years of the 1990s, however, the number of extended families decreased to 22.6%. Nonetheless, households shared by extended families remain strong story vehicles for telling stories about families. In many cases the extended family has been configured so as to replace a missing parent. Grandparents, or other relatives assume surrogate mother or father roles, depending on which parent is not present in the household.

In some cases, the extended family configuration has been transformed into multiple family configurations. Quite uncommon until the 1990s, the multiple family configuration has become a mainstay for writers creating scripts that focus on families. By changing extended families into multiple family configurations, the opportunity for idiosyncratic characters and differences and conflict is further enhanced. For example, with multiple family configurations, characters can differ in socioeconomic status, race, and a whole host of other characteristics that may or may not be plausible in an extended family configuration. The increase in prime-time soap operas that typically focus on families has also resulted in an increase in the use of the multiple family configurations. Childless parents and empty nest families are also common elements in the multiple family configuration series.

Although the numbers are not as dramatic, reconstituted families—those situations where two families are integrated into a single family—have also increased since the 1950s. During the first decade of television, reconstituted families represented 1.2% of all families. By the 1980s and 1990s, reconstituted families represented 6% of all the families on television.

The single-parent family represents another big change in family configurations on television. Although television has always employed the single parent as a major story vehicle, this number has grown steadily over the years. In the 1950s, single-parent families comprised 14% of the television families. By the 1980s, this number had grown to 22% of all families. During the first 5 years of the 1990s, the percentage remained over 20%. Increasingly, these single-parent families are the result of divorce that allows the use of the ex-spouse as a vehicle for conflict. During previous decades, widowhood was nearly the sole cause for single-parent familes on television.

Families on Television and Families Across America: A Comparison

Although few mass communication researchers embrace the notion that broad statistical categories comparing the television world to the real world are of any great value, policymakers and the general public frequently cite television images as indicators of change or influence. The agenda-setting consequences of these public debates cannot be easily overlooked. Statistics reflecting negative changes in family life such as double-digit divorce rates and the explosive increase of unwed mothers raising their children alone are just two of the many references regarding families that are tied to mediated imagery. In this section, the data on television families are presented in conjunction with Census Bureau data over the past 45 years. Comparisons are made between the head of household for families with children on television and the head of household for families with children as reported in the census across each decade. Although the link may not be causal, audience members can use television configurations of families as normative and comparative reference criteria.

As Table 7.5 indicates, families with children and headed by both parents have been underrepresented on television in every decade. The 1960 census indicated that nearly 88% of all families with children were headed by both parents. From 1950 through 1959, only 58% of the fictional families on television with children had both parents in the household. Whereas the census for the next 35 years showed a steady drop in the two-parent households with children (1970, 85%; 1980, 77%; 1990, 73%; 1995, 68%), television during this period was rather inconsistent. During the decade of the 1960s, 50% of television's families with children were headed by two parents—a 7-point drop. However, during the 1970s, the two-parent family with children returned to nearly the same level as the 1950s. The decade of the 1980s saw the two-parent family with children on television drop below the 50% level for the first time. This 9-point drop from the 1950s level may seem quite large, but it is no match for the 15-point drop of actual two-parent families with children that occurred during the same time period. In the first 5 years of the 1990s, TV families with children and headed by both parents remained at 49%—about what it had been during the 1980s.

Although two-parent families with children on television may have been below the actual percentages in the United States, there has been no shortage of single fathers on television. Single dads have been a dominant image on television since the very beginning and continue to remain so. Whereas the 1960 census reported that single fathers comprised just 1% of the U.S. households, 17% of TV families in 1950s and 28% in the 1960s had a father as the single head of household. The 1980 census revealed that single dads were heading 2% of America's families. From 1970 to 1979, 18% of television's families were directed by single fathers. Likewise, the 1990 census showed that 3% of families were headed by fathers. During the decade of the 1980s, television employed single dads in 22% of the family portrayals. In the first 5 years of the 1990s, 23.1% of the TV families were headed by single fathers, whereas the 1995 census indicated that only 3.5% of all households were headed by a single father.

Although single mothers have not been presented with the same level of exaggeration as fathers, during the decades of the 1950s and 1960s, single moms were seen in slightly greater numbers than their real world counterparts—14% versus 8% in the 1950s and 13% versus 11% in 60s.

TABLE 7.5

Head of Household for Families With Children: TV Versus U.S. Census by Decade

Head of House	TV 1950s	1960 Census	TV 1960s	1970 Census	TV 1970s	1980 Census	TV 1980s	1990 Census	TV 1990–1995	1995 Census
Parents	57.8%	87.7%	50.0%	85.2%	57.5%	76.6%	48.9%	72.6%	49%	68.71%
Father Only	17.2%	1.1%	28.4%	1.1%	17.9%	1.7%	22.0%	3.1%	23.1%	3.5%
Mother Only	14.1%	8.0%	13.5%	10.8%	14.2%	18.0%	20.6%	21.6%	18.3%	23.45%
Other Relatives	9.4%	2.5%	8.1%	2.2%	7.5%	3.1%	5.0%	2.2%	6.7%	3.35%
Nonrelatives	1.6%	0.7%	0.0%	0.7%	2.8%	0.6%	3.5%	0.5%	2.9%	0.097%
n	64	63.5[a]	74	68.9[a]	106	63.2[a]	141	63.9[a]	104	70.2[a]

[a] These numbers represent millions of households.

However, by the 1970s, real-life families headed by single moms surpassed the growing number of television shows featuring the same configuration. The 1970s had 14% of the TV families run by single mothers whereas the 1980 census reported 18%. The 1990 census was just one percentage point greater than the percentage of single mothers on television during the decade of the 1980s—21% on television versus 22% in the census. In the first 5 years of the 1990s, TV households headed by mothers dropped to 18.3% whereas the census indicated that 23% of all familes actually were headed by single moms. The increase of multiple family configurations may acount for some of this decrease in single mothers raising families on television. What is clear, however, is that in terms of heads of households, television clearly does not mirror the real world.

When the data regarding marital status of single parents are analyzed, there are few similarities between the real and fictional worlds. Across all decades on television, widows and widowers are the most frequent reason for single parenthood. When compared to the census data, the contrast is even greater. During the decade of the 1950s, 60% of the time single parenthood was due to the death of spouse. The census for 1960 indicated that such was the case for 26% of the single families in America—the highest of any decade in this study. Television programs during the 1960s employed the widow or widower in an incredible 84% of the single families. The census for 1970 indicated 20%, a 6 % decline in widowhood since the 1960 census. As television moved through the 1970s, widows and widowers accounted for 70% of the single families. The 1980 census reported 12%. Finally, in the decade of the 1980s, television's single families were headed by a modest 37% widows and widowers. However, in the 1990 census, the percentage of widows and widowers dwindled to just 7%. TV widows made a resurgence in the first 5 years of the 1990s—just over 13% of all households were headed by widows and widowers. It is interesting to note that only 4.3% of U. S. homes were headed by widows or widowers during that same time. Given the trends over the past 40 years, the data suggest that fictional television clearly prefers the death of a spouse as the predominant rationale for single parenthood. Even for the decade of the 1980s, with greater acceptance of divorce and single motherhood, the majority of single families on television were for reasons other than divorce, separation, or single motherhood. By contrast, the 1990 census reported that just 10% of the single-parent families were due to reasons other than divorce, separation, or single motherhood (see Table 7.6). According to the census, in the first 5 years of the 1990s, just over 8.2% of the single-parent families were due to reasons other than divorce, separation, or single motherhood. This is quite different than television where over 45% of all single-parent families are the result of things other than divorce, separation, or single motherhood.

TABLE 7.6

Marital Status of Single-Parent Households: TV Versus U.S. Census by Decade

Marital Status	TV 1950s	1960 Census	TV 1960s	1970 Census	TV 1970s	1980 Census	TV 1980s	1990 Census	TV 1990–1995	1995 Census
Widow/Widower	60%	26.4%	83.9%	20.1%	69.7%	11.8%	36.7%	7.1%	20.7%	4.38%
Other/Unclear	35%	18.7%	16.1%	12.6%	15.2%	4.6%	18.3%	3.4%	24.5%	3.85%
Unmarried	5%	4.2%	0%	6.8%	3%	14.6%	5%	30.6%	13.2%	34.63%
Divorced	0%	23.2%	0%	30.2%	12.1%	42.4%	31.7%	38.6%	37.7%	38.02%
Separated	0%	27.5%	0%	30.3%	0%	26.6%	8.3%	20.3%	3.8%	19.12%
n	20	5.8[a]	31	8.1[a]	33	12.4[a]	60	15.8[a]	53	18.9[a]

[a] These numbers represent millions of households.

Divorce and separation have been the predominant reasons for single-parent families for the last 40 years. The 1960 census reported that over 50% of the single-parent families were due to divorce or separation. The 1970 census indicated that over 60% of the single families were for the same reasons. Curiously, fictional television had no portrayals of families headed by a divorced or separated parent until December 1975, when CBS aired *One Day at a Time*. This series, which focused on the struggles of a single mother raising two daughters, starred Bonnie Franklin and lasted nearly 9 years on the prime-time schedule. The following August, ABC introduced *What's Happening*, which featured Mable King as a divorced African American woman raising two children in a working-class neighborhood.

With the introduction of these shows and a few others in the 1970s, divorced parents comprised 12% of the single heads of households on television. There were no incidents of separation between television spouses during this time. In reality, the 1980 census reported that 42% of the single households were headed by a divorced parent and 27% were headed by separated parents. As television moved into the decade of the 1980s, divorce (32%) and separation (8%) became a much more common reason for single parenthood—but it continued to lag behind the U.S. Census. The 1990 census actually reported a drop in the proportion of single households due to divorce (39%) and separation (20%). However, the total number of single-parent households did increase by over 3 million with single mothers doubling their proportional presence from 15% in 1980 to nearly 31% in 1990. During this same time frame, television increased its presentation of unmarried and single parenthood by just 2%—from 3% to 5% of the single-parent television families. During the first 5 years of the 1990s, the percentage of unmarried single-parent households doubled and the number of divorced single-parent households increased from 31.7% to 37.7%. TV series focusing on unmarried and divorced single-parent households—unheard of in the 1960s and uncommon in the 1970s—have become more commonplace in the 1990s. Although the actual divorce rate has declined slightly, the percentage of unmarried single-parent households still increased 4%. Clearly, television has become more comfortable with unmarried and divorced single parents as well as with multiple family configurations as frequent fictional story vehicles.

DISCUSSION

The findings of this investigation paint an interesting picture of what families look like on TV series employing one or more families as a central component of the story line. The predominant racial configuration of these families is White. Although the families on television are far from being racially or ethnically diverse, there have been significant changes over the past 45 years.

White families still outnumber other racial groups, although the percentage of White families has dropped from 97% to 90.5% during the first 45 years of television. Since first appearing in 1968, the number of African American families has increased to 14% in the 1990s. During that same time, however, families of other races have been nearly nonexistent. For many years, Asian or American Indian families were less likely to be found in a series featuring a family than was a family with an alien boarder from the planet Melmac.

It is interesting to note that African American families are configured somewhat differently than White families. African American families are more likely to be extended than nuclear and are more likely to be nuclear than a single-parent family. In White families, single-parent families, extended families, and nuclear families occur at a relatively equal rate.

In addition to changes in racial configuration, the size of families on television have also increased over the past 45 years. The number of children in prime-time families has increased from just under 2 children per show in the 1950s to nearly 2.5 children per program in the 1990s. This increase in average family size is not attributable to the dramatic decrease in the number of childless familes or to the increase in extended and reconstituted families on television. During the 1950s, the average nuclear family consisted of 1.84 children. By the 1980s and 1990s, the average number of children in nuclear families was about 2.5.

Examination of the gender of the children in these families over the first 45 years of television indicates that most of the kids on TV families were male. In fact, 53% of the children were male over this time frame. The disparity in gender had decreased from the 1950s until male and female children were equal in number during the 1980s. In the first 5 years of the 1990s, however, the trend reversed and once again, male children outnumber female children by about 5%.

Throughout the history of television, most of the families have been headed by married couples and the most common family configuration is nuclear. Whereas the percentage of nuclear families was higher during the 1950s, the percentage of nuclear families has been fairly stable at about 25% for the past 35 years. Most families on television are headed by both parents, although the percentage of such families has decreased from 43% to 38% over that time period.

The divorce rate of television families has jumped from 2.9% during the 1970s to 15% in the 1990s. If television is serving a normative reference function for audience members, it is clear that divorce is more common today than it was even 20 years ago. Similarly the percentage of married heads of households has dropped from 69% in the 1950s to 38.3% in the

1990s. Again, portrayals of single parenthood has increased significantly over a relatively short period of time. Heads of household are still more likely to be married than any other marital status configuration, but likelihood of divorced parents has increased and the likelihood of households being headed by adults who have lost a spouse has decreased considerably. Incidence of unmarried family heads, however, has remained stable across all years at a rate of about 5%. This means that unmarried family heads are still quite uncommon on television programs featuring families.

Single parents have been and remain significant factors in leading families on television, accounting for 24% in the 1950s, 32% in the 1960s, 24% in the 1970s, 34% in the 1980s, and 31% in the 1990s. Widowers and widows were most prominent in the 1960s heading up nearly 27% of the families. In the 1990s, however, that frequency dropped by two thirds to 8.4%. In single-parent families, nearly 38% of all household heads were divorced. This is a dramatic change in that single-parent families were once caused by forces other than choice. A spouse carrying on after the death of a spouse is a different story than a spouse electing to leave their family for reasons of personal choice and communicates a different message to the audience about family and marriage.

On television, fathers have always been more likely than mothers to be heading up a single-parent household. Although the number of single fathers has decreased and the number of single mothers has increased over the years, in the 1990s, 18% of the single-parent families were headed up by fathers and 14.4% by mothers. This is most discrepant when compared with the census figures of the 1990s.

Perhaps the biggest change in family configurations has been the advent of programs featuring multiple families. Nearly unheard of during the previous 40 years on television, during the first 5 years of the 1990s, 18% of all series employed more than one family as central to the story line. In several cases, this has been the result of an increase in prime-time soap operas such as *Dallas* or *Falcon Crest*. In other cases, however, the multiple family configuration has simply become another way families are organized on television.

Often such portrayals employ empty nest or childless families in conjunction with single-parent or nuclear families. In this way, writers have the opportunity to use a large number of diverse characters with disparate backgrounds. In many cases, economics necessitate families moving in together to make ends meet. Whether or not this trend will continue remains to be seen, but the multiple family configuration represents a significant departure from previous prime time-family configurations.

Exactly what these changes mean is impossible to discern from a descriptive study about the composition of television. However, it is clear that the changes in the portrayals of families provide audience members with a picture of families being more complex if nothing else. The increase in the number of different family configurations and marital configurations in families suggests that family members choose the composition of their families and can choose to change the configuration of their families in many cases.

Gerbner and his colleagues (1980) suggested that the images of family on television may be important touchstones by which real families might judge themselves. Given the diversity of the televised family models identified in this investigation and the complexity of their organization, it would not be difficult for real-life families to find numerous models of similar families in both better and worse shape than their own. There are many different family models depicted in prime time.

If televised portrayals of family are looked upon as social learning opportunities, information regarding the quality and context of family interaction are of central concern and importance. A number of investigations of this type are discussed at the beginning of this article. The missing component in many of these studies is the historical trend data relating to family images for the past 40 years of television. This current investigation should serve as a useful anchor for future studies of families on television and the audience responses to those images. Again, from this investigation, it is clear that there are many different models of family available.

Although real families may not completely mirror TV families, it is clear that TV portrayals of the family are becoming more complex and diverse. Although social critics have often voiced concern about the way television portrays the family, previous research into televised family portrayals and configurations has indicated that mediated images of family life tend to be conventional (Gerbner, et al., 1980; Skill & Robinson, 1994). Since the advent of the 1990s, however, television portrayals of the family have become less conventional. Whether that trend continues is a question that needs to be answered in the next few years.

Families can be configured in lots of different ways. As television programs become more sophisticated, writers will need additional complexity in their characters and story vehicles. To the extent that families are used as story vehicles, portrayals of the family can be expected to become more diverse. By using multiple family configurations, writers will be able to incorporate the traditional nuclear family as well as less conventional family configurations in the same programs.

The question is does TV endorse particular lifestyles or family configurations over others? We can't answer that question with the data presented, but it appears that the variety in family configurations provides viewers with different models of families. Unfortunately, such changes may be seen by some as depicting the traditional family as less important or less successful. With the increase in divorce and multiple family configurations and fewer childless families, widows and widowers, family configuration may be viewed as less of an act of God and more an act of choice made by heads of households.

For the 45-year span of this study, the overall structure and configuration of families on television indicates that few drastic or fundamental changes have occurred. Families on television have grown slightly larger over the years. In recent years, they were only somewhat more likely to be headed by a single parent. Children on television were more likely to grow up in a household that was shared with members of their extended family and, regardless of decade, children were far more likely to grow up in a home that was headed by a widow or widower than by a divorced or separated parent.

In the final analysis, this study of family portrayals suggests that television has been and remains clearly out of sync with the structural characteristics of real-world families. The data do not completely support the contention by critics that television promotes or overemphasizes any particular family configuration, but it is clear that the configurations of families are changing. If families in the real world were to conclude anything about families on television, it would have to be that different configurations of families are common and families are most desirable. In addition, audience members would also see that there is equifinality in the family structure and that there can be satisfaction with the family regardless of the configuration.

REFERENCES

Akins, G. (1986). An analysis of family interaction styles as portrayed on television (Doctoral dissertation, University of Georgia, 1986). *Dissertation Abstracts International, 47,* 2013A.

Brooks, T., & Marsh, E. (1988). *The complete directory to prime time network TV shows: 1946–present.* New York: Ballantine Books.

Brooks, T., & Marsh, E. (1992). *The complete directory to prime time network TV shows: 1946–present.* New York: Ballantine Books.

Comstock, J., & Strzyzewski, K. (1990). Interpersonal interaction on television: Family conflict and jealousy on prime time. *Journal of Broadcasting & Electronic Media, 34,* 263–282.

Coontz, S. (1992). *The way we never were: American families and the nostalgia trap.* New York: Basic Books.

Gerbner, G., Gross, L., Morgan, M., & Signorielli, N. (1980). *Media and the family: Images and impact.* Washington, DC: White House Conference on the Family, National Research Forum on Family Issues. (ERIC Document Reproduction Service No. ED 198919)

Greenberg, B., Buerkel-Rothfuss, N., Neuendorf, K., & Atkin, C. (1980). Three seasons of television family role interactions. In B. S. Greenberg (Ed.), *Life on television* (pp. 161–172). Norwood, NJ: Ablex.

Holland, H. (Ed.). (1991). *BIB Television programming source books: Vol. 4. Series.* Philadelphia: North American Publishing Co.

Holsti, O. L. (1969). *Content analyses for the social sciences and humanities.* Reading, MA: Addison-Wesley.

McNeil, A. (1984). *Total television.* New York: Penguin Books.

Moore, M. L. (1992). The family as portrayed on prime-time television, 1947–1990: Structure and characteristics. *Sex Roles, 26,* 41–61.

Signorielli, N. (1982). Marital status in television drama: A case of reduced options. *Journal of Broadcasting, 26,* 585–597.

Skill, T. (1994). Family images and family actions as presented in the media: Where we've been and what we've found. In D. Zillmann, J. Bryant, & A. Huston (Eds.), *Media, children, and the family: Social scientific, psychodynamic and clinical perspectives* (pp. 37–50). Hillsdale, NJ: Lawrence Erlbaum Associates.

Skill, T., & Robinson, J. (1994). Four decades of families on television: A demographic profile, 1950–1989. *Journal of Broadcasting & Electronic Media, 38,* 449–464.

Skill, T., Robinson, J., & Wallace, S. (1987). Family life on prime-time television: Structure, type and frequency. *Journalism Quarterly, 64,* 360–367, 398.

Skill, T., & Wallace, S. (1990). Family interactions on primetime television: A descriptive analysis of assertive power interactions. *Journal of Broadcasting & Electronic Media, 34,* 243–262.

Skill, T., Wallace, S. & Cassata, M. (1990). Families on prime-time television. Patterns of conflict escalation and resolution across intact, non-intact, and mixed family settings. In J. Bryant (Ed.), *Television and the American family* (pp. 129–163). Hillsdale, NJ: Lawrence Erlbaum Associates.

Sweeper, G. (1984). The image of the Black family and the White family in American prime-time television programming 1970 to 1980. (Doctoral dissertation, New York University, 1983). *Dissertation Abstracts International, 44,* 1964A.

Terrace, V. (1979). *Complete encyclopedia of television programs: 1947–1979.* Cranbury, NJ: A.S. Barnes and Co., Inc.

Thomas, S., & Callahan, B. P. (1982). Allocating happiness: TV families and social class. *Journal of Communication, 33,* 184–190.

U.S. Bureau of the Census. (1990). Marital status and living arrangement: March 1990. *Current Population Reports* (Series P-20, No. 450). Washington, DC: Government Printing Office.

U.S. Bureau of the Census. (1995). Marital status and living arrangement: March 1995. *Current Population Reports* (Series P-20, No. 491). Washington, DC: Government Printing Office.

Sibling Interaction in Situation Comedies Over the Years

Mary Strom Larson
Northern Illinois University

Concern about television's impact on values and behavior continues in both scholarly publications and the popular press. In scholarly publications, television's impact on the socialization of children has been described as much a potential source of influence as the home environment, the parents' behavioral style, and their socioeconomic milieu (Singer, Singer, & Rapaczynski, 1984).

In the popular press, a series in *TV Guide* cited a report from the National Institute of Mental Health stating that adults and children alike use TV to learn how to handle their own family roles (Kalter, 1988). Gary Goldberg, executive producer of *Family Ties*, stated that in terms of family values, television tells viewers, "Families are good, they are strong, they may make you crazy, but when push comes to shove, families are the best things we've got" (as cited in Kalter, 1988, p. 8). This chapter is concerned with what actually does occur in families on television sitcoms and asks about the nature of the sibling relationships portrayed.

The sibling relationship is of particular interest for several reasons. Irish (1964) described the sibling bond as the fundamental one of kinship. It is unique in that it is likely to be the longest lived relationship, predating one's relationship with a mate and outlasting one's relationship with parents. It is especially important because it is usually one's first relationship with a peer, and serves to socialize children in the ways of interpersonal relationships. Schvaneveldt and Ihinger (1979) also observed that sibling relationships have a profound effect on the development of interpersonal relationship skills. Thus, what television teaches one about how to be a sibling has the potential to influence one's interpersonal relationships both within and outside the family.

Descriptions of birth sibling relationships provide a useful basis for assessing television sibling interactions, although much of the research is limited to siblings of preschool age (e.g., Abramovitch, Corter, Pepler & Stanhope, 1986) or concerns families with such problems as a seriously ill or handicapped sibling (e.g., Grossman, 1972). Other sibling topics include the effects of birth order on personality (e.g., Schvaneveldt & Ihinger, 1979) and/or sibling rivalry (e.g., Merrell, 1995).

Among the existing research salient to this chapter is that of Bank and Kahn (1975). Although this work is relatively old, it continues to be cited by current writers as an important source of information about "normal" sibling relationships (e.g., Merrell, 1995). Bank and Kahn noted the importance of loyalty as the keystone of the sibling relationship and described four functions that siblings perform for each other. First, *identification* and *differentiation* are processes by which siblings see themselves in each other and distance themselves from each other. Identification occurs as one vicariously experiences life through a sibling. Differentiation serves to create self-identity by defining ways one is not like one's sibling. Second, in *mutual regulation,* siblings provide opportunities for trial runs for new roles and act as sounding boards for each other. The sibling relationship may provide a safe place for such experimentation. It may also offer critical feedback about ideas or behaviors. A third function is that of providing *direct services* such as teaching skills, loaning money, or introducing one to a new peer group. And last, *dealing with parents* includes forming coalitions in opposition to parents and threatening to tattle or reveal secrets to parents as leverage against a sibling.

The scope of this chapter is to describe the nature of sibling relationships in television families from the 1950s, beginning with *Ozzie and Harriet,* to the 1990s, ending with *The Simpsons.* All of these families feature more than one child. Larson conducted research on the 1950s families (Larson, 1991), the 1980s families (Larson, 1989), and on *The Simpsons* (Larson, 1993). The research on 1970s families and 1990s families was limited to those programs available in syndication. This chapter focuses on the proportions of positive/affiliative and negative/conflictive communication behavior, and where available, the functions siblings perform for each other.

SIBLING INTERACTION IN 1950s SITCOMS

From the 1950s, Larson (1991) studied nine episodes each of *Ozzie and Harriet* (1952–1965), *Father Knows Best* (1954–1960), and *Leave It to Beaver* (1957–1963), all of which featured an intact nuclear family with stay-at-home moms and two or three children. Sibling interactions was the unit of analysis.

The sample generated 803 sibling interactions. Larson found that significantly more communication behaviors were positive (74%) than were negative (26%) [X^2 (1, $N = 1,354$) $= 35.74$, $p < .01$]. In terms of the functions performed, the coder observed very few identification behaviors ($n = 21$, 2.6%); all were positive, and all were on *Leave It to Beaver*. A typical example would be a plot in which Beaver, trying to learn how to be a teenager, paid particular attention to the manner in which Wally grappled with the challenge of heading up the blind date committee (Larson, 1991).

Mutual regulation behaviors made up 29% of the communication behaviors ($n = 234$). Of those behaviors, 78% of them ($n = 183$) were negative. On *Father Knows Best,* for example, when Bud teased Betty about her upcoming blind date, her regulatory feedback was a threat, "Don't you dare open your big mouth" (Larson, 1991)!

Sixty-six percent of the communication behaviors ($n = 533$) were direct services, and 97% of those ($n = 517$) were positive. For example, when Wally drilled Beaver on his spelling words before a test, he did it in a positive, helpful way (Larson, 1991).

Only 2% of the communication consisted of dealing with parents ($n = 15$). Of that amount, 60% ($n = 9$) was positive communication. For example, Wally and Beaver broke a garage window while playing ball and worked together to get it repaired before their father came home (Larson, 1991). Negative communication was frequently threatening to tattle on a brother and get him in trouble with parents.

Thus, from the portrayal of siblings in these programs, we see primarily positive role models (see Table 8.1). However, although Bank and Kahn (1975) did not indicate what proportion of sibling interaction nor-

TABLE 8.1
Affiliative/Positive and Conflictive/Negative Communication

Years	Affil./Pos.	Conflict./Neg.
1950s	74%	26%
1960s/1970s	62%	38%
1980s	56%	44%
1990s	61%	39%

matively fell into each of the four functions, the distribution in these three programs seems atypical of real life. Only a total of 5% of the interactions concerned identification or dealing with parents, which seem like very important functions for real-life siblings. Further, 78% of the mutual regulation interactions were negative, hardly the safe place for trying out new roles as Bank and Kahn described (Larson, 1991).

SIBLING INTERACTIONS IN 1960s SITCOMS

All three of the 1950s sitcoms discussed earlier continued into the 1960s. Other popular family sitcoms with children were *My Three Sons* (1960–1972), *The Donna Reed Show* (1958–1966), *Here's Lucy* (1968–1974), and *The Brady Bunch* (1969–1974). But the changes in society in the last half of the 1960s brought changes in the family sitcom. Images of fragmentation of family life prevailed (Jones, 1992). Indeed, 1966 saw the demise of *The Donna Reed Show* and *Ozzie and Harriet. Father Knows* Best had left the air in 1960, and *Leave It to Beaver* was gone in 1963. *My Three Sons, Here's Lucy*, and *The Brady Bunch* all featured widowed parents and their families. Little, if any, research attention was given to these programs while they were on the air. Presently, only *The Brady Bunch* is in syndication. Thus, for this chapter on siblings, a content analysis of *The Brady Bunch* was conducted.

The Brady Bunch (1969–1974) featured a widowed mother and her three daughters who married a widowed father who had three sons. Nine episodes of the program were recorded and transcribed.

As with the earlier assessments, the unit of analysis was communication behavior between siblings. A communication behavior was defined as a verbal or nonverbal message directed toward a sibling, whether or not the receiving sibling was definitely aware of the message. A dirty look directed to a sibling, but not necessarily noticed by the intended sibling, was counted as a communication behavior. One behavior ended and another began when a change occurred in the sender, receiver, or type of message (e.g., affiliative or conflictive). Thus, it was possible (although rare) for two behaviors to occur in one uninterrupted statement.

An attempt was made to code for all four sibling functions, but this program appeared to feature only direct services and mutual regulation, so this coding scheme was abandoned for the following one used by Larson (1993), which assessed sibling interactions according to whether they were *affiliative* or *conflictive*. For affiliative, sibling interactions were assessed according to four categories: (a) Informing—seeking information giving information or opinion, clarifying facts; (b) Supporting—seeking support, encouragement or comfort, lamenting, giving support, indulging, assisting, accepting support, showing gratitude; (c) Directing—giving instructions, directing plans, accepting direction, cooperating, following orders; (d) Contributing—miscellaneous communication behaviors such as greetings, other phatic communication. For conflictive, sibling interactions were assigned to one of two categories; (a) Opposing—raising objections, threatening, refusing to cooperate or obey; (b) Attacking—criticizing, belittling, provoking, malicious teasing.

The principal investigator trained a graduate research assistant with the instrument for approximately 3 hours. Intercoder reliability of 89.5% was achieved using Holsti's formula (Wimmer & Dominick, 1997).

A total of 464 communication behaviors were coded between the siblings and step-siblings in the nine episodes of *The Brady Bunch*. There were significantly more affiliative behaviors ($n = 290$, 62%) compared to conflictive behaviors $n = 174$, 38%) [(X^2 $(1, N = 464)= 27.0, p < .001$].

Most of the affiliative communication was informing (see Table 8.2). For example, in one episode, Marcia lost her diary and the boys bought her a replacement. In an informing interchange, Greg asked, "What are you doing?" Peter replied, "Wrapping up a new diary for Marcia." The category of supporting often included seeking support, such as the youngest girl, Cindy, lamenting "Gee, I never had an innermost thought in my life." An example of offering support was Greg telling the youngest siblings, "You did a great job of acting scared last night!" in a scheme to prevent the sale of their house by pretending it was haunted.

The conflictive communication was predominantly opposing. For example, again in the diary episode, Marcia threatened Cindy with, "Cindy Brady, I'll never talk to you again as long as I live!"

Attacking communication often took the form of malicious teasing. For example, Greg sarcastically described to the boys (in Marcia's presence) why people write in a diaries: "So they can sit down and write stuff like,

TABLE 8.2
Affiliative and Conflictive Communication

Communication	Brady Bunch	Gimme a Break	Married With Children	Roseanne	The Simpsons
Affiliative					
Inform	49%	48%	32%	38%	27%
Support	7%	5%	13%	14%	23%
Direct	4%	2%	15%	0.6%	13%
Contribute	2%	3%	0.7%	—	8%
Conflict					
Oppose	25%	19%	14%	23%	21%
Attack	13%	23%	25%	25%	8%
Total *N*	464	120	154	159	207

'Dear Diary, at last I met him—my dream man—it was in the delicatessen and our fingers tingled as we both reached for the potato salad'" (he laughs).

Whereas this program featured more affiliative than conflictive communication, compared to the 1950 sitcoms, there were nearly 1½ times as much conflictive communications than in the 1950s programs (see Table 8.1). Furthermore, there was a very small proportion of supportive communication, which one can infer includes much of what Bank and Kahn (1975) called loyalty. Thus, *The Brady Bunch*, still widely viewed on Nickelodeon, offers primarily affiliative examples for modeling, but includes a rather large proportion of conflictive behaviors.

SIBLING INTERACTIONS IN THE 1970s SITCOMS

According to Jones (1992), the sitcom in general was fading in the 1970s. Situation comedies were being replaced with comedy-variety programs and crime and doctor shows. *The Brady Bunch* remained until 1974, and because neither *The Partridge Family* nor *Good Times* was available, it must remain the example, with just some general statements about siblings in these other two programs.

The fragmented family continued with *The Partridge Family* (1970–1974) that featured a widowed mother and her five children. They organized a rock group and toured the country in an old painted school bus, a premise that may be rather unrealistic as a model for family life or for peer interpersonal relationships.

Good Times (1974–1979) featured an intact family, but Mitz (1983) described the unlikely premise of a family living in the Chicago housing projects "struggling, struggling, struggling, but because there was so much love between them, these were good times" (p. 317). Mitz described the kids as good kids who loved and respected their parents and good-naturedly teased each other.

Greenberg, Buerkel-Rothfuss, Neuendorf, and Atkin (1980) studied communication in television families during the 1975 through 1978 seasons. But because they did not differentiate between sitcoms and dramas, or between families with adult siblings and those with dependent siblings, their work is not really pertinent to this chapter. Similarly, a study by Greenberg and Neuendorf (1980) that analyzed communication in African American television families, did not limit their analysis to families with dependent children in sitcoms, and thus is not included here. *All in the Family* (featuring adult siblings), *Little House on the Prairie*, and *The Waltons* (hour-long dramas) were also popular, but were not analyzed.

SIBLING INTERACTIONS IN THE 1980s SITCOMS

The family sitcom was a rare item during the early 1980s. Indeed, in 1983, only 3 of the top 22 shows were sitcoms of any kind. By 1986, they accounted for 12 of the 22 most popular programs (Jones, 1992).

Gimme a Break (1981–1987) was a 1980s family sitcom featuring another fragmented family, a single father raising his three daughters, Kate, Julie, and Samantha, with the help of an African American housekeeper. No research on this program was located, so a content analysis was done on nine episodes available in syndication in 1999. The method for analysis was the same as that described for *The Brady Bunch*.

The nine episodes featured 120 communication behaviors between siblings, and the communication tended to be more affiliative ($n = 68$, 55%) than conflictive ($n = 55$, 45%) [X^2 (1, $N = 120$) = 1.2, NS]. Compared to *The Brady Bunch* this is a rather large increase in conflictive communication (*The Brady Bunch*, 37% conflictive).

In this set of siblings, most of the affiliative communication was informing (see Table 8.2). For example, in an episode in which Samantha, who appears to be approximately 12 years old, is caught kissing her boyfriend, Samantha asked, "Well, how **do** mothers get babies?" Julie replied, "That's easy, from the male spermanzoa [sic]." Supporting communication was rare. An example would be Julie and Katie laughing together over a ridiculous dress Samantha has been forced to wear to a family party. In all nine episodes, a total of only six occurrences of supportive communication was found.

Conflictive communication was primarily attacking. Much of the attack was contained in a sarcastic tone of voice. For example, in the kissing episode, Julie and Katie taunted Samantha chanting, "Sam and Scottie sitting in a tree K-I-S-S-I-N-G. First comes love, then comes marriage, then comes Sam with a baby carriage." The opposing communication was also rather hostile, not merely disagreeing. For example, also in the kissing episode, Sam threatened Julie with, "Shut up Julie, or I'll tell everyone about the Kleenex in your bra!"

To the degree that supportive communication represents the "loyalty" element of the sibling relationship, which has been described as the keystone of the relationship (Bank & Kahn, 1975), these siblings do not seem to present a very good model for either sibling communication or interpersonal communication between friends.

During the mid- to late-1980s, the family sitcom again thrived. *The Cosby Show* (1984–1992), *Family Ties* (1982–1989), and *Growing Pains* (1985–1992) were all in the top 10 in the Nielsen ratings during the 1986–1987 season when Larson (1989) began her analysis. She coded for sibling functions as well as for positive and negative communication in the same manner as in her analysis of 1950s sitcoms. All three featured intact families, with working mothers. Nine episodes of each of the programs were coded. Sibling communication behavior was the unit of analysis.

Overall, 1,354 communication acts of sibling interaction were analyzed. *The Cosby Show* generated 424 interactions, *Family Ties*, 567, and *Growing Pains*, 363 interactions. In general, significantly more communication behaviors were positive ($n = 785$, 58%) than negative ($n = 569$, 42%) [X^2 $(1, N = 1,354) = 35.74, p < .001$]. However, chi square analysis revealed signifcant differences between programs [$X^2 (2, N = 1,354) = 43.67, p < .001$]. In both *The Cosby Show* and *Family Ties*, more sibling interactions (64% and 63% respectively) were positive than negative. For example, Theo, the older brother in *Cosby*, helped Rudy hide a stray dog she wanted to keep, even cleaning up the dog's messes on the kitchen floor. In another example, Alex, the older brother on *Family Ties*, tutored his sister's rather dull boyfriend so the boyfriend could earn his high school diploma (Larson, 1989).

On the other hand, in *Growing Pains*, the pattern of behavior was reversed. Significantly more sibling interactions were negative ($n = 323$, 57%) than were positive ($n = 244$, 43%) [$X^2 (1, N = 567) = 43.48 p < .01$]. Sibling behaviors were characterized by criticism and nasty barbs. For example, Mike, the older brother, told Carol that her new dress might be sexy enough for Bulgaria. In another instance, he said she shouldn't be allowed to skip a grade because his class had already exceeded its "nerd quota" (Larson, 1989).

Two functions, differentiation and dealing with parents, were eliminated from chi square analysis for lack of occurrence, leaving 1,315 communication behaviors for analysis. Analysis of the remaining functions (see Table 8.3) revealed that the most frequently performed function, in all three sets of siblings, was direct services (63%). Siblings were engaged in direct services such as giving information, negotiating arrangements, bargaining for favors, or threatening actions significantly more often than any other function. Furthermore, in all three sets of siblings, significantly more of this type of behavior was positive than was negative. For example, Sondra, on The Cosby Show asked her younger brother Theo to check out her blind date and signal his evaluation using a secret "code".

The mutual regulation function was the next most common, and significantly more regulatory behavior was negative ($n = 335$, 81.1%) than was positive ($n = 78$, 18.9%) in all three sets of siblings (see Table 8.3). Siblings appeared to criticize rather than encourage each other in their endeavors. It was interesting to note, however, that although the differences were not significant in terms of a quantitative differentiation, qualitative differences were apparent in the tone and style of mutual regula-

TABLE 8.3
Communication Behaviors by Function and Direction

Function	Direction	
	Positive	Negative
All Programs[a]		
Direct Services	74%	26%
Regulation	19%	81%
Identification	94%	6%
The Cosby Show[b]		
Direct Services	77%	23%
Regulation	25%	75%
Identification	92%	8%
Family Ties[c]		
Direct Services	82%	18%
Regulation	22%	78%
Identification	94%	6%
Growing Pains[d]		
Direct Services	60%	41%
Regulation	9%	91%
Identification	100%	—

[a] X^2 (2, $N = 1,315$) = 385.05, $p < .001$
[b] X^2 (2, $N = 400$) = 97.98, $p < .001$
[c] X^2 (2, $N = 559$) = 205.32, $p < .001$
[d] X^2 (2, $N = 356$) = 91.99, $p < .001$

Note. From "Interactions Between Siblings in Primetime Television Families," by M. S. Larson, 1989, Journal of Broadcasting & Electronic Media, 33, p. 310. Copyright 1989 by Journal of Broadcasting & Electronic Media. Reprinted with permission.

tion among the three programs. On Family Ties, Alex gently told 3-year-old Andy that he shouldn't remove the labels from the canned goods in the kitchen because Mom would be upset. On The Cosby Show, Vanessa aggressively chastised Theo and Rudy for horseplay in the living room and suggested that there would really be trouble when Mom and Dad got home. On Growing Pains, Carol criticized Mike, calling him "slime, just slime, like every other male!" and a "major wimp" (Larson, 1989).

In programs overall, significantly more identification behavior was positive than negative, but in total, it made up only 6% of all communication (see Table 8.3). That is, incidents in which siblingship was specifically mentioned or alluded to were more likely to be positive than negative. For example, Alex, in Family Ties, made a comment to Andy, the younger brother, about the "way Keaton men should act" in a positive way. Interestingly, almost all of the interactions involving identification occurred on The Cosby Show and Family Ties. The siblings on Growing Pains rarely referred to their siblingship or benefited vicariously from the experience of a sibling (Larson, 1989).

In sum, the 1980s, a decade of very popular family sitcoms, presents a view of siblings that is more positive than negative (see Table 8.1). Nevertheless, sibling interactions in the 1980s were the least positive of any decade to date. Indeed, little more than one half of the communication behaviors were positive. It would be difficult to argue that these programs offer good models of sibling behavior. Further, in terms of the functions described by Bank and Kahn (1975), there was remarkably little support or loyalty, very little identification, and the function dealing with parents failed to be exhibited in the programs examined.

SIBLING INTERACTIONS IN THE 1990s SITCOMS

In the 1990s, the family sitcom featuring children became rare. It was replaced by family sitcoms in which the children played minor roles and as sitcoms about adult relationships, such as *Friends, Seinfeld*, and *Frasier.*

Therefore, a content analysis was performed on nine episodes of *Married With Children* (1987–1997) that aired in syndication in 1998 to 1999. This program featured an intact family with a stay-at-home mom (but bearing no resemblance to 1950s moms), and two children.

The procedures and methodology for this analysis were the same as those for *The Brady Bunch*, discussed previously. The nine episodes yielded 154 communication behaviors between siblings. Of those, significantly more were affiliative ($n = 91$, 59%) than conflictive ($n = 63$, 41%) [X^2 (1, $N = 154$) = 5.0, $p < .05$].

Most of the affiliative communication was informing (See Table 8.2). For example, in an episode in which Bud planned to make a pinup calendar, Kelly asked, "You want to make a calendar of men's butts?" Later, Bud explained, "But I tell you, when I put out a casting call and say I'm making movies for HBO, beautiful women will come. Oh yes, they will come." Surprisingly perhaps, a greater percentage of their communication was supportive compared to the siblings on *The Brady Bunch* or *Gimme a Break.* For example, in the same episode, Bud asked for support, "Kelly please help me. Crystal's gonna be here any minute and I have no idea how to convince her to be in my calendar."

Most of the conflictive communication was attacking, such as criticizing, belittling, and teasing maliciously, and the tone of the communication was nasty. For example, an attacking exchange was, "Gee, Joey (who is really Bud), without your makeup you kind of look like my dorky brother, Bud." Bud replied, " I *am* Bud, you beach-blanket Bimbo! Yeah, you and the three slut-kateers thought you could just rip us off and leave us freezing in Chicago."

Thus, *Married With Children* continued to present a primarily affiliative pair of siblings, who are relatively supportive, but the attacking communication was remarkably harsh.

Nine episodes of another 1990s sitcom Roseanne (1988–1997), available in syndication, were also analyzed. *Roseanne* featured an intact family with a working mom and three children. In the episodes available, the children ranged in age from young adolescent to some episodes in which the eldest daughter was married. These episodes were also analyzed using the method described for *The Brady Bunch*, and yielded 159 sibling communication behaviors. No statistically significant differences between affiliative ($n = 83$, 52%) and conflictive ($n = 76$, 48%) behaviors ([X^2 (1, $N = 159$) = .308, NS] were found.

Most of the affiliative communication was informing (see Table 8.2). For example, Becky said to Darlene, "Dana did it! She got the concert tickets!" The supportive category was rather large, although much of it was seeking support rather than giving it. For example, Becky said to Darlene, "This is ridiculous, Mark is an hour and a half late. Where in the hell is he?"

Of all the programs analyzed, this one had the greatest proportion of conflictive communication (see Table 8.2) and was similar to *Married With Children* in terms of the level of hostility of it. Indeed, the second most frequent communication type was attacking, of which much was vitriolic. For example, Becky told DJ, the younger brother, "Hey pig, quit washing your hair in our sink!" The opposing communication, next most frequent, was similar. For example, Becky said to Darlene, "God, I hate you. Just go to school."

The Simpsons (1990-present) was analyzed earlier by Larson (1993) using the method described for *The Brady Bunch*. The program continues to be extremely popular and has met with both critical acclaim and disapproval. The program is in a cartoon format and features an intact family with a father, a stay-at-home mom, and three children, Lisa, Bart, and baby Maggie. Nine episodes of the program from its first season beginning in January 1990 were taped, transcribed, and coded. This analysis yielded 207 sibling interactions.

Significantly more sibling communication behaviors were affiliative ($n = 147$, 71%) than conflictive ($n = 60$, 29%) [X^2 (1, $N = 207$) = 34.9, $p < .001$]. Most of the affiliative communication was informing (See Table 8.2). For example, Lisa explained to Bart, "Oh, Bart, don't you see—this is what psychologists call overcompensation. Mom is racked with guilt because her marriage is failing." A remarkably large percentage of the communication was supportive. For example, Bart and Lisa were supportive of each other as they prepared breakfast-in-bed for Marge on her birthday. Lisa said, "This is gonna be the best birthday breakfast Mom ever had." And Bart earnestly replied, "Hey, Lise, you think that's enough for her?"

Most of the conflictive communication was opposing rather than *attacking*. An example occurred in an episode in which Bart cheated on an intelligence test. Lisa attacked with, "I don't care what that stupid test says,

Bart you're still a dimwit!" Bart *opposed* her with, "Maybe so, but from now on this dimwit is on Easy Street."

Although many critics of the program complain about hostile communication (e.g., an "antifamily sitcom, exploring the squalid underbelly of life . . . a grungy, bickering lot"; Zoglin, 1990, p. 85; a nagging, quarrelsome family, O'Connor, 1990), hostility is not prevalent between the siblings. Indeed these siblings very closely resemble the siblings of the 1950s, with the notable exception that their affiliative behavior was much more supportive than those siblings of yesteryear.

The 1990s, then, offer a mixed set of messages about siblings (see Table 8.1), in that *Married With Children* and *Roseanne* feature rather hostile sibling relationships whereas *The Simpsons* siblings are remarkably affiliative and supportive. Bart and Lisa appear to provide the loyalty described by Bank and Kahn (1975).

CONCLUSION

On average, the nearly 50 years of siblings on television present a primarily positive image (see Table 8.1). Sixty-three percent of the communication was coded as positive or affiliative. However, Bank and Kahn's (1975) description of siblings as loyal, helping each other try on new behaviors, and helping to shape one's self-identity suggest that 63% may not be enough.

Furthermore, there are implications regarding the functions that television siblings perform or do not perform for each other. In the sitcoms coded for function, very few of the behaviors fulfilled the identification and differentiation functions. As described by Bank and Kahn, birth siblings contribute to the creation of one's self-identity in important ways that are not reflected on television. Furthermore, insofar as one's identity is shaped by the regulatory responses of a sibling, a viewer of television siblings would have reason to be fearful of trying out new behaviors in the presence of a sibling, because it would be reasonable to anticipate a negative rather than a face-saving response.

Another function notably absent in these data is that of siblings dealing with parents. Indeed, in the sitcoms coded for function, this dimension was dropped from the statistical analysis for lack of occurrence. In real-world families, useful interpersonal skills are learned as siblings band together to negotiate with parents, or to teach younger siblings how to avoid wrath or to gain favor from parents. They also come to understand the power of such things as blackmail and extortion as they threaten to divulge damaging information as leverage to gain favors from a sibling.

Of the functions that were performed by television siblings, it is important to observe that the preponderance of mutual regulation behavior was negative or conflict producing. Bank and Kahn (1975) noted that in birth siblings, rivalry and conflict is minimal, and that siblings make efforts not to embarrass when regulating a sibling's behavior. Television siblings do not appear to share this face-saving motivation.

Siblings on television did negotiate for direct services in a positive way. They exchanged favors, bargained for goods and services, and asked for and received information in a positive manner. However, inasmuch as the coding of this function included many rather perfunctory exchanges such as greetings, the frequency of positive direct services may be deceptive.

In the sitcoms coded for affiliative and conflictive communication, the primary affiliative communication was informing. The loyal, supportive communication was only remarkably prevalent in *The Simpsons*. Further, the tone of the conflictive communication, especially in *Roseanne, Married With Children,* and *Gimme a Break*, all readily available in syndication, seem problematic as models for sibling communication as well as for other interpersonal communication.

In conclusion, over the 50 years of the portrayals of siblings in sitcoms, we do not find models that include many examples of siblings whose identities are shaped by siblings, nor do we find examples of siblings helping each other deal with parents. Furthermore, very few examples of the support and loyalty described as key elements in siblingship exist. The sitcom siblings observed do not appear to illustrate Goldberg's claim that television tells viewers "families are the best things we've got" (as cited in Kalter, 1988, p. 8).

REFERENCES

Abramovitch, R., Corter, C., Pepler, D., & Stanhope, L. (1986). Sibling and peer interaction—a final follow-up and comparison. *Child Development, 57,* 217–229.

Bank, S., & Kahn, M. (1975). Sisterhood–brotherhood is powerful: Sibling subsystems and family therapy. *Family Process, 14,* 311–337.

Greenberg, B., Buerkel-Rothfuss, N., Neuendorf, K., & Atkin, C. (1980). Three seasons of family role interactions. In B. Greenberg (Ed.), *Life on television: Content analyses of U.S. TV drama* (pp. 161–172). Norwood NJ: Ablex.

Greenberg, B., & Neuendorf, K. (1980). Black family interactions on television. In B. Greenberg (Ed.), *Life on television: Content analyses of U.S. TV drama* (pp. 173–181). Norwood NJ: Ablex.

Grossman, F. (1972). *Brothers and sisters of mentally retarded children.* Syracuse, NY: Syracuse University Press.

Irish, D. (1964). Sibling interaction: A neglected aspect in family life research. *Social Forces, 42,* 279–288.

Jones, G. (1992). *Honey, I'm home.* New York: St. Martin's Press.

Kalter, J. (1988, July 23). Television as value-setter. *TV Guide,* pp. 5–11.

Larson, M. (1989). Interaction between siblings in primetime television families. *Journal of Broadcasting & Electronic Media, 33,* 305–315.

Larson, M. (1991). Sibling interactions in 1950s versus 1980s sitcoms: A comparison. *Journalism Quarterly, 68,* 381–387.

Larson, M. (1993). Family communication on primetime television. *Journal of Broadcasting & Electronic Media, 37*, 349–357.

Merrell, S. (1995). *The accidental bond: The power of sibling relationships.* New York: Random House.

Mitz, R. (1983). *The great TV sitcom book.* New York: Perigree Books.

O'Connor, J. (1990, February 21). Prime-time cartoon of unbeautiful people. *New York Times,* p. C-13.

Schvaneveldt, J., & Ihinger, M. (1979). Sibling relationships in the family. In W. Burr, R. Hill, F. Nye, & I. Reiss (Eds.), *Contemporary theories about the family* Vol. 1 (pp. 453–467). New York: Free Press.

Singer, J., Singer, D., & Rapaczynski, W. (1984). Family patterns and television viewing as predictors of children's beliefs and aggression. *Journal of Communication, 34*(2), 73–79.

Wimmer, R., & Dominick, J. (1997). *Mass Media research: An introduction.* Belmont, CA: Wadsworth

Zoglin, R. (1990, April 16). Home is where the venom is. *Time,* pp. 85–86.

Balancing Acts: Work–Family Issues on Prime-Time TV

Katharine E. Heintz-Knowles
University of Washington

Television is a cultural storyteller. Its programming both reflects the values and ideals of American society and shapes the attitudes and beliefs of those who watch it. Heavy TV viewers tend to believe that the representations on TV programming reflect the state of the world outside TV, and thus develop perceptions about our world based on TV information. Through patterns of inclusion and exclusion, television content sends implicit messages about the relative cultural importance of different groups, behaviors, and ideologies (Gerbner, Gross, Morgan, & Signorielli, 1994).

TV has also been shown to be a powerful source of behavioral models. Through TV viewing, audience members can learn how to act in unfamiliar situations, how to dress, and different ways of speaking. Television characters—and the actors who play them—are often taken as role models by viewers, young and old alike. Television characters who are attractive, successful, and of high status are more likely to be imitated than those who are unattractive, unsuccessful, or ridiculed (Bandura, 1994).

Because of the dual role of TV as a reflection and an influence, it is critical to assess the messages sent incessantly into American homes. Prime-time broadcast entertainment programming reaches approximately

100 million Americans each night (Pope & Cauley, 1998). What is this medium telling us about one of the central dilemmas facing Americans today—finding a balance between work and family?

FAMILIES ON TV, WORK ON TV

Numerous previous studies have examined the representation of family structure, gender roles, and occupations on television. Families on television are quite diverse structurally and have been that way since the 1950s. In family situation comedies especially, history has shown a variety of forms (e.g., single parents, childless couples, two parents with children; Heintz, 1992).

TV family households are most often headed by a male wage earner, although in recent years it is not unusual for both partners in a TV marriage to work outside the home. According to Press and Strathman (1994), "Family women on early television were pictured almost exclusively in the domestic, or private, realm; rarely did they legitimately venture into the male, public, world of work" (p. 7). Indeed, early content analyses consistently discovered that overall, women on prime-time programs during the 1960s and 1970s were depicted as considerably younger than men, were less frequently shown in work situations, and had more restricted vocational roles than men (Feshbach, Dillman, & Jordan, 1979).

More recent content analyses suggest that women's roles on prime time during the 1980s and 1990s have become more varied, interesting, and vocationally involved (Davis, 1990; Huston et al., 1992; Meehan, 1988). Women's occupational roles represented, however, are not reflective of the working lives of real U.S. women. TV women are more likely than their real-life counterparts to occupy professional and entrepreneurial roles. Yet, despite the increased portrayal of working women, their traditional nurturing roles in the nuclear family are highlighted. For example, Clair Huxtable from *The Cosby Show* was rarely shown in her professional role as an attorney, and seemed to have ample time for domestic tasks (Press & Strathman, 1994). This point was echoed by Gail Collins in an article entitled "A Woman's Work is Never Shown" (*Working Woman,* 1994) in which she lamented prime time's lack of genuine images of women at work.

Studies of gender portrayals on TV show a shift in family role behaviors for fathers as well. Compared with TV fathers from the 1950s and the 1960s, TV dads in the 1980s and 1990s are more involved with parenting and domestic responsibilities (see Heintz, 1992). Indeed, one study concluded that TV fathers during the 1980s were shown in nontraditional ways, whereas TV mothers continued to be shown in traditional, stereotyped roles (Dail & Way, 1985). According to Huston et al. (1992), "Television families have mirrored other changes in society, but television tends to follow social change cautiously rather than leading it" (p. 38).

Work–Family Issues on Television

Previous content analyses suggest that current TV programming portrays mothers who participate in the workforce and fathers who participate in childrearing. Yet, how does TV programming represent the intersection of these two worlds? How does TV entertainment programming represent the challenges that American adults face each day in their attempts to balance work and family? What sorts of work–family issues arise for TV's working adults? How are these issues resolved? To examine these questions, the first ever content analysis of the representation of work–family challenges in prime-time entertainment programming was conducted.

METHODOLOGY

Two weeks of network-originated prime-time entertainment programming (Monday through Saturday: 8–11pm PST; Sunday: 7–11pm PST) from the six commercial broadcast networks (ABC, CBS, NBC, Fox, WB, UPN)[1] was recorded in early March 1998. All made-for-TV entertainment[2] airing March 1 to 14 was included for analysis. News magazines, award presentations, and reality programs were not considered entertainment for the purposes of this study. This selection process yielded 150 episodes of 92 different programs, including 6 made-for-TV movies. Total hours of programming examined was 119. See Appendix A for a complete list of programs examined.

All plot-relevant adult characters were identified and systematically analyzed to assess their marital, parental, occupational, and adult-care status. Adult characters were eligible for inclusion in the sample if they were either; (a) regular characters (identified as those characters who appear either visually or by name in the opening credit sequence of a series), or (b) plot-relevant characters in the episode (defined as those irregularly appearing, "special guest," or minor characters who appear in the episode and have some relevance to the plot). Excluded from analysis were adult characters who appeared as members of a group or crowd, who did not have speaking roles, or who were background characters

---

[1] Locally produced or syndicated programming airing during these hours was not included for analysis.

[2] Includes situation comedies, dramas, and made-for-TV movies. Excludes theatrical movies shown on TV.

(i.e., adults seen standing at reception desk on *ER* but whose case was not part of the episode).

Characters identified as parents were further examined to identify the number and ages of children, child-care arrangements, and performance of child-care activities. Characters identified as adult caregivers were further examined to assess the extent and nature of their care-giving activities. Finally, situations where work and family responsibilities collided were identified and examined for the type of conflict, whether or not it was recognized by the character(s) involved, and if and how the conflict was resolved.

All programs were analyzed by the author and three trained graduate students from the School of Communications at the University of Washington. Reliability between coders was assessed using randomly assigned pair-wise correlations. Agreement was achieved more than 90% of the time on all variables reported.

Description of the Sample

A total of 820 adult characters were identified for analysis. Tables 9.1 through 9.5 provide information about the demographic characteristics of the sample population.

TABLE 9.1
Gender of Prime-Time Adult TV Characters

Gender	Number	Percent of TV Population (%)
Male	508	62
Female	312	38
Total	820	100

TABLE 9.2
Race/Ethnicity of Prime-Time Adult TV Characters

Race/Ethnicity	Number	Percent of TV Population (%)
Caucasian	629	77
African American	134	16
Asian	14	2
Hispanic/Latino	27	3
Native American	4	0.5
Arab/Muslim	2	0.2
Other	9	1
Can't Tell	1	0
Total	820	100

TABLE 9.3
Age of Prime-Time Adult TV Characters

Age	Number	Percent of TV Population %
Young Adult (18–30)	261	32
Adult (30–50)	439	53
Older Adult (50–65)	98	12
Senior (over 65)	16	2
Not Sure	6	1
Total	820	100

TABLE 9.4
Occupational Status of Prime-Time Adult Characters by Gender

Occupational Status	Number of TV Males	Percent of TV Males (%)	Number of TV Females	Percent of TV Females (%)	Total	Percent of TV Population (%)
Working Full-Time	376	74	201	65	577	70
Working Part-Time	2	0.4	3	1	5	0.6
Unemployed	21	4	8	3	29	3.5
Retired	12	2	8	3	20	2.4
Student	8	2	9	3	17	2
Homemaker	0	-	11	3.5	11	1.3
Don't Know /Can't Tell	89	18	72	23	161	20
Total	508	100	312	100	820	100

KEY FINDINGS

Work and Family Obligations Rarely Collide for TV Characters

Coders identified all instances when characters' obligations to work and obligations to family would normally collide (e.g., character was asked to work late; character needed time off to attend birth of his child; character returns to work after being a stay-at-home caregiver). Each instance presented the potential for a conflict of responsibilities, but characters did not always perceive or react to the situation as a work–family conflict. For each instance, coders identified whether or not the character perceived it as a work–family conflict. Conflict recognition was defined as, either (a) verbal identification of a conflict of responsibilities (e.g., a character working overtime mentions that he is missing a family activity), or (b) visual or verbal depictions of attempts to resolve the conflict (e.g.,

TABLE 9.5
Occupations of Prime-Time Adult TV Characters With Full-Time Employment

Occupation	Male Characters	Male Characters %	Female Characters	Female Characters %	Total TV Population	Total TV Population %
Professional	51	14	30	15	81	14
Physician	25	7	16	8	41	7
Nurse	2	0.5	11	5.5	13	2
Writer/journalist	13	3.5	6	3	19	3
White collar/executive	15	4	9	4.5	24	4
White collar/mgmt/ business owner	51	14	19	9.5	70	12
White collar/clerical	7	2	25	12	32	5.5
School administrator	4	1	2	1	6	1
Teacher/child care	9	2	7	3.5	16	3
Service/retail	19	5	11	5.5	30	5
Technical/computer	8	2	-	-	8	1
Protective Service/ Military personnel	91	24	31	15	122	21
Skilled blue collar	10	3	2	1	12	2
Unskilled blue collar	3	1	1	0.5	4	0.7
Minister/other Religious	12	3	2	1	14	2
Agriculture	3	1	2	1	5	1
Art/performance	15	4	12	6	27	5
Other	28	7	9	4.5	37	6
No identifiable Occupation	10	3	6	3	16	3
Total	376	100.0	201	100.0	577	100.0

if character was shown asking for time off or actively searching for a substitute care giver). For those instances identified as recognized conflicts, coders identified how the conflict was handled and resolved.

For purposes of this chapter, each instance where work and family obligations would normally collide are referred to as a *conflict*. Those conflicts recognized by characters are referred to as *recognized conflicts*. Those conflicts not recognized by characters are referred to as *unrecognized conflicts*. The following examples illustrate this distinction:

> *Law and Order* (NBC): Assistant District Attorney Jamie Ross, a single parent, makes plans to work on the weekend and is shown at the office with no reference made to care arrangements for her daughter. (unrecognized conflict)

> *NYPD Blue* (ABC): Detective Greg Medavoy receives a phone call at work from his partner who has gone into labor. He talks with his supervisor and arranges to take time off so he can attend the birth of his child. (recognized conflict)

Out of 150 program episodes examined, only 22 episodes (15%) included any occurrences of potential or recognized work–family conflict (8 episodes contained more than one conflict).

Thirty-six work–family conflicts were identified, involving 36 different characters (4% of all characters). Six conflicts involved more than one character. Sixteen of these conflicts were recognized by 21 (3%) characters. Table 9.6 identifies the programs with work–family conflicts.

Three fourths of the conflicts ($n = 27$) occurred on dramatic programs, and nearly half ($n = 16$) on NBC (primarily due to the high number of conflicts on *Profiler*). See Appendix B for more information about genre and network breakdowns.

Although there were only 36 conflicts identified in the sample of programs, 8 involved more than one character. As well, 5 characters were involved in more than one conflict during the sample time period. For example:

> *Malcolm and Eddie* (UPN): When single parent, Paige, leaves her infant with her cousin and his roommate, a conflict is created involving three characters.

> *Profiler* (NBC): Single parent Samantha Waters, an FBI profiler, is shown in numerous situations that would normally create conflict for parents; she works late, gets called in early, and brings work home.

Because some conflicts involved more than one character, and some characters were involved in more than one conflict, the number of character-based work–family conflicts examined in this study was 44. Table 9.7 presents a list of all work–family conflicts identified in the sample broken down by gender of character involved.

TABLE 9.6
Prime-Time Programs Including Work–Family Conflicts

Program Title	Number of Unrecognized Conflicts	Number of Recognized Conflicts	Total Number of Conflicts
Brooklyn South (CBS)	1	2	3
Chicago Hope (CBS)	2	1	3
E.R. (NBC)	2	0	2
Ellen (ABC)	1	0	1
Everybody Loves Raymond (CBS)	0	1	1
Four Corners (CBS)	1	0	1
Homicide: Life on the Street (NBC)	1	0	1
JAG (CBS)	0	1	1
Law and Order (NBC)	2	0	2
Mad About You (NBC)	1	1	2
Malcolm and Eddie (UPN)	0	2	2
Millenium (Fox)	0	1	1
NYPD Blue (ABC)	1	2	3
The Pretender (NBC)	0	1	1
Profiler (NBC)	6	1	7
Seventh Heaven (WB)	0	2	2
Smart Guy (WB)	1	0	1
The Tom Show (WB)	1	1	2
Total	20	16	36

Work–Family Conflicts Are Rarely Featured as Primary Story Lines. For each conflict, coders identified the importance of the conflict to the story line of the episode. Less than 1% of episodes ($n = 5$) contained a work–family conflict as a primary story line. Five conflicts served as primary story lines in program episodes (14% of all conflicts). Another three conflicts were included as secondary story lines (8% of conflicts). The remaining conflicts ($n = 28$, 78% of conflicts) were either part of a tertiary story line or were unrelated to the plot of the episode. Often, the conflict was no more than a brief mention in a workplace conversation or received no comment in the course of the story line. For example:

> *The Pretender* (NBC): Technical Specialist Broots is called in to work. He sits down at a computer and says, "Truth is, I'd rather be home; I'm missing my daughter's dance class."

> *Smart Guy* (WB): T.J., a high school student, is learning the challenges of working on group projects. After a group meeting, he comes home to tell his father about his experiences. His father has brought work home, but T.J. interrupts him. Mr. Henderson stops working to talk with his son.

TABLE 9.7
Prime-Time Work–Family Conflicts by Gender of Character

Description of Conflict	Number of Characters Involved in Conflicts		Number of Characters with Recognized Conflicts	
	Male	*Female*	*Male*	*Female*
Dependent child needs basic care	5	5	2	3
Child gets sick	2	1	2	1
Parent/elder relative gets sick	1	-	-	-
Child's play, athletic event, etc. scheduled during work hours	2	-	1	-
Character or spouse/partner gives birth	1	-	1	-
Spouse/partner has medical emergency	-	1	-	-
Spouse/partner has non-emergency medical appointment	1	-	1	-
Child phones parent at office	-	1	-	-
Character needs to stay late/go in early/switch shifts	3	6	1	4
Character needs to travel for work	1	2	-	1
Character brings work home	1	1	-	-
Character brings child to workplace	1	1	-	-
Elderly parent drops in at character's office	1	-	1	-
Militia holds family for ransom unless character steals from workplace	1	-	1	-
Child custody hearing scheduled during work hours	1	-	-	-
Child is arrested and character needs to deal with criminal justice system during work hours	1	-	-	-
Child is killed and character needs to deal with FBI during work hours	1	-	-	-
Custody battle includes discussion of the challenges of balancing work and family	1	1	1	1
Character flees persecution leaving family without support	1	-	1	-
Total number of characters*	25	19	12	10

* Total characters adds to more than 36 because of multiple conflicts for some characters.

When conflicts were the primary or secondary story lines, they were defined as recognized conflicts by coders. Thus, when TV writers chose to focus on a situation where work and family obligations collide, characters were always shown as recognizing and dealing with the conflict. For example:

Mad About You (NBC): Jamie Buchman, a stay-at-home mom, decides to return to the workforce. The episode focuses on her mixed emotions about her decision.

Malcolm and Eddie (UPN): Paige, a single mother, leaves her infant in the care of her cousin while she goes out of town to a job interview. The challenges for two single men of balancing care of an infant with their work and social schedules dominate the story line.

The more casual inclusion of work–family conflicts may, in fact, be a more accurate reflection of the day-to-day challenges many working adults face as they manage their various responsibilities. For example, grabbing a quick call from a child while at your desk (*Chicago Hope*) is undoubtedly a common experience for many real working parents.

When Work and Family Obligations Collide, Family Obligations Created More Conflict Overall Than Work Obligations.
Approximately 60% of the characters involved in work–family conflicts on prime-time TV were male ($n = 22$, 4% of all male characters), whereas approximately 40% were female ($n = 14$, 4.5% of all female characters). Each conflict identified was labeled as either a *work-initiated conflict* (e.g., staying late at the office, *The Pretender*) or *family-initiated conflict* (e.g., Spouse/partner has a medical emergency, *Ellen*). Out of the 44 character-based work–family conflicts, 17 (39%) were work-initiated and 27 (61%) were family-initiated.

Men and Women Experienced Different Types of Work–Family Conflicts.
Even though family-initiated conflicts were more frequent overall, this type of conflict was felt much more by the male characters than by the female characters. For male characters, family was 2½ times more likely than work to cause conflict, whereas for female characters, work and family conflicted with each other equally. Table 9.8 presents the number of each type of conflict by gender of character.

For those conflicts that were recognized by characters, 60% were family-initiated and 40% were work-initiated. Table 9.9 presents the number of each type of recognized conflict by gender of character.

Again we see a great disparity by gender. For male characters, over 80% of their conflicts were initiated by family obligations. For female characters, on the other hand, 70% of their conflicts were initiated by work

TABLE 9.8
Type of Work–Family Conflict by Gender of Character

Type of conflict	Males	Females	Total
Work-initiated	7	9	16
Family-initiated	18	9	27
Total	25	18	43

TABLE 9.9
Type of Recognized Work–Family Conflict by Gender of Character

Type of conflict	Males	Females	Total
Work-initiated	2	7	9
Family-initiated	10	3	13
Total	12	10	22

obligations. In other words, when male characters perceived situations as conflictual, it was almost always when their families interfered with their work. But, for female characters, when a conflict of responsibilities was perceived, it was twice as likely to be work interfering with family obligations. For example:

> *Everybody Loves Raymond (CBS)*: Ray's young daughter has trouble sleeping at night and continually climbs into the parents' bed. This arrangement makes it difficult for Ray to sleep and he comments that the lack of sleep will impact on his performance at work. He and his wife develop strategies to solve the sleep problem.
>
> *Seventh Heaven (WB)*: Annie Camden, a married stay-at-home mom, starts her own baking business but quits because it does not allow her to spend enough time on family responsibilities without exhausting herself.

These differences indicate that on TV, women's worlds revolved around their families and men's worlds revolved around their work. When interference from outside these worlds was felt, it often resulted in conflict for the characters.

Characters With High-Status Occupations and Nonworking Spouses Recognized Fewer Conflicts Than Characters With Lower-Status Occupations and Working Spouses.   When examining the occupational characteristics of those characters who were involved in a work–family conflict, it was clear that characters with the highest status occupations perceived less conflict than those with lower status occupations. Professionals and physicians were involved in eight conflicts, but only recognized conflict in two instances (25%). On the other hand, police

TABLE 9.10
Occupation of Characters Involved in Work–Family Conflicts

Occupation	Conflict Unrecognized	Conflict Recognized	Total
Professional	3	1	4
Physician	3	1	4
Writer/Journalist		1	1
Business Owner/Middle Mgmt.	2	3	5
Teacher/Day Care	-	-	-
Technical	-	1	1
Protective	-	1	1
Service/Military	8	4	12
Minister	-	-	-
Art/Performance	-	1	1
Homemaker	2	2	4
Other	1	2	3
No identifiable occupation	-	1	1
	3	4	7

officers recognized conflict in three of six situations (50% of their conflicts were recognized). Table 9.10 presents the occupations of the characters involved in both unrecognized and recognized work–family conflicts.

Work–Family Conflicts Are Rarely Discussed in the Workplace. When These Conflicts Are Discussed at Work, They Rarely Include Mention of Policies Designed to Help out Working Parents. For each character involved in a recognized work–family conflict, coders identified with whom it was discussed. Characters most frequently sought out family members for discussion ($n = 10$). Characters were about equally likely to discuss the conflict with no one ($n = 6$) as with someone from their workplace ($n = 5$). Table 9.11 shows with whom characters discussed their conflicts.

In the few instances when characters did discuss their conflict with someone from the workplace ($n = 5$), neither the character nor his or her colleague or supervisor seemed uncomfortable or inhibited from talking about it. However, discussion of workplace or government policies to assist in conflicts was not a common topic of discussion. Just one workplace discussion included a mention of policies designed to help employees with work–family conflicts. For example:

On *NYPD Blue* (ABC) when Det. Martinez discusses with his boss, Lt. Fancy, his desire to accompany his partner to a doctor's appointment, Lt. Fancy instructs him to fill out the appropriate form and take some "lost time."

TABLE 9.11
With Whom Character Discussed Work–Family
Conflict by Gender of Character

With Whom Discuss Conflict	Male	Female
No one	3	3
Spouse/Partner	4	3
Parent/Older relative	2	-
Child	-	1
Employer/Supervisor	3	-
Coworker/Colleague	1	1
Friend	-	2
Other	2	1
Total	15	11

In four out of the five workplace discussions (80%), colleagues and/ or supervisors were coded as sympathetic to the character's situation. In one workplace discussion, the supervisor's response was coded as indifferent.

Work–Family Conflicts on TV Are Easily Resolved and Rarely Require Employer Involvement. For each recognized conflict, coders identified the strategies employed by the characters to resolve the conflict. Table 9.12 presents the resolution strategies employed in the 16 recognized conflicts.

The most common resolution strategy for parents in the sample was to find an alternative caregiver for their children. Six characters easily resolved their conflicts by calling on spouses, friends, or roommates to provide short-term care for their children.

Mad About You (NBC): When Jamie Buchman decides to return to the workforce after being a stay-at-home mom, husband Paul, a filmmaker, offers to stay home with the baby because he is between projects.

TABLE 9.12
Prime-Time Work–Family Conflict Resolution Strategies

Type of Resolution Strategy	Frequency of Occurrence	Percent of all Resolutions
Character finds alternative, short-term caregiver	5	31%
Character takes time off work	3	19%
Character quits work to stay home	1	6%
Other	5	31%
Conflict is not resolved	2	13%
Total	16	100%

Seventh Heaven (WB): Emory and Nel are having trouble managing their schedules with both working full-time and visiting their terminally ill son, Steve, in the hospital. They hire their minister's teenaged son to be a companion for Steve in the evenings.

Millenium (Fox): Katherine takes a job in the evening to supplement the family income. Her husband, Frank (from whom she is separated), readily agrees to take care of their daughter.

Three characters took time off from work to handle family-initiated conflicts. In all cases, there were no apparent barriers to this action. In one case, Chief of Cardiology, Dr. Kate Austin (*Chicago Hope,* CBS), chooses to skip an out-of-town conference in favor of some "mother–daughter time" with her school-age child. Both of the other time-off situations occurred on *NYPD Blue* (ABC) where Lt. Fancy readily accommodated the requests of Dets. Medavoy and Martinez for time off to attend to partner-related situations.

In two situations, the conflict went unresolved during the episode:

Pretender (NBC): Technical Specialist Broots is called in to work. He sits down at a computer and comments: "Truth is, I'd rather be home. I'm missing my daughter's dance class." After learning his boss' life might be in danger, he continues to work.

Everybody Loves Raymond (CBS): Ray's daughter has trouble sleeping in her own room and is causing Ray to have trouble getting enough sleep at night. Numerous strategies are tried out during the program to solve the problem, but it is still unresolved at the end of the episode.

The rest of the conflict resolutions involved a range of activities:

Brooklyn South (CBS): Sgt. Frank Donovan's father shows up unexpectedly at the station and wants to talk over a problem. Frank is in the midst of processing people involved in a prostitution bust, so he asks his father to wait in the sitting room until he has time to get back to him. The father agrees.

Brooklyn South (CBS): Lorraine, a prostitute, is jailed overnight, leaving her newborn baby home alone. After the police officers rescue the near-dead baby the next morning, Child Protective Services takes the baby away from Lorraine.

The Tom Show (WB): Maggie, Tom's ex-wife and a wildly successful talk show host, comes to visit their daughters and initiates a fight for custody. Tom explains to her the challenges of combining work and family responsibilities, and the trade-offs involved. She sees first-hand the day-to-day issues of her children's lives and realizes that her lifestyle is not compatible. At the end of the episode she decides to withdraw her petition for custody of their daughters.

JAG (CBS): Commander Douglass' family is held hostage by a militia organization. To secure the release of his family, he steals a Navy jet and agrees to undertake a deadly mission. Seconds before blowing up a passenger plane, he changes his mind. In the meantime, Navy forces have already rescued his family from the militia.

Profiler (NBC): A journalist from Nigeria flees persecution, leaving his family behind. To earn enough money to pay for their trip, he engages in an illegal boxing match.

Family Status Is not Clearly Identified for Characters on Prime-Time Programs

Marital, parental, and adult-care status were identified for each character using three main sources of information; visual and/or verbal information presented during program episodes, backstory knowledge of coders familiar with the program, backstory information provided by program representatives. The next three tables present information gathered only from what was clearly represented during the program episodes.

Out of 820 adult characters analyzed, just 151 (18%) were clearly identified as married and only 125 (15%) were identified as parents of dependent children.

Interestingly, marital and parental status were more evident for female characters than for male characters. For approximately 32% of female characters, marital status was unclear; for male characters, marital status was unclear more than 40% of the time. Similarly, parental status was evident for 47% of female characters, but for less than 40% of male characters. It appears that women more often than men are defined by their relationships to others. Tables 9.13 and 9.14 present the marital and parental status of the sample of TV adults.

In addition to the 115 custodial parents identified through on-screen information, an additional 8 characters were identified as custodial parents/legal guardians of dependent children (that is, adults with legal responsibility for minor children in the household) through the use of

TABLE 9.13
Marital Status of Adult TV Characters by Gender

Marital Status	Males (#)	Males (%)	Females (#)	Females (%)	Total (#)	Total (%)
Single	210	41	140	45	350	43
Married	79	16	72	23	151	18
Don't Know Can't Tell	219	43	100	32	319	39
Total	508		312		820	

TABLE 9.14
Parental Status of Adult TV Characters by Gender

Parental Status	Males (#)	Males (%)	Females (#)	Females (%)	Total (#)	Total (%)
Custodial parent/legal guardian	60	12	55	18	115	14
Noncustodial parent	7	1	3	1	10	1
Noncustodial grandparent	1		2	1	3	
Parent of adult children	36	7	20	6	56	7
Nonparent	94	19	68	22	162	20
Don't Know/Can't Tell	310	61	164	53	474	58
Total	508		312		820	

backstory information. Fifty-five percent of these parents ($n = 67$) appear on television dramas, and 67% ($n = 82$) appear on the "big three" networks. Probably due to their strategies of targeting younger viewers, Fox and the United Paramount Network featured the fewest parents.

Working Parents Are Scarce on Prime-Time Television

Occupational status and profession were identified where possible for each adult character in the sample. Whereas 70% of the total sample of TV adults were employed full-time, just 57% of TV parents were employed full-time ($n = 70$, 8.5% of total sample). Parents made up 12% of the full-time workers in the sample. Table 9.15 shows the employment status of parent characters.

Less than one third of TV mothers were shown engaging in full-time work outside the home. This is in sharp contrast to U.S. population statistics that show that more than two thirds of American mothers are

TABLE 9.15
Parental Employment Status by Gender of Character

Employment Status	Male (#)	Male (%)	Female (#)	Female (%)	Total (#)	Total (%)
Employed full-time	51	80	19	32	70	57
Employed part-time			1	2	1	1
Unemployed	1	2	3	5	4	3
Retired	1	2	2	3	3	2
Student			1	2	1	1
Homemaker			6	10	6	5
Don't Know/Can't Tell	11	17	27	46	38	31
Total	64		59		123	

employed full time (U.S. Department of Labor, 1996). Employment status was unclear for nearly half of TV mothers, because these moms were shown only in domestic situations and no discussion was made of possible employment.

TV Parents Are Rarely Shown Dealing With Child Care

More than half of TV parents ($n = 65, 53\%$) have just one dependent child living in the home. Approximately 40% ($n = 49$) have two or more children living with them. For 9 characters (7%), it was impossible to identify the number of dependent children (e.g., character referred to his or her children, but they were never seen or named).

Parents of Preschoolers. Twenty-six characters (13 males, 13 females—21% of all parents) were identified as parents of preschool children (including infants and toddlers). Of these parents, 92% of fathers ($n = 12$) and 39% of mothers ($n = 5$) were employed full-time (one mother is employed part-time). Three mothers (23% of mothers of preschoolers) were stay-at-home-moms.

While these parents worked, it was often unclear who took care of their children. For 42% of the characters ($n = 11$), child-care status is unclear. When child-care arrangements could be identified, parents were the

TABLE 9.16
Child-Care Arrangements for Preschool Children

Child-Care Provider	Number of Parents	Percent of Preschool Parents
Nonworking parent	10	39%
Grandparent not living in family home	2	8%
Nonrelative living in family home	2	8%
No one	1	4%
Don't Know/Can't Tell	11	42%
Total	26	100%

TABLE 9.17
Location of Care for Preschool Children

Location of Child Care	Number	Percent
In family home	13	50%
Caregiver's home	2	8%
Don't Know/Can't Tell	11	42%
Total	26	100%

most frequent caregivers; nearly 40% of parents of preschoolers ($n = 10$) had their preschool children being cared for by a parent (8 mothers, 2 fathers) in the family home. One couple relied on a grandfather living outside the family home (*NYPD Blue*), one couple had a nanny (*George and Leo*), and one infant was left unattended while her mother worked as a prostitute on the streets of Brooklyn (*Brooklyn South*). Tables 9.16 and 9.17 present the child-care arrangements for TV parents of preschoolers.

Parents of School-Age Children. Fifty-three males, 27 females (43% of all parents) were identified as parents of school-age children. Of these parents, 26 or 81% of fathers ($n = 21$) and 37% of mothers ($n = 10$) were employed full-time (1 mother was employed part-time). Five mothers (19% of mothers of school-age children) were stay-at-home-moms.

While these parents worked, it was often unclear who took care of their children. For 60% of the parents of grade schoolers ($n = 34$), child-care status was unclear. When child- care status could be identified, parents were again the most frequent caregivers. Nearly one third of all parents of grade schoolers ($n = 17$, 30%) had children being cared for by a parent (16 mothers, 1 father) in the family home. Two single fathers had nannies (*The Nanny, E.R.*); one couple relied on a live-in relative (*King of the Hill*); and one couple had a paid teenage companion for their terminally

TABLE 9.18
Child-Care Arrangements for School-Age Children

Child-Care Provider	Number of Parents	Percent of Grade School Parents
Nonworking parent	17	30%
Nonrelative living in family home	2	4%
Nonrelative not living in family home	2	4%
Relative living in family home	2	4%
Don't Know/Can't Tell	34	55%
Total	57	100%

TABLE 9.19
Location of Care for School-Age Children

Location of Child Care	Number	Percent of Grade School Parents
In family home	21	37%
Hospital	2	4%
Don't Know/Can't Tell	34	60%
Total	57	100%

ill child (*Seventh Heaven*). Tables 9.18 and 9.19 present the child-care arrangements for TV parents of grade schoolers.

It is interesting to note that not a single parent in this sample was identified as having a child attending a day-care center while the parent worked. This sharply contrasts with the experiences of working American parents. Twenty percent of U.S. parents have children who attend licensed day-care facilities (Bond, Galinsky, & Swanberg, 1998).

TV Adults Rarely Perform Child Care Activities.   Forty-seven men (9% of all male characters) and 46 women (15% of all female characters) were shown performing care-giving activities with children (total $N = 93$, 11% of all characters). Males and females performed an equal number of care-giving activities—both averaged two care-giving activities. Table 9.20 presents the frequency of care-giving activities for the male and female characters in the sample.

Even though there was an equal frequency of child-care activities performed by men and women, we see that women outnumbered men in the areas of cleaning and cooking for children, and men were more often called on to offer consolation to their children. For example:

> *Smart Guy* (WB): Mr. Henderson, a single father, consoles his school-age son and puts him to bed after T.J. has a near encounter with a pedophile.
>
> *George and Leo* (CBS): Alice is hired as a nanny for an infant. She is shown holding, feeding, and diapering the baby.
>
> *Everybody Loves Raymond* (CBS): Ray and Debra are shown performing a variety of child-care activities. He feeds, holds, and reads to their younger child. She dresses the younger child. Both are shown putting the children to bed and cleaning up after the children.

TABLE 9.20
Most Frequent Child-Care Activities Performed by Gender of Character

Child-Care Activity	Male	Female
Putting child(ren) to bed	8	6
Cleaning up after child(ren)	4	10
Consoling child(ren)	18	12
Driving child(ren)	8	7
Preparing food/feeding child(ren)	10	15
Holding child(ren)	8	10
Disciplining child(ren)	7	6
Total*	63	66

* Total adds to more than 93 because some characters performed more than one type of activity.

Adult Care Is Very Rarely Portrayed on Prime-Time Entertainment TV

Adult care giving is infrequently shown in prime-time entertainment. Out of 820 adult characters, just 26 had identifiable responsibilities for an adult relative, and fewer than half ($n = 12$) were caring for a relative over age 65. Table 9.21 presents the adult-care status of the TV characters in the sample.

Although 26 characters (3% of total sample) were identified as care-givers for an adult relative, just 7 of those (2 males, 5 females) were shown

TABLE 9.21
Adult-Care Status of Adult TV Characters by Gender

	Male		Female		Total	
Adult-Care Status	Number	Percent	Number	Percent	Number	Percent
Caregiver for elder parent	7	1.4%	3	1%	10	1.2%
Caregiver for elder in-law	2	0.4%			2	0.2%
Caregiver for adult sibling	5	1%	2	1%	7	1%
Caregiver for spouse			2	1%	2	0.2%
Caregiver for other adult relative	2	0.4%	3	1%	5	0.6%
No adults identified as needing care	492	96.8%	302	96%	794	96.8%
Total	508	100	312	100	820	100%

TABLE 9.22
Adult-Care Activities Performed by Gender of Character

Adult-Care Activity	Male	Female
Arranging schedule for relative	0	3
Driving relative	1	2
Preparing food/feeding relative	0	3
Administering medication	0	3
Helping relative to bed	1	2
Paying bills for relative	0	2
Helping relative with personal care (e.g., bathing, brushing hair)	0	1
Helping relative dress	0	1
Shopping for relative	0	1
Assisting relative with therapy	0	1
Total*	2	19

* Total adds to more than 7 because some characters performed more than one type of activity.

performing any adult-care activities. The females performed an average of four adult-care activities, whereas the males performed an average of one adult-care activity. Table 9.22 presents the frequency of adult-care activities for the characters in the sample.

One male character was shown driving an adult relative (Bailey on *Party of Five* drives his older brother, Charlie, who has leukemia) and one male character helped his elder father to bed (Frank Donovan on *Brooklyn South* visits his elder father in the hospital after surgery and helps him get out of bed).

Female characters were shown performing a range of adult-care activities. For example:

To Live Again (made-for-TV movie, CBS): Iris Sayer, a retired social worker becomes the guardian of an emotionally disabled woman who needs assistance eating, dressing, and doing other basic tasks.

Touched by an Angel (CBS): A terminally ill man in his 40s is cared for at home by his wife.

The Long Way Home (made-for-TV movie, CBS): Bonnie Gerrin cares for her retired father-in-law.

CONCLUSIONS

The world presented in prime-time entertainment programming is one in which work and family rarely come into contact, in which children—and their activities and care—are managed easily and mostly off-screen, and in which older adults are virtually nonexistent. It is a world heavily populated by single working adults with virtually no family responsibilities.

This world is in sharp contrast to the one many American adults face daily. Although TV entertainment is not expected to be an accurate reflection of the society in which it operates, it can send messages to viewers about the relative importance of different occupations, lifestyles, and activities in our culture. Those images and messages that viewers see repeatedly often get perceived as reflective of the real world. Similarly, those images and messages that are excluded can influence viewers to perceive these as less important and/or representative of the real world. Although entertainment television is not designed primarily to educate, one of the outcomes of viewing is social learning. Viewers around the world use television content—both informational and entertainment—to form perceptions about their worlds and to learn how to act in it.

In this way, television's representation of work and family as separate spheres that rarely intersect is not only a misrepresentation of the lives of most American adults, but it can send powerful messages to viewers struggling with these collisions, and to their employers and colleagues. Showing conflicts as primarily family-initiated for men and work-initiated for women reinforces traditional stereotypes that link men with work and women with family. Furthermore, showing conflicts as easily resolved without any involvement from employers can send the message that such conflicts are the sole responsibility of the employee and need not cause much concern, because they are so easily resolved.

Prime-time representations of child care giving shows a more egalitarian pattern than representations of adult care giving. Both types of care-giving activities are very infrequently portrayed, but when child care giving is shown, it is as likely to be performed by a man as a woman. Adult care giving, on the other hand, seems to be almost exclusively the domain of female adults. Showing male adults engaged in childrearing can provide valuable role models for fathers in the viewing audience. Conversely, the invisibility of adult care responsibilities can signal that this situation is uncommon or unimportant in the lives of many adults.

Television entertainment has never been a cultural trendsetter; rather, it lags behind in its representation of social change. Yet, other content analyses have shown that television entertainment has changed over time to reflect societal shifts in family lifestyles, women's and men's participation in the workforce, and women's and men's roles in the family. As issues of work and family continue to be paramount for U.S. adults, it is likely they will become more common in the world of TV adults as well. Such inclusion can provide opportunities for the viewing audience to more readily understand the nature of this balancing act, and to identify with and learn from the experiences of their TV counterparts.

ACKNOWLEDGMENTS

This project was made possible by a grant from the National Partnership for Women and Families, Washington, D.C. Many thanks go to University of Washington graduate students who worked on the coding and data entry phases of the project: Aaron Delwiche, Kristin Engstrand, Hilary Karasz-Dominguez, and Meredith Li-Vollmer. The author also thanks Lauren Asher, Communications Director for the National Partnership for Women and Families, for her insights and comments on earlier drafts of this chapter.

REFERENCES

Bandura, A. (1994). Social cognitive theory of mass communication. In J. Bryant & D. Zillmann (Eds.), *Media effects: Advances in theory and research* (pp. 61–90). Hillsdale, NJ: Lawrence Erlbaum Associates.

Bond, J. T., Galinsky, E., & Swanberg, J. E. (1998). *1997 National study of the changing workforce*. Families and Work Institute, New York.

Collins, G. (1994, September). A woman's work is never shown. *Working Woman, 19*(9), 102.

Dail, P., & Way, W. (1985). What do parents observe about parenting from prime-time television. *Family Relations, 34*, 491–499.

Davis, D. (1990). Portrayals of women in prime-time network television: Some demographic characteristics. *Sex Roles, 23*(5/6), 325–332.

Feshbach, N., Dillman, A., & Jordan, T. (1979). Portrait of a female on television: Some possible effects on children. In C. B. Kopp (Ed.), *Becoming female: Perspectives on development* (pp. 363–385). New York: Plenum.

Gerbner, G., Gross, L., Morgan, M., & Signorielli, N. (1994). Growing up with television: The cultivation perspective. In J. Bryant & D. Zillmann (Eds.), *Media effects: Advances in theory and research* (pp. 17–42). Hillsdale, NJ: Lawrence Erlbaum Associates.

Heintz, K. (1992). *Children, television, and families: A content analysis of prime-time family programs and an examination of the influence of children's family structure on their perceptions of TV and real families.* Unpublished Doctoral Dissertation, University of Illinois at Urbana-Champaign.

Huston, A., Donnerstein, E., Fairchild, H., Feshbach, N., Katz, P., Murray, J., Rubinstein, E., Wilcox, B., & Zuckerman, D. (1992). *Big world, small screen.* Lincoln: University of Nebraska Press.

Meehan, D. (1988). The strong–soft woman: Manifestations of the androgyne in popular media. In SQ Oskamp, (Ed.), *Applied social psychology annual: Television as a social issue* (pp. 103–122). Newbury Park, CA: Sage.

Pope, K., & Cauley, L. (1998, May 6). In battle for TV ads, cable is now the enemy. *The Wall Street Journal.* p. B1.

Press, A., & Strathman, T. (1994). Work, family, and social class in television images of women: Prime-time television and the construction of postfeminism. *Women and Language, 16*(2), 7–15.

U.S. Department of Labor. (1996). *Employment characteristics of families.* Washington, DC: Bureau of Labor Statistics.

APPENDIX A: PROGRAM LIST

The following list includes all programs for which one or more episodes were analyzed.

Program Title	Network	Program Title	Network
Ally McBeal	FOX	King of the Hill	FOX
Alright Already	WB	Law and Order	NBC
Beverly Hills, 90210	FOX	Mad About You	NBC
Boy Meets World	ABC	Magnificent Seven	CBS
Brooklyn South	CBS	Malcolm and Eddie	UPN
Buffy the Vampire Slayer	WB	Melrose Place	FOX
Caroline in the City	NBC	Michael Hayes	CBS
Chicago Hope	CBS	Millennium	FOX
Clueless	UPN	Moesha	UPN
Cosby	CBS	Nash Bridges	CBS
Cybill	CBS	New York Undercover	FOX
Dawson's Creek	WB	NewsRadio	NBC
Dharma and Greg	ABC	Nick Freno	WB
Diagnosis Murder	CBS	Nothing Sacred	ABC
Dr. Quinn, Medicine		NYPD Blue	ABC
Woman	CBS	One Hot Summer Night	ABC
Drew Carey Show	ABC	Parent 'Hood	WB
e.r.	NBC	Party of Five	FOX
Earth: Final Conflict	WB	Players	NBC
Ellen	ABC	Police Academy: Series	WB
Everybody Loves		Pretender	NBC
Raymond	CBS	Prey	ABC
Four Corners	CBS	Profiler	NBC
Frasier	NBC	Promised Land	CBS
Friends	NBC	Sabrina, Teenage Witch	ABC
George and Leo	CBS	Seinfeld	NBC
Goldrush	ABC	Sentinel	WB
Good News	UPN	Seventh Heaven	WB
Hiller and Diller	ABC	Significant Others	FOX
Home Improvement	ABC	Silencing Mary	NBC
Homicide: Life on Street	NBC	Simpson's	FOX
House Rules	NBC	Sister, Sister	WB
In the House	UPN	Sleepwalkers	NBC
JAG	CBS	Smart Guy	WB
Jamie Foxx Show	WB	Something So Right	ABC
Just Shoot Me	NBC	Sparks	UPN

Program Title	Network	Program Title	Network
Spin City	ABC	To Live Again	CBS
Star Trek: Voyager	UPN	Tom Show	WB
Steve Harvey Show	WB	Touched by an Angel	CBS
Suddenly Susan	NBC	Two Guys, a Girl, and a	
That's Life	ABC	Pizza Place	ABC
The Closer	CBS	Unhappily Ever After	WB
The Long Way Home	CBS	Veronica's Closet	NBC
The Naked Truth	NBC	Walker, Texas Ranger	CBS
The Nanny	CBS	Wayans Brothers	WB
The Practice	ABC	X-Files	FOX
Third Rock From the Sun	NBC	The Young and the	
Three	WB	Restless	CBS

APPENDIX B: NETWORK AND GENRE INFORMATION

This appendix provides information about the distribution of characters
and conflicts across program genres and networks. The first set of tables
(B1–B10) refers to the entire set of characters coded ($n = 820$). The second set of tables (B11–B18) refers to the set of characters identified as
parents of dependent children ($n = 123$). The final set (B19–B20) refers
to the set of conflicts identified ($n = 36$).

TABLE B1
Gender of Characters by Program Genre

Gender	Situation Comedy	Drama	Made-for-TV Movie	Total
Male	183	299	26	508
Female	126	171	15	312
Total	309	470	41	820

TABLE B2
Gender of Characters by Network

Gender	ABC	CBS	NBC	FOX	WB	UPN	Total
Male	98	142	126	45	64	33	508
Female	60	78	90	31	38	15	312
Total	158	220	216	76	102	48	820

TABLE B3
Marital Status of Characters by Program Genre

Marital Status	Situation Comedy	Drama	Made-For-TV Movie	Total
Single	164	164	22	350
Married	61	85	5	151
Don't Know/Can't Tell	84	221	14	319
Total	309	470	41	820

TABLE B4
Marital Status of Characters by Network

Marital Status	ABC	CBS	NBC	FOX	WB	UPN	Total
Single	62	97	80	43	39	29	350
Married	33	42	34	11	26	5	151
Don't Know/Can't Tell	63	81	102	22	37	14	319
Total	158	220	216	76	102	48	820

TABLE B5
Parental Status of Characters by Program Genre

Parental Status	Situation Comedy	Drama	Made-For-TV Movie	Total
Custodial parent/legal guardian	55	59	1	115
Non-custodial parent	6	4	-	10
Non-custodial grandparent	3	-	-	3
Parent of adult children	22	26	8	56
Non-parent	70	76	16	162
Don't Know/Can't Tell	153	305	16	474
Total	309	470	41	820

TABLE B6
Parental Status of Characters by Network

Parental Status	ABC	CBS	NBC	FOX	WB	UPN	Total
Custodial parent/legal guardian	22	30	21	12	22	8	115
Non-custodial parent	2	3	2	-	3	-	10
Non-custodial grandparent	-	1	1	1	-	-	3
Parent of adult children	12	26	11	1	3	3	56
Non-parent	36	36	31	28	19	12	162
Don't Know/Can't Tell	86	124	150	34	55	25	474
Total	158	220	216	76	102	48	820

TABLE B7
Occupational Status of Characters by Program Genre

Occupational Status	Situation Comedy	Drama	Made-For-TV Movie	Total
Working Full Time	211	342	24	577
Working Part Time	5	-	-	5
Unemployed	11	16	2	29
Retired	9	8	3	20
Student	7	4	6	17
Homemaker	7	4	-	11
Don't Know/Can't Tell	59	96	6	161
Total	309	470	41	820

TABLE B8
Occupational Status of Characters by Network

Occupational Status	ABC	CBS	NBC	FOX	WB	UPN	Total
Working Full Time	107	135	166	62	70	37	577
Working Part Time	1	2	1	1	-	-	5
Unemployed	6	10	6	1	4	2	29
Retired	7	8	3	1	-	1	20
Student	5	4	6	1	-	1	17
Homemaker	2	5	2	1	1	-	11
Don't Know/Can't Tell	30	56	32	9	27	7	161
Total	158	220	216	76	102	48	820

TABLE B9
Adult Care Status of Characters by Program Genre

Adult Care Status	Situation Comedy	Drama	Made-for-TV Movie	Total
Caregiver for elder parent	3	4	3	10
Caregiver for elder in-law	1	1	-	2
Caregiver for adult sibling	4	3	-	7
Caregiver for spouse	-	2	-	2
Caregiver for other adult relative	4	-	1	5
No adults identified as needing care	281	460	37	794
Total	309	470	41	820

TABLE B10
Adult Care Status of Characters by Network

Adult Care Status	ABC	CBS	NBC	FOX	WB	UPN	Total
Caregiver for elder parent	1	4	4	1	-	-	10
Caregiver for elder in-law	1	1	-	-	-	-	2
Caregiver for adult sibling	-	-	3	4	-	-	7
Caregiver for spouse	-	1	1	-	-	-	2
Caregiver for other adult relative	-	1	-	1	3	-	5
No adults identified as needing care	156	213	208	70	99	48	794
Total	158	220	216	76	102	48	820

Parents Only

The following tables include only the characters identified as parents or legal guardians of dependent children (*n*=123).

TABLE B11
Gender of TV Parents by Program Genre

Gender	Situation Comedy	Drama	Made-for-TV Movie	Total
Male	61	33	-	64
Female	24	34	1	59
Total	55	67	1	123

TABLE B12
Gender of TV Parents by Program Genre

Gender	ABC	CBS	NBC	FOX	WB	UPN	Total
Male	12	17	12	6	13	4	64
Female	12	15	11	7	10	4	59
Total	24	32	23	13	23	8	123

TABLE B13
Marital Status of TV Parents by Program Genre

Marital Status	Situation Comedy	Drama	Made-For-TV Movie	Total
Single	19	16	1	36
Married	32	44	-	76
Don't Know/Can't Tell	4	7	-	11
Total	55	67	1	123

TABLE B14
Marital Status of TV Parents by Network

Marital Status	ABC	CBS	NBC	FOX	WB	UPN	Total
Single	55	8	7	7	6	3	36
Married	19	23	10	6	16	2	76
Don't Know/Can't Tell	-	1	6	-	1	3	11
Total	24	32	23	13	2	8	123

TABLE B15
Occupational Status of TV Mothers by Program Genre

Occupational Status	Situation Comedy	Drama	Made-For-TV Movie	Total
Working Full Time	3	16	-	19
Working Part Time	1	-	-	1
Unemployed	1	2	-	3
Retired	1	-	1	2
Student	1	-	-	1
Homemaker	4	2	-	6
Don't Know/Can't Tell	13	14	-	27
Total	24	34	1	59

TABLE B16
Occupational Status of TV Fathers by Program Genre

Occupational Status	Situation Comedy	Drama	Made-For-TV Movie	Total
Working Full Time	24	27	-	51
Unemployed	-	1	-	1
Retired	-	1	-	1
Don't Know/Can't Tell	7	4	-	11
Total	31	33	-	64

TABLE B17
Occupational Status of TV Mothers by Network

Occupational Status	ABC	CBS	NBC	FOX	WB	UPN	Total
Working Full Time	3	6	4	3	2	1	19
Working Part Time	-	-	-	1	-	-	1
Unemployed	-	1	-	1	-	1	3
Retired	1	1	-	-	-	-	2
Student	1	-	-	-	-	-	1
Homemaker	1	2	1	1	1	-	6
Don't Know/Can't Tell	6	5	6	1	7	2	27
Total	12	15	11	7	10	4	59

TABLE B18
Occupational Status of TV Fathers by Network

Occupational Status	ABC	CBS	NBC	FOX	WB	UPN	Total
Working Full Time	9	15	10	5	8	4	51
Unemployed	-	1	-	-	-	-	1
Retired	-	-	1	-	-	-	1
Don't Know/Can't Tell	3	1	1	1	5	-	11
Total	12	17	12	6	13	4	64

TABLE B19
Work-Family Conflicts by Network

Type of Conflict	Situation Comedy	Drama	Made-for-TV-Movie	Total
Potential Conflict	4	16	-	20
Recognized Conflict	5	11	-	16
Total	9	27	-	36

TABLE B20
Work-Family Conflicts by Program Genre

Type of Conflict	ABC	CBS	NBC	FOX	WB	UPN	Total
Potential Conflict	2	4	12	-	2	-	20
Recognized Conflict	2	5	3	1	3	2	16
Total	4	9	15	1	5	2	36

Portrayals of Families
of Color on Television

Jannette L. Dates
Carolyn A. Stroman
Howard University

Works from the mid- to late 1990s (e.g., Hill, 1998; McCubbin, 1998; Zambrana, 1995) attest to scholars' enduring interest in the family and the diversity of family life in America. Likewise, earlier works by Greenberg and Atkin (1978), Greenberg and Neuendorf (1980), Cummings (1986), Sweeper (1987), Dates (1993), and Merritt and Stroman (1993) are indicative of communication scholars' continual interest in television families.

A number of theories (e.g., social learning theory, cultivation theory, expectancy theory) undergird scholars' long-standing interest in televised families. Emanating from these theories is the proposition that frequent exposure to distorted televised images of families may result in viewers' distorted perceptions of families reflecting those portrayed on television rather than those in real life. The implications of this proposition is captured in the assertion that family interactions on television are an "important class of environmental stimuli available for attitude formation and change and for behavioral modeling by a child" (Greenberg, Hines, Buerkel-Rothfuss, & Atkin, 1980, p. 150).

The notion that televised family portrayals are a source of socialization is intuitively appealing. Television teaches us about us, as we talk about ourselves. As we tell our stories to each other, we gain a better

understanding of our past, present, and future. For this reason, it is important that the stories reflect multiple perspectives from those inside and
outside of cultural, racial, and ethnic groups.

The experiences of people of color in U. S. society differ from White
America's experiences because prejudice and discrimination have profoundly affected almost all people of color. Therefore, it is reasonable to
expect television programs about people of color to reflect aspects of
those unique experiences, including the needs, interests, concerns, or
perspectives written by, for, or about the group. In fact, however, the
mainstream values and beliefs of people of color seen on prime-time
commercial television have not revealed unique African, Latino, Native
or Asian American experiences, but rather the stories and perceptions
of White producers, sponsors, writers, and owners.

The current study examines and analyzes dramatic and comedic prime-
time television family programs as we interpreted the stories about
African, Latino, Native and Asian Americans. Recognizing that the experiences of ethnic groups are varied and unique, we chose to focus, for
expediency sake,on one group—African Americans. Using Gerbner's (as
cited in Jensen, 1998) building blocks concept of storytelling, we examined the "casting and fate" of African American television family programs
to focus on the social roles and messages that emerged. We examined
these programs, asking questions such as the following: Who does what
to whom? Who is powerful, successful, in control of whom? Who are the
victims or victimizers? What are the messages being conveyed? Who are
the targeted viewers? How are they courted? Is there a recognizable pattern of casting and fate in the messages conveyed in the stories about
African Americans?

We focused on conventional and nonconventional African American
families portrayed on fictional, weekly, entertainment television programs. A conventional African American television family is an African
American family with or without children. It could also be a family made
up of a single parent, be she or he divorced, widowed, or separated, with
children. A nonconventional African American television family is one
made up of nonfamilial African American adults who share a domicile.

We examined original airings of series that fit this definition, that aired
between the 1950–1951 and 1998–1999 seasons on NBC, CBS, ABC, Fox,
WB, and UPN. A comprehensive listing of the programs that fit the criteria is found in Appendix A.

In order to provide as complete a picture as possible, this chapter
considers a number of issues related to how people of color and their
families are portrayed on television. We gathered historical, qualitative,
and quantitative data, and divided the chapter into four main sections.
The first section provides an historical context for the discussion to fol-

low. In the second section, we critically analyze how people of color have been portrayed from the 1950s through the end of the 20th century. In the third section, we review the literature on the portrayal of people of color and their families. The final section contains a research agenda that suggests issues and questions warranting consideration in future research.

HISTORICAL ANALYSIS

Between 1950 and 1990, television as a broadcasting phenomenon offered a common shared experience for America's television viewers. Media decision makers sought the largest possible number of viewers from the "mainstream" of society. This changed after the early 1990s. Then, networks targeted television programming toward "segments" of the American viewing public. This change affected African American and other family shows from traditionally underrepresented groups.

Before this segmenting, *Roots* (1970s) and *The Cosby Show* (1980–1990s) were the African American family programs that many believed would finally usher in a new era of television where more family programs would air, based on a variety of African American experiences and culture, and that would appeal to a broad audience of viewers from all segments of society. Like *Roots* a dramatic family miniseries, *The Cosby Show* a weekly, family comedy, achieved extraordinary success, excellent ratings, and critical acclaim. But neither of the two series was able to generate the "goodwill" among decision makers to carry African American family programming to the next level of acceptance by mainstream viewers and more importantly, by the decision makers who decide to air or not to air more shows with similar themes and characterizations.

Usually, programs with the "reach and pull" to bring in the types of viewers advertisers most covet spawn other programs like them that are granted strong support. But, after the success of *Roots,* even the paired genius of Alex Haley and Norman Lear could not convince decision makers to give weekly African American dramatic family series, such as *Palmerstown, USA* and *Frank's Place,* a chance to succeed. And even the success of *The Cosby Show* could not create an atmosphere where African American family shows such as *South Central* and *The Gregory Hines Show* were given a chance to find their audiences—as mainstream targeted programs were consistently allowed to do.[1]

Beginning in the 1990s, the segmenting of the American viewing audience yielded a targeted viewership that placed a predominant number of African American family shows—aimed at African American audiences—

---

[1] Mainstream programs that had been given this latitude include *Northern Exposure* and *Cheers.*

on a few specific networks. The Fox network pioneered the trend of targeting African American viewers, who had been consistently neglected by the big three networks. Then Warner Brothers (WB) followed, with United Paramount Network (UPN) jumping in later. Targeting African American viewers was a short-lived programming strategy. By the 1998 to 1999 television season, each of the three newest networks had begun to shift their targeted programming from African American viewers to mainstream viewers. The big three networks (NBC, ABC, CBS) continued all along to cater to mainstream tastes that they argued responded to African American music, culture, and ethnic nuances to sell products, but responded mainly to White faces on programs.

Producers did little to attract "outsiders" to programs that appeared to be designed for appeal within the group. As a result, an African American television "ghetto" emerged where nearly all the African American family shows were placed. In 1997, Los Angeles Times critic Greg Braxton (1997) observed that

> the 1990s' biggest hit television series depicted voluntary segregation. In the top rated shows by White viewers the core casts (*Mad About You, Friends, Ellen, Murphy Brown, Frasier, Seinfeld, Caroline in the City, Cybill, Life's Work,* and *Wings*) and several other comedies are exclusively White, while in the top rated shows by Black viewers (*Family Matters, Martin, Living Single, Sparks, Malcolm and Eddie, In the House, The Wayans Brothers, The Jamie Foxx Show*) the core casts are almost exclusively Black (p. F-1).

This is partially explained because, until the mid-1970s, very few African American family dramas or comedies had aired. Twenty years later, a multiplicity of types of African American characters and programs were resonating well with African American viewers.

For nearly 10 years (1990–1998), African American viewers had a distinctly different top network program favorites list from that of White viewers. Top favorites for White and African American viewers had increasingly differed, from 1990 until the fall 1998 season, when CBS was the top rated network among both White and African American viewers. African American viewers' former favorite (UPN) in 1997 plummeted to last place in 1998. As late as 1996, African Americans White viewers had shared only *Monday Night Football* across their top 20 lists; but in the 1998 fall season, they shared six favorites; *ER, 60 Minutes, Monday Night Football, Touched by an Angel, NYPD Blue* and CBS's Sunday Movie (de Mornes, 1999).

By 1998, activists and African American professionals managed to topple some political and social barriers, and a moderate amount of significant gains had been made by African Americans in some areas of television. More African Americans were seen on network broadcast and cablecast television entertainment programs, and as anchors and reporters for the news (local and national). People of color served as presidents, vice presidents, directors, and more of the major production houses and networks.

Yet, the decision makers in the industry were still 95 to 98% White and male. And with this power concentrated in the hands of "people like us" (PLUs as they were coined), views and perspectives of those who were not White or male often did not "make the cut." In 1996, *People* magazine conducted a 4-month study of this issue (Lambert, 1996). They argued that although African Americans made up 12% of the U.S. population and 25% of the moviegoing audience, they were not represented in Academy Award nominations or among those who chose Oscar awardees; nor were they found in representative numbers among the Directors Guild membership. With Hollywood as the primary locale where films and television programs were produced by many of the same White, male producers, directors, and writers, People viewed this identified underrepresentations of African American decision makers as a major barrier to balanced programming about and targeted to people of color.

Regardless of their racial or ethnic origins, however, the writers and producers usually followed the patterns set by those who came before them and who most often surrounded them—or they were not allowed into the game at all. With some rare exceptions, when a few African American creative types were brought into the mix, they were rendered powerless to make substantive changes from the status quo or to create different images and messages that might resonate as more authentic or give a different perspective than that seen before.

CRITICAL ANALYSES

Dramas

The 50 years of commercial television's depictions of America's symbolic images included people of color mainly in comedic, not dramatic, offerings. Consistently, African Americans were cast in stories designed to make people laugh—not to think seriously about issues. Most weekly African American family dramas aired a few per year—usually staying on for less than a year—or as sidebar stories in ensemble series. Latinos, and Asian and Native Americans were rarely depicted at all as central characters in dramatic programs.

From the early years to the most current television offerings of serious dramatic programming, African American talents have most often been showcased on occasional specials and miniseries (*Roots, A Woman Called Moses, The Women of Brewster Place, The Jacksons, The Piano Lesson, Queen, There Are No Children Here*), as adjunct themes to a mainstream storyline within a series (*Baretta, Mod Squad, Dynasty, St. Elsewhere, ER*), or in daytime serials (*All My Children, One Life to Live*).

Thus, in 50 years, only 30 weekly dramatic programs were shown on television that featured African Americans, carried an African American focus to viewers and had significant impact or received critical acclaim. Twenty of the 30 dramas were family shows. Of these family shows, 10 aired for a year or less, while the others aired as follow:

2 dramas aired for 2 years (*I'll Fly Away, New York Undercover*)

2 dramas aired for 3 years (*Roc, 21 Jump Street*)

1 drama aired for 4 years or more (*ER*)

3 dramas aired for 5 years or more (*Fame, NYPD Blue, Homicide*)

2 dramas aired for 6 years (*St. Elsewhere, In the Heat of the Night*)

From this group, we briefly examine shows that were short lived and ones that had a long run. *Frank's Place* aired less than a year, whereas *Roc* lasted 2 years on the air, and *In the Heat of the Night* lasted 6 years on the air. Each of these shows had high viewership and explored topics of great significance to African Americans.

In the Fall of 1987 when *Frank's Place* began airing, Tim Reid and Hugh Wilson were fulfilling their dream of presenting to the American public a weekly network series focused on culturally grounded African American story lines and addressing diverse interests and concerns of the group. They used authentic folklore and story ideas to produce "dramedy"—part comedy and part drama. Reid particularly wanted to tell stories about being African American in America from the African American perspective.

With its vignettes about African American New Orleans, each week *Frank's Place* unveiled themes to help viewers understand the characters— their motivations, concerns, weaknesses, and strengths. Revealed within the context of evolving tales, there were victims and victimizers, heroes and cowards in carefully crafted plots that addressed the human condition through the eyes of African Americans. The richness that the series brought to American audiences was unprecedented in its authentic dramas about Black America then and remains so—with few exceptions— even today.

Within a few weeks of the premiere, *Frank's Place* was moved about on the CBS schedule. Despite glowing reviews about its high quality from the beginning, the series was not promoted or strongly marketed and remained in limbo while its creators contended with persistent rumors that the program would fail.

In the series, the messages conveyed in recurring themes were that: (1) African Americans people have developed strategies to survive and thrive in a hostile environment where their intelligence, skills, and talents created a world in which they had a measure of control of their lives; (2) they used these skills as they interacted with each other and outsiders to the culture to help meet their needs; (3) they did not see themselves as powerless victims, despite the prejudice toward the group; and (4) their fate lay in their own hands when they seized and wielded the available power.

With Tim Reid cast as "the fish out of water" in a city that was foreign to him, *Frank's Place* reflected the languor of New Orleans—its flavor, mood, and tone. Its mixture of characters with colorful names (Shorty LaRoux, Big Arthur, Tiger, and The Right Reverend Tyrone Deal) was among the 11 regular members of the ensemble group. *Frank's Place* did not focus on the extremes in society (super people or pimps and hookers) but on people in the middle of the continuum of humankind. The honest characterizations included respect for older people, respect for different spiritual experiences, and respect for Whites and African Americans. No racial or sitcom stereotypes cropped up in the program. Developed with smart crispness, the characters seemed to reflect a slice of life—as daring sociological and racial points were made with subtlety.

Like *Frank's Place,* the series *Roc* addressed many issues of serious concern to those in the African American community. And like *Frank's Place, Roc* was a dramedy. Often, audiences had to "reach" to discern whether the segment was playing for laughs or for tears. Award-winning Broadway actor Charles Dutton played Roc, with an ensemble group brought in from the highly regarded and highly successful August Wilson plays, "The Piano Lesson" and "Ma Rainey's Black Bottom." The series appealed to Dutton because it allowed him to reach, teach, and preach. Although created and written (Stan Daniels) and directed (James Burrows) by White men as an HBO independent production that aired weekly on Fox, Dutton could exert creative control to focus, with sensitivity, on issues that were a part of his views of African American experiences.

The producers had Roc trying to intercede in his neighborhood when he saw problems. With some credibility, the show tried to teach viewers who were in similar situations how they might handle bullies, con artists, drug dealers, and other nefarious types—without endangering themselves. A tricky dilemma, at best.

Although Roc was a garbage man, his character was not portrayed as a hapless victim of society. Admittedly poor, he and his wife (a nurse) had values that kept them proudly in control of their own fate. Roc consistently vied with his younger brother about the brother's behaviors that crossed over into lawlessness from time to time.

The series was typical of other sitcoms on commercial television—usually with predictable plots and themes, but the African American family setting allowed for different nuances. After just 2 years, as the series wound down to go off the air, it became preachy, losing its predominantly African American audience to the faster paced raucousness of other comedies of the day. Still, to their credit, it was an attempt by HBO and Fox to offer viewers a more balanced representation of the African American experience, at least for a while.

During the 1988–1989 season, four African American-focused dramatic programs premiered. Only one was scheduled for a second season, *In the Heat of the Night*. This had been a successful film of 1967, starring Sidney Poitier as Virgil Tibbs, a Philadelphia homicide detective, and Rod Steiger as Chief of Police William Gillespie. Set in the town of Sparta, Mississippi, the movie allowed Gillespie and returning city-son, Tibbs to slowly work out their differences about racial issues and moral rights and wrongs. In the television series, with Howard Rollins as a thoughtful, consistent, but less commanding Tibbs, and Carroll O'Connor as a softened Gillespie, the protagonists resolved their differences within the allotted 60 minutes each week, with varying degrees of credibility. During the first season, O'Connor had a heart attack and Rollins had to carry much of the weight of each episode. The series maintained steady high ratings and was usually found among the top 20 programs each week. O'Connor returned in good health in the 1989–1990 season and the series had a good run for 5 more years. Rollins' strength in pulling in viewers while the recuperating O'Connor held a lesser role, was an important but unheralded milestone in network television. Rarely in its 40-year history had African Americans and their issues been addressed in a serious framework with a strong, African American male lead—and with viewers watching in large numbers.

In the Heat of the Night conveyed messages to viewers about civil rights, human rights, the terrible cost of prejudice and discrimination, generational conflicts, male/female conflicts, age conflicts, as well as a theme about human beings being drawn to each other across the racial divide because of a growing respect, a physical attraction, human concern, and more. Most significantly, in the series, African American issues and concerns as the focus of attention revealed African American perspectives with a sensitivity that was as noteworthy as it was largely unnoticed by media watchers, critics, and viewers alike. As African American and White viewers continued to support the show over a 6-year period, few took note of this milestone in American television history.

COMEDIES

Comedies can tell stories that have serious messages. Unfortunately, from the early years of television to the present, many comedies involving African Americans did not base their humor on honesty and respect but rather on demeaning caricatures that borrowed heavily from the minstrel show tradition. Many who produced or starred in some comedies failed to understand how the characters they portrayed became a permanent, damaging part of the American popular culture that was transmitted around the world.

Although these stereotypes restricted the way African Americans perceived themselves, within the American culture, they further encouraged other Americans and the world to see African American people as extremes and not as real people. And the perception of African Americans as frivolous, menial, foolhardy, or unworthy helped move other Americans to retreat on racial fairness issues.

Of the 70 African American comedies that aired after 1950 that carried an African American focus, had significant impact, or received critical acclaim, 60 of them can be categorized as family shows. Twenty-four of the family comedies aired for a year or less (see Appendix A). The other shows aired as follows:

6 aired for 2 years	0 aired for 7 years
12 aired for 3 years	1 aired for 8 years
4 aired for 4 years	1 aired for 9 years
9 aired for 5 years	1 aired for 10 years
2 aired for 6 years	

Of this group, we analyzed shows that had modest and long on-air lives. *Martin* aired for 4 years, *Family Matters* for 9 years, and *Fresh Prince of Bel-Air* aired for 6 years. These shows were selected for analysis to reveal variations in comedic programming.

The series *Martin* (Fox) centered on the life of an African American talk show host played by standup comedian Martin Lawrence. In the series, the producers took risks with some outlandish slapstick humor, but in Lawrence they also introduced viewers to a skilled comedian, who dared expose the confusion and vulnerability many young African American men of the 1990s felt about their role in society. In addition to the lead male character, Lawrence took on other roles. He played the part of his own mother, a caricatured female neighbor, and a raucous, male neighborhood roustabout. The ensemble cast of (mostly) young actors gave Lawrence strong support. In its first few years, the series was most striking because of its focus on some of the compelling issues that young adults cared about. For one of the few times on network television, viewers saw a young African American couple who were in a serious, committed relationship, who had good jobs, and who went beyond the usual mainstream story lines to focus on problems and issues found in urban African American communities.

Still, the series left some things to be desired. It was often side-splittingly funny but tasteless and bawdy. In a recurrent theme, cast members were characterized as silly, powerless, and without control of their own emotions. Women and men engaged in fistfights; sometimes women pulled off their shoes and began to uncontrollably pummel each other, and men had to be separated before they landed a knock-out punch on a friend or acquaintance. Although some serious issues emerged (class, race, age, male/female domination), they were reduced to a slapstick comedic context. Therefore, the issues were easily dismissed by viewers.

With Topper Carew, an African American as executive producer, and Stan Lathan (another African American man) as director, the series had promise, because these veterans had extensive experience in producing quality programming. They should have been able to help the series escape the minstrelsy of other comedies, but they were less and less able to control the minstrellike, slapstick characterizations.

The recurring themes that the mainly African American viewers received from the series were mixed. For example, one message that was promulgated was that young adult African Americans had found a way to obtain an education and mainstream employment and move beyond the poverty of their youth. However, this message was countered with the image of African Americans as perpetually immature, insecure, and powerless.

The series *Family Matters* (ABC) stayed on the air for 9 years. What factors made it the second longest running African American family television comedy series in history, after *The Jeffersons,* which aired for 10 years? The two shows have some similarities that made them attractive to mainstream and African American viewers alike. They each used miscommunication between family members or friends and innocuous plots that were silly escapist fare. The only factor that differentiated these series from other mainstream silly plots lay in the fact that the casts were predominantly African American. Often for a Black history month segment, there was a story line that focused on the need for more inclusiveness and less racial prejudice, but that was the exception. Usually, *Family Matters* focused attention on plots such as Steve Urkel staying with the Winslows for a period of time where he caused great confusion and problems for others, but in the end the right "family values" prevailed so that he could continue to be a frequent guest in their home and have numerous plots revolve around him.

While these two shows (*The Jeffersons* and *Family Matters*) probably did no real harm, the void that they could have helped to fill was left wanting. Some comedies teach and inspire within the contexts of their funny scripts.

The series *The Fresh Prince of Bel-Air* starred Will Smith as a breezy, nonconfrontational, charming, lovable teenager forced by his mother to go live with his rich uncle. The mother believed that the uncle and his family would help to straighten the youngster out.

Distinctive because it marked the first time a rap/hip-hop star was seen on weekly television, the series used tried and true plots and story lines revolving around Smith as a fish out of water. "Clash of cultures" issues, African American class distinctions, generated conflicts, sibling rivalry, and gender clashes evolved as the show's plots. Power plays between Will and Uncle Phil, and Will and cousin Carlton were also typical fare. African American and White viewers alike watched this escapist comedy, where few heavy messages were conveyed.

The mainstream series *MASH* taught something about human resiliency in times of great stress, about man's ability to rise above awful circumstances, and more. The *Dick Van Dyke Show, The Mary Tyler Moore Show, Coach, Cheers, Frasier,* and *The Cosby Show* each offered viewers compelling stories, with characters who were in control of their own fates, even if they sometimes lost control of their emotions. They addressed current events, political and social issues, and the characters grew and developed as human beings. More African American family comedies can rise to these levels, and in a unique, engaging, but funny way focus on some aspects of issues, concerns, or interests of those in their communities. When they fail to do so, then we have inaccurate, distorted representations, which are reflected to us weekly.

The foregoing critique represents our reading and interpretation of the stories conveyed about African American families in television presentations. What has empirical research revealed about the portrayals of people of color and their families? We focus on that question in the following section.

EMPIRICAL RESEARCH

In reviewing the literature about television and African Americans, Poindexter and Stroman (1981) listed four propositions that summarize the portrayals of African Americans from the 1950s to the end of the 1970s:

1. Historically, African Americans have been underrepresented in television portrayals.
2. There has been a trend toward increased visibility of African Americans on television.

3. African Americans are generally presented on television in minor roles and in low-status occupational roles.

4. Stereotyping and negative connotations of African Americans continue to be presented in television programs.

These propositions served as baseline data for later research; they have been supported numerous times in the literature.

Research on African American families and television provides some specificity for these propositions. For example, Berry (1980) characterized African American families on television as follows:

- Female-dominated households
- Conflictual family interactions
- Children not valued and loved

Research by Greenberg and Atkin (1978) supported these observations. Their examination of the families appearing on *What's Happening?, Sanford and Son, Good Times,* and so forth revealed that the African American mother is the dominant figure when critical family decisions are made.

In a longitudinal comparison of the roles, family structures, and interactive behavior of African American and White television families, Greenberg and Neuendorf (1980) also found conflictual relations between and among African American family members. In shows such as *That's My Mama* and *The Jeffersons,* African American sons were portrayed as being especially dominant, initiating much of the family interaction. Also, in contrast to African American families in real life, extended kinship was minimal, and role portrayals were centered on spouses, parents, children, and siblings.

In summarizing the portrayal of African Americans and their families during the period of 1969 to 1982, Stroman (1986) noted that few television shows featured a husband, wife, and children living together and few of them portrayed a lifestyle other than that of a poor struggling African American family. Images such as these support James Comer's (1982) observation that the impression often received from television is that African Americans cannot care for their families adequately, that they are not responsible, and that they are not competent.

Later research found a more palatable portrayal of African American families. Stroman, Merritt, and Matabane (1989–1990) and Dates (1993) found that African American characters were likely to appear in a situation comedy as a generally competent member of a middle-class, two-parent family. Similarly, Merritt and Stroman (1993) examined intact African American nuclear families on *The Cosby Show, 227,* and *Charlie & Co.* In their role-by-behavior description of verbal interaction among family members, Merritt and Stroman found that African American families on these shows were comprised of both a husband and a wife who interacted frequently, equally, and lovingly with each other, and who treated their children with respect and dignity. They interpreted this to mean that a more positive portrayal of African American families was emerging.

While some might argue that a more favorable portrayal of African Americans and their families has evolved, the same cannot be said for Latinos. Early research revealed propositions about Latinos that were similar to those about African Americans: They were underrepresented and when portrayed, they appeared in unflattering or stereotypical roles. In what may be the first systematic analysis of Hispanics on television, Greenberg and Baptista-Fernandez (1980, p. 11) provided the following qualitative analysis of Hispanic Americans:

- They're hard to find.
- They're gregarious and pleasant, with strong family ties.
- Half work hard, half are lazy, and very few show much concern for their futures.
- Most have very little education, and their jobs reflect that fact.

More recent research suggests that little has changed. As late as 1994, Latinos were represented in about 2% of the sampled television shows and the few characters that appeared were shown in low-status occupational roles. A 1996 report by the Center for Media and Public Affairs noted that their report card of the best and worst shows in portrayals of Latinos included:

FAVORABLE	UNFAVORABLE
ABC, *NYPD Blue*	CBS, *Walker, Texas Ranger*
Fox, *New York Undercover*	Synd., *Pointman*
NBC, *John Larroquette Show*	Synd., *Renegade*
UPN, *Star Trek, Voyager*	Synd., *Thunder in Paradise*
NBC, *Sea Quest DSV*	Synd., *Baywatch*

The unfavorably cited *Walker* and *Baywatch* shows were set in Texas and Southern California—where there were huge Latino populations—with almost no Latinos in continuing roles (Braxton, 1996). The latest research (Dixon, 1998) reported that Latinos continue to be underrepresented and are more likely than Whites to be portrayed as lawbreakers.

Tan, Fujiola, and Lucht (1997) suggest that televised portrayals of Native Americans reflect some of the same characteristics as those of

African Americans and Latinos. In addition to being shown infrequently, Native Americans are portrayed as alcoholics and poor. Also, the portrayals give the impression that although Native Americans are family-oriented, their families are dysfunctional.

Iiyama and Kitano (1982) spoke to the invisibility of Asian Americans when they noted that "Asian Americans are seldom seen, seldom heard, seldom felt on American television" (p. 151). When Asians are portrayed, it is in an unflattering manner. For example, in one of the few studies of its kind, Shu (1979) analyzed the portrayal of Chinese on television and found that in comparison to White characters, Chinese were more likely to be poor, teenage, and criminals.

In commenting on African American portrayals, Stroman et al. (1989–1990) observed that the casting of African American characters generally remains governed by many of the dominant myths about preferred social roles for African Americans. They wrote "Research identifying some of the demographic characteristics and role attributes associated with African-American television characters suggests a departure from reality in line with the defined social preferences of the television industry" (p. 46).

Dates (1993) argued that African American television images were distorted, as African American talents were exploited and as African Americans were systematically denied opportunities to act as full participants in the television industry. She observed that "What evolved were mass media that favored black stereotypes created by Whites over the more authentic and positive black characters by black image makers (p. 16).

The same thing can be said about the televised portrayals of people of color generally. The social realities of African Americans, Asian Americans, Native Americans, and Latinos families are still not portrayed accurately; rather, their portrayals reflect the myopic lens through which people of color are viewed by decision makers in the television industry.

A RESEARCH AGENDA

As the foregoing literature review reveals, there has been sustained interest in researching African American television families. However, the review also demonstrates that we need more research on televised families of color. Especially needed is research that focuses on Asian American, Native American, and Latino television families.

In providing suggestions for future research, it may be instructive to briefly review how researchers have quantitatively analyzed television content. Variables coded generally include two types of information; (a) characteristics of individual characters, and (b) characteristics of individual programs. Character attributes include demographic information such as age, gender, socioeconomic status, and occupation. Researchers also generally code the kind of role played by characters (major, supporting, or minor); whether the character was in a serious or comic role; and whether the character was a member of a family. Program attributes include the type of program (situation comedy, drama, or action-adventure) and the type of setting (home, work, and other).

As indicated earlier, much of the previous quantitative research has had a rather narrow demographic focus. As a result, little attention has been paid to the latent content of the shows. Therefore, future research should focus more attention on the latent content of shows featuring people of color, for example, investigations that explore the more subtle messages about and meanings of relationships and interactions in families of color.

Future research should be concerned with what people acquire from both fictional and nonfictional television content. Of particular relevance to African American and other families is the role of television in the formation of ideas about how families should operate or interact. We know very little, for example, about attitudes toward family life acquired from or reinforced by programs such as *Cosby*, *Living Single*, and *PJs*. An equally important question is what effect the lack of people of color in dramas has on the formation of perceptions about people of color and their families.

The notion that televised portrayals influence perceptions is paramount in the effects literature. However, little empirical research exists that clearly demonstrates the process by which the outcome variable occurs. Therefore, a great need in future research is the need to understand how people process family portrayals of people of color. Especially useful would be studies in which participants describe how they conceptualize and process television portrayals of African Americans. Recent research that may serve as a model for this type of research is work, which used reception analysis to obtain an understanding of the meanings that the African American situation comedy has for African Americans (Means, 1996; Coleman 1998). Similarly, a question posed by Greenberg and Brand (1994) may serve as a guide for future research: Do African Americans alter or shape their behavior toward Whites on the basis of anything they see on television and vice-versa? It would be highly appropriate to conduct such research developmentally, selecting cohorts of children, adolescents, and young adults, and the elderly for examination.

More critical analyses in the vein of Gandy's (1998) recent work are needed. Future research in this area should be guided by the premise that portrayals of African American families must be examined in the context of a number of variables, including audience characteristics and preferences, media ownership, technological advances, and market conditions (Gandy, 1998).

Past research suggested that the portrayals of African Americans in prime-time advertising have steadily increased over the years. How do these portrayals compare with portrayals in other programming venues? Future research may want to focus attention on televised portrayals of people of color in advertising.

Other relevant questions to be asked in future research include: Have increased portrayals changed perceptions of African Americans; has increased ownership by people of color changed their portrayals; and lastly, we must continue to wrestle with question of how to use the media to "socially construct" a society in which portrayals of families of color will no longer be an issue. Over a decade ago, Stroman, et al. (1989–1990) noted that questions pertaining to the role of television in the resolution of urban problems should be a starting point for future inquiries in this area. This is still timely advice.

Needless to say, a wide variety of approaches should be used in future research. In discussing various content analysis research designs, Stroman and Jones (1998) recommended more content analysis studies in which both quantitative and qualitative research are integrated. Clearly, multi-method approaches combining qualitative and quantitative techniques would be particularly appropriate for the study of televised families featuring people of color. Earlier, we recommended studies of how people process televised portrayals of African Americans. Such studies are particularly amedable to both qualitative and quantitative techniques.

More rigorous, sophisticated approaches to the conduct of content analyses are needed. Instead of conducting content analyses as outlined at the beginning of this portion of the chapter, communication researchers should move beyond existing ways of doing. Increasingly, they should incorporate the use of theory and hypothesis testing in their research designs. Conducting longitudinal research would also be useful.

Future content analyses should be conducted in conjunction with other research methodologies. For example, experiments and surveys on reactions to televised portrayals of people of color would be very insightful. Doswell's (1994) examination of White viewers' perceptions of African American television images and Rada's (1997) study of the effects of news portrayals are exemplars for future research combining content analysis with other methodologies.

Finally, we must emphasize the need for longitudinal studies that trace the consequences accruing to families of people of color as a result of repeated exposure to White-dominated media content; and perceptions of people of color and their families that are fostered in the minds of both people of color and White people as a result of the inclusion of people of color in television programming.

The proposed research agenda suggests areas that, if thoroughly studied, would contribute greatly to our understanding of the more subtle messages presented by television about people of color and their families. Furthermore, by conducting studies proposed herein communication scholars might begin to move toward a sustained, systematic research program that places analyses of portrayals of families of color in a context that ultimately affects both media policy and public policy.

SUMMARY

Diverse sociological perspectives on families of color provide us with varied interpretations of these families. These diverse sociological perspectives flow to and from the mass media. The question with which we were concerned was which of these perspectives or views flow from television to audiences. In order to address this question, we provided historical, qualitative, and empirical data that shed light on televised portrayals of people of color and their families.

Our analyses revealed that, in general, the majority of the images of families of color emerging from television are those of African Americans. Other families of color are relatively absent from television presentations.

In general, the portrayals of African American families can be characterized as having gone through several phases. Quantitatively, African American families have gone from seldom appearing to appearing at levels representative of their numbers in the population. Qualitatively, their portrayals have become more expansive to include a variety of family roles and structures, income levels, educational levels, and so forth.

Indeed, it can be argued that at times, the portrayals have been positive and worthy of being seen as role models for African American youth. However, portrayals of African Americans have never been static; instead, they have flowed and ebbed with the times. And while we have more images, they are not necessarily more accurate images. What is still missing after 50 years of portrayals is the emergence of a variety of images that is sustained over time.

During the 1970s and 1980s, it was quite popular for communication researchers to analyze televised portrayals of people of color, especially African Americans. However, this trend seems to have abated much too early. We still need information about portrayals of people of color. Furthermore, we need firm documentation of whether and how portrayals of people of color have affected both individual decisions and media policies. In fact, what is needed is a planned, theory driven approach to the study of the portrayals of people of color.

A research agenda has been provided that can be used as a starting point for research on the portrayal of families of color on television. The topics that could be researched are unlimited; so, too, are the theoretical frameworks and perspectives that could be used to guide research in this area. What is clear is that there is still more research to be conducted if we are ever to obtain a firm understanding of televised portrayals of people of color and their effects.

ACKNOWLEDGMENTS

Data for this chapter were collected with the assistance of Howard University graduate students Laura Dorsey, Cheryl Jenkins, and Rockell Brown.

REFERENCES

Berry, G. L. (1980). Television and Afro-Americans: Past legacy and present portrayals. In S. B. Withey & R. P. Abeles (Eds.), *Television and social behavior: Beyond violence and children* (pp. 231–248). Hillsdale, NJ: Lawrence Erlbaum Associates.

Braxton, G. (1996, April 16). Latinos on TV: Mixed findings. *The Los Angeles Times*, p. F1.

Braxton, G. (1997, January 27). Black and white TV: Though the casts of many dramatic series represent a racial mix, most sitcoms show little integration—A fact that has some observers troubled. The Los Angeles Times, p. F-1.

Coleman, R. R. M. (1998). *African American viewers and the Black situation comedy: Situating racial humor.* New York: Garland.

Comer, J. (1982). The importance of television images of Black families. In A W. Jackson (Ed.), *Black families and the medium of television*. Ann Arbor: Bush Program in Child Development and Social Policy, University of Michigan.

Cummings, M. S. (1986). The changing image of the Black family. *Journal of Popular Culture, 22* (2), 75–85.

Dates, J. L. (1993). Fly in the buttermilk. In J. L. Dates & W. Barlow (Eds.), *Split image: African-Americans in the mass media* (pp. 267–329). Washington, DC: Howard University Press.

de Mornes, L. (1999, February 2). Maureen Bunyan returns. *The Washington Post*, p. C01.

Dixon, T. L. (1998). *Overrepresentation and underrepresentation of African Americans and Latinos as lawbrakers on television news*. Unpublished doctoral dissertation, University of California, Santa Barbara.

Doswell, C. M. (1994). *White viewers' perceptions of Black television images.* Unpublished doctoral dissertation, Howard University, Washington, DC.

Gandy, O. H. (1998). *Communication and race: A structural perspective.* New York: Oxford University Press.

Greenberg, B. S., & Atkin, C. K. (1978, August). *Learning about minorities from television.* Paper presented at the annual conference of the Association for Education in Journalism, Seattle, WA.

Greenberg, B. S., & Baptista-Fernandez, P. (1980). Hispanic-Americans—The new minority on television. In B. S. Greenberg (Ed.), *Life on television: Content analysis of U.S. TV drama* (pp. 173–181) . Norwood, NJ: Ablex.

Greenberg, B. S., & Brand, J. E. (1994). Minorities and the mass media: 1970s to 1990s In J. Bryant & D. Zillman (Eds.), *Media effects: Advances in theory and research* (pp. 273–314). Norwood, NJ: Ablex.

Greenberg, B. S., Hines, N., Buerkel-Rothfuss, N., & Atkin, C. (1980). Family role structure and interactions of commercial television. In B. S. Greenberg (Ed.), *Life on television: Content analysis of U.S. TV drama* (pp. 149–160). Norwood, NJ: Ablex.

Greenberg, B. S., & Neuendorf, K. (1980). Black family interactions on TV. In B. S. Greenberg (Ed.), *Life on television: Content analysis of U.S. TV drama* (pp. 173–181). Norwood, NJ: Ablex.

Hill, R.B. (1998). *The strengths of African American families: Twenty-five years later.* Lanham, MD: University Press of America.

Iiyama, P., & Kitano, H. H. L. (1982). Asian Americans and the media. In G. Berry & C. Mitchell-Kernan (Eds.), *Television and the socialization of the minority child* (pp. 151–186). New York: Academic Press.

Jensen, D. (1998). Telling stories: How television skews our view of society and ourselves. *CEM Monitor, 2,* 5–7.

Lambert, P. (1996, March). What's wrong with this picture? *People.*

McCubbin, H. I. (Ed.). (1998). *Resiliency in African-American families.* Thousand Oaks, CA: Sage.

Means, R. R. (1996). *Satire or stereotype? A reception analysis of African-American portrayals in Black situation comedies.* Unpublished doctoral dissertation, Bowling Green State University, Ohio.

Merritt, B., & Stroman, C. A. (1993). Black family imagery and interactions on television. *Journal of Black Studies, 23,* 492–499.

Poindexter, P. M., & Stroman, C. N. (1981). Blacks and television: a review of the research literature. *Journal of Broadcasting, 25,* 103–122.

Rada, J. A. (1997). *Effects of television news portrayals of African Americans:The consequent altruism of viewers.* Unpublished doctoral dissertation, University of Georgia.

Shu, J. I. (1979). *The portrayal of Chinese on network television as observed by Chinese and White raters.* Unpublished doctoral dissertation, State University of New York at Stony Brook, New York.

Stroman, C. A. (1986). *Black families and the mass media* (Occasional Paper No. 23). Washington DC: Howard University, Institute for Urban Affairs and Research.

Stroman, C. A., Merritt, B. D., & Metabane, P. W. (1989–1990). Twenty years after Kerner: The portrayal of African Americans on prime-time television. *The Howard Journal of Communication, 2,* 44–56.

Stroman, C. A., & Jones, K. E. (1998). The analysis of television content. In J. K. Asamen & G. L. Berry (Eds.), *Research paradigms, television, and social behavior* (pp. 271–285) Thousand Oaks, CA: Sage.

Sweeper, G. W. (1983). *The image of the Black family and the White family in American prime time television programming 1970 to 1980.* Unpublished doctoral dissertation, New York University.

Tan, A., Fujiola, Y., & Lucht, N. (1997). Native American stereotypes, TV portrayals, and personal contact. *Journalism and Mass Communication Quarterly, 74,* 265–284.

Zambrana, R. E. (Ed.) (1995). *Understanding Latino families: Scholarship, policy and practice.* Thousand Oaks, CA: Sage.

APPENDIX A

Dramas

    *1). *Harris & Co.,* CBS, 1979

    *2). *Palmerstown, USA,* CBS, 1980

    3). *Fame,* NBC/Syndicated, 1982–1987

    4). *St. Elsewhere,* NBC, 1982–1988

    5). *In the Heat of the Night,* NBC, CBS, 1988–1994

    6). *21 Jump Street,* NBC, 1987–1990

    *7). *A Man Called Hawk,* ABC, 1989

    *8). *Frank's Place,* CBS, 1987

    *9). *Equal Justice,* ABC, 1990

    10). *I'll Fly Away,* NBC, 1991–1993

    11). *Roc,* Fox, 1991–1994

   *12). *Angel Street,* CBS, 1992

    13). *NYPD Blue,* ABC, 1993–present

    14). *Homicide: Life on the Streets,* NBC, 1993–present

    15). *ER* NBC, 1994–present

   *16). *Sweet Justice,* NBC, 1994

    17). *South Central,* FOX, 1994

   *18). *Under One Roof,* CBS, 1995

    19). *New York Undercover,* Fox, 1995–1997

   *20). *413 Hope Street,* Fox, 1997

Comedies

    1). *Amos and Andy,* CBS, 1951–1953

    2). *Julia,* NBC, 1968–1971

    3). *The Bill Cosby Show,* NBC, 1969–1971

   *4). *Barefoot in the Park,* ABC, 1970–1971

    5). *Sanford & Son,* NBC, 1972–1977

    6). *Good Times,* CNS, 1974–1979

   *7). *That's My Mama,* ABC, 1974–1975

    8). *The Jeffersons,* CBS, 1975–1985

    9). *What's Happening?,* ABC, 1976–1979

---

*Aired for a year or less.

*10). *Sanford Arms,* NBC, 1977

*11). *One in a Million,* ABC, 1980

12). *New Odd Couple,* ABC, 1980–1983

*13). *Open All Night,* ABC, 1981–1982

14). *The Cosby Show,* NBC, 1984–1992

15). *What's Happening Now?,* ABC, 1985–1988

16). *227,* NBC, 1985–1990

17). *Charlie & Co.,* CBS, 1985–1990

18). *Amen,* NBC, 1986–1991

*19). *Frank's Place,* CBS, 1987–1988

20). *A Different World,* NBC, 1987–1993

*21). *Snoops,* CBS, 1989–1990

22). *Family Matters,* ABC, 1989–1998

23). *Fresh Prince of Bel-Air,* NBC, 1990–1996

*24). *You Take the Kids,* CBS, 1990–1991

25). *True Colors,* Fox, 1990–1992

*26). *The Royal Family,* CBS, 1991–1992

*27). *Rhythm & Blues,* NBC, 1992

*28). *Here & Now,* NBC, 1992–1993

*29). *Out All Night,* NBC, 1992–1993

30). *Martin,* Fox, 1992–1996

31). *Hangin' With Mr. Cooper,* ABC, 1992–1997

32). *Getting By,* ABC, 1993–1994

*33). *Where I Live,* ABC, 1993

*34). *Thea,* ABC, 1993–1994

*35). *George,* ABC, 1993–1994

36). *Living Single,* Fox, 1993–1998

*37). *South Central,* Fox, 1994

*38). *On Our Own,* ABC, 1994–1995

39). *Me and the Boys,* ABC, 1994–1997

40). *Sister, Sister,* ABC/WB, 1994–present

41). *In the House,* NBC/WB, 1994–present

42). *The Parenthood,* WB, 1995–present

43). *The Wayans Brothers,* WB, 1995–present

44). *Moesha,* UPN, 1995–present

---

*Aired for a year or less.

45). *Homeboys in Outer Space,* UPN, 1996–present

46). *Malcolm & Eddie,* UPN, 1996–present

47). *Sparks,* UPN, 1996–1998

48). *Cosby,* CBS, 1996–present

49). *The Steve Harvey Show,* WB, 1996–present

50). *Goode Behavior,* UPN, 1996–present

51). *The Jamie Foxx Show,* WB, 1996–present

52). *Built to Last,* NBC, 1997–present

*53). *The Gregory Hines Show,* CBS, 1997–1998

54). *Between Brothers,* Fox, 1997–present

*55). *Good News,* UPN, 1997–1998

*56). *The Secret Diary of Desmond Pfeiffer,* UPN, 1998

57). *The Hughley's,* ABC, 1998–present

58). *Living in Captivity,* Fox, 1998–present

59). *Mercy Point,* UPN, 1998–present

60). *Linc's,* Showtime, 1998–present

---

*Aired for a year or less.

Subversion of the American Television Family

William Douglas
University of Houston

There are competing and quite divergent opinions regarding the state of the television family. Following her extensive review of the family in domestic comedy, Cantor (1991) concluded that television spouses continued to share a noncompetitive relationship based on shared concern and love. Indeed, although television family relationships may commonly be conflictual, Cantor reported that such conflict is easily resolved through negotiation and, in a larger sense, observed that "the love of parents for one another and for their children are central facts of life" (p. 214). Others have taken a similar position, maintaining that television families articulate an ideology of achievement and relational maturity; they are affluent and live in explicit ease and comfort, and their relationships are characterized by mutual affection, involvement, and cooperation (Frazer & Frazer, 1992; Lichter, Lichter, Rothman, & Amundson, 1988; Moore, 1992; Newcomb, 1974; Skill & Wallace, 1990; Taylor, 1989). Moreover, although some minority families may be presented in stereotypic and comparatively unfavorable ways (Cummings, 1988; Greenberg & Neuendorf, 1980; Sweeper, 1984), Merritt and Stroman (1993) declared that, in modern African American families, "spouses interact frequently, equally, and lovingly with each other; and children are treated with respect and taught achievement-oriented values. All of this takes place in an atmosphere that harbors little conflictual behavior" (pp. 497–498), suggesting that, on television, prosperity and happiness are not limited by ethnicity.

At the same time, of course, there is a clear sense among many people that the television family is in decline. Critics have argued that comparison of the Nelsons and Cleavers with the Conners and Bundys reveals in an almost commonsense way that the family has altered fundamentally (Buck, 1992; Fields, 1994; Hoffman, 1994). It is not simply that the Conners and Bundys look different, it is that to many they appear less able to function effectively, less able to socialize family members appropriately, less able to interact in supportive and nonconflictual ways, less interested in each other, and less able to manage the day-to-day routine of family life. To some, parent–child relations appear particularly impoverished. Both Zoglin (1990) and Waters (1993) argued that, in modern television families, parents provide inappropriate and unhelpful role models to children who have become undisciplined and hostile whereas Blanco (1998) described the relationship between modern television parents and children as one in which "parents . . . are most often either absent ogres or idiots . . . If they're in the same house as their children, they're tolerated. If they live elsewhere, their occasional visits provoke an almost paralyzing dread" (p. 1D).

It might be supposed that such opposing views arise because different researchers are examining different kinds of television families. However, although some aspects of interaction do differ systematically across television genres (Comstock & Strzyzewski, 1990; Greenberg, Buerkel-Rothfuss, Neuendorf, & Atkin, 1980; Haefner & Comstock, 1990), most analyses have focused on domestic comedy. Perhaps because the family is fundamental to domestic comedy (Mitz, 1980; Skill & Robinson, 1994), families like the Nelsons, Bunkers, Huxtables, and Conners have commonly been at the center of television family research. Besides, observers disagree substantially even when discussing the same family. In her summary of *Roseanne*, for example, Cantor (1991) described the Conner parents as "friends and lovers" who work together "in a loving and cooperative way" and "accept their working-class status with good humor" although they look to their children to do better (p. 211). In contrast, Rowe (1995) concluded that, unlike earlier working-class couples, the Conners do not gracefully accept their lot in life, and they rarely express affection for each other, and Rapping (1994) described the children as unruly and unmotivated.

Why, then, does opinion vary so dramatically and what, in fact, does television "say" about the American family? The position to be explored in this chapter is that researchers' points of view are affected significantly by the way in which they examine the television family and that a "received view" of life and relations in the television family offers considerable evidence of decline, especially in the experience of television children.

MAKING SENSE OF THE TELEVISION FAMILY: I. A VIEW FROM THE SCREEN

There is little doubt that television promotes a traditional family model. Not only are marriage and parenthood routine (Abelman, 1990; Cantor, 1991; Frazer & Frazer, 1992), but intact families are presented as less conflictual and more conforming than nontraditional families (Skill & Wallace, 1990; Skill, Wallace, & Cassata, 1990), although even nontraditional families appear to subscribe to conventional and, so, generally conservative family values (Cantor, 1991; Cantor & Cantor, 1992; Harrington & Bielby, 1991; Newcomb, 1974).

Spouses on Television

A traditional family model not only describes family structure but also implies the rights and responsibilities of family members. As such, the relationship between television spouses is often seen to be one in which husbands are dominant and act in instrumental ways and wives are dependent and act in expressive ways (Dail & Way, 1985; Durkin, 1985; Livingstone & Liebes, 1995; Shaner, 1982). Consistent with this view, analyses of the television family have indicated variously that, compared to wives, husbands are more talkative (Honeycutt, Wellman, & Larson, 1997); less likely to engage in avoidance and more likely to seek conflict resolution (Comstock & Strzyzewski, 1990; Skill et al., 1990); more likely to rely on reasoning (Skill et al., 1990); more likely to blame others and more willing to act unilaterally (Comstock & Strzyzewski, 1990); and more likely to seek compliance from other family members (Haefner & Comstock, 1990). Additionally, husbands more often hold high status positions (Durkin, 1985) and are more likely to be presented as the primary provider (McNeil, 1975), whereas wives are more frequently rooted in the home (Signorielli, 1982).

Recent analyses suggest little or no need to revise this model. Although television fathers have become more involved in meal preparation (Cantor, 1991) and modern mothers are more likely to pursue professional careers outside the home (Cantor, 1991; Lichter et al., 1988; Moore, 1992; Pingree & Thompson, 1990), Frazer and Frazer (1992) compared *Father Knows Best* and *The Cosby Show* and concluded that the portrayal of gender roles was "essentially the same" (p. 166) and functioned to place women in a domestic and subservient role.

Although the provider-husband/caregiver-wife model appears robust across time, there is evidence to suggest that it is unstable across social class. Based on their categorization of family series during the period of 1946 to 1978, Glennon and Butsch (1982) concluded that working-class husbands are commonly presented as bumbling and inept. This position has been reiterated by Butsch (1992) who argued that, in contrast to their middle-class counterparts, working-class males are portrayed as inept, immature, stupid, lacking in good sense, and emotional; at the same time, working-class wives are more likely to be portrayed as relatively intelligent, rational, and responsible. Thomas and Callahan (1982) also argued that working-class families are more cohesive, more helpful, and both friendlier and happier than middle-class families, suggesting that, although gender status may be "inverted" (Butsch, 1992, p. 397) in low SES families, the general effectiveness of the traditional spousal model is unaffected.

Finally, there is mixed evidence concerning the affective trajectory of television spousal relations. Some researchers have reported that modern spouses are comparatively more likely to express their love (Akins, 1986) and sexuality (Cantor, 1991; Cantor & Cantor, 1992), whereas others have concluded that modern spousal relations are more conflictual (Akins, 1986; Comstock & Strzyzewski, 1990; Heintz, 1992) and more likely to involve a variety of negative conversational acts, such as ignoring, evading, and withdrawing from each other (Akins, 1986).

In sum, a substantial body of research suggests that, although spousal relations may have become more volatile and although contemporary wives are more likely to engage in work outside the home, television husbands and wives continue to share a generally effective relationship in which rights and responsibilities are partitioned on the basis of gender. Although working-class spouses are portrayed in somewhat opposite ways, the distribution of functions remains gender based and, in a more general sense, working-class husbands and wives appear to subscribe to a conservative, middle-class family ideology.

Parents and Children on Television

The prevailing view is that, in television families, parent–child relations adhere to traditional principles. Mothers are most likely to enact expressive behaviors (Dail & Way, 1985) and, during conflict, invoke strategies that emphasize commonality and empathy and serve to reduce disagreement and reestablish family unity (Comstock & Strzyzewski, 1990). Fathers, meanwhile, are "centers of authority . . . practiced in decision-making" (Newcomb, 1974, p. 48) and, as such, more frequently act instrumentally (Dail & Way, 1985) and in ways that produce negative affect (Comstock & Strzyzewski, 1990).

Together, parents function to offer information and direction (Greenberg et al., 1980), exhibit concern and provide reassurance and support (Greenberg et al., 1980; Shaner, 1982; Skill et al., 1990), and resolve a variety of problems that infiltrate the lives of television children (Lichter et al., 1988; Newcomb, 1974). Children are posited to behave in complementary ways, seeking parental attention (Shaner, 1982) and conforming to parental authority (Skill & Wallace, 1990).

That is, the widely accepted view of parent–child relations is one in which both parents and children perform traditional roles. Television mothers are commonly associated with emotionality and family togetherness whereas television fathers are more often linked to decision making and discipline in the family. Consistent with this model, television children occupy a dependent status that is confirmed by their use of subordinate conversational behaviors, their recurrent inability to resolve problems, their obedience to parental authority, and so on. According to this view, television parents and children share an abundantly positive relationship. Conflict is resolved, mutual affection is apparent, and social and professional achievement is encouraged and maintained, again suggesting the effectiveness and desirability of the traditional family model.

Siblings on Television

Examination of the few studies of television siblings often encourages a familiar conclusion; siblings share a traditional and rewarding relationship. Compared to males, female children appear less likely to exhibit aggression, more likely to show affection, and more likely to succeed when performing goal-related sexual and/or romantic acts (Heintz-Knowles, 1995). Likewise, sisters more frequently seek information and give reassurance, less frequently use reasoning and commands, and less frequently disparage and attack another's motives (Skill et al., 1990). That is, like their adult counterparts, children are often seen to be portrayed in stereotypically feminine or masculine ways.

The same body of research suggests, as well, that children behave in generally prosocial ways. Indeed, antisocial behavior is usually shown to be ineffective and children are often motivated by their concern for other family members, especially when they are young (Heintz-Knowles, 1995). Sibling relations also appear to be a source of positive affect. Larson (1991) compared sibling interactions in *Leave it to Beaver*, *Ozzie and Harriet*, and *Father Knows Best* with those in *The Cosby Show*, *Growing Pains*, and *Family Ties* and concluded that, whereas earlier interactions were more positive, relations between siblings remained supportive and friendly.

Summary and Observations

While extended and single-parent families have become more common (Cantor & Cantor, 1992; Skill & Robinson, 1994), a substantial volume of research suggests that television continues to celebrate and promote the traditional family. Not only does "mother, father, and dependent children" remain a common family template, especially in domestic comedy, but life and relations in the traditional family appear to many to be prosperous and orderly.

This position can be criticized for at least two reasons. First, the research on which it is based adopted a generally narrow view of television family life and television family relations. In particular, prior studies often focused on salient aspects of interaction, such as conflict, but ignored associated features, in this case, conflict resolution, so that conclusions about family relations are potentially biased. As well, there has been little or no explicit examination of essential family functions, such as child socialization and ability to manage the routine of day-to-day life, nor has there been much research on significant family outcomes, such as relational satisfaction and family stability. These are important omissions because such issues are fundamental to family functioning and, therefore, are implicated in both description of the television family's development and evaluation of the modern family's performance.

Second, because prior examinations of the television family tended to rely on content analysis, they are unlikely to reflect a received view of family life and family relations and, in particular, may underestimate the attributional impact of negative family action. Although content analysis yields a clear indication of the objective aspects of television family life, viewers often infuse portrayals with information that is not explicit but, nonetheless, affects their interpretations (Dambrot & Reep, 1988; Livingstone, 1990). For example, the meanings that persons construct may be influenced by the extent to which they judge the content realistic, by their own related experiences, by their ambitions for the characters, or even by their general mood. Moreover, whereas content analysis implicitly treats all coded acts as attributionally equivalent, viewers are likely to be more influenced by some acts than by others and, in particular, are likely to be substantially affected by negative acts. In interpersonal situations, negative information exerts significantly more effect than does positive information on the judgments that persons make about others (e.g., Fiske, 1980; Hamilton & Huffman, 1971; Hamilton & Zanna, 1972), and both Abelman (1986) and Comstock and Strzyzewski (1990) speculated that the same effect occurs during television viewing. As such, viewers may develop negative impressions of television families even though the majority of family action is prosocial. That is, viewers may define families as distressed even if family members often act in nondistressed ways. At the very least, limitations associated with content analysis suggest that the method may provide only limited access to the impressions that audiences develop about television families.

MAKING SENSE OF THE TELEVISION FAMILY: II. A VIEW FROM THE CHAIR

In a series of analyses, Douglas and Olson (Douglas, 1996; Douglas & Olson, 1995, 1996; Olson & Douglas, 1997) examined viewer attributions about a variety of families presented in domestic comedy. In overview, these researchers studied television families that had appeared in the "top 20" annualized viewer ratings during the period of 1950 to 1997; that is, families were selected on the basis of prominence. This criterion yielded a group of 17 families; Ricardos (*I Love Lucy*), Andersons (*Father Knows Best*), Douglases (*My Three Sons*), Clampetts (*Beverly Hillbillies*), Stevenses (*Bewitched*), Bunkers (*All in the Family*), Sanfords (*Sanford and Son*), Cunninghams (*Happy Days*), Jeffersons (*The Jeffersons*), Huxtables (*The Cosby Show*), Keatons (*Family Ties*), Bower-Micellis (*Who's the Boss?*), Conners (*Roseanne*), Winslows (*Family Matters*), Tanners (*Full House*), Seavers (*Growing Pains*), and Taylors (*Home Improvement*).

Participants in the studies were shown sample episodes, determined by viewer "experts" to be representative of the program as a whole, and were required to make judgments about family power and affect, family performance, and family satisfaction and stability. These measures are described fully in Douglas and Olson (1995) but, in general, were organized around the familial framework proposed by Fitzpatrick and Badzinski (1985, 1994). As such, the measure of family power and affect involved more specific measures of dominance, equality, similarity of function, involvement, attraction, receptivity—trust, influence, and formality; the broad measure of family performance involved more specific measures of amount of conflict, conflict management, socialization of family members, cultivation of stable personalities, and management of the daily routine; and the measure of family satisfaction and stability involved separate measures of relational satisfaction and relational stability. Participants made separate judgments about the spousal, parent–child, and sibling relationships.

Spouses on Television

For the most part, spousal relations are seen as positive. Wives and husbands are judged to have become more equal and, although modern couples are comparatively more conflictual, they are also more likely to articulate positive emotions and, so, appear more generally expressive. That is, partners are more informal and explicitly emotional so that their interactions are more spontaneous and more likely to include expressions of both positive and negative affect. Such relations are usually associated with nontraditional sex roles, suggesting that, in modern television families, spousal rights and responsibilities are more often shared than divided as a function of gender.

Similarly, both modern couples, such as the Huxtables, as well as earlier couples, such as the Andersons, appear to have established open relationships in which spouses communicate honestly and openly and are willing to listen to each other. In those relationships, couples are seen as comparatively involved, satisfied, and trusting, and able to manage both the daily routine, in general, and conflict episodes, in particular.

The generalizability of these conclusions is limited in two ways. First, working-class spouses are seen to establish relationships that are significantly less rewarding and gratifying than those shared by their middle-class counterparts. In contrast to previous research that suggested that, in television families, socioeconomic status was inversely related to relational satisfaction and relational stability (Thomas & Callahan, 1982), the Ricardos, Bunkers, Jeffersons, and Conners, all of which are rooted in something lower than middle-class America, were seen to involve spousal relationships that were relatively closed, conflictual, and unsatisfying. That is, across families, the lowest levels of mutual fulfillment were attributed to working-class couples.

Second, in two families in particular, the Taylors and Conners, spousal relations seemed to be governed by an essentially traditional model in which rights and responsibilities were gender based. What is more, both couples appeared to share a relatively distressed relationship characterized by frequent attempts by one spouse to exert control over the other, high levels of conflict, low ability to manage the relationship, low levels of relational satisfaction and relational stability, and, in the case of the Taylors, extremely low supportiveness.

There is, then, broad convergence between these studies that focus on viewers' attributions, and other research that is concerned most often with content features. Both approaches suggest that spousal relations remain generally positive although contemporary partners appear more expressive and more likely to violate traditional gender roles. Attributional analyses do suggest, however, that working-class spousal relations are comparatively impoverished and, so, imply that television portrayals reinforce the desirability of middle-class life not simply as a function of domestic artifacts, such as the level of consumption, but as a consequence of relations inside the family.

Parents and Children on Television

Viewer attributions about the relationship between television parents and children appear complex. On the one hand, parent–child relations are judged more conflictual in contemporary families and contemporary parents are seen to socialize children less effectively than their earlier counterparts. At the same time, parent–child relations appear to have become generally more cohesive; that is, modern parents and children are perceived as more mutually involved, more trusting of each other, more attracted to each other, more able to manage the day-to-day routine of family life, and more relationally satisfied. Finally, according to viewers, parents and children perform increasingly similar functions in the family.

Notably, two families, the Conners and Taylors, again violated this general model. Relations between parents and children in these families appeared not only highly conflictual but characterized by levels of cohesiveness and role similarity more like early television families. The analyses suggested that the Conners, in particular, were substantially unable to perform functions associated with child socialization and family management and that relations between parents and children were flagrantly hostile, nonsupportive, and unsatisfying. Parents and children in *Home Improvement* were evaluated in similar ways, although the level of distress was considerably lower than in *Roseanne*.

In general, these findings imply that rights and responsibilities in the television family have been redistributed such that parent–child relations have become more symmetrical and more egalitarian. This is consistent with the pattern of increased conflict and role ambiguity (Parks, 1977) and suggests that television family life is more often a function of parent–child negotiation than of parental mandate. Despite these changes, most parents and children appear to like and support each other and to derive mutual satisfaction from their relationship. Nonetheless, the exceptions to this covering model are significant for a variety of reasons. First, the Conners and Taylors offer a single, coherent alternative so that it is difficult to dismiss them as unrelated and/or trivial "outliers." Second, the model of parent–child relations implicit in these presentations deviates dramatically and negatively from that available in other families and is not simply a variant of the primary model. Third, the relational distress shared by these families cannot be explained as a function of socioeconomic status in that, whereas the Conners are explicitly working-class, the Taylors clearly reflect all of the visible trappings of middle-class life. Finally, the Conners, in particular, are frequently applauded as a reflection of life and relations in real families (Berkman, 1993; Lee, 1995; Mayerle,

1991; Rapping, 1994; Rowe, 1995), suggesting that these portrayals may have a larger significance to audiences.

Attributional studies, then, support two versions of parent–child relations. One coincides, at least in tone, with studies of television content and suggests emotional closeness, although, even in this model, modern parents are seen to exert less authority and to be less effective socializing agents than earlier couples; the other proposes a substantially distressed model in which parent–child relations have become oppositional so that modern parents and children are not only affectively remote from each other but also significantly less able to achieve outcomes normally expected of families, such as those associated with child socialization and family management.

Siblings on Television

In overview, attributional analyses suggest that sibling relations have evolved along a trajectory of increasing distress. According to viewers, contemporary siblings, such as those in the Conner, Winslow, and Taylor families, are less trusting, more hostile, less able to manage and resolve conflict, and less able to socialize each other appropriately than were siblings in families like the Andersons, Douglases, Cunninghams, Huxtables, and Keatons. Modern siblings also appear not only to like one another less and to be less happy in their relationships but less involved in each other and less likely to become or remain close and supportive in the future. That is, sibling relations are judged to have become relatively ineffective, emotionally unrewarding, and unlikely to endure.

Relations between television siblings also appear more impoverished than do other family relationships. Spouses, for example, are seen as more involved and more attracted to each other, less fixed on dominating or influencing each other, more trusting and more open, less conflictual, and more able to manage conflict than are children. Spousal relations are also rated as more satisfying and more stable. Likewise, compared to sibling relations, those between parents and children are seen as significantly less conflictual and more cohesive, implying that relations between siblings are moderated by parental involvement. Modern parents are also judged as more effective role models than siblings and as more likely to encourage academic and social success in children. Specifically, parents' perceived socializing ability has remained stable whereas that of siblings has decayed sharply across time so that, in earlier families (i.e., the Andersons to the Keatons), siblings are seen to outperform parents whereas, in more contemporary families (i.e., the Conners to the Taylors), that pattern is reversed.

Clearly, attributional analyses suggest that, in television families, sibling relations have deteriorated and have become considerably distressed. Modern siblings score relatively poorly on a variety of performance measures and are judged less able than both other family members and earlier generations of television children to construct and maintain mutually satisfying relationships. This contrasts with content-based studies that suggest that children are often motivated by concern for each other and continue to share generally positive relations inside the family.

Summary and Observations

Attributional studies suggest that the relational context of television families varies systematically between adults and children. Whereas the family on television appears to have become generally more conflictual, spousal relations are seen to involve a concurrent increase in expressions of attraction so that contemporary couples appear, on the one hand, relatively argumentative but, on the other, more overtly affectionate to each other. Moreover, whereas spousal relations are judged uniformly satisfying, relational satisfaction seems especially high in more modern marriages, reinforcing the sense that the aggregate change in many television families is toward more positive spousal relations. In contrast, the relational experience of television children appears to have worsened substantially across time. Parent–child relations are not only more hostile in modern families but, in some families, are defined by lower levels of mutual trust, lower liking for each other, lower supportiveness, lower relationship management skills, and lower relational satisfaction and stability. At the same time, sibling relations are rated as more conflictual, less supportive, less trusting, less satisfying, and less stable in contemporary families than in families like the Andersons and Douglases. As well, modern families appear less able to socialize children effectively, a deficit that is especially acute among siblings.

Significantly, children are fundamental to the modern television family. Children have become an increasingly common feature of television families (Skill & Robinson, 1994) and typically initiate and dominate family conversations (Abelman & Ross, 1986). Domestic comedy, in particular, narrates a child-centered culture (Rapping, 1992) in which children exert an increasingly profound influence on family relations as they grow older (Heintz-Knowles, 1995). As such, parent–child and sibling interactions are not only commonplace but often form the focus of television portrayals, suggesting that the diminished experience of television children may be especially salient to viewers and, so, may affect their understanding of the television family in important (and negative) ways. This is particularly likely because modern childhood is seen by many as a relatively unregulated and impoverished experience. Large majorities of people, for example, believe that parents' willingness to discipline children has decreased during the past decade (Marks, 1996) and that children are less well cared for now than in the past (Mellman, Lazarus, & Rivlin, 1990; Whitman, Ito, & Kost, 1996). What is more, like the television family, the American family has become more child centered (Calhoun, 1945; May, 1988; Mintz & Kellogg, 1988) so that evaluation of real family performance frequently focuses on responsibilities associated with childrearing and the provision of affection (Blankenhorn, 1995; Popenoe, 1988, 1993a, 1993b). At the very least, such convergence between television family life and family relations and public concerns and priorities about the real family may become mutually reinforcing so that persons are predisposed to interpret the family experience, both on and off television, disapprovingly.

Attributional studies also suggest that working-class versions of the television family are consistently presented in ways that imply distress. Not only do these families involve troubled parent–child and sibling relations but, in contrast to those of middle-class families, like the Ricardos, Bunkers, Jeffersons, and Conners involve spouses that are seen as unreceptive, hostile, and dissatisfied with each other. This contradicts earlier research that proposed an inverse relationship between SES and such factors as sympathy, cooperation, and happiness (Thomas & Callahan, 1982) and implies, instead, that established failings in working-class fathers (Andreasen, 1990; Butsch, 1992; Glennon & Butsch, 1982; Marc, 1989) may be attached to more extensive family problems. At the very least, because working-class families are comparatively rare on television, comprising about 1 in every 10 families in domestic comedy (Butsch, 1992), and because they are, by definition, less economically successful, such relational shortcomings can be viewed as further evidence of a bias toward a middle-class family model on television.

CONCLUSIONS

The significance of television portrayals derives substantially from the growing belief that they may influence viewers' family cognition and/or reflect on the real family experience. There is widespread agreement that popular presentations, especially those on television, affect the way in which people think about the family (Andreasen, 1990; Fitzpatrick, 1987; Haefner & Comstock, 1990; Harrington & Bielby, 1991; Meadowcroft & Fitzpatrick, 1988; Perse, Pavitt, & Burggraf, 1990; Rothschild & Morgan, 1987). Moreover, although television families are demographically unlike real families (Fuller, 1990; Skill & Robinson, 1994) and often enjoy an unusually high level of good fortune (Frazer & Frazer, 1992; Heintz-Knowles,

1995; Jones, 1992; Moore, 1992; Pingree & Thompson, 1990), television has been posited to present the family in ways that viewers deem realistic (Buck, 1992; Hoffman, 1994; Mayerle, 1991; Rapping, 1994; Spigel, 1992) and in ways that reflect the changes in American family life (Buck, 1992; Lewis, 1991; Marc, 1989; Zoglin, 1990). This is not to suggest that television portrayals correspond in detail to the lived family experience. Because they are generally constructed and consumed as entertainment, television families often exhibit a variety of characteristics that violate viewers' expectations about the family. Nonetheless, television families habitually behave in ways that make sense to viewers and routinely involve characters, contexts, relationships, and events that are mundanely familiar. Even early television families are seen to have offered a realistic portrayal of "family relations and domestic space" (Haralovich, 1989, p. 61), a view shared by contemporary audiences who judged shows like *Leave it to Beaver* to be reflective of their own family circumstances (Leibman, 1995), perhaps because the shows were frequently based on the real experiences of the writers and cast (Haralovich, 1989; Jones, 1992; Spigel, 1992). Indeed, realism of character and situation is often explicitly mandated and collaboratively imposed in domestic comedy (McCrohan, 1987) so that the articulated television family environment is commonly intended to be authentic.

To the extent that television families do, in some way, inform viewers about the real family, attributional studies suggest not simply that the family has changed but that, in many ways, it has become distressed. Although, in some modern families, spousal relations are more rewarding than in the past, that effect does not extend to working-class families and, in the Conners and Taylors, is contradicted by a model of disagreement, disunity, and relational instability. Likewise, the experience of television children appears to have followed a downward trajectory, in part, because parent–child relations seem to have become more hostile and, in part, because children, themselves, seem to have become less involved with each other. Most obviously, neither parents nor siblings appear to function effectively as socializing agents in contemporary television families.

Notably, this overall pattern of distress is consistent, in all critical respects, with criticism of the contemporary American family. Public opinion polls routinely reveal that large majorities of respondents are substantially dissatisfied with the family, in general (e.g., National Family Opinion, Inc., 1994; The Gallup Poll, 1992), and the experience of children, in particular (e.g., Marks, 1996; Mellman et al., 1990; Whitman et al., 1996). More specifically, Popenoe (1988, 1993a, 1993b, 1995) argued that factors such as increased divorce rate, decreased fertility rate, and the disappearance of the two-parent family reveal the erosion of the family. According to this position, the family has become less able to socialize children effectively, in part, because of reduced parental authority, and is less able to provide care, affection, and companionship to its members. Blankenhorn (1995), meanwhile, proposed that the family has been undermined by a "me-first" egotism that places priority on personal fulfillment and, so, reduces partners' commitment to family and marginalizes children.

Although it might be supposed that general perceptions of family decline accrue from persons' investigation of their own (relatively impoverished) family experience, available evidence suggests otherwise. Although 81% of respondents in a recent poll (National Family Opinion, Inc., 1994) expressed the view that the American family has become weaker, 77% described their own family as "loving," 70% percent described their family as "supportive," and 66% described their family as "happy." Only 5% described their family as "unstable" and even fewer described their family as "neglected." That is, respondents appeared satisfied with their own family life even though convinced that the family, in general, is in a state of decay.

Clearly, beliefs about the American family are likely to be influenced by information about divorce rates, fertility rates, rates of spousal and child abuse, and so on. Such information promotes a negative view of modern family life and receives pointed and widespread attention. However, attributional studies of the family on television suggest that those portrayals may also contribute to viewers' real-world beliefs. First, television portrayals appear ideologically consistent with other public information about the family. Although abuse and divorce may be rare on television, and absent from domestic comedy, viewers seem to place television families on a deteriorating relational trajectory, certainly one in which separation and divorce are seen as increasingly likely. Second, unlike demographic and sociological indices, television presentations narrate the routine of family life and do so in uninterrupted detail. When they watch the Huxtables, Conners, and others, viewers enter "the living room within the living room, the mirror of family life, the barometer of the normal thing" (Marc, 1989, p. 127). That is, television allows viewers to intrude unobtrusively on a host of mundane but connected family activities that, together, yield an integrated and frequently realistic set of relational vignettes that may elaborate on otherwise pallid information about family distress and divorce.

Although attributional studies of the television family can be criticized because they have relied on college student samples or because they provide limited exposure to the families being studied, they clearly are more likely to map consensus audience readings than are studies that depend on content analysis or on a researcher's own, and potentially idiosyncratic, understanding. What is more, unlike other analyses, attributional studies generate a view of the television family that is consistent with both extant family theory and current criticism of the family. In real families, siblings construct a unique relational environment (Fitzpatrick & Badzinski, 1994) that is less affiliative and more conflictual than that developed by children and parents (Baskett & Johnson, 1982). Moreover, both formal criticism and public opinion have often focused on the depleted experience of children as the fundamental shortcoming of the modern family. In the same way, contemporary television children appear to establish an especially hostile environment for each other that contrasts not only with earlier generations of siblings but also, in many television families, with the relationship between parents. At the very least, attributional studies suggest that a substantial number of viewers may interpret the modern television family in comparatively negative ways and may define the evolution of the family on television as a record of diminishing success.

REFERENCES

Abelman, R. (1986). Children's awareness of television's prosocial fare: Parental discipline as an antecedent. *Journal of Family Issues, 7*, 51–66.

Abelman, R. (1990). From "The Huxtables" to "The Humbards": The portrayal of family on religious television. In J. Bryant (Ed.), *Television and the American family* (pp. 165–184). Hillsdale, NJ: Lawrence Erlbaum Associates.

Abelman, R., & Ross, R. (1986). Children, television, and families: An evolution in understanding. *Television & Families, 9*, 2–55.

Akins, G. (1986). An analysis of family interaction styles as portrayed on television. (Doctoral dissertation, University of Georgia, 1986). *Dissertation Abstracts International, 47*, 2013A.

Andreasen, M. S. (1990). Evolution of the family's use of television: Normative data from industry and academe. In J. Bryant (Ed.), *Television and the American family* (pp. 3–55). Hillsdale, NJ: Lawrence Erlbaum Associates.

Baskett, L. M, & Johnson, S. M. (1982). The young child's interaction with parents versus sibling: A behavioral analysis. *Child Development, 53*, 643–650.

Berkman, D. (1993). Sitcom reality. *Television Quarterly, 26*, 63–69.

Blanco, R. (1998, December 17). The disappearance of mom and dad: Parents lose grip on TV families. *USA Today*, pp. 1D, 2D.

Blankenhorn, D. (1995). *Fatherless America: Confronting our most urgent social problem*. New York: Basic Books.

Buck, J. (1992, September 27). Television's versions of family values. *The Witchita Eagle*, p.6E.

Butsch, R. (1992). Class and gender in four decades of television situation comedy: Plus ça change. *Critical Studies in Mass Communication, 9*, 387–399.

Calhoun, A. W. (1945). *A social history of the American family* (Vol. 3). New York: Barnes & Noble.

Cantor, M. G. (1991). The American family on television: From Molly Goldberg to Bill Cosby. *Journal of Comparative Family Studies, 22*, 205–216.

Cantor, M. G. & Cantor, J. M. (1992). *Prime-time television: Content and control*. Newbury Park, CA: Sage.

Comstock, J., & Strzyzewski, K. (1990). Interpersonal interaction on television: Family conflict and jealousy on primetime. *Journal of Broadcasting & Electronic Media, 34*, 263–282.

Cummings, M. S. (1988). The changing image of the Black family on television. *Journal of Popular Culture, 22*, 75–85.

Dail, P. W., & Way, W. L. (1985). What do parents observe about parenting from prime-time television? *Family Relations, 34*, 491–499.

Dambrot, F. H., & Reep, D. C. (1988). In the eye of the beholder: Viewer perceptions of TV's male/female working partners. *Communication Research, 15*, 51–69.

Douglas, W. (1996). The fall from grace? The modern family on television. *Communication Research, 23*, 675–702.

Douglas, W., & Olson, B. M. (1995). Beyond family structure: The family in domestic comedy. *Journal of Broadcasting & Electronic Media, 39*, 236–261.

Douglas, W., & Olson, B. M. (1996). Subversion of the American family: An examination of children and parents in television families. *Communication Research, 23*, 73–99.

Durkin, K. (1985). Television and sex-role acquisition: Vol. 1. Content. *British Journal of Social Psychology, 24*, 101–113.

Fields, S. (1994, October 11). Ozzie and Harriet did provide moral s in our complex world. *Houston Post*, p. A–17.

Fiske, S. T. (1980). Attention and weight in person perception: The impact of negative and extreme behavior. *Journal of Personality and Social Psychology, 38*, 889–908.

Fitzpatrick, M. A. (1987). Marital interaction. In C. R. Berger & S. H. Chaffee (Eds.), *Handbook of communication science* (pp. 564–618). Newbury Park, CA: Sage.

Fitzpatrick, M. A., & Badzinski, D. M. (1985). All in the family: Interpersonal communication in kin relationships. In M. L Knapp & G. R. Miller (Eds.), *Handbook of interpersonal communication* (pp. 687–736). Beverly Hills, CA: Sage.

Fitzpatrick, M. A., & Badzinski, D. M. (1994). All in the family: Interpersonal communication in kin relationships. In M. L Knapp & G. R. Miller (Eds.), *Handbook of interpersonal communication* (pp. 726–771). Beverly Hills, CA: Sage.

Frazer, J. M., & Frazer, T. C. (1992). "Father Knows Best" and "The Cosby Show": Nostalgia and the sitcom tradition. *Journal of Popular Culture, 27*, 163–172.

Fuller, T. (1990, March). *Television vs. the real world: A content analysis of family configuration.* Paper presented at the annual convention of the Texas Association of Broadcast Educators, Dallas, TX.

Gallup Poll. (1992, September). *The Gallup Poll Monthly*, p. 4. (Survey GO 322014**)

Glennon, L., & Butsch, R. (1982). The family as portrayed on television 1946–1978. In D. Pearl, L. Bouthilet, & J. Lazar (Ed.), *Television and behavior: Ten years of scientific progress and implications for the eighties: Vol. 2. Technical reviews* (DHHS Publication No. ADM 82–1196, pp. 264–271) Washington, DC: U.S. Government Printing Office.

Greenberg, B. S., Buerkel-Rothfuss, N. L., Neuendorf, K., & Atkin, C. K. (1980). Three seasons of television family role interactions. In B. S. Greenberg (Ed.), *Life on television: Content analyses of U.S. TV drama* (pp. 161–172). Norwood, NJ: Ablex.

Greenberg, B. S., & Neuendorf, K. (1980). Black family interactions on television. In B. S. Greenberg (Ed.), *Life on television: Content analyses of U. S. TV drama* (pp. 173–181). Norwood, NJ: Ablex.

Haefner, M. J., & Comstock, J. (1990). Compliance gaining on prime time family programs. *Southern Communication Journal, 55*, 402–420.

Hamilton, D. L., & Huffman, L. F. (1971). Generality of impression-formation processes for evaluative and nonevaluative judgments. *Journal of Personality and Social Psychology, 20*, 200–207.

Hamilton, D. L., & Zanna, M. P. (1972). Differential weighting of favorable and unfavorable attributes in impression formation. *Journal of Experimental Research in Personality, 6*, 204–212.

Haralovich, M. B. (1989). Sitcoms and suburbs: Positioning the 1950s homemaker. *Quarterly Review of Film & Video, 11*, 61–83.

Harrington, C. L., & Bielby, D. D. (1991). The mythology of modern love: Representations of romance in the 1980s. *Journal of Popular Culture, 24*, 129–144.

Heintz, K. E. (1992). Children's favorite television families: A descriptive analysis of role interactions. *Journal of Broadcasting & Electronic Media, 36*, 443–451.

Heintz-Knowles, K. E. (1995). *The reflection on the screen: Television's image of children* (Report commissioned by Children Now) Oakland, CA.

Hoffman, A. (1994, February 4–6). Reality check: Roseanne vs. Donna. *USA Weekend*, p. 24.

Honeycutt, J. M., Wellman, L. B., & Larson, M. S. (1997). Beneath family role portrayals: An additional measure of communication influence using time series analyses of turn at talk on a popular television program. *Journal of Broadcasting & Electronic Media, 41*, 40–57.

Jones, G. (1992). *Honey, I'm home! sitcoms: Selling the American dream.* New York: Grove Weidenfeld.

Larson, M. S. (1991). Sibling interactions in 1950s versus 1980s sitcoms: A comparison. *Journalism Quarterly, 68*, 381–388.

Lee, J. (1995). Subversive sitcoms: Roseanne as inspiration for feminist resistance. In G. Dines & J. M. Humez (Eds.), *Gender, race, and class in media* (pp. 469–475). Beverly Hills, CA: Sage.

Leibman, N. C. (1995). *Living room lectures: The fifties family in film and television.* Austin, TX: University of Texas Press.

Lewis, J. (1991). *The ideological octopus: An exploration of television and its audience.* New York: Routledge.

Lichter, S. R., Lichter, L. S., Rothman, S., & Amundson, D. (1988). TV and the family: The parents prevail. *Public Opinion, 10*, 19, 51–54.

Livingstone, S. M. (1990). Interpreting a television narrative: How different viewers see a story. *Journal of Communication, 40*, 72–85.

Livingstone, S., & Liebes, T. (1995). Where have all the mothers gone? Soap opera's replaying of the Oedipal story. *Critical Studies in Mass Communication, 12*, 155–175.

Marc, D. (1989). *Comic visions: Television comedy and American culture.* Boston: Unwin Hyman.

Marks, J. (1996, April 22). The American uncivil wars. *US. News & World Report*, pp. 66–72.

May, E. T. (1988). *Homeward bound: American families in the Cold war era.* New York: Basic Books.

Mayerle, J. (1991). Roseanne—How did you get inside my house? A case study of a hot blue-collar situation comedy. *Journal of Popular Culture, 24*, 71–88.

McCrohan, D. (1987). *Archie & Edith, Mike & Gloria: The tumultuous history of All in the Family.* New York: Workman Publishing.

McNeil, J. (1975). Feminism, femininity, and the television series: A content analysis. *Journal of Broadcasting, 19*, 259–269.

Meadowcroft, J. J., & Fitzpatrick, M. A. (1988). Theories of family communication: Toward a merger of intersubjectivity and mutual influence processes. In R. P. Hawkins, J. M. Wiemann, & S. Pingree (Eds.), *Advancing communication science: Merging mass and interpersonal processes* (pp. 253–275). Newbury Park, CA: Sage.

Mellman, M., Lazarus, E., & Rivlin, A. (1990). Family time, family values. In D. Blankenhorn, S. Bayme, & J. B. Elshtain (Eds.), *Rebuilding the nest: A new commitment to the American family* (pp. 54–66). Milwaukee: Family Service America.

Merritt, B., & Stroman, C. A. (1993). Black family imagery and interactions on television. *Journal of Black Studies, 23*, 492–499.

Mintz, S., & Kellogg, S. (1988). *Domestic revolutions: A social history of American family life.* New York: The Free Press.

Mitz, R. (1980). *The great TV sitcom book.* New York: Richard Marek.

Moore, M. L. (1992). The family as portrayed on prime-time television, 1947–1990: Structure and characteristics. *Sex Roles, 26*, 41–60.

National Family Opinion, Inc. (1994, March). American families today: How they feel about personal issues, (Study commissioned by Kraft Cheese). *Good Housekeeping, 218,* 80–84.

Newcomb, H. (1974). *TV: The most popular art.* New York: Anchor Press.

Olson, B. M., & Douglas, W. (1997). The family in television: Evaluation of gender roles in situation comedy. *Sex Roles, 5/6,* 409–427.

Parks, M. (1977). Relational communication: Theory and research. *Human Communication Research, 3,* 372–381.

Perse, E. M., Pavitt, C., & Burggraf, C. S. (1990). Implicit theories of marriage and evaluations of marriage on television. *Human Communication Research, 16,* 387–408.

Pingree, S., & Thompson, M. E. (1990). The family in daytime serials. In J. Bryant (Ed.), *Television and the American family* (pp. 113–127). Hillsdale, NJ: Lawrence Erlbaum Associates.

Popenoe, D. (1988). *Disturbing the nest: Family change and decline in modern societies.* New York: Aldine de Gruyter.

Popenoe, D. (1993a April 14). Scholars should worry about the disintegration of the family. *Chronicle of Higher Education, 39,* p.A48.

Popenoe, D. (1993b). American family in decline, 1960–1990: A review and appraisal. *Journal of Marriage and the Family, 55,* 527–542.

Popenoe, D. (1995). The American family crisis. *National Forum, 75,* 15–19.

Rapping, E. (1992, April). A family affair. *The Progressive,* pp. 36–38.

Rapping, E. (1994, July). In praise of Roseanne. *The Progressive,* pp. 36–38.

Rothschild, N., & Morgan, M. (1987). Cohesion and control: Adolescents' relationships with parents as mediators of television. *Journal of Early Adolescence, 7,* 299–314.

Rowe, K. (1995). *The unruly woman: Gender and the genres of laughter.* Austin: University of Texas.

Shaner, J. (1982). Parental empathy and family role interactions as portrayed on commercial television (Doctoral dissertation, The University of North Carolina, Greensboro). *Dissertation Abstracts International, 42,* 3473A.

Signorielli, N. (1982). Marital status in television drama: A case of reduced options. *Journal of Broadcasting, 26,* 585–597.

Skill, T., & Robinson, J. D. (1994). Four decades of families on television: A demographic profile, 1950–1989. *Journal of Broadcasting & Electronic Media, 38,* 449–464.

Skill, T., & Wallace, S. (1990). Family interactions on prime-time television: A descriptive analysis of assertive power interactions. *Journal of Broadcasting & Electronic Media, 34,* 243–262.

Skill, T., Wallace, S., & Cassata, M. (1990). Families on prime-time television: Patterns of conflict escalation and resolution across intact, nonintact, and mixed-family settings. In J. Bryant (Ed.), *Television and the American family* (pp. 129–163). Hillsdale, NJ: Lawrence Erlbaum Associates.

Spigel, L. (1992). *Make room for TV: Television and the family ideal in postwar America.* Chicago: University of Chicago Press.

Sweeper, G. (1984). The image of the Black family and the White family in American prime-time television programming 1970 to 1980 (Doctoral dissertation, New York University, 1984). *Dissertation Abstracts International, 44,* 1964A.

Taylor, E. (1989). *Prime-time families: Television culture in postwar America.* Berkeley: University of California Press.

Thomas, S. & Callahan, B. P. (1982). Allocating happiness: TV families and social class. *Journal of Communication, 33,* 184–190.

Waters, H. F. (1993, August 30). Fractured family ties. *Newsweek,* pp. 50–52.

Whitman, D., Ito, T. M., & Kost, A. (1996, March 4). A bad case of the blues. *U.S. News & World Report,* pp. 54–56, 59–60, 62.

Zoglin, R. (1990, April 16). Home is where the venom is. *Time,* pp. 85–86.

How Psychologically Healthy Are America's Prime-Time Television Families?

Jennings Bryant
University of Alabama

J. Alison Bryant
University of Southern California

Charles F. Aust
Kennesaw State University

Gopakumar Venugopalan
University of Alabama

One of the surprising developments of the 1990s was that American presidents and vice presidents developed more than a passing interest in the psychological well-being of America's television families. As the decade began, former President George Bush advised American families to be a lot more like "the Waltons" and a lot less like "the Simpsons" ("Bush Derides Simpsons," 1991). Shortly thereafter, then Vice President Dan Quayle launched his often parodied criticism of the single-parent lead character of *Murphy Brown*—an attack that seemingly unleashed a fusillade of acerbic exchanges about the impact of television characters' behavior on the family ("Dan Quayle vs. Murphy Brown," 1992). As the decade came to a close, President Clinton temporarily chilled studios and production houses by holding White House conferences on media violence and family values. And most of the leading candidates to be the first American president of the 21st century proclaimed in key positioning statements that they would restore family values, each addressing the role of television in this process (e.g., "Bradley Offers Plan to Help Families," 1999; "Bush Returns to Familiar Theme of Family Values," 1999; "Gore Stresses Family Values," 1999).

DO TELEVISION'S FAMILIES AFFECT OUR FAMILIES?

Implicit in such expressions of concern is an assumption about media impact. Specifically, the critics assume that family portrayals modeled in fictional media fare are assimilated into the psychological reality of the viewing public. A number of communication theories, such as social cognitive theory (e.g., Bandura, 1994) and cultivation theory (e.g., Gerbner, Gross, Morgan, & Signorielli, 1994), offer models that can be called on in support of such a contention of direct media effects, especially from repeated, prolonged exposure to television's family fare.

Many more specific statements from various scholars have underscored these theories' propositions regarding the potential of television's families to influence real families. For example, Singer, Singer, and Rapaczynski (1984) argued that television has as much potential to influence the family as does the home environment, parental behavior, and the socioeconomic milieu of the family. Greenberg (1980), Stroman (1984), and Kalter (1988), among others, noted that viewers use television families as models.

Moreover, several influential research summaries have endorsed the theoretical contentions of the impact of television's families on our families. For example, the National Institutes of Mental Health, in their summary of research about television's impact, concluded that the behaviors in "television families almost certainly influence viewers' thinking about real-life families" (as cited in Pearl, Bouthilet, & Lazar, 1982, p. 70).

In other words, assumptions that fictional portrayals in popular culture influence everyday perceptions of reality—or that art influences life— appear to be more than assumptions. Extant theory and evidence would seem to rather consistently support these claims.

ARE PRIME-TIME TELEVISION'S FAMILIES PSYCHOLOGICALLY HEALTHY?

An equally important assumption implicit in claims that dysfunctional family values are at least partially caused by television viewing is that television programs typically depict psychologically unhealthy family interactions and behaviors, thereby serving as flawed role models for real families. Such claims generally lack compelling supportive evidence and often appear to be made based on casual observations and on selective anecdotal accounts rather than on systematic assessments. Over the years, prime-time programs such as *Married With Children, Roseanne, The Simpsons, Beavis and Butt-head, Dharma and Greg, Will and Grace, Dawson's Creek*, and *That '70s Show* have been exemplar cases used to accompany more general or even blanket condemnations of prime-time television as being harmful to family values and as having deleterious effects on family functioning (Farah, 1990; Hatch, 1999; Zoglin, 1990).

Other voices have reflected a different point of view. For example, Dr. Joyce Brothers publicly promoted specific shows that she claims demonstrate effective parenting skills worthy of imitation (Larson, 1989). Television's programmers, distributors, and exhibitors have spoken out in their own defense also. For example, John Leonard of CBS noted that prime-time television families feature "more hugging than mugging," and he specifically asked television's vocal critics to include estimates of how much hugging is portrayed on prime-time television in addition to all those assessments of muggings ("Experts Speak Out," 1992, p. 18).

Occasionally, more objective social commentators have offered collusive comments. For example, Zoglin (1992) noted that even in television's most controversial family programming, the sanctity of the family is emphasized. Stanley (1996) commented that very positive family values were presented in CBS's *Touched by an Angel*, in Fox's *Party of Five*, and in WB's *Seventh Heaven*. And Katz (1997) commended WB's family programming as presenting many wholesome family models.

THE RESEARCH QUESTION

Other contributors to the chapter of this volume entitled "Portrayals of the American Family on Television" examined how television's families are depicted and reviewed and synthesized diverse research traditions in the process. Despite the diversity of approaches, perspectives, and protocols taken by our peers, our fundamental question remains unanswered by their treatments: Just how psychologically healthy or unhealthy are the families and family interactions that are portrayed in family-oriented, prime-time television programming? To what extent do the actions portrayed model optimal versus problematic family functioning?

To address this research question, we utilized two standard clinical approaches to analyzing psychological well-being. The first approach, discussed in the next section, was family centered and examined family interactions on prime-time television. The second approach, discussed under "The Mental Health of Individual Members of Prime-Time Television's Families," examined the family members depicted on prime-time television from a psychodynamic perspective and looked for serious mental illness (SMI) at an individual level.

The Circumplex Model of Marital and Family Systems

Our examination of television families from a clinical perspective, looking at family interactions rather than at individual behavior, is not unique, although it is unusual. Aust (1988, 1992) used communication models of relationship enhancement employed by family therapists to examine selected popular situation comedies. He found that many relationship-enhancing communication skills are practiced in sitcoms, not only in programs such as *The Cosby Show*, *Major Dad*, and *Who's the Boss?*, but also in the often maligned *Roseanne* and *The Simpsons*. And Douglas (1996) examined relational difficulties in television's families, reporting that although most families were rated comparatively positively, two families (the Conners from *Roseanne* and the Taylors from *Home Improvement*) were rated in ways that indicated significant relational difficulties. We utilized a different approach to analyze prime-time television families across the decade of the 1990s.

In order to employ standard clinical perspectives to assess the healthiness of television's families, the circumplex model of marital and family systems developed by Olson and his associates (e.g., Olson, Russell, & Sprenkle, 1989) was employed. The circumplex model takes a family system—rather than an individual—perspective for assessing and treating families. According to one expert on family therapy, the circumplex model "sets a new standard for integrating family theory, research, measurement, and clinical practice" (Guerney, 1989, p. 1). The circumplex model (Fig. 12.1) has three primary dimensions; family cohesion, family adaptability (change), and family communication. Each dimension is composed of several key concepts that define it, which are assessed on several rating scales typically utilized during a clinical assessment.

The circumplex model includes a variety of variables within the three major themes of family cohesion, family change (adaptability), and family communication. Family cohesion is defined in the model as "the emotional bonding that family members have toward one another" (Olson, 1989, p. 9). Specific variables of the family cohesion theme include emotional bonding, family involvement, marital relationship, parent–child relationship, internal boundaries, external boundaries, and an overall global cohesion measure. The scale for each variable in the family cohesion dimension ranges from disengaged (1 or 2), to separated (3 or 4), to connected (5 or 6), to enmeshed (7 or 8). The extreme levels of cohesion (disengaged and enmeshed) are considered problematic to family functioning. The central levels of cohesion (separated and connected) are deemed ideal for family functioning.

Family adaptability (change) is defined as "the ability of a marital or family system to change its power structure, role relationships, and relationship rules in response to situational and developmental stress" (Olson, 1989, p. 12). Specific variables of the family adaptability theme include leadership, discipline, negotiation, roles, rules, and an overall global adaptability (change) rating. The levels of the scales on the adaptability dimension range from rigid (1 or 2), to structured (3 or 4), to flexible (5 or 6), to chaotic (7 or 8). The model considers the central levels of adaptability (structured and flexible) to be most healthy for family

CIRCUMPLEX MODEL
OF MARITAL & FAMILY SYSTEMS

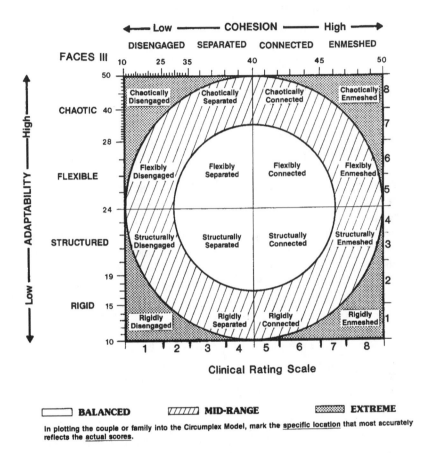

FIG. 12.1. Circumplex model of marital and family systems. Reprinted by permission of D. H. Olson, *Circumplex Model of Marital and Family Systems.* University of Minnesota, Minneapolis, MN: Life Innovations.

functioning, whereas the extremes (rigid and chaotic) are considered most problematic for family functioning.

The third dimension of family communication "is considered critical for facilitating couples and families to move on the other two dimensions" (Olson, 1989, p. 13). Specific variables of the family communication construct include empathy, attentive listening, speaking for self, speaking for others (reverse scored), self-disclosure, clarity, continuity/tracking, respect/regard, and an overall global communication rating. The level of the scales on the family communication dimension range from low (1 or 2), to moderate (3 or 4), to high (5 or 6). The model considers the highest levels of communication to be optimal for family functioning and the lowest levels to be the most problematic. These communication skills "enable couples and families to share with each other their changing needs and preferences as they relate to (the other themes of) cohesion and adaptability" (Olson, 1989, p. 13).

The Mental Health of Individual Members of Prime-Time Television's Families

Some extant research evidence seems applicable to discussions of the mental health and well-being of individual members of television's families. The richest research tradition in this area deals with the way people with mental disorders are depicted on television. Cassatta, Skill, and Boadu (1979) examined health in daytime serial dramas. Using printed synopses of the programs found in *Soap Opera Digest*, the authors found 25 instances of "mental problems" in descriptions of each of 13 daytime serial dramas broadcast in 1977. They concluded, "These 25 instances of various 'mental problems' make psychiatric disorders the number one specific health-related problem in the soap opera world" (p. 77).

Fruth and Padderud (1985) subsequently examined 5 episodes from each of the 14 serials broadcast on network television in the mid-1980s. In the 70 soap opera episodes they examined, eight characters were considered to represent true portrayals of mental illness. Their summary assessment was, "Overall, results of this study support the conclusion that daytime serials perpetuate a negative image of mental illness through frequent presentations which emphasize dangerous behaviors and minimize the effectiveness of psychiatric intervention" (p. 387).

Gerbner (1980) summarized portrayals of mental disorders from 11 years of content analyses of television presentations. He concluded that each year, approximately 2% of television's major characters were identified as having some mental disorder.

Wahl and Roth (1982) examined 385 prime-time programs from 1981. They reported finding 35 characters with mental disorders. In terms of evaluation of the nature of the portrayals of characters with mental disorders, they indicated that many characters did have positive traits such as loyalty and friendliness; however, they were more frequently described by using such negative terms as "'confused,' 'aggressive,' 'dangerous,' and 'unpredictable'" (p. 604).

Finally, Signorelli (1989) examined the portrayal of the mentally ill on entertainment television and confirmed earlier findings of a negative and generally stigmatizing image. She also noted that most common portrayals showed characters as violent and victimized.

In considering the applicability of this research tradition to the present investigation, three caveats are in order: Some of these content analyses have been conducted on soap operas, not on prime-time programming; the vast majority of this research considered any character, not just members of recurring families; and much of the research on the psychological health of characters utilized informal and/or nonstandard classifications of mental disorders.

Because the psychological well-being of a family can be affected quite dramatically if individual family members suffer from serious mental illness, we thought it would be valuable to continue the tradition of searching for mental disorders exhibited by television characters. Because of the focus of our interest, we limited our content analyses to recurring families on prime-time television, however. Also, we utilized the same criteria for mental disorders used by the most highly trained mental health professionals, the criteria for mental disorders defined in the *Diagnostic and Statistical Manual of Mental Disorders* (American Psychiatric Association, 1987, 1994), to identify behaviors of program characters within television's prime-time families that could be considered antisocial or otherwise detrimental.

The various tests for specific disorders feature numerous specific diagnostic criteria, which are very clearly delineated and easily understood. The following are the potentially serious mental disorders we assessed; specific developmental disorders, disruptive behavior disorders, eating disorders, gender identity disorders, tic disorders, reactive attachment disorder, organic mental disorders, psychoactive substance use disorders, psychotic disorders, mood disorders, anxiety disorders, posttraumatic stress disorder, dissociative disorders, sexual disorders, sleep disorders, factitious disorders, impulse control disorders, and personality disorders.

RESEARCH METHODOLOGY

Samples for these content analyses were drawn from the universe of all primetime commercial fare aired during the fall seasons of 1991, 1996, and 1999 on U.S. network television that featured either nuclear, extended, blended, single-parent, or a combination of two or more of these constellations of family units. Using *TV Guide* descriptions and the programming knowledge of more than a dozen mass communication doctoral research assistants, 86 programs were identified as having such family constellations—26 from 1991, 26 from 1996, and 34 from 1999. Those programs are listed in Table 12.1.

TABLE 12.1

Family-Sited Prime-Time Television Programs 1991, 1996, 1999

Broadcast Network	1991	1996	1999
ABC	Baby Talk Davis Rules Dinosaurs Doogie Howser Family Matters Full House Home Improvement Life Goes On Roseanne Step by Step Who's the Boss Wonder Years	Boy Meets World Family Matters Grace Under Fire Home Improvement Life's Work Roseanne Second Noah	Boy Meets World Brother's Keeper Dharma and Greg Home Improvement The Hughleys Two of a Kind
CBS	Brooklyn Bridge Evening Shade Major Dad	Cosby Dave's World Everybody Loves Raymond	Cosby Everybody Loves Raymond King of Queens The Nanny Promised Land Turks
Fox	Beverly Hills 90210[1] Married with Children Roc The Simpsons True Colors	Married with Children Ned & Stacey The Simpsons	Family Guy King of the Hill Party of Five The PJs The Simpsons That 70s Show
NBC	Blossom Empty Nest Fresh Prince I'll Fly Away Sisters The Cosby Show	Third Rock from the Sun Frasier Jeff Foxworthy Mad About You Something So Right Wings	Third Rock from the Sun Frasier Jesse Mad About You Providence
UPN			Between Brothers DiResta Guys Like Us Legacy
WB		Seventh Heaven Brotherly Love Kirk Sister, Sister The Parent 'Hood The Wayans Brothers Unhappily Ever After	Seventh Heaven Charmed Jamie Foxx Sister, Sister Smart Guy Wayans Brothers Unhappily Ever After

[1] *Beverly Hills 90210* was included in 1991 because at that time, the action frequently was centered on the family. By 1996, and certainly by 1999, the program was no longer family-oriented and was excluded from the analysis.

254

As can be seen from examining Table 12.1, the face of prime-time network television programming changed dramatically during the 1990s. Each new wave of assessments featured an additional network—WB in 1996, UPN in 1991—and these new networks offered a large number of family programs. It might also be noted that the specific programs analyzed during each of the three seasons varied substantially. In fact, only two programs, *Home Improvement* and *The Simpsons*, were aired on a first-run basis during all three seasons we content analyzed.

Three episodes of each of the programs examined were taped during the 1991, 1996, and 1999 television seasons. Typically, a few lower rated programs were exempted so frequently—typically by holiday specials, sports specials, or blockbuster movies—that videotaping had to be extended over the course of several weeks to obtain the requisite three episodes. In all, 258 episodes (78 in 1991, 78 in 1996, 102 in 1999) of prime-time family-sited programs were videotaped and systematically examined.

CAVEATS ABOUT USING CLINICAL TOOLS IN CONTENT ANALYZING TELEVISION PROGRAMS; CONSIDERATIONS OF RELIABILITY AND VALIDITY

Circumplex Model

The circumplex model was not designed to evaluate television families. In fact, the "Instructions for the Use of the Clinical Rating Scale" indicated that assessments should take place in a clinical interview. Obviously, that is not possible in content analyzing or otherwise evaluating families on television. On the other hand, clinicians rarely have an opportunity to witness holistic family interactions and other behaviors over the course of extended periods, a luxury that is afforded by content analyses of serial television programs. Nevertheless, because the content analytic approach we utilized was so different from that for which high reliability and validity had been established for the circumplex model (e.g., Olson, 1990, 1991), the use of the clinical rating scale for the family profile (see Fig. 12.2) was approached cautiously.

We established the procedures used for the coding and determined the reliability of the procedures and instruments prior to coding the 1991 sample. After reviewing literature on the use of the circumplex model of marital and family systems, two doctoral students independently coded a sample of 14 episodes as a pilot study. Overall, intercoder reliability was $\alpha = .87$. After obtaining this estimate of intercoder reliability, we carefully examined every instance in which the coders differed in their ratings. Working with the supervising investigator (who on two occasions

FAMILY PROFILE
Based on the Circumplex Model

	DISENGAGED		SEPARATED		CONNECTED		ENMESHED	
COHESION	1	2	3	4	5	6	7	8
Emotional Bonding	•	•	•	•	•	•	•	•
Family Involvement	•	•	•	•	•	•	•	•
Marital Relationship	•	•	•	•	•	•	•	•
Parent-Child Relationship	•	•	•	•	•	•	•	•
Internal Boundaries	•	•	•	•	•	•	•	•
External Boundaries	•	•	•	•	•	•	•	•
GLOBAL RATING	•	•	•	•	•	•	•	•

	RIGID		STRUCTURED		FLEXIBLE		CHAOTIC	
CHANGE	1	2	3	4	5	6	7	8
Leadership	•	•	•	•	•	•	•	•
Discipline	•	•	•	•	•	•	•	•
Negotiaton	•	•	•	•	•	•	•	•
Roles	•	•	•	•	•	•	•	•
Rules	•	•	•	•	•	•	•	•
GLOBAL RATING	•	•	•	•	•	•	•	•

	LOW ←		Facilitation		→ HIGH	
COMMUNICATION	1	2	3	4	5	6
Listener's Skills	•	•	•	•	•	•
Empathy						
Attentive Listening						
Speaker's Skills	•	•	•	•	•	•
Speaking for Self						
Speaking for Others						
(*Reversed Scoring)						
Self-Disclosure	•	•	•	•	•	•
Clarity	•	•	•	•	•	•
Continuity/Tracking	•	•	•	•	•	•
Respect and Regard	•	•	•	•	•	•
GLOBAL RATING	•	•	•	•	•	•

FIG. 12.2.   Family profile based on the circumplex model. Reprinted by permission of D. H. Olson, *Circumplex Model of Marital and Family Systems.* University of Minnesota. Minneapolis, MN: Life Innovations.

consulted with members of the Family Inventory Project of the University of Minnesota—the research group that developed and licensed the circumplex model), the coders refined their interpretations of the circumplex model and its application to our content analyses. During the process of these discussions, we decided that the pair of coders would achieve more valid results if they worked together rather than independently in viewing and coding. This collaborative process was utilized in all three waves of coding.

Additionally, two licensed family therapists, each of whom had employed the circumplex model in his or her work, utilized the same procedures as the two coders and analyzed two of the same episodes that had been analyzed by the regular coders. The results from the therapists were highly similar to those from the regular coders (α = .91 for the two programs combined). Because the therapists had used the circumplex model successfully in their work, these results offer some face validity to applying the model in content analyses of television.

DSM-III-R and DSM-IV

The third revised edition of the *Diagnostic and Statistical Manual of Mental Disorders* (American Psychiatric Association, 1989) is typically referred to as DSM-III-R, and the fourth edition of the same manual (American Psychiatric Association, 1994) is referred to as DSM-IV. Our idiosyncratic use of these clinical guides presents a caveat similar to that of using the circumplex model to evaluate television's families. That is that the *Diagnostic and Statistical Manual of Mental Disorders* was designed primarily for use in clinical practices with real patients. Nevertheless, because the tool is designed to be used by many different types of clinicians, and because it contains classification-rule definitions of every "official" mental disorder, it proved to be imminently practical for usage in content analysis. A hint of this potential can be found in the introduction to the fourth edition (DSM-IV):

> An official nomenclature must be applicable in a wide diversity of contexts. DSM-IV is used by clinicians and researchers of many different orientations (e.g., biological, psychodynamic, cognitive, behavioral, interpersonal, family/systems). . . . It must be usable across settings. (American Psychiatric Association, 1994, p. xv)

A second caveat is that our research spanned two editions of DSM (III-R and IV). We studied the fourth edition carefully, and although it did include adjusted criteria and even a couple of "new" mental disorders, we decided that, for consistency, we would stick with the criteria and disorders identified in DSM-III-R for the content analyses of the 1996 and 1999 samples.[2]

---

[2] In 1996, when we decided to conduct assessments of a second season of family-sited prime-time programming, we discovered that we had not retained the videocassettes of the television programs from 1991; therefore, we could not reevaluate the earlier programs using the criteria of DSM-IV.

PROCEDURES

Coder pairs watched each of the 258 episodes in its entirety. Following their joint viewing of each episode, the coders discussed the episode in terms of the circumplex model and completed a single Family Profile Rating Sheet (purchased from the Family Inventory Project of the University of Minnesota) for the primary family that was featured in that episode. A copy of the rating sheet we employed was presented previously as Fig. 12.2.

After completing the coding for the circumplex model, the pair of coders considered every individual family member to determine whether his or her behavior in the episode undergoing scrutiny qualified as exhibiting a mental disorder. As a reference guide, the pair of coders utilized a four-page summary sheet of the 36 mental disorders presented in DSM-III-R; the first page of that summary sheet is presented as Fig. 12.3. If the coders had any questions about whether a character met the criteria for one or more mental disorders, they referred to the portion of the manual in which the criteria are delineated in great detail and then summarized in tabular form. The page on which each disorder was described in DSM-III-R was included in the summary sheet at the end of the synopsis of each disorder.

RESULTS

The Circumplex Model of Marital and Family Systems

The three major dimensions of the circumplex model of marital and family systems are first considered separately. Because the most crucial determination is the psychological well-being of prime-time television's families, rather than differences between television seasons, more general normative findings are emphasized first. Then, if difference testing via analyses of variance yielded statistically significant differences between years (1991, 1996, 1999), those findings are presented.

Cohesion. For the dimension of cohesion, it should be recalled that disengaged and enmeshed families are considered problematic for optimal family functioning, and separated and connected families are considered to indicate psychologically healthy families. Seven scales contribute to this factor. All of these scales are numbered 1 through 8, and 1 and 2 correspond to disengaged, 3 and 4 to separated, 5 and 6 to connected, and 7 and 8 to enmeshed.

For emotional bonding, 251 of the 258 episodes (97.3%) featured families that were rated either as separated ($n = 49$) or connected ($n = 202$),

---

DSM-III-R Coding Categories

Disorders Usually First Evident in Infancy, Childhood, or Adolescence

___ **1. Conduct Disorder** – 'six months, 3+) Stealing or forgery; run away from home overnight; lies; fire-setting; truant from school; has broken into a house, building or car; deliberately destroyed others' property, physically cruel to animals; forced someone into sexual activity; used a weapon in more than one fight; initiates physical fights; physically cruel to people. (Begins on p. 55).

___ **2. Oppositional Defiant Disorder** – (six months, 5+) Often loses temper; argues with adults; actively refuses or defies adult requests or rules; deliberately acts to annoy people; blames others for own mistakes; touchy or easily annoyed by others; angry and resentful; spiteful and vindictive; swears or uses obscene language. (Begins on p. 57).

___ **3. Overanxious Disorder** – (six months, 4+) Excessive or unrealistic anxiety or worry, with these indications: excessive or unrealistic worry about future events, about the appropriateness of past behavior, about competence in one or more areas (e.g., athletic, academic, social); somatic complaints for which no physical basis can be found; marked self-consciousness; excessive need for reassurance about a variety of concerns; marked feelings of tension or inability to relax. (Begins on p. 64).

___ **4. Anorexia Nervosa** – Refusal to maintain body weight over a minimal normal weight for age and height (15% below that expected); intense fear of gaining weight or becoming fat, even though overweight; perception of one's body weight is disturbed (e.g., feeling fat when emaciated or when obviously underweight); in females, absence of at least three consecutive menstrual cycles. (Begins on p. 67).

___ **5. Bulimia** – Recurrent episodes of binge eating (i.e., rapid consumption of a large amount of food in a discrete period of time); lack of control of binge eating; self-induced vomiting; excessive use of laxatives or diuretics; compulsively strict dieting, fasting, or vigorous exercise to prevent weight gain; minimum average of two binge eating episodes a week for at least three months; persistent overconcern with body shape and weight. (Begins on p. 68).

Organic Mental Syndromes and Disorders

___ **6. Intoxication** – Substance-specific syndrome due to recent ingestion of a psychoactive substance (can include more than one). Maladaptive behavior during the waking state due to the effect of the substance on central nervous system (e.g., belligerence, impaired judgment or social or job functioning). (Begins on p. 117).

___ **7. Manic Episode** – Distinct period of abnormally and persistently elevated, expansive, or irritable mood with (3+) inflated self-esteem or grandiosity, decreased need for sleep, more talkative than usual or pressure to keep talking, flight of ideas or racing thoughts, distractibility, increased goal-directed activity or psychomotor agitation, excessive pleasurable acts having high potential for painful consequences (e.g., sexual, shopping, investments). Sufficiently severe to impair social, job functioning, or require hospitalization to prevent harm to self or others. (Begins on p. 217).

___ **8. Depressive Episode** – (2 weeks). Depressed mood most of day, nearly every day (n.e.d.). Loss of interest or pleasure and at least four of the following: significant weight or appetite loss or gain when not dieting; insomnia or hypersomnia n.e.d; psychomotor agitation or retardation n.e.d; fatigue or loss of energy n.e.d.; worthless or excessive/inappropriate guilt feelings n.e.d.; indecisiveness or lack of concentration n.e.d.; recurrent thoughts of death or suicidal ideation w/ or w/out specific plan or concrete attempt at such. (Begins on p. 222).

FIG. 12.3.   Page 1 from our summary sheet of mental disorders in DSM-III-R (American Psychiatric Association, 1987).

with a mean score of 5.09 ($SD = .27$), which corresponds to connected. In the circumplex model, this typically translates to emotional closeness, with a healthy degree of separation between family members. Loyalty to the family is typical with such ratings.

On the dimension of family involvement, 240 of the 258 episodes (93.0%) featured separated ($n = 34$) or connected ($n = 206$) families, with a mean of 5.45 ($SD = .35$). This scoring is interpreted as emphasizing involvement but with appropriate space for personal distance, and affective interactions by family members are encouraged.

Regarding marital relationship, in 197 of the 212 episodes (92.9%) in which married couples were presented, the relationships were either separated ($n = 40$) or connected ($n = 157$), with a scale mean on this factor of 5.14 ($SD = .29$), corresponding to connected. This rating is exemplified by emotional closeness, with some separateness.

For the item parent–child relationship, in 234 of the 243 (96.3%) episodes that featured one or more parents and one or more children, the relationships were evaluated either as separated ($n = 44$) or connected ($n = 190$). The mean score on this scale was 5.40 ($SD = .31$). This indicates clear generational boundaries and high parent–child closeness.

Regarding internal boundaries, 39 episodes featured families depicted as separated, and 204 were judged to be connected, for a total of 243 of the 258 episodes (94.2%). The mean score on this item was 5.46 ($SD = .37$), which corresponded to connected. In the circumplex model, this generally describes a family in which time together is important but time alone is permitted; although space typically is shared among family members, private space is respected. Moreover, joint decisions regarding internal boundaries are preferred.

Analysis of the external boundaries scale yielded a similar profile, with an identical mean score of 5.46 ($SD = .16$). A total of 251 of the 258 episodes (97.3%) were judged to have separated or connected families, with $n = 39$ evaluated as separated and $n = 214$ rated as connected. These ratings indicate that individual friendships are shared with the family, that the family has more shared than individual activities, and that family members often have joint interests.

Of the 258 episodes, 69 were rated as separated, and 189 were rate as connected (combined; $258/258 = 100.0\%$). The mean score for the "global cohesion" scale was 5.17 ($SD = .14$). This is considered to correspond to a moderate to high rate of family cohesion. In terms of overall cohesion, clearly none of the prime-time television programs examined featured disengaged or enmeshed families. Not even a single episode of a prime-time program depicted the central family as dysfunctional in terms of global cohesion.

To assess differences in cohesion in time in the manner in which prime-time television families were depicted, analyses of variance were conducted on the data for each scale that made up the cohesion dimension, with year of assessment (1991, 1996, 1999) as the independent variable. A couple of statistically significant differences were found. For all analyses, subsequent comparisons were by Student Newman-Keuls procedures.

No statistically significant differences were found for the global cohesion measure, which featured mean scores by year as follows; 1991 = 5.20 (SD = .16), 1996 = 5.23 (SD = .19), and 1999 = 5.11 (SD = .17). Nor were statistically significant differences found for the following scales; emotional bonding, marital relationship, internal boundaries, and external boundaries.

Statistically significant differences by year were found on the data for two measures. For family involvement, the analysis of variance yielded $F(2, 255) = 5.33$, $p < .005$; 1999's prime-time families were rated higher in family involvement ($M = 5.73$, $SD = .30$) than 1991's ($M = 5.26$, $SD = .41$) or 1996's ($M = 5.29$, $SD = .35$) prime-time television families. The analysis of variance performed on the data for parent–child relationship also yielded statistically significant differences, $F(2, 141) = 30.75$, $p < .001$; the mean score from 1999 (5.88, $SD = .23$), was significantly higher than that from 1996 (5.28, $SD = .29$), which in turn was significantly higher than that from 1991 (4.93, $SD = .31$).

Adaptability and Change.   In the circumplex model, six items from the Clinical Rating Scale contribute to the concept of couple and family adaptability and change. For all items, rigid corresponds to ratings of 1 and 2, structured to 3 and 4, flexible to 5 and 6, and chaotic to 7 and 8. The model conceptualizes the internal levels of adaptability (structured and flexible) as more conducive to marital and family functioning and family well-being. The rigid and chaotic domains are considered to describe problematic psychological well-being for the family.

For leadership (control), 250 of the 258 episodes (96.9%) were found to feature families that were structured ($n = 55$) or flexible ($n = 195$). The mean score on this scale was 5.19 ($SD = .24$), which falls within the flexible portion of the scale. According to the circumplex model, this indicates a family with egalitarian leadership that engages in fluid changes.

For the discipline factor, 247 of the 258 episodes (95.7%) presented families that were structured ($n = 48$) or flexible ($n = 199$). The mean score was 5.10 ($SD = .28$), corresponding with flexible. Such families are typically considered to be democratic, to negotiate consequences, and to be somewhat lenient.

On the dimension of negotiation, 39 of the episodes featured structured families, and 216 depicted flexible families, for a combined total of 255 of 258 (98.8%). The mean score on this scale was 5.45 ($SD = .25$), which falls roughly at the midpoint of flexible. According to the circumplex model, such families are flexible in their negotiations and reach decisions via consensus building.

Regarding roles, 244 of 258 episodes (94.6%) were either structured ($n = 48$) or flexible ($n = 196$). The mean score for roles was 5.48 ($SD = .34$), which corresponds to flexible. This is interpreted to mean that the families engage in role sharing and role making and have fluid changes of roles.

Rules yielded 50 episodes presenting structured families and 200 episodes featuring flexible families (combined; 250/258 = 96.9%). The mean score on this item was 5.39 ($SD = .26$), which corresponds to moderately flexible. Families with these characteristics typically offer some rule changes and enforce rules flexibly.

The global change ratings for television's prime-time families were similar; 61 episodes received low to moderate adaptability ratings, and 187 received moderate to high adaptability scores (combined; 248/258 = 96.1%). The mean score for the global adaptability and change item was 5.19 ($SD = .25$), corresponding to a moderate change or adaptability rating overall.

As with the cohesion factors, the data for the individual adaptability and change factors were also treated by analyses of variance, with year of presentation (1991, 1996, 1999) as the independent variable. Four of the six scales exhibited differences over time.

Statistically significant differences were found for the leadership factor, with $F(2, 255) = 4.98$, $p < .005$. Subsequent tests revealed that the mean for 1991 episodes ($M = 4.91$, $SD = .26$) was significantly lower than those for 1996 ($M = 5.27$, $SD = 24$) or 1999 ($M = 5.35$, $SD = .21$). The same pattern of results occurred for the factor of negotiation, $F(2, 255) = 17.36$, $p < .001$, with the mean score for 1991 ($M = 4.99$, $SD = .21$) being significantly different from the means for 1996 ($M = 5.63$, $SD = .19$) and 1999 ($M = 5.72$, $SD = .21$). Roles and rules also yielded statistically significant F-ratios at $p < .001$; for roles, $F(2, 255) = 9.46$, with the mean score for 1991 ($M = 4.67$, $SD = .14$) being lower than those for 1996 ($M = 5.73$, $SD = .21$) or 1999 ($M = 5.97$, $SD = .27$); for rules, $F(2, 255) = 23.88$, with the 1991 mean score of 4.82 ($SD = .23$) being significantly lower than those for 1996 ($M = 5.62$, $SD = .17$) or 1999 ($M = 5.65$, $SD = .19$). No statistically significant differences were found for the global change measure (for 1991, $M = 4.94$, $SD = .23$; for 1996, $M = 5.26$, $SD = .26$; for 1999, $M = 5.32$, $SD = .21$), although the F-ratio approached conventional levels of acceptable statistical significance ($p = .056$).

Family Communication. Seven measures of the Clinical Rating Scale make up the family communication factor of the circumplex model. Two of the seven scales can be subdivided, which we did for our analyses, yielding nine measures in all. All scales are numbered from 1 through 6, with 1 and 2 identified as low facilitating, 3 and 4 as moderate facilitating, and 5 and 6 as high facilitating.

The dimension of listener's skills is divided into empathy and attentive listening. For empathic listener skills, 53 episodes featured families moderate in empathy skills, and 199 featured families high in these skills, for a combination of 252 of 258 episodes (97.7%). The mean score on this scale was 4.83 (*SD* = .19), which falls between "empathy is sometimes evident" and "empathy is often evident." For attentive listening, 66 episodes were rated as moderate and 175 as high (combined; 241/258 = 93.4%). The mean on this item was 4.55 (*SD* = .17). In the circumplex model, this is located near the midpoint between "attentive listening is sometimes evident" and "attentive listening is often evident."

The factor of speaker's skills is also subdivided; in this instance, into speaking for self and speaking for others (the latter is reverse scored). In speaking for self, 40 episodes were rated as having families that were moderate in this skill and 216 as having families high in this regard (combined; 256/258, or 99.2%). The mean for this scale was 4.92 (*SD* = .23), falling between "speaking for self sometimes evident" and "speaking for self often evident." In speaking for others, 79 episodes had families that were moderate on this communication factor, and 170 episodes were rated high (combined; 249/258 = 96.5%). The mean score was 4.55 (*SD* = .26). According to the circumplex model, this means that prime-time television's families show skill in speaking for others at a rate that falls between "sometimes" and "often."

The study of self-disclosure has a rich history in the communication discipline. On this factor, a total of 253 of 258 episodes (98.1%) feature families either moderate (*n* = 36) or high (*n* = 217). The mean score of 4.88 (*SD* = .17) falls between "some" and "open" discussion of self, feelings, and relationships.

On clarity of communication, a total of 257 of 258 episodes (99.6%) depict families either moderate (*n* = 71) or high (*n* = 188) in communication clarity. The mean score was 4.69 (*SD* = .21). This is interpreted within the context of the circumplex model as indicating that prime-time television's families engage in communication that typically is rather clear, and many if not most of the messages seemingly have congruous meanings for different family members.

The element of continuity/tracking of communication deals with competence in negotiating the complex process of interpersonal exchanges (or sharing symbols, or making meaning) among and between family members. On this factor, 91 of the episodes were found to feature families who were moderately proficient, and in 166 episodes, the families were deemed to be quite good in tracking (combined; 257/258 = 99.6%). The mean score of 4.51 (*SD* = .26) falls between the circumplex model's interpretation of "moderately" and "highly" consistent tracking, with few irrelevant or distracting asides and facilitative nonverbal communication, and with most topic changes being appropriate and easily followed.

In terms of respect and regard, in 249 of the 258 episodes (96.5%) the coders rated prime-time television's families as moderate (n = 55) or high (n = 194). The circumplex model interprets the mean score of 4.75 (SD = .21) as meaning that the families depicted rather consistently appear to be respectful of other's feelings and messages.

The global family communication rating scores for prime-time television's families were quite high, as might be anticipated from the previous findings on family communication. In fact, 100% (258/258) of the episodes were deemed to feature families either moderate (n = 59) or high (n = 199) in global family communication skills.

On six of the nine scales or subscales, depictions of prime-time families appear not to have changed measurably over time, at least during the 1990s. For the global family communication factor, empathy, speaking for self, clarity, continuity/tracking, and respect and regard, the analyses of variances failed to reveal statistically significant differences. The mean scores for the global family communication factor by year were as follows; for 1991, M = 4.65, SD = .17; for 1996, M = 4.61, SD = .21; and for 1999, M = 4.91, SD = .19.

Analyses of variance performed on the data from the remaining three scales did reveal statistically significant differences across the factor of time (1991, 1996, 1999). For empathy, $F(2, 255) = 5.13, p < .005$, with mean scores by year for 1991 (M = 4.49, SD = .41), 1996 (M = 4.79, SD = .46), and 1999 (M = 5.05, SD = .47). The Student Newman Keuls (SNK) test revealed that only the two most extreme mean scores are significantly different. For speaking for others, $F(2, 255) = 5.26, p < .005$, with mean scores of 1991 (M = 4.31, SD = .36), 1996 (M = 4.53, SD = .39), and 1999 (M = 4.79, SD = .37). Again the SNK test revealed that only the two outlying values were significantly different statistically. Finally, the results for self-disclosure were, $F(2, 255) = 3.11, p < .05$, with mean scores for 1991 of 4.69 (SD = .24), for 1996 of 4.86, SD = .25), and for 1999 of 5.07 (SD = .29). As with the other two subsequent tests from the statistically significant ANOVAs for family communication measures, only the 1999 and 1991 mean scores are reliably different by SNK test.

Overview.   Perhaps the best way to summarize the results of the findings of this content analysis is to plot the findings by year on a graphic representation of the circumplex model. As can be seen in Fig. 12.4, which presents the coordinates of the mean scores of cohesion and change by year, prime-time television's families of the 1990s are extremely healthy clinically. In fact, this provides a graphic image of family health. Furthermore, Fig. 12.4 illustrates that prime-time television's archetypical family has been consistently healthy throughout the 1990s.

CIRCUMPLEX MODEL
OF MARITAL & FAMILY SYSTEMS

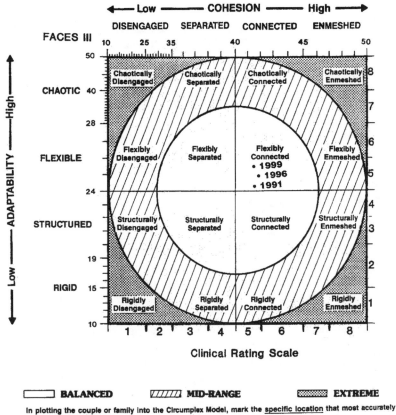

BALANCED   MID-RANGE   EXTREME

In plotting the couple or family into the Circumplex Model, mark the **specific location** that most accurately reflects the **actual scores.**

FIG. 12.4.   Coordinates of cohesion and change for prime-time families as shown on circumplex model. Reprinted by permission of D. H. Olson, *Circumplex Model of Marital and Family Systems.* University of Minnesota. Minneapolis, MN: Life Innovations.

DSM AND THE MENTAL HEALTH OF INDIVIDUAL MEMBERS OF PRIME-TIME TELEVISION'S FAMILIES

We turn from the family system perspective of the circumplex model to a clinical assessment of the mental health of individual members of prime-time television's families, as determined by the criteria of the *Diagnostic and Statistical Manual of Mental Disorders (DSM)* of the American Psychiatric Association. Now we ask, do individual members of prime-time television's families get a clean bill of mental health? Looked at another way, do healthy family systems mask diseased individual family members?

Because television's dramatic conventions include assigning recurring members (including essential family members) of a program's cast roles that may occasionally have them exhibit aberrant behaviors to carry out a story line, we decided to attribute a mental disorder to a family member if he or she exhibited a comprehensive set of symptoms of that mental disorder (i.e., met the *DSM* criteria for that disorder) in any two of the three episodes of the program examined during any year. It should also be remembered that because our focus was on television's families, we examined the behavior of the members of a program's central family only. With these restrictions in mind, our coders engaged in a detailed assessment of potential mental disorders of every family member as exhibited in the 258 episodes screened.

Although a great deal of time and effort went into the coding of the mental health of prime-time television's family members according to *DSM* criteria, not a single member of any television prime-time family was found to fit the criteria for a mental disorder. Quirky? You bet! Mental disorder? No. Not according to strict clinical criteria.

Occasionally the plot line of a program would call for a family member to engage in a conduct disorder (e.g., breaking into a building, destroying someone's property), exhibit symptoms of intoxication, or the like on a one-time basis, but by the end of the program, some miraculous therapeutic process would seem to have produced a return to good mental health, as well as family well-being. The purpose of these isolated manifestations of a disorder appears to be to set up a temporary family conflict, which typically is resolved during the course of the episode through healthy family communication strategies, appropriate mediation, standing coping mechanisms, or the like. In other words, aberrant behavior that may seem to indicate an underlying mental disorder may be exhibited by a family member in an episode (albeit very rarely), but typically that behavior's antecedents ultimately are explained in such a way that the viewer is led to understand the "good reasons" why the family member behaved as he or she did. It may have been a lapse in judgment, but it was not a "real" mental disorder, and the audience does not need to worry.

As we coded and coded without finding exemplar cases of mental disorders by prime-time television's family members, we began to look informally to see whether recurring nonfamily cast members might be depicted as having a mental disorder, perhaps one of the more "sensational" mental disorders, such as Tourette's Disorder, Hallucinogen Persisting Perception Disorder (Flashbacks), or Hypomanic Episodes. Our future working hypothesis is that this is a more common occurrence. What seems to be even more common is for "guest talent" (i.e., characters that last for one or, at most, a few episodes) to have mental disorders. But that is for future research to determine.

DISCUSSION AND CONCLUSIONS

The overarching finding of this investigation is that America's pime-time television families of the 1990s appear to be quite healthy psychologically. Evidence from the content analysis that employed the circumplex model of marital and family systems indicates that prime-time families were almost ideally "centered" on the dimensions of cohesion and adaptability and were at least moderately high in communications skills.

Cohesion is defined in the circumplex model as "the emotional bonding that family members have toward one another" (Olson, 1989, p. 9). The content analysis revealed that on the nine scales measuring cohesion, the percentage of prime-time families that exemplified ideal emotional bonding ranged from 92.9% to 100%, with a mean of 95.9%. Obviously, that means that of the 258 television episodes examined, 4.1% were judged to be less than ideal in emotional bonding by well-established clinical criteria; that is, they were rated either as disengaged or enmeshed—the two extremes of the cohesion dimension.

The dimension of family adaptability and change of the circumplex model is defined as "the ability of a marital or family system to change its power structure, role relationships, and relationship rules in response to situational and developmental stress" (Olson, 1989, p. 12). On the six scales of this dimension, between 94.6% to 98.8% of prime-time television's families were found to fall into the ideal range of adaptability, with a mean score on this dimension of 96.5%. Of course, this means that 3.5% of prime-time television's families were rated as overly rigid or overly chaotic in terms of their potential to change.

Family communication is somewhat different than the cohesion and adaptability in the circumplex model, in that it is considered to be the facilitator of the other two dimensions of healthy families. Communication "is considered critical for facilitating couples and families to move on the other two dimensions" (Olson, 1989, p. 13). From the perspective of communication scholars, this may be an overly limiting view of communication, but this restriction comes with this clinical model. Nevertheless, in the episodes examined, on the seven dimensions (with two subscales) of communication examined, television's families do very well, with a range of the percentages of episodes that fall into moderate and high facilitation varying from 93.4% to 100%, and with an overall communication mean of 97.8%. Looked at conversely, this means that 2.8% of prime-time television families are considered to be low in this critical attribute of family well-being.

Moreover, the analyses of differences in family portrayals over time generally indicate that on most scales that make up the three dimensions of the circumplex model, prime-time television's families are getting better over time. In general, 1999's prime-time television families were better connected emotionally, more suited to change, and better in communication skills than those of the 1991 and 1996 samples.

What results, then, from this examination using clinical family systems criteria is rather high marks for television's families, at least those that were presented during prime time during the decade of the 1990s. As far as we could tell, no research has attempted to determine a comparative picture of the psychological well-being for America's real families. But the statistics on domestic violence alone would suggest that the families on the screen are at least as healthy as those in front of the screen. There is always room for improvement, of course, but it appears that those who attempt to denigrate the "family values" of American television should focus on areas other than the psychological health and well-being of television's prime-time families.

If the findings from content analyses of television characters during the 1980s (e.g., Gerbner, 1980) hold true for the 1990s, then approximately 2% of television's talent would be depicted as having a mental disorder. Our clinical analysis of mental disorders among individual members of prime-time television's families during the 1990s suggests that those characters are not recurring family members.

More importantly, the use of the criteria of the *DSM* to examine individual members of prime-time families provides further support for the findings of the circumplex model. The absence of Serious Mental Illness can be taken as another marker of psychologically healthy families.

Undoubtedly, families on prime-time television can accurately be accused of exhibiting a plethora of negative characteristics that potentially could lead audience members to engage in deviant and antisocial behaviors. No doubt many find prime-time television's families overly and unnecessarily gross, vulgar, trivial, sexual, and otherwise unseemly. As far as the psychological health and well-being of the family systems and individual family members depicted, however, when judged by standard clinical criteria, most prime-time families are models that the real American family could well follow.

REFERENCES

American Psychiatric Association. (1987). *Diagnostic and statistical manual of mental disorders* (3rd ed. rev.). Washington, DC: Author.

American Psychiatric Association. (1994). *Diagnostic and statistical manual of mental disorders* (4th ed.). Washington, DC: Author.

Aust, C. F. (1988, January). *Relationship-enhancing communication skills in "The Cosby Show."* Paper presented at the meeting of the Georgia Speech Communication Association, Macon, GA. [ERIC Document Reproduction Service No. ED321 330]

Aust, C. F. (1992, April). *Relationship-enhancing communication skills in prime time television programs about families.* Paper presented at the meeting of the Southeastern Council on Family Relations, Mobile, AL.

Bandura, A. (1994). Social cognitive theory of mass communication. In J. Bryant & D. Zillmann (Eds.), *Media effects: Advances in theory and research* (pp. 61–90). Hillsdale, NJ: Lawrence Erlbaum Associates.

Bradley offers plan to help families. (1999, October 8). *The Tuscaloosa News*, p. 3A.

Bush derides Simpsons. (1991, March 7). *The Tuscaloosa News*, p. 5A

Bush returns to familiar theme of family values. (1999, November 18). *The Tuscaloosa News*, p. 4B.

Cassata, M. B., Skill, T. D., & Boadu, S. O. (1979). In sickness and in health. *Journal of Communication, 29* (4), 73–80.

Dan Quayle vs. Murphy Brown. (1992, June 1). *Time*, p. 20.

Douglas, W. (1996). The fall from grace? The modern family on television. *Communication Research, 23*, 675–702.

Experts speak out. (1992, August 22). *TV Guide*, pp. 12–22.

Farah, J. (1990, November). TV's assault on families is not joke. *Focus on the Family*, 9–11.

Fruth, L., & Padderud, A. (1985). Portrayals of mental illness in daytime television serials. *Journalism Quarterly, 62*, 384–387, 449.

Gerbner, G. (1980). Dreams that hurt: Mental illness in the mass media. In R. C. Baron, E. D. Rutman, & B. Klaczynska (Eds.), *The community imperative* (pp. 19–23). Philadelphia: Horizon House Institute.

Gerbner, G., Gross, L., Morgan, M., & Signorielli, N. (1994). Growing up with television: The cultivation perspective. In J. Bryant & D. Zillmann (Eds.), *Media effects: Advances in theory and research* (pp. 17–41). Hillsdale, NJ: Lawrence Erlbaum Associates.

Gore stresses family values in presidential announcement. (1999, June 17). *The Tennessean*, p. 1.

Greenberg, B. S. (1980). *Life on television: Content analyses of U.S. TV drama.* Norwood, NJ: Ablex.

Guerney, G. G., Jr. (1989). *Circumplex model: Systematic assessment and treatment of families* (Promotional piece). Binghamton, NY: Haworth.

Hatch, D. (1999, March 8). A good TV dad is hard to find. *Electronic Media*, pp. 19, 23.

Kalter, J. (1988, July 23). Television as value-setter. *TV Guide*, pp. 5–11.

Katz, R. (1997, May 12). WB values families. *Mediaweek*, pp. 6–7.

Larson, M. S. (1989). Interaction between siblings in primetime television families. *Journal of Broadcasting & Electronic Media, 33*, 305–315.

Olson, D. H. (1989). Circumplex model of family systems VIII: Family assessment and intervention. In D. H. Olson, C. S. Russsell, & D. H. Sprenkle (Eds.), *Circumplex model: Systemic assessment and treatment of families.* New York: Haworth.

Olson, D. H. (1990). *Clinical rating scale (CRS) for the circumplex model of marital and family systems.* Minneapolis: Family Social Science, University of Minnesota.

Olson, D. H. (1991). *Uses of FACES II versus FACES III.* Minneapolis: Family Inventory Project, University of Minnesota.

Olson, D. H., Russell, C. S., & Sprenkle, D. H. (Eds.). (1989). *Circumplex model: Systemic assessment & treatment of families.* New York: Haworth.

Pearl, D., Bouthilet, L., & Lazar, J. (Eds.). (1982). *Television and behavior: Ten years of scientific progress and implications for the Eighties, Vol. 1* (DHHS Publication No. ADM 82-1196). Washington, DC: U.S. Government Printing Office.

Signorielli, N. (1989). The stigma of mental illness on television. *Journal of Broadcasting & Electronic Media, 33,* 325–331.

Singer, J. L., Singer, D. G., & Rapaczynski, W. S. (1984). Family patterns and television viewing as predictors of children's beliefs and aggression. *Journal of Communication, 34*(2), 73–79.

Stanley, T. L. (1996, February 5). Prime-time family values. *Mediaweek,* pp. 9–12.

Stroman, C. (1984). The socialization influence of television on Black children. *Journal of Black Studies, 15,* 79–100.

Wahl, O. F., & Roth, R. (1982). Television images of mental illness: Results of a Metropolitan Washington media watch. *Journal of Broadcasting & Electronic Media, 26,* 599–605.

Zoglin, R. (1990, April 16). Home is where the venom is. *Time,* pp. 85–86.

Zoglin, R. (1992, June 1). Where fathers and mothers know best. *Time,* p. 33.

V

Meanings and Effects

The Meaning of Television in the American Family

Alison Alexander
University of Georgia

"What is the meaning of television to the American family?" is an important question indeed. Whose meanings structure the use, mediation, and influence of the medium goes to the heart of psychological, family system, and cultural approaches to the study of the meaning of television within the family. Whether seen as an object of perception, a subject of conversation, or an instrument of social control, these views grant considerable importance to media within the family, despite their differences in epistemology.

Researchers working within the psychological paradigm have tended to focus on viewing within the family; parental mediation, control, and rules; and contingent cognitive, affective, or behavioral consequences. The "meaning" of television is an implicit aggregate of individual responses to its stimulus. Researchers working with a family system paradigm, on the other hand, tend to theorize about the generative power of communication in creating family systems that contextualize media and create the meaning of media for that family. Variables are at the level of the family unit and are frequently expressed as "patterns." Researchers within the culturalist paradigm are sensitized to the symbolic role of media and families in sustaining cultural myths and social power. The meaning of television content is located in a complex process of inter-action between text and reader, but the larger meaning of television is located in the production of popular culture and perpetuation of domi-nant social forces.

This chapter sets out to briefly review some of these influential approaches to the study of television within the family in the belief that each contributes improved understanding of the mechanisms linking media to larger social patterns of perception, of family systems, and of cultural power—that is, the meaning of television. Using questions con-cerning how we (individuals, families, society) think about the meaning of television is a starting point to organize insights and to theorize about media and its place in the family.

PSYCHOLOGICAL PARADIGMS

Viewing and Coviewing

Television viewing with family members is common. Lawrence and Woz-niak (1989) reported that children ages 6 to 17 spend 65% of their view-ing time with family members. Viewing with others is the most frequent mode of media exposure of 5-year-olds according to Field (1987), who estimated that 85% of their viewing was coviewing: 45% with parents and the remaining with siblings and friends. Other studies offer a note of cau-tion. One study of 3- to 5-year-olds (St. Peters, Fitch, Huston, Wright, & Eakins, 1991) found that the majority of shows were watched without parents and that coviewing declined with age. Alternatively, Dorr, Kovaric, and Doubleday (1990) found that coviewing occurred least often with younger children, who need it most, and reflected similar preferences rather than explicit mentoring. Coviewing with siblings is arguably the most common viewing situation (Van Evra, 1998). Viewing with siblings clearly influences the younger child: They "watch up" to the older chil-dren's preferences (Wright, St. Peters, & Huston, 1990), and are the recip-ient of older siblings' interpretation of content (Alexander, Ryan, & Munoz, 1984). Yet, this interpretation of content does not improve their under-standing (Haefner & Wartella, 1987). Unfortunately, coviewing does not equal interaction, and it is interaction with children that most clearly influences their interpretation of the medium.

Discussions of coviewing versus solitary viewing should not obscure other variability in the viewing context. Family members often engage in concurrent activities while viewing, relegating television to the back-ground. Individuals may vary considerably in how they experience view-ing, depending on mood and social situation. Certainly, the history of uses and gratifications research points to the multiplicity of gratifica-tions that can be obtained from the same content. The experience sampling method (ESM) of Kubey and Csikszentmihalyi (1990) provides insight into the quality of life for families, and thus provides a hint about the meaning of television within that life. They measured self-reports of perceived activity, involvement, mood, and physical state in situations where the individual was with the family without television, watching with the family, and watching alone. Watching television with the family was relaxing and cheerful. Watching alone was also relaxing, although less cheerful and challenging than viewing with the family. Kubey and Csikszentmihalyi concluded that family viewing is both significantly less activating and less challenging than family time spent in other activities.

Parental Commentary and Mediation

A number of studies convincingly demonstrate the potential for family interaction to mediate the impact of television. In experimental settings, parental or adult comments have been found to aid children's understanding of program content (Collins, Sobol, & Westby, 1981), to shape perceptions of families in the real world (Austin, Roberts, & Nass, 1990), to foster critical viewing skills (Corder-Bolz & O'Bryant, 1978), and to increase recall of information from educational programs (Wright et al. 1990). Thus, parents may increase the amount children learn from programs, may help kids better understand plots, and may counteract the negative effects of violence and antisocial content through expression of disapproval or discussions of values. Despite these potential benefits, little evidence exists to suggest that parents actually engage in these behaviors. Coviewing in a context of limited interaction tends to be the norm, restricting the learning that interaction could promote (Anderson & Collins, 1988; Field, 1987).

There is a growing body of observational research that describes how interpretation of meaning is accomplished within the family viewing context. Most of the research in this area has focused on the development of children's understanding of the television medium.

Lemish (1987) observed the home television viewing behavior of 16 children between 6 and 30 months of age. She found that viewing—although attention was sporadic—was shared with adults. Much of the interaction during viewing involved considerable language interaction including naming or identifying familiar objects, repeating labels, asking questions, and relating television content to the child's experience. Amount of talk was related to the program being watched, with *Sesame Street* eliciting the most verbal interaction. Vocabulary teaching appeared to be a major focus of these interactions and Lemish speculated that those interactions may enrich vocabulary learning from television. Alexander, Ryan, and Munoz (1984) observed siblings in the viewing situation. Only 40% of the interaction was about television. But the majority of that was interpretive in function. Younger children asked about character's identification, problematic visual devices, narrative conventions, and the medium per se.

Interview and observational data reinforce these conclusions. McLeod, Fitzpatrick, Glynn, and Fallis (1982) noted that a majority of mothers report frequent use of interpretive or evaluative statements. Messaris (1986) interviewed over 100 mothers about their responses to questions concerning television realism. Mothers described a variety of interactions in which they told children about things that could not happen in real life, including making some complex distinctions between the improbable and the impossible and explaining certain disturbing images of immorality, poverty, and so forth. Messaris noted his fundamental assumption that audience members are creative, and one consequence is the "interpersonal calibration of interpretations among members of a social network" (p. 104).

In summary, although empirical observation of interaction is sparse, the existing research suggests that children as well as adults create television-related interactive sequences. These sequences fulfill functions as diverse as the interpretation and evaluation of programming content, generation of conversation, and creation of nonmedia-related social actions.

Control

In many families, television gives rise to issues involving control of how much and what is viewed. Families adopt strategies or enact ritual practices to control the effect of the medium. Television viewing per se can create conflict within the home as parents voice concern about the amount of time spent with TV and the other activities that television displaces. Television content can create similar conflicts when members squabble over program choices, or parents are concerned about the effects of content, and helping children understand what they see.

Control of television viewing has been studied in terms of explicit rules about amount and content of exposure. The most consistent finding is the paucity of rules, with estimates ranging from 19 to 69% of families that report any rules, varying due to age of children, class, and by whether mother or child responded (McLeod et al., 1982; Mohr, 1979). Rules are typically viewed as mediating variables: attempts by parents to moderate the potential impact of television on children through control of viewing. The rules are also, however, constructions. They're the account offered by children or parents to describe the explicit rules about television viewing that operate within that family system. As such, these research studies uncover the explicit rules and inevitably underestimate the power that existing structures impose on media consumption. At the family level, it is easy to miss the implicit rules that govern viewing. For example, in one family, the television may never be on during weekend days because children have learned that if parents find them "goofing off too much," they will be assigned chores. Although it is doubtful that anyone would describe this as a family rule, such practices have the force of limiting viewing contexts.

Perception and Social Cognition

Perception functions in the interpretation and organization of experience. Television is a complicated object of perception. How do we as individuals, as family members, and as members of a larger culture make sense of it as a physical object? Is not television inescapably a thing? A large object in our family, living and bedrooms? Then, how do we make sense of its content, which is inarguably more important than its physical size, and which is blatantly part of a larger social context in a way that the coffee table or even our newest fashionable outfit never is. (There is much room to examine television as a subject, but that is beyond the scope of this chapter. But we do quite rightly attribute agency or autonomy to program content, placing media in a space separate from other objects). In contemplating the meanings of television for the American family, one question that emerges is, "What does it mean to think about television as a social object?"

Some foundational truths about television seem banal. First, television is an object. Second, it is an object of perception. And finally, it is an object with important social attributes. These observations allow us to pair the insights of both perception research and research in the area of social cognition, the psychological study of how we think about other people and their motivations (Fiske, 1995). It forces us to think about how we think about people versus how we think about things. And, to consider the uneasy space that the television medium occupies, firmly a thing, but with many attributes of a social object. Perhaps the term "media cognition" describes the activity of thinking about such a space, neither an object nor an "other." (Although I suspect that the space so described may be larger than media alone. Perhaps pets?)

What are the differences between thinking about television in our lives, as compared to our parents or siblings? It would be hard to argue that we ever devote the time or strategic planning to television that we devote to our interpersonal relationships within the family. With others, we act as a "motivated tactician" (Fiske, 1995), actively involved in cognizing our own intentions, as well as those of others. Alternatively, television really is different from our coffee table. And the differences echo, even if faintly, the distinctions between thinking about others and thinking about objects. Television, conceived as both medium and message, as both an object and an event, is seen as causal, mutable, and—in the larger sense of the industry—capable of receiving feedback. Its consumption implicates the self and its content is extensively variable, perhaps more variable even than interaction with other people. We even have an area of research dedicated to understanding individuals who substitute parasocial (i.e., televisual) for interpersonal interactions (e.g., Anderson & Collins, 1988).

If television in the American family is to be understood, at least one perspective asks us to contemplate the schemas by which we dissect its place in our lives. These cognitive schemas are cognitive structures that represent knowledge about a stimulus or concept, as well as its perceived attributes. These schemas direct attention, guide memory, and influence judgment. Although quite specifically studied, particularly by Schank and Abelson (see Fiske, 1995, for discussion), schema theory has not been a major area of research within mass communications. Nonetheless, if one goes back to the fundamental premise that schemas are cognitive structures that aid understanding and enable us to operate as "cognitive misers," taking short cuts in our routine perceptions, one can see that a number of loosely defined schemas exist for television. The content of these schemas can be understood by looking at the metaphors for the place of television within our lives.

One group of metaphors paints television as a drug or an addiction. Television is seductive, and individuals fear becoming couch potatoes. In these cases, the lure of an activity that may not be controllable defines the category. When Foss and Alexander (1996) explored the metaphors used by heavy and nonviewers, they found both embraced the metaphor of addiction. Heavy viewers concentrated on the literal falseness of "television-as-drug" metaphor, and talked freely of the addictive qualities of the medium precisely because they do not buy it as anything other than a metaphor, in which there is never a direct correspondence between two compared objects. Thus, they hold the medium harmless and view it as mere entertainment, except for vulnerable audiences who should be protected. Nonviewers operate in just the reverse fashion, avoiding that which they cannot control. Television is treated with fear for its seductive and potentially harmful consequences.

Related to the addiction metaphor are other metaphors that stigmatize television viewing and television viewers. Not only is television viewing per se considered unworthy, but certain texts such as soap operas, talk shows, stock car racing, or wrestling occupy a special low status. Time is being wasted; self-worth can be called into question. It is hard to see such terms as "couch potatoes" or "dead heads" who spend their time consuming "mind candy" being viewed as positive assessments. Yet, just such metaphors reveal what is probably the most pervasive social construction for television in our culture: that television is mindless entertainment. We—the people—see through television, a statement Miller (1988) called the "jeering gaze" of the contemporary audience. This attitude fosters an illusion of "knowing" that we wrongly assume protects us from any consequences of consumption. In fact, Salomon (1977) convincingly demonstrated how just such a perception diminishes learning from educational programming. In short, the meaning we accord television has important consequences for its influence.

One particularly powerful metaphor compares television to a babysitter. To this metaphor apparently adheres all the negative connotations of television within the family: isolating children, replacing family interaction, absentee parenting, unsupervised viewing, and so on. This is in contrast to the relatively few metaphors that portray television as a positive influence: television as an electronic hearth, as conversational currency, and as a social glue.

Questions as to how cognitive schemas, even ones disguised as simple metaphors, direct attention, guide encoding and memory, or influence judgment challenge researchers to examine the content and process of our understanding of the meaning of television. Lest the reader feel (correctly) that this perspective slights affect and behavior, note that other chapters in this book deal with existing research programs that study the importance of affect and explore our understanding of behavior, and understanding cognition is important to forging the links among cognition, affect, and behavior.

Questions about the meaning of television in the American family have not been used to organize our knowledge, but much of the existing literature, particularly in the areas of mediation, metaphor, and perceived reality, could contribute to our understanding of the answers to the following. A first question is: What is the nature of our perceptions of the meaning of television as a social object within the American family? Second: What are the consequences of how we perceive it?

We find ourselves arrayed along an interesting continuum, ranging from the jeering gaze of the cognitive miser who uses the least elaborated strategies to process the medium, to the motivated tactician, who treats television in the home as something to be studied, carefully monitored, and managed. Are we, then, arrayed along a media-cognition dimension ranging in terms of its social importance from object to other?

FAMILY SYSTEMS PERSPECTIVES

Family systems-based media research uses a communicative perspective on the role of television in family interaction and begins by examining the family as the context in which viewing is performed and made meaningful. Of the many contexts that influence meaning and behavior, none is more ubiquitous than the family. And it is through communication that the structure and processes that regulate a family are created. This interactionist perspective from family process research has been modified by communication researchers with a strong symbolic orientation to become the predominant position in the field of communication (Meadowcroft & Fitzpatrick, 1988). Families share a set of enduring assumptions about the social world. Understanding the dimensions of the family system can help us understand the social reality constructed within the family. Because communication is seen as fundamental to family process, researchers have attempted to identify dimensions of family interaction that illuminate the processes whereby communication operates within the family to create family systems (Fitzpatrick & Ritchie, 1994).

This perspective assumes that there are patterns and regularities in marriage and family communication. Uncovering these patterns, their characteristics, causes, and consequences has long been the primary focus of family research. These patterns can appear to be contradictory. They can seem to be fragile when, as is the case of classical drama, an outsider can easily disrupt family systems. Yet, for family therapists these patterns can be robust enough to withstand profound attempts to change unwanted patterns of interaction within families. Although interactionists agree that communication is the process whereby families create a social reality, such agreement has not led to common research strategies or perspectives. Research has conceptualized the family as a system, as a small group, as a type, as part of a network, in a life stage, in family therapy, or negotiating power. Similarly, the examined outcomes of communication are quite varied. Concepts such as conflict, dominance, intrusion, and influence are frequently studied. More rarely, support or encouragement is examined.

The most frequently used paradigmatic description of family communication in mass communication research comes from the work of McLeod and Chaffee (1973). Their schema is based on two communicative dimensions (socio and concept orientation) in which parents stress harmony and obedience on the one hand, and negotiation and self-reliance on the other. Although it has been linked to differences in political knowledge, exposure to types of programming, social adaptability, and family rules (Van Evra, 1998), important dimensions of family interaction are not tapped by this measure.

With the emergence of interest in qualitative investigations of how media are used in everyday life, researchers began to observe the nature and consequences of television-related interaction in the home (cf. Lindlof, 1987, 1991). One major conclusion from this line of research is that television may serve an almost limitless range of diverse uses and functions. Family members can watch television to be together, or to get away from each other; as a basis for talk or to avoid interaction; as a source of conflict, or an escape from it. Because much of the time that family members spend together is in the presence of television, television at least partially defines the context within which family interaction occurs and therefore helps determine the meaning of that interaction. From this perspective, family themes, roles, or issues are carried out in a variety of contexts, and the television viewing context becomes one in which it is useful to study patterns of family interaction in general (Lull, 1980). As such, media are implicated in the accomplishment of numerous family functions, including defining role expectations, articulating the nature of relationships, and using economic and relational currencies in the negotiation of intimacy and power.

Such a perspective foregrounds the recognition that television can influence family interaction even when family members are not watching (Bryce, 1986). Media influence is embedded in people's lives. The effects of media are not contained within the primary exposure context but are seen in numerous ongoing and communicative contexts (Fry, Alexander, & Fry, 1990). These contexts are separated spatially and temporally from the primary exposure context, but are, nonetheless, important for understanding media influence. Such a focus acknowledges the range and complexity of different ways in which media texts and individuals can come together to create the meaning of media content and of the medium itself. If communication can be defined as a process of creating and sharing meanings, then mass communication scholars might profitably focus their attentions on the ways in which media affect the process of creating and sharing meanings within the family, as well as on the ways in which the process of creating and sharing meanings within the family affects the place of media within the family.

In many studies on media and the family, the family communication pattern has been studied as a variable mediating the effect of exposure to media (Fitzpatrick & Ritchie, 1994). It is, however, the social patterning of family communication, rather than the aggregate effect of types of comments, that places this research in the family systems perspective. It is clear that television and its content are social objects and take on contextual meaning based on the actions of those around it. Yet, the television viewing context is not easily defined. In one family, viewing may contextualize the family interaction. Thus, when viewing, families are focused on the television and define their activity as watching television. Alternatively, some families may have the television on, but define their activity much differently, perhaps as sharing time together, completing routine work, or even making family decisions. Nor should we assume that viewing routines are analogous to family types. The television context may also be variable within the family, changing as a function of both media content and the constellation of viewers.

Family systems paradigms have rightfully been criticized for ignoring larger cultural patterns that also shape family interactions. One cannot naively assume a solely communicatively generated family system. For although families do jointly create rules, roles, and systems, that creation occurs within a larger cultural context that provides frames and boundaries, just as media texts and technologies are associated with social values in everyday life that affect how, when, and where they are used in the domestic sphere (Lindlof, 1987, 1991). These questions of larger social structures are taken up by individuals working within the critical/cultural perspective.

Those exploring the question of the meaning of television within the American family may profit from careful examination of communication patterns about media within the family. By analogy from the family communication pattern literature, one could ask, what is the nature of the media communication patterns (MCPs)? Does there exist a reasonably identifiable pattern of interaction about media within famililes? Is it a subset of larger family communication patterns? How does its status as a social object get created in these interactions? Does this pattern relate to how the media is interpreted, discussed, and evaluated within the home? And what are the consequences of these communication patterns for the family system and for the impact of media on and within the family? If family patterns of interaction are both robust and fragile, is the same true of media communication patterns? What are the consequences?

CRITICAL/CULTURAL PERSPECTIVES

To date, the vast majority of literature on children and the family has been approached from two perspectives: a psychological tradition that examines individual cognition and development, and a sociological family systems perspective that looks at communicatively constructed social or familial systems. Studies that approach children from a critical perspective constitute a relatively small body of research within the realm of children and mass communication. Critical/cultural studies examine the role of media in maintaining and changing the structure of power within society (Fejes, 1984). They see society as deeply divided by class, and perhaps as well by gender and race. Feeling constrained by traditional linear transportation models of communication, cultural studies refer to schools of thought that examine the place of media in the situated production of meaning within society. Although meaning is overdetermined by cultural hegemony and the ability of those in control to naturalize meanings (what Hall, 1980, called "dominant meanings"), the reproduction of ideology in individuals requires their willing consent. Hence, a struggle for meaning ensues wherein dominant forces create normative subject positions (that is, "normal" ways of interpreting messages that support the interest of the powerful). Yet, individuals can resist these dominant ideologies and negotiate their own meanings based at least in part on local perceptions (Hall, 1980). Thus, media texts are referred to as polysemic or open to multiple interpretations that may vary from "dominant readings." Hall (1980) used the terms "negotiated" and "oppositional" readings.

The issue of where meaning is located—in the message, in the audience, in some interaction between the two, or elsewhere, has been significant to researchers. Textual analysis opens the possibility of displaying ideologies or interpretations that are embodied within the text, with an emphasis on how meaning is constructed through complex processes of signification and subject positioning, although researchers tend to differ on the weight they place on the structural components of the text and on the interpretive act of actually reading a particular text. It is just as possible, however to encounter a text—a film, a program—through talk about the text as it is to encounter it as a definable physical object. These two uses of the term text parallel the contexts in which the text is encountered: Consumption context is used to describe the reader's engagement with the physical object, and communicative context to refer to the myriad encounters one can have with the same text as a object of talk. In short, the existence of the television medium is a necessary, although not sufficient, condition for the production of meaning. It is not wise to assume that meaning is merely reproduced with no alteration, in either the consumption or the communicative context. The meaning of text is woven from fabric created by every aspect, use, and implication related to the consumption of text. Communicative contexts are significant because the meaning produced in these contexts may differ from those produced during the media consumption context. Viewers most likely produce a more elaborate and critical reading during the communicative context. Immediate experience with a program may well deviate significantly from the rational explanations that occur after the fact. Elaborated meaning may not occur unless or until audience members discuss the content in communication contexts.

Following the broad classification scheme of Curran, Gurevitch, and Woollacott (1982), critical communications research can be divided into three areas: (a) political economy examinations of the infrastructure of media; (b) structuralist approaches that use textual analysis and draw from semiotics, psychoanalysis, and literary theory; and (c) cultural studies, referring to schools of thought that examine the place of media in the situated production of meaning within society. Political economy analysis undergirds our understanding of how media are created. Structuralist and cultural approaches are most useful in understanding the creation of meaning in the home.

Coming from the political economy perspective, Kline (1993) examined the role of children in the marketplace, arguing that we seldom acknowledge the "marketplace as a part of the matrixes of contemporary socialization that reinforce the consumer culture" (p. 13). Kline analyzed the evolution of children's consumerism, framing it within the overall structural forces of the marketplace. Yet he noted that the public is adept at pretending that what is wrong with children's television is anything but a structural issue. Hence, his analysis of structural issues does not directly study the meaning of television within the family, but provides a cogent analysis of one important system of meanings and representation. Using a structuralist perspective to address issues of children's television advertising, Seiter (1993) asserted that television is a communication system that, in its combination of verbal and visual signs presents a formidable but worthy challenge to analysis. She viewed children as active in their appropriation of consumer good and media, creating their own meanings from the stories and symbols of consumer culture. Her analysis focused on the themes, characters, and strategies of ads that facilitate certain patterns of cultural appropriation.

Increasingly, researchers are asking questions about the polysemic nature of texts (i.e., multiple possible meanings, a perspective that sees that the act of individual interpretation may vary from "dominant readings"). For example, Morley (1986) argued that patterns of television viewing can only be understood in the overall context of family leisure activity. His in-depth interviews investigated how television is used within different social classes of families and how television material is interpreted by its audience, with particular attention to gendered patterns of selections, preference, enjoyment, and integration into everyday life.

Buckingham (1993, 1998) took a media literacy approach to studying the meaning of television for children. He suggested that children are being exposed to extensive information about television, including the views of parents. Yet, he found that children are able to construct and create their own interpretations of events and formulate their own opinions, which may be different from their parents. Kids have their own unique interpretations of the events occurring around them.

His extensive analysis of rich interview data revealed a displacement finding that children present themselves as "knowing," "mature" consumers of television products, but they detach themselves from the harmful effects of television. Knowing something was "not real" seemed important in their evaluation of self-competence. He found that interaction with parents was important as a "reality test," and that talking with parents about television fulfilled several functions for children. These included asserting their own power, defining their position, entering adult conversations about issues, and affiliating with others (Buckingham, 1993, 1998).

Again, we see that the critical cultural tradition has been struggling with questions of meaning. Whether dominant messages or resistant readers get the upper hand, their focus is much broader than the meaning of an individual text. These scholars are concerned with the larger social forces that create meanings for society at large. Rather than locating all social power within the consciousness of the individual or the activities of a small group, critical/cultural scholars ponder the consistencies of the social order, and ask how these meanings are created and maintained.

CONCLUSION

On the basis of this review, it seems that psychological, family systems, and cultural approaches need to inform our research on the meaning of television with the family. The psychological focus on the individual effects of usage and interventions that produce outcomes is necessary to understand how learning and gratifications occur. The psychological paradigm has equipped researchers less well to examine the social creation of meaning within the family, which in turn has slighted the larger questions of cultural myth and popular culture.

The lines between these approaches are not fixed. For example, the work in family patterns of interaction about media shares much with culturalist readings of gender and power in the work of Morley (1986). Research would profit from sharing a recognition of the importance of individual differences and the weight of the complex dynamics of the creation of social power. There is scope to pursue in the future the ways in which these perspectives can inform each other. By examining the interrelationships of perception and family structures as they interact in the production and reproduction of meaning, the examination of the meaning of television with the American family can be greatly enhanced.

Television is more than an object of perception, but not quite "another"—not an object of social cognition. Occupying an uneasy space between the two, television occupies what might be termed in the cultural tradition a *contested space*. Throughout this review a number of heuristic contradictions have emerged as we consider the questions of the meaning of television and what it means to view television as a social object. We have a cognitive miser, who is also a motivated tactician when engaging in important social interactions, operating within a family system of communicatively created patterns that are robust and fragile, and within a social system in which social power and dominance create normative patterns of seeing the world to which some offer a measure of resistance.

Ironically, in all three levels of analysis, we have intriguing opposites. Like metaphors that are both obviously false and intriguingly true, these provide us with a useful heuristic for exploring how to think about the meaning of television.

REFERENCES

Alexander, A., Ryan, M. S., & Munoz, P. (1984). Creating a learning context: Investigations on the interaction of siblings during television viewing. *Critical Studies in Mass Communication, 1,* 354–364.

Anderson, D. R., & Collins, P. (1988). *The impact of children's education: Television's influence on cognitive development.* Washington, DC: U.S. Department of Education.

Austin, E. W., Roberts, D. F., & Nass, C. I. (1990). Influences of family communication on children's television-interpretation processes. *Communications Research, 17,* 545–565.

Bryce, J. (1986). Family time and television use. In T. Lindlof (Ed.), *Natural audiences: Qualitative research of media uses and effects* (pp. 121–138). Norwood, NJ: Ablex.

Buckingham, D. (1993). *Children talking television: The making of television literacy.* London: Falmer Press.

Buckingham, D. (Ed.). (1998). *Teaching popular culture.* London: UCL Press.

Collins, W. S., Sobol, B. L., & Westby, S. (1981). Effects of adult commentary on children's comprehension and inferences about a televised aggressive portrayal. *Child Development, 52,* 158–63.

Corder-Bolz, C. R., & O'Bryant, S. (1978). Can people affect television: Teacher vs. program. *Journal of Communication, 28*(1), 97–103.

Curran, J., Gurevitch, M., & Woollacott, J. (1982). The study of the media: Theoretical approaches. In M. Gurevitch, T. Bennett, J. Curran, & J. Woollacott (Eds.), *Culture, society and the media* (pp. 11–29). London: Methuen.

Dorr, A., Kovaric, P., & Doubleday, C. (1990). Television literacy for younger children. *Journal of Broadcasting & Electronic Media, 34*(4), 377–397.

Fejes, F. (1984). Critical mass communications research and media effects: The problem of the disappearing audience. *Media, Culture and Society, 6,* 210–232.

Field, D. (1987). *Child and parent coviewing of television: Relationships to cognitive performance.* Unpublished doctoral dissertation, University of Massachusetts, Amherst MA.

Fiske, S. (1995). Social cognition. In A. Tessler (Ed.), *Advanced social psychology* (pp. 149–193). New York: McGaw-Hill.

Fitzpatrick, M. A., & Ritchie, L. D. (1994). Communication schemata within the family: Multiple perspectives on family interaction. *Human Communication Research, 20,* 275–301.

Foss, K., & Alexander, A. (1996). Exploring the margins of television viewing. *Communication Reports, 9,* 61–67.

Fry, V., Alexander, A., & Fry, D. (1990). Textual status, the stigmatized self, and media consumption. In J. Anderson (Ed.), *Communication yearbook 13* (pp. 519–544). Newbury Park, CA: Sage.

Haefner, M., & Wartella, E. (1987). Effects of sibling coviewing on children's interpretation of television programs. *Journal of Broadcasting & Electronic Media, 31,* 153–168.

Hall, S. (1980). Encoding/decoding. In S. Hall, D. Hobson, A. Lowe, & P. Willis (Eds.), *Culture, media, language* (pp. 128–138). London: Hutchinson.

Kline, S. (1993). *Out of the garden.* London: Verso.

Kubey, R., & Csikszentmihalyi, M. (1990). *Television and the quality of life: How viewing shapes everyday experience.* Hillsdale, NJ: Lawrence Erlbaum Associates.

Lawrence, F., & Wozniak, L. (1989). Children's television viewing with family members. *Psychological Reports, 65,* 395–400.

Lemish, D. (1987). Viewers in diapers. In T. Lindlof (Ed.), *Natural audiences: Qualitative research of media uses and effects* (pp. 33–57). Norwood, NJ: Ablex.

Lindlof, T. (Ed.). (1987). *Natural audiences: Qualitative research of media uses and effects.* Norwood, NJ: Ablex.

Lindlof, T. (1991). The qualitative study of media audiences. *Journal of Broadcasting & Electronic Media, 35,* 15–30.

Lull, J. (1980). The social uses of television. *Human Communication Research, 6,* 197–209.

McLeod, J. M., & Chaffee, S. (1973). Interpersonal approaches to communication research. *American Behavioral Scientist, 16,* 469–499.

McLeod, J. M., Fitzpatrick, M. A., Glynn, C. J., & Fallis, S. F. (1982). Television and social relations: Family influences and consequences for interpersonal behavior. In D. Pearl, L. Bouthilet, & J. Lazar (Eds.), *Television and behavior: Ten years of scientific progress and implications for the eighties* (Vol. 2, pp. 272–286). Washington, DC: U.S. Government Printing Office.

Meadowcroft, J. M., & Fitzpatrick, M. A. (1988). Theories of family communication: Toward a merger of intersubjectivity and mutual influence process. In R. P. Hawkins, J. Wiemann, & S. Pingree (Eds.), *Advancing communication science: Merging mass and interpersonal processes* (pp. 253–275). Newbury Park, CA: Sage.

Messaris, P. (1986). Mothers' comments to their children about the relationship between television and reality. In T. Lindlof (Ed.), *Natural audiences: Qualitative research of media uses and effects* (pp. 33–57). Norwood, NJ: Ablex.

Miller, M. C. (1988). *Boxed in: The culture of TV.* Evanston, IL: Northwestern University Press.

Mohr, P. J. (1979). Parental guidance of children's viewing of evening television programs. *Journal of Broadcasting, 23,* 213–228.

Morley, D. (1986). *Family television: Cultural power and domestic leisure.* London: Comedia.

Salomon, G. (1977). Effects of encouraging Israeli mothers to co-observe "Sesame Street" with their five-year-old child. *Child Development, 48,* 1146–1151.

Seiter, E. (1993). *Sold separately.* New Brunswick, NJ: Rutgers University Press.

St. Peters, M., Fitch, M., Huston, A. C., Wright, J. C., & Eakins, D. J. (1991). Television and families: What do young children watch with their parents? *Child Development, 62,* 1409–1423.

Van Evra, J. P. (1998). *Television and child development* (2nd ed.). Mahwah, NJ: Lawrence Erlbaum Associates.

Wright, J. C., St. Peters, M., & Huston, A. C. (1990). Family television use and its relations to children's cognitive skills and social behavior. In J. Bryant (Ed.), *Television and the American family* (pp. 227–251). Hillsdale, NJ: Lawrence Erlbaum Associates.

Conflicts and Resolution Strategies Associated With Television in Marital Life

Walter Gantz
Indiana University

In contemporary society, television viewing is an important component of daily life. Most viewing occurs at home, within the context of family activities and relationships. Although a majority of American households now have at least two television sets, television viewing still commonly involves use of a single set and multiple family members, including husbands and wives. Negotiation and subsequent accommodation centers on a number of potentially contentious issues, including the following; the amount of time devoted to watching television, when the television is turned on and off, the specific programming viewed, and the way in which television programs and commercial matter are watched (e.g., uses of the remote control when commercials are aired). Gender differences associated with these issues (e.g., program preferences and viewing styles) can be dramatic.

The way and extent to which spouses resolve conflicts often is reflected in their satisfaction with and commitment to their marital relationship (Fitzpatrick & Badzinski, 1994). Television viewing—and the conflicts and accommodation strategies related to it—may affect the ways in which spouses evaluate their marital relationships. Given the value placed on intact families and the increased recognition of the fragility of contemporary families (e.g., marital relationships), it is important to understand the dynamics of television's fit in the home.

Relatively little is known about the ways in which marital partners negotiate and accommodate each other's potentially disparate television viewing interests and behaviors. Because differences between partners are likely, husbands and wives must learn about each other's television viewing needs and habits and then negotiate appropriate resolutions, much as is done in other domains of their lives. Active negotiation and intentional patterns of accommodation are likely to occur early in the relationship, as partners observe each other's behaviors on a daily basis and try to reconcile differences probably rooted in television habits developed before marriage. But, negotiation and accommodation is almost certainly an on going process as demands within the household fluctuate, available content changes, and new technologies become available. With older married couples, the processes may be more subtle, as spouses respond on a more intuitive, anticipatory basis. As is the case with other differences between marital partners, television viewing differences are not always resolved to each partner's satisfaction. Television, then, may be a source of ongoing conflict, particularly among those who are dissatisfied with other aspects of their relationship. Direct comparisons between married and divorced adults may be instructive here. Among divorced adults, television may have been a source of conflict and/or of inadequately enacted attempts to accommodate differences. Alternatively, television viewing may have been a source of shared experiences and comfort in otherwise incompatible marital relationships (Rosenblatt & Cunningham, 1976).

Because the literature has little to offer in terms of detailed descriptions of the accommodation and negotiation processes over TV, it is difficult to make reasoned predictions about the ways in which programs are selected, alternative activities are considered, and spouses are satisfied with the process and outcomes. Television may exacerbate existing conflicts or may create conflicts of its own. Spouses may be unhappy and argue with one another about the amount of time spent watching television. And, with cable and its highly segmented programming, television can easily trigger discord about the programming viewed. As a result, television may be divisive. Differing interests separate husbands and wives from one another, each going to a TV set to watch the programming of their choice. Even coviewing may be disquieting, as there often is less conversation and interaction than when the set is off (Comstock, 1982). Remote control devices serve as a source of coviewing tension as well, as varying patterns of use (sometimes deliberately) create friction among coviewers (Walker, Bellamy, & Traudt, 1993). Gender matters here, as males make more frequent use of this technology than do females

(Copeland & Schweitzer, 1993; Hetter, 1988; Heeter & Greenberg, 1988; Perse & Ferguson, 1993). Gantz, Wenner, Carrico, and Knorr (1995) found that spouses appeared to easily resolve selected viewing differences related to televised sports although a power differential did emerge. When one partner wanted to watch televised sports and the other wished to watch something else at the same time, far more often than not, the woman went to the second set. This study was limited in two important ways. First, its sample was skewed in that most respondents had been married for many years. As a result, strategies used to accommodate initial differences may no longer have been seen as accommodation. Second, the authors made no use of qualitative research strategies. Gantz (1995) described a survey that pointed to a relationship between marital length and the extent to which TV-related disagreements occurred within the marital relationship. But, this effort also offered a snapshot limited by the methods used and respondents interviewed (e.g., only one spouse per household). Consequently, recent efforts may have only skimmed the surface of the negotiation and accommodation processes.

Whereas qualitative research efforts often leave social scientists hungering for a more generalizable database, such efforts do bring a contextual richness that traditional survey research procedures often are unable to provide. Relevant work in this domain includes Lull's classic but now dated observational study of the control exerted by family members in the selection of television programs (Lull, 1982) as well as Krendl's intensive examination of the ways in which three families watched and imposed television viewing rules (Krendl, Troiano, Dawson, & Clark, 1993).

This study was designed to fill an important void in our understanding of television viewing by placing television viewing within the setting in which most viewing occurs (home) and within the context of ongoing relationships (marriages) central to our culture. In order to maximize understanding of the negotiation and accommodation processes associated with television viewing, this study employed both qualitative and quantitative methods. Additionally, this study focused on three potentially distinct groups of adults; newlyweds, older married couples, and divorced individuals.

The following research questions were addressed:

1. What issues related to TV use generate communication and/or conflict? To what extent do they involve differences in time management (e.g., amount of television watched; when it is watched), programming preferences, or viewing styles (e.g., use of the remote control)?

2. How do married adults resolve conflicts that arise as a result of differential interest in television programs and/or different patterns and styles of viewing found in the relationship?

Beyond this, studies on the representation of families in television programs (Douglas & Olsen, 1996) have suggested that life for the modern TV family can be characterized by conflict and a lack of cohesiveness. Because television programming can serve to transport culture (Taylor, 1989), it is possible that these representations are serving as models, which are then incorporated into marital relationships (Robinson, Skill, Nussbaum, & Moreland, 1985). As a result, this study also was guided by the following question:

3. To what extent do married adults find themselves using relational strategies at home employed by those on television?

METHODS

There were four stages of data collection. The first three stages, primarily qualitative in nature, were designed to provide the rich, thick description so often missing from purely quantitative studies. The final stage was designed to provide the quantitative response to the research questions at hand. All the data were collected between November 1996 and March 1997.

Stage 1 utilized existing newsgroups on Usenet. Six unmoderated Usenet newsgroups were identified as likely to have readers interested in the topic: alt.feminism, alt.romance, rec.arts.tv, alt.support.divorce, soc.singles, and alt.support marriage. A single message was simultaneously posted to each newsgroup under the header "Television and Relationships." The message described the study and asked readers who were currently married, living with someone, or divorced to share their insights and experiences. The single posting generated responses from 30 individuals situated across the United States, Canada, and the United Kingdom[1] Follow-up questions directed to individuals resulted in an additional 9 responses.

Stage 2 involved intensive, face-to-face interviews conducted with 11 couples, one couple at a time. Participation was solicited on the telephone using random digit dialing techniques for numbers in Marion County, Indiana. Interviews were audiotaped and ran approximately 75 minutes. Each couple was paid for their participation.[2]

---

[1] About half of those who responded were female. Based on the evidence presented, most appeared to be in their 20s or 30s.

[2] Participants ranged in age from 18 to 69. Eight couples had been married to their present partner for no more than 8 years. Most were well educated. Nine of the couples were White, two were African-American.

In Stage 3, six focus groups were conducted. Separate sessions were held with newlywed males, newlywed females, males in long-standing marriages, females in long-standing marriages, divorced males, and divorced females. For these groups, newlywed was operationalized as married for no longer than 3 years. Participants were recruited on the telephone using random digit dialing techniques for numbers in Marion County, Indiana. In order to increase the potential diversity of responses, one adult from each couple (or former couple) was asked to participate. Each focus group was audiotaped. Sessions ran approximately 1 hour and 45 minutes each, with each participant paid at the end of their session. A total of 43 people participated in the focus groups.[3]

Stage 4 involved telephone interviews with 145 adults residing in 49 counties in Indiana, using the Genesys random digit dialing method and the University of California Computer Assisted Survey Methods software (CASES).[4] The questionnaire relied on close-ended questions. Nonetheless, it included several open-ended questions designed to provide the illustrations and texture often difficult to tap with close-ended questions. The average interview took 34 minutes to complete.

RESULTS

Issues Generating Communication and Conflict

Face-to-Face Interviews.   Couples were asked if they had talked, wanted to talk, or had disagreements about 12 issues related to TV. These were the amount of TV watched; how late one or the other watched TV; the shows watched; who picked the shows that got watched; who watched on the best set in the household; how loud the TV was; whether TV interfered with meals, chores, talking with each other, doing something with friends or doing something else together; and, for those with children, what and

---

[3] Participants ranged in age from 19 to 72. Ten men and 7 women participated in the long-standing married groups. Marital length ranged from 4 to 51 years. Five men and 4 women participated in the newlywed groups. Marital length ranged from less than a month to 2 years. Eight men and 9 women participated in the divorced groups. They had been married for 1 to 16 years. Most (74%) of the participants were White.

[4] A majority of those interviewed (63%) were female. Nine of 10 (91%) were currently married. Nearly half (42%) had been married to their present spouse for no more than 10 years. Slightly more than half (54%) were between the ages of 18 and 44. Most (63%) had at least some post high school education. Almost all of the respondents (95%) were White. Respondents in the telephone survey appeared to be fairly satisfied with their marriages. On the nine-item marital satisfaction index, respondents averaged 69. (Responses ranged from 14 to 90, the maximum possible score. Cronbach's alpha for this index was .90.)

how much TV their children watched. Respondents also were asked if they had disagreements about use of their TV's remote control device.

Responses to these questions pointed to widespread but generally limited disagreements. Whereas differences existed, their importance often was minimized by the participants. On occasion, however, these differences surprised and rankled participants. It was clear that some couples either had not confronted each other about the issue or had been unable to resolve it to the satisfaction of both.

Most had no objections to the amount of television the other currently watched. Two participants acknowledged that whereas it had been a problem earlier in the relationship, it had been addressed (e.g., the heavy viewer watched less than before). For one young couple, though, the issue triggered an argument in front of the interviewer:

> **W (Wife)**:   I think he watches too much television. He says he doesn't but to me it's a psychological crutch for him to function through the house. I don't think he can stand silence. He can't. So, I do think it's a crutch and I wish he could just go without it sometimes. But, that was an issue when we first got married because I had dust on my TV set. I still have a television set I have had for over 15 years and he always said "God, you never turn on your TV." . . . He'll stop and make a point of "I don't need this television on. Turn it off." And it will be [off] that day. But, a lot of times the argument is really that he's watching TV and not really doing something I want him to do.
>
> **H (Husband)**:   I disagree totally with what she has to say . . . I don't really watch TV as much as she thinks I watch. When she gets back from school, then I decide to watch TV. But, she thinks I've been watching TV from the time I get home until the time she gets back plus the time she's home seeing me watch TV. So, she thinks I've been watching for 4 hours when I probably have only been watching for 30 minutes. . . . So, I don't agree with her saying I watch a lot of TV. It's fizzling out and the computer is becoming the big issue in the household. . . ., TV is not like a magnet. She thinks it is and that it suckers me into it. I gotta have it, you know. Well, I don't have to have TV. That is something I have been trying to convince her. If you think I watch TV a lot now which I don't, you should have known me 4 or 5 years ago . . .
>
> **W**:   I did know you.
>
> **H**:   All right. Let's go.

Most acknowledged that they or their spouse often watched television later at night than the other. This period of viewing alone amounted to about an hour per day. In general, such viewing was not regarded as problematic. Several participants said their spouse did not object to their late night viewing because the spouse was asleep. Others said their spouse accepted or encouraged late night viewing, even in the bedroom, as it provided the spouse with a sense of security, comfort, and togetherness. As one young woman noted, "Just knowing that he is lying there in bed watching TV, that he's there, makes me more relaxed and I can go to sleep a lot quicker. If he's not home, then I worry."

Some participants simply noted that when they watched later than their spouse, they made efforts to accommodate their nonviewing spouse's needs (e.g., by making the sound lower so the spouse could sleep). For several female participants, however, late night viewing was problematic. One complained because, as a light sleeper, she had difficulty sleeping with the set on. Another disapproved because her husband was not going to bed at the same time as she.

Disagreements about late night viewing were not always resolved, as exemplified by this difference of opinion between a husband and wife, married for 1 year:

W: I usually go to bed and he follows about an hour later. We don't fight about it too much. If I pull on his arm and I say, "You know, it's late. You have to get up even earlier than I do so don't complain tomorrow."
H: She gives me a guilt trip if I try to stay up.
W: Maybe 30–40 minutes and then I just give up and go to bed. It usually doesn't work.
H: Actually, it usually does work.
W: Only after I'm pouting.
H: After that 30 or 40 minutes.
W: After your show [*Stark Trek*] is over.
H: I don't always stay up if it's an episode that I have seen before.
W: (Interrupting) I beg to differ.
H: If she harks on me enough I'll just turn it off anyway and go to bed.
W: Only if it's a rerun. If it's one he hasn't seen, there is nothing I can do to get him to come to bed.

There appeared to be little discord about the shows participants wanted to watch, the way in which shows were selected for viewing, or claiming the household's best set for personal use. Between shared interests, a willingness to compromise, and easy access to a second set, most respondents quickly dismissed these issues as not germane in their households. Similarly, those with children tended to discount discrepant viewpoints with regard to their children's viewing behavior. One male did recall his wife's ire at his willingness to let his children extend their bedtimes in order to watch TV.

More often than not, these participants felt TV did not interfere with meals, talking with one another, doing something else together, or being with friends. One couple had "strict rules" about television and dinner; meals were to be eaten as a family, without distractions. Others ate dinner every night in front of the set, husband and wife content with TV's place alongside their table. Several couples said they were ready to override the set and listen when their partner had something to say. One couple agreed that TV did take away from talking with one another. And, although they had talked about it, they didn't have a "specific plan to say this is how we're going to talk instead of watching TV." Television was occasionally blamed for delaying visits to relatives or to the nearest mall. More often, though, television was a valued activity, filling in nicely for a lack of funds and, for one couple, relatively few friends.

Six participants expressed some annoyance with how loud the TV was when their partner watched. Some said they complained, with mixed results.

> Yes. Yes. The TV is always too loud. When he's watching it's always too loud. [And] he complains that it's too loud when I have the TV.

> W: It's so loud we can't hear anyone outside knocking on the door. I say "Turn it down. Turn that TV down." (And, does he turn it down?) Yes.
> H: In a minute. In a heartbeat.
> W: He turns it down a little bit but I think he eases it back up. (Laughter.)

When pressed, one couple quietly acknowledged that they had not talked with each other about the issue, even though both thought the volume was too loud when the other watched. Indeed, it was clear to the interviewers that, prior to the interview, a number of participants either had not thought about the issues under consideration or had not shared their concerns with their spouse.

Half of the couples said they had no qualms or disputes about how the remote control was used in their household. In these instances, the husband almost always controlled the device. One woman noted she lived in a traditional household and seldom challenged her husband. Another ceded the remote to her husband because she always had: "You know, this is the way we always did it. I just let him have it [the remote control] and go on. I'll sit there and look at whatever he's got on TV." Other couples clearly battled over the remote, sometimes compromising, other times not. Nonetheless, in the course of the interview, several couples were able to laugh about their actions.

H: She takes over that control and I can't find it.
W: It's a fight really.
H: I try to hang on [to the remote control] cause I know what's going to happen if she gets it. It's going to be click, click, click, click, click every time.
I: And, when that happens?
W: He gets mad. He says I can't take it.
H: Yeah, I get mad.
W: And gets up and walks out.
H: [She] abuses the television. I try to sit down and watch TV with her and she's flipping channels every second. I don't have a problem when the commercials are on. I do that. But, she keeps on flipping, you know. I get it if I can. Yeah, I kind of take that male role of controlling the remote control. I admit that. I hold that remote control and keep it on the head of the waterbed next to me.
W: If I get a chance, I grab it. He's a flicker and that just shatters my nerves.
H: We tease about it all the time. But, I don't think it's a serious problem.

Focus Groups.   As was the case with the intensive interviews, focus group participants were asked if they had talked or ever wanted to talk with their spouse about a series of issues related to TV. All but three of the issues used in the intensive interviews were pursued here as well. (The issues omitted were the shows each spouse wanted to watch; who picked the shows watched; and, what and how much TV their children watched.)

A handful of participants said they were concerned about the amount of television their spouse watched. Two women said they talked about it with their spouse. A third said she had wanted to talk about it with her ex-spouse but was "scared" to raise the issue; she was "from that generation where you just kept still." Women in long-standing marriages were most likely to say the topic merited conversation with their spouse. But, even they appeared generally content to accommodate their husband. As one noted:

> I sometimes think my husband watches too much but I think it's also as if he has had a real hard day. I think he just kind of stares at it and just lets his mind go dead for awhile. And I

> think it's his way of unwinding so I don't ever tell him one way or another. I just think he needs to do that.

Late night viewing was not a contentious issue. For a few participants, late night viewing was valued in that it kept the two apart.

> Toward the end of our marriage I was staying up a lot later. She went to bed and I just didn't want to join her so I stayed up and watched TV.

> It gives me a chance to fall asleep before he comes in and starts messing with me and if I'm sleeping he won't bother me.

No one complained about use of the best set at home. And, almost no one expressed concern about television interfering with meals. Many appeared content to eat and talk with their spouse while the set was on. One male in a long-standing marriage said he based his mealtime viewing on the effort his wife put into preparing the meal.

> If there's a full spread on the table I just go right into the seat. If I come home and it's like something she cooked in the micro-wave, I'll sit in front of the TV and eat my dinner on the coffee table. But, I will give her courtesy if she cooks dinner and sits it on the table. If she slaves over the stove I can tell as soon as I come in the front door from work. It's time to sit down and have a family meal. If there's no aroma and I see my stuff on a paper plate, she don't care.

Two women in long-standing marriages were unhappy here. One blamed herself for buying TV trays when she was redoing her kitchen. Her husband never gave up the habit of watching while they ate dinner. The other was bothered because, given the configuration of their break-fast table, her husband was able to see the TV but she was not. Asked if she didn't ever change seats, she said "No. No. That's his seat." Almost no one thought television really interfered with household chores. Several women said they took care of chores (e.g., cleaning, laun-dry, balancing the checkbook) while they watched television. A few men said they deliberately took care of chores before viewing so that their wives wouldn't nag. No woman said her husband reminded her about chores that needed to be accomplished.

> My wife has a "to do" list and I know if I want to watch or view the football game or something like that then I know I got to get it done or I'm going to hear about it. And she is going to

come in and say "Hey, the garage isn't done." And you know I
don't want to hear "Oh honey after this football game is over
you promised me you were going to get it done."

Others acknowledged chores sometimes took a back seat to viewing.
They appeared confident, though, chores would get done.

If there is a race that he wants to see, he will do that instead of
the grass or something. But, it will get done. I know it will get
done. (By whom?) Not me. I don't do the yard. (Laughter.) He'll
do it. It will just be next week.

Almost no one said television interfered with spending time with
friends. And, no more than one or two in each focus group thought TV
interfered with doing other things together. One divorced male noted that
televised sports interfered with church activities his ex-wife favored. A
newly married man recognized TV sports interfered with doing things
with friends. Fortunately for him, his wife appeared comfortable spending time with friends while he watched sports. Two women, one newlywed, the other divorced, expressed frustration with the difficulty they
had getting their husbands away from the set:

My [ex-]husband was just plain lazy. He was one to relax and
don't have to get up and go nowhere unless it's very, very special. He wanted to go to work, wanted to get through with that
and that's it. And he was just lazy. And to lay down and watch
TV was all that he desired to do. Unless on very special occasions. . . . He just liked to lie and watch TV. And that was it and
having some treats.

None of the newly married men thought that TV interfered with talking with their spouse. In every other group, at least two participants
admitted this was the case for them. One divorced male seemed thank-
ful; TV spared them from embarrassing silence. "[It was] something to
do rather than looking at each other with nothing to say." More often,
particularly among women, TV was blamed for stifling conversation.

If he's watching something, you don't talk . . . until a commercial. But sometimes there would be something on my mind
right then and there and I would want to say it. Then he would
jump up and snap at me to wait until a commercial. And then
it was like he had spoiled it to where I didn't even want to talk
with him because he made me feel like, God, you know.

One elderly divorced woman went further. Her ex-husband appeared tyrannical, permitting no intrusions when he watched TV.

> My husband wouldn't even allow the kids to walk in front of the TV when they had to go to the bathroom. It's "You go over there and sit down and don't walk in front of that TV again." It really dominated our life once he got in and turned the TV on. We lived differently before he got home.

On the other hand, a number of participants said there was plenty of time for talk. Several men noted that when their spouse really wanted to talk, even when the set was on, she got their attention.

> My wife stands in front of the TV or very close. She can yell at me while I'm watching TV. She has to get right in front of the set. "I want to talk with you." She makes sure I see her.

In all but one group, two or three participants acknowledged they had talked with their spouse about how loud the television was. (None of the women in long-standing marriages said loudness was an issue in their households.) Those in the newlywed groups were quite vocal here, noting easily resolved disagreements.

> I like it loud and he doesn't. He's like "That is so loud. Can you turn it down?" It's usually loud because I'm doing stuff in the kitchen or something so I turn it up. . . . I will just lower it . . . though . . . to his level.

Many participants noted frequent battles over the remote control. Here, participants offered a mix of humor, feistiness, and resignation. Differences in usage patterns appeared to create a mix of playful banter and good-natured roughhousing to annoyance and resignation. Occasionally, men complained about or admired their spouse's use of the remote control. As one male in a long-standing marriage noted, "They say most guys are like channel surfers [but] I'll put my old lady up against anybody." More often, they talked about the remote control as theirs.

> When you're married long enough [6 years], your wife and you understand there are certain things that are yours. My wife has a couple of things that I don't touch. They're hers. The remote control is mine. When I walk into the living room and my wife has the remote control, she hands it to me. And when I get done with my remote control I put it on top of my TV every night.

> Mine is an unspoken rule. I don't go in there and use her curling iron and the waffle maker because I can't and I don't know how to use them. There are just certain things in our life that my wife understands that are mine and hers and even though we've been married for 16 years, they are still ours separate.

Many men appeared to accommodate their spouse's viewing style, using the remote less frequently when they watched TV with their spouse than when they watched alone. When one group of men was asked if they used the remote more often, almost all immediately and quite vocally said "Yes!" As one noted:

> I can appreciate my wife because she can watch a whole TV show for an hour and never touch the remote control and watch the commercials and everything. I can't. When it comes to commercial time, I have to see what else is on.

Bantering and jousting over the remote were commonplace. Generally, these scraps appeared to be well contained. On occasion, though, participants grew wary with these battles. As noted below, one divorced male said the problem was addressed when he purchased a second set for the household. More often, women appeared to yield ground, resigned to more channel flipping than they cared to see.

> We argued about [who controlled the remote]. So we got a universal remote which became the battle because she would have one and I would have one. (Laughter) It was funny and then it became really not funny. We said "This is getting us nowhere" because I play channel select in between commercials and she hated it. "Can't you just watch a commercial?" "No, I don't want to watch the commercials. I don't need any hair products, OK?" Yeah, that was a bad thing. We never ever agreed on it. I always thought I should have it and she always thought she should have it. So, that's when we got another TV that had a remote. I really couldn't afford it but I was too stressed out.

> We've never talked about it but I doubt it would do any good. Especially when commercials come on, he's just going to flip.

Telephone Survey.   Two lengthy series of close-ended questions were used to tap communication and conflict related to television viewing. In the first set of questions, respondents were asked to estimate the frequency with which nine potentially disruptive viewing behaviors occurred in their household. Estimates were initially provided on a days per week basis. Respondents who said the behavior occurred less than once a week were asked if the behavior occurred at all in the preceding year. Those who said the behavior occurred at least once a week or at least once in the preceding year were asked if the behavior ever "bothered" them or bothered their spouse.

Almost everyone acknowledged that, in the preceding year, one of the spouses watched TV while the other went to sleep (88%); one watched on one set while the other watched a different show at the same time on another set (86%); and both watched TV while eating dinner together (83%; see Table 14.1). Although each of these behaviors occurred two to three times a week, relatively few respondents (maximum = 14% of the entire sample) said they were bothered by them. Four other widely acknowledged behaviors, each occurring between once and twice a week, bothered a larger proportion of respondents (maximum = 41% of the entire sample). These were one wants to talk while a show is on and the

TABLE 14.1
Occurrence of Potentially Disruptive Activities Related to Television

Item	Days/Week	Happens At least 1/year (%)	Percent Bothered[a]	
			You	Spouse
One of you watches TV while the other goes to bed	3.1	88	15/13	23/20
You and your spouse watch TV while eating dinner together	2.9	83	17/14	06/05
Both of you watch different shows on different sets at the same time	1.9	86	12/08	15/10
One of you watches a show the other thinks is a waste of time	1.7	72	31/22	33/23
One of you wants to talk while a show is on and the other doesn't	1.6	75	54/41	50/37
One of you watches TV instead of taking care of chores	1.3	68	46/31	39/27
One of you watches TV when the other wants to do something else	1.1	72	31/22	39/28
Both of you watch the same show at the same time on different sets	0.7	52	10/04	10/04
One or both of you watch TV to get away from a disagreement you were having	0.3	27	56/15	49/13

[a] In each column, the first figure is the percentage among respondents who noted that the behavior happened at least once in the preceding year. The second figure is the percentage among all respondents.

other doesn't; one watches TV instead of doing chores; one watches TV while the other wants to do something else; and one watches a show the other thinks is a waste of time. About one in four respondents (27%) said they or their spouse had used TV to get away from a disagreement the two of them were having. Because most respondents said that had not happened with them, this behavior bothered relatively few of the entire sample. However, it did bother over half the respondents (56%) who said TV had been used in their house as an escape from disagreements.

Two indices were constructed here using seven of the nine behaviors presented to respondents.[5] The first (BOTHERR) summed the number of situations that respondents said bothered them. The second (BOTHERSP) summed the number of situations respondents thought bothered their spouse. Scores on both indices ranged from 0 to 7. Both had means of 1.4, with modest reliability estimates (Cronbach's alpha of .70 and .63, respectively). Women were more likely to report being bothered by these behaviors ($M = 1.8$, $SD = 1.7$ for women; $M = 0.7$, $SD = 1.3$ for men; $t = [140] = 4.0$, $p < 01$). Men were marginally more likely to say their spouses were bothered by the behaviors ($M = 1.6$, $SD = 1.7$ for men; $M = 1.3$, $SD = 1.4$ for women; $t [140] = 1.2$; $p > .05$). Those in longer standing marriages had lower scores on these indices than did their counterparts. Pearson correlation coefficients were $-.31$ with BOTHERR and $-.30$ with BOTHERSP, both $p < .01$.

In the second set of questions, respondents were asked if they had ever talked with their spouse in the preceding year about each of 16 issues. Respondents who said they had not talked with their spouse about an issue were asked if they had "wanted" to talk about it. A large majority (85%) said they had talked with their spouse about the shows they watched together, after the shows were over (see Table 14.2). Such conversations seem more likely to be pleasant than contentious. Two other frequently cited topics seem more likely to involve congenial conversation as well, the shows one wanted to watch (66%) and the shows watched separately, after the shows were over (59%).

Nearly two thirds of the respondents (63%) said they had talked with their spouse about how loud their TV was; nearly half discussed control (46%) and use (43%) of the remote control device. One in three said they talked about TV interfering with chores (35%), the amount of TV watched

---

[5] The items were one of you wants to watch TV while the other wants to do something else; one of you watches a show the other thinks is a waste of time; you and your spouse watch TV while eating together; one of you watches TV while the other goes to bed; one of you wants to talk while the show is on and the other doesn't; one or both of you watch TV to get away from a disagreement you were having; and one of you watches TV instead of taking care of chores.

TABLE 14.2
Communication About Television

In the Past Year, Have You and Your Spouse Ever Talked About	1	2	3
the shows that you watch together, after the shows are over	85	09	86
the shows one of you wants to watch	66	02	67
how loud the TV is	63	02	64
the shows you watch separately, after the shows are over	59	02	60
who controls the remote control	46	01	46
who chooses the show that gets watched on the main set	45	05	48
how the remote control is used	43	03	45
how late one of you stays up to watch TV	39	00	39
TV interfering with chores	35	04	37
the amount of TV one of you watches	32	04	35
TV interfering with talking with each other	32	01	33
who watches TV on the best set where you live	29	00	29
TV interfering with doing something else together	23	02	24
TV interfering with meals	17	01	17
TV interfering with resolving a disagreement	15	01	16
TV interfering with doing something with friends	05	00	05

Note. 1 = percent of respondents who said they had talked with their spouse about the issue in the preceding year; 2 = percent of respondents who said they wanted to talk with their spouse about the issue among those who did not talk about the issue; and 3 = percent of respondents who either talked or wanted to talk with their spouse about the issue in the preceding year.

(32%), and TV interfering with talking with each other (32%). Fewer than one in four noted they had talked with their spouse about TV interfering with doing other things together (23%), with meals (17%), or with resolving disagreements (15%). Almost no one (5%) said they talked with their spouse about TV interfering with doing something with friends. Those who had not talked with their spouse about the issues covered did not express a desire to do so. When asked if they had wanted to talk with their spouse about the issue, no more than 9% said that they had. More often, and this certainly was the case with the potentially contentious issues, the figure dropped below 5%. Apparently, almost everyone who wanted to talk with their spouse about television did just that.

One index was constructed using responses to 12 of the 16 issues addressed in the preceding set of questions. It was designed to measure the number of potentially contentious issues respondents talked about or wished they had talked about with their spouse.[6] Scores on the index

---

[6] Issues included were the amount of TV one of you watches; the shows one of you wants to watch; how loud the TV is; how late one of you stays up to watch TV; who controls the remote control; how the remote control is used; TV interfering with doing something with friends; TV interfering with doing something else together; TV interfering with meals; TV interfering with talking with each other; TV interfering with chores; and TV interfering with resolving a disagreement you were having.

ranged from 0 to 12. The mean response was 4.3. Cronbach's alpha for the index was .80. Scores on this index were not related to gender. However, the index was related to respondent age ($-.44$, $p < .01$) as well as to marital longevity ($-.37$, $p < .01$): Older respondents as well as those married for longer periods of time were less likely to talk about these issues or express an interest in talking about this with their partner.

A third set of open-ended questions addressed three areas anticipated to be sources of conflict; viewing television when one spouse does not want to watch anything; TV set use when both spouses want to watch different shows at the same time; and, use and control of the remote control device.

Most respondents (64%) said they would watch TV when both were home even if their spouse did not want to watch. A larger proportion (83%) said their spouse would do the same. Conversely, one in three respondents (34%) said they would not watch TV if their partner wasn't interested in watching. Fewer (15%) thought their spouse would be as magnanimous. When one or the other did watch television in this circumstance, the spouse not interested in viewing typically did something else around the house (62% when the respondent would watch TV, 78% when the spouse would watch). Responses here reflected those recorded earlier when one wanted to watch a program the other did not want to watch.

When asked what happened when the respondent and their spouse wanted to watch two different shows at the same time, most (58%) said they simply went to different sets with the spouse more likely than the respondent to watch on the main set (46% to 32% among those going to two sets). Few (8%) said they'd tape one of the shows. Respondents were more likely to say they would watch their spouse's show (12%) than report their spouse stayed to watch the respondent's favorite (3%). Decisions on who watched on the main set frequently appeared to be based on show- and time-specific needs and interests. Nonetheless, territoriality came into play, too. One in five (20%) said they watched on the set considered to be theirs. An additional 16% said the person who was watching first got the main set when both wanted to watch different shows at the same time.

A majority (53%) said their spouse generally controlled the remote control device when respondent and spouse were watching television together. Nearly one in three (31%) acknowledged that they controlled the device. Nearly half (45%) estimated their use of the remote control was likely to bother their spouse at least once a week ($M = 1.5$ days/week). Slightly more (53%) said their spouse's use of the remote control bothered them at least once weekly ($M = 1.9$ days/week). Those who reported disagreeing with their spouse about the remote control were asked to describe the typical disagreement and the way in which the conflict was resolved. The most prevalent disagreement centered on one partner's use of the device to change channels too frequently and/or at inopportune times. Fewer than a dozen complained about the volume. About a handful were annoyed with the programming their spouse selected and chose to watch.

> Well, he just flips it so fast that he'll flip it in midsentence so that you don't get to hear the whole sentence.

> He'll change the channel during a commercial. And then he doesn't change it back when I think he should. So, I either ask him to change it back or, if the remote is nearby, I take the remote.

Respondents reported an array of conciliatory responses. Many said their spouse (at least temporarily) stopped flipping channels or settled on a single channel that both would watch. A good number of respondents, though, claimed their options were to concede or go elsewhere, either to watch on another TV set or to do something else around the house. For these people, almost always women, use of the remote control remained a contentious issue.

> He channel surfs and never spends enough time to even find out what the program content is about let alone begin to view the program before he changes. Generally, I tell him to stop it. If he continues to do it I go to another set.

> It's never worked out. He just switches channels a lot and that aggravates me. If we're trying to sit down and watch TV together and there's a commercial, he'll switch to another station and make me miss what's going on on the other channel. It never gets worked out.

> We're not able to work it out. He controls it and if I complain, he doesn't listen. It's not a democracy when it comes to controlling the remote control.

Strategies Used to Resolve TV-Related Conflicts

Usenet. A good number of those who expressed complaints did not describe strategies they used to resolve the conflicts. Instead, the conflicts presented seemed to be ones respondents had yet to resolve. One respondent recognized that her efforts to talk about the problem were not working. When she spoke to her spouse about her frustration with his viewing, he "would give me the look on his face. . . He would say I bug him" and then go back to his viewing. At its worst, one respondent wrote that the conflicts she experienced played a role in the dissolution of her marriage:

> I don't have problems with going to the movies, but when they're on a TV-sized screen in my small apartment, for some reason I find it very unpleasant. I've found myself getting angry at the poor guy just for watching a movie once in a while. On the two occasions when I actually watched a movie with him, I felt so drugged and "sick" afterward that I had to go out and walk for a couple of hours to "get my head back." I wouldn't say it's the main reason I don't live with him now, but it was definitely on the list.

Others described an array of strategies that seemed to work well for them. In an effort to curtail a spouse's viewing, respondents said they got rid of the second set in their house or refused to purchase a second set, particularly if had been earmarked for the bedroom. Those with different viewing preferences relied on VCRs or multiple television sets so that each could view their favorites; took turns selecting shows; swapped media, with one watching television, the other using the computer; watched two shows at the same time; and left the room to pursue other activities.

> The only time TV causes problems is Saturday night, when I want to watch *Dr. Quinn* and my husband wants to watch *Hockey Night in Canada*. Usually, we compromise by watching hockey during the commercials of *Dr. Quinn*.

Generally, these strategies seemed to represent a compromise acceptable to both partners. Those who disliked their spouse's use of the remote control said they complained, grabbed the remote, or left the room. There appeared to be less compromise here, although the complaints at times seemed to reduce the offending behaviors.

> I simply got very serious one day and explained how obnoxious it was that he seemed to think it was his God-given right to be the holder of the remote control for some reason. I explained how it annoyed me that he would choose to just aimlessly channel surf when there was something genuinely interesting on. So, I let him channel surf and watch whatever he wants most of time and then if there's something I really want to watch I say "Hey, there's something on next that I really want to watch."

Intensive Interviews and Focus Groups.   When asked to describe strategies they used to resolve TV-related conflicts, nearly half of the couples in the intensive interviews said they did not have any specific strategies. Several said strategies were not needed as each partner's habits were so well known or schedules were so fixed. With her spouse nodding in agreement, one woman noted "We have no strategy. We just know each other well." For these couples, the strategy appeared to be implicit tolerance of each other's viewing or an experience-based understanding of the spouse's likes and dislikes.

Those who articulated strategies frequently talked about compromises, with a second television set often part of the solution. Argumentation was not among the strategies described. Instead, several participants talked about quiet capitulation, perhaps because viewing differences did not merit discussion. Ironically, one woman gently chided her husband for backing away as quickly as he did. She sought discussion while he sought tranquility.

H: [My strategy is to say] I love you honey just a little bit. (Laughter)

W: He doesn't like to argue. But, every now and then I feel like I have to flare up. You've got to have, they tell me for a healthy relationship, you've got to have arguments or disagreements or something.

H: All of our arguments, if we have any, she initiates them. I just shrug them off because if she gets angry and I get angry we get into a fight. The best way is to walk away.

W: Well, I don't like that too well. I like to talk about it and come to some kind of understanding. It's communicating. . . . You've got to talk.

Most of those in the focus groups had to pause before answering the question, as though they had not consciously considered the issue beforehand. With or without pause, many acknowledged they had no set strategy or "game plan" as one male described. In actuality, their strategy appeared to be one based on habit, shared understanding, compromise, and "common courtesy" worked out on a situation-specific basis. Implicit, too, was a sense of respect for the partner's wishes.

I call it balance. Say we'll cut you your hour out for *Dr. Quinn Medicine Woman*, you know you can't miss that. You know if I have to watch a sitcom and my favorite is *Married With Children*. So, pretty much I get my half hour without the children hanging off my legs and she'll answer the phone and give me that space in time. So, it's not something we've really spoken about. It's just worked out through the years that I know what she likes and when she likes not to be disturbed and vice versa.

[I handle TV-related conflicts] the same way I try to handle any conflict that we have with each other. It's just think of common courtesy toward the other person. I mean if it boils down to it's going to create a serious problem because I'm going to watch something she isn't going to want to watch, then I'm going to just go ahead and watch whatever [she wants] to watch or just shut the TV off or whatever. Just, you know, common courtesy to avoid any problems in the relationship that are silly problems. Who cares about TV that much, you know?

Several participants made use of proactive, preventative strategies. One said he and his wife would read through the television listings together to see if there was anything both were interested in watching. If not, they compromised, with each watching the other's favored show throughout the evening. One talked about making sure his wife had something to do so he could watch TV:

I encourage her to go and do her shopping. Saturday and Sunday afternoons I make sure she has some activity planned. Normally there is something that she hasn't done and this is a reminder that this is a good time to go and take care of it and, uh, "Why don't you go and do it."

Telephone Survey.   Respondents were asked to describe the strategies they used when they disagreed with their spouse's use of television as well as with the strategies they employed when their spouse disagreed with the respondent's own use of television. Interviewers probed here as both items seemed to catch many respondents off-guard, much as seemed to be the case when the questions were posed to those who participated in the intensive interviews and focus groups. Up to three different strategies were coded for each respondent although only a handful of respondents offered more than two.

When asked what strategies they had when they disagreed with their spouse's use of television, one in three (33%) said they had none. From their perspective, no strategy was needed, either because they did not disagree with their spouse's viewing or because the disagreement did not merit a strategy. Such differences were unimportant. A few respondents, however, noted they had no strategy because none worked.

> We don't have too many disagreements. She doesn't watch that much TV [and] we usually watch it together. It's rare that she watches something that I don't like.

> We work 12 hours a day, 6 days a week so whatever she wants to watch is fine with me. I'm not going to argue with her about TV. She feels the same. We're not going to argue about TV. We have lives.

> I have none. TV isn't worth fighting about and he's going to watch it. That's an argument that I'm not going to win so I just go on.

About one in four (26%) said they talked with their spouse about disagreements related to TV. Some did this merely to express their feelings; others acknowledged that they were interested in persuading their spouse to watch something else or turn the set off.

> I usually tell him that it's boring or if there's something else on, maybe we can watch something different.

> Believe it or not, if we disagree about a TV show, I'd try to persuade him that my [show] is morally superior and ask what he thinks he's supporting by watching what he's watching.

The most commonly used single strategy (18%) involved using a second television set. One in seven (14%) said they simply yielded to their spouse's interests. As many (14%) said they did something around the house while their spouse watched TV.

> If he wants to watch TV, I generally do something else, work on a crossword puzzle or get up and do something. I don't make a big issue of it and neither does he.

> I just do something else. She has the right to watch what she wants. If I don't like it, I go play the computer or read.

When the situation was reversed, that is, when the spouse disagreed with the respondent's use of television, responses reflected but did not completely mirror those just described. Again, a plurality (in this case, 39%) said no strategy was needed. Most who took that position did not think their spouse disagreed with the respondent's viewing.

> He never disagrees with me and we agree to disagree. We've been married so long that we know what each other will do before they do it.

> This kind of thing is really insignificant. If it is something one of us really wants to watch, we go ahead and watch it.

Again, about one in four (26%) suggested they mentioned, discussed, or even joked about the disagreement with their spouse. At times, though, these conversations seemed a bit more deliberately persuasive and one-sided with the respondent calling for their right to use television as they wished.

> I usually talk real nice to him and most of the time I get my way.

> I tell him he gets to watch more shows than I do so he gets to watch what he wants. So, he can be polite when I watch my one. When my show is over, he can have the remote back.

One in five (20%) said they simply continued to watch, occasionally ignoring their spouse's complaints. One in nine (11%) said they went to another TV set to watch or they taped their show. Conversely, 15% yielded to their spouse's objections or compromised and somehow modified their behaviors.

> I usually tell him that if he doesn't like it he can go find something else to do.

> I usually try to modify a little bit. If he tells me I'm watching too much, I try to modify the amount of TV I'm watching and look critically at what I'm doing.

Emulation of Conflict Resolution Strategies Seen on TV

Intensive Interviews and Focus Groups.   Those who participated in the intensive interviews as well as those in the focus groups were asked if they ever found themselves using strategies to solve conflicts at home that they had observed on television entertainment shows. Many participants responded with a smile, quick laugh, or look of modest incredulity, dismissing television as a source of conflict resolution. Others responded with a quick and terse "No!" When asked to consider talk shows, too, in this light, almost everyone still answered in the negative. As one married woman noted, "I don't think anything I watch on TV is that significant." Another middle-aged married woman mirrored that sentiment when she said that while she watched TV for 2 years from "morning until night," she found nothing on that she might use in real relationships. One couple took the position that while they watched talk shows like *Jerry Springer* and *Montel Williams*, the issues on those shows just didn't apply to their relationship:

H: Montel's interesting [in terms of] how other people get into those situations. [But] I never use any of their answers or anything because I've never had problems like any other girlfriend or abusing my wife.

W: They've got some weird stuff going on in their lives.

H: Most of that stuff is for the younger generation. I've been around those corners, did that and done that. Doesn't mean anything to me now.

About 12 participants responded affirmatively to the question, recognizing that television content at least occasionally stimulated them to reflect and integrate strategies into their married lives. Women were more likely than men to say they emulated or integrated into their own relationships relational strategies seen on television.

One woman who participated in the intensive interviews noted that the talk shows constantly reinforced the importance of communication, that couples needed to "communicate, communicate, communicate, to be open" with each other. Another, married for 3 years, said she used infomercials and specials such as *Making Love Work* and *One Thousand and One Ways to be Romantic* as a stimulus for her relationship. They offered techniques she then tried at home on her husband. One middle-aged African American couple that made judicious use of television spoke of frequently learning from television. The husband cited *The Cosby Show*, recalling how Cosby frequently reasoned with his (television) children. Without mentioning a specific show, the wife talked about watching relationships on shows, comparing them with her own and trying what seemed valuable at home with her spouse and children. *Home Improvement* served to remind one man that he needed to listen more often and to do more things for his spouse.

H: *Home Improvement* typifies the male and female battle of communication. . . . You know where he's got his brain's set, grunting and scratching and building and watching sports and that sort of thing. And he forgets to be sensitive to his wife's needs. Watching that reminds me that my wife needs me to listen to her more often. She needs me to do special things for her.

W: (Interjecting) I tell him, though. I let him know.

H: When something like that comes on and we're watching together she'll look at me like, Did you see that? I hope you did, you know.

One woman said she picked up phrases from TV and used them against her husband: "I can throw them out when I'm arguing. I can throw them out and he can't argue too much with them."

Five of the eight focus group participants who said they had picked up conflict resolution strategies from television were men. One male participant in the newly married group recalled watching a show that struck an emotional chord:

I can remember one specific instance watching television [which] struck me in a very emotional way and I had a hard time dealing with it. And in discussing it and then understanding it I was able to convey to my wife how I felt about my father's passing away several years ago. . . . It was something we had never really discussed before and it was a way to bring something to the surface, deal with it and share it and that was brought on by a television program.

While this appeared to be an important breakthrough for the participant, it also seemed to be an isolated event for him. Two other males, both divorced, noted that entertainment programs such as *The Simpsons* and *Married With Children* served as sources of insight and inspiration particularly when, as one noted, "I had no words of my own."

[On *The Simpsons*] Homer was doing his normal Homer and Marge had kicked him out of the house. Lisa [Homer's daughter] was trying to get them back together. And she was being the proliberal woman of the 90s and she went to tell her father that he needed to go back to mom. "Don't you remember anything out of the marriage that you'll miss her for? Can't you tell her something? All she wants to do is feel special." And he says "No." And she says "Well, tell her you love her." And he says "I have." And she goes "Well, tell her why." And he says "I can't." And she goes "Well, love is where two people find that one person and no other person can give them that." And, every so often on TV, I'll hear something like that and I'll use it to my best advantage.

One woman mentioned *Oprah* and segments of the *Today* show but could not recall a strategy acquired from those shows. A second woman talked about Martha Stewart but the lesson learned from her show was that violets could be used on salads and with ice cubes in drinks, an insight more likely to stimulate conversation than to resolve relational conflict. One newly married woman thought that shows such as *I Love Lucy* gave her helpful ideas:

> Like maybe if you're angry . . . sometimes it calms you down or gives you a strategy . . . something you were going to make a big deal but now it's not a big deal. So you think about what someone did [with] maybe a similar problem and it's like that's how that person approached that problem and I'm not going to do that.

Usenet and Telephone Survey.   None of the Usenet exchanges touched on emulation. And, given responses from those in the intensive interviews and focus groups, the issue was not formally pursued with those who participated in the telephone interviews. All told, relatively few of the adults in this study turned to television for relational advice or made a conscious effort to emulate the conflict resolution strategies presented in entertainment and talk show programming.

CONCLUSIONS

For the most part, husbands and wives appear willing to yield to each other's viewing patterns. Few are disturbed by late night viewing differences. Some are content to have their spouse watch TV nearby while they sleep. Others appreciate the reprieve from an otherwise frisky spouse! Relatively few think that television interferes with meals or partaking in other activities together and with others. Somehow, television viewing fits reasonably well into their daily schedules and lives.

Disagreements related to TV are frequently downplayed, a function perhaps of the ease with which spouses are able to accommodate each other. Little bother, little fuss although differences at times rankle a spouse. On occasion, feelings are hurt when one wants to watch while the other wants to talk. And, on occasion, annoyance is felt when one watches TV instead of doing chores or turns to a show the other thinks is a waste of time.

Thanks to the remote control, differences in viewing styles appear to be somewhat disruptive. As documented by other researchers, wives often object to their husband's inclination to surf and then lose these battles. For the most part, husbands control the remote and surf as needed while wives joke, fight, scheme, yield, or abandon coviewing. Discrepancies here may trigger the most widespread irritation and, as a result, serve to depress coviewing.

In general, television-related conflicts are resolved quickly and quietly. Indeed, proactive accommodation appears to be the rule. Knowing each other well, couples almost instinctively cede to each other's viewing preferences, giving each other the opportunity to watch what they want. This appears to happen quite often without either set rules or much conscious thought. Relatively few have well formulated, clearly articulated strategies related to TV viewing that they consciously employ. Perhaps this should not be surprising. After all, television viewing, a patterned activity, is predictable. Over the course of shared lifetimes, couples anticipate each other's interests and behaviors and adjust accordingly. Beyond this, most couples appear quite willing to compromise. The give and take that lubricates smooth relationships operates in this domain as well. Out of courtesy and respect for one another, and perhaps the expectation of reciprocity, spouses let each other view. In this sense, television-related conflicts are resolved with the same spirit that marks conflict resolution elsewhere in marital relationships. Of course, a live-and-let-live accommodation strategy is easy when chores can be pushed back, the remote control temporarily dropped, the sound slightly lowered, and the second set made available when all else fails. Differences in viewing interests and styles may be more problematic in single set households and cramped living conditions as well as with those whose leisure time is severely constrained.

REFERENCES

Comstock, G. (1982). Television and American social institutions. In D. Pearl, L. Bouthilet, & J. Lazar (Eds.), *Television and behavior: Ten years of scientific progress and implications for the eighties* (pp. 334–348). Rockville, MD: National Institute for Mental Health.

Copeland, G. A., & Schweitzer, K. (1993). Domination of the remote control during family viewing. In J. R. Walker & R.V. Bellamy, Jr. (Eds.), *The remote control in the new age of television* (pp. 155–168). Westport, CT: Praeger.

Douglas, W., & Olsen, B. M. (1996). Subversion of the American family? *Communication Research, 23,* 73–99.

Fitzpatrick, M. A., & Badzinski, D. M. (1994). All in the family: Interpersonal communication in kin relationships. In M. Knapp & G. R. Miller (Eds.), *Handbook of interpersonal communication* (2nd ed., pp. 726–771). Thousand Oaks, CA: Sage.

Gantz, W. (1995, April). *Television and marriage: Patterns of conflict and accommodation.* Paper presented at the meeting of the Broadcast Education Association, Las Vegas, NV.

Gantz, W., Wenner, L. A., Carrico, C., & Knorr, M. (1995). Televised sports and marital relationships. *Sociology of Sport Journal, 12,* 306–323.

Heeter, C. (1988). Gender differences in viewing styles. In C. Heeter & B. S. Greenberg (Eds.), *Cableviewing* (pp.151–166). Norwood, NJ: Ablex.

Heeter, C., & Greenberg, B. S. (1988). Profiling the zappers. In C. Heeter & B. S. Greenberg (Eds.), *Cableviewing* (pp. 67–73). Norwood, NJ: Ablex.

Krendl, K. A., Troiano, C., Dawson, R., & Clark, G. (1993). "OK, where's the remote?" Children, families, and remote control devices. In J. R. Walker & R. V. Bellamy, Jr. (Eds.). *The remote control in the new age of television* (pp. 137–153). Westport, CT: Praeger.

Lull, J. (1982). How families select television programs: A mass observational study. *Journal of Broadcasting, 26,* 801–811.

Perse, E. M., & Ferguson, D. A. (1993). Gender differences in remote control use. In J. R. Walker & R. V. Bellamy, Jr. (Eds.), *The remote control in the new age of television* (pp. 169–186). Westport, CT: Praeger.

Robinson, J., Skill, J. D., Nussbaum, J., & Moreland, K. (1985). Parents, peers, and television characters: The use of comparison others as criteria for evaluating marital satisfaction. In E. C. Lange (Ed.), *Using the media to promote knowledge and skills in family dynamics* (pp. 11–15). Dayton, OH: Center for Religious Telecommunications.

Rosenblatt, P. C., & Cunningham, M. R. (1976). Television watching and family tensions. *Journal of Marriage and the Family, 38,* 105–111.

Taylor, E. (1989). *Prime-time families: Television culture in postwar America.* Berkeley: University of California Press.

Walker, J. R., Bellamy, R. V., Jr., & Traudt, P. J. (1993). Gratifications derived from remote control devices: A survey of adult RCD use. In J. R. Walker & R. V. Bellamy, Jr. (Eds.), *The remote control in the new age of television* (pp. 103–112). Westport, CT: Praeger.

Effects of Television on Child and Family Emotional Well-Being

Joanne Cantor
Marie-Louise Mares
University of Wisconsin–Madison

Television has an enormous capacity to affect viewers' moods and emotions. It can stimulate the bored, distract the distressed, and excite the thrill-seeker, with no more effort on the part of the viewer than a touch of the remote (see, for example, Kubey, 1986; Zillmann & Bryant, 1994). Television has always provided a wide array of programming, but now that cable television is received in 85% of American homes (Labaton, 1999), the assortment of available televised images is more diverse than ever. What are the emotional effects of television on children and families? How do families counteract the effects of mass media content? This chapter reports the research in this area. Some of the research to be reviewed has not made a distinction between movies and television programs. However, given the fact that in the current media environment, most theatrical films are ultimately seen on TV either by being telecast or by being replayed on videotape, the distinction between movie- and television-induced emotions may no longer be important.

Television has the potential to generate the whole gamut of emotions. A number of studies, primarily with adults, have examined emotional responses such as sadness (Oliver, 1993; Oliver, Sargent, & Weaver, 1998), anger, and happiness (Choti, Marston, Holston, & Hart, 1987). Other research has examined viewers' use of mass media as a way to "tune out the world" and reduce stress (Larson, 1995) or to provide a framework for unstructured time (Kubey, 1986). However, most of the research that has been conducted on the emotional responses of children and families to television content has dealt with the emotion of fear. Indeed, fear is a common emotional consequence of watching television. In contrast to Signorielli and Morgan (chap. 16, this volume), who report on the more cognitive, "cultivation" effects, and examine the relationship between television viewing and perceptions of the world as a mean and dangerous place, this chapter explores emotional effects, ranging from mild feelings of anxiety to acute and overwhelming feelings of terror.

Over the years that the effects of the mass media have been studied, many researchers have reported fear as a prominent outcome of viewing (see Cantor, 1994, for a review). For example, as far back as the 1930s, Blumer (1933) reported that 93% of the children in his sample said they had been frightened or horrified by a motion picture. More recently, about 75% of the respondents in two separate samples of preschool and elementary school children said that they had been scared by something they had seen on television or in a movie (Wilson, Hoffner, & Cantor, 1987). Cantor and Nathanson (1996) reported that in a random sample of parents of elementary school children in Madison, Wisconsin, 43% said that their child had experienced enduring fright as a function of exposure to television. In the first random national survey of its kind in the United States, Gentile and Walsh (1999) reported that 62% of parents with children between the ages of 2 and 17 said that their child had become scared that something they saw in a TV program or movie might happen to them. Finally, in a random national survey of 7- to 12-year-old children in the Netherlands, 31% of the respondents reported having been frightened by television during the preceding year (Valkenburg, Cantor, & Peeters, 2000).

To the extent that mass media depictions prevent children from sleeping or carrying out everyday activities, they impinge on the quality of the child's life, and the life of the family as a whole. An experimental study explored the impact of witnessing scary media events on children's subsequent behavioral choices (Cantor & Omdahl, 1991). In this experiment, exposure to dramatized depictions of a deadly house fire or a drowning increased children's self-reports of worry about similar events in their own lives. More importantly, these fictional depictions affected the children's preferences for normal, everyday activities that were related to the tragedies they had just witnessed: Children who had seen a movie depicting a drowning expressed less willingness to go canoeing than did other children; those who had seen the program about a house fire were less eager to build a fire in a fireplace. Although the duration of such effects was not measured, the effects were undoubtedly short-lived, especially because debriefings were employed and safety guidelines were taught so that no child would experience long-term distress (Cantor & Omdahl, 1999).

There is growing evidence, in fact, that the fear induced by mass media exposure is often intense and long lasting, with sometimes debilitating effects (Cantor, 1998). In a study designed to assess the severity of enduring fright reactions to mass media, Johnson (1980) asked a random sample of adults whether they had ever seen a motion picture that had disturbed them "a great deal." Forty percent replied in the affirmative, and the median length of the reported disturbance was 3 days. Respondents also reported on the type, intensity, and duration of symptoms such as nervousness, depression, fear of specific things, and recurring thoughts and images. Based on these reports, Johnson judged that 48% of these respondents (19% of the total sample) had experienced, for at least 2 days, a "significant stress reaction." Johnson argued that

> it is one thing to walk away from a frightening or disturbing
> event with mild residue of the images and quite another thing
> to ruminate about it, feel anxious or depressed for days,
> and/or to avoid anything that might create the same unpleas-
> ant experience. (p. 786)

On the basis of his data, he concluded that such reactions were more prevalent and more severe than had previously been assumed.

Recent retrospective studies of adults' detailed memories of having been frightened by a television show or movie provide more evidence of the severity and duration of media-induced fear (Harrison & Cantor, 1999; Hoekstra, Harris, & Helmick, 1999). In these studies, involving samples of undergraduates from three universities, the presence of vivid memories of enduring media-induced fear was nearly universal. All of the participants in the Hoekstra et al. research reported such an incident. In the Harrison and Cantor study, 90% reported an intense fear reaction to something in the media, in spite of the fact that the respondents could receive full extra credit for participating if they simply said "no" (meaning "I never had such an experience"), and thereby avoid writing a paper and filling out a three-page questionnaire.

As for the effects reported, both studies revealed a variety of intense reactions. In Hoekstra et al.'s (1999) study, 61% reported a generalized fear or free-floating anxiety after viewing, 46% reported what they called "wild imagination" ("monsters under the bed" or "someone sneaking up on you"), 29% reported a specific fear (e.g., sharks, power tools, spiders), and more than 20% reported a variety of sleep disturbances, including fear of sleeping alone, nightmares, insomnia, or needing to sleep with the lights on. Of the students reporting fright reactions in Harrison and Cantor's (1999) samples, 52% reported disturbances in eating or sleeping,

22% reported mental preoccupation with the disturbing material, and 35% reported subsequently avoiding or dreading the situation depicted in the program or movie. Moreover, one third of those reporting having been frightened said that the fear effects had lasted more than a year. Indeed, more than one fourth of the respondents said that the emotional impact of the program or movie (seen an average of 6 years earlier) was still with them at the time of reporting!

The most extreme reactions reported in the literature come from psychiatric case studies in which acute and disabling anxiety states enduring several days to several weeks or more, are said to have been precipitated by the viewing of horror movies such as *The Exorcist, Invasion of the Body Snatchers*, and *Ghostwatch* (Buzzuto, 1975; Mathai, 1983; Simons & Silveira, 1994). Most of the patients in the cases reported had not had previously diagnosed psychiatric problems, but the viewing of the film was seen as occurring in conjunction with other stressors in the patients' lives.

A recent large-scale survey documented the association of heavy television viewing with negative emotional consequences. Singer, Slovak, Frierson, and York's (1998) survey of more than 2,000 third through eighth graders in Ohio public schools revealed that as the number of hours of television viewing per day increased, so did the prevalence of symptoms of psychological trauma, such as anxiety, depression, and posttraumatic stress. Although these survey data cannot rule out the alternative explanation that children experiencing trauma symptoms are more likely to turn to television for distraction, they are consistent with the notion that exposure to frightening and disturbing images on television contributes to a child's level of stress and anxiety, particularly in light of other research that demonstrates the impact of exposure to specific frightening depictions on acute fear levels.

Together, these studies suggest that enduring emotional disturbances occur in a substantial proportion of children and that these responses can sometimes be intense and debilitating.

DEVELOPMENTAL DIFFERENCES AND MEDIA-INDUCED FEAR

A large body of research has examined two major developmental issues in fright reactions to media: (a) the types of mass media stimuli and events that frighten children at different ages, and (b) the strategies for preventing or reducing unwanted fear reactions that are most effective for different-aged children. Experiments and surveys have been conducted to test expectations based on theories and findings in cognitive development research. The experiments have had the advantage of testing rigorously controlled variations in program content and viewing conditions, using a combination of self-reports, physiological responses, the coding of facial expressions of emotion, and behavioral measures. For ethical reasons, only small excerpts from relatively mild stimuli are used in experiments. In contrast, the surveys have investigated the responses of children who were exposed to a particular mass media offering in their natural environment, without any researcher intervention. Although less tightly controlled, the surveys permit the study of responses to much more intensely frightening media fare.

Developmental Differences in the Media Stimuli That Produce Fright

It is not true that as children get older they become less and less susceptible to all media-produced emotional disturbances. As children mature cognitively, some things become less likely to disturb them, whereas other things become potentially more upsetting. This generalization is consistent with developmental differences in children's fears in general. According to a variety of studies using diverse methodologies, children from approximately 3 to 8 years of age are frightened primarily by animals, the dark, supernatural beings, such as ghosts, monsters, and witches, and by anything that looks strange or moves suddenly. The fears of 9- to 12-year-olds are more often related to personal injury and physical destruction and the injury and death of family members. Adolescents continue to fear personal injury and physical destruction, but school fears and social fears arise at this age, as do fears regarding political, economic, and global issues (see Cantor, Wilson, & Hoffner, 1986, for a review).

Perceptual Dependence. The findings regarding the media stimuli that frighten children at different ages are consistent with observed changes in children's fears in general. Broad generalizations are summarized here. The first generalization is that the relative importance of the immediately perceptible components of a fear-inducing media stimulus decreases as a child's age increases. Research on cognitive development indicates that, in general, very young children react to stimuli predominantly in terms of their perceptible characteristics and that with increasing maturity, they respond more and more to the conceptual aspects of stimuli (see Flavell, 1963; Melkman, Tversky, & Baratz, 1981). Research findings support the generalization that preschool children (approximately 3 to 5 years old) are more likely to be frightened by something that looks scary but is actually harmless than by something that looks attractive but is actually harmful; for older elementary school children (approximately 9 to 11 years), appearance carries much less weight, relative to the behavior or destructive potential of a character, animal, or object.

One set of data that supports this generalization comes from a survey (Cantor & Sparks, 1984) asking parents to name the programs and films that had frightened their children the most. In this survey, parents of preschool children most often mentioned offerings with grotesque looking, unreal characters, such as the television series *The Incredible Hulk* and the feature film *The Wizard of Oz*; parents of older elementary school children more often mentioned programs or movies (like *The Amityville Horror*) that involved threats without a strong visual component, and that required a good deal of imagination to comprehend. Sparks (1986) replicated this study, using children's self-reports rather than parents' observations, and reported similar findings. Both surveys included controls for possible differences in exposure patterns in the different age groups.

A second investigation that supports this generalization was a laboratory study involving an episode of *The Incredible Hulk* (Sparks & Cantor, 1986), a program that 40% of parents of preschoolers spontaneously mentioned when asked which programs had frightened their child (Cantor & Sparks, 1984). The laboratory study concluded that preschool children's unexpectedly intense reactions to this program were partially due to their overresponse to the visual image of the Hulk character. When participants were asked how they had felt during different parts of the program, preschool children reported the most fear after the attractive, mild-mannered hero was transformed into the monstrous-looking Hulk. Older elementary school children, in contrast, reported the least fear at this time, because they understood that the Hulk was really the benevolent hero in another physical form, and that he was using his superhuman powers on the side of "law and order" and against threats to the well-being of liked characters.

Another study (Hoffner & Cantor, 1985) tested the effect of appearance more directly, by creating a story in four versions, so that a major character was either attractive and grandmotherly looking or ugly and grotesque. The character's appearance was factorially varied with her behavior—she was depicted as behaving either kindly or cruelly. In judging how nice or mean the character was and in predicting what she would do in the subsequent scene, preschool children were more influenced than were older children (6–7 and 9–10 years) by the character's looks and less influenced than older children by her kind or cruel behavior. As the age of the child increased, the character's looks became less important and her behavior carried increasing weight. A follow-up experiment revealed that all age groups engaged in physical appearance stereotyping in the absence of information about the character's behavior.

Fantasy Versus Reality.   A second generalization that emerges from the research is that as children mature, they become more responsive to realistic, and less responsive to fantastic dangers depicted in the media. The data on trends in children's fears suggest that very young children are more likely than older children and adolescents to fear things that are not real, in the sense that their occurrence in the real world is impossible (e.g., monsters). The development of more "mature" fears seems to presuppose the acquisition of knowledge regarding the objective dangers posed by different situations. One important component of this knowledge includes an understanding of the distinction between reality and fantasy, a competence that develops only gradually throughout childhood (see Flavell, 1963; Kelly, 1981; Morison & Gardner, 1978).

This generalization is supported by Cantor and Sparks' (1984) survey of parents. In general, the tendency to mention fantasy offerings, depicting events that could not possibly occur in the real world, as sources of fear, decreased as the child's age increased, and the tendency to mention fictional offerings, depicting events that could possibly occur, increased. Again, Sparks (1986) replicated these findings using children's self-reports. Further support for this generalization comes from a study of children's fright responses to television news (Cantor & Nathanson, 1996). A random survey of parents of children in kindergarten, second, fourth, and sixth grades showed that although fear produced by fantasy programs decreased as the child's grade increased, fear induced by news stories increased with age. Valkenburg et al. (2000) also found a decrease between the ages of 7 and 12, in fright responses to fantasy content.

Abstract Thinking. Thirdly, as children mature, they become frightened by media depictions involving increasingly abstract concepts. This generalization is clearly consistent with the general sources of children's fears, cited earlier. It is also consistent with theories of cognitive development (e.g., Flavell, 1963), which indicate that the ability to think abstractly emerges relatively late in cognitive development.

Data supporting this generalization come from a survey of children's responses to the television movie, *The Day After* (Cantor, et al., 1986). Although many people were concerned about young children's reactions to this movie, which depicted the devastation of a Kansas community by a nuclear attack (Schofield & Pavelchak, 1985), developmental considerations led to the prediction that the youngest children would be the least affected by it. In a random telephone survey of parents conducted the night after the broadcast of this movie, children under 12 were reportedly much less disturbed by the film than were teenagers, and parents were the most disturbed. The very youngest children were not upset or frightened at all. More parents of younger than older children could think of other shows that had frightened their child more during the preceding year. The findings seem to be due to the fact that the emotional impact of the film comes from the contemplation of the potential annihilation of the earth as we know it—a concept that is beyond the grasp of the young child. The visual depictions of injury in the movie were quite mild compared to what most children have become used to seeing on television.

A study of children's reactions to television coverage of the war in the Persian Gulf also supports the generalization that children become increasingly responsive to abstract as opposed to concrete aspects of frightening media (Cantor, Mares, & Oliver, 1993). In a random survey of parents of children in public school in Madison, Wisconsin, there were no significant differences between first, fourth, seventh, and eleventh graders in the prevalence or intensity of negative emotional reactions to television coverage of the war. However, children in different grades were upset by different aspects of the coverage. Parents of younger children, but not of adolescents, stressed the visual aspects of the coverage and the direct, concrete consequences of combat in their descriptions of the elements that had disturbed their child the most (e.g., the missiles exploding). As the child's age increased, the more abstract, conceptual aspects of the coverage (e.g., the possibility of the conflict spreading) were cited by parents as the most disturbing.

In summary, research on the relationship between cognitive development and emotional responses to television can be very helpful in predicting the types of television programs that are more or less likely to frighten children of different ages. Parents and other family members may be able to make more sensible viewing choices for children by heeding these developmental findings (Cantor, 1998).

Developmental Differences in the Effectiveness of Coping Strategies

No matter how well intentioned or careful or sensitive families are to the emotional vulnerabilities of their children, children are likely to be frightened at one time or another by what they see on television. Research in cognitive development has also been used to determine the best ways to help children cope with fear-producing stimuli or to reduce their children's fear reactions once they occur.

Developmental differences in children's information-processing abilities yield differences in the effectiveness of strategies to prevent or reduce their media-induced fears (Cantor & Wilson, 1988). The findings of research on coping strategies can be summed up in the following generalization: In general, preschool children benefit more from "noncognitive" than from "cognitive" strategies; both cognitive and noncognitive strategies can be effective for older elementary school children, although this age group tends to prefer cognitive strategies.

Noncognitive Strategies. Noncognitive strategies are those that do not involve the processing of verbal information and that appear to be relatively automatic. The process of visual desensitization, or gradual exposure to threatening images in a nonthreatening context, is one such strategy that has been shown to be effective for both preschool and older elementary school children. In one experiment, gradual visual exposure to filmed footage of snakes tended to reduce fear reactions to the "snake pit" scene from the action-adventure film *Raiders of the Lost Ark* (Wilson & Cantor, 1987). In a second experiment (Wilson, 1987), exposure to a realistic rubber replica of a tarantula reduced the emotional impact of a scene involving tarantulas from *Kingdom of the Spiders*. In a third experiment (Wilson, 1989a), exposure to a live lizard reduced children's expression of fear while watching a scene involving deadly lizards in *Frogs*. In a fourth experiment (Weiss, Imrich, & Wilson, 1993), exposure to graphic photographs of worms taken from the horror film *Squirm* reduced children's self-reports of fear during a scene from that movie. Finally, fear reactions to the Hulk character in *The Incredible Hulk* were reduced by exposure to footage of Lou Ferrigno, the actor who plays the character, having his make-up applied so that he gradually took on the menacing appearance of the character. None of these experiments revealed developmental differences in the technique's effectiveness.

Other noncognitive strategies involve physical activities, such as clinging to an attachment object or having something to eat or drink. Although these techniques are available to viewers of all ages, there is reason to believe they are more effective for younger than for older children. First, it has been argued that the effectiveness of such techniques is likely to diminish as the infant's tendency to grasp and suck objects for comfort and exploration decreases (Bowlby, 1973). Second, it seems likely that the effectiveness of such techniques is partially attributable to distraction, and distraction techniques should be more effective in younger children, who have greater difficulty allocating cognitive processing to two simultaneous activities (e.g., Manis, Keating, & Morison, 1980).

Children seem to be intuitively aware that physical techniques work better for younger than for older children. In a study of children's perceptions of the effectiveness of strategies for coping with media-induced fright, preschool children's evaluations of "holding onto a blanket or a toy" and "getting something to eat or drink" were significantly more positive than those of older elementary school children (Wilson et al., 1987).

Another noncognitive strategy that has been shown to have more appeal and more effectiveness for younger than older children is covering one's eyes during frightening portions of a presentation. In an experiment by Wilson (1989b), when covering the eyes was suggested as an option, younger children used this strategy more often than did older children. Moreover, the suggestion of this option reduced the fear of younger children, but actually increased the fear of older children. Wilson noted that the older children recognized the limited effectiveness of covering their eyes (while still being exposed to the audio features of the program) and may have reacted by feeling less in control, and therefore more vulnerable, when this strategy was offered to them.

Cognitive Strategies. In contrast to noncognitive strategies, cognitive (or "verbal") strategies involve verbal information that is used to cast the threat in a different light. These strategies involve relatively complex cognitive operations, and research consistently finds such strategies to be more effective for older than for younger children. When dealing with fantasy depictions, the most typical cognitive strategy seems to be to provide an explanation focusing on the unreality of the situation This strategy should be especially difficult for preschool children, who do not have a full grasp of the implications of the fantasy–reality distinction. In an experiment by Cantor and Wilson (1984), older elementary school children who were told to remember that what they were seeing in *The Wizard of Oz* was not real showed less fear than their classmates who received no instructions. The same instructions did not help preschoolers, however. A more recent study (Wilson & Weiss, 1991) again showed developmental differences in the effectiveness of reality-related strategies.

Children's beliefs about the effectiveness of focusing on the unreality of the stimulus have been shown to be consistent with these experimental findings. In the study of perceptions of fear-reducing techniques, preschool children's ranking of the effectiveness of "tell yourself it's not real" was significantly lower than that of older elementary school children (Wilson et al., 1987). In contrast to children, who apparently view this strategy accurately, parents do not seem to appreciate the inadequacy of this technique for young children. Eighty percent of the parents of both the preschool and elementary school children who participated in another study (Wilson & Cantor, 1987) reported that they employed a "tell them it's not real" coping strategy to reduce their child's media-induced fear.

For media depictions involving realistic threats, the most prevalent cognitive strategy seems to be provide an explanation that minimizes the perceived severity of the depicted danger. This type of strategy is not only more effective with older children than with younger children, in certain situations it has been shown to have a fear-enhancing rather than an anxiety-reducing effect with younger children. In the experiment involving the snake-pit scene from *Raiders of the Lost Ark* mentioned earlier (Wilson & Cantor, 1987), a second experimental variation involved the presence or absence of reassuring information about snakes (e.g., the statement that most snakes are not poisonous). Although this information tended to reduce the fear of older elementary school children, kindergarten and first-grade children seem to have only partially understood the information, focusing more on "poisonous" than on "not." For them, negative emotional reactions were more prevalent if they heard the supposedly reassuring information.

Data also indicate that older children use cognitive coping strategies more frequently than do preschool children. In the survey of reactions to *The Day After* (Cantor et al., 1986), parents' reports that their child had discussed the movie with them after viewing it increased with the age of the child. And, in a laboratory experiment involving exposure to a scary scene (Hoffner & Cantor, 1990), significantly more 9- to 11-year-olds than 5- to 7-year-olds reported spontaneously employing cognitive coping strategies (thinking about the expected happy outcome or thinking about the fact that what was happening was not real).

Studies have also shown that the effectiveness of cognitive strategies for young children can be improved by providing visual demonstrations of verbal explanations (Cantor, Sparks, & Hoffner, 1988), and by encouraging repeated rehearsal of simplified, reassuring information (Wilson, 1987). In addition, research has explored some of the specific reasons for the inability of young children to profit from verbal explanations, such as those involving relative quantifiers (e.g., "some are dangerous, but most are not," Badzinski, Cantor, & Hoffner, 1989) and probabilistic terms ("this probably will not happen to you," Hoffner, Cantor, & Badzinski, 1990). It is clear from these studies that it is an extremely challenging task to "explain away" threats that have induced fear in a child, particularly when there is a strong perceptual component to the threatening stimulus, and when the reassurance can only be partial or probabilistic, rather than absolute (see Cantor & Hoffner, 1990).

IMPLICATIONS FOR FAMILY INTERACTION AND PARENTAL GUIDANCE

Parental Knowledge and Children's Exposure

It has been noted that parents often are not aware of the frequency or severity of their children's fright reactions. For example, Cantor and Reilly (1982) found that parents' estimates of the frequency of their children's media-induced fright reactions were significantly lower than their children's self-reports. This finding may be due in part to children's reluctance to admit to their parents that they have been scared, in an attempt to appear mature or to avert parental restrictions over their future viewing. Parents also underestimate their children's exposure to scary media. Research suggests that children often experience fright reactions to programs that many parents would not expect to be scary (Cantor, 1998). Nevertheless, there is evidence that children are widely exposed to televised stimuli that were originally intended for adults and that are considered frightening by a large proportion of adult moviegoers. Sparks (1986), for example, reported that almost 50% of the 4-to-10-year-olds he interviewed had seen *Poltergeist* and *Jaws*, and substantial proportions of his sample had seen *Halloween* and *Friday the 13th*. Most of this viewing was done in the home, on cable television.

When Family Members Watch Together

What are the emotional implications of family members watching television together? Most studies touch on this question only indirectly, by describing the types of interactions that occur in front of the television set. Lemish and Rice (1986) observed that television viewing fit into a stream of interactions between infants and their mothers. Infants watched television while they played, had their diapers changed, ate, and went about their ordinary routines. In contrast, being read to required special time and the cessation of other activities by both mother and child. Other researchers studied preschoolers and found that although families didn't talk or interact as much when watching television as they did during other play activities, television time involved more affectionate cuddling and touching (Brody, Stoneman, & Sanders, 1980).

The trend toward having more than one television set per household has resulted in less family coviewing (Comstock, 1990). The exception to this trend is that siblings often watch together, even if another set is available. Alexander, Ryan, and Munoz (1984) observed that siblings in front of the television set played games, ate, fought, read, and did homework while they "watched" together. Discussions about the content of the program included explanations for younger sibling about the plot, predictions of what would happen next, and debates about whether the program was interesting or "dumb." The same patterns were observed in a study by Jordan (1990) of families' interactions around the videocassette recorder. Parents used the VCR to create a quiet time when they could leave their children unattended without too much concern about the content. Siblings generally watched together and incorporated the content of the video into their discussions and activities.

What about research specifically on coviewing and emotional responses? Such research has focused primarily on fright reactions and on the role that siblings can play in reducing the fear. Hoffner and Haefner (1997) asked first-through sixth-grade children to recall a time when they watched a television show with someone who became scared and to describe how (if at all) they had attempted to comfort the frightened coviewer. Almost 40% said that they recalled watching a program with a frightened sibling (indeed, 5% said they remembered watching a program during which their mother had become frightened!). Approximately 50% of the girls and 30% of the boys said that they had tried to comfort the frightened coviewer. Comforting messages ranged from simple attention diversion to a discussion and explanation of the coviewer's fear. Even the youngest children adjusted the sensitivity of their comforting strategy based on the intensity of the coviewer's fright response.

How effective are siblings at providing comfort for one another? Wilson and Weiss (1993) studied preschoolers' reactions to a scary television program when viewed with or without an older sibling. More than half of the sibling pairs talked about how scary the program was while watching the movie, and more than a third of the older siblings actively tried to provide comfort by offering reassurance, a hug, or a hand to hold. Compared to children who watched the scary program alone, preschoolers who viewed with an older sibling were less emotionally aroused and liked the program more.

SUMMARY AND CONCLUSIONS

In summary, the research presented here suggests that television content can have substantial negative effects on children's emotional well-being, and that these effects can sometimes endure for years. Moreover, effects on a child can affect the whole family. When children are suddenly reluctant to sleep alone (or to sleep at all) or to engage in everyday activities, the tenor of family life changes for the worse. Most importantly, children do not respond at random to mass media content or to attempts to alleviate its effects. There are strong developmental changes in the types of content that frighten different age groups, and equally strong changes in the effectiveness of different coping strategies. By knowing which material is most scary for each age group, and how best to deal with it, families can avoid or reduce many of the potential negative emotional effects of viewing (Cantor, 1998).

REFERENCES

Alexander, A., Ryan, M. S., & Munoz, P. (1984). Creating a learning context: Investigations on the interaction of siblings during television viewing. *Critical Studies in Mass Communication, 1,* 345–364.
Badzinski, D. M., Cantor, J., & Hoffner, C. (1989). Children's understanding of quantifiers. *Child Study Journal, 19,* 241–258.
Blumer, H. (1933). *Movies and conduct.* New York: Macmillan.
Bowlby, J. (1973). *Separation: Anxiety and anger.* New York: Basic Books.
Brody, G. H., Stoneman, Z., & Sanders, A. K. (1980). Effects of television viewing on family interactions: An observational study. *Family Relations, 29,* 216–220.
Buzzuto, J. C. (1975). Cinematic neurosis following *The Exorcist. Journal of Nervous and Mental Disease, 161,* 43–48.
Cantor, J. (1994). Fright reactions to mass media. In J. Bryant & D. Zillmann (Eds.), *Media effects: Advances in theory and research* (pp. 213–245). Hillsdale, NJ: Lawrence Erlbaum Associates.
Cantor, J. (1998). *"Mommy, I'm scared": How TV and movies frighten children and what we can do to protect them.* San Diego, CA: Harcourt Brace.

Cantor, J., & Hoffner, C. (1990). Children's fear reactions to a televised film as a function of perceived immediacy of depicted threat. *Journal of Broadcasting & Electronic Media, 34*, 421–442.

Cantor, J., Mares, M. L., & Oliver, M. B. (1993). Parents' and children's emotional reactions to televised coverage of the Gulf War. In B. Greenberg & W. Gantz (Eds.), *Desert Storm and the mass media* (pp. 325–340). Cresskill, NJ: Hampton Press.

Cantor, J., & Nathanson, A. (1996). Children's fright reactions to television news. *Journal of Communication, 46*(4), 139–152.

Cantor, J., & Omdahl, B. (1991). Effects of fictional media depictions of realistic threats on children's emotional responses, expectations, worries, and liking for related activities. *Communication Monographs, 58*, 384–401.

Cantor, J., & Omdahl, B. (1999). Children's acceptance of safety guidelines after exposure to televised dramas depicting accidents. *Western Journal of Communication, 63*(1), 1–15.

Cantor, J., & Reilly, S. (1982). Adolescents' fright reactions to television and films. *Journal of Communication, 32*(1), 87–99.

Cantor, J., & Sparks, G. G. (1984). Children's fear responses to mass media: Testing some Piagetian predictions. *Journal of Communication, 34*(2), 90–103.

Cantor, J., Sparks, G. G., & Hoffner, C. (1988). Calming children's television fears: Mr. Rogers vs. The Incredible Hulk. *Journal of Broadcasting & Electronic Media, 32*, 271–288.

Cantor, J., & Wilson, B. J. (1984). Modifying fear responses to mass media in preschool and elementary school children. *Journal of Broadcasting, 28*, 431–443.

Cantor, J., & Wilson, B. J. (1988). Helping children cope with frightening media presentations. *Current Psychology: Research & Reviews, 7*, 58–75.

Cantor, J., Wilson, B. J., & Hoffner, C. (1986). Emotional responses to a televised nuclear holocaust film. *Communication Research, 13*, 257–277.

Choti, S. E., Marston, A. R., Holston, S. G., & Hart, J. T. (1987). Gender and personality variables in film-induced sadness and crying. *Journal of Social and Clinical Psychology, 5*, 535–544.

Comstock, G. (1990). *Television and the American child*. New York: Academic Press.

Flavell, J. (1963). *The developmental psychology of Jean Piaget*. New York: Van Nostrand.

Gentile, D. A., & Walsh, D. A. (1999). *MediaQuotient*[tm]: *National survey of family media habits, knowledge, and attitudes*. Minneapolis, MN: National Institute on Media and the Family.

Harrison, K., & Cantor, J. (1999). Tales from the screen: Enduring fright reactions to scary media. *Media Psychology, 1*(2), 97–116.

Hoekstra, S. J., Harris, R. J., & Helmick, A. L. (1999). Autobiographical memories about the experience of seeing frightening movies in childhood. *Media Psychology, 1*(2), 117–140.

Hoffner, C., & Cantor, J. (1985). Developmental differences in responses to a television character's appearance and behavior. *Developmental Psychology, 21*, 1065–1074.

Hoffner, C., & Cantor, J. (1990). Forewarning of a threat and prior knowledge of outcome: Effects on children's emotional responses to a film sequence. *Human Communication Research, 16*, 323–354.

Hoffner, C., Cantor, J., & Badzinski, D. M. (1990). Children's understanding of adverbs denoting degree of likelihood. *Journal of Child Language, 17*, 217–231.

Hoffner, C., & Haefner, M. J. (1997). Children's comforting of frightened coviewers: Real and hypothetical television-viewing situations. *Communication Research, 24*, 136–152.

Johnson, B. R. (1980). General occurrence of stressful reactions to commercial motion pictures and elements in films subjectively identified as stressors. *Psychological Reports, 47*, 775–786.

Jordan, A. B. (1990). A family systems approach to the use of the VCR in the home. In J. Dobrow (Ed.), *Social and cultural aspects of VCR use* (pp. 163–179). Hillsdale, NJ: Lawrence Erlbaum Associates.

Kelly, H. (1981). Reasoning about realities: Children's evaluations of television and books. In H. Kelly & H. Gardner (Eds.), *Viewing children through television* (pp. 59–71). San Francisco: Jossey-Bass.

Kubey, R. W. (1986). Television use in everyday life: Coping with unstructured time. *Journal of Communication, 24*, 35–47.

Labaton, S. (1999, March 8). Cable rates rising as industry nears end of regulation. *New York Times*, pp. A1, A12.

Larson, R. (1995). Secrets in the bedroom: Adolescents' private use of the media. *Journal of Youth and Adolescence, 24*, 535–550.

Lemish, D., & Rice, M. (1986). Television as a talking picture book: A prop for language acquisition. *Journal of Child Language, 13*, 251–274.

Manis, F. R., Keating, D. P., & Morison, F. J. (1980). Developmental differences in the allocation of processing capacity. *Journal of Experimental Child Psychology, 29*, 156–169.

Mathai, J. (1983). An acute anxiety state in an adolescent precipitated by viewing a horror movie. *Journal of Adolescence, 6*, 197–200.

Melkman, R., Tversky, B., & Baratz, D. (1981). Developmental trends in the use of perceptual and conceptual attributes in grouping, clustering and retrieval. *Journal of Experimental Child Psychology, 31*, 470–486.

Morison, P., & Gardner, H. (1978). Dragons and dinosaurs: The child's capacity to differentiate fantasy from reality. *Child Development, 49*, 642–648.

Oliver, M. B. (1993). Exploring the paradox of the enjoyment of sad films. *Human Communication Research, 19*, 315–342.

Oliver, M. B., Sargent, S. L., & Weaver, J. B. (1998). The impact of sex and gender role self-perception on affective reactions to different types of film. *Sex Roles, 38*, 45–60.

Schofield, J., & Pavelchak, M. (1985). "The Day After": The impact of a media event. *American Psychologist, 40*, 542–548.

Simons, D., & Silveira, W. R. (1994). Post-traumatic stress disorder in children after television programmes. *British Medical Journal, 308*, 389–390.

Singer, M. I., Slovak, K., Frierson, T., & York, P. (1998). Viewing preferences, symptoms of psychological trauma, and violent behaviors among children who watch television. *Journal of the American Academy of Child and Adolescent Psychiatry, 37*(10), 1041–1048.

Sparks, G. G. (1986). Developmental differences in children's reports of fear induced by the mass media. *Child Study Journal, 16*, 55–66.

Sparks, G.G., & Cantor, J. (1986). Developmental differences in fright responses to a television program depicting a character transformation. *Journal of Broadcasting & Electronic Media, 30*, 309–323.

Valkenburg, P. M., Cantor, J., & Peeters, A. L. (2000). *Fright reactions to television: A child survey. Communication Research, 27*(1), 82–99.

Weiss, A. J., Imrich, D. J., & Wilson, B. J. (1993). Prior exposure to creatures from a horror film: Live versus photographic representations. *Human Communication Research, 20*, 41–66.

Wilson, B. J. (1987). Reducing children's emotional reactions to mass media through rehearsed explanation and exposure to a replica of a fear object. *Human Communication Research, 14*, 3–26.

Wilson, B. J. (1989a). Desensitizing children's emotional reactions to the mass media. *Communication Research, 16*, 723–745.

Wilson, B. J. (1989b). The effects of two control strategies on children's emotional reactions to a frightening movie scene. *Journal of Broadcasting & Electronic Media, 33*, 397–418.

Wilson, B. J., & Cantor, J. (1987). Reducing children's fear reactions to mass media: Effects of visual exposure and verbal explanation. In M. McLaughlin, (Ed.), *Communication Yearbook 10* (pp. 553–573). Beverly Hills, CA: Sage.

Wilson, B. J., Hoffner, C., & Cantor, J. (1987). Children's perceptions of the effectiveness of techniques to reduce fear from mass media. *Journal of Applied Developmental Psychology, 8*, 39–52.

Wilson, B. J., & Weiss, A. J. (1991). The effects of two reality explanations on children's reactions to a frightening movie scene. *Communication Monographs, 58*, 307–326.

Wilson, B. J., & Weiss, A. J. (1993). The effects of sibling coviewing on preschoolers' reactions to a suspenseful movie scene. *Communication Research, 20*, 214–248.

Zillmann, D., & Bryant, J. (1994). Entertainment as media effect. In J. Bryant & D. Zillmann (Eds.), *Media effects: Advances in theory and research* (pp. 437–461). Hillsdale, NJ: Lawrence Erlbaum, Associales.

Television and the Family: The Cultivation Perspective

Nancy Signorielli
University of Delaware

Michael Morgan
University of Massachusetts-Amherst

To one degree or another everyone has first-hand knowledge of being a member of a family. Some families are larger or more cohesive, whereas others are smaller or seemingly disjointed. We get our ideas about family life from numerous first-hand sources—our own family and extended family as well as the families of our friends and neighbors. We also learn about families and family life from mediated sources such as television and the movies and, in turn, may judge our own families through the prism of these mass mediated messages.

The importance of television's messages in shaping peoples' conceptions about families and family life is not trivial. Television is one of the major players in the socialization process. Television is seen by just about everyone practically every day. Few escape daily exposure to the vast and seemingly limitless amount of programming available around the clock. Whether watching network broadcast programming, premium cable channels, superstations, cable networks (e.g., Nickelodeon), other broadcast and cable services, or using the VCR, the images provide a wealth of information about families and family life. This chapter explores how television contributes to people's conceptions about families and family life, through the theoretical perspective of cultivation analysis.

Cultivation analysis is the third part of the cultural indicators research paradigm, a three-pronged empirical approach that examines the social consequences of growing up and living with television (e.g., Gerbner, 1973). This perspective suggests that our understanding of the unique role that television plays in our lives should be based on an understanding of (a) the institutions that create television's messages (institutional process analysis), (b) the most stable, pervasive, and recurrent images that we find in media content (message system or content analysis), and (c) how exposure to the world of television contributes to viewers' conceptions about the real world (cultivation analysis).

Cultivation analysis is not concerned with the "impact" of any particular television program, genre, or episode, because television viewing is a cumulative process. It is not concerned with formal aesthetic categories, style, artistic quality, issues of high culture versus low culture, or specific, selective "readings" or interpretations of media messages. Rather, cultivation researchers approach television as a *system* of messages, made up of aggregate and repetitive patterns of images and representations to which entire communities are expose—and that they absorb—over long periods of time.

The concept of "storytelling" is central to the theory of cultivation. Gerbner (1967) contended that the basic difference between human beings and other species is that we live in a world created by the stories we tell. All living organisms exchange energy with their environments, and many creatures exchange information and change their behavior as a result of learning. But only humans communicate by the manipulation of complex symbol systems. Humans therefore uniquely live in a world experienced and constructed largely through many forms and modes of storytelling. We have never personally or directly experienced great portions of what we know, or think we know; we "know" about many things based on the stories we hear and the stories we tell.

Television has transformed the cultural process of storytelling into a centralized, standardized, market-driven, advertiser-sponsored system. In earlier times, the stories of a culture were told face-to-face by members of a community, by parents, teachers, or the clergy. Today, television tells most of the stories to most of the people, most of the time. Therefore, the cultural process of storytelling is now in the hands of global commercial interests who have something to sell, and who in effect operate outside the reach of democratic decision making.

THE THEORETICAL UNDERPINNINGS OF CULTIVATION

We are a mass mediated society. The mass media, especially television, play important roles in our daily lives. Television is the source of the most broadly shared images and messages in history, both in the United States and around the world. As the number of people who have always lived with television continues to grow, the medium is increasingly taken for granted as an appliance, a piece of furniture, a storyteller, a member of the family. Few can remember, or care to remember, what life was like before television.

Television sets, with their cable or satellite dish hookups, VCRs, and perhaps Internet connections are usually placed in prominent positions in our homes, whether in the family room, the living room, the kitchen, the bedroom, or all of these locations. Furniture is arranged to provide the best "sight lines" to the TV, not to foster conversation. Today, most homes have two or more sets, and more and more viewing has become a solitary rather than a family activity. For most viewers, expanded delivery systems such as cable, satellite dishes, and VCRs signal even further penetration and integration of established viewing patterns into everyday life.

Television has thus become our nation's (and increasingly the world's) most common and constant learning environment. It both mirrors and leads society. It serves, however, first and foremost as our storyteller and has become the wholesale distributor of images that form the mainstream of our popular culture. The world of television shows and tells us about life—people, places, striving, power, fate, and family life. It presents the good and bad, the happy and sad, the powerful and the weak, and lets us know who or what is a success or a failure.

As with the functions of culture in general, the substance of the consciousness cultivated by television is broad, underlying, global assumptions about the "facts" of life rather than specific attitudes and opinions. Nevertheless, television is only one of the many things that explain the world to us and our children. Television, however, is special because its socially constructed version of reality bombards all classes, groups, and ages with the same perspectives at the same time. More importantly, these images are presented primarily in the guise of entertainment, whether in sitcoms, drama, action-adventures, TV movies, or even news and information programs (as the lines between entertainment and information formats continue to erode).

The views of the world embedded in television drama do not differ appreciably from images presented in other media, and its rules of the social hierarchy are not easily distinguishable from those imparted by other powerful agents of socialization. What makes television unique, however, is its ability to standardize, streamline, amplify, and share with virtually all members of society these common cultural norms.

Although television has a great deal in common with other media, it is different in some important ways. For one thing, people spend far more time with television than with other media; more time is spent watching television than doing any other activity except working and sleeping. Most people under 50 have been watching television since before they could read or probably even speak. Unlike print media, television does not require a formal literacy; unlike theatrical movies, television runs almost continuously, and can be watched without leaving one's home; unlike radio, television can show as well as tell. Each of these characteristics is significant in and of itself; their combined force is unprecedented and overwhelming.

Television is different from other media in its centralized mass production and ritualistic use of a coherent set of images and messages produced to appeal to the entire population. Therefore, exposure to all television viewing (broadcast, cable, or VCRs) rather than only to specific genres or programs is what accounts for the historically new and distinct consequences of living with television—the cultivation of shared conceptions of reality among otherwise diverse publics.

The variety of viewing choices is limited by the fact that many programs designed for the same broad audience tend to be similar in their basic make-up and appeal and are often broadcast during the same time slots (Signorielli, 1986). Most programs are, by commercial necessity, designed to be watched by nearly everyone. Even the "Black situation comedies" of the 1990s (e.g., *Sister, Sister; Malcolm and Eddy; Smart Guy*) broadcast on the newer networks are similar to the earlier genre of "Black situation comedies" (*The Jeffersons, Sanford and Son*) in that they incorporate the same basic storytelling elements of situation comedies in general. Amount of viewing typically follows the lifestyle of the viewer and is relatively insensitive to specific programs. The audience is always the group available at a certain time of the day, the week, and the season, regardless of the programs. Most viewers watch by the clock and follow established routines rather than choose each program as they would choose a book, a movie, or a magazine. Moreover, those who start by watching a specifically selected program, often continue watching once their program is over. The increased offerings of cable systems facilitate this process as viewers, through the use of the remote control, try to watch two of more programs simultaneously or "surf" through the available channels searching for something to watch. Consequently, the more people watch, the less selective they can be. Series and fads come and go, yet for the past 15 to 20 years, viewing has stabilized at about 7 hours a day for the average household and 3 hours a day for the average person (Nielsen, 1990; Vivian, 1999).

Of course, cable and especially VCRs have obviously and dramatically changed the home media environment, and the Internet seems to promise to continue these transformations. The family without a VCR is now the exception, especially when children are present. VCRs have contributed to the drop in audience share (and revenue) among the three major broadcasting networks (Lawrence, 1989), and have profoundly altered the marketing and distribution of "theatrical" films. Likewise, cable's increased channel capacities, movie channels, and "pay-per-view" have also changed the nature of home viewing. The Internet, at least in much popular or commercial discourse, is poised to render television an obsolete dinosaur.

It may appear then that technological developments such as cable, the VCR, and computer networks strongly challenge or even negate some assumptions of cultivation theory. Armed with a VCR, for example, the viewer may be more selective than ever. Instead of being limited to whatever happens to be on the air, viewers can pick and choose what they want to record or rent from a vast range of alternatives. This scenario, however, assumes that the specific content seen by VCR users (especially heavy VCR users and those who are heavy television viewers in general) presents alternative worldviews, values, and stereotypes from most network-type programs. This assumption seems unlikely, especially because available evidence suggests that cable and VCRs serve mainly to intensify rather than undercut cultivation; most regular and heavy viewers use cable and VCRs to watch more of the most popular fare, and cultivation patterns are even more pronounced among those who use these delivery systems more often (Morgan & Rotschild, 1983; Morgan & Shanahan, 1991; Morgan, Shanahan, & Harris, 1990). Meanwhile, rather than bestowing upon us an interactive democracy, the largest media conglomerates are devoting their web sites to the promotion of greater exposure to their most popular television programs and channels.

None of this should be too surprising. Given the tight links among the various industries involved in the production and distribution of media content, and the fact that all these sources are trying to attract the same overlapping, heterogeneous audiences, the most popular program materials tend to present consistent and complementary messages. For example, in regard to violence, a comparison of cable and broadcast dramatic programming (Gerbner, 1993) found similar levels of violence overall. Consequently, from an economic standpoint, the industry's programming practices are geared to reproduce what has already proven to be profitable (Gitlin, 1983). Hence, the reliance on "spin-offs," formulaic scriptwriting, and cable's as well as independent stations' use of recently syndicated or "classic TV" programs. Despite all the socalled alternatives of the new media, the bulk of the audience is still living in the TV world and seems likely to stay there for the foreseeable future.

Therefore, from the point of view of the cultivation of relatively stable and common images, what counts is the total pattern of programming to which total communities are regularly exposed over long periods of time. The pattern of settings, casting, social typing, actions, and related outcomes cuts across most program types and viewing modes and defines the world of television—a world in which many viewers live so much of their lives that they cannot avoid absorbing or dealing with its recurrent patterns. Nowhere is this more apparent than in images relating to families and family life on television.

FAMILY AND FAMILY LIFE ON TELEVISION

Cultivation studies must be based on an understanding of what kinds of images are seen on television. There is an existing body of research about television's families that clearly illustrates both the constancy and derivative nature of television programming (see Skill, 1994; Skill, Wallace, & Cassata, 1990; and chap. 7, this volume). Home and family is one of the most common themes in network dramatic programs. It is found in more than 8 out of 10 programs (Signorielli, 1991) and many titles reflect this focus (e.g., *Home Improvement, Family Matters*). Most of the programs that feature families on television are situation comedies with problems that are easily solved, within a 22-minute format, and typically in a humorous manner (Moore, 1992; Skill & Robinson, 1994).

In the early days of television, families were intact, perfect, and often antiseptic (e.g., *Donna Reed, Leave it to Beaver, Ozzie and Harriet*). Glennon and Butsch (1982) found that most shows were about glamorous and successful middle-class families while under- and misrepresenting the lower class. In most cases, the parents effectively and quickly dealt with any problem that came their way. Fathers were all knowing, and mothers took care of everything (Bundy, Thompson, & Strapp, 1997). Moreover, the children in these comedies interacted positively, although not every frequently (Larson, 1991). The second generation of television families, broadcast in prime time during the 1970s, had no dominant family structure—programs featured nuclear families as well as divorced and/or single (widowed) parents (Greenberg, Buerkel-Rothfuss, Neuendorf, & Atkin, 1980). Few of these television families had financial problems, children who had problems at school, or other real life, day-to-day problems (Barcus, 1983). African American television families during the mid-1970s were twice as likely as White families to have one parent and few extended family members. These programs exhibited more family conflict, and the sons in these families (e.g., J.J. in *Good Times*) were often the most active family members (Greenberg & Neuendorf, 1980).

During the 1980s programs continued to feature traditional and nuclear families (e.g., *The Cosby Show, Growing Pains, Family Ties*) as well as single-parent and other permutations that endorsed nontraditional families (e.g., *Who's the Boss, Kate and Allie*). Sibling relationships, particularly those between younger sisters and older brothers, also became somewhat more conflictual in these programs (Larson, 1991). Yet, in the programming from the 1980s, family members were more supportive of each other even though children initiated and exhibited more parent–child interactions (Akins, as cited in Skill et al., 1990). Situation comedies with positive portrayals of African American families were also found during the mid-1980s (e.g., *The Cosby Show, 227, Charlie & Company*). Merritt and Stroman (1993) found that these programs contained little conflictual behavior and focused on intact families whose spouses interacted equally, lovingly, and frequently, and whose children were taught achievement-oriented values and were treated respectfully. The dominant family programming of the 1980s thus presented conservative or moderate families (Skill, Robinson, & Wallace, 1987) in which intact families were a little more supportive and harmonious than nonintact families (Skill et al., 1990).

During the 1990s, despite stylistic changes, many programs continued to reflect the traditional and conservative values of family life seen in preceding decades (e.g., *Home Improvement, Boy Meets World, Family Matters*). As in preceding decades, the story lines of family situation comedies of the 1990s typically focused on the children and on common emotions (fear, anger) and emotional situations (Weiss & Wilson, 1996). Although negative emotions often appear in the major plot line, they usually are presented in a humorous context. The plot typically revolves around a child who has a problem or is in trouble, the resolution of this problem, and a happy ending. The late 1980s and the 1990s also spawned a group of programs, quite popular with viewers, whose families are presented as psychotic and dysfunctional, and, at times, almost "antifamily" (e.g., *Roseanne, Married With Children, The Simpsons*; cf. chap. 12, this volume). Bundy et al. (1997) found that whereas both types of programing in the 1990s contained parenting behaviors that were detrimental in nature, the controversial antifamily series had more of these problematic behaviors. Others, however, say the representation of the family in programs such as *Roseanne* is closer to reality than most situation comedies and provides a glimpse about survival in a blue-collar community (Lee, 1995).

Television families, overall, remain more likely to be conventional than nonconventional. Skill et al. (1987), in an analysis of television families broadcast between 1979 and 1984, found that two thirds of the program hours focused on conventional families and one third on nonconventional families. Moreover, these families typically reinforced traditional family values, often within a comic frame of reference. Similarly, Moore (1992), in an analysis of family series broadcast between 1947 and 1990, found that more than 6 out of 10 of these families were conventional whereas 4 out of 10 were nonconventional (single-parent). Although the ratio of conventional to nonconventional families varied from decade to decade, by the end of the 1980s, the ratio remained at 60% to 40%.

Compared to U.S. census figures, television actually tends to under-represent two-parent families (Skill & Robinson, 1994). More important, television's single-parent families are often idealized and differ from actual single-parent families in several ways. First, on television the single parent typically is a man who has a good job (Moore, 1992; Skill & Robinson, 1994). Second, television characters are single parents because they never married in the first place or because their spouse died, not because of divorce. Third, television's single-parent households frequently enjoy live-in domestic help (Moore, 1992). In reality, most single-parent households are headed by women either because of divorce or from having children out-of-wedlock, who do not have high-paying jobs and cannot afford domestic help. In short, television programs do not focus on the significant problems and real difficulties faced by most single-parent households on a day-to-day basis.

Similarly, television's presentation of marriage does not adequately reflect reality. In an analysis of programming of the 1970s, Signorielli (1982) found that themes of romance and marriage were pervasive during prime time, especially for women. When compared to men, more women, especially women of color, could be classified by marital status and, in general, were more likely to be portrayed as married or formerly married. In addition, during the 1970s, prime-time television overwhelmingly presented husbands and wives in traditional roles. Married women had children and were seen as happy, nurturing, and feminine but were less likely to work outside the home than were single or divorced women. Moreover, those married women who were presented as successful in the work world, typically had problems with marital and family relationships (Roberts, 1982; see chap. 9, this volume).

Signorielli and Kahlenberg (1999), in an analysis of prime-time programing of the 1990s, found that women of color were less likely to be married than were White women, and that race was not a predictor of marital status for men. Moreover, in the 1990s programming, as was true of earlier programming, single and formerly married female characters continued to dominate the television women's work force, whereas married women were less likely to be seen working outside the home. For married males in 1990s programming, on the other hand, themes of romance, home, marriage, and family did not necessarily influence whether or not they were depicted in the work force. More than three quarters of the married males, as compared to only two fifths of the married women, were portrayed as working. In fact, about the same percentage of married males, single males, and formerly married males were depicted as working, which continues to reinforce the stereotype of men as the breadwinners. As in the programs broadcast during the 1970s, the television programs of the 1990s continued to portray married women with reduced options, for, unlike men, women on television can rarely combine marriage and employment with any success.

Marriage on television is also likely to be depicted as conventional and happy (Perse, Pavitt, & Burggraf, 1990). Marital partners tend to be supportive and avoid conflict. Moreover, when Perse et al. (1990) examined marriages using Fitzpatrick's (1977, 1984) schema, the majority of the television marriages turned out to be traditional in nature, with husbands and wives performing traditional gender-typed behaviors.

Whether conventional or nonconventional, the television family is, above all, happy, and whereas each week's episode brings problems and conflicts, these are rarely very serious and certainly can be solved relatively easily and within a short period of time (Cantor, 1990; Moore, 1992). Most family interactions are affiliative rather than conflictive and positive rather than negative, with the most harmonious relationships in conventional families (Comstock & Strzyewski, 1990; Greenberg, Buerkel-Rothfuss, et al., 1980; Skill & Wallace, 1990; Taylor, 1989). Similarly, most verbal interactions between husbands and wives, during prime time, are positive and help build the relationship (Greenberg, Hines, Buerkel-Rothfuss, & Atkin, 1980).

In a recent series of studies, college students rated family situation comedies broadcast during the 1950s through the early 1990s on a number of dimensions relating to conflict, parent–child relationships, gender roles, and so forth. Douglas and Olson (1996) found that families in more recent situation comedies (1980s and 1990s) were rated as more conflictual and less cohesive than families in the situation comedies of the 1950s, 1960s, and 1970s. In these series, the experience of the children seemed to have deteriorated over time—parent–child relationships were less stable, less satisfactory, and less supportive in the more recent situation comedies (e.g., *Roseanne*) and the families were seen as less able to manage day-to-day life. In another study using many of the same programs, Douglas and Olson (1995) found that working class families were less functional than families with higher socioeconomic status. Finally, Olson and Douglas (1997) examined gender-role depictions in these programs, finding a curvilinear pattern with peaks in stability and satisfaction in the programs of the 1950s and the 1980s. The more recent situation comedies (e.g., *Roseanne, Grace Under Fire, Home Improvement*), however, were less positive than earlier situation comedies in their depictions because the characters exhibited more patterns of dominance but less stability and satisfaction in their relationships.

An analysis of three seasons of programming broadcast between 1975 to 1976 and 1977 to 1978 found the highest levels of verbal aggression between characters in situation comedies and the least in family dramas (Greenberg, Edison, Korzenny, Fernandez-Collado, & Atkin, 1980). This analysis also found that verbal aggression (insults, rejections, hostility) occurred in situation comedies roughly 30 times an hour. Other subsequent analyses found that, compared to the sitcoms of the 1960s and 1970s, situation comedies broadcast during the 1980s and 1990s have more negative communication behaviors and express more conflicts (Heintz, 1992; Larson, 1991).

Marriage and especially the family are clearly important elements of television programming. On television, marriage is often presented ambivalently—intimate and harmonious on the situation comedies whereas fractured and less positive in dramas, especially the evening serial dramas and the daytime soap operas. Families, especially those in situation comedies broadcast during prime time, tend to be more affiliative and harmonious than conflictual, even though, in more recent programs, many verbal interactions consist of wisecracks, and "humorous" insults. In more recent years, although family constellations have become more nontraditional, many programs, again mostly situation comedies, revolve around conventional, traditional, and nuclear families.

THE CULTIVATION OF FAMILY VALUES

How do these images affect viewers? Although there is not a very large body of literature to answer this question, the available data tend to suggest that television's images about marriage, the family, and family life influence the conceptions that children and adults hold about marriage and the family. A number of scholars (see, e.g., Brown & Bryant, 1990; Greenberg, 1982) provide evidence that television influences people's beliefs about marriage and family life as well as the types of behaviors that are appropriate and desirable in marriage and in the family.

The existing studies fall into two categories; studies that examined respondents' perceptions of the realism of television families, and studies conducted in the tradition of cultivation analysis. The first group of studies examined how realistic television families appear to different groups of people. Although these studies are not directly relevant to cultivation theory because they do not examine relationships between television viewing and conceptions about families, they have produced interesting results and shed additional light on this area of study. We briefly discuss these studies and then examine those that have a direct bearing on cultivation theory.

Perceptions of Families and Family Life

Berry's (1992) examination of low income African American teenagers' perceptions of the characters in two television shows (*Good Times* and *The Cosby Show*) illustrates the potential power of television to influence conceptions of social reality. Most of the teens in this sample said that they thought these two shows accurately reflected reality because the images they saw were similar to their own experiences and knowledge. Many of these teens said they thought the father (James Evans) in *Good Times* provided a stronger image of manhood than the father (Heathcliff Huxtable) in *The Cosby Show* because Evans was authoritarian, often threatened to use physical punishment, typically took control of situations, and generally dominated the family (perceptions consistent with the behavior of men these youngsters typically encounter in their everyday life). These teens also evaluated the oldest son in both situation comedies. J.J. Evans in *Good Times* was seen by more than half of these teens as having positive characteristics, whereas one fifth of the sample categorized J.J. as having negative qualities. Two thirds of these teens perceived Theo Huxtable (*The Cosby Show*) as having a positive image, whereas more than one fourth saw Theo as having both positive and negative qualities. Very few of these teens saw Theo as having mostly negative traits. To some extent, these young people may have perceived J.J. Evans as a more realistic character than Theo Huxtable (and thus judged him as having both positive and negative traits, rather than as a negative character), because Theo's upper middle-class lifestyle did not reflect the way in which most of these teens lived. This analysis thus shows that television may give African American adolescents conflicting messages about families and family interactions.

Dorr, Kovaric, and Doubleday (1990) also examined children's perceptions of the realism of television families. Overall, the children judged the demographics of traditional families as more realistic than the demographics of nontraditional families. The degree of realism in these two types of family series was judged to be similar in regard to the feelings and actions expressed by the characters. There were, however, differences by age. More specifically, second graders judged the television families, whether traditional or nontraditional, as realistic. Sixth and tenth graders, on the other hand, rated the traditional television families as more realistic than the nontraditional families. Overall, these children said that about half of real-life American families are similar to the families they see on television and that the way the television families handle feelings and emotions was very realistic.

Children may also perceive negative emotions in family situation comedies, and these perceptions may influence their conceptions about similar emotional events in their own lives. Weiss and Wilson (1998), in a study of boys and girls in kindergarten and second grade, found that the younger children and all the boys had a more difficult time understanding a negative plot (expression of fear or anger) in a popular family sitcom

(*Full House*) when the action included a positive, humorous subplot. The children, in this case, downplayed the main character's negative feelings even though the primary plot of the program revolved around the character's expression of anger or fear. Moreover, the children typically rated *Full House* as very realistic and believed that most families were like the family and children in this show.

Research also indicates that viewers' implicit theories of marriage may be related to how they perceive television marriages. Perse et al. (1991) examined relationships between college students' perceptions of television couples' marital satisfaction with the students' implicit theories of marriage (marital schemata), using Fitzpatrick's (1977, 1984) typology of marital relationships (traditional, independent, or separate). They found similarities between the students' marital schemata and their judgments of whether television couples had traditional, independent, or separate marriages, which were related to the students' evaluations of the degree of success or satisfaction in the television marriages. Specifically, those students who had traditional marital schemata rated traditional television couples as more satisfied than independent television couples. Contrary to the authors' expectations, however, those students whose own marital schemata were independent rated independent television couples as less satisfied than the traditional or separate television couples. Similarly, those students who had separate marital schematas rated the marriages of the separate television couples as the least satisfied relationships. Finally, married and divorced viewers use television's images about marriage to guide how they behave in their own marriage (Robinson, Skill, Nussbaum, & Moreland, 1985). Interestingly, viewers in this study indicated that they often relied on these images even though they thought that television's presentation of marriage was inaccurate, unrealistic, and sometimes even inappropriate.

The Cultivation of Conceptions About Families and Family Life

The portrayal of marriage and family life on television is related to the way in which people think about them. Buerkel-Rothfuss and Mayes (1981), for example, found that college students who viewed more soap operas had views about marriage and the family that reflected the way these themes were presented in the soaps. Students who were heavy viewers of soap operas, compared to those who were light viewers of the soaps, gave higher estimates of the proportion of both men and women who engage in extramarital affairs, get divorces, and have illegitimate children. These students also overestimated the number of women who had abortions. Soap opera viewing was not related to college students' perceptions about the number of people who had happy marriages but those who were habitual viewers of the soaps were more likely to believe that marriages were fragile.

Wober and Gunter (1987) found that married people who frequently watched soap operas, compared to those who did not watch the soaps, believed that, in reality, a husband's prolonged absence would be an important source of marital discord. Among unmarried respondents, however, the reverse was true—those who watched soap operas infrequently, compared to heavy viewers of the soaps, said that a husband's absence was a realistic source of marital discord.

Morgan and Harr-Mazar (1980) and Morgan (1980) found, in a 3-year panel of 200 adolescents, a positive relationship between television viewing and expressing the views that "families are good," "being single is bad," and that "families are large." These adolescents also expressed ambivalence about what they believed were the appropriate options and roles for women. Moreover, although the young women in this sample said that they wanted to get married at an earlier age, to have children early in life, and to have large families, they also indicated that they had high career aspirations and expectations.

Buerkel-Rothfuss, Greenberg, Atkin, and Neuendorf (1982) found that fourth-, sixth-, and eighth-grade children who watched more family situation comedies, whether these television families were affiliative or conflictual, were more likely to believe that real-life families were affiliative (supportive and concerned about each other). This was particularly true if the children felt that they could learn a lot from watching these programs on television. Moreover, the more realistic these television families seemed to the children, the stronger they believed that members of actual families were supportive of each other. The children who were heavy viewers of family situation comedies also believed that families in real life were less likely to experience strife and conflicts. The idealized image of family affinity may have different repercussions for adults, however, as Baran and Courtright (1980) found a negative relationship between viewing programs with family or marriage orientations and self-reported marital happiness. Compared to the happy families of the TV world, our own families may thus appear to be lacking.

Signorielli's (1991) analysis of data from the monitoring the Future Survey of high school seniors illustrated that television viewing cultivates profamily sentiments as well as conceptions that reflect the ambivalent presentation of marriage on television. This analysis found that adolescents who watched more television were more likely to say "they wanted to get married, to stay married to the same person for life, and to have children" (p. 145). High school students who were heavy viewers were also likely to disagree with the statement that "having a close intimate relationship with only one partner is too restrictive for the average person" (p. 144). Nevertheless, there was a positive relationship between viewing and expressing the opinion that one sees so few good or happy marriages that one could question marriage as a way of life.

Television viewing may also be related to learning how to handle marital problems. Fallis, Fitzpatrick, and Friestad (1985), using Fitzpatrick's (1977, 1984) typology of marital relationships, postulated that, after watching television portrayals of married life, couples would have better conversations with each other. Key to this position was whether or not the spouses perceived the television shows as relevant to their own marriages. Particularly, discussion should be higher among viewers who saw programs with marriages that were relevant but inconsistent with their own expectations. The findings indicated that viewing was related to increased discussions about topics relevant to the relationship only among those in marriages categorized as separates (those in marriages that may be emotionally divorced and who often express dissatisfaction with the marriage). These groups did not talk any more than the traditionals or independents about other topics (politics, the children, jobs).

Because many of television's families, particularly those broadcast during the late 1990s, are nontraditional in nature, it is conceivable that those who watch more television have views about marriage and the family that reflect nontraditional or antinuclear family alternatives. Morgan, Leggett, and Shanahan (1999), in testing this hypothesis, looked specifically at two issues, illegitimacy and single parenthood, using data from the 1988 and 1994 General Social Surveys. Two indices were calculated such that higher scores indicated more support for traditional values (disapproval of illegitimacy and single parenthood). The data showed little change between 1988 and 1994 in overall beliefs about illegitimacy and single parenthood; these respondents, by and large, indicated support for traditional family values. Yet, there was solid support for the hypothesis that heavy viewers were more likely than light viewers to endorse nontraditional family values. Moreover, the relationship withstood controls for important background factors (education, age, race, gender, marital status, parenthood, political party, religiosity). Furthermore, the results indicated that age was the strongest predictor of having traditional family values—younger respondents were less insistent that one should be married before having children and were more accepting of single parenthood. Women, non-Whites, and those who were less religious also expressed greater support for nontraditional family values; education was not related to having either traditional or nontraditional views about marriage and the family.

Morgan et al. (1999) noted that although these data may be interpreted as supporting the notion that television viewing contributes to the decay of "traditional family values" rather than espousing them, the overall implications are far from simple. The data clearly indicated that heavy television viewers were more accepting of single parenthood and of having children out of wedlock and that the relationship was more pronounced for younger respondents (both "Boomers" and "Gen-Xers"). Moreover, these findings were quite consistent with how television overrepresents and normalizes single-parent families. In interpreting these findings, however, it is important to remember that television's single-parent families have few of the problems these families face in reality. Although television content clearly presents the message that a single parent can raise a child as easily as two parents, the single parent on TV bears little resemblance to single-parent households in reality. On television, the single parent typically is a well-off male with full-time, live-in domestic help (e.g., *The Nanny*). Heavy viewers may thus be more accepting of a highly fantasied and luxurious notion of single parenthood; not the stark reality of single parenthood, which is seen in the feminization of poverty, limited access to health care, and widening gaps in income.

Consequently, the findings of this study cannot be interpreted as saying that television is "causing" the breakup of the nuclear family or that the "liberal media" are out to undermine the family. Rather, television's images are most likely reflecting and buttressing the changes that have occurred in society and in the family (Elkind, 1993). This position clearly fits within the perspective and assumptions of cultivation theory. Television viewing and conceptions about the world are mutually reinforcing; certain cultural, social, and ideological lifestyles and outlooks lead people to watch more television, and the messages they absorb tend to help sustain these outlooks. In short, media portrayals reflect and reinforce (i.e., cultivate) but do not cause changes in views about the nature of the family in society.

CONCLUSION

The family as presented on television cannot be pigeonholed into one image and often the images we see are more ambivalent than consistent. Television families reflect both traditional and nontraditional structures. Like most things on television, however, the images are far from the stark reality of life. This is particularly true in the case of television's non-traditional families. Most single parents, contrary to what we see on television, do not live comfortably; most are young, single mothers, often women of color, who do not have the luxury of high paying jobs or a comfortable lifestyle complete with live-in help. Similarly, the problems faced by television's traditional families do not necessarily reflect those that face today's families. Certainly, most day-to-day problems cannot be solved in 22 minutes or with humor that perhaps explains the popularity of the dysfunctional or television families of the 1990s (e.g., *Simpsons, Roseanne, Married With Children*).

Although there is not an overwhelming body of evidence, the studies that exist clearly indicate that what is seen on television is related to viewer's conceptions about families and marriage. Ambivalence is seen in the conceptions of high school students who watch a lot of television who indicate that they want to get married, have children, and stay married to the same person for life but who also question marriage as a way of life because they see so few good or happy marriages. Similarly, college students who watch more soap operas overestimate the number of people who are divorced or who have extramarital affairs, elements that are central to the story lines of many soap operas. Indeed, college students, particularly those whose implicit theories of marriage are traditional in nature, view traditional television couples as having greater marital satisfaction.

Most interestingly, those who watch more television, particularly those who are younger, seem to be more accepting of single parenthood and of having children out of wedlock. Unfortunately, the conceptions of non traditional families as seen on television may be at odds with the harsh realities of this lifestyle. The cultivation of a glorified, rosy image of single-parent families may actually contribute to the promotion of conservative policies that will ultimately hurt rather than help those less fortunate. If people believe that most single-parent families are doing ok, then the reality of the obstacles faced by many single women in the position of caring for their families, is obliterated. If most people's conceptions of single parenthood reflect that single parents have all the support they need, then special social programs to provide day care, improve skills, enhance income, or provide other forms of societal help may be perceived as a waste of tax dollars. The end result of nontraditional images on television may paradoxically be to further isolate those in nonconventional families rather than to lessen the likelihood that they will be accepted as part of mainstream culture.

In sum, as the family has undergone profound changes in the last half of the 20th century, so too have television's images of families become complex and multifaceted. This is not a simple relationship, however; television's representations are not a straightforward mirror of changes in the real world of families. Changes in television's images mainly reflect the search for narrative novelty or the need to generate compelling (if conventional) conflicts. But whatever portrayals are to come in the future, televison will continue to provide us with broadly shared, collective models of how families are structured and how their members behave toward each other. And this will continue to affect real families in significant ways.

REFERENCES

Baran, S., & Courtright, J. (1980, May). *The relationship between television portrayals of marriage and married and divorced people's perceptions of marriage.* Paper presented at the International Communication Association convention, Acapulco, Mexico.

Barcus, F. E. (1983). *Images of life on children's television.* New York: Praeger.

Berry, V. T. (1992). From *Good Times* to *The Cosby Show*: Perceptions of changing televised images among black fathers and sons. In S. Craig (Ed.), *Men, masculinity, and the media* (pp. 111–123). Newbury Park, CA: Sage.

Brown, D., & Bryant, J. (1990). Effects of television on family values and selected attitudes and behaviors. In J. Bryant (Ed.), *Television and the American family* (pp. 253–274). Hillsdale, NJ: Lawrence Erlbaum Associates.

Buerkel-Rothfuss, N., Greenberg, B. S., Atkin, C. K., & Neuendorf, K. (1982). Learning about the family from television. *Journal of Communication, 32*(3) 191–201.

Buerkel-Rothfuss, N., & Mayes, S. (1981). Soap opera viewing: The cultivation effect. *Journal of Communication, 31*(3), 108–115.

Bundy, K. A., Thompson, K. L., & Strapp, C. M. (1997). Parenting behaviors: A content analysis of situation comedies based on TV fictional families. *Psychological Reports, 80,* 1123–1137.

Cantor, M. (1990). Prime-time fathers: A study in continuity and change. *Critical Studies in Mass Communication, 7,* 275–285.

Comstock, J., & Stryzewski, K. (1990). Interpersonal interaction on television: Family conflict and jealousy on prime time. *Journal of Broadcasting & Electronic Media, 34,* 263–282.

Douglas, W., & Olson, B. M. (1995). Beyond family structure: The family in domestic comedy. *Journal of Broadcasting & Electronic Media, 39,* 236–261.

Douglas, W., & Olson, B. M. (1996). Subversion of the American family? An examination of children and parents in television families. *Communication Research, 23,* 73–99.

Dorr, A., Kovaric, P., & Doubleday, C. (1990). Age and content influences on children's perceptions of television families. *Journal of Broadcasting & Electronic Media, 34,* 377–397.

Elkind, D. (1993). Adolescents, parenting, and the media in the 21st century. *Adolescent Medicine: State of the Art Reviews, 4,* 599–606.

Fallis, S. F., Fitzpatrick, M. A., & Friestad, M. S. (1985). Spouses' discussion of television portrayals of close relationships. *Communication Research, 12,* 59–81.

Fitzpatrick, M. A. (1977). A typological approach to communication in relationships. In B. D. Rubin (Ed.), *Communication yearbook I* (pp. 263–278). New Brunswick, NJ: Transaction Books.

Fitzpatrick, M. A. (1984). A typological approach to marital interaction: Recent theory and research. In L. Berkowitz (Ed.), *Advances in experimental and social psychology* (pp. 1–47). New York: Academic Press.

Gerbner, G. (1967). Mass media and human communication theory. In F. E. X. Dance (Ed.), *Human communication theory:Original essays* (pp. 40–60). New York: Holt, Rinehart & Winston.

Gerbner, G. (1973). Cultural indicators: The third voice. In G. Gerbner, L. Gross, & W. H. Melody (Eds.), *Communications, technology and social policy* (pp. 555–573). New York: Wiley.

Gerbner, G. (1993). *Violence in cable-originated television programs.* Philadelphia, PA: The Annenberg School for Communication.

Gitlin, T. (1983). *Inside prime time.* New York: Pantheon.

Glennon, L. M., & Butsch, R. (1982). The family as portrayed on television: 1946–1978. In D. Pearl, L. Bouthilet, & J. Lazar (Eds.), *Television and behavior: Ten years of scientific progress and implications for the eighties* (Vol. 2, pp. 264–271). Washington, DC: Government Printing Office.

Greenberg, B. S. (1982). Television and role socialization: An overview. In D. Pearl, L. Bouthilet, & J. Lazar (Eds). *Television and behavior: Ten years of scientific progress and implications for the eighties* (Vol. 2, pp. 179–190). Washington, DC: Government Printing Office.

Greenberg, B. S., Buerkel-Rothfuss, N., Neuendorf, K. A., & Atkin, C. K. (1980). Three seasons of television family role interactions. In B. S. Greenberg (Ed.), *Life on television: Content analyses of U.S. TV drama* (pp. 161–172). Norwood, NJ: Ablex.

Greenberg, B. S., Edison, N., Korzenny, F., Fernandez-Collado, C. & Atkin, C. (1980). Antisocial and prosocial behaviors on television. In B. S. Greenberg (Ed.), *Life on television: Content analyses of U.S. TV drama* (pp. 99–128). Norwood, NJ: Ablex.

Greenberg, B. S., Hines, M., Buerkel-Rothfuss, N., & Atkin, C. K. (1980). Family role structure and interactions on commercial television. In B. S. Greenberg (Ed.), *Life on television: Content analyses of U.S. TV drama* (pp. 129–136). Norwood, NJ: Ablex.

Greenberg, B. S., & Neuendorf, K. A. (1980). Black family interactions on television. In B. S. Greenberg (Ed.), *Life on television: Content analyses of U.S. TV drama* (pp. 173–182). Norwood, NJ: Ablex.

Heintz, K. E. (1992). Children's favorite television families: A descriptive analysis of role interactions. *Journal of Broadcasting & Electronic Media, 36,* 443–451.

Larson, M. (1991). Sibling interactions in the 1950s versus 1980s sitcoms: A comparison. *Journalism Quarterly, 68,* 381–387.

Lawrence, R. (1989). Television: The battle for attention. *Marketing and Media Decisions, 24* (2), 80–82.

Lee, J. (1995). Subversive sitcoms: Roseanne as inspiration for feminist resistance. In G. Dines & J. M. Humez (Eds.), *Gender, race and class in media: A text reader* (pp. 469–475). Thousands Oaks, CA: Sage.

Merritt, B., & Stroman, C. A. (1993). Black family imagery and interactions on television. *Journal of Black Studies, 23,* 492–499.

Moore, M. L. (1992). The family as portrayed on prime-time television, 1947–1990: Structure and characteristics. *Sex Roles, 26,* 41–60.

Morgan, M. (1980, May). *Television and role socialization.* Paper presented at the International Communication Association convention, Acapulco, Mexico.

Morgan, M., & Harr-Mazar, H. (1980). *Television and adolescents' family life expectations.* Unpublished manuscript, The Annenberg School of Communications, University of Pennsylvania, Philadelphia.

Morgan, M., Leggett, S., & Shanahan, J. (1999). Television and "family values": Was Dan Quale right? *Mass Communication and Society, 2*(1/2), 47–63.

Morgan, M., & Rothschild, N. (1983). Impact of the new television technology: Cable TV, peers, and sex-role cultivation in the electronic environment. *Youth and Society, 15,* 33–50.

Morgan, M., & Shanahan, J. (1991). Do VCRs change the TV picture? VCRs and the cultivation process. *American Behavioral Scientist, 35*(2), 122–135.

Morgan, M., Shanahan, J., & Harris, C. (1990). VCRs and the effects of television: New diversity or more of the same? In J. Dobrow (Ed.), *Social and cultural aspects of VCR use* (pp. 107–123). Hillsdale, NJ: Lawrence Erlbaum Associates.

Nielsen, A. C. (1990). *Nielsen report on television.* New York: Nielsen Media Research.

Olson, B., & Douglas, W. (1997). The family on television: Evaluation of gender roles in situation comedy. *Sex Role, 36*(5-6), 409–427.

Perse, E. M., Pavitt, C., & Burggraf, C. (1990). Implicit theories of marriages and evaluations of marriage on television. *Human Communication Research, 16,* 387–408.

Roberts, E. J. (1982). Television and sexual learning in childhood. In D. Pearl, L. Bouthilet, & J. Lazar (Eds.), *Television and behavior: Ten years of scientific progress and implications for the eighties* (Vol. 2, pp. 209–223). Washington, DC: Government Printing Office.

Robinson, J., Skill, T., Nussbaum, J., & Moreland, K. (1985). Parents, peers, and television character: The use of comparison as criteria for evaluating marital satisfaction. In E. C. Lange (Ed.), *Using the media to promote knowledge and skills in family dynamics* (pp. 11–15). Dayton, OH: Center for Religious Telecommunications.

Signorielli, N. (1982). Marital status in television drama: A case of reduced options. *Journal of Broadcasting, 26*(2), 585–597.

Signorielli, N. (1986). Selective television viewing: A limited possibility. *Journal of Communication, 36*(3), 64–75.

Signorielli, N. (1991). Adolescents and ambivalence towards marriage: A cultivation analysis. *Youth & Society, 23*, 121–149.

Signorielli, N., & Kahlenberg, S. (1999, November). *Television's world of work in the nineties.* Paper presented at annual convention of the National Communication Association, Chicago, IL.

Skill, T. (1994). Family images and family actions as presented in the media: Where we've been and what we've found. In D. Zillmann & J. Bryant (Eds.), Media, children, and the family: Social scientific, psychodynamic and clinical perspectives. (pp. 37–50). Hillsdale, NJ: Lawrence Erlbaum Associates.

Skill, T., & Robinson, J. D. (1994). Four decades of families on television: A demographic profile, 1950–1989. *Journal of Broadcasting & Electronic Media, 38*, 449–464.

Skill, T., Robinson, J., & Wallace, S. (1987). Family life on prime-time television: Structure, type and frequency. *Journalism Quarterly, 64*, 360–367, 398.

Skill, T., & Wallace, S. (1990). Family interactions on prime time television: A description analysis of assertive power interactions. *Journal of Broadcasting & Electronic Media, 34*(3), 243–262.

Skill, T., Wallace, S., & Cassata, M. (1990). Families on prime-time television: Patterns of conflict escalation and resolution across intact, nonintact, and mixed-family settings. In J. Bryant (Ed.), *Television and the American family* (pp, 129–163). Hillsdale, NJ: Lawrence Erlbaum Associates.

Taylor, E. (1989). *Prime-time families: Television culture in postwar America.* Los Angeles: University of California Press.

Vivian, J. (1999). *The media of mass communication* (5th ed.). Boston: Allyn & Bacon.

Weiss, A. J., & Wilson, B. J. (1996). Emotional portrayals in family television series that are popular among children. *Journal of Broadcasting & Electronic Media, 40*, 1–29.

Weiss, A. J., & Wilson, B. J. (1998). Children's cognitive and emotional responses to the portrayal of negative emotions in family-formatted situation comedies. *Human Communication Research, 24*, 584–609.

Wober, J. M., & Gunter, B. (1987). *Television and social control.* Aldershot, Great Britain: Gower.

VI

Mediating Television's Impact

Family Mediation

Nancy L. Buerkel-Rothfuss
Rick A. Buerkel
Central Michigan University

Television continues to evolve. With the advent of cable TV and the availability of hundreds of new channels, TV programming has become more and more outrageous in attempting to capture the attention of an increasingly fickle audience. Although nudity is still taboo on network television, more than one television actor has bared his or her behind on the small screen, and depictions of sexual activity are on the upswing (Greenberg, Brown, & Buerkel-Rothfuss, 1993). The heroic crew of the Enterprise has given way to grisly depictions of flesh-eating netherworld creatures on the *X-Files* and Satan's soul-baiting entourage on *Millennium*. *Oprah*'s folksy brand of human interest still collects its market share, but viewers are turning in increasing numbers to shock talk TV hosts such as Jerry Springer. Two of today's most popular animated programs, *South Park* and *The Simpsons*, are not broadcast on Saturday morning with the other cartoons because they are not intended for a young audience. The language is raw, the behaviors are crude, and some of the characters are socially unacceptable. There are no Smurfs.

In spite of the demise of Ellen Degeneres' sitcom after the "coming out" of its main character, television has opened the door at least a crack to alternative relationships with shows such as *Friends* and *Mad About*

You, which feature lesbian partners in minor roles, and *Will and Grace*, a show depicting two male homosexual friends. Gay males are seen on TV holding down responsible jobs and working side by side and even being friends with straight men. There are few limp-handed handshakes, feigned swoons, or other stereotypical portrayals.

Not everything has changed, however. Violence continues to be a staple on action-adventure shows, as well as on the evening news. Minorities (mostly teenagers) are represented somewhat more than they were in the late 1980s, thanks to cable channels, but most characters on the major networks are still White, young, male, and middle class. Members of African American families are more likely to come from broken homes headed by single females; education level and social class are also likely to be lower for African American characters than for White (Greenberg & Brand, 1994; Sweeper, 1984). An occasional strong woman (even doctors!) can be found on shows such as *ER*, but many depictions of sex roles still reflect stereotypical male-dominant images (e.g., Daphne, the "health care worker" from *Frasier* mostly cooks and wears pretty dresses; the two female angels on *Touched by an Angel* are the helpers and caregivers, whereas the "Angel of Death" is a man).

No debate remains as to whether or not television affects children. Forty years and thousands of studies later, we can say with assurance that children are influenced by what they see on TV (see Gantz, chap. 14, this volume). Some children are affected more than others and the range of effects is large, but no one is immune to television's ubiquitous influence, not even adults.

To comprehend the complexity of the relationship between exposure to television and the effects TV watching can have on children and adolescents, it is necessary to first identify those effects. A review of this literature takes us back to the 1950s, when the earliest television broadcasts began. It is also necessary to identify the variables that intervene in the learning process. For example, research suggests that television effects might be a function of why a child "uses" the medium (Cantor & Nathanson, 1997). Thus, the predispositions a child brings to the viewing experience may be a factor. Likewise, significant others may influence what is learned and retained, making family mediation a process worthy of attention.

The focus of this chapter is on the mediation process more than on cognitive or affective processes that precede and/or shape the television viewing experience. We begin with a discussion of TV effects in general and then identify variables that can alter the exposure–effects relationship. Three types of parental mediation activities are discussed; *social coviewing, restrictive mediation*, and *strategic* and *nonstrategic active mediation* (labels based on work by Valkenburg, Krcmar, Peeters, & Marseille, in press). This section also discusses a less linear, cause–effect approach for understanding television's influence by examining possible family system and family interaction variables that may predispose children to outcomes. The chapter concludes with a model of the mediation process.

EFFECTS OF TELEVISION EXPOSURE

Some of the earliest studies on television and children were based on social learning theory, which argues that children imitate behaviors seen as rewarding, realistic, and principled (Bandura, 1986). Of particular interest is the link between viewing televised violence and subsequent aggressive behavior. The conclusions drawn about TV violence research are almost unequivocal: Children learn physical aggression and other antisocial behaviors from watching television (Andison, 1977; Dorr & Kovaric, 1980; Hearold, 1986).

Aggressiveness is not the only consequence of television viewing, however. Repeated exposure to violence can lead to desensitization for both adults and younger viewers (Donnerstein & Berkowitz, 1983; Thomas, Horton, Lippincott, & Drabman, 1977). Once one is accustomed to seeing blood and gore, real human suffering can lose its urgency and impact.

Children and adolescents are also susceptible to what has been called the "cultivation effect" (Hawkins & Pingree, 1983; Signorielli & Morgan, 1990). Television can shape a person's view of the "real" world and his or her expectations about the people in it. For example, cultivation researchers have found links between watching TV news and perceptions of personal danger (Perse, 1990; Sparks & Cantor, 1986). Other cultivation studies have linked soap opera viewing with beliefs about relationship difficulties in the real world (Buerkel-Rothfuss & Mayes, 1981), sex on television with beliefs about real-world sexual activity (Buerkel-Rothfuss & Strouse, 1993), and sex-role portrayals on TV with beliefs about sex roles in real life (Morgan, 1982).

Television contains a wealth of distorted depictions. Content analyses suggest under representation of minorities in high-status roles (Baptista-Fernandez & Greenberg, 1980; Greenberg, & Brand, 1994; Sweeper, 1984), a tendency to portray men as problem solvers and women as caregivers (Henderson, Greenberg, & Atkin, 1980), and depictions of elderly persons on television as sad, lonely, and/or weak (Aronoff, 1974; Bishop & Krause, 1984; Greenberg, Korzenny, & Atkin, 1980). Viewing this distorted world of television reality can shape a child's view of society, especially if the depictions are believable and not directly contradicted by real-life experience (Austin, Roberts, & Nass, 1990). Furthermore, television can affect an adolescent's construction of social reality, including development of moral judgment and beliefs about sexual activity (Bryant & Rockwell, 1994).

Exposure to television can also lead to consumerism. Commercials aimed at young children can create desire for specific products (Moore, 1990; Moschis, 1987). Programming that includes use of substances such as alcohol has been linked with positive attitudes toward alcohol (Atkin, Hocking, & Block, 1984; Austin & Meili, 1994; Einspruch & Pollard, 1993), even in nondrinking populations, such as Mennonites (Umble, 1990).

Finally, television can be a powerful teacher (Liebert & Sprafkin, 1988). Young children learn their numbers and the alphabet with Barney and Big Bird, but they may also learn about more adult topics if tuned into adult programming. Likewise, adolescents may learn about interpersonal and sexual relationships from television, and those lessons could differ significantly, based on the programming consumed. Heavy doses of *Jerry Springer* might suggest a different view of intimacy and sexuality than *The Cosby Show* or *Chicago Hope*.

In short, television affects children and young adult viewers—at least some of them, at some time in their lives, in some way. The weight of evidence is enormous, but the equation is not simple cause–effect or stimulus–response (S–R). Many variables influence this process, and the equation is not linear.

INTERVENING AND MEDIATING VARIABLES

Intervening variables disrupt simple S–R relationships by affecting how the information is received, processed, and acted on by the audience. Mediating variables may precede exposure and predispose viewers to some effects and not others. Some of these variables are demographic, such as the child's age (Atkin, Greenberg, & Baldwin, 1991; Lin & Atkin, 1989) and gender (Brown, Childers, Bauman, & Koch, 1990; Desmond, Hirsch, Singer, & Singer, 1987). Others are tied to parental attitudes (Brown & Linneé, 1976), family characteristics (McLeod & Brown, 1976; Meadowcroft & Fitzpatrick, 1988) and/or the way family members view the world (Reiss & Oliveri, 1983). Perceived reality (Austin et al., 1990), identification with the characters in the program (Hoffner, 1996), personal experience with similar characters, and reasons for watching a particular show (Rosengren, Wenner, & Palmgreen, 1985) may all alter the effects television exposure produces.

Of particular interest to this chapter is the nature of family mediation and the ways family members and others act to break the link between exposure and attitudes or behaviors in children and young adults.

Desmond, Singer, Singer, Calam, and Colimore (1985) defined television mediation as "some form of active effort by parents and others to translate the complexities of the physical and social environment, as well as the television medium, into terms capable of comprehension by children at various levels of cognitive development" (p. 463). According to Messaris (1982), mediation involves helping children with three processing tasks; categorization, validation, and supplementing. Categorization involves discussing how mediated portrayals reflect the real world, validation deals with supporting or condemning the accuracy of mediated portrayals, and supplementing involves adding material to mediated portrayals to illustrate the usefulness of televised information.

Mediation can be a deterrent to television exposure effects. For example, adult mediation can influence children's judgments of minorities and certain dimensions of ethics (Roberts, 1981; Robertson, 1979). Parental mediation can also counteract the persuasive effects of television advertising (Prasad, Rao, & Sheikh, 1978; Robertson, 1979). According to Desmond et al. (1990), "the child whose family imposes no limits on viewing . . . shows greater confusion between reality and fantasy, more restlessness and aggression, and a poorer acquisition of general information than the child of a mediating family" (p. 301).

Bybee, Robinson, and Turow (1982) studied the parental guidance provided by mass media scholars with children ages 3 to 18 and identified three dimensions of guidance; restrictive, evaluative, and unfocused. Restrictive mediation involves limiting the child's amount of viewing time and the programs watched. Evaluative guidance involves discussions with the child to assist in evaluating the meanings behind portrayed messages. Unfocused guidance involves general discussion of television programming. These three dimensions have been shown to be used by American parents of fourth-grade children (Abelman & Pettey, 1989) and by Dutch parents (van der Voort, Nikken, & van Lil, 1992). A fourth category, social coviewing, involves watching television with a child.

Some research suggests that characteristics of the children may influence the guidance employed by parents. Abelman and Pettey (1989), for example, showed that parents of "gifted" children were more likely to employ evaluative guidance than were other parents. This finding suggests that parents of gifted children are more likely to exert the time and effort involved to explain aspects of programs to contribute to their children's understanding of television. Furthermore, parents of gifted children were more likely to perceive television as affecting their child's thought processes. Parents of nongifted children, on the other hand, perceived television's effects to be behavioral and responded by removing the child from the source of the offensive message.

Several studies have shown that age is another consideration in determining mediation (Lin & Atkin, 1989; St. Peters, Fitch, Huston, Wright, & Eakins, 1991). Bybee et al. (1982) found that children under the age of 13 receive more restrictive parental guidance than children ages 13 to 18 years. This conclusion was supported by St. Peters et al. (1991), who found that younger children are more likely than older children to have a parent present when watching television and by Atkin et al. (1991), who found that younger children receive more supervision than adolescents.

Several studies have illustrated differences in boy's and girl's television viewing habits (Brown et al., 1990; Lyle & Hoffman, 1972; McLeod & Brown, 1976). However, gender has received little support as a determinant of parental mediation (Abelman, 1985; Desmond et al., 1987; Singer, Singer, & Rapaczynski, 1984). One study conducted by Lin and Atkin (1989), however, found that male children were more likely to have rules placed on VCR usage than were female children.

Social class may also be related to parental guidance. Saloman (1977), in a study of 5-year-old Israeli children, determined that lower SES mothers' coviewing of *Sesame Street* was related to the amount of time their children watched the program and their program enjoyment. No significant coviewing effects were found in the middle SES sample.

Several studies have illustrated the effectiveness of mediation in influencing the way children respond to mass media messages (Atkin et al., 1991; Austin, 1993; Austin et al., 1990; Corder-Bolz, 1980; Desmond et al., 1985). Adult mediation can influence learning about people, places, careers, and politics (Corder-Bolz, 1980; Corder-Bolz & O'Bryant, 1978) and can influence the acquisition of attitudes and norms (Roberts, 1981; Robertson, 1979).

As suggested by the previous discussion, family mediation may take at least three forms; social coviewing; restrictive mediation, which involves establishing rules and exerting control over what is watched; and strategic or nonstrategic active mediation, which involves making deliberate evaluate judgments about TV (strategic) or casual comments about TV in general or about specific shows or events (nonstrategic). These strategies, alone or in combination, can influence the effects of television viewing. A fourth category of mediating variables, family characteristics, may also affect what and how a child learns from television and/or how a child is affected. Each of these mediating variables deserves a closer examination.

Social Coviewing

Social coviewing refers to the act of sitting with a child and watching the same show he or she is watching. The conclusions about the value of this activity are mixed, based on what is being viewed and the parental comments that accompany viewing. Coviewing may be an interactive activity, as when parents and children discuss what is happening on TV (a form of active mediation), or it may be a passive activity where all parties sit silently together in the same room, eyes focused on the screen. Through coviewing, parents can monitor the programs children watch and intervene if undesirable content is broadcast (Desmond et al., 1985; Dorr, Kovaric, & Doubleday, 1989). In this way, coviewing allows parents to turn the television off, change the channel, or discuss the offensive content, if they are so inclined. But coviewing can also have a reinforcing effect for TV content.

Many researchers over the last 20 years have argued that children's learning of knowledge and attitudes from television can be influenced by the presence of a coviewing adult (Bybee et al., 1982; Huston & Wright, 1996; Huston, Zillmann, & Bryant, 1994; Messaris & Sarett, 1981; St. Peters et al., 1991; Valkenburg, Krcmar, & dee Roos, 1998). Martin and Benson (1970), for example, found that over half of the parents they interviewed reported that the television was used as a means to educate their children. Coviewing creates an environment where adults can offer comments that aid learning (Desmond et al., 1985; Dorr et al., 1989). When parents coview child-oriented, educational programming, the child's understanding of the subject matter portrayed has been shown to increase (Ball & Bogatz, 1970; Corder-Bolz, 1980; Collins, 1983; Friedrich & Stein, 1975; Saloman, 1977; Singer & Singer, 1976; Watkins, Calvert, Huston-Stein, & Wright, 1980). Coviewing can enhance children's understanding of characters and plots in action-adventure programs (Collins, Sobol, & Westby, 1981) and influence attitudes toward violence (Corder-Bolz, 1980; Corder-Bolz & O'Bryant, 1978). Negative parental comments about TV violence can help children understand the reasons behind that violence and the unrealistic nature of such portrayals. Thus, parental coviewing can help children interpret television behaviors.

The impact of coviewing is not always positive, however. Because social coviewing can have a television-enhancing effect, watching TV with children can magnify the negative impact of the medium. A parent who consumes violent or sexually oriented television fare with children is likely to reinforce those portrayals through the very nature of his or her attention to them. Even nondirective comments such as "Wow" or "Look at that!" serve to highlight aspects of the TV viewing experience for children, thus reinforcing what is viewed (Nathanson, 1998).

Silent acceptance can be a mediator in that the silence implies tacit approval of a show and its contents. Chaffee & Tims (1976), for example, found that social learning was highest in instances in which a coviewing adult was present, even when nothing was said. Thus, the parent who watches a show every week in rapt attention conveys a positive message about the characters and events depicted therein. The mere presence of an adult in the room can enhance the viewing experience. Watkins et al. (1980), for example, demonstrated that children can recall more information when viewing with an experimenter present than children who view alone. Likewise, research on coviewing suggests that the presence of a parent in the room is positively associated with children's aggression (Nathanson, 1998), stereotyped attitudes toward gender roles (Rothschild & Morgan, 1987), and a belief that television is similar to real life (Messaris & Kerr, 1983). Thus, parental approval in the form of watching a program with a child can enhance the exposure–effects relationship.

Austin et al. (1990) proposed a model of the television coviewing process that compliments the cultivation approach. Their model suggests that children use television and other information sources as referents for anchoring themselves in social reality. This reality is constructed by comparing televised information with messages from other sources (e.g., parents, older siblings, teachers). When televised information contradicts what is commonly seen in the home or social environment, children will generally reject the television portrayal as unrealistic. However, the model also suggests that unrealistic portrayals may be embraced by children if they are perceived to be highly attractive. Children are more likely to reject televised portrayals as unrealistic if a coviewing adult illustrates how a portrayal differs from real life.

Austin and Meili (1994) tested this model in the context of alcohol portrayals. They determined that children's expectancies are based on a logical and emotional interpretation process that makes use of real-life and televised sources of information. Austin and Meili (1994) argued that helping children develop skepticism toward televised portrayals of alcohol could help prevent abuse later in life. Coviewing by parents or significant others who comment on the dangers of alcohol consumption may help to develop that skepticism.

The amount and kind of coviewing that occurs in American households varies, based on a number of child and family variables. Some research suggests that the presence of technology in the household may influence the amount of coviewing that occurs. Bower (1973), for example, found that the time spent coviewing was associated with the number of television sets in a household. In families with two television sets, 80% of all respondents reported spending some time viewing with their children. This figure dropped to 66% in households with three televisions. Other research suggests that coviewing happens frequently, especially with younger children (Carpenter, Huston, & Spera, 1989; McDonald, 1986). Wright, St. Peters, and Huston (1990) found parental coviewing to be high (69–81%) but only for general interest and adult-oriented programs. The implication is that young children frequently watch child-oriented programs alone or with siblings (Bower, 1973) and adult-oriented programs with parents (Wright et al., 1990). McDonald (1985, 1986) determined that coviewing occurred when programs appealed to both parents and children but not when a program appealed only to children. This conclusion was supported by Dorr et al. (1989), who found that coviewing was likely to occur in instances where parents and children reported similar viewing habits and program preferences.

Some research suggests that coviewing is a rare occurrence. Mohr (1978, 1979), for example, determined that about 70% of parents reported never having watched Saturday morning programming consumed by their children. Eighty-five percent of all parents reported offering "no guidance" to children when choosing television content.

Overall, coviewing has been shown to be an effective mediating activity for a variety of reasons, but it is not clear what percentage of parents use this form of mediation. When watching television with their children, parents are able to turn off objectionable shows, discuss the social construction of reality depicted on television in comparison to the real world, and reward or sanction depicted behaviors. As such, coviewing can reduce negative effects of television viewing. Conversely, approval of televised content can highlight that material as salient and valuable, thus increasing the magnitude of a variety of exposure effects. Finally, coviewing of educational programs or prosocial fare can enhance children's learning of prosocial attitudes and behaviors.

Restrictive Mediation

The use of rules to control viewing, known as restrictive mediation (Atkin et al., 1991; Valkenburg et al., in press), can have important effects on children. For example, Desmond et al. (1985) found that family control of television, the presence of rules regulating television use, and discipline increased kindergarten and first-grader's abilities to determine what is real. Lin and Atkin (1989) found that parents' regulation of television and VCR usage predicted higher academic performance.

Restrictive mediation can focus children's attention on television programs parents deem appropriate and away from others. However, research suggests that relatively few households have explicit rules restricting television viewing (Comstock, 1975; Corder-Bolz, 1980; Lyle & Hoffman, 1972). Bower (1973), for example, found that only 43% of parents reported having rules to guide children's television viewing.

Atkin et al. (1991) showed that the presence of cable television may lead to more restrictive mediation by parents but could also lead to more unsanctioned viewing on the part of adolescents. The presence of VCRs has also been shown to influence viewing. Krendl, Clark, Dawson, and Troiano (1993), for example, found that children reported family rules regarding both the amount of time spent using the VCR (60%) and the content of the programming (50%). However, 30% of the research participants were unable to identify what the rules regarding amount of time viewing were, and 22% could not identify the content rules in the family. Finally, 62% reported being instructed to use the VCR when their parents were busy.

Other researchers warn that self-reports of viewing rules may not be reliable. Kim, Baran, and Massey (1988) found that parents and children offer conflicting reports about rules dictating VCR usage. This finding is consistent with research by Greenberg, Ericson, and Vlahos (1971), who found a lack of agreement in parents' and children's reporting of rules regarding television viewing. Rossiter and Robertson (1975) offered further support by identifying discrepancies in parents' and children's reports of total viewing time, amount of coviewing, control, and parent–child discussion of televised information. According to their research, children's reports of rule making are probably more reliable than parents' reports. Parental reports of rules governing exposure to mediated messages are greater than that reported by children in grades one through five, presumably a social desirability response.

Rules about viewing may not be the only way to provide restrictive mediation, however. The strategic scheduling of alternative events (e.g., church on Sunday morning, soccer games on Saturday afternoons, family dinners during the evening news) can also serve rule functions without direct parental control over viewing. To what degree the scheduling of family activities is based on a desire to remove children from in front of the TV is undocumented to date, but further consideration of the behaviors that lead to restriction and, thus, to mediation of television, are worthy of consideration. In the grand scheme of family interaction, restrictive mediation may take many forms.

Strategic and Nonstrategic Active Mediation

Active coviewing, which involves making comments about what is being viewed, requires less interpretation on the part of the child than silent coviewing, because it is overt and so has the capacity for communicating specific value judgments about aspects of the program. Active coviewing results in conversation about the parent's interpretation and evaluation of what is being viewed.

Of course, the nature of the comments made by parents will affect the outcome of influence attempts. Atkin and Greenberg (1977) argued that parental mediation would have greatest impact when perceived reality of portrayals is noted, consequences of actions are discussed, motives for behaviors are explained, parents evaluate those behaviors, and parents either encourage or discourage similar behaviors from the child. According to Desmond, Singer, and Singer (1990)

> it is moral judgment and explanation about issues presented on television, rather than the simple act of underlining or

> pointing out content in a neutral manner, that characterizes
> the families of children who are skillful at comprehending . . .
> the medium. Children who dwell in such a positive atmos-
> phere of family communication are less fearful of being
> harmed, less aggressive, and more willing to wait patiently
> than are children from families who simply comment on tele-
> vision's array of people and events. (p. 304)

Conversation about television, even when it does not occur during coviewing, has been shown to influence children's learning from adult-
oriented programs. Atkin and Gantz (1974), for example, showed that
children are better able to recall the content of news programming when
parents expand on the televised information. Other research suggests
that discussion about TV content can increase the knowledge children
gain about a television program's plot (Desmond et al., 1985). Furthermore, comments by parents, older siblings, and teachers can increase
children's understanding of television portrayals (Bogatz & Ball, 1971;
Corder-Bolz & O'Bryant, 1978; Saloman, 1977; Singer & Singer, 1976).

Program-related communication between family members can influence how children use television to construct an image of reality (Corder-
Bolz, 1980; McLeod, Fitzpatrick, Glynn, & Fallis, 1982; Messaris & Sarett,
1981). Austin et al. (1990) found that children place more emphasis on
their own family experiences than on media portrayals when assessing
perceptions of reality.

According to Atkin, Heeter, and Baldwin (1989), content-related discussion increases when values portrayed in media contradict those held
by the family. Mothers report frequent use of comments about the over-
simplification of problems on television (McLeod et al., 1982). Messaris
(1986) found that the mothers made comments to their children about
the improbability and lack of reality depicted on TV. Furthermore, parental reassurances can help children overcome their fears when faced with
frightening programs such as *The Wizard of Oz* (Cantor & Wilson, 1984;
Messaris, 1982).

Not all parental commentary is strategic, however, which may lead to
underreporting of this mediation activity. Bryce and Leichter (1983)
argued that an ethnographic approach to studying parental mediation
can contribute to our understanding of unintentional and nonverbal mediating influences. Parents may discuss television portrayals with their
children indirectly or may think of such discussions as merely conversations when, in fact, such conversation could have mediatory impact.
Similarly, families in which there is an open exchange of ideas and a perception that the environment is safe for the exploration of a variety of
topics may produce children who are less influenced by TV. Thus, mediation may occur as an outcome of family interaction. For example, Bryant

and Rockwell (1994) found that teens were less likely to adopt televised portrayals of sexual morality when they were raised in a family system that held clear family values and when they were able to discuss personal topics with parents. Although not mediation per se, family communication variables can affect the television–exposure relationship.

Family Characteristics

Family types and family communication styles have been conceptualized in a variety of ways, few of which have been applied to investigations of television use. Paradigmatic family theorists argue that families share a set of enduring perceptions about the real world and that understanding these family paradigms can illuminate how families construct their social realities (Reiss & Oliveri, 1983). From this approach, researchers have attempted to develop family typologies that stress an orientation to values and beliefs about the world. A constructionist perspective focuses on communication processes in families as the method for development and modification of a family's worldview (Meadowcroft & Fitzpatrick, 1988). Central to this perspective is the assumption that families develop patterns of interaction, and understanding families involves identifying those patterns and the symbols that create and sustain them. Meaning is negotiated, not absolute. Structural family communication researchers look for the configuration of role relationships and the power issues implied in the nature of the hierarchy to understand how a family functions. Beliefs about the social world are tied to beliefs about the roles individuals are expected to play in family life (Yerby, Buerkel-Rothfuss, & Bochner, 1995).

Family types could affect the exposure–effects relationship. First of all, family type could affect how parents choose to mediate television use, if at all. Authoritarian families might experience more restrictive mediation than democratic families due to the top-down power structure. Some family forms could influence the viewing experience by providing values and beliefs for their children apart from and instead of television exposure. For example, families with strong moral values who attend church regularly have been shown to influence their children's learning about sexuality and morality from the media (Strouse & Buerkel-Rothfuss, 1987). The quantity and quality of family interaction, in combination with the relative strength or weakness of family values, can shape perceptions, attitudes, and beliefs. Thus, family communication can mediate learning from television before, during, and after exposure.

The best known schema of family communication (Chaffee, 1978; Chaffee & Tims, 1976) differentiates between two dimensions in families; one in which parents stress harmony and obedience (socioorientation) and one in which parents stress negotiation and self-reliance (concept orientation).

These dimensions relate to children's selection of and learning from television in a variety of ways (Abel, 1976; Fry & McCain, 1980; Lull, 1980).

Another family characteristic that has been linked to television viewing is family cohesion (Olson, Sprenkle, & Russell, 1979). Cohesive families demonstrate closeness to one another and family members perceive adequate amounts of shared time and attention. Overly cohesive families perceive themselves to be enmeshed and smothered by family members; noncohesive families perceive themselves to be distanced and separated from one another. In general, cohesiveness is related to high parental interaction with children (Kantor & Lehr, 1976; Olson et al., 1979) and, by implication, mediation of television. Noncohesive or chaotic families would tend not to engage in either parental discussion of television or regulation of viewing.

Kantor and Lehr's (1975) differentiation of family systems into three forms—open, closed, and random—suggests yet another way to use family characteristics to predict mediation influence. In closed families, information is tightly regulated; access to media influences is controlled by parents (Kantor & Lehr, 1975). Open families allow for more access to inputs from outside the system, and unrestricted television consumption would be highest in random families, where rules are antithetical to the value system of the family (Kantor & Lehr, 1975). Open families are characterized by an equal balance of cohesiveness and adaptability. Closed families, on the other hand, tend to be overly cohesive and tend to resist change.

Reiss (1981; Reiss & Oliveri, 1983) developed a family typology based on the family's belief and value system and their problem-solving orientation. Underlying this model is the assumption that "each family develops its own shared set of constructs or principles about how the world operates and about the relationship of the family to its social environment" (Yerby et al., 1995, p. 273). Consensus-sensitive families perceive the world as hostile, threatening, and chaotic, an orientation that could enhance cultivation effects with regard to real-world violence and danger, because family values reinforce the perception life is dangerous. The likelihood of parental mediation is especially high in this family, especially restrictive mediation, based on the value that the family's role is to protect one another (Reiss, 1981). In a second of Reiss' family forms, interpersonal distance-sensitive families, the potential for mediation is low. According to Yerby et al. (1995), "Any agreement among members seems to provoke resistance. Family members express little value of one another's opinions and make little effort to exchange information" (p. 274). One would expect little social coviewing and little strategic active mediation under those circumstances.

A final family variable that has received virtually no attention in the family mediation literature is the degree to which male and female parents differ in their mediation activities and the degree to which gender of parent interacts with gender of child to impact the exposure–effects relationship. Research on parent–child interaction suggests that fathers interact differently with their daughters than they do with their sons and have different expectations for sons than for daughters (Buerkel-Rothfuss, Fink, & Buerkel, 1995), but similar claims about differential female parenting styles have received less research attention (Stafford & Bayer, 1993). These gender differences could affect the methods of mediation selected (if any), the types of shows coviewed, and the types of discussions between parent and child about television and the real world.

Clearly, the application of family forms to our understanding of children and television has yet to be explored in any significant way. Nevertheless, characteristics of families might be an important intervening variable, especially given the overall importance of families for child socialization (Noller & Fitzpatrick, 1993).

A MODEL OF FAMILY MEDIATION VARIABLES

The relationship between viewing and effects is not simple, nor is it linear. Many variables help to structure the experience for children and determine which shows will be selected. These variables make up the previewing experience and help to influence selective exposure and attention. Other variables operate during viewing to shape the learning that will occur. These variables pertain to elements of the message, the context, and receiver variables felt during the viewing situation. Still other variables pertain to strategic and nonstrategic communication that may affect viewing choices and outcomes. These mediation attempts could occur before, during, and/or after the viewing experience. Last but not least, the children themselves bring characteristics to the viewing experience that help determine what, if anything, they will take away. Many of these variables are embedded in family system values and norms.

Table 17.1 presents a list of variables that might play a role in the mediation process. In spite of the linear appearance of the list, it should be clear from this chapter that there are many reciprocal and or spiral-like relationships between and among those variables. The overall research picture is complex—and incomplete.

SUMMARY AND CONCLUSION

Parental mediation of television exposure can provide a number of positive outcomes for children. Mediation can enhance learning from children's television and development of prosocial attitudes and behaviors. Mediation can reduce potentially harmful effects of watching TV violence

TABLE 17.1
Variables in the Parental Mediation Process

Pre-Viewing Variables

Family Variables
beliefs, values, orientation toward world (paradigms)
social reality(ies)
hierarchy, roles, power relationships (structural elements)
social and economic status (demographic variables)
nature of the family system; open, closed, random
gender of parent(s)
number and gender of sibling(s)

Contextual Variables
number of television sets in the household
constraints on the television (lock-out boxes, etc.)
number of VCRs
access to cable channels
layout of living space relative to television
availability of other activities during television viewing

Child Variables
intelligence, gender, age, physical/emotional/cognitive ability, experience with real-world
activities and structures
perceived reality of television
identification and parasocial interaction with TV characters
uses and gratifications related to television viewing

Types of Mediation

Passive Coviewing
with siblings
with parent
with more than one adult

Restrictive Mediation
limits on hours of viewing
limits on types of shows or direction toward prosocial shows
use of other activities as distracter from television

Strategic Mediation
comments about specific programming while viewing
comments about aspects of television in general
comments about real life, family values, etc.

Nonstrategic Mediation
comments about television in general
comments about media in general
comments about life in general

Viewing Variables

Television Characteristics
type of television message (news, sports, situation comedy, etc.)
time of day
network/cable channel
volume, color, room distractions

(Continued)

369

TABLE 17.1
(Continued)

Viewing Variables

Viewer Characteristics While Engaged in Exposure
selective attention to the message
cognitive and affective processing of the message
parasocial interaction with television characters
participation (e.g., singing along with jingles, reciting with speakers, etc.)

Outcomes/Effects for Children

---

learning
changes in/shaping of attitudes and behavior
social reality construction
consumerism
selection of future television choices

---

and other negative portrayals, and it can interfere with the cultivation effect by providing information that negates the reality of television depictions. Mediation can help children make good choices for their own viewing later in life, when parents are not there to intervene.

Some families do not mediate children's television viewing at all, however (Austin et al., 1990; Ward, Wackman, & Wartella, 1977), and when parental mediation does occur, it may be nonstrategic. This apparent lack of mediation may be an artifact of the research methods used to assess the activity. Perhaps parents do not recognize the impact conversations with their children can have on what children learn and retain from television and, as a result, do not report mediation activities. Likewise, single-item assessments of mediation may not tap the multiplicity of forms actually used by parents to exert influence (Bryce & Leichter, 1983).

Those would be the noncynical interpretations of the data presented. However, a more cynical writer could conclude that parents simply do not understand, do not believe in, or do not care about the potential for television to affect their children. In fact, Mills and Watkins (1982) found that one reason for a lack of parental mediation was that many parents view television as a benign presence, not a source of either good or evil. However, according to Greenberg, Abelman, and Cohen (1990), even when informed of the negative impact of TV on children and provided with strategies for effective parental mediation, the majority of parents in their sample were not likely to participate in their children's viewing behavior to any important degree.

Perhaps adults are so taken with the medium themselves that they fail to see the potential problems. Perhaps they are so convinced that television has no effect on them that they cannot fathom deleterious effects on others. Or maybe the demands of 21st century living are so great that, in the grand scheme of things, a little misinformation from TV doesn't seem too serious.

Whatever the reason, parental mediation appears to be no more active or rigorous at beginning of the new millennium than it was shortly after the introduction of the medium to American homes 50 years ago. Clearly, more research is warranted into not only the characteristics of mediation but also into ways to motivate parents to play a more substantive role in this process.

REFERENCES

Abel, J. D. (1976). The family and child television viewing. *Journal of Marriage and the Family, 38*, 331–335.

Abelman, R. (1985). Sex differences in parental disciplinary practices: An antecedent of television's impact on children. *Women's Studies in Communication, 8*, 51–61.

Abelman, R., & Pettey, G. R. (1989). Child attributes as determinants of parental television-viewing mediation: The role of child giftedness. *Journal of Family Issues, 10*, 251–266.

Andison, F. S. (1977). TV violence and viewer aggression: A cumulation of study results 1956–1976. *Public Opinion Quarterly, 41*, 314–331.

Aronoff, C. (1974). Old age in prime time. *Journal of Communication, 24*, 86–87.

Atkin, C. K., & Gantz, W. (1974). *How children use television news programming: Patterns of exposure and effects.* Paper presented at the meeting of the International Communication Association, New Orleans.

Atkin, C. K., & Greenberg, B. S. (1977). Parental mediation of children's social behavior learning from television. *CASTLE Report.* Washington, DC: US Office of Child Development.

Atkin, C., Hocking, J., & Block, M. (1984). Teenage drinking: Does advertising make a difference? *Journal of Communication, 34*(2), 12–20.

Atkin, D. J., Greenberg, B. S., & Baldwin, T. F. (1991, Summer). The home ecology of children's television viewing: Parental mediation and the new video environment. *Journal of Communication, 41*(3), 40–52.

Atkin, D., Heeter, C., & Baldwin, T. (1989, Autumn). How presence of cable affects parental mediation of TV viewing. *Journalism Quarterly, 66*, 557–563.

Austin, E. W. (1993). Exploring the effects of active parental mediation of television content. *Journal of Broadcasting & Electronic Media, 37*, 147–158.

Austin, E. W., & Meili, H. K. (1994). Effects of interpretations of televised alcohol portrayals on children's alcohol beliefs. *Journal of Broadcasting & Electronic Media, 38*, 417–435.

Austin, E. W., Roberts, D. F., & Nass, C. I. (1990, August). Influences of family communication on children's television-interpretation processes. *Communication Research, 17* 545–564.

Ball, S., & Bogatz, G. A. (1970). *The first year of "Sesame Street:" An evaluation.* Princeton, NJ: Educational Testing Service.

Bandura, A. (1986). *Social foundations of thought and action: A social cognitive theory.* Englewood Cliffs, NJ: Prentice-Hall.

Baptista-Fernandez, P. & Greenberg, B.S. (1980). The contexts, characteristics, and communication behaviors of Blacks on television. In B. S. Greenberg (Ed.), *Life on television* (pp. 13–22). Norwood, NJ: Ablex.

Bishop, J. M., & Krause, J. M. (1984). Depictions of aging and old age on Saturday morning television. *The Gerontologist, 24*, 91–94.

Bogatz, G. A., & Ball, S. (1971). *The second year of "Sesame Street": A continuing evaluation.* Princeton, NJ: Educational Testing Service.

Bower, R. T. (1973). *Television and the public*. New York: Holt, Rinehart & Winston.

Brown, J. D., Childers, K. W., Bauman, K. E., & Koch, G. G. (1990, February). The influence of new media and family structure on young adolescents' television and radio use. *Communication Research, 17*, 65–82.

Brown, J. R., & Linne , O. (1976). The family as a mediator of television's effects. In R. Brown (Ed.), *Children and television* (pp. 184–198). Beverly Hills, CA: Sage.

Bryant, J., & Rockwell, S. C. (1994). Effect of massive exposure to sexually oriented prime-time television programming on adolescents' moral judgment. In D. Zillmann, J. Bryant, & A. C. Huston (Eds.), *Media, children and the family* (pp. 183–198). Hillsdale, NJ: Lawrence Erlbaum Associates.

Bryce, J. W., & Leichter, H. J. (1983, June). The family and television: Forms of mediation. *Journal of Family Issues, 4*(2), 309–328.

Buerkel-Rothfuss, N. L., Fink, D. S., & Buerkel, R. A. (1995). In T. J. Socha & G. H. Stamp (Eds.), *Parents, children, and communication: Frontiers of theory and research* (pp. 63–86). Mahwah, NJ: Lawrence Erlbaum Associates.

Buerkel-Rothfuss, N. L., & Mayes, S. (1981). Soap opera viewing: The cultivation effect. *Journal of Communication, 31*(3), 108–115.

Buerkel-Rothfuss, N. L., & Strouse, J. S. (1993). Media exposure and perceptions of sexual behaviors: The cultivation hypothesis moves to the bedroom. In B. S. Greenberg, J. D. Brown, & N. L. Buerkel-Rothfuss (Eds.), *Media, sex and the adolescent* (pp. 225–247). Cresskill, NJ: Hampton Press.

Bybee, C., Robinson, D., & Turow, J. (1982). Determinants of parental guidance of children's television viewing for a special subgroup: Mass media scholars. *Journal of Broadcasting, 16*, 697–710.

Cantor, J., & Nathanson, A. I. (Spring, 1997). Predictors of children's interest in violent television programs. *Journal of Broadcasting & Electronic Media, 41*, 155–167.

Cantor, J., & Wilson, B. J. (1984). Modifying fear responses to mass media in preschool and elementary school children. *Journal of Broadcasting, 28*, 431–443.

Carpenter, C. J., Huston, A. C., & Spera, L. (1989). Children's use of time in their everyday activities during middle school. In M. N. Block & A. D. Pellegrini (Eds.), *The ecological context of children's play* (pp. 232–244). Norwood, NJ: Ablex.

Chaffee, S. H. (1978, November). *Communication patterns in the family: Implications for adaptability and change*. Paper presented at the Speech Communication Association convention, Minneapolis.

Chaffee, S. H., & Tims, A. R. (1976). Interpersonal factors in adolescent television use. *Journal of Social Issues, 32*, 98–115.

Collins, W. A. (1983). Interpretation and inference in children's television viewing. In J. Bryant & D. R. Anderson (Eds.), *Children's understanding of television* (pp. 125–150). New York: Academic Press.

Collins, W. A., Sobol, B. L., & Westby, S. (1981). Effects of adult commentary on children's comprehension and inferences about a televised aggressive portrayal. *Child Development, 52*, 158–163.

Comstock, G. (1975). The evidence so far. *Journal of Communication, 25*(4), 25–34.

Corder-Bolz, C. R. (1980). Mediation: The role of significant others. *Journal of Communication, 30* (3), 106–118.

Corder-Bolz, C. R., & O'Bryant, S. (1978). Teacher vs. program: Can people affect television? *Journal of Communication, 28*(1), 97–103.

Desmond, R. J., Hirsch, B., Singer, D. G., & Singer, J. L. (1987). Gender differences, mediation, and disciplinary styles in children's responses to television. *Sex Roles: A Journal of Research, 16*, 375–389.

Desmond, R. J., Singer, J. L., & Singer, D. G. (1990). Family mediation: Parental communication patterns and the influence of television on children. In J. Bryant (Ed.), *Television and the American family* (pp. 293–309). Hillsdale, NJ: Lawrence Erlbaum Associates.

Desmond, R. J., Singer, J. L., Singer, D. G., Calam, R., & Colimore, K. (1985, Summer). Family mediation patterns and television viewing: Young children's use and grasp of the medium. *Human Communication Research, 11*, 459–460.

Donnerstein, E., & Berkowitz, L. (1983). *Effects of film content and victim association on aggression behavior and attitudes.* Unpublished manuscript, University of Wisconsin-Madison.

Dorr, A., & Kovaric, P. (1980). Some of the people some of the time—But which people? Televised violence and its effects. In E. L. Palmer & A. Dorr (Eds.), *Children and the faces of television: Teaching, violence, selling* (pp. 183–199). New York: Academic Press.

Dorr, A., Kovaric, P., & Doubleday, C. (1989). Parent–child coviewing of television. *Journal of Broadcasting & Electronic Media, 33*, 35–51.

Einspruch, E. L., & Pollard, J. P. (1993). *Washington State survey of adolescent health behaviors 1988–1992.* Portland, OR: Northwest Regional Educational Laboratory.

Friedrich, L. K., & Stein, A. H. (1975). Prosocial television and young children: The effects of verbal labeling and role playing on learning and behavior. *Child Development, 46*, 27–38.

Fry, D., & McCain, T. (1980, August). *Controlling children's television viewing: Predictors of family television rules and their relationship to family communication patterns.* Paper presented at the annual meeting of the Association for Education in Journalism, Boston, MA.

Greenberg, B. S., Abelman, R., & Cohen, A. (1990). Telling children not to watch television. In R. J. Kinkel (Ed.), *Television and violence: An overview* (pp. 2–22). Detroit, MI: Mental Health Association of Michigan.

Greenberg, B. S., & Brand, J. E. (1994). Minorities and the mass media: 1970s to 1990s. In J. Bryant & D. Zillmann (Eds.), *Media effects: Advances in theory and research* (pp. 273–314). Hillsdale, NJ: Lawrence Erlbaum Associates.

Greenberg, B. S., Brown, J. D., & Buerkel-Rothfuss, N. L. (1993). *Media, sex and the adolescent.* Cresskill, NJ: Hampton Press.

Greenberg, B. S., Ericson, P. M., & Vlahos, M. (1971). *Children's television behaviors as perceived by mother and child.* Michigan State University. (ERIC Document Reproduction Service No. ED 058 750)

Greenberg, B. S., Korzenny, F., & Atkin, C. K. (1980). Trends in portrayals of the elderly. In B. S. Greenberg (Ed.), *Life on television* (pp. 23–34). Norwood, NJ: Ablex.

Hawkins, R. P., & Pingree, S. (1983). Television's influence on social reality. In D. Pearl, L. Bouthillet, & J. Lazar (Eds.), *Television and behavior* (Vol. 2, pp. 224–247). Washington DC: US Government Printing Office.

Hearold, S. (1986). A synthesis of 1,043 effects of television on social behavior. In G. Comstock (Ed.), *Public communications and behavior Vol. 1,* pp. 65–133). New York: Academic Press.

Henderson, L., Greenberg, B. S., & Atkin, C. (1980). Sex differences in giving orders, making plans, and needing support on television. In B. S. Greenberg (Ed.), *Life on television* (pp. 49–64). Norwood, NJ: Ablex.

Hoffner, C. (1996). Children's wishful identification and parasocial interaction with favorite television characters. *Journal of Broadcasting & Electronic Media, 40*, 389–402.

Huston, A. C., & Wright, J. C. (1996). Television and socialization of young children. In T. M. MacBeth (Ed.), *Tuning into young viewers: Social science perspectives on television* (pp. 37–60). Thousand Oaks, CA: Sage.

Huston, A. C., Zillmann, D., & Bryant, J. (1994). Media influence, public policy, and the family. In D. Zillmann, J. Bryant, & A. Huston (Eds.), *Media, children, and the family* (pp. 3–18). Hillsdale, NJ: Lawrence Erlbaum Associates.

Kantor, D., & Lehr, W. (1975). *Inside the family.* San Francisco: Jossey-Bass.

Kim, W. Y., Baran, S. J., & Massey, K. K. (1988). Impact of VCR on control of television viewing. *Journal of Broadcasting & Electronic Media, 32*, 351–358.

Krendl, K. A., Clark, G., Dawson, R., & Troiano, C. (1993). Preschoolers and VCRs in the home: A multiple methods approach. *Journal of Broadcasting & Electronic Media, 37*, 293–312.

Liebert, R. M., & Sprafkin, J. (1988). *The early window: Effects of television on children and youth* (3rd ed.). New York: Pergamon.

Lin, C. A., & Atkin, D. J. (1989). Parental mediation and rulemaking for adolescent use of television and VCRs. *Journal of Broadcasting & Electronic Media, 33*, 53–67.

Lull, J. (1980). The social uses of television. *Human Communication Research, 6*, 120–136.

Lyle, J., & Hoffman, H. R. (1972). Children's use of television and other media. In E. A. Rubinstein, G. A. Comstock, & J. P. Murray (Eds.), *Television and social behavior: Television in day-to-day life*, (Vol. 4, pp. 129–256). Rockville, MD: National Institute of Mental Health.

Martin, C. A., & Benson, L. (1970). Parental perceptions of the role of television in parent–child interaction. *Journal of Marriage and the Family, 32*, 410–414.

McDonald, D. G. (1985). Spousal influences on television viewing. *Communication Research, 12*, 530–545.

McDonald, D. G. (1986). Generational aspect of television coviewing. *Journal of Broadcasting & Electronic Media, 30*, 75–85.

McLeod, J., & Brown, J. D. (1976). The family environment and adolescent television use. In R. Brown (Ed.), *Children and television* (pp. 199–234). Beverly Hills, CA: Sage.

McLeod, J. M., Fitzpatrick, M. A., Glynn, C. J., & Fallis, S. F. (1982). Television and social relations: Family influences and consequences for interpersonal behavior. In D. Pearl, L. Bouthillet, & J. Lazar (Eds.), *Television and behavior: Ten years of scientific progress and implications for the eighties* (DHHS Publication NO. ADM 82-1196, Vol. 2, pp. 272–286). Washington, DC: U.S. Government Printing Office.

Meadowcroft, J. M., & Fitzpatrick, M. A. (1988). Theories of family communication: Toward a merger of intersubjectivity and mutual influence processes. In R. P. Hawkins, J. M. Wiemann, & S. Pingree (Eds.), *Advancing communication science: Merging mass and interpersonal processes* (pp. 253–275). Newbury Park, CA: Sage.

Messaris, P. (1982). Parents, children, and television. In G. Gumpert & R. Cathcart (Eds.), *Inter/Media* (3rd ed., pp. 519–536). New York: Oxford University Press.

Messaris, P. (1986). Mothers' comments to their children about the relationship between television and reality. In T. Lindlof (Ed.), *Natural audiences: Qualitative research of media uses and effects* (pp. 95–197). Norwood, NJ: Ablex.

Messaris, P., & Kerr, D. (1983). Mothers' comments about TV: Reaction to family communication. *Communication Research, 10*, 175–194.

Messaris, P., & Sarett, C. (1981, Spring). On the consequences of television-related parent–child interaction. *Human Communication Research, 7*, 226–244.

Mills, S., & Watkins, B. (1982). *Parents' perception of television's effects and its relationship to televiewing restrictions.* Paper presented at the Midwestern Association for Public Opinion Research Conference, Chicago.

Mohr, P. J. (1978). *Television, children and parents.* Unpublished report, Department of Speech Communication, Wichita State University.

Mohr, P. J. (1979). Parental guidance of children's viewing of evening television programs. *Journal of Broadcasting, 23*, 213–228.

Moore, R. L. (1990). Effects of television on family consumer behavior. In J. Bryant (Ed.), *Television and the American family* (pp. 275–292). Hillsdale, NJ: Lawrence Erlbaum Associates.

Morgan, M. (1982). Television and adolescents' sex-role stereotypes: A longitudinal study. *Journal of Personality & Social Psychology, 43*, 947–955.

Moschis, G. P. (1987). *Consumer socialization: A life-cycle perspective.* Lexington, MA: Lexington Books.

Nathanson, A. I. (1998). Identifying and explaining the relationship between parental mediation and children's aggression. *Communication Research, 26*, 124–143.

Noller, P., & Fitzpatrick, M. A. (1993). *Communication in family relationships.* Englewood Cliffs, NJ: Prentice-Hall.

Olson, D. H., Sprenkle, D., & Russell, C. (1979). Circumplex model of marital and family systems I: Cohesion and adaptability dimension, family types, and clinical applications. *Family Process, 18*, 3–28.

Perse, E. M. (1990). Cultivation and involvement with local television news. In N. Signorielli & M. Morgan (Eds.), *Cultivation analysis: New directions in media effects research* (pp. 51–70). Newbury Park, CA: Sage.

Prasad, V. K., Rao, T. R., & Sheikh, A. A. (1978, Winter). Mother vs. Commercial. *Journal of Communication, 28* (1), 91–96.

Reiss, D. (1981). *The family's construction of reality.* Cambridge, MA: Harvard University Press.

Reiss, D., & Oliveri, M. E. (1983). The family's construction of social reality and its ties to its kin network: An exploration of causal direction. *Journal of Marriage and the Family, 45*, 81–91.

Roberts, C. (1981). Childrens' and parents' television viewing and perceptions of violence. *Journalism Quarterly, 58*, 556–564.

Robertson, T. S. (1979, Winter). Parental mediation of television advertising effects. *Journal of Communication, 29* (1), 12–26.

Rosengren, K. E., Wenner, L. A., & Palmgreen, P. (Eds.) (1985). *Media gratifications research: Current perspectives.* Beverly Hills, CA: Sage.

Rossiter, J., & Robertson, T. (1975). Children's television viewing: An examination of parent–child consensus. *Sociometry, 38*, 308–326.

Rothschild, N., & Morgan, M. (1987). Communication and control: Adolescents' relationships with parents as mediators of television. *Journal of Early Adolescence, 7*, 299–314.

Saloman, G. (1977). Effects of encouraging Israeli mothers to co-observe Sesame Street with their five-year-olds. *Child Development, 48*, 1146–1151.

Signorielli, N., & Morgan, M. (1990). *Cultivation analysis: New directions in media effects research.* Newbury Park, CA: Sage.

Singer, J. L., & Singer, D. G. (1976, July). Family television viewing habits and the spontaneous play of preschool children. *American Journal of Orthopsychiatry, 46*, 496–502.

Singer, J. L., Singer, D. G., & Rapaczynski, W. S. (1984). Family patterns and television viewing as predictors of children's beliefs and aggression. *Journal of Communication, 34* (2), 73–89.

Sparks, G. G., & Cantor, J. (1986). Developmental differences in fright responses to a television program depicting a character transformation. *Journal of Broadcasting & Electronic Media, 30*, 309–323.

St. Peters, M., Fitch, M., Huston, A. C., Wright, J. C., & Eakins, D. J. (1991). Television and families: What do young children watch with their parents? *Child Development, 62*, 1409–1423.

Stafford, L., & Bayer, C. L. (1993). *Interaction between parents and children.* Newbury Park, CA: Sage.

Strouse, J. S., & Buerkel-Rothfuss, N. L. (1987). Media exposure and the sexual attitudes and behaviors of college students. *Journal of Sex Education and Therapy, 13*, 43–51.

Sweeper, G. (1984). The image of the black family and the white family in American prime time television programming 1970 to 1980 (Doctoral dissertation, New York University, 1983). *Dissertation Abstracts International, 44*, 1964a.

Thomas, M. H., Horton, R. W., Lippincott, E. C., & Drabman, R. S. (1977). Desensitization to portrayals of real-life aggression as a function of exposure to television violence. *Journal of Personality and Social Psychology, 35*, 450–458.

Umble, D. Z. (1990). Mennonites and television: Application of cultivation analysis to a religious subculture. In N. Signorielli & M. Morgan (Eds.), *Cultivation analysis: New directions in media effects research* (pp. 141–156). Newbury Park, CA: Sage.

Valkenburg, P. M., Krcmar, M., & de Roos, S. (1998). The impact of a cultural children's program and adult mediation on children's knowledge of and attitudes towards opera. *Journal of Broadcasting & Electronic Media, 42*, 315–326.

Valkenburg, P. M., Krcmar, M., Peeters, A. L., & Marseille, N. M. (in press). Developing a scale to assess three styles of television mediation: "Active mediation," "restrictive mediation," and "social coviewing." *Journal of Broadcasting and Electronic Media.*

van der Voort, T. H. A., Nikken, P., & van Lil, J. E. (1992). Determinants of parental guidance of children's television viewing: A Dutch replication study. *Journal of Broadcasting & Electronic Media, 36,* 61–74.

Ward, S., Wackman, D. B., & Wartella, E. (1977). *How children learn to buy.* Beverly Hills, CA: Sage.

Watkins, B., Calvert, S., Huston-Stein, A., & Wright, J. C. (1980). Children's recall of television material: Effects of presentation mode and adult labeling. *Developmental Psychology, 16,* 672–674.

Wright, J. C., St. Peters, M., & Huston, A. C. (1990). Family television use and its relation to children's cognitive skills and social behavior. In J. Bryant (Ed.), *Television and the American family* (pp. 227–252). Hillsdale, NJ: Lawrence Erlbaum Associates.

Yerby, J., Buerkel-Rothfuss, N. L., & Bochner, A. P. (1995). *Understanding family communication* (2nd ed.). Scottsdale, AZ: Gorsuch.

Effects of Family Communication on Children's Interpretation of Television

Erica Weintraub Austin
Washington State University

Common sense tells us the media have a major influence on children's lives and that parents are in the best position to shape media effects into positive influences. How parents can and do intervene is less obvious, because, for the most part, parents do not affect media influences directly. Instead, parents affect the ways in which children use and interpret media such as television. The media do not have *effects* as much as their use has *results*, and parents have the potential to shape those results in both positive and negative ways.

CHILDREN'S ROLE IN THEIR OWN MEDIA EFFECTS

Decades of research has shown conclusively that children help control both how and what they learn, participating in their own socialization process from the time they are infants. For example, an infant in a baby seat in a room with voices coming from different directions will purposefully look toward a voice that makes baby talk sounds, called "parentese," because infants can make sense of large swings in pitch better than less exaggerated speech patterns (Fernald, 1984; Fernald & Kuhl, 1987; Kuhl

377

et al., 1997). Even at such a young age, children make decisions about which things merit their attention.

Nevertheless, research also has shown that children have to learn how to gain control over the continuous and massive amounts of information that beg for their attention every day. For example, children are naturally drawn to sudden noises, bright colors, and laughter (Anderson & Collins, 1988), which can attract them to *Sesame Street* but also to ads for things their parents may not want them to have. With experience, children learn to pay attention if information seems relevant, if the content is understandable, and if the presentation style seems interesting (Austin, 1995), with their interests changing somewhat with age (Lyle & Hoffman, 1972). If children never learned control, they would be bound by the TV stimulus from infancy, by what's called an orienting reflex—the reflex that makes us pay attention to sudden noises (Malcuit, Bastien & Pomerlau, 1996; Sostek & Brackbill, 1976).

Because this means children learn to make choices about where to direct their attention, one important way parents influence children's interpretations of media messages is by helping them develop the ability to make good ones. Attention to messages alone, however, does not explain how children learn from them. This makes it important to tease out the process by which children draw conclusions from media messages.

How Children Use Information

Children want to grow up to become competent adults, and to do this, they look for information that will help them achieve success. When children use the media, they often are trying to learn about the world. What they want to know is (a) *What is real*, such as what exists, and how to organize things into categories; (b) *What is right and wrong*, that is, values; (c) *What is important*, such as how to rank smartness, money, and glamour as priorities; and (d) *What is related to what*, to determine cause and effect relationships such as whether drinking beer makes you popular (Gerbner, 1973). In short, they search for ways to act successfully on the world as they see it (O'Keefe & Reid-Nash, 1987).

Mature use of mass media requires the ability to pay attention selectively, to understand implicit as well as explicit information, to understand the perspective and intentions of programmers and characters, and to understand the meaning behind techniques such as slow motion and flashbacks (Dorr, 1980). Although these skills must be learned, children nevertheless do not accept or act on everything they see suggested by the media. Overall, children tend to believe and emulate portrayals seen frequently that seem relevant, useful, realistic, normative, desirable, and rewarding (e.g., Reeves, 1978; Hawkins & Pingree, 1982; Austin & Meili, 1994). Reinforcement of messages by real-life people and experiences

(DeFleur & Ball-Rokeach, 1982; Austin & Meili, 1994) can make media portrayals appear more desirable or attractive. On the other hand, a lack of information from real-life referents can magnify television's potential to serve as a primary source of information (Rosengren & Windahl, 1972).

A THEORY OF MESSAGE INTERPRETATION PROCESSES

Because children take an active role in their socialization and decision making, the ways they interpret messages will affect the ways they consider options, possible consequences, and obstacles to their decisions (Fischhoff & Quadrel, 1991). A model of information processing we have been developing, called the message interpretation process model (MIP), focuses on some of the important benchmarks that take an individual from message exposure to later behavior. The model has been tested in a series of studies with individuals ranging from third grade to college age and has demonstrated that the process used to interpret television messages may have "bugs" that parents can help fix.

The MIP model holds that acceptance of a television portrayal occurs via a causal sequence that takes place at a number of increasingly rigorous levels, or "zones of relevance" (Adoni & Mane, 1984). To the extent children apply logic to their analysis of media messages, they compare real-world and television-world reference groups.

First, a child will determine whether a portrayal seems realistic or normative—that is, "like most people" (Austin & Meili, 1994; Austin, Roberts, & Nass, 1990; Gitlin, 1990). If perceived as realistic, a logically processed message is more likely to survive yet a tougher test. This test is to determine how closely the portrayal reflects personal experiences, called "perceived similarity" (Austin & Meili, 1994). Even children as young as third grade make distinctions between what is true for "most people" and what is true for their own family (Austin & Meili, 1994; Austin et al., 1990).

When portrayals survive the tougher "similarity" test, a child is more likely to want to be like (identify with) the portrayal, which can lead to changes in social reality construction or behavior. Identification tends to lead to the expectation that doing something consistent with that seen on television will bring positive results (expectancies), a belief that strongly and consistently predicts behavior (Austin & Johnson, 1997a, 1997b; Austin & Knaus, 1998; Austin & Meili, 1994; Austin, Pinkleton, & Fujioka, 1999). Similarity, however, depends not just on media-related variables such as perceived realism, but also on personal experience and direct communication from significant others such as parents (Austin & Freeman, 1997; Austin & Meili, 1994). This means that parents can play an especially important role in the child's logic-based decision-making process by shaping children's perceptions of similarity.

Of course, decisions are not purely logical, as shown in Fig. 18.1. Desir-

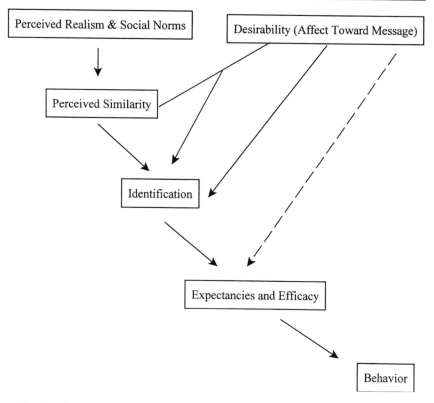

FIG. 18.1.   The message interpretation process (MIP) model. Solid lines indicate strong relationships demonstrated across a number of studies. Dotted line indicates a weaker relationship, found less consistently in studies.

ability of a portrayal or its perceived attractiveness (Austin & Meili, 1994) can also influence identification, both on its own and in interaction with similarity (the two together magnify each other's effects). Desirability also has the potential to affect expectancies directly, particularly in combination with similarity (Austin & Johnson, 1997a, 1997b; Austin, Pinkleton, & Fujioka, 1999, 2000). Desirability appears to have less impact in the context of influences such as parents (e.g., Austin & Meili, 1994). This means that parents may have the potential to mute the effects of desirability by directly affecting expectancies (Austin et al., 2000; Austin & Meili, 1994) and efficacy (Austin & Freeman, 1997).

Parents do not seem as successful at influencing desirability and identification as at influencing variables such as similarity, expectancies, and skepticism. Skepticism, however, can affect nearly every media interpretation variable, including point-of-entry variables such as desirability (Austin & Johnson, 1997a, 1997b) and important predictors of behavior such as expectancies (Austin & Chen, 1999; Austin & Johnson, 1997a, 1997b).

When parents discuss television critically, they seem to enhance children's skepticism and can motivate children to be more involved in public affairs (Austin, 1993). In addition, the ways parents and children communicate can affect children's health-related behaviors by affecting the child's perceived social resistance skills, which predict self-efficacy, which predicts the salience of risky issues, which predicts preventive behavior (Austin, 1996). Thus, to the extent parents can cultivate skepticism and social resistance skills, they can soften the effects of desirability and reduce the likelihood of risky behavior.

Cultivating skepticism means teaching children that every message has a motive, and that the motives can call a source's trustworthiness into question. Tests of the MIP model have suggested that benchmark beliefs such as desirability, identification, and expectancies develop sometimes years before the behaviors they can predict, such as alcohol use (Austin & Knaus, 1998; Austin et al., 2000). Children's understanding of persuasive intent, however, appears to increase more gradually than beliefs such as desirability and identification (see Fig. 18.2.) This means

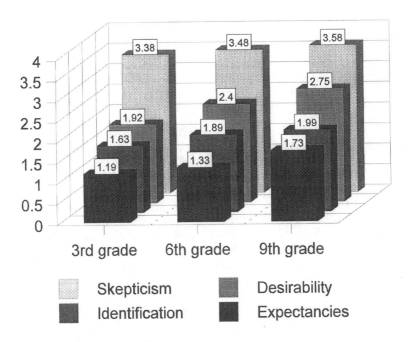

FIG. 18.2.   Age differences in beliefs about media and alcohol. Bars represent mean scores on indices standardized to 4-point scales. Data collected in 1997 from third (n=87), sixth (n=146), and ninth graders (n=40) in Washington State, with mean differences examined via Student-Newman-Keuls tests.

that children need extra help to resist the appeal of well-produced media messages that may provide appealing but disagreeable ideas. Figure 18.2 shows that third and ninth graders differ significantly on skepticism, but sixth graders do not differ significantly from either third graders or ninth graders. All other variables increase significantly between third and sixth grade, with desirability and expectancies continuing to increase between sixth and ninth grade (Austin & Knaus, 2000).

A number of common themes have emerged across age groups and samples from the tests of the MIP model to date. First, individuals' decision-making processes are somewhat logical and somewhat emotional. Wishful thinking—or denial (Knaus & Austin, 1999)—can corrupt sensible logic. In addition, because people look to role models and reference groups to determine how they should behave, the desire to emulate a media portrayal can be a powerful motivator. Because parents are an extremely important reference group and model for children's behaviors, they can help strengthen the logical aspects of children's decision making and can counterbalance the emotion-based beliefs that can overwhelm logic. Finally, although longitudinal research is needed on this point, existing research suggests that early input into children's uses of the media for decision making can have long-term protective effects.

Conceptualizing the Parents' Role

Scholars have suggested that the media serve as a bridge between the home to the larger society (Chaffee & Yang, 1990), and without parental guidance, the media can become a child's most authoritative source of information (Austin & Freeman, 1997; Austin & Meili, 1994; Rosengren & Windahl, 1972). Young children in particular place a lot of trust in television, believing that it exists to entertain, educate and, finally, to tell them the truth (Dorr, 1980, 1983). Meanwhile, adolescents use media to guide them through a period of enormous uncertainty as they begin to focus on developing their own identities and independence (Christenson & Roberts, 1990). Parents initially comprise children's most frequent and authoritative sources of information, but children increasingly rely on television and other media as they get older. As they approach adolescence, children begin to choose media sources—and particularly music— to facilitate their relationships with their peers (Christenson, DeBenedittis, & Lindloff, 1985; Christenson & Roberts, 1990), who are becoming increasingly important sources of information. The media, meanwhile, seem to act as a special form of peer influence (Austin & Freeman, 1997; van der Voort, 1986).

This means that by adolescence, parents are no longer as dominant a source of direct information and reinforcement. As the tests of the MIP model have demonstrated, however, parents still can provide an important counterbalancing influence to the media even when parental influences at times seem limited and indirect. In addition, over the long term, parents guide children's development of one of their most important skills, that of "functional communication competence," or the ability to use communication resources, such as the media, strategically (Burleson, Delia, & Applegate, 1995). Research on the effects of parent–child interaction on children's peer acceptance, academic achievement, and moral development has indicated that parents' communication styles affect the child's social skills and cognitive competence in a variety of ways (Burleson, et al., 1995; Chaffee, McLeod, & Atkin, 1971; Chaffee, McLeod, & Wackman, 1973; Dornbusch, Ritter, Leiderman, Roberts, & Fraleigh, 1987). As a result, how parents interact with their children both in general and regarding the media in particular will affect the messages to which a child pays attention along with how the child interprets the messages received.

Parents' Routes to Influence

Parents have four major routes by which they can mediate the influences of television messages. Some types of guidance require more effort than others, and some frequently happen quite unintentionally. These four routes include (a) *general communication norms* that influence children's information seeking patterns; (b) *rule making*, or the encouragement or prohibition of certain media experiences by the parent for the child; (c) *modeling*, or behaving in ways that confirm or disconfirm media messages in everyday behavior along with coviewing, the shared experience of media exposure by parent and child; and (d) *mediation*, or the active discussion of media content (Austin, 1993). Terminology among scholars has varied, making research findings occasionally confusing, but findings across studies generally support the idea that coviewing, discussion, rule making, and general communication style are distinct yet interrelated parenting activities that affect the ways children use and interpret media messages.

General Communication Style.   Parents differ in the ways they communicate with their children; some parents focus more on the interplay of ideas and others focus more on rule making. Some parents, for example, stress deference and avoid controversial ideas, whereas others stress the value of challenging discussion without much concern about generating controversy (Chaffee et al., 1971). Similarly, parenting styles may stress authoritarian leadership, with less communication overall, or more democratic decision making, leading to more communication (Baumrind, 1966, 1967).

One especially useful model of family communication styles for the study of media effects has been called the family communication patterns (FCP) model, which locates parents on two dimensions of communication norms (McLeod & Chaffee, 1972). Socio-orientation indicates parental emphasis on conformity among family members, and the avoidance of controversy and disagreement, even at the cost of individual personal feelings. Concept orientation, on the other hand, places value on individual ideas and opinions, with family members encouraged to express themselves and engage in an open discussion even if it produces disagreement. The irony of FCP research has been that although socio-oriented families emphasize conformity to the family norm, in the end, children from concept-oriented families are the ones more likely to do so.

In relating parenting style to discussion of television specifically, Austin (1993) found communication warmth and the emphasis on a democratic decision-making style positively related to the discussion of television content. Similarly, Krcmar's (1996) study on family communication patterns found that parents who perceive themselves as high in control (socio-oriented) were less likely to exhibit positive affect (warm expression) toward their child. Austin (1993), meanwhile, found that those high on concept orientation exhibit more warmth.

The FCP model parallels research in psychology and child development that has explored family communication styles, such as Baumrind (authoritarian vs. authoritative; 1968), Hoffman (power-assertive vs. inductive/reasoning; 1977), and Bernstein (position centered vs. person centered; 1974). Authoritarian parents, for example, expect strict obedience from the child and discourage give-and-take, whereas authoritative parents might set controls but are more open to the child's opinions and willing to adjust their behavior in response (Baumrind, 1968). According to Bernstein (1974), the position-centered orientation focuses on social roles and status, whereas the person-centered orientation places individual psychological states (e.g., motivations, feelings) at the center of communication, leading parents to offer reasons and explanations to guide the child's conduct.

The communication styles emphasizing open discussion have been found to help children achieve academic success, avoid substance abuse and resist persuasive media messages (Burleson et al., 1995; Chaffee et al., 1971, 1973; Dornbusch et al., 1987). Similarly, research has found that socio-orientation positively associates with great amounts of television viewing by family members (Chaffee et al., 1971; McLeod & Chaffee, 1972) and more affirmation of what is presented on television (Messaris & Kerr, 1983). Concept orientation positively associates with negations of television messages in general, and with greater involvement in critical discussion and information giving (Austin, 1993; Messaris & Kerr, 1983).

Rule Making. Rule making, however helpful, generally is insufficient as a strategy for controlling media effects. Children not permitted to watch a particular program at home frequently hear about it from their friends anyway, or even watch or listen to it at someone else's house. Moreover, parents historically have enacted few rules about media use (Alexander, 1990; Bower, 1973; Comstock, 1975; Corder-Bolz, 1980; Lyle & Hoffman, 1972). According to a Gallup poll (Moore, 1997), 80% of parents reported that they were familiar with the television advisory ratings system, but only 43% of them considered it helpful in making decisions about the television shows they would allow their children to watch.

Research assessing rule-making patterns, however, appears to underestimate parental control of media and of media content (Alexander, 1990). Some recent research has suggested that rules themselves may matter less than how rules are developed (Andreason, 1990), reflecting broader communication patterns within the household. Krcmar (1996), for example, reported that parents and children used a consultative style to select a TV program to watch if they came from families emphasizing open discussion, whereas parents emphasizing conformity in the household made the decision themselves. Carlson, Grossbart, and Walsh (1990) also found that control-oriented (socio) parents tended to restrict children's exposure to television, and Fujioka and Austin (1999) found that control-oriented (socio) parents consulted with the television ratings system more frequently than did others to set guidelines for the child. Abelman (1986), meanwhile, found that a rule-making style characterized by open discussion was associated with children's awareness of prosocial messages on television. Andreason (1990) noted that the research on rule making indicates primarily that family rules appear to matter more than do television-specific rules.

Coviewing.   Having parents watch television with children seems like it should be helpful. Scholars, however, have suggested that coviewing may not be sufficient to mediate children's perceptions of television (Alexander, 1990; Austin, 1993; Bower, 1973; Desmond, Singer, Singer, Calam, & Colimore, 1985). Coviewing with children tends to decrease with the age of the child (Austin, Knaus, & Meneguelli, 1998; Wright, St. Peters, & Huston, 1990), and it does not appear to relate to parent's levels of concern about television content (Austin et al., 1998). Instead, it seems to relate mainly to more viewing time overall (Alexander, 1990). Greater viewing time tends to be associated with less rule making and less critical viewing (Atkin, Greenberg, & Baldwin, 1991; Chaffee et al., 1971, 1973; Desmond et al., 1985; Medrich, 1979).

Indeed, parents frequently watch with their children without actually discussing media content, doing so because they *like* the content, not because they plan to provide commentary. Parents who make heavier use of television are more likely to watch with their children, talk positively about television content, and report that television is a useful tool (Austin,

Fujioka, Bolls, & Engelbertson, 1999). Although more coviewing occurs when parents value television content and view education as a primary benefit of television (Bower, 1973; Dorr, Kovaric, & Doubleday, 1989), global perceptions of television's usefulness do not seem to transfer into deliberate use of television. Bybee, Robinson, and Turow (1982), for example, found that whereas negative views predicted the use of both content-related discussion and rule making by parents, positive views predicted only discussion. Parents who discuss television more critically appear to use television less and more selectively (Atkin et al., 1991; Chaffee et al., 1971, 1973; Desmond et al., 1985; Medrich, 1979) and do not necessarily coview more than other parents (Austin, et al., 1998). This suggests that parents who often use television as a tool use it to reinforce positive lessons, rather than to discuss examples of what not to do. Indeed, Austin and Pinkleton (1997), for example, found more frequent coviewing of news associated with positive reinforcement instead of with critical discussion.

It has become increasingly clear that coviewing and critical or analytical parental discussion of content are conceptually distinct behaviors (Austin, Fujioka, et al., 1999; Valkenburg, Krcmar, Peeters, & Marseille, 1999) and that coviewing can occur without concurrent discussion (Austin, 1993; Chaffee et al., 1971). When discussion occurs in conjunction with coviewing, it tends to be positive in tone instead of critical or analytical (Austin, Fujioka, et al., 1999). Thus, coviewing by parents appears unlikely without other influences to develop critical viewing skills in children. Among these, one particularly important type of influence is parental mediation.

Mediation. Parental mediation is the active discussion of television content with a child (Austin, 1993). Parents may discuss whether and how television represents the actual world (categorization), endorse or condemn television messages (validation), and provide additional information to show how television messages can be applied in real life (supplementation) (Austin, 1993; Messaris, 1982). All three of these tasks can refute or reinforce television content by suggesting that television messages either are or are not realistic; are right or wrong, and are or are not applicable to real-life situations.

Most research examining the role of parents has assumed they create a buffer or counterbalance to media messages to the extent they coview or discuss the media. Increased general knowledge of domains such as politics or geography have found to be outcomes of parent or teacher mediation of television content (Corder-Bolz, 1980). Similarly, attitudes toward minorities and certain modes of normative or ethical behavior have been improved when parents have been directed to mediate their children's viewing (Roberts, 1981; Robertson, 1979). Unfortunately, the literature suggests that parents also demonstrate the potential to exacerbate potentially deleterious effects of television content (Austin & Chen, 1999; Austin, Fujioka, et al., 1999; Austin & Nach-Ferguson, 1995. As a result, some research has begun to examine whether endorsement of media content ("positive mediation") has different effects than discussion that cultivates skepticism, often emphasizing counterargument of television messages ("negative mediation").

As Table 18.1 shows, "negative mediation" as measured by Austin et al.

TABLE 18.1
Recent Indices Used to Assess Parent–Child Discussion
Patterns Regarding Television

Positive Mediation: Used with children of varied ages and with parents (e.g., Austin & Chen, 1999, alpha = .83)
How often parents or guardians said:
  They like a product in TV ad
  They like a person or character seen on TV
  They agree with something seen on TV
  Say that something on TV happens in real life
  Repeat something heard on TV
  Say that something seen on TV is OK

Negative Mediation: Used with children of varied ages and with parents (e.g., Austin, Fujioka, et al., 1999, alpha = .74)
How often parents or guardians:
  Say that something seen on TV is not OK
  Say that something in a TV ad is not OK
  Say that something on TV is not real
  Say that something in a TV ad is not true
  Tell more about something seen on TV
  Explain what ads are trying to do

Negative Mediation: Used with older children (alpha = .75; Austin, Pinkleton, & Fujioka, 2000)
How often parents or guardians:
  Speak up when they see something on TV they dislike
  Say something in a TV ad looks better than it really is
  Say something on TV is not true
  Tell more about something seen on TV
  Talk about what ads are trying to do
  Say they disagree with something shown on TV

Instructive Mediation: Used with parents (alpha = .80, Valkenburg et al., 1999)
How often do you:
  Try to help the child understand what he or she sees on TV?

(Continued)

TABLE 18.1

(Continued)

Point out why some things actors do are good?
Point out why some things actors do are bad?
Explain the motives of TV characters?
Explain what something on TV really means?

Social Coviewing: Used with parents (alpha = .79, Valkenburg et al., 1999)
How often do you:
　Watch together because you both like a program?
　Watch together because of a common interest in a program?
　Watch together just for the fun?
　Watch your favorite program together?
　Laugh with your child about the things you see on TV?

Restrictive Mediation (rule making): Used with parents (Valkenburg et al., 1999,
　alpha = .79)
How often do you:
　Say to your child to turn off the TV when s/he is watching an unsuitable program?
　Set specific viewing hours for your child?
　Forbid your child to watch certain programs?
　Restrict the amount of child viewing?
　Specify in advance the programs that may be watched?

Note: Coviewing without assumed concurrent discussion has been measured as an index by Fujioka and Austin (1999) for various genres such as sports, educational shows, news programs, movies, and prime time (alpha = .66), but single measures have been used most frequently (e.g., Abelman & Pettey, 1989; Dorr et al., 1989; Gross & Walsh, 1980).

(1999, or "instructive mediation" as measured by Valkenburg et al., 1999) does not always appear explicitly negative in tone, but the terminology reflects the critical tone that analytical comments tend to take. Even comments intended to supplement media content (i.e., "telling more about") provide children with more potential to critically analyze portrayals. As others have noted (e.g., Austin et al., 1990; Bandura, 1986; Roberts, 1989), children tend to analyze content more critically when they have life experience or previous information with which to compare new information received. "Positive" mediation, on the other hand, tends to be explicitly reinforcing rather than explanatory.

According to Austin et al. (1999), parents may use either positive or negative mediation, or a combination of the two mediation styles. In general, parents tend to engage in negative mediation when strongly concerned with media influence on their child or when skeptical about media messages. In contrast, parents tend to use positive mediation when they possess a low level of skepticism and when they have positive attitudes toward television in general. Positive mediators watch more television and coview more with the child (Austin et al., 1999). In some cases, positive mediation seems to occur out of a concern that condemning or countering messages might threaten family harmony. Fujioka and Austin (1999) found that the extent to which parents embrace the socio orientation's emphasis on conformity and harmony in the household associates with positive mediation, whereas the extent to which parents welcome controversy and open discussion correlates with negative mediation.

SUMMARIZING HOW MEDIATION PATTERNS RELATE TO OTHER COMMUNICATION PATTERNS

Demographic differences appear to explain little about parental communication about the media (Austin et al., 1998). Instead, parents' attitudes about the media tend to direct their discussion patterns regarding the media. In general, when parents hold positive attitudes toward television (Dorr et al., 1989; van der Voort, Nikken, van Lil, 1992) or use television as a socialization tool (Dorr et al., 1989) or a learning tool for the child (Austin et al., 1999), parents tend to watch television more with the child. In contrast, when parents possess negative opinions about television content, either being skeptical about (Austin et al., 1999), concerned with (Bybee et al., 1982), or disagreeing with (Atkin et al., 1991) television messages, they tend to engage in critical discussion with the child. Those who consume a great deal of television tend to be the least skeptical (Chaffee, et al., 1971, 1973).

Negative mediators tend to be more critical viewers, and they watch less television. As Gallup (1989) found, parents tend to turn off the television when content offends them, but as Dorr et al. (1989) found, parents discuss television more when their values appear threatened. In other words, although parents may turn off what they don't like, they may nevertheless continue discussing it. Desmond, Singer, and Singer (1990) suggested that the most effective critical discussions about television probably occur in the car, around bedtime, and during other times when watching television is not the focus of activity.

Whereas negative mediation seems to have protective effects on the child's interpretation processes, positive mediation seems to have worrisome results. In a study with third, sixth, and ninth graders, for example, positive mediation predicted higher expectancies for alcohol use, a greater desire to emulate characters who consumed alcohol on television, and a stronger belief in the realism of such portrayals. Negative mediation, on the other hand, predicted lower levels of expectancies for alcohol use (Austin & Knaus, 2000). Negative mediation also has been shown to predict skepticism (Austin, 1993) with socio and concept orientation unrelated, whereas positive mediation has been shown to predict lower levels of skepticism (Austin & Chen, 1999). Positive mediation also has been shown to associate with higher levels of desirability and expectancies, even among college students presumably more distant from parental communication effects than younger children would be (Austin & Chen, 1999).

TREATING TELEVISION AS A TOOL

Television and other media seem like toys. They provide entertainment and an opportunity to share enjoyable experiences with others. But TV is a *tool*. It is a tool that message producers use to sell both products and ideas. It is a tool that brings strangers who do not always behave well into our houses (Meyrowitz, 1985). In a capitalistic culture, it also is a tool by which strangers sell us and our children to other strangers every time we watch.

Every message has a motive behind it, and children's welfare usually does not rate as the message producer's highest priority. Because we learn something from everything we watch, children need to realize that we cannot necessarily trust the teachers of these lessons. Every media message includes the potential for children to learn things that parents agree with, disagree with, or that may be dangerous. Loving parents would never sell their child to a stranger, so the Center for Media Literacy advised parents about television, "Love it or hate it, but you can't ignore it!" (Center for Media Literacy, 1988).

In the absence of messages from those who care, children will fill themselves with messages from those who don't. This doesn't necessarily doom them to deleterious media effects, but it puts them at a definite disadvantage. Consider that a popular baby book, called *Baby's First Words* (Wik, 1985), features "television" among the first words significant to a baby, along with "bottle" and "potty." In the chunky board book, the baby's entire day consists of getting up, getting dressed, eating, watching TV without any parents present, getting ready for bed, and going to bed. *Baby's First Words* illustrates the prominence of media, and especially TV, from babyhood; it also illustrates the potential for television to supercede the parents as a socialization influence.

Evidence suggests that this does occur. For example, children and adolescents appear to learn more about alcohol from television and beer advertising than from more balanced sources such as parents, leaving them more knowledgeable about beer brands than about potential health risks associated with drinking (Austin & Nach-Ferguson, 1995; CSPI, 1988; Wallack, Cassady, & Grube, 1990). Although controversy continues among scholars and policymakers, many think it no coincidence that 45% of high school seniors report having been drunk by tenth grade, 80% report having tried alcohol, and 74% continue to use it, making alcohol unquestionably the drug of choice among adolescents (Johnston, O'Malley, & Bachman, 1996).

Fortunately, the research reviewed here also demonstrates that parents can help children use the media instead of letting the media use them. Treating television as a toy, however, suppresses the vigilance required of the tool. Watching television together is fine, but discussing television after the TV has been turned off seems much more important. Rules are fine, but rules by themselves do not address the decision-making process that children must develop, with or without the parent's direct assistance. Children use the media to make sense of and decisions about their world, making their ability to use the media well an essential skill. Because this skill set evolves in the context of children's most important influence, the family, parents who allow their children to live in a world like *Baby's First Words* risk becoming unwitting coproducers of media-influenced results they may regret.

REFERENCES

Abelman, R. (1986). Children's awareness of television's prosocial fare: Parental discipline as an antecedent. *Journal of Family Issues, 7*, 51–66.

Abelman, R., & Pettey, G. R. (1989). Child attributes as determinants of parental television-viewing mediation. *Journal of Family Issues, 10*, 251–266.

Adoni, H., & Mane, S. (1984). Media and the social construction of reality: Toward an integration of theory and research. *Communication Research, 11*, 323–340.

Alexander, A. (1990). Television and family interaction. In J. Bryant (Ed.), *Television and the American Family* (pp. 211–226). Hillsdale, NJ: Lawrence Erlbaum Associates.

Anderson, D., & Collins, P. (1988). *The impact on children's education: Television's influence on cognitive development.* Washington, DC: U.S. Department of Education, Office of Educational Research and Improvement.

Andreason, M. S. (1985). How people use media in home learning. In N. M. Miller (Ed.), *The home as a learning center, American Home Economics Association yearbook 5* (pp. 239–265). Peoria, IL: Bennett & McKnight.

Andreason, M. S. (1990). Evolution in the family's use of television: Normative data from industry and academe. In J. Bryant (Ed.), *Television and the American family* (pp. 3–55). Hillsdale, NJ: Lawrence Erlbaum Associates.

Atkin, D., Greenberg, B. S., & Baldwin, T. F. (1991). The home ecology of children's television viewing: Parental mediation and the new video environment. *Journal of Communication, 41*, 40–52.

Austin, E. W. (1993). Exploring the effects of active parental mediation of television content. *Journal of Broadcasting & Electronic Media, 37*, 147–158.

Austin, E. W. (1995). Reaching young audiences: Developmental considerations in designing health messages. In E. Maibach & R. Parrott (Eds.), *Designing Health Messages: Approaches from Communication Theory and Public Health Practice* (pp. 114-144). Beverly Hills: Sage Publications.

Austin, E. W. (1996). Direct and indirect influences of parent–child communication norms or adolescent's tendencies to take preventive measures for AIDS and drug abuse. In

G. Kreps & D. O'Hair (Eds.), *Relational communication and health outcomes* (pp. 163–183). Cresskill, NJ: Hampton Press.

Austin, E. W., & Chen, Y. J. (1999, August). *The relationship of parental reinforcement of media messages to college students' alcohol-related behaviors, age of experimentation and beliefs about alcohol.* Paper presented to the Communication Theory & Methodology Division of the Association for Education in Journalism & Mass Communication, New Orleans.

Austin, E. W., & Freeman, C. (1997). Effects of media, parents and peers on African-American adolescents' efficacy toward media celebrities. *Howard Journal of Communication, 8,* 275–290.

Austin, E. W., Fujioka, Y., Bolls, P., & Engelbertson, J. (1999). Taking on the tube: An examination of parents' media behavior, attitudes and discussion regarding television. *Journal of Broadcasting & Electronic Media, 43,* 83–100.

Austin, E. W., & Johnson, K. K. (1997a). Immediate and delayed effects of media literacy training on third graders' decision making for alcohol. *Health Communication, 4,* 323–349.

Austin, E. W., & Johnson, K. K. (1997b). Effects of general and alcohol-specific media literacy training on children's decision making about alcohol. *Journal of Health Communication, 2,* 17–42.

Austin, E. W., & Knaus, C. S. (2000). Predicting the potential for risky behavior among those "too young" to drink, as the result of appealing advertising. *Journal of Health Communication, 5,* 13–27.

Austin, E. W., Knaus, C., & Meneguelli, A. (1998). Who talks how to their kids about TV: A clarification of demographic correlates of parental mediation patterns. *Communication Research Reports, 14,* 418–430.

Austin, E. W., & Meili, H. K. (1994). Effects of interpretations of televised alcohol portrayals on children's alcohol beliefs. *Journal of Broadcasting & Electronic Media, 38,* 417–435.

Austin, E. W., & Nach-Ferguson, B. (1995). Sources and influences of young school-age children's general and brand-specific knowledge about alcohol. *Health Communication, 7,* 1–20.

Austin, E. W., & Pinkleton, B. E. (1997, May). *Parental mediation as information source use: Effects on attitudes and behaviors in the political socialization process.* Paper presented to the Political Communication Division of the International Communication Association, Montreal, Canada.

Austin, E. W., Pinkleton, B. P., & Fujioka, Y. (1999). Assessing pro-social message effectiveness: Effects of message quality, production quality and persuasiveness. *Journal of Health Communication, 4,* 195–210.

Austin, E. W., Pinkleton, B. E., & Fujioka, Y. (2000). The role of interpretation processes and parental discussion in the media's effects on adolescents' use of alcohol. *Pediatrics, 105,* 343–349.

Austin, E. W., Roberts, D. F., & Nass, C. I. (1990). Influences of family communication on children's television-interpretation processes. *Communication Research, 17,* 545–564.

Bandura, A. (1986). *Social foundations of thought & action: A social cognitive theory.* Englewood Cliffs, NJ: Prentice-Hall.

Baumrind, D. (1966). Effects of authoritative parental control. *Child Development, 37,* 887–907.

Baumrind, D. (1967). Child care practices anteceding three patterns of preschool behavior. *Genetics Psychological Monograph, 75,* 43–88.

Baumrind, D. (1968). Authoritarian vs. authoritative parental control. *Adolescent, 3,* 255–272.

Bernstein, B. (1974). *Class, codes, and control: Theoretical studies toward a sociology of language* (rev. ed). New York: Schocken.

Bower, R. T. (1973). *Television and the public.* New York: Holt, Rinehart & Winston.

Burleson, B. R., Delia, J. G., & Applegate, J. L. (1995). The socialization of person-centered communication: Parents' contributions to their children's social-cognitive and communication skills. In M. A. Fitzpatrick & A. L. Vangelisti (Eds.), *Explaining family interactions* (pp. 34–76). Thousand Oaks, CA: Sage.

Bybee, C., Robinson, D., & Turow, J. (1982). Determinants of parental guidance of children's television viewing for a special subgroup: Mass media scholars. *Journal of Broadcasting & Electronic Media, 26*, 697–710.

Carlson, L., Grossbart, S., & Walsh, A. (1990). Mothers' communication orientation and consumer socialization tendencies. *Journal of Advertising, 19*, 27–39.

Center for Media Literacy; (1988). (Slogan) www.medialit.org.

Center for Science in the Public Interest (CSPI). (1988). *Kids are as aware of booze as president, survey finds* [News release]. Washington, DC: Author.

Chaffee, S. H., McLeod, J. M., & Atkin, C. K. (1971). Parental influence on adolescent media use. *American Behavioral Science, 14*, 323–340.

Chaffee, S., McLeod, J., & Wackman, D. (1973). Family communication patterns and adolescent political participation. In J. Dennis (Ed.), *Socialization to politics: Selected readings* (pp. 349–364). New York: Wiley.

Chaffee, S. H., & Yang, S. (1990). Communication and political socialization. In O. Ichilov (Ed.), *Political socialization for democracy* (pp. 137–158). New York: Columbia University Teachers College Press.

Christenson, P., DeBenedittis, P., & Lindloff, T. (1985). Children's use of audio media. *Communications Research, 12*, 327–343.

Christenson, P. G., & Roberts, D. F. (1990). *Popular music in early adolescence.* Washington, DC. Carnegie Council on Adolescent Development.

Comstock, G. (1975). The evidence so far. *Journal of Communication, 25*(4), 25–34.

Corder-Bolz, C. R. (1980). Mediation: The role of significant others. *Journal of Communication, 30*(3) 106–118.

DeFleur, M. L., & Ball-Rokeach, S. (1982). *Theories of mass communication* (4th ed.). New York: David McKay.

Desmond, R. J., Singer, J. L., & Singer, D. G. (1990). Family mediation: Parental communication patterns and the influences of television on children. In J. Bryant (Ed.), *Television and the American family* (pp. 293–309). Hillsdale, NJ: Lawrence Erlbaum Associates.

Desmond, R. J., Singer, J. L., Singer, D. G., Calam, R., & Colimore, K. (1985). Family mediation patterns and television viewing: Young children's use and grasp of the medium. *Human Communication Research, 11*, 461–480.

Dornbusch, S. M., Ritter, P. L., Leiderman, P. H., Roberts, D. F., & Fraleigh, M. J. (1987). The relation of parenting style to adolescent school performance. *Child Development, 58*, 1244–1257.

Dorr, A. (1980). When I was a child, I thought as a child. In S. Withey & R. Abeles (Eds.), *Television and social behavior: Beyond violence and children* (pp. 191-230). Hillsdale, NJ: Lawrence Erlbaum Associates.

Dorr, A., Kovaric, P., & Doubleday, C. (1989). Parent–child coviewing of television. *Journal of Broadcasting & Electronic Media, 33*, 33–51.

Fernald, A. (1984). The perceptual and affective salience of mothers' speech to infants. In L. Feagans, C. Garvey, R. Golinkoff, M. T. Greenberg, C. Harding, & J. N. Bohannon (Eds.), *The origins and growth of communication* (pp. 5–29). Norwood, NJ: Ablex.

Fernald, A., & Kuhl, P. (1987). Acoustic determinants of infant preference for motherese speech. *Infant Behavior and Development, 10*, 279–293.

Fischhoff, B. B., & Quadrel, M. M. (1991). Adolescent alcohol decisions. *Alcohol Health and Research World, 15*, 43–51.

Fujioka, Y., & Austin, E. W. (1999, May). *The relationship of family communication patterns to parental mediation styles.* Paper presented to the Mass Communication Division of the International Communication Association, San Francisco.

Gallup, G. J. (1989, April 10). Parents disturbed by TV shows. *San Francisco Chronicle*, p. B4.

Gerbner, G. (1973). Cultural indicators: The third voice. In G. Gerbner, L. P. Gross, & W. H. Melody (Eds.), *Communications technology and social policy* (pp. 555–573). New York: Wiley.

Gitlin, T. (1990). On drugs and mass media in America's consumer society. In H. Resnick, S. E. Gardner, R. P. Lorian, & C. E. Maccus (Eds.), *Youth and drugs: Society's mixed messages* (OSAP Prevention Monograph No. 6, pp. 31–52). Rockville, MD: Office of Substance Abuse Prevention.

Gross, L. S., & Walsh, R. P. (1980). Factors affecting parental control over children's television viewing: A pilot study. *Journal of Broadcasting, 24*, 411–419.

Hawkins, R., & Pingree, S. (1982). Television's influence on social reality. In D. Pearl, L. Bouthilet, & J. Lazar (Eds.), *Television and behavior: Ten years of scientific progress and implications for the eighties, Technical reviews* (pp. 224–247). Rockville, MD: National Institute of Mental Health.

Hoffman, M. L. (1977). Moral internalization: Current theory and research. In L. Berkowitz (Ed.), *Advances in experimental social psychology (Vol. 10, pp. 85–133)*. New York: Academic Press.

Johnston, L. D., O'Malley, P. M., & Bachman, J. G. (1996). *National survey results on drug use from the monitoring the future study, 1975–1995*. Rockville, MD: National Institute on Drug Abuse.

Krcmar, M. (1996). Family communication patterns, discourse behavior, and child television viewing. *Human Communication Research, 23*, 251–277.

Knaus, C., & Austin, E. W. (1999). The AIDS Memorial Quilt as preventative education: A developmental analysis of the Quilt. *AIDS Education and Prevention, 11*, 525–540.

Kuhl, P., Andruski, J. E., Chistovich, I. A., & Chistovich, L. A., E. V. Kozhevnikova, V. L. Ryskina, E. I. Stolyarova, U. Sundberg, & F. Lacerda (1997). Cross-language analysis of phonetic units in language addressed to infants. *Science, 277*, 684–686.

Lyle, J., & Hoffman, H. R. (1972). Children's use of television and other media. In E. A. Rubinstein, G. A. Comstock, & J. P. Murray (Ed.), *Television and social behavior: Vol. 4. Television in day-to-day life: Patterns of use,* (pp. 129–256). Washington, DC: U.S. Government Printing Office.

Malcuit, G., Bastien, C., & Pomerleau, A. (1996). Habituation of the orienting response to stimuli of different functional values in 4-month-old infants. *Journal of Experimental Child Psychology, 62*, 272–291.

McLeod, J. M., & Chaffee, S. H. (1972). The construction of social reality. In J. Tedeschi (Ed.), *The social influence process* (pp. 50–59). Chicago: Aldine-Atherton.

Medrich, E. A. (1979, Summer). Constant television: A background to daily life. *Journal of Communication, 29*, 171–176.

Messaris, P. (1982). Parents, children, and television. In G. Gumpert & R. Cathcart (Eds.), *Inter/Media* (2nd ed., pp. 580–598). New York: Oxford University Press.

Messaris, P., & Kerr, D. (1983). Mothers' comments about TV: Relation to family communication patterns. *Communication Research, 10*, 175–194.

Meyrowitz, J. (1985). *No sense of place: The impact of electronic media on social behavior*. New York: Oxford University Press.

Moore, D. W. (1997, March). Parents give mixed reviews to new TV ratings system. *The Gallup Poll Monthly, 378*, 18–19.

O'Keefe, G. J., & Reid-Nash, K. (1987). Socializing functions. In C. R. Berger & S. H. Chaffee (Eds.), *Handbook of communication science* (pp. 419–445). Newbury Park, CA: Sage.

Reeves, B. (1978). Perceived reality as a predictor of children's social behavior. *Journalism Quarterly, 55*, 682–689, 695.

Roberts, D. C. (1981). Children's and parents' television viewing and perception of violence. *Journalism Quarterly, 58*, 556–564.

Roberts, D. F. (1989). The impact of media portrayals of risky driving on adolescents: Some speculations. *Alcohol, Drugs and Driving, 4*, 149–156.

Robertson, T. (1979, Winter). Parental mediation of television advertising effects. *Journal of Communication, 29*, 12–26.

Rosengren, K. E., & Windahl, S. (1972). Mass media as a functional alternative. In D. McQuail (Ed.), *Sociology of mass communications* (pp. 166–194). Middlesex, England: Penguin.

Sostek, A., & Brackbill, Y. (1976). Stability of motor OR and heart rate habituation rates of infancy. *Developmental Psychology, 9*, 353–358.

Valkenburg, P. M., Krcmar, M., Peeters, A. L., & Marseille, N. M. (1999). Developing a scale to assess three styles of television mediation: "Instructive mediation," "restrictive mediation," and "social coviewing." *Journal of Broadcasting & Electronic Media, 43*, 52–66.

van der Voort, T. H. A. (1986). *Television violence: A child's eye view.* Amsterdam: North-North-Holland.

van der Voort, T. H. A., Nikken, P., & van Lil, J. E. (1992). Determinants of parental guidance of children's television viewing: A Dutch replication study. *Journal of Broadcasting & Electronic Media, 36*, 61–74.

Wallack, L., Cassady, D., & Grube, J. (1990). *TV beer commercials and children: Exposure, attention, beliefs and expectations about drinking as an adult.* Washington, DC: AAA Foundation for Traffic Safety.

Wik, L. (1985). *Baby's first words.* New York: Random House.

Wright, J. C., St. Peters, M., & Huston, A. C. (1990). Family television use and its relation to children's cognitive skills and social behavior. In J. Bryant (Ed.), *Television and the American family* (pp. 227–251). Hillsdale, NJ: Lawrence Erlbaum Associates.

Mediating Advertising Effects

David M. Boush
University of Oregon

At 7:00 p.m. on a Thursday, two teenagers and a 7-year-old watch *The Simpsons* in the family room. Upstairs, their parents watch *CNN Headline News* in their bedroom. During the next 30 minutes, they will each see about 17 television commercials. If they are average in viewing behavior, they will see over 120 television commercials that day, and 40,000 that year (Comstock & Paik 1991). How will these television advertisements affect them, as a family, and as developing young family members? How will characteristics of their family, of the way family members interact, and of the way they think as individuals affect the way advertising persuades? How will the advertisements influence what they buy? Answers to these questions are far from complete, and to a large extent, are subject to constant change along with the culture in which they are embedded. However, a substantial body of research has accumulated over the past 25 years that helps us at least start to understand the relationship between television advertising and the family. The purpose of this chapter is to summarize what we know and then to suggest some of what we need to find out about this relationship.

At least since the 1960s, parents and public policymakers have expressed the fear that television advertising can have detrimental effects, particularly on children. Potential effects include; (a) long-term cumulative exposure to advertising leading to harmful attitudes and behavior developing over time, (b) inadequate cognitive defenses leading to advertising deception, (c) undesirable child–parent interaction, leading to conflict, and (d) the purchase of undesirable products, especially candy and junk food (Adler et al., 1980). Perhaps the most extreme vision of advertising would be that television commercials flow unfiltered into viewers' heads resulting directly in the purchase of bad products. However, the effects of television advertising on the family are not simple and direct. Advertising effects are mediated and moderated[1] by a host of variables. Effects on the brand knowledge, attitudes, and behavior of children and adolescents are mediated by a filter of skepticism that can be nurtured by parents, peers, and exposure to the media themselves. The effects of television advertising on family decisions are mediated by the roles and influence strategies that different family members adopt. These, in turn, are influenced by product class and stage of the purchase process. Demographic characteristics of the family, such as socioeconomic status and presence of both parents in the household may moderate those relationships.

Three different, but related, models are implicated in the question of mediating advertising effects on families. The first is a model of the way television commercials are processed as information. The second is a model of socialization, or how children within a family develop into knowledgeable consumers with appropriate defenses against advertising techniques. The third is a model of family decision making, or how family members interact when buying household items or trying to influence other household members to buy things. We examine each of these models in turn and show how they build on each other.

HOW TELEVISION ADVERTISING INFORMATION IS PROCESSED

The processing of a television commercial may be usefully considered as a series of stages; exposure, attention, interpretation, and memory (Hawkins, Best, & Coney, 1995). Because the stages by which a commercial is processed are sequential, each mediates the final effect. As the first stage, exposure is perhaps the most predictable. Advertisers care-

---

[1] Baron and Kenny (1986) noted several important distinctions between mediator and moderator variables in social-psychological research. Mediators play a causal role in the relationship between the independent and dependent variables (e.g., between exposure to advertising and persuasion). Moderators, in contrast, influence the degree or direction of the relationship but are not responsible for causing it. Treatment throughout this chapter attempts to reflect the language of the original studies.

fully match their target markets to television audience profiles. The probability of exposure to television commercials goes up on average with television viewing time, and exposure to a particular television commercial depends on the nature of associated programming. As stated earlier, the number of television advertising exposures per year numbers in the tens of thousands, making the medium so cluttered that most ads are ignored. Television and direct mail are rated by viewers as the media highest in perceived clutter (Elliott, Speck, & Surgi, 1998) and the situation is getting progressively worse (Teinowitz, 1999). Advertising clutter has also increased with the number of commercials lasting 15 seconds rather than 30 seconds. The communication environment for television is even more competitive if you consider the total number of commercial exposures from all media.

Attention is the strongest mediator of advertising effects or, stated somewhat differently, selective attention is considered by advertisers to be their greatest challenge (O'Guin, Allen, & Semenik, 1998). Television is an intrusive medium by virtue of the combination of sight, sound, and motion so it is more likely to be noticed than other advertising media. Attention to particular commercials is influenced by the personal relevance of the message to the viewer, which is, in turn, influenced by their needs and goals (MacInnis & Jaworski, 1989). Attention to particular parts of a commercial also can be influenced by various television production tactics (MacKenzie, 1986). It is important to note that viewers tend to keep watching and listening to the same stimulus unless interrupted, a phenomenon known as attentional inertia (Anderson, Alwitt, Lorch, & Levin, 1979). Attentional inertia is useful because it helps children get through the less interesting parts of a program. However, inertia implies that television viewers continue attending from program to commercial, even if the commercial is irrelevant to their goals.

Interpretation is the process by which television commercials are comprehended and then integrated with the viewer's previous knowledge. Greenwald (1968) first noted that a critical element in the processing of advertisements was the mental response that is evoked when ads are viewed. These cognitive responses have since been classified in various ways, notably as support arguments, counterarguments, source derogations, and curiosity (Wright, 1973). Advertisements also evoke feelings such as anger, sadness, and elation (Batra & Ray, 1986). An important aspect of cognitive response categories is that they are mutually exclusive at any single moment. For example, it is extremely difficult for a viewer to generate support and counterarguments at the same time.

The viewers' responses to advertising result in the formation of attitudes toward the product, brand, and even the ad itself. Attitude toward the ad has been shown to mediate attitude toward the advertised brand

(MacKenzie, Lutz, & Belch, 1986). In cases where an attitude already exists, the advertisement may either strengthen or change it. Research on advertising persuasion was for decades dominated by the message learning approach (Hovland & Janis, 1959), focusing on the question "who said what to whom with what effect?" Specifically, the preceding question addresses aspects such as source credibility, message complexity, and viewer persuasibility (McGuire, 1968). A more recent approach posits that advertising essentially takes two routes to persuasion (Petty & Cacioppo, 1986). One route occurs when viewers are highly involved with the message; that is, motivated and able to think carefully about a commercial. When that happens, they elaborate on the message and change their beliefs in a lasting way. Persuasion takes a different route when viewers care less about the message. In that case, attitude change depends on peripheral cues like pretty music or attractive models, and tends to be less enduring. Note that this elaboration likelihood model (ELM) relates interpretation to memory. Associations with existing knowledge make commercials more memorable, and memory for television commercials is generally aided by the associations across modalities of sight and sound.

The persuasion knowledge model (PKM) views television advertising and other persuasion attempts as an active strategic interaction between viewer and advertiser (Friestad & Wright, 1994). Viewers, as targets of an advertiser's attempt to persuade them to buy a product, are equipped with personal knowledge about the product, the advertiser as persuasive agent, and the way persuasion works. Advertisers, as persuasive agents, similarly have knowledge about the product, the viewers, and the way they think persuasion works. According to the PKM, advertisers select strategies to persuade viewers, and viewers select strategies to cope with those attempts. Coping does not necessarily, or even typically, entail resistance. It simply means that the viewer tries to control the interaction and achieve whatever goals are salient. The PKM therefore focuses on viewer knowledge about advertisers and persuasion itself as key mediators of its effects. As we discuss later, such a model seems potentially fruitful for studying television advertising and the family.

Many of the issues raised about television advertising's impact can be mapped directly on to stages of processing. The next section looks at how people develop processing skills.

ACQUISITION OF PROCESSING SKILLS

Television advertising's influence on the family has most often been studied in the context of consumer socialization—the process by which viewers, especially young people, acquire skills, knowledge, and attitudes relevant to their effective functioning as consumers in the marketplace

(Moschis, 1987). This perspective emphasizes developmental limitations in processing ability (Piaget, 1963), consistent with concerns that deceptive advertising is particularly problematic for children. Although the process is lifelong, it can be usefully subdivided according to developmental categories such as childhood, adolescence, and adulthood. Most research has employed the individual family member as the principal unit of analysis. The most common dependent measures are knowledge, attitudes, and behavior concerning products and brands. Predictor variables include the extent of television viewing and the viewer's age. The research in this area has also examined family characteristics, such as communication patterns, as mediating variables.

Children and Adolescents

Among the first issues raised regarding advertising effects on families concerned the way children were influenced by television advertising. Television represented an unprecedented potential for intrusion and young viewers seemed particularly vulnerable. Consumer advocacy groups such as Action for Children's Television (ACT) and the Council on Children, Media, and Merchandising, generally viewed children as victims and television advertisers as seducers (Young, 1990). Many of the concerns with television advertising and the research in response to those concerns can be mapped onto the information processing stages discussed earlier. In general, television advertising effects are greater for younger children, especially heavy viewers, and for those who lack the influence of an educated parent or knowledgeable peer (Robertson & Rossiter, 1977).

Exposure.   The first line of defense for families who are concerned about advertising to their children is to limit exposure. Advertisers trying to maximize efficiency of exposure to children created the Saturday morning cartoon time slot, a particular concern because content analyses show that much of the advertising during that time is for high sugar breakfast and snack foods (Barcus & McLaughlin, 1978). Effects of increased exposure to advertising have been difficult to document, however. In Ward, Wackman, and Wartella's (1977) study of 615 mother–child pairs, increased exposure to television advertising neither facilitated nor hindered children's skill development and had only a small impact on consumer learning. It was also reassuring that, despite television's substantial role in providing product and brand information to children, parents remained the major influence.

Attention.   Earlier, the phenomenon of attentional inertia was discussed. One of the faculties that develops during childhood and into adolescence, is the ability to overcome this inertia and focus attention deliberately.

Adolescents are better than children at this but not as good as young adults (Manis, Keating, & Morrison, 1980). Older children tend to pay less attention throughout a commercial than younger children, and older children's attention within a series of commercials also tends to decline toward the end of a block (Ward & Wackman, 1973).

Interpretation. Research shows that even children as young as 5 years old can filter television messages and discriminate persuasive intent from regular programming, especially when taught how by parents (Ward et al., 1977). Less reassuring findings argue that although some kindergarteners can understand the persuasive intent of advertising, many children do not acquire that understanding until age 8 or so. After a number of studies, the preponderance of evidence is that some children may acquire the ability to differentiate advertising from other television programming by the age of 4 and that the ability is universal by age 11 (Young, 1990). When a child attributes persuasive intent to commercials, he believes them less, likes them less, and is less likely to want the advertised products (Robertson & Rossiter, 1974).

Children's comprehension of messages and the resultant categories that they form are at first dominated by perceptual attributes. As they mature, they are increasingly able to see and use more abstract dimensions (John & Sujan, 1990). Between preschool and second grade, for example, children begin to make inferences about people based on the products they buy (Belk, Bahn, & Mayer, 1982). As children move from preschool age to preadolescent, they develop abilities to use more controlled strategies for storing and retrieving information (Roedder, 1981). They increase their ability to accumulate experience and acquire new marketplace information (John & Whitney, 1986). By combining sight and sound, television is well suited to overcome some of the information processing deficits of young children, particularly their inability to spontaneously elaborate on audio information (Peracchio, 1993). Macklin (1994) found that preschool children were able to recall product-related information only when the audio presentation of information was combined with appropriate visuals.

Increased knowledge of advertising may not be accessed when actually viewing a commercial. In a study of responses to television commercials by 9- to 10-year-old children, Brucks, Armstrong, and Goldberg (1988) found that knowledge of advertising did not result in counterarguments against commercials unless children were prompted in some way to activate that knowledge. Viewing commercials with parents may cue those counterarguments. Moore and Moschis (1980) also found that family discussions of television commercials influenced the development of adolescent ability to distinguish fact from exaggeration.

As children move into and through adolescence, they develop greater sophistication and understanding regarding a great variety of issues, including advertising. For example, they improve in their ability to take a variety of perspectives on the same issue (Selman, 1980) and to make good decisions (Mann, Harmoni, & Power, 1989). Their persuasion knowledge also improves. Boush, Friestad and Rose (1994) conducted a longitudinal study of attitudes toward television advertising and knowledge of television advertiser tactics among middle school students (Grades 6–8) during one school year. Knowledge of tactics was measured as the extent to which respondents understood the intended effects of such things as use of a celebrity spokesperson or product demonstration. Attitudes toward advertising revealed a level of skepticism among sixth graders that was high enough to constitute a ceiling effect. Knowledge of advertiser tactics was quite limited however, but moved in the direction of the adult comparison sample over Grades 6 through 8. Apparently adolescents develop a general, if uninformed, attitude of skepticism that is gradually augmented with more precise schematic persuasive knowledge. Adolescent processing of advertising is limited in other ways as well. Linn, Delucci, and Benedictus (1984) reported that seventh and eighth graders lose track of their own criteria for evaluating products when confronted with advertising claims and become overloaded with information.

Adult viewers comprehend both the message and its commercial nature, and realize that it represents at best a one-sided portrayal of reality. Children first develop an understanding that television advertisements are different from other programs and are therefore not to be trusted. From there, they continue to elaborate organized knowledge about persuasion, and to improve their ability to focus attention, and to actively process the information in commercials. Active, strategic processing of commercials can be facilitated by education directed at acquiring those skills (Ploghoft & Anderson, 1982). The ability to recognize puffery is also better for families with higher socioeconomic status (Moschis & Churchill, 1979) and television advertising has less impact when parents talk with their children about consumption matters (Moschis & Moore, 1982). *How* parents talk about consumption with their children is also important.

Communication Style

The family communication environment is an important influence on the way children develop an understanding of television advertising. This environment can be thought of as having two unrelated dimensions, sociooriented and concept-oriented communication (Carlson & Grossbart, 1988; Rose, Bush, & Kahle 1998). Sociooriented messages from parents are generally aimed at monitoring and controlling children's consumption behavior and at promoting deference to parents. Concept-oriented messages foster the child's autonomy and development of their own skills and competencies as consumers. When parents tell a child that he cannot have a candy bar because parents know best what kids should eat, they are giving a socioriented message. When parents tell a child that advertisers make candy bars look better on television than they look in real life, they are giving a concept-oriented message. Concept orientation is related to coviewing and discussing television commercials, as well as to shopping together and yielding to children's requests. Socioorientation is related to limiting children's television exposure and to refusing requests (Carlson, Grossbart, & Walsh, 1990). Mothers who generally respect and solicit children's opinions also tend to communicate in ways that foster the ability of children to make intelligent consumption decisions (Carlson, Grossbart, & Stuenkel, 1992).

As children move into and through adolescence, their communication patterns regarding consumption shift from the family toward peers (Churchill & Moschis, 1979). Susceptibility to peer influence therefore becomes of increasing interest. Notions of persuasibility and yielding have long been central to attitude change (McGuire, 1968), and have usually been seen as a tendency to conform. Bearden, Netemeyer, and Teel (1989) defined consumer susceptibility to interpersonal influence (CSII) as "a willingness to conform to the expectations of others regarding purchase decisions" (p. 473), which is correlated with low self-esteem (Rosenberg, 1986). CSII has both an informational component, which is a tendency to seek information from others, and a normative dimension, which is a desire to comply with the expectations of others. Bearden and Rose (1990) reported that subjects who attended more closely to social comparison information were more likely to comply with normative consumer influences. Mangleburg and Bristol (1998) found important differences between normative and informational peer influence as it relates to skepticism. Normative peer influence is essentially conformity, and was negatively related to skepticism. On the other hand, susceptibility to informational peer influence could be characterized as openness to expertise. In their study, the information that friends provided to teens seemed to help them develop a critical orientation toward commercials.

Media Use.   The number of hours spent in front of a television set has usually served as the surrogate measure for the number of commercials watched (Moschis, 1987). Seeing more commercials may have conflicting effects, however. On the one hand, television may have the kind of negative impact on attitudes and behavior that were outlined earlier. However, media exposure, including exposure to television, is one of the ways children learn about persuasion tactics. Therefore, television viewing can teach people to be more skeptical and to recognize the complex narrative conventions of persuasion. Mangleburg and Bristol (1998) found that concept-oriented communication, susceptibility to informational peer influence, and the extent of television viewing all increase skepticism of television commercials. Furthermore, they found that marketplace knowledge mediates the effects of all three of those variables on skepticism. Specifically, the kinds of interactions with peers, parents, and the media that increase their marketplace knowledge lead teens to be more skeptical.

In order to be effective, the viewer has to act in some way based on the television commercial. The action may be delayed and almost certainly requires the accumulation of many similar advertising messages. The action may be either to buy the product or to influence someone else to buy the product. In the latter case, family members contribute to a decision at the household level.

FAMILY DECISION MAKING

Understanding the effects of television advertising on household purchasing requires that we first understand something about that process and the roles of different family members in it.

Stages of Household Decision Making

Most studies examining relative influence of family members have divided the stages into initiation (problem recognition), information search, and choice. Children and adolescents have the greatest impact as initiators of purchase decisions (Beatty & Talpade, 1994; Foxman, Tansuhaj, & Ekstrom, 1989; Mangleburg, 1990). Product purchase also involves a variety of subdecisions, such as where to buy a product, how much to spend, and what brand, model, or color to buy. Children's influence seems to be lowest in subdecisions involving where to purchase, and how much to spend, however children are more involved in selection of color, make, or model, and brand choice (Belch, Belch, & Ceresino, 1985).

Spouses too, have different amounts of relative influence depending on the purchase category and the stage of the decision. The study of relative influence has always been complicated by the question of direct versus indirect influence. For example, a wife and mother may make what appears to be an autonomous decision to buy a product that she thinks her husband and children prefer. Their influence would then be powerful, but mediated by her beliefs about their needs and perceptions of her role.

Product Type. Different family members take a more or less active role at each stage depending on the nature of the family and of the product under consideration. As might be expected, children have the greatest influence in purchase decisions for products for which they are the primary consumer. These include breakfast cereal, snack food, toys, school supplies, and children's clothing (Mangleburg, 1990). Although several of these product categories dominate Saturday morning television, it is impossible to say whether television advertising increases children's influence or simply reflects their interests. However, one study showed that children who were exposed to television ads made more attempts to influence their parents than those not exposed to ads (Brody, Stoneman, Lane, & Sanders, 1981). Children also have some influence over decisions regarding leisure activities, such as movie attendance and vacation destinations. In contrast, they have little influence over decisions about buying products that the whole family uses, especially durable goods such as furniture and cars (Foxman et al., 1989).

Influence Strategies.   Children ages 3 to 11 are likely to simply ask for a product (Isler, Popper, & Ward, 1987). However, adolescents use a variety of strategies to try and influence parental purchase behavior. Palan and Wilkes (1997) recently developed a typology of influence tactics used by adolescents and of response tactics used by their parents. Based on in-depth interviews with adolescents, mothers, and fathers, their classification included three principal categories beyond that of making a simple request. *Bargaining* techniques consisted of reasoning, negotiation, and deal making, such as offers to pay for all or part of the purchase. *Persuasion* techniques included a number of techniques that are unpleasant from the parent's perspective, such as whining, begging, and manipulation. *Emotional* techniques consisted of things like anger, pouting, and humor. Parents and children agreed that the more adultlike techniques such as negotiation were most effective for adolescents, whereas begging and whining were least effective.

SUMMARY

The stages by which television commercials are processed as information mediate advertising effects. Cognitive defenses are implicated at each phase, and are affected by socialization and development. Children acquire some cognitive defenses at a very young age. By early adolescence, they evidence a high level of general skepticism about commercials but lack the kind of knowledge about persuasion that adults have. As they move though adolescence, they continue to improve their understanding about what advertisers are trying to do and how. They also continue to improve their ability to deliberately focus attention, so they can break away from television advertising more easily. However, adolescents may not actually evoke very sophisticated cognitive defenses even if they have the potential to do so. One of the ways that children develop knowledge about persuasion is by exposure to media, so television advertising has the potential to teach skepticism. Parents, peers, and teachers can accelerate the development of this kind of knowledge, and of the ability to counterargue. Parental communication style has been identified as an important mediator of the way children and adolescents develop these skills. A parental style that promotes the child's autonomy leads to better understandings of persuasion than one that emphasizes control. Communication with peers and parents generally promotes an informed skepticism about advertising claims.

It is not clear whether television advertising significantly increases parent–child conflict. However, television seems to have the potential for increasing the child's influence over the purchase decision. This influence occurs largely through the child's role as initiator of a purchase, especially something the child consumes as an individual, such as a toy, cereal, or snack food. Children and their parents use a variety of influence tactics on each other, and children are most effective when these tactics resemble those their parents use.

FUTURE RESEARCH

A number of weaknesses in past research have been suggested, including inadequate measurement and sampling (Mangleburg, 1990) and the lack of underlying theory (Young, 1990). The three streams of research described to this point suggest that advertising effects are mediated by information processing stages, the development of persuasion knowledge skills, and characteristics of the family decision process. Future studies may continue both to tackle those areas separately and to integrate them. Future research also needs to take a longitudinal perspective to discover the effects of repeated advertising exposure over time. Particularly fruitful areas of research are to be found by applying the persuasion knowledge model, which broadens the scope of persuasive interaction, and by taking a broader view of the meaning of family.

Acquisition and Use of Persuasion Knowledge

One area of research that is needed concerns the complex belief structures that people develop about how persuasion works. The persuasion knowledge model, described earlier, suggests that both advertisers and viewers have complex beliefs about each other and about persuasion. The development of those beliefs has not been fully explored. Past research usually has inferred advertiser knowledge from behavior. Presumably television advertisers think that attractive young people are useful for getting attention, for example. What do advertisers believe about families in America? Particularly, how do they think families interact in response to their influence attempts?

One might also envision research into how family members use the tactics of television advertisers to influence family decisions. A point of inflection occurs when the viewer of a commercial attempts to influence a family decision. The viewer changes from persuasion target to persuasion agent, a shift in roles that would be interesting to explore. Do viewers replicate some of the tactics used by the advertiser? Perhaps the tactics used depend on the nature of the ad. Informative commercials give viewers arguments to use. However, the viewer as persuasive agent would likely take into consideration the characteristics of the family members who are persuasive targets. It is also possible that persuasive tactics differ according to product type, stage of the decision process, and characteristics of the family structure itself. Patterns of persuasive family interaction may be identifiable, making it possible to develop measures at the family level. Given that virtually all prior research in persuasion uses the individual as the unit of analysis, measures using the family as the unit of analysis would have great potential for enriching this literature.

Effects of Alternative Family Structure

Nearly all the studies to date on effects and interactions among family members have involved a traditional two-parent family (Rindfleisch, Burroughs, & Denton, 1997). In one of the few exceptions, Ahuja and Stinson (1993) replicated many of the effects described for two-parent households using a sample of female single-parent families. Children's influence varied according to the product type, stage of household decision, and mother's education and income. The children's influence increased with the age of the oldest child but perhaps surprisingly, decreased with the mother's level of education and sex role autonomy. It seemed that more confident mothers shouldered more of the decision-making responsibility.

Given the dramatic changes in family structure over the past 30 years, the dearth of research on the consumer behavior of alternative families leaves us with a very incomplete picture. Cherlin (1992) estimated that more than half of today's children will spend some time growing up in a single-parent family. This has direct implications for a variety of family characteristics. Single-parent families have access to substantially fewer economic resources than traditional families, which is reflected in household expenditures of only about half those for two-parent families (Wilkes, 1995). Approximately 90 % of single-parent households are headed by the mother, who also frequently has severe demands placed on her time.

Children in single-parent families are reported to have less parental supervision, emotional support, practical help, role modeling and guidance than children in two-parent families (Cherlin,1992; McLanahan & Booth, 1989).

We can speculate on what some of these changes might mean. Single-parent families may have less time available for teaching the kind of processing skills that enable children to filter commercial messages. If the television is used more as a babysitter, the children may spend more time watching television. A lack of skepticism may be combined with more influence on purchase decisions. Older children, especially girls, may have an increased role in a variety of household purchases.

CONCLUSION

Returning to the family with which this chapter began, we can describe a few of the most prominent variables mediating the effect of a particular commercial. When a commercial for a snack food that "tastes like real fruit" interrupts *The Simpsons,* the 7-year-old is more likely than the teenagers to keep watching, but it depends on the skill of the advertiser and both the motivation and ability of the children. The commercial may induce some mental counterargument, especially from the teenagers, but it depends on their level of involvement and their beliefs about advertisers. If the younger child expresses desire for the product, he may be told that it only looks good to eat on television, but that depends on how much the siblings have developed knowledge of advertiser tactics and on whether they are more concept oriented than sociooriented in communication style. (Such development depends in part on how much the parents have watched television with them in the past.) If more sociooriented, the teenagers may just say that the parents won't let him have it. Depending on the use of visual cues in the commercial and how many times he has seen it before, the child may recognize the product when he gets to the store. He may persuade his mother to buy it, depending on the development of his influence tactics. If he just whines, the effect will probably be conflict.

The effects of any particular commercial, and of television advertising more generally, are mediated by a long string of contingencies. Although much has been learned about the way individuals cope with commercials, much of that must be constantly reinterpreted as the American family changes.

REFERENCES

Adler, R. P., Lesser, G. S., Meringoff, L. K., Robertson, T. S., Rossiter, J. R., & Ward, S. (1980). *The effects of television advertising on children: Review and recommendations.* Lexington, MA: Lexington Books.

Ahuja, R. D., & Stinson, K. N. (1993). Female-headed single parent families: An exploratory study of children's influence in family decision making. *Advances in Consumer research, 20*, 469–474.

Anderson, D. R., Alwitt, L. F., Lorch, E. P., & Levin, S. R. (1979). Preschool children's visual attention to attributes of television. *Human Communication Research, 7*, 52–67.

Baron, R. M., & Kenny, D. A. (1986, December). The moderator–mediator variable distinction in social-psychological research: Conceptual, strategic, and statistical considerations. *Journal of Personality and Social Psychology, 51*, 1173–1182.

Barcus, F. E., & McLaughlin, L. (1978). *Food advertising on children's television: An analysis of appeals and nutritional content.* Newtonville, MA: Action on Children's Television.

Batra, R., & Ray, M. (1986, September). Affective responses mediating acceptance of advertising. *Journal of Consumer Research, 13*, 234–249.

Beatty, S. E., & Talpade, S. (1994, September). Adolescent influence in family decision making: A replication with extension. *Journal of Consumer Research, 21*, 332–341.

Bearden, W. O., Netemeyer, R. G., & Teel, J. E. (1989, June). Measurement of consumer susceptibility to interpersonal influence. *Journal of Consumer Research, 15*, 473–481.

Bearden, W. O., & Rose, R. L. (1990, March). Attention to social comparison information: An individual difference factor affecting consumer conformity. *Journal of Consumer Research, 16*, 461–471.

Belch, G. E., Belch, M. A., & Ceresino, G. (1985). Parental and teenage child influences in family decision making. *Journal of Business Research, 13*, 163–176.

Belk, R. W., Bahn, K. D., & Mayer, R. (1982). Developmental recognition of consumption symbolism. *Journal of Consumer Research, 9*, 4–17.

Boush, D. M., Friestad, M., & Rose, G. M. (1994, June). Adolescent skepticism toward V advertising and knowledge of advertiser tactics. *Journal of Consumer Research, 21*, 165–175.

Brody, G. H., Stoneman, Z., Lane, S., & Sanders, A. K. (1981). Television food commercials aimed at children, family grocery shopping and mother–child interactions. *Family Relations, 30*, 435–439.

Brucks, M., Armstrong, G. M., & Goldberg, M. E. (1988, March). Children's use of cognitive defenses against television advertising: A cognitive response approach. *Journal of Consumer Research, 14*, 471–482.

Carlson, L., & Grossbart, S. (1988, June). Parental style and consumer socialization of children. *Journal of Consumer Research, 15*, 77–94.

Carlson, L., Grossbart, S., & Stuenkel, K. J. (1992). The role of parental socialization types on differential family communication patterns regarding consumption. *Journal of Consumer Psychology, 1* (1), 31–52.

Carlson, L., Grossbart, S., & Walsh, A. (1990). Mothers' communication orientation and consumer-socialization tendencies. *Journal of Advertising, 19* (3), 27–38.

Cherlin, A. (1992). *Marriage, divorce, remarriage.* Cambridge, MA: Harvard University Press.

Churchill, G. A., Jr. & Moschis, G. P. (1979, June). Television and interpersonal influences on adolescent consumer learning. *Journal of Consumer Research, 6* 23–35.

Comstock, G., & Paik, H. (1991). *Television and the American child.* San Diego, CA: Academic Press.

Elliott, M., Speck, T., & Surgi, P. (1998). Consumer perceptions of advertising clutter and its impact across various media. *Journal of Advertising Research, 38* (1), 29–41.

Foxman, E. R., Tansuhaj, P. S., & Ekstrom, K. M. (1989, March). Family members' perceptions of adolescents' influence in family decision-making. *Journal of Consumer Research, 15*, 482–491.

Friestad, M., & Wright, P. (1994, June). The persuasion knowledge model: How people cope with persuasion attempts, *Journal of Consumer Research, 21*, 1–31.

Greenwald, A. G. (1968). Cognitive learning, cognitive response to persuasion, and attitude change. In A. G. Greenwald, T.C. Brock, & T.M. Ostrom (Eds.), *Psychological foundations of attitudes* (pp. 147–170). New York: Academic Press.

Hawkins, D. I., Best, R. J., & Coney, K. A. (1995). Consumer behavior: Implications for marketing strategy (6th ed.). Chicago: Irwin.

Hovland, C., & Janis, I. L. (1959). *Personality and persuasibility.* New Haven: Yale University Press.

Isler, L., Popper, E. T., & Ward, S. (1987, October–November). Children's purchase requests and parental responses. *Journal of Advertising Research, 27*, 28–39.

John, D.R., & Sujan, M. (1990, March). Age differences in product categorization. *Journal of Consumer Research, 16*, 452–460.

John, D. R., & Whitney, J. C., Jr. (1986, March). The development of consumer knowledge in children: A cognitive structure approach. *Journal of Consumer Research, 12*, 406–417.

Linn, M. C., Delucci, K. L., & Benedictus, T. (1984, Winter). Adolescent reasoning about advertisements: Relevance of product claims. *Journal of Early Adolescence, 4*, 371–385.

MacInnis, D. J., & Jaworski, B. J. (1989, October). Information processing from advertisements: Toward an integrative framework. *Journal of Marketing, 53*, 1–23.

MacKenzie, S. B. (1986, September). The role of attention in mediating the effect of advertising on attribute importance. *Journal of Consumer Research, 13*, 174–195.

MacKenzie, S. B., Lutz, R. J., & Belch, G. E. (1986, May). The role of attitude toward the ad as a mediator of advertising effectiveness: A test of competing explanations. *Journal of Marketing Research, 23*, 130–143.

Macklin, M. C. (1994). The impact of audiovisual information on children's product-related recall. *Journal of Consumer Research, 21*(1), 154–164.

Mangleburg, T. F. (1990). Children's influence in purchase decisions: A review and critique. *Advances in Consumer Research, 17*, 813–825.

Mangleburg, T. F., & Bristol, T. (1998). Socialization and adolescents' skepticism toward advertising. *Journal of Advertising, 27*(3), 11–20.

Manis, F. R., Keating, D. P., & Morrison, F. J. (1980). Developmental differences in the allocation of processing capacity. *Journal of Experimental Child Psychology, 29*, 156–169.

Mann, L., Harmoni, R., & Power, C. N. (1989, September). Adolescent decision making: The development of competence. *Journal of Adolescence, 12*, 265–278.

McGuire, W. J. (1968). Personality and susceptibility to social influence. In E. F. Borgatta & W. W. Lambert (Eds.), *Handbook of personality theory and research* (pp. 1130–1187). Chicago: Rand McNally.

McLanahan, S. S., & Booth, K. (1989, August). Mother-only families: Problems, prospects, and politics. *Journal of Marriage and the Family, 51*, 557–580.

Moore, R. L., & Moschis, G. P. (1980). Social interaction and social structural determinants in adolescent consumer socialization. *Advances in Consumer Research, 7*, 757–759.

Moschis, G. P. (1987). *Consumer socialization: A life-cycle perspective.* Lexington, MA: Heath.

Moschis, G. P., & Churchill, G. A., Jr. (1979, Summer). An analysis of the young consumer. *Journal of Marketing, 43*, 43–48.

Moschis, G. P., & Moore, R. L. (1982, December). A longitudinal study of televison advertising effects. *Journal of Consumer Research, 9,* 279–286.

O'Guin, T. C., Allen, C. T., & Semenik, R. (1998). *Advertising.* Cincinnati: Southwestern Publishing.

Palan, K. M., & Wilkes, R. E. (1997, September). Adolescent–parent interaction in family decision-making. *Journal of Consumer Research, 24*, 159–169.

Peracchio, L. A. (1993). Young children's processing of a televised narrative: Is a picture really worth a thousand words? *Journal of Consumer Research, 20*(2), 281–293.

Petty, R. E., & Cacioppo, J. T. (1986). The elaboration likelihood model of persuasion. In E. L. Berkowitz (Ed.), *Advances in experimental social psychology* (Vol. 19, pp. 123–205). New York: Academic Press.

Piaget, J. (1963). *The origins of intelligence in children.* New York: Newton.

Ploghoft, M. E., & Anderson, J. A. (1982). *Teaching critical television viewing skills: An integrated approach.* Springfield, IL: Thomas.

Rindfleisch, A., Burroughs, J. E., & Denton, F. (1997, March). Family structure, materialism, and compulsive consumption. *Journal of Consumer Research, 23,* 312–325.

Robertson, T. S., & Rossiter, J. R. (1974, June). Children and commercial persuasion: An attribution theory analysis. *Journal of Consumer Research, 1,* 13–20.

Robertson, T. S., & Rossiter, J. R. (1977). Children's responsiveness to commercials. *Journal of Communication, 27*(1), 101–106.

Roedder, D. L. (1981, September). Age differences in children's responses to television advertising: An information processing approach. *Journal of Consumer Research, 8,* 144–153.

Rose, G., Bush, V. D., & Kahle, L. (1998). The influence of family communications on parental reactions toward advertising: A cross-national examination. *Journal of Advertising, 27*(4), 71–88.

Rosenberg, M. (1986). Self-concept from middle childhood through adolescence. In J. Suis & A. G. Greenwald (Eds.), *Psychological perspectives on the self* (pp. 101–135). Hillsdale, NJ: Lawrence Erlbaum Associates.

Selman, R. L. (1980). *The growth of interpersonal understanding.* New York: Academic Press.

Teinowitz, I. (1999, April 12). Net prime-time clutter worsens. *Advertising Age, 70* (16), p. 36.

Ward, S, & Wackman, D. (1973). Children's information processing of television advertising. In P. Clark (Ed.), *New models for communication research* (pp. 119–146) Beverly Hills, CA: Sage.

Ward, S., Wackman, D., & Wartella, E. (1977). *How children learn to buy: The development of consumer information processing skills.* Beverly Hills, CA: Sage.

Wilkes, R. E. (1995). Redefining family in America: Characteristics and expenditures of single-parent families. In D. Stewart & N. Vilcossin, *Marketing theory and application* (Vol. 6, pp. 270–276). Chicago American Marketing Association.

Wright, P. (1973, February). The cognitive responses mediating the acceptance of advertising. *Journal of Marketing Research, 10,* 53–62.

Young, B. (1990). *Television advertising and children.* Oxford, England: Clarendon.

VII

Public Policy Issues

Curriculum-Based Preschool Television Programming and the American Family: Historical Development, Impact of Public Policy, and Social and Educational Effects

J. Alison Bryant
University of Southern California

James F. McCollum
Lipscomb University

Jennings Bryant
Lisa Mullikin
University of Alabama

Curtis C. Love
University of Nevada-Las Vegas

The American family has changed dramatically since the 1940s (see Andreasen, chap. 1, this volume). In the 1940s and 1950s, a stay-at-home mom and an on-the-job dad typified the internal structure of the family. The external structure was grounded in a close-knit community in which neighbors looked after each other's kids, and grandma and grandpa often lived nearby and served as supplementary caregivers. During the 1960s, these dominant community and family patterns began to change, and by the 1970s, a major internal and external restructuring of the prototypical American family had taken place. In many instances, close-knit communities had been replaced by urban or suburban anonymity. Moreover, volatile job markets and shifting societal norms and expectations for success and well-being influenced families to move away from their roots, creating a U-Haul generation. By the mid-1980s, half of all U.S. marriages were ending in divorce, contributing to a substantial increase in the

415

number of single mothers in the workforce. In addition, the rampant consumerism of this decade created a perceived need in dual-parent households for both parents to be gainfully employed. If the parents were not at home, younger children typically were in day care, and professional child-care providers became one of the fastest growing occupational categories of the recent era.

These social, economic, and demographic changes deeply affected the experience of childhood and the shape of contemporary society. No longer were extended families and neighbors the only—or even the primary—sources of the preschool education and socialization of America's children. In addition to external child-care providers, a "new community" emerged to fill the void in family caregiving—the families, friends, and neighbors portrayed on children's television.

As the role of television in the preschooler's life expanded from entertainer to educator and pseudocaregiver, a critical need developed for television programs that would be consciously and conscientiously designed to teach many of the essential lessons required for successful child development. Fortunately, a handful of tele-educators rose to the occasion.

The first program to accept the challenge to creatively and successfully combine education and socialization with entertainment was the venerable *Sesame Street* (e.g., Fisch & Truglio, 2000). Offering a genuine revolution in children's television, *Sesame Street* combined the talents, expertise, and wisdom of child-development specialists, television producers, and in-house researchers. This team created, piloted, evaluated, refined, and then widely disseminated episodes of this innovative program, which was designed to help children navigate the complex pathways of childhood and emerge from their preschool experience ready to learn in the formal educational environment. In addition to addressing these educational and prosocial goals, the myriad successes of *Sesame Street* precipitated a new genre of television programming; curriculum-based preschool television.

CURRICULUM-BASED PRESCHOOL TELEVISION: HISTORICAL DEVELOPMENT AND THE IMPACT OF PUBLIC POLICY

Sesame Street turned 30 years old in 1999, and during the 30+ years of its continuing evolution, the landscape of curriculum-based preschool programming changed dramatically. To place this important transition in perspective, we provide a brief history of children's television prior to *Sesame Street*. Then we focus more specifically on the evolution of curriculum-based preschool programming and its impact on the American family.

The 1940s, 1950s, and 1960s were tumultuous times for children's television programming. In the early years, children's programming was used as a market development tool. Many early promotional efforts of television set manufacturers emphasized what television could do for the youngsters, and high quality programs for children were aired during prime time (Lesser, 1977). As television penetration increased, the perceived importance and, concomitantly, the status of children's programs declined. In the early 1960s, family programs, which had greater audience potential, moved into the prime-time slots, and children's programs were moved to afternoon time periods. Soon after their move to the afternoon, a new wave of programs targeted to the American housewife (e.g., soap operas and game shows) once again displaced children's programs. This time children's programs were amassed in a time slot ideal for advertisers looking to direct their efforts—Saturday morning.

Moving the majority of children's programming to the weekend might have been acceptable for school-age children, who spent the majority of their day at school, but what about preschoolers? With few exceptions, a void existed in terms of preschool programming. *Mister Rogers' Neighborhood*, a feel-good safe-haven for preschoolers, was produced by WQED-Pittsburgh, but at the time it was not aired nationally. In fact, the only nationally airing weekday program for preschoolers during this era was *Captain Kangaroo*, a positive, kid-friendly show on CBS. There was a need for something else, something different.

Enter *Sesame Street*. An early advocate of curriculum-based preschool television programming (Morrisett, 1989) provided a valuable context for the emergence for this breakthrough program:

> I'd like to recall for you the conditions in the late 1960s when *Sesame Street* was born. . . . We had a President who had a belief in education, Lyndon Johnson. We had had the Civil Rights Act, signed in 1964, and there was a generally felt crisis in education. . . . There was a concern about disadvantaged children who were entering school at a loss and falling further and further behind. And there was the realization that this was an extreme handicap, not only to the individual child but to the nation as a whole; we were losing talent, regularly. There was a shortage of preschool teachers and classrooms, and of course, we were in the midst of Viet Nam and the Cold War. (p. 78)

In addition, Congress created the Corporation for Public Broadcasting (CPB) in 1967, with children's programs designated as an important piece of the programming and public service puzzle. These conditions allowed for the creation of the Children's Television Workshop (CTW). With the initiative and guidance of Joan Ganz Cooney, a producer at WNET in New

York, and Lloyd Morrisett, an executive at the Carnegie Foundation, and the financial support of several government agencies and private foundations, CTW was launched in 1968. Its primary mission was to provide an oasis in the underserved area of preschool children's programming.

Sesame Street was the first product of CTW's innovative efforts. *Sesame Street* was formulated as an "edutainment" show. "[CTW] did not want it to be didactic and pedantic; they did not want to put a camera in a classroom" (Truglio, 1999). Therefore, *Sesame Street* combined the forces of academicians and producers to form a curriculum that would be weighted heavily toward cognitive development and a program format that would be catchy. After much formative research, the attention-getting format turned out to be a broadcast magazine, initially featuring segments that were roughly the same length as children's commercials. The educational content was delivered via Muppets and engaging humans who sang and laughed and taught in ways that generally were lots of fun. The formula worked, and *Sesame Street* became a huge success. The 1960s closed with great public hope for the potential of educational television.

In the 1970s, a public and governmental movement began championing educational programming for children. Much of this programming was supported by federal Equal Education Opportunity funds, private foundations, and government public broadcasting money (Kunkel, 1991). *Sesame Street* was demonstrating anew each season that quality, educational, curriculum-based preschool programming could be produced, would be watched, and could be marketed. Those new programs developed with the government and foundation funding did not target preschoolers, however. It appears that other public broadcasting programmers thought that preschoolers were now taken care of by *Sesame Street* so no additional programming was needed. Commercial broadcasters also continued to ignore the needs of preschoolers.

The prevailing tone of deregulation in the U.S. government in the 1980s allowed commercial networks to discontinue any earlier efforts for educational television (Kunkel, 1991). When the Reagan Administration gained control in 1980, the FCC quickly took on a staunch marketplace competition stance on all issues of regulation. This deregulatory position by the regulatory body deeply hurt the cause of children's educational programming. Commercial broadcasters who had been struggling to keep educational programs on the air quickly abandoned their efforts in favor of more profitable forms of children's programming. Cartoons strongly tied to children's toys proliferated during this decade. These "program-length commercials" were inexpensively acquired by stations, because they were subsidized by the toy companies and meant sizable profits for broadcasters. From the insipid *Smurfs, Rainbow Brite,* and *My Little Pony*, to the brutish *Transformers, He-Man,* and *Thundercats*, television programmers showed little or no interest in edifying children, particularly preschoolers, through television.

The FCC's change of heart and the subsequent drop in educational programming for children did not go unnoticed. Although the social and political climate of the 1980s was not as activist charged as that of the 1970s, segments of the public, particularly those with children, and the press took notice of the shift. By the middle of 1980, 8,000 complaints had been filed by the public about the state of children's programming, and 130 formal comments had been filed about proposed FCC rules (Shaw, 1983).

In 1988, Congress made an attempt to remedy some of the damage done to children's television by passing the Children's Television Act (CTA). The Act limited commercials within children's programming and required the FCC to consider the amount of educational programming provided by the broadcaster when deciding license renewals. But the bill was not in line with President Reagan's deregulatory economics and was killed by a pocket veto.

In contrast to the deregulatory tone of this decade, a positive step for children's programming came in the introduction and rapid popularity of Nickelodeon and The Disney Channel. Both of these cable networks offered programming exclusively for children. Their introduction did not, however, resolve the children's programming issue. First, both were available only in selected markets, so vast areas of the country could not access them. In addition, initially both were available only at an added price to viewers, effectively taking them out of reach of many of the families in need of their programming. Moreover, Nickelodeon was targeting school-age children, not preschool children. And, finally and most importantly, neither network was following the example of *Sesame Street* and programming curriculum-based shows.

Nevertheless, small positive steps were being taken by federal agencies and private foundations to improve the state of children's television programming. For example, the National Endowment for the Humanities offered small grants to both commercial and public television stations to support programs with a strong humanities content (Molotsky, 1982). But in the face of a void in demand for programs by networks, and in competition with the money to be made from noneducational programming, these awards seemingly had little effect. Other private funding was sparse. Even CTW, which had proven itself with *Sesame Street*, struggled to find funding for new ventures in preschool educational programming (Daley, 1984). Apparently, only federal regulation with "teeth" could generate beneficial preschool programming.

Public pressure for Congress to enact the Children's Television Act (CTA) was substantial. A revised version of the Act was developed and promoted. This one renounced the deregulatory stance of the FCC, stating that, in order for there to be adequate educational programming for children, a more hands-on approach must be taken by the Federal Communications Commission (Kunkel, 1998). Moreover, the CTA "mandate[d] that, as a public service condition for license renewal, broadcast television stations provide a minimal amount of educational and informative programming for children" (Anderson, 1998, p. 25). The CTA became law with more than a two-thirds vote on October 17, 1990, very noticeably lacking the signature of President Bush.

With these requirements for children's programming now law, Congress stepped back to let the FCC change the children's television environment; however, Congress promised to keep watch over what happened and assured programmers that they would step in if need be. In 1991, the FCC passed rules to implement the CTA. The rules deeply disappointed children's educational television advocates, parents, and legislators. Although they did deem that program-length commercials were advertisements and limited commercials to 10.5 minutes per hour on weekdays and 12 minutes on weekends, the FCC did not significantly strengthen regulations on educational/informational programming. Instead, the FCC defined educational programming overly broadly as "programming that furthers the positive development of the child in any respect, including the child's cognitive/intellectual and emotional/social needs" (Federal Communications Commission, 1996) and did not establish a minimum amount of educational programming for broadcasters (Farhi, 1991).

Without the FCC bite added to the CTA bark, there was little reason for commercial broadcasters to increase or improve their educational programming—and they did not. Fortunately, this was not the case with public broadcasting and some cable channels. In 1991, PBS responded to the doldrums of children's programming by scheduling *Barney & Friends, Shining Time Station,* and *Lamb Chop's Play-Along. Barney,* in particular, was a huge success, and PBS took steps to add more preschool programming.

Then, in 1992, a major congressional initiative helped change the shape of children's educational programming. In attempting to address the educational needs of preschoolers, Congress passed the Ready-to-Learn (RTL) Act, commissioning the Corporation for Public Broadcasting (CPB) to conduct a study to guide the formation of a national Ready-to-Learn network. Prompted by a report produced by the Carnegie Foundation, the RTL Act was an attempt to remedy the situation in America's kindergartens, where more than half the children entering were not prepared for formal education (Corporation for Public Broadcasting, 1993). According to the report, two factors in preschoolers' everyday lives had affected the decline in readiness to learn; the changing family structure and the increase in poverty. In order to remedy the situation, and with the understanding that the second greatest influence in a preschool child's life is the family television set, the Corporation for Public Broadcasting told Congress that they were up to the challenge of preparing preschoolers throughout the nation to learn. But because cable was still only at a 60% rate of penetration, instead of a *new* network, it was more feasible to use the existing national network, PBS (S. Petroff, personal communication, March 19, 1999).

After 18 months of development, Ready to Learn was launched in July 1994, with 10 PBS affiliate stations participating. The project met with considerable success, and the program grew rapidly. Today, RTL is available to 94% of the nation (S. Petroff, personal communication, March 19, 1999). Funded by the U.S. Department of Education and administered by the Corporation for Public Broadcasting, the goals of the RTL programs are legislated, and each program must have an advisory group of educators and specialists. Sixty percent of the federal money is used for programming, whereas 40% is reserved for outreach to communities.

PBS's Ready to Learn combines 11 hours of educational programming throughout the day with community and parent outreach and resources to address social and emotional development, physical well-being and motor development, approaches to learning, language skills, cognitive skills, and the general knowledge level of 2- to 8-year-olds. In order for a program to be part of RTL, it must have curriculum goals, as well as a formative and summative research plan, either in- or out-of-house. For several of the programs already on PBS, this meant a change of production strategy. *Barney & Friends*, for example, was not curriculum based when it first aired on PBS. Now, every episode has a lesson, and every season is planned and evaluated with specific goals in mind. PBS works directly with the producers to create pilots and outline curricula. In addition to a curriculum, every program must have a parenting component (J. Chase, personal communication, April 28, 1999; S. Petroff, personal communication, March 19, 1999).

The effect of RTL on public preschool programming was tremendous. The average number of children's programming hours (the vast majority aimed at preschoolers) per public broadcast station per year nearly doubled between 1990 and 1994 (Corporation for Public Broadcasting, n.d.).

During that time, cable programming and delivery companies also introduced significant new preschool programming initiatives. In 1993, Nickelodeon decided to invest $30 million to overhaul its preschool programming, in part because PBS was capturing the younger audience with its revamped programming (Anderson, 1998). Nickelodeon subsequently held a 2-day seminar to discuss this new venture, deciding that any programs that they developed internally would be based on a curriculum. They realized that many preschoolers were watching a lot of television, and that they had a responsibility to make the time spent watching

Nickelodeon positive, educationally, or at least to encourage positive growth and development (M. Williams, personal communication, April 2, 1999). With a new mission in hand, Nickelodeon launched their Nick Jr. programming, a 9:00 a.m. to 2:00 p.m. time block for preschoolers. The programs are shown without commercial interruption, and the advertising is separated from the shows by "Face," a full-screen, transformable, jocular pair of eyes and a mouth that explains to the child what is going on.

> The goal of Nick Jr. is to promote "flexible thinking" in pre-schoolers. Flexible thinking provides the foundation for *adaptive behavior.* . . . [It] depends upon learning that is characterized by openness, authenticity, and a plurality of viewpoints and styles. It requires the ability to examine information independently, critically, from many perspectives, and to be sensitive to the opinions of others and the social context within which learning is taking place. It assumes that the "right answer" is not right for every situation. Feelings, values, and facts are mixed in the social construction of reality by pre-schoolers. (Nick Jr., n.d., sec. III)

The Nick Jr. curriculum emphasizes three skill areas; partnership, problem solving, and information management. Like PBS's commitment to preschool preparation for school (i.e., Ready to Learn), every program on Nick Jr. is designed to fit into this "flexible thinking" framework. When choosing new programming or creating an original show, Nick Jr. looks at the flexible thinking goals of their current lineup and tries to fill in the gaps (M. Williams, personal communication, April 2, 1999). Nickelodeon's first two coproductions, *Allegra's Window* and *Gullah, Gullah Island*, as well as its first in-house production, *Blue's Clues*, introduced curriculum-based programming to cable.

The networks, however, remained antagonists in the eyes of children's programming advocates. A 1994 study by the Center for Media Education (CME), which interviewed 50 producers and network executives, found that most "FCC-friendly" shows programmed by the networks were given lower budgets than were other children's programs, were placed in pre-dawn time slots or during prime sports coverage slots where they were consistently preempted, and were insufficiently promoted (Aufderheide & Montgomery, 1994).

In 1995, 80 groups joined in writing a letter to FCC Chair Reed Hundt, urging him to strengthen the FCC rules on children's television (Center for Media Education, 1995b). The letter was a reaction to the lack of improvement in overall children's programming since the Children's Television

Act. A 1992 study by CME found that many broadcasters were labeling cartoons such as *The Jetsons* and *The Flintstones* as educational. Many children's advocates worried that, unless regulations on what could be considered "educational" were improved, shows that were responding to the Act, such as *Cro* and *Bill Nye the Science Guy*, would vanish. Public opinion was ripe for stronger regulation, with 82% of adults believing that not enough educational children's programming was on commercial broadcast television (Center for Media Education, 1995a).

In 1996, the FCC reacted to the lack of broadcaster initiatives in improving children's educational programming by releasing the "Policies and Rules Concerning Children's Television Programming: Revision of Programming Policies for Television Broadcast Stations" (Federal Communications Commission, 1996). These new guidelines furthered outlined the CTA obligation of broadcasters to serve the "educational and informational needs of children through . . . overall programming" (The Children's Television Act of 1990, sec. 103a). According to the new rules, broadcasters must schedule at least 3 hours of core educational programming during the week.

> Specifically, we proposed to define core educational programming as those programs that meet the following requirements: (1) the program has education as a significant purpose; (2) the educational objective of the program and the target child audience are specified in writing in the children's programming report; (3) the program is aired between the hours of 6:00 a.m. and 11:00 p.m.; (4) the program is regularly scheduled; (5) the program is of a substantial length (e.g., 15 or 30 minutes); and (6) the program is identified as educational children's programming at the time it is aired, and instructions for listing it as educational programming are provided by the licensee to program guides. (Federal Communications Commission, 1996, para. 75)

In the immediate wake of the FCC 3-hour rule, "high quality" programs were not attracting the large audiences that "low quality" shows were (Jordan, 1996). Many felt that that was due to a self-fulfilling prophecy within broadcasting. Broadcasters feared those shows would fail, so they shied away from placing them in prime-time slots. But the intervening years since the FCC's 3-hour rule have proven those fears wrong. As FCC Chair Hundt stated, the FCC ruling "started a feeding frenzy among producers and creators of potentially educational programming" (Davis, 1997, p. 8). These producers are finding varied outlets for their programming.

Considering the entire spectrum of children's programming, basic cable provides 40% of the programs, PBS provides 22%, premium channels provide 19%, small networks (FOX, UPN, WB) provide 17%, and the big three networks only provide 2% (Jordan & Woodward, 1997). Of this programming, approximately 23% is targeted toward preschoolers (Jordan, 1998).

The Annenberg Public Policy Center rated the quality of the preschool programs in 1996. They found 75% to be of high quality, 13% moderate, and 12% low in 1996 (Jordan, 1996).[1] By 1998, 85% of preschool programming was rated as high quality (Jordan, 1998). These numbers may seem more impressive than they are, however, considering that 97% to 99% of the programs on PBS were rated as high quality, leaving much lower percentages for the other exhibitors.

During the closing years of the 1990s, an explosion of high quality, educational (and even curriculum-based) television programs for children, especially preschoolers, has occurred. Two major factors have contributed to this growth; the realization that children are a diverse and economically influential group; and the sheer number of programs available from which children, and parents, can choose (Mifflin, 1999). The former has been demonstrated by Nickelodeon and its preschool time block, Nick Jr. No longer can educational programming be "defined as series aired on public television stations" (Crane, 1980, p. 35).

Cable networks and broadcasters quickly realized that there was a huge market in children's television programs and product spin-offs. Advertisers likewise soon took heed of the success of the Nickelodeon programs. From 1996 to 1999, the amount of advertiser revenue increased "at a double-digit rate annually, and it exceeded $1 billion for the 1998–99 season" (Mifflin, 1999, paragraph 3). This raised the status of educational programming in the eyes of those in charge of the production pocketbooks, in turn raising the children's programming budgets. The success of this all-kids, all-the-time network has spurred several other large media corporations to take the plunge. The Cartoon Network by Time-Warner; Fox Kids Network by Fox; Noggin, a joint venture in educational television by CTW and Nickelodeon; and the Kids Channel by PBS are examples of the very recent boom. The firestorm of new cable channels from golf to gardening is definitely including the youngest viewers.

In addition, the vertical integration of the entertainment corporations has allowed easier access to programming for some of the networks. ABC, for example, is saturated with programming from its owner Disney; WB can program any Warner Brothers cartoons from its vast archive—and

---

[1] The criteria for judging the quality of the programs were, lesson clarity, lesson salience, lesson involvement, and lesson applicability. Each quality was rated on a scale of 0 (*not at all*) to 2 (a *lot*), and a final score was reached by summing the four scores to obtain the "educational strength" of the program.

all at a huge profit margin. This has increased the number of programs available for children and therewith raised the level of competition for viewers. In order to stay on top, the producers and channels must give parents what they want, and they currently seem to want prosocial, non-violent fare.

The media coverage of the Children's Television Act and the 3-hour rule apparently have had an impact on the way the public, especially parents, view children's programming. When given the choice, parents will choose those programs they see as positive, or at least as less negative, for their children. This is especially true of preschool children's parents, who still retain strict control over the remote control. But there is some question as to what parents will accept as educational. Rick Siggelkow, Vice President of Children's Programming for BBC Worldwide Americas, thinks there is a new definition of educational programming.

> People's concept of educational TV has changed. Not many producers look to *Sesame Street* for inspiration. There is a drift toward softer things. But parents are just as happy to get lots of shows that don't model violence and anti-social behavior. If it's prosocial, they think it's educational. (Mifflin, 1999, paragraph 2)

One recent and potentially disturbing trend in educational programming seems to be a shift away from so-called "cognitive content" to socio-emotional content. According to one source, only 3 of the 28 broadcast educational children's programs focus on cognitive/intellectual content (Center for Media Education, 1999). "Given the choice between offering more rigorous curriculum-based programming and softer, more entertaining fare, the networks opt for the latter nearly nine times out of ten" (p. 2). Within broadcast commercial preschool programming, the focus is even more skewed. Of the two programs offered for preschoolers (ABC's *The New Adventures of Winnie the Pooh* and CBS's *Rupert*), neither focus on cognitive content, nor are they curriculum based.

Looking at the overall educational programming picture—including public and commercial broadcasting, as well as basic and premium cable channels—in 1996, preschool programs focused on very diverse lessons. Some were cognitive (17%); others were knowledge oriented; 30% were social in nature; and 19% of the lessons were physical in nature (Jordan, 1996). But these "lessons" are not necessarily curriculum based. The FCC mandates that broadcasters describe how their programs meet "core" programming standards in their children's programming reports, but that is the extent to which they must be accountable on paper for those programs. For other programmers, with the exception of PBS's Ready-to-

Learn block, there is no one to whom they report on the content of their "educational" programs. But as the choices for high-quality preschool programming have increased, this lack of a watchdog seems to have become less of a problem. By 1998, 84.2% of preschool programming had a clear and well-integrated lesson (Jordan, 1998). But according to Susan Petroff (personal communication, March 19, 1999), Chief Program Officer for Children's Programming at RTL, not every show has to be "hard," cognitive content. "Kids need to have their 'popcorn shows' too"; the key is to keep them substantive, and the main objective should be to offer something all day.

The combined forces of cable and public stations have greatly improved those offerings for preschool children over the past decade. Just as PBS's revamped services for preschoolers forced Nickelodeon to reposition its programming for the younger audience, cable entering the market got public broadcasting "off their laurels" (J. Chase, personal communication, April 21, 1999). Nickelodeon was adept at branding its shows; if PBS was to survive, they had to bring in more programs (S. Petroff, personal communication, March 19, 1999). And although the commercial networks have been slow and hesitant in targeting preschoolers with their programming, the recent success of *Blue's Clues* in ratings and in merchandising may yet make them rethink their stance.

"After thirty years, curriculum-based preschool programming is finally beginning to hold its own as a public good *and* a private product. Its current state, however, is neither static nor stable. Instead, it remains a fertile ground for academic research, government debate, and industry initiative" (J. A. Bryant, 1999, p. 35).

THE EDUCATIONAL AND SOCIAL IMPACT OF CURRICULUM-BASED PROGRAMS ON CHILDREN AND FAMILIES

Sesame Street

The vast majority of the research into the impact of curriculum-based programs on children and families has been conducted on CTW's *Sesame Street*. In fact

> *Sesame Street* is the most heavily researched series in the history of television. More than 1,000 studies have examined *Sesame Street* and its power in areas such as literacy, number skills, and promoting prosocial behavior, as well as formal features pertaining to issues such as children's attention. This body of literature has not only contributed to our understanding of children's interaction with *Sesame Street*, but also con-

stitutes a significant portion of the literature on the educational impact of television in general. It is safe to say that, if not for *Sesame Street*, the research literature on children and television would be very different than it is today, as would the shape of educational television itself. (Truglio & Fisch, 2000, p. xvii).

Because of the obtrusiveness of *Sesame Street*, academic scholars seeking to understand various facets of the process and effects of television have conducted a substantial amount of research on the educational and prosocial impact of this program. In this chapter, however, we focus on a relatively small number of large-scale evaluation studies designed to assess the impact of this innovative program in a relatively comprehensive manner.

"Before any production had begun, CTW arranged for the Educational Testing Service (ETS) of Princeton, New Jersey to design and conduct the summative evaluation for the premiere and second seasons of *Sesame Street*" (Mielke, 2000, p. 85). In this landmark project, Ball and Bogatz (1970; Bogatz & Ball, 1971) compared a large sample of *Sesame Street's* preschool viewers with a matched sample of nonviewers on several goal-based topics featured in the series. Cognitive skills (e.g., knowledge of the alphabet, sorting and classification skills) were stressed in the evaluation. Mielke (2000) summarized the most general findings of this research as follows:

- Children 3 to 5 years of age who watched the most learned the most; their "gain scores" increased stepwise upward as viewing went stepwise upward.
- Topics getting more screen time on the show (e.g., letters) were learned better than topics receiving less screen time.
- Children viewing in the informal home setting gained as much as children viewing in school under the supervision of a teacher. (p. 87)

Cook et al. (1975) reanalyzed the data from these pioneering studies, removing what they perceived to be "encouragement to view" dimensions of the design, and they reached more modest conclusions about the impact of the early seasons of *Sesame Street*. A generation of critical-viewing studies has rendered somewhat naïve the perspectives of Cook et al., because scholars now realize that viewing context is inseparable from the uses and effects of educational television. In fact, CTW and other educational television organizations now go to great efforts (e.g., Ready-to-Learn workshops, *Sesame Street Parents* magazine) to actively promote parents to coview with their preschoolers.

Three other major investigations have contributed greatly to our understanding of the impact of *Sesame Street* on the sorts of learning skills that are deemed essential for academic success (cf. Mielke, 2000).

1. Investigators at the Center for Research on the Influences of Television on Children (CRITC) found that viewing *Sesame Street* was positively correlated with subsequent performance in reading, math, vocabulary, and school readiness. When the researchers controlled for a variety of potentially contributing effects (e.g., socioeconomic status, educational quality of the home environment), the positive correlations between academic indicators and *Sesame Street* viewing remained (Wright, Huston, Scantlin, & Kotler, 2000).

2. Zill (2000) analyzed data from a national survey conducted for the U.S. Department of Education and reported significant correlations between viewing of *Sesame Street* and preschoolers' school readiness as measured by alphabet recognition and knowledge and storytelling abilities. Moreover, when these *Sesame Street* viewers entered the first and second grades, they were more likely than their nonviewing peers to read books independently and less likely to require remedial reading instruction.

3. Finally, CRITC and a team from the University of Massachusetts at Amherst "recontacted" high school students whose television viewing as preschoolers had been assessed 10 to 15 years earlier. They found that the high school students who had watched *Sesame Street* frequently as preschoolers had significantly better grades in English, science, and math, and that they read more books and were higher in achievement motivation (Huston, Anderson, Wright, Linebarger, & Schmitt, 2000).

The curriculum goals of *Sesame Street* have evolved rather strikingly over the years (Lesser & Schneider, 2000). Many of these goals—especially in certain seasons—have been more prosocial than cognitive in nature. Mielke (2000) reviewed the studies that assessed the prosocial impact of *Sesame Street* and concluded the following:

> Together, these studies suggest that *Sesame Street* can exert a significant impact on children's social behavior, but the research evidence is not as strong as it is with cognitive effects, nor are there as many studies in the literature. Some studies have found exposure to *Sesame Street* to affect social behavior only in situations comparable to those shown on the series (e.g., Leifer, 1975), while others have also found effects on children's social behavior in other situations (e.g., Zielinksa & Chambers, 1995). (pp. 92–93).

Allegra's Window and Gullah, Gullah Island

As previously discussed, Nick Jr. (Nickelodeon's preschool programming block) entered the realm of curriculum-based preschool programming with the launch of *Allegra's Window* and *Gullah Gullah Island* in the fall of 1994. Investigators at the Institute for Communication Research of the

University of Alabama (in collaboration with the University of Rhode Island and the University of California, Santa Barbara) were charged with leading a major 2-year investigation into the impact of regularly viewing these programs on preschoolers' flexible thinking, problem solving, and prosocial behaviors (e.g., Bryant & Maxwell, 1997).

Employing a national sample and a longitudinal experimental design that featured viewers versus nonviewers and nine waves of assessments (a pretest and eight posttests), the investigators asked parents or other caregivers to report their perceptions of the preschoolers' behaviors relating to the key dependent measures. The preschool children's viewing was assessed regularly via diaries, and the parents also intermittently reported their own perceptions of and attitudes toward various aspects of preschool television. To supplement the caregivers' evaluations, a set of more objective behavioral tests of flexible thinking was administered at the end of 9 months of viewing *Allegra's Window* and *Gullah Gullah Island*.

The results revealed that regular viewers of *Allegra's Window* and *Gullah Gullah Island* performed better than nonviewers on flexible thinking. Moreover, the reported differences between viewers and nonviewers continued to increase throughout the 2-year evaluation period. Some statistically significant improvements in problem solving were observed for viewers when compared to nonviewers, but those findings were much less robust than were those for flexible thinking. Regarding prosocial behaviors, regular viewers of *Allegra's Window* and *Gullah Gullah Island* were evaluated as exhibiting more prosocial behaviors that nonviewers, and these differences were particularly robust during the second year of the evaluation.

Parents and other regular caregivers were also affected when their children regularly viewed these curriculum-based shows. The caregivers whose children regularly viewed Nick Jr.'s curriculum-based programming reported increasing levels of satisfaction with preschool television, and the parents' esteem for Nick Jr. improved steadily with their children's regular viewing of *Allegra's Window* and *Gullah Gullah Island*.

Blue's Clues

During the fall of 1996, Nick Jr. launched an innovative "think-along, play-along" series that "changed the way preschool children watch television" ("Nick Jr.'s *Blue's Clues* top dog," 1997, p. 1). This program enticed young children to be collaborative, active problem solvers with the program's lead characters Steve and Blue. By the end of its second season, *Blue's Clues* was the top rated program in children's television (J. Bryant et al., 1999). *Blue's Clues* also had one of the most carefully designed and rigorously adhered to curricula in the history of children's television (J.A. Bryant, 1999).

As with *Allegra's Window* and *Gullah Gullah Island*, Nickelodeon commissioned an in-depth 2-year investigation of the impact of viewing *Blue's Clues*. A consortium of five universities conducted this research, with coordination by the Institute for Communication Research of the University of Alabama. The design employed in this massive field experiment utilized two types of control; a pretest and a nonviewing control group. Viewing condition (viewers, nonviewers) was an independent factor, and time of assessment was a repeated-measures factor (a pretest, eight posttests). Among the dependent measures employed were the following; viewing level, attention while viewing, character identification and liking, and information acquisition; a battery of standardized measures of flexible thinking and self-esteem; and a variety of caregiver ratings of their children's behaviors related to flexible thinking, problem solving, and social behaviors.

The results revealed that the preschool *Blue's Clues* viewers performed better than their peers in the control condition in terms of information acquisition during each wave of the assessment. The results of the standardized measures of flexible thinking also revealed that regular viewers of the program with its heavy doses of curriculum became much more proficient in flexible thinking than did their nonviewing peers. Although there was a tendency toward higher self-esteem scores for viewers than for nonviewers, those differences were not statistically reliable.

The conclusions of the longitudinal investigation of *Blue's Clues* were summarized by the investigators (J. Bryant et al., 1999):

> The results of the longitudinal investigation of the effects of *Blue's Clues* in accomplishing its curriculum goals are extremely clear: Regular viewing of this breakthrough Nick Jr. program contributed substantially to preschoolers' problem-solving abilities and flexible-thinking skills. Gains shown during the first season were accentuated during the second season. (p. 35)

CONCLUSIONS

The evolution of public policy in children's television has finally resulted in a fertile environment for curriculum-based programming for preschoolers. Not only is the entire PBS preschool block now guided by curricula, the success of commercial ventures in curriculum-based programming bodes very well for the continuation if not accentuation of this important programming genre in realms other than public television.

A review of the most substantial research efforts to examine the impact of curriculum-based programming to date strongly supports the claim that a thoughtful curriculum conveyed in an engaging program can make a positive difference in the lives of children.

> In many ways these findings return us to the promises made in the early days of television—promises that so often seemed to fall by the wayside: Television can make a positive difference in the lives of children! However, the defining conditions must be that this television features a novel, appropriate, developmentally correct curriculum and be presented in the form of enticing programming that attracts, entertains, and engages the young viewer as it unobtrusively teaches its lessons. (J. Bryant et al., 1999, p. 35)

REFERENCES

Anderson, D. R. (1998). Educational television is not an oxymoron. In A. B. Jordan & K. H. Jamieson (Eds.), *The Annals of the American Academy of Political and Social Science, 557: Children and television* (pp. 24–38). Thousand Oaks, CA: Sage.

Aufderheide, P., & Montgomery, K. (1994). *The impact of the Children's Television Act on the broadcast market.* Washington, DC: Center for Media Education. www.epn.org/cme/ctact.html [1999, September].

Ball, S., & Bogatz, G. (1970). *The first year of Sesame Street: An evaluation.* Princeton, NJ: Educational Testing Service.

Bogatz, G., & Ball, S. (1971). *The second year of Sesame Street: A continuing evaluation.* Princeton, NJ: Educational Testing Service.

Bryant, J. A. (1999). *Big Bird, Barney, and Blue: The evolution and current state of national curriculum-based preschool television programming.* Unpublished master's thesis, The University of Alabama, Tuscaloosa.

Bryant, J., & Maxwell, M. (1997, July). *Executive summary: Longitudinal assessment of the effects of viewing Allegra's Window and Gullah Gullah Island.* Tuscaloosa, AL: Institute for Communication Research.

Bryant, J., Mullikin, L., Maxwell, M., Mundorf, N., Mundorf, J., Wilson, B., Smith, S., McCollum, J., & Owens, J. W. (1999, June). *Effects of two years' viewing of Blue's Clues.* Tuscaloosa, AL: Institute for Communication Research.

Center for Media Education. (1995a). *In a new poll, public backs more educational TV for kids* [online]. Available: www.epn.org/cme/cme pubs.html [1999, September]

Center for Media Education. (1995b). *More than 80 groups sign a letter urging FCC to strengthen children's TV rules.* [online]. Available: www.epn.org/cme/cta/pr80ctagroups.html [1999, September]

Center for Media Education. (1999, Spring). The Children's Television Act in its second year [online]. *Infoactive Kids.* Available: www.epn.org/cme/infoactive/iakspr99.pdf [1999, September]

The Children's Television Act of 1990, Pub. L. No. 101-437 [online]. Available: www.thomas. loc/gov/cgi-bin/query/C?c101:/temp/~c101ORLt8a [1999, September]

Cook, T. D., Appelton, H., Conner, R. F., Shaffer, A., Tamkin, G., & Weber, S. J. (1975). *Sesame Street revisited.* New York: Russell Sage Foundation.

Corporation for Public Broadcasting. (1993). *Public broadcasting: Ready to teach: How public broadcasting can serve the Ready-to-Learn needs of America's children.* Washington, DC: Author.

Corporation for Public Broadcasting. (n. d.). *Research Note #87.* Washington, DC: Author.

Crane, V. (1980). Content development for children's television programs. In E. Palmer & A. Dorr (Eds.), *Children and the faces of television: Teaching, violence, selling* (pp. 33–48). New York: Academic Press.

Daley, S. (1984, December 16). Children's programming remains TV's poor relation [Lexis/Nexis]. *The New York Times,* pp. 2, 31.

Davis, S. M. (1997). *The Second Annual Annenberg Public Policy Center's Conference on Children and Television: A Summary* (Report No. 21) [online]. Philadelphia: Annenberg Public Policy Center, University of Pennsylvania. Available: www.appcpenn.org/kidstv/appc/reports/rep21.pdf [1999, September]

Farhi, P. (1991, April 10). FCC issues tighter rules on kid's TV [Lexis/Nexis]. *The Washington Post,* p. C1.

Federal Communications Commission. (1996). *Policies and rules concerning children's television programming: Revision of programming policies for television broadcast stations* [online]. MM Docket No. 93–48. Available: www.fcc.gov/Bureaus/Mass Media/Orders/1996/fcc96335.wp [1999, September]

Fisch, S. M., & Truglio, R. T. (Eds.). (2000). *G is for growing: Thirty years of research on children and Sesame Street.* Mahwah, NJ: Lawrence Erlbaum Associates.

Huston, A. C., Anderson, D. R., Wright, J. C., Linebarger, D. L., & Schmitt, K. L. (2000). *Sesame Street* viewers as adolescents: The recontact study. In S. M. Fisch & R. T. Truglio (Eds.), *G is for growing: Thirty years of research on children and Sesame Street.* Mahwah, NJ: Lawrence Erlbaum Associates.

Jordan, A. B. (1996). *The state of children's television: An examination of quantity, quality and industry beliefs* (Report No. 2) [online]. Philadelphia: Annenberg Public Policy Center, University of Pennsylvania. Available: www.appcpenn.org/kidstv/appc/reports/rep2.pdf [1999, September]

Jordan, A. B. (1998). *The 1998 state of children's television report: Programming for children over broadcast and cable television* (Report No. 23) [online] Philadelphia: Annenberg Public Policy Center, University of Pennsylvania. Available: www.appcpenn.org/kidstv/appc/reports/rep23.pdf [1999, September]

Jordan, A. B., & Woodard, E. H. (1997). *The 1997 state of children's television report: Programming for children over broadcast and cable television* (Report No. 14). [online]. Philadelphia: Annenberg Public Policy Center, University of Pennsylvania. Available: www.appcpenn.org/kidstv/appc/report/rep14.pdf [1999, September]

Kunkel, D. (1991). Crafting media policy. *American Behavioral Scientist, 35,* 181–202.

Kunkel, D. (1998). Policy battles over defining children's educational television. In A. B. Jordan & K. H. Jamieson (Eds.), *The Annals of the American Academy of Political and Social Science, 557: Children and television* (pp. 39–53). Thousand Oaks, CA: Sage.

Leifer, A. (1975, July). *How to encourage socially valued behavior.* Paper presented at the biennial meeting of the Society for Research in Child Development, Denver, CO.

Lesser, G. S., & Schneider, J. (2000). Creation and evolution of the *Sesame Street* curriculum. In S. M. Fisch & R. T. Truglio (Eds.), *G is for growing: Thirty years of research on children and Sesame Street* (pp. 25–38). Mahwah, NJ: Lawrence Erlbaum Associates.

Lesser, H. (1977). *Television and the preschool child: A psychological theory of instruction and curriculum development.* New York: Academic Press.

Mielke, K. W. (2000) A review of research on the educational and social impact of *Sesame Street.* In S. M. Fisch & R. T. Truglio (Eds.), *G is for growing: Thirty years of research on children and Sesame Street.* (pp. 83–95). Mahwah, NJ: Lawrence Erlbaum Associates.

Mifflin, L. (1999, April 19). A growth spurt is transforming TV for children [online]. *The New*

York Times, Available: *www.nytimes.com/yr/mo/day/early/041999kids-tv.html* [1999, September]

Molotsky, I. (1982, September 27). Surge in aptitude scores termed nothing to cheer [Lexis/Nexis]. *The New York Times,* p. A13.

Morrisett, L. (1989). Challenges met and to be met. *Sesame Street 20th Anniversary Research Symposium.* New York: Children's Television Workshop.

Nick, Jr. (n.d.). *Nick Jr. flexible thinking curriculum statement* [Partial document, facsimile transmission]. New York: Nick Jr./Nickelodeon.

"Nick Jr.'s *Blue's Clues* top dog." (1997, July 18). Associated Press Newswire [Nexis/Lexis], pp. 1–2.

Shaw, S. (1983, December 14). *FCC expected to act soon on proposals to control children's TV programs* [Lexis/Nexis]. United Press International.

Truglio, R. (1999, April 29). Phone interview with J. Alison Bryant.

Truglio, R. T., & Fisch, S. M. (2000). Introduction. In S. M. Fisch & R. T. Truglio (Eds.), *G is for growing: Thirty years of research on children and Sesame Street* (pp. xv–xxi). Mahwah, NJ: Lawrence Erlbaum Associates.

Wright, J. C., Huston, A. C., Scantlin, R., & Kotler, J. (2000). The Early Window project: *Sesame Street* prepares children for school. In S. M. Fisch & R. T. Truglio (Eds.), *G is for growing: Thirty years of research on children and Sesame Street* (pp. 97–114). Mahwah, NJ: Lawrence Erlbaum Associates.

Zielinska, I. E., & Chambers, B. (1995). Using group viewing of television to teach preschool social skills. *Journal of Educational Television, 21,* 85–99.

Zill, N. (2000). Does *Sesame Street* enhance school readiness?: Evidence from a national survey of children. In S. M. Fisch & R. T. Truglio (Eds.), *G is for growing: Thirty years of research on children and Sesame Street* (pp. 115–130). Mahwah, NJ: Lawrence Erlbaum Associates.

The Effect of Television Policy on Children and Families

Marina Krcmar
University of Connecticut

The passage of the Children's Television Act (CTA) of 1990 marked the beginning of a decade fraught with philosophical changes in the Federal Communication Commission (FCC), legal battles over FCC regulations, and, ultimately, policy changes regarding children's television. In view of such legislative changes, it is important to ask how children and their families have responded to them and what impact these policy changes have had on audiences. In this chapter, I first briefly review the policy changes that have occurred in the last decade regarding children's programming. Second, I examine the impact that those changes have had on the landscape of children's educational programming and children's responses to educational programs. Third, I review the research that asks what impact policy changes have had on parents' and children's attitude toward and use of programs that are potentially harmful to children.

A BRIEF LOOK AT REGULATION REGARDING CHILDREN'S PROGRAMMING

In 1990, Congress passed legislation known as the CTA. This act required, in part, that broadcasters provide programming to serve the educational needs of children. However, the initial ruling was vague, specifying neither the amount of time that had to be devoted to the educational needs of children, nor the content that should be considered "educational." Due to the vagueness of the CTA's wording, little was done by broadcasters to actually provide for the educational needs of children. By 1997, broadcasters were in fact claiming an average of 3.4 hours of educational programming per week (Kunkel, 1998); however, these educational programs included shows such as the *Flintstones*, which one station reported, taught history. Due to embarrassments such as these, as well as extensive pressure applied by child advocacy groups, the FCC instated processing guidelines known as "the 3-hour rule." This rule requires broadcasters to supply child audiences with 3 hours of programming per week that "furthers the positive development of . . . the child's intellectual/cognitive needs or social/emotional needs" (FCC, 1996, C.F.R. 47 73.671). Furthermore, intellectual/cognitive and social/emotional needs are said to be met by a program only if the program has education as a specific purpose.[1] It is likely, therefore, that the CTA, especially in its more stringent form, may have an impact not only on the face of educational television but also on the children and families who make up the audience.

Another major policy change that may have an impact on children and families is the Telecommunications Act of 1996. This Act mandated that within 2 years of the Act's passage, all newly manufactured television sets contain a V-chip. This device would allow viewers and parents of young viewers to block objectionable content. In addition, the Act mandated that broadcasters must label programs to provide information that could be read by the V-chip. Thus, in January of 1997, networks[2] began using a rating system, based on the one utilized by the Motion Picture Association of America (MPAA). These parental guidelines used an age-based rating system; that is, the rating indicated for what age group the program might be suitable, but provided no content information about the program.

Once again, child advocacy groups were quick to respond, indicating that the rating system did not provide the type of information to parents that would help them make decisions regarding their children's television viewing. In fact, several national polls indicated that a majority of parents did prefer content ratings for television programs rather than age-based ratings (e.g., Cantor, Stutman, & Duran, 1996; Mifflin, 1997). As a result, content indicators were added to the existing age-based system in October of 1997. These include V, for violent content; FV, for fantasy violence (such as might appear in programs for children); L for language; D for

---

[1] Broadcasters may provide less than 3 hours if they demonstrate service to children in other areas; however, they will not then be guaranteed a license renewal.

[2] With the notable exception of NBC, all networks used the rating system.

sexual dialogue. In addition to these advisory ratings, educational programs are identified with an E/I to specify their educational/informational content.

Overall, the CTA and the Telecommunications Act of 1996 had largely different intents and emphasized different aspects of children's television. Whereas the intent of the CTA was to improve children's educational television, the intent of the Telecommunications Act of 1996 was to deregulate the telecommunications industry—not necessarily to improve television aimed at young children. However, a relatively small portion of the Act was in fact intended to impact children's television. By enforcing the 3-hour rule, and by requiring broadcasters to label problematic as well as educational television content, the Telecommunications Act of 1996 could potentially affect children's television and parents' and children's responses to that content (FCC, 1996).

THE EFFECT OF THE CTA AND THE TELECOMMUNICATIONS ACT ON CHILDREN AND FAMILIES

The Impact of Policy Changes on Educational Offerings

As mentioned earlier, the original CTA seemed to have little impact on children's programming content. Currently, however, the CTA is armed with greater specificity concerning both the amount of educational programming that broadcasters must present for child audiences and a greater specificity in the definition of "educational programming." It seems likely, therefore, that strengthening the original CTA would result in increased quality in children's educational programs and, subsequently, an increase in the amount of exposure that children have to quality programming. Is this the case? Is there better programming, and are children attracted to it?

To answer this question, it is important to take somewhat of an historical perspective, that is, to examine the content of children's television in the years following the original CTA of 1990 and in those years following the new, stricter guidelines set for children's educational television in 1996. In the following section, I review the research conducted in the last decade that has examined what impact, if any, the educational television policy changes have had.

In the days subsequent to the passage of the 1990 CTA, it seemed promising that children's television would be improved. Perhaps new educational programs would be designed; broadcasters would see merit in providing positive programming for children; and the selection available to children and their parents would be improved. However, Kunkel and Canepa (1994), in a systematic effort to identify any changes that may have occurred in children's television after the passage of the CTA, found that, despite broadcasters' claims of meeting the spirit of the act, children's television was no better than it had been prior to its passage. Programs like the *Jetsons*, which supposedly taught about life in the future, and *Yogi Bear*, which taught ethical values, were claimed by broadcasters as "educational" programs. Kunkel and Canepa's research lead Kunkel to conclude that "the principal impact of the CTA had been to force broadcasters to creatively relabel their existing program offerings as educational, rather than to generate many new shows of value to youths" (Kunkel, 1998, p. 44). Similarly, Bryant and Bryant (1995) found a small increase in the number of educational programs from 1990 to 1993, but the difference was not statistically significant.

Shortly thereafter, the industry responded that the study had been conducted too early, before broadcasters had a solid understanding of the new regulations and the responsibilities that the regulations entailed. Therefore, the study was replicated. This time, Kunkel and Goette (1997) focused on the 1994 to 1995 television season, reasoning that by this time, broadcasters would have a better understanding of the new regulations and would be more likely to be adhering to them. Again, they found that not only were broadcasters still citing blatantly frivolous programs as educational, but that they were doing so with a full understanding of the CTA of 1990 and how that law was intended to affect children's educational programming.

Based on the research conducted by Kunkel and his colleagues, the CTA was viewed as unsuccessful in terms of improving children's educational programming. But what of the new, stricter regulations? As described previously, the new 3-hour law regulates *how much* time should be devoted to educational programming for children, and, is more specific about the content of that educational programming. Research conducted by the Annenberg Public Policy Center (APPC) during the television season of 1997 to 1998 provides some information regarding the television landscape during that season. In addition, because APPC conducted similar studies in the preceding two television seasons as well, results from the 1997 to 1998 season could be compared to those of earlier seasons. In this way, conclusions could be drawn regarding the impact of the Telecommunications Act of 1996 on the quality of programming aimed at children.

During the 1997 to 1998 season, the APPC conducted a content analysis that identified programs that were listed by broadcasters as educational (i.e., had an E/I rating); then coded those programs for their intended audience (preschoolers, elementary school children, preteen or teen) and last rated each program as minimally, moderately, or highly educational. Overall, they found that although the 3-hour rule was being met by a majority of broadcasters, a significant proportion of the programs being labeled by them with an "E/I" still fell short of being "highly educational" as indicated by the standards set by the researchers. Although improvements do seem to have been made in the programs being offered to children, some programs, such as *Wheel of Fortune 2000,* still received poor marks and were, in fact, labeled by APPC as "minimally education."

Specifically, the 1997 to 1998 season showed a line-up of programs in which 36.4% of the programs were highly educational, 27.3% of the programs were moderately educational, and 36.3% were minimally educational. Variations occurred, however, when quality of program was analyzed by intended audience. The best programming seems to be created for preschoolers. Of all of the E/I programs targeted at this age group, 85.3% was found to be highly educational; whereas only 1.5% of the programs were minimally educational. Elementary school children fare worse, with only 21.1% of their E/I programs identified as highly educational and 47.7% as minimally educational. Preteens and teens fall in the middle with 28.3% of their programs identified as highly educational and 37.4% identified as minimally educational.

What do these results mean? According to the ongoing research conducted by the APPC, it appears that although children's network television has improved in some ways, it remains decidedly lacking in others. For example, the 1997 to 1998 season saw an increase in programs created for the long-ignored teen population, and preschoolers were still offered a good variety of well-produced educational programs. However, there has not been a substantial increase in the number of educational programs for children overall.[3] A bright spot in this research was that, unlike Kunkel and his colleagues, Jordan (1998) found no evidence of clear mendacity by broadcasters. In other words, programs that were of no educational value by even the most lax standards were no longer being claimed as educational. Although some programs were identified by APPC as minimally educational, the programs could at least be said to have been designed to be educational. Perhaps then, there is a growing respect among broadcasters and producers for the idea of children's educational programming. Forced by the new rating system to label their educational programs and hence, "go public" with their claims of meeting the educational needs of children, broadcasters perhaps are slowly making a more reasonable attempt to provide decent children's programming.

---

[3] Keep in mind, however, that the results reported in this study were from commercial network programming. PBS typically does an excellent job of providing educational programs for children. Cable stations may also provide educational programs that were not included in these results.

The Impact of Policy Changes on Parents' and Children's Responses to Educational Television

To understand the effect of policy changes regarding children's television, it is important to look not only at changes in the content of children's educational programs, but at parents' use of those ratings and their effect on children. In the early days of the rating system, when only age-based ratings (e.g., TV-Y7) and not content ratings (e.g., "S" for sex) were assigned to programs, parents seemed to approve of the efforts being made by networks to employ ratings, but they didn't necessarily use the ratings. In a study conducted by *The New York Times* (Mifflin, 1997), 86% of the parents approved of the ratings, although 69% said that programs should get two ratings, one for content and one for intended age group. Despite this approval, only 39% of the parents reported using the ratings. Keep in mind that these results referred to parents' use of the ratings overall, and not only their attention to the E/I ratings.

When Jordan (1998) asked parents specifically about their use of the E/I ratings, the results look dramatically different. Slightly under 5% of the parents were aware of the FCC guidelines regarding children's educational television. Similarly, less than 5% of the parents regularly used the E/I rating to help children make their selections. These results indicate, that at least for the E/I ratings, parents are not gaining too much from the presence of E/I labels. Why is this the case? It is possible that parents are neither aware of the E/I nor using it because parents are simply not in the room when children are watching this kind of programming. Because they are not present, they don't see the E/I symbols; thus, awareness among parents of these ratings has been slow to occur. In fact, research that examines patterns of parent–child coviewing corroborates this hypothesis. Overall, parents and children tend to coview programs that have a family, or general audience focus, not those that indicate children as their intended audience (Huston & Wright, 1996). Because children's educational programming, by definition, identifies children as its primary audience, it is likely that parents are not using the E/I because they simply do not see it. This hypothesis is offered some support by the fact that parents are, in general, woefully unaware of the educational offerings of commercial broadcasters (Stanger, 1997). This study suggests, too, that parents are probably not exposed to children's programs, and consequently, may not be exposed to the E/I.

So, if parents are not using the E/I symbol, who is making use of it? Recent research indicates that children, especially older children, are making use of the E/I ratings, but not always in the way that is intended (Krcmar, 1999). A sample of 169 children between the ages of 5 and 11 were shown an educational program, then asked to rate their liking of the program; they were also tested for recall. The four experimental conditions included three variations on the manipulation and a no E/I control group. The first group was shown the program with an E/I; the second group was shown the program with an E/I that was then pointed out to them by the experimenter; the third group was shown an E/I and prior to the program, the new rating system was explained to them; the fourth group was shown the program with no E/I.[4]

Overall, children did not differentially prefer the program based on the E/I; however, there was an age by gender by condition interaction. Specifically, older girls liked the program more when it had an E/I and older boys liked it less. In addition, recall was affected by the E/I, again, for older children. Specifically, children recalled less when the program contained an E/I, except in the condition in which the E/I was pointed out to them by the researcher. In this latter condition, children's attention was drawn to the E/I, and consequently to the screen, likely causing increases in attention, and thus, recall. The researcher argued that the "pointing" done by the experimenter, and not the E/I itself, was responsible for the increase in the children's attention. In sum, then, for older boys, the E/I caused them to devalue the program, but not so for older girls. In terms of recall, the simple presence of an E/I seemed to decrease the amount of recall for older children, perhaps because they "tuned out" the program after realizing it was intended to be educational.

These studies suggest that the E/I rating may not be working as intended. Adults are not using the E/I symbol, most likely because they are unaware of it, or, as Jordan and Woodard (1998) argued, they do not know what it is because the symbols are somewhat obtuse and idiosyncratic. Children, on the other hand, are using the symbol, but not always with the intended outcome. It is likely that the difference between adults' awareness and children's awareness of the E/I rating has to do primarily with their actual exposure to it. Simply put, children see the E/I rating when they are watching TV and therefore have become familiar with it. Adults, who are not present during the airing of these programs and the airing of the associated rating, simply have not become familiar with the system yet. It is important to note, however, that due to the relative newness of the E/I rating on television, it is possible that both the parents' and the children's responses will change as familiarity increases for the former and novelty of the symbol decreases for the latter.

What, then, has been the impact of policy regarding educational television on children and families? We might conclude that there has been

---

[4] In this study, 60% of the children reported having seen the E/I rating; however, older children reported having seen it more than younger children. The hypotheses were tested on the entire sample.

minimal—very minimal—improvement in the offerings of educational television for children. Improving the face of educational television aimed at children was an uphill battle from the early 1990s (Kunkel, 1998). Also, although policy changes have forced commercial broadcasters to be more forthcoming about their educational offerings, it has not improved what is on television to any great extent (Jordan, 1998). In addition, parents don't seem to be aware of the policy changes or of the resulting E/I ratings that were put in place largely for their use. Alternately, it is children who are seeing and making use of the E/I rating, not always in the way that we would hope. The results, therefore, seem poor. However, it is worth noting that educational policy changes have really been enforced for only one season. As always, audiences and broadcasters may acclimate slowly to the new environment, making change a slow process.

The Impact of the New Advisory System on Parents and Children

It is not just children's educational television that has been affected by changes in telecommunications policy. In fact, there was more ferment between producers and policymakers over the advisory rating system than over the E/I rating. It is understandable, perhaps, that broadcasters would not object to labeling their educational programs with an E/I. Labeling, for example, sexual content with an S, however, created discomfort in the industry. Fear over potential loss of advertising revenues was likely the cause of networks' resistance to labeling problematic and objectionable content.

Despite resistance from within the industry, in January of 1996, broadcasters were required to begin labeling programs. The early system was based on the MPAA ratings and programs were categorized by the age group for whom the program was considered appropriate. However, parents, as well as child advocacy groups, were displeased with the rating system developed by the networks. In fact, research repeatedly demonstrated that parents wanted a rating system that looked quite different from the one being used. What is it that parents wanted? Several studies conducted by various organizations, and conducted independently, suggested that parents wanted content information so that they could make informed decisions themselves about their children's television viewing. In September of 1996, a sample of 679 parents was randomly selected and asked about their views on the new rating system. Of the parents sampled, 80% preferred a content-based system. Just 3 months later, 1,000 adults participated in a national poll conducted by the Media Studies Center and the Roper Organization. This study found that 79% of the parents in the sample preferred a content to age-based rating system (Media Studies Center & Roper, 1996). The results of these and other similar studies overwhelmingly indicated that parents wanted more information about the programming their children were being offered. What they clearly did not want was an age-based rating system that simply classified programs by appropriate target audience.

The fact that parents wanted more information about the content of the programs their children might watch seemed reason enough for the networks to agree to provide it to them. But even more reason exists to avoid age-based rating systems in favor of content-based ones: Some children seem to be attracted to programs that contain age-based ratings. Research conducted by Cantor and Harrison (1996) and by Krcmar and Cantor (1997) suggests that whereas parents are disparaging of programs with cautionary advisories (e.g., Contains Some Violence; Parents Strongly Cautioned), some children are likely to approve of such warnings and are likely to be attracted to programs with more restrictive ratings.

Two studies, each conducted as part of the National Television Violence Study examined the effect of ratings on parents' and children's attitudes toward programs with various advisories and ratings. In the first study, Cantor and Harrison (1996) examined the effect of ratings and advisories on a group of 297 children between the ages of 5 and 14. The children were randomly assigned to one of four conditions. In each condition, children read identical descriptions of programs and were asked to select the one they most wanted to watch. What was manipulated about the programs was simply the rating that appeared at the end of the description. The program was rated either "G: general audiences," "PG: parental guidance suggested," "PG-13: parents strongly cautioned," or "R: restricted." Although there was no main effect for the condition, there was an interesting interaction effect: Boys, especially older boys, were significantly more likely to select the program when it contained an "R" rating. Older boys were also more attracted to programs when the advisory mentioned parents (e.g., "Parental discretion advised") than when viewers were simply mentioned (e.g., "Viewer discretion advised"). What these results suggest is that programs seem more appealing to some children, especially older boys, when they perceive the program to be restricted from them by parents and other adults. When they simply perceive that audiences in general are being cautioned, this boomerang effect does not occur. Therefore, Cantor and Harrison (1996) concluded that it was the restrictive nature of the program advisory or rating, and not simply the mention of violence that seemed to attract older boys.

In a second study, conducted by Krcmar and Cantor (1997), parents and children were asked to jointly make decisions about and choices from a TV Guide booklet shown to them. Again, the program descriptions in the booklets were identical; however, some descriptions contained cautionary advisories (e.g., Contains some violence; Parental discretion advised) whereas others did not. While parents and children looked over the booklet and made their selections, they were unobtrusively video-taped. The findings of this study were similar to those of Cantor and Harrison (1996); however, because parents' and children's comments were recorded, some insight was gained into why children made the selections they did and, also, why parents made the selections they did.

The first set of findings regarding the parent–child study are perhaps unsurprising. When parents and children made decisions together, they overwhelmingly avoided programs with violence advisories and with more restrictive MPAA ratings. However, the second set of findings, those that focused on what parents and children said about the advisories and ratings, are interesting. Almost half of the parents made reference to the advisory that they saw, and all of those comments were disparaging. Specifically, parents said things like "parental discretion. I'd say proba-bly not." Alternately, they interpreted the advisory for their children in such a way as to make the program seem less desirable (e.g., "that means it's too scary"). Children, on the other hand, were less likely than their parents to make comments about the advisories, but when they did, chil-dren made positive as well as negative comments about the advisories. For example, one older child excitedly exclaimed "that's awesome," after she read the advisory. Overall, older children made more positive com-ments about the advisories and more restrictive MPAA ratings than did younger children.

In addition to examining what parents and children said about the pro-grams and the associated ratings, this study also looked at the negotia-tion process that parents and children engaged in in order to arrive at a decision. The presence of an advisory or more restrictive MPAA rating also seemed to increase the level of conflict between the parent and child. Specifically, negative affect increased when an advisory was present, espe-cially among the parents

The results described in these studies suggest that advisories and re-strictive MPAA ratings may have a boomerang effect, especially when children feel that they are being restricted from the content by adults. It is for this reason that Cantor, Harrison, and Krcmar (1998) argued that "parental discretion" advisories, and not "viewer discretion" advisories are particularly attractive to some children. And based on the positive comments made by some of the children in the Krcmar and Cantor (1997) study, it seems that some children do feel favorably about some tele-vision content precisely because it is restricted. What might be concluded, then, is that the advisories and ratings that had been implemented by broadcasters, particularly those ratings that are age based and those advisories that warn parents of potentially harmful content, may have un-intended harmful consequences.

Despite the fact that research has demonstrated a clear link between use of age-based advisories and ratings and children's attraction to potentially problematic content, network executives were reluctant to instate a purely content-based rating system. Whereas most advocacy groups recommended that programs be designated with three different levels of different contents, the industry preferred a system that employed age guidelines. Therefore, a compromise was reached whereby programs receive both a single content indicator and an age-based rating. In this system, euphemisms such as "D" for dialogue about sexual matters and "FV" for violence that appears in children's programs are also utilized. This system is considered a compromise, and not a victory for child advocacy groups for two reasons. First, the age-based system may still cause some children to be attracted to programs that they consider restricted and that their parents might consider inappropriate. Second, because there is an age-based rating, only one content rating is given, rather than three, even if the program has, for example, sexual dialogue *and* violence (Cantor, 1998). This compromise may present problems for parents. In addition to concerns over the attraction that the age-based ratings may have for their young children, Jordan (1998) and Kunkel (1998) argued that the euphemistic use of D and FV is particularly confusing to parents. And, these ratings (D and FV) are precisely those that appear frequently in children's programming and in the situation comedies that children may watch.

Who Is Using the Advisories?

It seems possible, therefore, that the rating and advisory system may not be as useful to parents as it could be, were it more interpretable and unambiguous. It is perhaps because the rating system is not completely effective in keeping children away from potentially harmful content or in informing parents about the content, that all parents are not making use of the system. For example, by 1997, only 41% of parents reported using the rating system (Stanger, 1997). The use of the rating system does, however, tend to vary with characteristics of the parents. Surveys conducted in December of that year offered some insight into questions regarding parents' use of the newly implemented system.

Krcmar (1998) asked parents of children between the ages of 5 and 13 to report on their use of the networks' rating system. She reasoned that parents who had monitored and restricted their children's television viewing in the past might continue to do so simply by utilizing the new tools that were available to them. Alternately, parents who had not monitored their children's viewing would probably continue this pattern, despite the fact that television programs now contained ratings to help them make decisions. Previous research had shown that several factors predicted parents' tendency to restrict and guide their children's television. Specifically, parents of younger children were more likely than parents of older children to restrict their viewing (St. Peters, Fitch, Huston, Wright, & Eakins, 1991). Similarly, those who believed that television negatively impacted their child's behavior and cognitive development were more likely to restrict television viewing than parents who did not hold this view (Abelman, 1987). Consistent with earlier research, prior to the days of television advisories and ratings, Krcmar (1998) found that parents of younger children were more likely to report using the rating system than parents of older children. In addition, parents who thought television negatively affected children's behavior were more likely to report using the system, as were parents who thought that television negatively affected children's cognitive development. What this research suggests is that the new rating and advisory system provided a new tool for parents who had been vigilant about their children's viewing in the past, but the system did not necessarily encourage all parents to begin monitoring the television viewing done by their child.

In sum, then, what can be said about the impact of policy changes on parents and children? How has educational television changed? How have parents' and children's attitudes toward educational television changed as a result of changes in public policy? And what of the potentially problematic content to which children are exposed? How has policy changed the nature of that content, and how has it impacted parents' and children's attitudes toward it? Although some of these questions have been answered over the past few years, and have been reviewed as part of this chapter, other important questions remain, although unanswered. We know, for example, that educational television has not improved drastically as a result of the 3-hour rule. But, perhaps improvements will occur over time as producers learn the art of creating quality children's programs. For this reason, it will be important to continue to track the progress of children's educational television. We know, too, that the E/I rating may turn some children away from the program. But this might also change as the E/I symbol loses its novelty. It is also possible that if the quality of children's educational programming does improve, the E/I might come to stand for something that is particularly attractive to children, and not something they devalue. At any rate, it is crucial to consider children's responses to the E/I rating as potentially variable, and not fixed in its current context.

In terms of the advisory system, which is intended to warn parents and children of potentially harmful content, we know that the ratings that restrict children's access to certain content actually serve to make some children more attracted to the program. Parents, unsurprisingly, are not influenced in a similar way. In fact, they tend to avoid programs with advisories and more restrictive MPAA ratings when they are selecting programs with their children. What we do not know about the advisory system is if and how it has affected the content of programs targeted at children and families. For example, it is conceivable that producers might decrease the amount of harmful content in a program for young children in order to obtain a more favorable rating for that program. In addition, it may be interesting to see if more parents, and not just those who monitor their children's viewing in the first place, begin to use the rating system as it becomes more familiar to them. Questions such as these remain to be investigated. In doing so, we continue to gain an understanding of the translation of public policy into private practice.

REFERENCES

Abelman, R. (1987). Child giftedness and its role in parental mediation of television. *Roper Review, 9* (4), 217–220.

Bryant, J. A., & Bryant, J. (1995, June). *Does public policy affect children's television programming?* Paper presented at a conference on Cynicism and the media: Is our ability to govern being eroded? New York Department of Humanities, Albany, NY.

Cantor, J. (1998). Ratings for program content: The role of research findings. In A. Jordan & K. H. Jamieson (Eds.), *The Annals of the American Academy of Political and Social Science: Television and Children* (pp. 54–69). Thousand Oaks, CA: Sage.

Cantor, J., & Harrison, K. (1996). Ratings and advisories for television programming. In *National Television Violence Study* (Vol. 1, pp. 361–397). Thousand Oaks, CA: Sage.

Cantor, J., Harrison, K., & Krcmar, M. (1998). Ratings and advisories: Implications for the new rating system for television. In J. Hamilton (Ed.), *Television violence and public policy* (pp. 179–212). Ann Arbor: University of Michigan Press.

Cantor, J., Stutman, S., & Duran, V. (1996). *What parents want in a television rating system: Results of a national survey.* Report released by the National PTA, the Institute for Mental Health initiative, and the University of Wisconsin-Madison.

Federal Communication Commission, (1996). *In the matter of policies and rules concerning children's television programming: Report and order.* 11 F.C.C. Record 10660.

Huston, A., & Wright, J. (1996). Television and socialization of young children. In T. MacBeth (Ed.), *Tuning in to young viewers* pp. (37–60). Thousand Oaks, CA: Sage.

Jordan, A. (1998). The 1998 state of children's television report: Programming for children over broadcast and cable television [Annenberg Public Policy Center Survey Series, no. 23]. Philadelphia: University of Pennsylvania, Annenberg Public Policy Center.

Jordan, A., & Woodard, E. H. (1998). Growing pains: Children's television in the new regulatory environment. In A. Jordan & K. H. Jamieson (Eds.), *The Annals of the American Academy of Political and Social Science: Television and Children* (pp. 83–95). Thousand Oaks, CA: Sage.

Krcmar, M. (1998, November). *Television advisories and the V-Chip: New tools for vigilant parents.* Paper presented at the annual conference of the National Communication Association, New York.

Krcmar, M. (1999). *The effect of E/I ratings on children's liking of and learning from an educational program.* Paper presented at the annual conference of the Society for Research in Child Development, Albuquerque, NM.

Krcmar, M., & Cantor, J. (1997). The role of television advisories and ratings in parent–child discussion of television viewing choices. *Journal of Broadcasting & Electronic Media, 41,* 393–411.

Kunkel, D. (1998). Policy battles over defining children's educational television. In A. Jordan & K. Hall Jamieson (Eds.), *The Annals of the American Academy of Political and Social Science: Television and Children* (pp. 39–53). Thousand Oaks, CA: Sage.

Kunkel, D., & Canepa, J. (1994). Broadcasters' license renewal claims regarding children's educational programming. *Journal of Broadcasting & Electronic Media, 38,* 397–416.

Kunkel, D., & Goette, U. (1997). Broadcasters' response to the children's television act. *Communication Law and Policy, 2,* 289–308.

Media Studies Center & Roper Organization. (1996, December). *Poll finds public support for content over age-based TV rating system.* Arlington, VA: Freedom Forum.

Mifflin, L. (1997, February 22). New ratings codes for television get mixed reviews from parents. *New York Times,* p.?

Stanger, J. (1997). *Television in the home: The 1997 survey of parents and children* [Annenberg Public Policy Center Survey Series, no. 2]. Philadelphia: University of Pennsylvania, Annenberg Public Policy Center.

St. Peters, M., Fitch, M., Huston, A., Wright, J. C., & Eakins, D. (1991). Television and families: What do young children watch with their parents? *Child Development, 62,* 1409–1423.

Author Index

Subject Index